THE EUROPEAN ENCYCLOPEDIA

First taking shape during the seventeenth century, the European encyclopedia was an alphabetical book of knowledge. For the next three centuries, printed encyclopedias in the European tradition were an important element of culture and people's lives, initially just among Europe's educated elite but ultimately through much of the literate world. Engaging with printed encyclopedias – now largely extinct and the object of nostalgia – as well as the global phenomenon of Wikipedia, Jeff Loveland brings together encyclopedias from multiple languages (notably English, French, and German, amongst others). Organized around themes such as genre, economics, illustration, and publishing, *The European Encyclopedia* is the first comprehensive survey of encyclopedias to be written in English in more than fifty years. This book will be of interest to anyone, from academics in the humanities to non-academic readers, with an interest in encyclopedias and their history.

JEFF LOVELAND is Professor in Romance and Arabic Languages and Literatures at the University of Cincinnati. He is the author of numerous articles on encyclopedias as well as *Alternative Encyclopedia? Dennis de Coetlogon's Universal History of Arts and Sciences* (2010). With Frank Kafker, he also co-edited *The Early Britannica (1768–1803): The Growth of an Outstanding Encyclopedia* (2009).

THE EUROPEAN ENCYCLOPEDIA

From 1650 to the Twenty-First Century

JEFF LOVELAND

University of Cincinnati

CAMBRIDGE
UNIVERSITY PRESS

University Printing House, Cambridge CB2 8BS, United Kingdom

One Liberty Plaza, 20th Floor, New York, NY 10006, USA

477 Williamstown Road, Port Melbourne, VIC 3207, Australia

314–321, 3rd Floor, Plot 3, Splendor Forum, Jasola District Centre, New Delhi – 110025, India

79 Anson Road, #06-04/06, Singapore 079906

Cambridge University Press is part of the University of Cambridge.

It furthers the University's mission by disseminating knowledge in the pursuit of
education, learning, and research at the highest international levels of excellence.

www.cambridge.org
Information on this title: www.cambridge.org/9781108481090
DOI: 10.1017/9781108646390

© Jeff Loveland 2019

First published 2019

Printed in the United Kingdom by TJ International Ltd. Padstow Cornwall

A catalog record for this publication is available from the British Library.

Library of Congress Cataloging-in-Publication Data
Names: Loveland, Jeff, author.
Title: The European encyclopaedia from 1650 to the
twenty-first century / Jeff Loveland, University of Cincinnati.
Description: Cambridge; New York, NY: Cambridge University Press, [2019] |
Includes bibliographical references and index.
Identifiers: LCCN 2019000698 | ISBN 9781108481090 (hardback) |
ISBN 9781108703802 (paperback)
Subjects: LCSH: Encyclopedias and dictionaries – History and criticism.
Classification: LCC AE1.L68 2019 | DDC 030.94–dc23
LC record available at https://lccn.loc.gov/2019000698

ISBN 978-1-108-48109-0 Hardback

Contents

Figures

Tables

Chronological List of Printed Encyclopedias

In general, these are the works mentioned in three or more chapters of my book.

Moréri, Louis. *Le Grand Dictionaire historique; ou, Le Mélange curieux de l'histoire sainte et profane*. 1st edn. Lyon: Girin and Rivière, 1674. Further editions through 1759.

Furetière, Antoine. *Dictionaire universel contenant généralement tous les mots françois tant vieux que modernes, et les termes de toutes les sciences et des arts*. 1st edn. 3 vols. The Hague: Leers, 1690. Further editions through 1727, one highlighted below.

Corneille, Thomas. *Dictionnaire des arts et des sciences*. 2 vols. Paris: Coignard, 1694. Further editions through 1732.

Bayle, Pierre. *Dictionaire historique et critique*. 1st edn. 2 vols. Rotterdam: Leers, 1697. Further editions through 1820.

Furetière, Antoine, and Henri Basnage de Beauval. *Dictionaire universel contenant généralement tous les mots françois tant vieux que modernes, et les termes des sciences et des arts*. Rev. edn. 3 vols. The Hague: Leers, 1701.

Coronelli, Vincenzo. *Biblioteca universale sacro-profana, antico-moderna*. 7 vols. Venice: 1701–6.

[*Dictionnaire de Trévoux*]. 1st edn. *Dictionnaire universel françois et latin*. 3 vols. Trévoux: Ganeau, 1704. Further editions through 1771, one highlighted below.

Harris, John. *Lexicon Technicum; or, An Universal English Dictionary of Arts and Sciences*. 1st edn. 2 vols. London: Brown *et al.*, 1704–10. Further editions through 1744.

Reales Staats- und Zeitungs-Lexicon (later *Reales Staats- Zeitungs- und Conversations-Lexicon*, etc.). 1st edn. Leipzig: Gleditsch, 1704. Further editions through 1828.

Chomel, Noël. *Dictionnaire oeconomique, contenant divers moyens d'augmenter et conserver son bien, et même sa santé.* 2 vols. Lyon: Thened, 1709. Further editions through 1767.

[Marperger, Paul Jacob]. *Curieuses Natur- Kunst- Gewerck- und Handlungs-Lexicon* (later *Curieuses und reales Natur- Kunst- Berg- Gewerck- und Handlungs-Lexicon*, etc.). 1st edn. Leipzig: Gleditsch, 1712. Further editions through 1792.

Corvinus, Gottlieb Siegmund. *Nutzbares, galantes und curiöses Frauenzimmer-Lexicon.* Leipzig: Gleditsch, 1715. Further editions through 1773.

[*Dictionnaire de Trévoux*]. 2nd edn. *Dictionnaire universel françois et latin.* 5 vols. Trévoux: Delaulne *et al.*, 1721.

[Jablonski, Johann Theodor]. *Allgemeines Lexicon der Künste und Wissenschafften.* Leipzig: Fritsch, 1721. Further editions through 1767.

Savary des Bruslons, Jacques, *et al. Dictionnaire universel de commerce.* 3 vols. Paris: Estienne, 1723–30. Further editions through 1765.

Dyche, Thomas, and William Pardon. *A New General English Dictionary.* London: Ware, 1735. Further editions through 1794.

Chambers, Ephraim. *Cyclopaedia; or, An Universal Dictionary of Arts and Sciences.* 1st edn. 2 vols. London: Knapton *et al.*, 1728. Further editions through 1753.

Grosses vollständiges Universal-Lexicon aller Wissenschafften und Künste. 64 vols. Halle and Leipzig: Zedler, 1732–50.

Coetlogon, Dennis de. *An Universal History of Arts and Sciences.* 2 vols. London: Hart, 1745. Revised edition in 1759.

Pivati, Gianfrancesco. *Nuovo dizionario scientifico e curioso sacro-profano.* 10 vols. Venice: Milocco, 1746–51.

Encyclopédie; ou, Dictionnaire raisonné des sciences, des arts et des métiers. Ed. Denis Diderot and Jean Le Rond D'Alembert. 28 vols. [Paris]: [Briasson *et al.*], 1751–72. Further editions through 1780, one highlighted below.

De Felice, Fortunato Bartolommeo, ed. *Encyclopédie; ou, Dictionnaire universel raisonné des connoissances humaines.* 58 vols. Yverdon: [Société Typographique], 1770–80.

Encyclopaedia Britannica. 1st edn. 3 vols. Edinburgh: Bell and Macfarquhar, 1771. Further editions through 2012, some highlighted below.

Krünitz, Johann Georg *et al.*, eds. *Oeconomische Encyclopädie; oder, Allgemeines System der Land- Haus- und Staats-Wirthschaft* [later *Oeconomisch-technologische Encyklopädie*]. 242 vols. Berlin: Various, 1773–1858.

Encyclopaedia Britannica. 2nd edn. 10 vols. Edinburgh: J. Balfour *et al.*, 1778–83.

Rees, Abraham, ed. *Cyclopaedia; or, An Universal Dictionary of Arts and Sciences.* 5 vols. London: Strahan *et al.*, 1778–88.

[First *Deutsche Encyclopädie*]. *Deutsche Encyclopädie; oder, Allgemeines Real-Wörterbuch aller Künste und Wissenschaften.* 24 vols. Frankfurt: Varrentrapp and Wenner, 1778–1807.

Encyclopédie méthodique. Around 200 vols. Paris: 1782–1832.

Encyclopaedia Britannica. 3rd edition. 18 vols. Edinburgh: Bell and Macfarquhar, [1788]–97.

Encyclopaedia Britannica. 3rd edn. Irish edn. 20 vols. Dublin: Moore, 1790–8.

[*Grosse Brockhaus*]. *Conversationslexikon mit vorzüglicher Rücksicht auf die gegenwärtigen Zeiten.* 1st edn. 6 vols. Leipzig: 1796–1808. Further printed editions through 2006.

Edinburgh Encyclopaedia. Ed. David Brewster. 18 vols. Edinburgh: Blackwood *et al.*, [1808]–30. Further editions through 1832.

Supplement to the Fourth, Fifth, and Sixth Editions of the Encyclopaedia Britannica. Ed. Macvey Napier. 6 vols. Edinburgh: Constable, 1824.

Encyclopaedia Metropolitana. 29 vols. London: Fellowes *et al.*, [1817]–45.

Allgemeine Encyclopädie der Wissenschaften und Künste. Ed. Johann Samuel Ersch *et al.* 167 vols. Leipzig: 1818–89.

Rees, Abraham, ed. *The [New] Cyclopaedia; or, Universal Dictionary of Arts, Sciences, and Literature.* 45 vols. London: Longman *et al.*, 1819–20.

[*Grosse Brockhaus*]. 5th edn. 1st printing. *Allgemeine deutsche Real-Encyclopädie für die gebildeten Stände (Conversations-Lexikon).* 10 vols. Leipzig: Brockhaus, 1819–20.

[*Pierer's Universal-Lexikon*]. 1st edn. *Encyclopädisches Wörterbuch der Wissenschaften, Künste und Gewerbe.* 26 vols. Altenburg: 1824–36. Further editions through 1879.

Encyclopédie progressive; ou, Collection de traités sur l'histoire, l'état actuel et les progrès des connaissances humaines. Paris: Bureau de l'Encyclopédie Progressive, 1826.

[*Grosse Brockhaus*]. 7th edn. *Allgemeine deutsche Real-Encyclopädie für die gebildeten Stände (Conversations-Lexikon).* 12 vols. Leipzig: Brockhaus, 1827.

Encyclopaedia Americana: A Popular Dictionary of Arts, Sciences, Literature, History, Politics and Biography. 1st edn. Ed. Francis Lieber. 13 vols. Philadelphia: Carey *et al.*, 1829–33.

Encyclopaedia Britannica. 7th edn. 21 vols. Ed. Macvey Napier. Edinburgh: Black, 1842.

Dictionnaire de la conversation et de la lecture. 52 vols. Paris: Belin-Mandar, 1832–9. Further editions through 1878.

Encyclopédie des gens du monde, répertoire universel des sciences, des lettres et des arts. 22 vols. Paris: Treuttel and Würtz, 1833–44.

Penny Cyclopaedia of the Society for the Diffusion of Useful Knowledge. 27 vols. London: Knight, 1833–43.

Encyclopédie nouvelle [originally *Encyclopédie pittoresque à deux sous*]. Ed. Pierre Leroux and Jean Reynaud. 8 vols. Paris: 1834–42.

Encyclopédie du dix-neuvième siècle: Répertoire universel des sciences, des lettres et des arts. 26 vols. Paris: Bureau de l'Encyclopédie du XIXe siècle, 1838–53.

[*Pierer's Universal-Lexikon*]. 2nd edn. *Universal-Lexikon der Gegenwart und Vergangenheit oder neueste encyclopädisches Wörterbuch der Wissenschaften, Künste und Gewerbe.* 36 vols. Altenburg: Pierer, 1840–8.

[*Meyer's Konversations-Lexikon*]. "oth" edn. [*Wunder-Meyer*]. *Das Grosse Conversations-Lexicon für die gebildeten Stände.* 46 vols. Hildburghausen: Bibliographisches Institut, 1840–53. Further editions through 1986, some highlighted below.

Encyclopaedia Britannica. 8th edn. 22 vols. Ed. Thomas Stewart Traill. Edinburgh: Black, 1853–60.

[*Grosse Brockhaus*]. 9th edn. *Allgemeine deutsche Real-Encyklopädie für die gebildeten Stände: Conversations-Lexikon.* 15 vols. Leipzig: Brockhaus, 1843–8.

[*Grosse Herder*]. 1st edn. *Herders Conversations-Lexikon.* 5 vols. Freiburg: Herder, 1854–7. Further editions through 1968.

English Cyclopaedia. 22 vols. London: Bradbury and Evans, 1854–62. Second edition through 1873.

Larousse, Pierre. *Nouveau Dictionnaire de la langue française.* Paris: Larousse and Boyer, 1856.

[*Meyer's Konversations-Lexikon*]. 1st edn. *Neues Conversations-Lexikon für alle Stände.* 15 vols. Hildburghausen: Bibliographisches Institut, 1857–60.

Larousse, Pierre, ed. *Grand Dictionnaire universel du XIXᵉ siècle.* 15 vols. Paris: [Larousse], 1866–76.

Chambers's Encyclopaedia. 1st edn. 10 vols. London: Chambers, 1868. Further editions through 1973.

Johnson's New Universal Cyclopaedia (later *Johnson's Universal Cyclopaedia*). Ed. Frederick A. P. Barnard and Arnold Guyot. 4 vols. New York: Johnson, 1875–7. Further editions through 1899.

[*Grosse Brockhaus*]. 12th edn. *Conversations-Lexikon: Allgemeine deutsche Real-Encyklopädie*. 15 vols. Leipzig: Brockhaus, 1875–9.

Encyclopaedia Britannica. 9th edn. 25 vols. Ed. Thomas Spencer Baynes and W. Robertson Smith. Edinburgh: Black, 1875–89.

La Grande Encyclopédie: Inventaire raisonné des sciences, des lettres et des arts. 31 vols. Paris: Lamirault, 1885–1902.

Enciklopedičeskij slovar'. 86 vols. St. Petersburg: Efron, 1890–1907.

Nouveau Larousse illustré. Ed. Claude Augé. 7 vols. Paris: Larousse, 1897–1904.

[*Encyclopaedia Britannica*]. 10th edn. *The New Volumes*. 11 vols. London: Black, 1902–3.

New International Encyclopaedia. 17 vols. New York: Dodd, Mead, and Co., 1902–4. Further editions through 1935.

Encyclopedia Americana. Ed. Frederick Converse Beach. 16 vols. New York: Americana, 1903–4. Further editions through 2006.

Nelson's Encyclopaedia (later *Nelson's Perpetual Loose-Leaf Encyclopaedia*, etc.). 23 vols. London: Nelson, 1905. Further editions through 1940.

Funk and Wagnalls Standard Encyclopedia (later *Funk and Wagnalls New Standard Encyclopedia*, etc.). 25 vols. New York: Funk and Wagnalls, 1912. Further editions through 1996.

Petit Larousse illustré. Paris: Larousse, 1905. Further editions through the present.

[*Espasa*]. *Enciclopedia universal ilustrada europeo-americana*. 72 vols. Madrid: Espasa *et al.*, 1908–30.

Encyclopaedia Britannica. 11th edn. Ed. Hugh Chisholm. 29 vols. Cambridge: Cambridge University Press, 1910–11.

[*World Book*]. *The World Book: Organized Knowledge in Story and Picture*. Ed. M. V. O'Shea. 8 vols. Chicago: World Book, 1918. Further editions through the present.

[*Great Soviet Encyclopedia*]. *Bolshaia sovetskaia entsiklopediia*. 1st edn. 65 vols. Moscow: Sovetskaia Entsiklopediia, 1926–47. Further editions through 1978, one highlighted below.

Der kleine Herder: Nachschlagebuch über alles für alle. Freiburg: Herder, 1925. Further editions through 1933.

[*Grosse Brockhaus*]. 15th edn. *Der grosse Brockhaus: Handbuch des Wissens*. 20 vols. Leipzig: Brockhaus, 1928–35.

Encyclopaedia Britannica. 13th edn. 3 vols. London: Encyclopaedia Britannica, 1926.

Compton's Pictured Encyclopedia (later *Compton's Encyclopedia*, etc.). 8 vols. New York: Compton's, 1922. Further editions through 2008.

Australian Encyclopaedia. 2 vols. Sydney: Angus and Robertson, 1925–6. Further editions through 1996.

Encyclopaedia Britannica. 14th edn. Ed. James Louis Garvin. 24 vols. London: Encyclopaedia Britannica, 1929.

Britannica Junior. 12 vols. New York: Encyclopaedia Britannica, 1934. Further editions through 1996.

Enciclopedia italiana. Ed. Giovanni Gentile and Calogero Tumminelli. 36 vols. Rome: Treccani, 1929–39.

[*Grosse Herder*]. 4th edn. *Der grosse Herder: Nachschlagewerk für Wissen und Leben*. 12 vols. Freiburg: Herder, 1931–5.

The Columbia Encyclopedia. 1st edn. Ed. Clarke F. Ansley. Morningside Heights: Columbia University Press, 1935.

Encyclopédie française. 20 vols. Paris: 1935–66.

[*Great Soviet Encyclopedia*]. *Bolshaia sovetskaia entsiklopediia*. 2nd edn. 53 vols. Moscow: Bolshaia Sovetskaia Entsiklopediia, 1949–58.

Collier's Encyclopedia. 20 volumes. New York: Collier and Son, 1950.

[*Grosse Brockhaus*]. 16th edn. *Der grosse Brockhaus*. 14 vols. Wiesbaden: Brockhaus, 1952–63.

[*Grosse Brockhaus*]. 17th edn. *Brockhaus Enzyklopädie*. 20 vols. Wiesbaden: Brockhaus, 1966–74.

Merit Students Encyclopedia. 20 vols. New York: Cromwell-Collier, 1967. Further editions through 1991.

Encyclopaedia universalis. 1st edn. Ed. Claude Grégory. 20 vols. Paris: Encyclopaedia Universalis France, 1970–5. Further editions through 2012.

[*Meyer's Konversations-Lexikon*]. 9th edn. *Meyers enzyklopädisches Lexikon*. 25 vols. Mannheim: Bibliographisches Institut, 1971–9.

New Encyclopaedia Britannica. 30 vols. Chicago: Encyclopaedia Britannica, 1974.

[*Grosse Brockhaus*]. 18th edn. *Der grosse Brockhaus*. 12 vols. Wiesbaden: Brockhaus, 1977–81.

Academic American Encyclopedia. 21 vols. Princeton: Arête, 1980. Further editions through 1998.

[*Grosse Brockhaus*]. 19th edn. *Brockhaus Enzyklopädie*. 25 vols. Mannheim: Brockhaus, 1986–94.

[*Grosse Brockhaus*]. 21st edn. *Brockhaus Enzyklopädie*. 30 vols. Mannheim: Bibliographisches Institut and Brockhaus, 2005–6.

Acknowledgments

As a child, I was, if not fascinated by encyclopedias, then at least interested in them. Besides using my parents' old set of the *Encyclopaedia Britannica* for browsing, writing reports, and looking for information, I was bemused by mother's use of the encyclopedia to press and keep flowers, and delighted by my grandmother's habit of storing money in her own edition of the *Britannica* – as she did in other books too. I mention these experiences as a way of paying tribute to my parents and relatives for giving me all that they did in my childhood – and not just an encyclopedia.

My academic interest in encyclopedias is in large measure due to the influence of my former colleague at the University of Cincinnati, Frank Kafker. Frank introduced himself to me when I was hired at the University of Cincinnati, and quickly adopted me as a collaborator on projects related to encyclopedias. Without his guidance and mentoring, I am not sure I would have succeeded as a researcher or academic. In our two decades of collaboration, I developed ever greater affection and respect for him. Although he did not have the chance to read more than a small part of this book, I would like to acknowledge him here as a friend and mentor.

Otherwise, I am grateful to fellow scholars for making suggestions and corrections concerning my research. Some did so anonymously when I submitted articles for publication. Others did so at conferences. Of particular benefit to me were four: "From Text to Publication," in Nancy in June 2012; "Translation and Transfer of Knowledge in Encyclopedic Compilations," in Los Angeles in April 2013; "Shaping the Sciences of the Ancient World," in Paris in June 2013; and the conference for the Edition Numérique Collaborative et Critique de l'*Encyclopédie* ("Collaborative, Critical, Digital Edition of the *Encyclopédie*") in Marseille in October 2015. I would like to thank the organizers for inviting me, and the participants for sharing their ideas with me.

John Considine and Kathleen Doig were kind enough to read the whole manuscript – then considerably longer – before publication. I am deeply grateful to them for their encouragement and detailed criticism. In addition, a handful of colleagues and friends read and commented on specific chapters: David Eick, Linn Holmberg, Marie Leca-Tsiomis, Liz Liebman, Joseph Reagle, Rose Roberto, and Stéphane Schmitt. I thank them all for finding time to give me feedback. The book is better for their suggestions, though none of them should be held responsible for what I have written.

The Charles Phelps Taft Memorial Fund at the University of Cincinnati has been generous in its support of my research on this project. Numerous librarians in the United States and Europe went out of their way to assist with my work and arrange for illustrations, but I am particularly grateful to the office of inter-library loans at the University of Cincinnati.

Finally, I would like to thank my wife Olimpia and daughter Lee – with profound love – for their support through the project. Among other acts of selflessness, they helped me carry a nearly complete set of the *Nouveau Larousse illustré* (1897–1904) away from a flea market in a hot French village in 2015. Lee would have preferred that I write an encyclopedia instead of a book about encyclopedias, but I hope that she and her mother will be proud of the outcome.

Introduction

This book is a history of the European encyclopedia, an alphabetical book of knowledge that took shape in the seventeenth century. For three centuries afterward, printed encyclopedias in the European tradition were an element of culture and peoples' lives, initially just among Europe's educated elite but ultimately through much of the literate world. In the late nineteenth century, a blurb from a physician and contributor to *Johnson's New Universal Cyclopaedia* (1875–7) proclaimed *Johnson's* the best book for families short of the Bible.[1] As gigantic books, encyclopedias invited hyperbole, and one should be skeptical about testimonials, especially from contributors. Still, the notion that encyclopedias, by this time, stood at the forefront of books is corroborated elsewhere. In 1899, for example, a survey by a German newspaper identified the *Konversations-Lexikon*, or conversational dictionary – a kind of German encyclopedia – as the most influential book of the preceding century, ahead of the Bible and the naturalist Charles Darwin's writings.[2] By the mid twentieth century, encyclopedias were present in a large percentage of households in the rich world. Many were little used, but it would be tendentious to deny that they often informed and occasionally educated.

Living as we do in an age in which information is available for nearly effortless access, we tend to underestimate the importance of the ponderous precursors to our present devices and systems for finding information. If a link to the internet can now fulfill all the functions of a library in the eyes of some people, it is not unreasonable to imagine, in accordance with the 1759 edition of Louis Moréri's *Grand Dictionaire historique* (1674), that there were once "people for whom the Moréri takes the place of everything."[3]

---

[1] "Testimonials," 13.
[2] Kochanowska-Nieborak, "Konversationslexika," 183.
[3] "… des personnes à qui le Moréri tient lieu de tout." Moréri, *Grand Dictionnaire*, new edn., 1: iii.

The European encyclopedia, as conceived here, is approaching extinction. The age of alphabetical encyclopedias is almost entirely over, as is the age of encyclopedias printed on paper. Still, they enjoy an afterlife in electronic encyclopedias. At a minimum, electronic encyclopedias have borrowed from their content. More subtly, the organizing devices of the European encyclopedia – the keyword, the article, and the cross-reference, above all – were taken up by electronic encyclopedias. In fact, nearly all my book's themes remain pertinent to electronic encyclopedias. Questions of authorship, copyright, and economics, for example, are central to today's debates about Wikipedia. Can an encyclopedia be written without control by experts? Is it plagiarism to quote from Wikipedia without bothering to cite it? Does an accurate, up-to-date encyclopedia necessarily cost money? Familiarity with the questions' background can help us come up with answers.

Beyond this intrusion of the past on our own times, the European encyclopedia has a story worth telling. Viewed against the backdrop of all written history, it corresponds to a phase of an age-old endeavor: encyclopedism, or the recording of knowledge. The story of this endeavor comes close to forming a history of literate civilization itself, within which my episode covers a heyday. At the same time, while a tension between dreams and realities pervades the history of encyclopedism, it is especially fascinating in the case of the European encyclopedia, which was both a commodity and a storehouse of knowledge. This tension at the heart of the European encyclopedia could manifest itself variously. Sometimes it surfaced in the same person, as in the hard-nosed but utopian Charles-Joseph Panckoucke, the editor and publisher of the *Encyclopédie méthodique* (1782–1832).[4] At other times it was a tension between associates – for example, between the businessmen Horace Hooper, a visionary, and Walter Jackson, a pragmatist, who together ran the *Encyclopaedia Britannica* around 1900.[5] Whether for good or for ill, it was a motor for creativity.

The European Encyclopedia Defined

The European encyclopedia, as understood here, was never a single encyclopedia suitable for all of Europe. A mid-eighteenth-century supplement pronounced Moréri's *Grand Dictionaire* a book "of all nations," a claim

---

[4] Loveland, "Why Encyclopedias Got Bigger," 243.
[5] Kogan, *Great EB*, 146, 206–7; Kruse, "Story," 257.

reflecting its adaptation into English, German, Dutch, and Spanish.[6] Yet despite cascades of translation and imitation across borders, the localism remarked on by an Italian observer in 1771 never disappeared: "Each nation has its own particular encyclopedia because each nation has its own language, has its own ideas, has its own maxims, has its own arts, has … its own prejudices …. a European encyclopedia … is impossible."[7] Instances of such localism will be noted throughout this book.

Nor was the European encyclopedia necessarily an encyclopedia published in Europe, though before the twentieth century the majority were. Rather, it was an encyclopedia growing out of a European tradition in the late seventeenth and early eighteenth centuries, primarily in Britain, France, and the German states – that is, in western or even northwestern Europe. Shortly after its inception, the European encyclopedia took root in European colonies such as New England and New Spain (later Mexico). Then, in the eighteenth and early nineteenth centuries, it began to be adapted and translated for use on the peripheries of Europe and in other places, charting a course toward internationalization.[8]

It is probably futile to try to define what an encyclopedia is with much precision. A better approach is to recognize that encyclopedias have always existed on a continuum with other works of reference, notably dictionaries, and that they are seen as encyclopedias because of their relationship to models and prototypes.

Here I define the European encyclopedia loosely as having two characteristics, neither one distinguishable with perfect clarity. First, it was alphabetical – though my book brings in non-alphabetical works when they seem relevant. Second, it covered knowledge on a grand scale. Indeed, certain encyclopedists claimed to have treated all knowledge. Beyond the megalomania and self-promotion underpinning such claims, conceptions of what knowledge was differed with historical context. The expected scope of an encyclopedia was nonetheless stable from the end of the eighteenth century to the end of the twentieth. This was the period of what I will be calling the modern encyclopedia. Modern encyclopedias varied considerably – in size, most conspicuously – but they were distinctive in

---

[6] *Supplément au Dictionnaire*, 1: *2r. For the foreign-language adaptations see Miller, "Louis Moréri's *Grand Dictionnaire*," 49–50.

[7] "Ogni nazione ha la sua particolare enciclopedia perché ogni nazione ha il suo linguaggio, ha le sue idee, ha le sue massime, ha le sue arti, ha … i suoi pregiudizi; ed in consequenza che un'enciclopedia europea … è impossibile." Abbattista, "Folie," 428.

[8] See for example Denny and Mitchell, "Russian Translations"; Proust, "Encyclopédie," 414–15; Proust, "De quelques dictionnaires"; Herren and Prodöhl, "Kapern," 48–9.

their coverage relative to preceding and following works. Specifically, they treated the arts and sciences as well as places, events, and individuals, but not the myriad details of practical know-how and popular culture, two aspects of coverage that only came into their own with Wikipedia.

Before 1750, in contrast, some alphabetical works were devoted to the arts and the sciences, while others were devoted to history and geography, or narrower fields such as chemistry or law. Only a handful of such proto-encyclopedias came close to the coverage of the modern encyclopedia, chief among them the so-called dictionary of the arts and sciences, the universal dictionary, and the historical dictionary. As their generic names indicate, these works were not called encyclopedias. Instead, they were assimilated to the genre of the dictionary or lexicon, as shown below in Chapter 1. Regardless of their titles and lack of generality, they are crucial for understanding the modern European encyclopedia. For this reason, they play a big role in the following chapters.

Beginning with such seventeenth-century proto-encyclopedias, my book is thus devoted to an originally and markedly European phenomenon that lasted around 300 years. These limitations, geographical and temporal, reflect my conviction that the tradition of encyclopedia-making that developed in Europe was different from other traditions of encyclopedism. Such traditions were multiple, for many cultures have aspired toward a mastery of knowledge. Since the invention of writing some 6,000 years ago, these aspirations have given rise to texts summarizing knowledge. Among them were wide-ranging Sumerian lists from around 2500 BC and canonical religious books such as the Vedas and the Bible. All of these works have been characterized as encyclopedias.[9] As written texts proliferated in Greek and Roman antiquity, another form of encyclopedism developed to help make sense of them. Like annotation and bibliography, this was a distinctively secondary kind of literature, that is, one superposed on an established framework of text-making.[10] Likewise, during the medieval period, European, Arabic, and Chinese culture all engendered works posthumously labeled encyclopedias.

With regard to geography, a distinction between traditions of encyclopedism is easy to draw, but it deserves defense and nuance. Encyclopedism in China dates back to the third century AD, and encyclopedism in India

---

[9] See for example Michel and Herren, "Unvorgreifliche Gedanken," 14; McArthur, *Worlds*, 37. On encyclopedism see also Becq, *Encyclopédisme*; Schaer, *Tous les savoirs*.
[10] König and Woolf, "Encyclopaedism," 31–2.

to perhaps a thousand years earlier.[11] Interactions with European encyclopedism were insignificant, however, before the nineteenth century in India and the twentieth in China. Chinese *leishu*, or "categorized books," are often assimilated to the European encyclopedia, but the comparison points to differences as well as similarities. Whether organized thematically or by rhymes or calligraphic strokes, *leishu* were collections of quotations. They resembled the so-called "florilegium," or book of extracts, a robust genre in Europe through the time of the Renaissance, but they differed from the European encyclopedias under scrutiny here, in which borrowed material was more regularly adapted.[12] Before 1900, moreover, though China had other forms of encyclopedism – some concerned with domestic and everyday life – many Chinese encyclopedic works were written to help candidates pass tests leading to jobs as civil servants.[13] A comparable specificity of purpose is hard to find for European encyclopedias.

The case of Arabic encyclopedism is more ambiguous.[14] Arabic scholarship flourished in the medieval period and was sometimes European, since the Iberian peninsula was one of its centers. In part as a relay to Greek antiquity, it exerted a huge influence on scholars writing in Latin and thus on Latin encyclopedic works. In Richard McKeon's abstract formulation, the medieval encounter between the scientific, principle-driven Arabic "encyclopedia" and the discipline-based Latin "encyclopedia" pushed European intellectual culture toward modern science.[15] Still, it is unclear if the term "encyclopedia" applies to medieval Arabic works, or at least to the most prestigious ones, the so-called classifications of the sciences. As this modern name indicates, they were focused on the structure of knowledge, not knowledge itself. Co-existing with them was the more encyclopedia-like *adab* – a term originally meaning something like "etiquette" or "decency." Mostly by administrative secretaries, *adab* communicated shallow knowledge on a wide range of subjects to fellow administrators and to anyone aspiring to cultivation. Their impact on European encyclopedism was undoubtedly minor. In any event, the great age of Arabic encyclopedism

---

[11] On Indian encyclopedism see Filliozat, "Encyclopédies." On Chinese encyclopedism see Bauer, "Encyclopaedia"; Bretelle-Establet and Chemla, *Qu'était-ce qu'écrire une encyclopédie?*; Diény, "Encyclopédies."

[12] Blair, "Florilège," 185–97; Drège, "Des ouvrages," 19–20; Bauer, "Encyclopaedia," 668.

[13] Zurndorfer, "Passion," 505–27; Elman, "Collecting," 131–53; Bauer, "Encyclopaedia," 666, 677–8, 690.

[14] On Arabic encyclopedism see Biesterfeldt, "Medieval Arabic Encyclopedias," 77–98; Chapoutot-Remadi, "Encyclopédie"; Fierro, "Saber"; Pellat, "Encyclopédies."

[15] McKeon, "Organization," 183–6.

was long past by the time the European encyclopedia developed in the seventeenth century.

Soon after that time, European encyclopedism became an item of export, a trend that accelerated in the nineteenth and twentieth centuries. By the mid twentieth century, one can speak of global encyclopedism. For this reason, my account includes European-inspired encyclopedias in other countries, though Europe and its former colonies retain a dominant role. Even within Europe, I return again and again to encyclopedias in English, French, and German. These encyclopedias were the most original and influential in all of Europe, the models and sources for other encyclopedias. In part, nonetheless, my emphasis corresponds to my linguistic competence, or rather, its limits. A broader scope might be preferable, but it is worthwhile integrating scholarship on English-, French-, and German-language encyclopedias – as I do here, with a sprinkling of material from other languages – since most histories of encyclopedias remain bound to exclusive national and linguistic traditions.

Chronologically speaking, I have chosen the mid seventeenth century for the start of my study. Like histories of European or "western" civilization, most histories of encyclopedias begin with Greek and Roman antiquity and go on to lavish attention on the Middle Ages if not also the Renaissance. In this narrative, the first encyclopedia is often a title from the first century AD, Pliny the Elder's *Naturalis historia*, a vast survey of knowledge. If nothing else, the *Naturalis historia* was a source for encyclopedias through the end of the eighteenth century. Other candidates for ancient encyclopedias are known largely in fragments.[16] Then come medieval "encyclopedias," among which figure prominently Isidore of Seville's *Origines seu etymologiae* (*Origins or Etymologies*), from the seventh century, and Vincent of Beauvais's *Speculum maius* (*Great Mirror*), from the thirteenth.[17] All these texts can be considered as embodying encyclopedism – as can many others from the ancient and medieval world – but were they encyclopedias? Crucially, little indicates that contemporaries saw them as forming a genre, let alone one approximating that of the encyclopedia.[18]

Furthermore, while continuities can be found between encyclopedic works from before 1650 and those that came after, the differences are striking.

---

[16] Naas, "*Histoire*"; Schmitt and Loveland, "Scientific Knowledge," 339; Doody, *Pliny's Encyclopedia*, 1–6, 51–8. On ancient "encyclopedias" see also Grimal, "Encyclopédies"; König and Woolf, "Encyclopaedism."

[17] On medieval "encyclopedias" see Meier, "Grundzüge," 467–92; Beyer, "Encyclopédies," 9–40; Draelants, "Siècle."

[18] Doody, *Pliny's Encyclopedia*, 12–13, 40–58; Draelants, "Siècle," 104–6.

First, alphabetical order only became widespread as the primary order for encyclopedic works in the late seventeenth century.[19] Second, encyclopedic works in Latin declined in the seventeenth century, while those in living languages proliferated, a tendency corresponding to a broadening readership. Third, the market for encyclopedias took off in the second half of the seventeenth century. Above all, Moréri's *Grand Dictionaire* (1674) boasted nine editions or reprints by 1700.[20] Indeed, the *Grand Dictionaire* is sometimes seen as having triggered the vogue for alphabetical encyclopedias.[21] Fourth, with the exception of Pliny's *Naturalis historia*, general encyclopedic works from before 1650 had little direct influence on those published afterward, though they did establish tools for making texts consultable.[22] By contrast, a tradition of trans-European encyclopedia-making emerged in the late seventeenth century, characterized by exchanges of ideas and texts.

Organization and Methodology

Unlike many histories of encyclopedias, this book is not organized around historical periods. Among large-scale histories, Robert Collison's *Encyclopaedias* (1964) exemplifies this approach.[23] In Collison's book and others, a chronological framework makes for orderliness and lends itself to a comprehensive survey of titles. It can also lead to choppiness and a lack of focus, however. Here I aim for thematic coherence without providing a chronicle of titles or milestones. Instead of advancing from epoch to epoch, I will analyze the European encyclopedia from a variety of perspectives corresponding to my chapters. Only within chapters do I resort, intermittently, to chronological or geographical order. While this arrangement reduces zigzagging between different themes – a pitfall of chronological order – it risks creating its own zigzags by bringing together material from different places and times. The risk is outweighed, in my judgment, by the gain in comparative knowledge, but to minimize confusion, I reidentify encyclopedias when it seems necessary, resupplying their dates and, at times, other attributes. In addition, in the front matter, I have provided a chronological list of the encyclopedias most often mentioned here.

---

[19] Headrick, *When Information Came of Age*, 160–7; Yeo, "Encyclopedism," 670.
[20] Miller, "Louis Moréri's *Grand Dictionnaire*," 13.
[21] See for example Sullivan, "Circumscribing Knowledge," 319.
[22] On the lack of influence of medieval encyclopedic works see for example Twomey, "Inventing," 75–92. On tools for consulting developed in the Middle Ages see Draelants, "Siècle," 84; Blair, *Too Much*, 33–4, 88–9.
[23] Large-scale chronological histories of encyclopedias include Collison, *Encyclopaedias*; Rey, *Miroirs*, 87–234; Wendt, *Idee*.

In studying encyclopedias in three languages over more than three centuries, I have chosen to privilege synthesis and breadth. In other words, while my research leads to generalizations about linguistic traditions and change over time, it glosses over details. In fact, every encyclopedia was published in a particular time and place, and through the early twentieth century, they were almost all sold in a limited region. In addition, the switch to publication in Europe's vernaculars corresponded to a geographical narrowing of markets and thus to a certain localism. Unlike a Latin encyclopedic work, an encyclopedia in Dutch could not be expected to sell in Britain or Italy. Even as late as 1900, most contributors to an encyclopedia lived close to the region where it was published, which further encouraged local biases in coverage. On a trivial level, nearly every encyclopedia devoted extra space to the geography of the area where it was published. At one extreme, the article on Spain in the *Enciclopedia universal ilustrada europeo-americana* (1908–30) – nicknamed the *Espasa* after its publisher – took up a whole volume. Still, the localism of encyclopedias should not be exaggerated. From the seventeenth century onward, encyclopedists used other encyclopedias as sources, and not just encyclopedias from neighboring areas. Publishers, for their part, were familiar with encyclopedias from other regions and countries, which they regularly opted to translate or adapt.

My book also stresses continuity in the history of encyclopedias. In some ways, it makes little sense to compare an encyclopedia from 1970, say, with one from 1820. Among other things, book-making had changed, the market for encyclopedias had grown and democratized, and illustrations had become a normal part of any encyclopedia. Yet commonalities can be found between the old and the new. These are not so much on the pages of encyclopedias themselves, though it is easy to find articles that were copied or paraphrased from articles published more than fifty years earlier. Rather, many of the tasks facing encyclopedists in 1970 were still the same ones faced by encyclopedists in 1820. Prominent among them were the tasks of ordering material for alphabetical presentation, creating authoritative articles, and appealing to non-specialists. Such commonalities of purpose motivate my comparisons among encyclopedias of different periods.

To appreciate my comparative approach, consider, for instance, the question of whether encyclopedias were agents of change and liberation or whether they were stockpiles of old information, rendered all the more conservative by their support for established ideologies such as nationalism and communism. On the one hand, a first lesson of any overview is that the question requires more than a simple answer. As shown below in Chapter 5, it would be wrong to imagine that encyclopedias were inherently liberating. Nor, as the example of Denis Diderot and Jean Le Rond D'Alembert's anti-religious *Encyclopédie* (1751–72) proves, were they always orthodox or conservative. Indeed, since the very categories of the liberating and conservative are tied to our ideas of what ought to change, it would be better to recognize that encyclopedias all had a political aspect but that these varied widely, even if nationalism was a recurring element.

On the other hand, it is striking that the best examples of encyclopedias anticipating future knowledge come from the century from 1750 to 1850. In no encyclopedia was every article or more than a smattering of articles ahead of the times, but during this period – as noted below in Chapter 2 – scholars occasionally used encyclopedias to present or explore developing knowledge. In this sense, the period witnessed a distinctive convergence between encyclopedias and scholarly interests.

As this example indicates, my survey is meant to point to trends in the history of encyclopedias, some of them spanning centuries and linguistic boundaries. Only by assigning chronology a subordinate role can I hope to do them justice.

The chapters below, then, are thematically defined. They are both independent and intertwined. Chapter 1 analyzes kinds of encyclopedias, including varieties of proto-encyclopedias as well as such enduring variants as the linguistically oriented encyclopedic dictionary. Chapter 2 deals with the contents of encyclopedias from an abstract point of view – specifically, with respect to the notions of progress, practicality, objectivity, and nationalism. Chapters 3 to 6 deal with topics related to encyclopedias' contents as well: Chapter 3 with their size and economic viability, Chapter 4 with their preparation by authors and editors, Chapter 5 with their organization, and Chapter 6 with illustrations. The following three chapters then consider encyclopedias from a social point of view, reflecting on the people and institutions around them. Chapter 7 thus examines authorship in relation to encyclopedias; Chapter 8 encyclopedia-publishers and their ways of publishing; and Chapter 9 how people read and made use of encyclopedias. Chapter 10 is an epilogue, on the rise of electronic encyclopedias in the late twentieth century and afterward.

Portions of several chapters could have been moved to a different one. Chapter 3, for example, covers the price of encyclopedias, a topic related to both their economic situation – the focus of the chapter – and their owners and users, the subject of Chapter 9. Chapter 10 treats promotional discourse in printed encyclopedias as well as in Wikipedia, though the subject also relates to my examination of objectivity in Chapter 3. In such instances, I recapitulate material when it is once again pertinent.

My research here is indebted to the fields of intellectual history and the history of the book. Encyclopedias have long been studied from the perspective of intellectual history, namely as vessels for knowledge and ideas. True to this inspiration, I devote much of the book to what is contained in encyclopedias. It would be rash to assume that encyclopedias simply reflected what was known at the time they were published. Beyond the idiosyncrasies of compilers and editorial staffs, the knowledge they offered could be dated or up-to-date, established or speculative, popularized or scholarly, and otherwise distinctive. Regardless, it would be a poor history of encyclopedias that neglected their content, particularly in its relation to contemporary knowledge and discourse.

At the same time, drawing inspiration from historians of the book, I see encyclopedias as objects that not only record knowledge but are also compiled, manufactured, advertised, bought, consulted, ignored, and so on. In short, encyclopedias take their place in a network of people and processes. This view of encyclopedias tempers my debts to intellectual history. In particular, unlike many intellectual histories of encyclopedias, mine places more emphasis on the practicalities of encyclopedia-making than on philosophical ideals, whether latent in the etymology of the word "encyclopedia" or spelled out in prefaces or manifestos. No doubt such philosophical ideals merit attention, especially when formulated by thinkers as famous as Gottfried Leibniz, Samuel Coleridge, or H. G. Wells. Still, their impact on actually published encyclopedias was less than one would guess from how much they are studied. In Diderot and D'Alembert's *Encyclopédie*, for example, a handful of philosophical and programmatic texts have been studied exhaustively, illuminating the thinking of the two editors but shedding little light on the encyclopedia as a whole or the experience of using it.

In a perfect world, my book would be premised on a reading of all European-style encyclopedias from the late seventeenth century onward, as well as their advertisements, the correspondence of their authors, the archives of encyclopedia-publishers, and citations of encyclopedias in reviews and other texts. The corpus could even be broadened to include, say, texts influenced by encyclopedias or texts into which encyclopedias were copied or paraphrased. Such a mastery of available resources is impossible, unfortunately.

First, the amount of material is too large to assimilate. Since 1650, there have been hundreds of encyclopedias and thousands of editions of them, too many to study in a meaningful way. Already toward 1700, observers were astounded at the number being published, though they lumped together encyclopedias, dictionaries, and more specialized works of reference.[24] From then on, the perception that an "age of encyclopedias" was under way resurfaced intermittently through the twentieth century. As late as 1989, for example, the *New York Times* evoked a "boom" for encyclopedias in the United States.[25] Indeed, from 1800 onward, it is difficult to find a year in which an encyclopedia was not being published.

For pre-modern times especially, scholars have correlated the production of encyclopedic works with the state of a civilization, whether with its confidence and certainty, its entry into crisis, its exit from a creative period, or its decline.[26] Beyond the difficulty of judging the state of a civilization, the near ubiquity of encyclopedias in the years after 1800 suggests that any such correlations had become weak by this time. In fact, though encyclopedias were advertised as being necessitated by recent happenings and changing knowledge, and though publishers desisted from launching them in the direst of times, they were published for reasons that went beyond those of contemporary cultural and political circumstances.

Second, and more subtly, the boundaries between encyclopedias and non-encyclopedias are poorly defined – and always have been. Here, for the most part, I will restrict the term "encyclopedia" to alphabetically arranged works with a certain generality and with explanatory articles on non-linguistic topics. For works with similar contents that are not necessarily alphabetical, I will use the expression "encyclopedic work."

Necessary as they are as a point of departure, these definitions are inadequate for delimiting the class of "encyclopedias" with any exactness. As noted above, it is difficult to pinpoint the requisite generality for an encyclopedia. It would be counter-productive, moreover, to exclude non-alphabetical encyclopedic works such as the *Encyclopédie méthodique* (1782–1832) and the *Encyclopaedia Metropolitana* (1817–45) from scrutiny here, since they were frequently alphabetical beneath a thematic framework, and since they competed with alphabetical encyclopedias. Once some non-alphabetical works are included, however, it becomes harder to rationalize excluding any work of reference. Studying works of reference

---

[24] Considine, *Academy Dictionaries*, 1–2.
[25] *New York Times*, May 28, 1989: F15.
[26] See for example Rey, *Miroirs*, 160–1, 169; Zucker, *Encyclopédire*, 16; Michel and Herren, "Unvorgreifliche Gedanken," 20; Gómez Aranda, "Enciclopedias," 107; Gluck, "Fine Folly," 243; Godin, "Des encyclopédies," 33.

as a group could be productive and worthwhile, as it already has been for other researchers.[27] I have chosen instead, though, to use the three criteria of general scope, significant reliance on alphabetical order, and direct competition with alphabetical encyclopedias to open my narrative to some non-alphabetical works without accepting all of them.

Nor is the distinction between dictionaries and encyclopedias any clearer than those between explanation and definition or between linguistic and non-linguistic topics. In fact, dictionaries and encyclopedias have always existed on a continuum. Brief works of reference, with their minimal entries and haphazard coverage, particularly strain the limits of any definition of an encyclopedia. In the end, given the indeterminacy of the potential field of encyclopedias, I have chosen which works to focus on partly in response to existing scholarship on the subject. As a result, my book overemphasizes big encyclopedias relative to small ones, though the big ones probably influenced the small ones more than vice versa.[28] To a degree, then, I will be studying encyclopedias that have already been studied as such – and for precisely this reason. At the same time, however, my decisions about which encyclopedias to study, and in what proportions, are meant to shift the way the story of encyclopedias is told, if only a little.

To cope with the size of my corpus of encyclopedias and related works, I have made as much use as possible of scholarly literature. Doing so created a bias toward the period before 1800. In view of my research and specialization, I myself am more familiar with eighteenth-century British and French encyclopedias than with any others. Regardless of my own bias, less has been written on nineteenth- than eighteenth-century encyclopedias, while the secondary literature on twentieth-century encyclopedias is smaller still. Ironically, more has been written about "encyclopedias" in a period in which their very existence is doubtful – that is, the Middle Ages – than about the abundance of examples from the nineteenth and twentieth centuries. Worse still, even research on eighteenth-century encyclopedias remains concentrated on a single unusual work, Diderot and D'Alembert's *Encyclopédie*, though scholarly interest has broadened since the publication of Frank Kafker's *Notable Encyclopedias of the Seventeenth and Eighteenth Centuries* (1981).

For both of these reasons, my book is more thorough regarding earlier than later periods. Indeed, the disparity is worse when we recall the

---

[27] See for example Blair, *Too Much*; Headrick, *When Information Came of Age*; Lynch, *You Could Look It Up*; McArthur, *Worlds*.
[28] Hass, *Grosse Lexika*, 6.

growing number of encyclopedias per century. I hope, nonetheless, to have encouraged further scholarship on the nineteenth and twentieth centuries. Even if the majority of twentieth-century encyclopedias were formulaic commodities rather than intellectual monuments, they still deserve scholarly attention as such.

A second reaction on my part to the size of my topic has been to concentrate my primary research on foregrounded texts – encyclopedias' prefaces, reviews, advertisements, and so on – and to delve into the main text of encyclopedias only occasionally. This strategy, though common, has limitations. Prefaces can be philosophical and disconnected from what follows. Like advertisements, they often mislead or exaggerate. Considered in light of their goals, though, prefaces and advertisements can be informative, especially when contrasted with texts representing different perspectives and purposes.

My third means of dealing with the bulk of encyclopedias has been quantification. Here and there, I have resorted to numerical measurements – whether of articles' lengths, contributors' professions, or the density of cross-references. For the most part, I use sampling rather than exhaustive enumeration. Besides acting as a control on claims from prefaces and advertisements, quantitative analysis provides insight into aspects of encyclopedias that are not usually noticed. In my sampling, I have not drawn on formal statistical techniques. Because the character of an encyclopedia can vary from volume to volume as policies change, I have chosen samples away from a work's beginning or end. The middle pages are likelier than the first or the last ones to represent the whole work, but my extrapolations can still only be seen as indicative. In any event, this book should not be taken as an embodiment of the "digital humanities," in which computers are used to analyze texts. This approach holds promise for the study of encyclopedias, since it allows quantification to be extended beyond sampling. For the moment, however, computers' ability to recognize and interpret patterns of text remains limited, and the full text of many encyclopedias cannot be searched electronically. Accordingly, while I have taken advantage of scanned encyclopedias available online, my use of electronic searching and analysis has been heuristic: that is, confined to helping guide research conducted by traditional means.

A Few Conventions

To facilitate reading, I have modernized spelling, punctuation, and capitalization in quotations. In titles, by contrast, I respect older spelling – but not necessarily accents, capitalization, or punctuation – since it may be difficult, otherwise, to locate or recognize the works in question. For this reason, for example, the modern German word *Enzyklopädie* appears in titles both as "Encyclopädie" and "Encyklopädie," and the expression *Konversations-Lexikon*, usually unhyphenated in modern German, appears in titles as "Conversations-Lexicon," "Conversations-Lexikon," and "Conversationslexikon." For the characters "&," "&c.," "æ," "œ," and "β," I have substituted "and" (or its non-English equivalent), "etc.," "ae," "oe," and "ss." When referring to an edition of encyclopedia, I have spelled the title as it was spelled for the editions most referred to in my book, so that Moréri's encyclopedia, for instance, is his *Grand Dictionaire*, not his *Grand Dictionnaire* (the later spelling).

When encyclopedias have nicknames that have all but eclipsed their real titles, I use them as formal titles, italicizing the nicknames. The *Dictionnaire universel françois et latin* (1704) is thus the *Dictionnaire de Trévoux*, the "zeroth" edition (1840–53) of Joseph Meyer's *Konversations-Lexikon* is the *Wunder-Meyer*, and the *Enciclopedia universal ilustrada europeo-americana* (1908–30) is the *Espasa*.

Translations from foreign languages are my own unless otherwise indicated.

To minimize bibliographical references, I have adopted two policies. First, in footnotes, I have cited works under authors' last names and an abbreviated title – even when citing a work the first time. Second, for texts in encyclopedias, newspapers, and popular magazines, I have cited the encyclopedia or periodical as a whole, not crediting an individual – even when identified – for what was written.

In my bibliography, similarly, I have listed most encyclopedias by their titles, not their editors. The main exceptions are encyclopedias credited to a handful of people, and encyclopedias that I cite with respect to an editor alone.

Lastly, in measuring the lengths of articles, I count pages inclusively, so that an article beginning on p. 3 and ending on p. 5 will be three pages long.

CHAPTER I

Genres of Encyclopedias

Genre can be understood in complementary ways. On the one hand, in taxonomical terms, it is something resulting from a classification of literature, whether with respect to current reasoning or with respect to the past. On the other hand, in a more recent outlook, it is a dynamic communicative link between producers and consumers of texts. In particular, it is partly through genre that writers and publishers market their texts, and partly through genre that audiences choose what to buy, what to read, and how to read it.

Before the late eighteenth century, genre was less clearly defined for encyclopedias than it was for other texts, since so few were published. Specialized encyclopedias proliferated before 1750, but general encyclopedias did not. As a result, the genres against which they defined themselves were less deeply entrenched and less subtly distinguished than those of novels, for example, hundreds of which had been published by 1700. Through the mid eighteenth century, the publication of each new encyclopedia was capable of shifting expectations about the genre in a significant way.

Nebulous though they may have been, genres of encyclopedias were already forming in the second half of the seventeenth century, as indicated, for instance, by the presence of standardized expressions in titles. Like other genres, they were subject to transformation and mixing. Indeed, it was just such experimentation that led to the genre of the modern encyclopedia in the mid eighteenth century. In the century before then – that is, from 1650 to 1750 – encyclopedias were considered "dictionaries," and almost none of them approached the generality of the modern encyclopedia. Instead, as I show below in the first section of the chapter, three genres of "dictionaries" – the dictionary of the arts and sciences, the universal dictionary, and the historical dictionary – disseminated distinct kinds of encyclopedic information. Each contributed in its own way to the modern encyclopedia.

With the merger of the three genres toward 1750, the modern encyclopedia came into being, but it did not put an end to questions of genre. To begin with, it was never a tightly defined genre. Beyond the criteria of broad coverage and alphabetical order, it remained open for tinkering. While cautious authors and publishers contented themselves with perpetuating its better-known models, the more innovative among them played with its boundaries, creating new combinations, and in some cases models and sub-genres. Three of the more important sub-genres will be examined below: the encyclopedic dictionary, the *Konversations-Lexikon*, and the children's encyclopedia. None had sharp boundaries, a characteristic they shared with the modern encyclopedia itself. The *Konversations-Lexikon*, in particular, is hard to define as a coherent sub-genre except in a limited temporal framework. My analysis of the sub-genres adds concreteness to the idea of the modern encyclopedia, but it also points to complexity and tension within the genre. Specifically, while the case of the encyclopedic dictionary highlights the interchange between encyclopedias and dictionaries, those of the *Konversations-Lexikon* and the children's encyclopedia draw attention to the pressures of popular versus learned culture within encyclopedism.

Three Kinds of Proto-Encyclopedias and Their Posterity

In its modern, one-word form, "encyclopedia" was a neologism coined by European humanists before 1475.[1] It derived from a two-word expression in ancient Greek, *enkyklios paideia*, inherited through Roman times and mistranscribed as one word. We do not know precisely what *enkyklios paideia* meant to the Greeks or the Romans, in part because the expression was rarely used.[2] While *paideia* referred to education in Greek, it is unclear how an education could be seen as recurrent or circular – the basic meanings of *enkyklios* – and it was apparently unclear to ancient writers.[3] One common view is that *enkyklios paideia* designated a usual or general education, one that preceded more specialized training, though the ancient Greeks probably understood it in several competing senses as well.[4] By the time of the Roman empire, allusions in Latin to *enkyklios paideia* suggest that it was considered an education covering requisite disciplines,

[1] Fowler, "Encyclopaedias," 27–9.
[2] Doody, *Pliny's Encyclopedia*, 45.
[3] Vogelgsang, "Zum Begriff," 17–18.
[4] Zucker, *Encyclopédire*, 14.

but the disciplines were variable.[5] Eventually, the expression gave rise to the Latin *orbis disciplinarum*, or circle of disciplines, and was associated with the liberal arts.

When "encyclopedia" emerged as a single word during the Renaissance, it referred to a range of disciplines an educated person should be familiar with. Soon after 1500 it began to appear in the titles of a variety of books. The most important for encyclopedism was Johann Heinrich Alsted's *Encyclopaedia* (1630), a survey of knowledge organized around disciplines. Only in the 1700s did "encyclopedia" start to signify a book as much as an educational ideal.

By the end of the seventeenth century, a few alphabetical proto-encyclopedias were associated with the word "encyclopedia." A friend called Moréri's *Grand Dictionaire* (1674) an "encyclopedia of history," just as Antoine Furetière called his own *Dictionaire* (1690) an "encyclopedia of the French language."[6] In published titles as well, the word "encyclopedia" cropped up occasionally, though not for encyclopedias. In the early eighteenth century, for example, it was used in editions of Johann Doläus's *Encyclopaedia chirurgica* (*Encyclopedia of Surgery*, 1689), a non-alphabetical survey of surgery, and in Gottfried Rogg's *Encyclopaedia, oder: Schau-Bühne curieuser Vorstellungen* (*Encyclopedia, or: Theater of Curious Images*, 1726), a book of templates for artists.

Still, "encyclopedia" remained unusual as a term and a title until Ephraim Chambers revived a variant for his *Cyclopaedia* (1728).[7] In choosing a title signifying a program of learning, Chambers sought to emphasize his work's interconnectedness. Twenty years later, as editors of the *Encyclopédie*, Diderot and D'Alembert took inspiration from Chambers's title. Henceforth, "encyclopedia" was used as a title for books covering a wide range of topics in a consultable format. Besides the *Encyclopédie* in its original and revised forms, the following works were entitled encyclopedias in the late eighteenth century: the first three editions of the *Encyclopaedia Britannica*, the first *Deutsche Encyclopädie* (*German Encyclopedia*, 1778–1807), and Johann Georg Krünitz and others' *Oeconomische Encyclopädie* (*Economic Encyclopedia*, 1773–1858). By the end of the century, "encyclopedia" was being used as a generic name for any encyclopedia, though

---

[5] Doody, *Pliny's Encyclopedia*, 47–8.

[6] Moréri, *Grand Dictionaire*, 1st edn., á1v; Furetière, *Essais*, a1*v*.

[7] Schneider and Zedelmaier, "Wissensapparate," 349–50; Blair, "Revisiting," 391–2; Henningsen, "Enzyklopädie," 285–7. For seventeenth-century titles with the word "encyclopedia" see Dierse, *Enzyklopädie*, 24–5n; Henningsen, "Enzyklopädie," 302–3. On "cyclopedia" versus "encyclopedia" see Henningsen, "Enzyklopädie," 302–3, 310.

it co-existed with "lexicon" in German usage. From this point onward, we can legitimately speak of the genre of the encyclopedia, within which sub-genres continued to appear, and around which hybrids continued to thrive.

Before the second half of the eighteenth century, however, there was no specific term for encyclopedias. Instead, Europeans used other terms, notably "dictionary" and "lexicon," to refer to works now subsumed in the category of encyclopedias. In keeping with their titles, discourse about encyclopedias from 1650 to 1750 assigned them, first and foremost, to the genre of the dictionary or lexicon. A theme in the prefaces to the period's encyclopedias was the recent profusion of alphabetical works, the diversity of which hints again at the dominance of the basic category of the dictionary or lexicon. In his preface to the *Grosses vollständiges Universal-Lexicon* (*Great, Complete Universal Lexicon*, 1732–50), for example, the professor Johann Peter von Ludewig wrote that the title "lexicon" was used for almost any alphabetical work, and went on to enumerate twenty sub-genres. These dealt with such varied subjects as history, the Bible, politics, arts and crafts, geography, the household, and even thieves and scoundrels.[8]

The primacy of the genre of the dictionary or lexicon did not mean that people were unaware of the possible distinction between lexical and encyclopedic works. On the contrary, the opposition between dictionaries of words and things was ubiquitous. In German, for instance, the use of the adjective "real" after "lexicon" indicated a focus on things.[9] The same opposition undergirded the Académie Française's decision to sponsor two dictionaries, the lexical *Dictionnaire de l'Académie françoise* (1694) and Thomas Corneille's encyclopedic *Dictionnaire des arts et des sciences* (1694). Similarly, the preface to the lexical dictionary (1726–39) of Real Academia Española promised a separate dictionary of the liberal and mechanical arts. The promise went unfulfilled, but in 1745, the Italian Accademia della Crusca complemented its own dictionary with an encyclopedic companion.[10]

Nevertheless, despite the apparent clarity of the dichotomy between lexical and other dictionaries, it was frequently obscured in discourse about encyclopedias, not to mention in practice. First, French theorists of the universal dictionary contended that ordinary and technical language must

---

[8] *Grosses vollständiges Universal-Lexicon*, 1: 2.
[9] See for example Conrad, *Lexikonpolitik*, 43. For a similar characterization of "real" dictionaries in English see review of *Supplement*, 51.
[10] Considine, *Academy Dictionaries*, 26–7, 115–16.

not be separated. They were thus advocating dictionaries of both things and words.[11] Indeed, the editors of the first edition (1704) of the *Dictionnaire de Trévoux*, a self-proclaimed universal dictionary, associated its universality with the fact of its containing everything "with some connection to language," its only omissions being "purely historical facts."[12] Second, it was difficult distinguishing between entries on words and those on things. Chambers, for instance, posited three kinds of dictionaries: grammatical dictionaries (in which definitions were limited to a one-word equivalent), philosophical dictionaries (which explained words' general meanings), and technical dictionaries (which gave specialized meanings). Only his third type focused wholly on things. One might expect him to have identified his *Cyclopaedia* (1728) as a work of this type. Instead, he wrote that he and other dictionary-writers used definitions "promiscuously," blending the three types, and that the "art" of lexicography was not reducible to rules.[13]

Another sign that encyclopedists saw their works as dictionaries in the broad sense is their identification of lexical dictionaries as models or rivals. In his *Dictionnaire françois* (1680), for example, César-Pierre Richelet promised entries on both things and words, but he categorized his work as having the same "nature" as the gestating *Dictionnaire de l'Académie françoise*.[14] Likewise, in the *Cyclopaedia*'s preface, Chambers listed eight of his encyclopedia's ancestors.[15] One was the *Dictionnaire de Trévoux*, which styled itself a dictionary of everything related to language. Elsewhere in the preface, Chambers criticized an unnamed "dictionary which few people are without." The work in question was Nathan Bailey's *Universal Etymological English Dictionary* (1721), a largely lexical work.[16] Chambers, in short, saw his *Cyclopaedia* as belonging to a broader class than that of the dictionary of the arts and sciences.

Seventeenth- and eighteenth-century encyclopedists were thus familiar with the opposition between dictionaries of things and those of words, but before 1750, they did not see firm borders between their works and other dictionaries. The overarching genre in which they were working was that of the dictionary, within which they recognized various sub-genres. Between 1650 and 1750, three of these came closest to the generality of the

[11] Behnke, *Furetière*, 22–5; Leca-Tsiomis, *Ecrire*, 17–21, 257–65.
[12] [*Dictionnaire de Trévoux*], 1st edn., 1: éiir.
[13] Chambers, *Cyclopaedia*, 1: xxi–xxiv.
[14] Richelet, *Dictionnaire*, **1r, **2r.
[15] Chambers, *Cyclopaedia*, 1: i.
[16] Loveland, "Encyclopaedias," 162.

modern encyclopedia: the historical dictionary, the dictionary of the arts and sciences, and the universal dictionary.

The historical dictionary grew out of sixteenth-century dictionaries of proper names, a genre exemplified by Charles Estienne's *Dictionarium historicum* (1553). By the eighteenth century, such precursors had been eclipsed by two international successes, Moréri's *Grand Dictionaire* (1674) and Pierre Bayle's *Dictionaire historique et critique* (1697). These works supplied opposing models of what a historical dictionary should be. Bayle's *Dictionaire* treated history through biographical notices, while Moréri's *Grand Dictionaire* had geographical as well as historical keywords. The majority of Moréri's non-geographical articles were in fact biographies, but a minority were on other subjects such as sects, feasts, and social groups. Amplifying the encyclopedia's historical coverage, many of the work's geographical articles were historical too. The breadth of the historical dictionary in Moréri's lineage was further expanded with the *Supplément* of 1689. Here the anonymous authors highlighted their inclusion of new kinds of articles – for example, on arts and sciences, and on notable entities such as chocolate and canals. The additions, they argued, would make the encyclopedia useful to more people.[17]

Consequently, though followers of both Moréri's and Bayle's approaches identified their encyclopedias as historical dictionaries, it would be more accurate to speak of two kinds of historical dictionaries: the historico-geographical dictionary and the biographical dictionary. Yet in another sense, the two kinds of historical dictionaries did form a group, one to which the purely geographical dictionary also belonged. Specifically, their keywords were nearly all proper names, and their articles were devoted to particulars and historical facts, neither of which were considered as part of science.[18] Even entries on the disciplines of history and geography were usually lacking.

Unlike the historical dictionary, the dictionary of the arts and sciences was supposed to treat knowledge with a systematic component. On a practical level, its mission was to explain terminology from the arts and sciences. With its unambiguous title, Corneille's *Dictionnaire des arts et des sciences* (1694) inaugurated the genre. In German, two similar works were the *Curieuses Natur- Kunst- Gewerck- und Handlungs-Lexicon* (*Curious Dictionary of Nature, Art, Trades, and Business*, 1712) and Johann Theodor Jablonski's *Allgemeines Lexicon der Künste und Wissenschafften* (*General*

---

[17] *Ibid.*, 166; Burrell, "Pierre Bayle's *Dictionnaire*," 90–1.
[18] Kossmann, "Deutsche Universallexika," 1559; Yeo, *Encyclopaedic Visions*, 14–18.

Lexicon of the Arts and Sciences, 1721). All three are often overlooked in favor of the genre's most famous models, both of them British: the *Lexicon Technicum* (1704) and the *Cyclopaedia* (1728).

Dictionaries of the arts and sciences and historical dictionaries were complements, in principle, with mutually exclusive collections of keywords. The dictionary of the arts and sciences dealt with disciplines and their vocabulary, while the historical dictionary dealt with the particulars of history and geography. History itself was not generally considered an art or a science. Instead, it was a literary genre and a collection of facts. Corneille's *Dictionnaire*, by this logic, had no entry on history. By putting in entries on religious sects, though, Corneille set a precedent for encroaching on historical material, a tendency that was magnified in other dictionaries of the arts and sciences.

Let us turn now to the period's third proto-encyclopedia, the universal dictionary. What constituted a universal dictionary was a little unclear. Some dictionaries were called universal because of their cosmopolitanism or fitness for different readers or purposes.[19] The term could also be reserved for a work containing all knowledge. A universal dictionary was thus sometimes depicted as something impossible. More pragmatically, Ludewig rationalized the title of the *Grosses vollständiges Universal-Lexicon* by pointing out that it was more universal than a university, since its contents went beyond the university's curriculum. Universality, in this context, was a matter of comparative breadth.[20]

In eighteenth-century France, a universal dictionary was a dictionary with entries on a language's entire vocabulary. It therefore included both everyday and technical words, though not proper names, which were seen as outside normal language.[21] Furetière produced his "universal dictionary" with this understanding, as did subsequent editors of his *Dictionaire* (1690) as well as the authors of the *Dictionnaire de Trévoux* (1704). In the following paragraphs, I will be dealing with universal dictionaries in this particular French sense.

Like dictionaries of the arts and sciences, universal dictionaries had an uncertain border with historical dictionaries. For some of their authors, the addition of historical material was unproblematic. In the preface to the first edition, the *Dictionnaire de Trévoux* was identified as a universal

---

[19] See for example Loveland, *Alternative Encyclopedia?*, 70; Bernard *et al.*, *General Dictionary*, 1: a1v ("Preface").
[20] *Grosses vollständiges Universal-Lexicon*, 1: 5–6. See also Savary *et al.*, *Dictionnaire*, 1: xvi.
[21] Rey, *Miroirs*, 39; Quemada, *Dictionnaires*, 310–11.

dictionary but vaunted as having features that were lacking in others, including coverage of religious sects, much of it historical.[22] The presence of the latter material in the Catholic encyclopedia provoked outcries from supporters of its commercial and religious rival, Furetière's Dutch-published *Dictionaire*. Furetière too had been reproached for his coverage of sects, albeit because he treated some but not others.[23] Historical material in universal dictionaries was not always condemned, then, for being out of place but also, at times, for being brought in inconsistently. Regardless, Furetière's successor as editor, Henri Basnage de Beauval, criticized the *Dictionnaire de Trévoux* for transgressing genres: "Each dictionary has its prescribed boundaries."[24]

Not everyone was convinced. In a mixed review of the *Dictionnaire de Trévoux* in 1704, one commentator pronounced the articles on religious history a worthwhile addition.[25] Perhaps reacting to such sentiments, the *Dictionnaire de Trévoux* went further in its second edition (1721), now adding articles under numerous geographical and personal names. The authors defended their additions, judging them convenient for readers, justified by precedent, and consistent with the mission of the universal dictionary, since proper names were an element of grammar and language.[26] Their arguments point to the difficulty of resisting the attractions of greater comprehensiveness.

As these descriptions indicate, the dictionary of the arts and sciences and the universal dictionary were closely related. Both covered the terminology of arts and sciences, while the universal dictionary also defined everyday language, including merely grammatical words such as prepositions and articles. Both kinds of encyclopedias stood opposed to the historical dictionary, at least in theory. In fact, they appropriated historical material throughout the century from 1650 to 1750. For the most part, the process was not reciprocal. Instead, after the expansion of Moréri's *Grand Dictionaire* toward the arts and sciences in 1689, historical dictionaries offered more and more material on historical or geographical particulars, but not on other subjects.

As the drift of the universal dictionary and the dictionary of the arts and sciences toward history shows, their rationales were ineffective at stabilizing

22 [*Dictionnaire de Trévoux*], 1st edn., 1: eiir–eiiiv.
23 [Le Clerc], review of *Dictionaire*, 124–5.
24 "Chaque dictionnaire a ses bornes prescrites." See Basnage, review, 319. See also Furetière, Basnage, and Brutel, *Dictionnaire*, 1: *****1r.
25 Behnke, *Furetière*, 124.
26 [*Dictionnaire de Trévoux*], 2nd edn., 1: viii.

their contents. First, it was possible to imagine new genres with equally compelling rationales. In particular, some contemporaries welcomed the prospect of merging extant genres into something with the approximate scope of the modern encyclopedia. Second, the dictionary of the arts and sciences was almost by definition disposed to expansion in view of the flexibility of the terms "art" and "science." To a lesser extent, the universal dictionary as well carried the seeds of its destruction in its own definition, for as the *Dictionnaire de Trévoux* argued, proper nouns could be seen as inextricable from the system of language.

For both of these reasons, hybrids of the three genres were already appearing in the seventeenth century, and they became increasingly common in the eighteenth. Among them were Johann Jacob Hofmann's Latin *Lexicon universale* (1677), Vincenzo Coronelli's *Biblioteca universale* (1701–6), and Gianfrancesco Pivati's *Nuovo dizionario scientifico e curioso* (*New Scientific and Curious Dictionary*, 1746–51). Hofmann's *Lexicon* began as a historico-geographical dictionary, but a supplement (1683) expanded the coverage to natural history and other domains. The *Biblioteca universale* was dominated by geographical and biographical entries. In addition, however, it had entries on everyday language and some arts and sciences.[27] Lastly, much of Pivati's *Nuovo dizionario* was devoted to geography, but it also treated arts and sciences and a certain amount of ordinary vocabulary.

Overall, the three encyclopedias' departures from the historico-geographical dictionary were erratic and tentative. Indeed, the works of Hofmann and Coronelli can be interpreted as historical dictionaries intruding on the territory of the universal dictionary and the dictionary of the arts and sciences rather than as something thoroughly hybrid. An even more specialized dictionary that evolved by encroachment was Johann Christoph Nehring's *Manuale juridico-politicum* (1684), a political and legal dictionary, which grew into a *Historisch- politisch- juristisches Lexicon* (1706) promising coverage of history, medicine, theology, and other disciplines. Likewise, the *Biblioteca universale* was a product of Coronelli's determination to improve on the historical dictionaries of Moréri and Bayle as well as two geographical dictionaries.[28] Pivati, for his part, emphasized his coverage of the arts and sciences in the preface.[29] Perhaps he was striving for something like the *Dictionnaire de Trévoux* from its second edition

[27] Fuchs, "Vincenzo Coronelli," 222–3, 225–8. Notice Coronelli's commitment to explaining the terms of all arts and sciences in Coronelli, *Biblioteca*, 1: [unnumbered page after the title page], †2v. See also Arato, "Savants," 70–1.

[28] Fuchs, "Vincenzo Coronelli," 176–82.

[29] Pivati, *Nuovo dizionario*, 1: 1, LXXVIII.

onward. Certainly the two encyclopedias had similar scope, though Pivati's *Nuovo dizionario* was less predictable in its contents.

A more serious challenge to contemporary genres of encyclopedias was the *Grosses vollständiges Universal-Lexicon*. If it had to be placed in one of the genres above, it would fit best among historical dictionaries, for two-thirds of its entries were on history and geography. Yet the remaining third were the longest, and they were mainly on the arts and sciences.[30] In addition, it had entries on everyday language.[31] In the front matter, the only genre it was associated with was that of the simple dictionary of things. In this class, it was touted as the first to transcend specialization and encompass all knowledge. Similarly, an announcement of its publication in 1731 presented it as containing everything in twenty-two varieties of specialized dictionaries, including, near the end of the list, historical and geographical ones.[32] Nor did the publisher Johann Heinrich Zedler or his associates defend their "transgression" of extant genres of encyclopedias. A newcomer to encyclopedias, and a confident, self-made businessman, Zedler was perhaps a natural candidate for upending conventions about genres of encyclopedias, but he was also astute enough to doubt the public would care.[33]

In an independent development, by pursuing its encroachment on geographical and historical material, the dictionary of the arts and sciences attained a comparable scope. The process culminated with the second edition (1778–83) of the *Encyclopaedia Britannica*, which offered biographies as well as entries on places. Entries on places had already appeared in the *New and Complete Dictionary of Arts and Sciences* (1754–5), and entries on individuals had appeared in the *Modern Dictionary of Arts and Sciences* (1774). The expansion of the *Britannica* away from its origins as a dictionary of the arts and sciences was registered in titles. The publishers of the second edition added "etc." to the first edition's sub-title, making it a *Dictionary of Arts, Sciences, etc.*, while the third edition (1797) was sub-titled a *Dictionary of Arts, Sciences, and Miscellaneous Literature*. Also reflective of the expansion of the dictionary of arts and sciences was its designation as a "scientific dictionary" or a "dictionary of science" from the

---

[30] Dorn, Oetjens, and Schneider, "Sachliche Erschliessung," 99, 102–3. On the *Universal-Lexicon*'s coverage see also Carels and Flory, "Johann Heinrich Zedler's *Universal Lexicon*," 174–95.

[31] Dorn, Oetjens, and Schneider, "Sachliche Erschliessung," 119. The need for a dictionary of German is mentioned in *Grosses vollständiges Universal-Lexicon*, 1: 3–4.

[32] Schneider, "Konstruktion," 86.

[33] See Dreitzel, "Zedlers 'Grosses vollständiges Universallexikon,'" 118–19.

late eighteenth century onward.[34] These titles nudged science away from an identifiable collection of disciplines toward knowledge in general.

As the general coverage of the modern encyclopedia grew into a standard, the three kinds of proto-encyclopedias that dominated the period from 1650 to 1750 became less important, but they did not disappear. Nor did the reasoning that had helped to support them. Even in the late eighteenth century, the editor of the first *Deutsche Encyclopädie* refused to include entries having proper names for their keywords, insisting they belonged in historical or geographical dictionaries.[35] Allowing keywords to be proper names did create problems. To merit inclusion, how big did a village or a river have to be? How famous should a person be?

These problems were akin to those of choosing keywords in general, but other problems were not. Especially but not exclusively before 1800, many encyclopedists balked at offering biographies of the living, considering it indiscreet or impossible to do so fairly.[36] In his *Grand Dictionaire* (1674), Moréri placed a tribute to France's reigning monarch under "Louis XIV," but otherwise, he kept his promise to cover only the dead, at least overwhelmingly.[37] Bayle did the same in his *Dictionaire* (1697). Exceptionally, he inserted material on living members of the Basnage family, albeit in an article on their deceased ancestor Benjamin Basnage, and with this excuse: "Although these gentlemen remain full of life, it was necessary to speak of them in order to prevent people from continuing to mistake them for one another."[38]

The first encyclopedia to feature biographies of living individuals as a matter of policy was the *Grosses vollständiges Universal-Lexicon*. Such biographies began to appear, belatedly, in volume xviii when Carl Günther Ludovici took over as editor. Henceforth they were numerous. Of roughly 100 biographies under the surname Wagner, for instance, around half were devoted to still-living subjects. Another of Ludovici's innovations was to invite readers to send in biographical articles. I will return to this invitation in Chapter 4, but it is worth noting here that many articles on the living may have been autobiographies or the reminiscences of relatives.[39]

---

[34] See for example Rees, *Cyclopaedia*, 1: i; Howard *et al.*, *New Royal Cyclopaedia*, 1: iii; *British Encyclopaedia*, 1: viii. See also Yeo, *Encyclopaedic Visions*, 13.

[35] Goetschel, Macleod, and Snyder, "*Deutsche Encyclopädie*," 257, 270–1, 288.

[36] See for example *Supplément au Grand Dictionnaire*, 1: á1v.

[37] Moréri, *Grand Dictionaire*, 1st edn., á4r, 817–18.

[38] "Quoique ces messieurs soient pleins de vie, il a fallu nécessairement parler d'eux, afin d'empêcher qu'on ne continue de les prendre les uns pour les autres." Bayle, *Dictionaire*, 1: 494; Leca-Tsiomis, *Ecrire*, 42n.

[39] Schneider, *Erfindung*, 40–1, 101–11.

In the early nineteenth century, biographies of the living became one of the hallmarks of the German *Konversations-Lexikon*. Influential as it was, the *Konversations-Lexikon* brought such biographies to much of Europe and elsewhere. In France, for example, the *Encyclopédie des gens du monde* (*Encyclopedia of People of the World*, 1833–44) – modeled on the *Konversations-Lexikon* – became an early adopter. Many encyclopedists remained wary, though. One odd solution was that of the first edition of the *Encyclopaedia Americana* (1829–33) – another offshoot of the *Konversations-Lexikon* – which had biographies of living Europeans but not Americans.[40] A notable laggard was the *Encyclopaedia Britannica*, where the living only gained entrance in the early twentieth century.[41]

Another problem for encyclopedists involved proper names for things other than people and places. This was less a moral than a logistical problem. Most modern encyclopedias had a minority of keywords of this variety – names of festivals, months, or stars, for example – but the list risked expanding beyond manageability. Extending the logic that led to coverage of mythical individuals in historical dictionaries, Pierre Larousse announced that his *Grand Dictionnaire universel du XIXe siècle* (*Great Universal Dictionary of the Nineteenth Century*, 1866–76) would cover fictional characters in general. Accordingly, it included entries on Caliban from William Shakespeare's *The Tempest* (1610–11) and Félix Grandet from Honoré de Balzac's *Eugénie Grandet* (1834), among many others. Larousse expanded the range of keywords in his *Grand Dictionnaire* in another way too, inserting entries on works of art such as Germaine de Staël's novel *Corinne* (1807) and Eugène Delacroix's painting *Liberty Guiding the People* (1830).[42] Finding the right keywords for artworks could be a challenge, since titles had variants. While some encyclopedias followed the *Grand Dictionnaire* in offering articles on specific artworks, many more dealt with artworks in broader articles, whether under the name of an artist or of an esthetic movement.

Allowing proper names to be keywords burdened encyclopedists with concerns about naming and what was worthy of coverage, but refusing such keywords became increasingly untenable. Even latter-day scientific and technical encyclopedias such as *Van Nostrand's Scientific Encyclopedia* (1938) often had biographies of famous scientists. For this reason, neither the dictionary of the arts and sciences nor the universal dictionary had

⁴⁰ *Encyclopaedia Americana*, 1st edn., I: vii.
⁴¹ Runte and Steuben, "*Encyclopaedia*," 84. See also Einbinder, *Myth*, 60.
⁴² Larousse, *Grand Dictionnaire*, I: LXX–LXXI, LXXIII, III: 147, V: 137–8, VIII: 1446, X: 474.

much posterity in their pure forms, though these had always been ideals as much as realities. In their impure forms, by contrast – that is, with the acceptance of proper names as keywords – both genres led into the modern encyclopedia.

According to Richard Yeo, the dictionary of the arts and sciences was the most direct ancestor of the modern encyclopedia.[43] Thanks to Chambers' *Cyclopaedia* (1728), this was the genre first associated with the word "encyclopedia." Yeo's genealogy works well for the anglophone world, as the *Encyclopaedia Britannica* – easily depicted as the epitome of encyclopedias – grew out of the eighteenth century's dictionaries of the arts and sciences.

The universal dictionary, for its part, is harder to discern in the modern encyclopedia, though it reigned supreme in eighteenth-century France. The *Encyclopédie* itself covered everyday language, but scholarly encyclopedias rarely did so in the nineteenth and twentieth centuries.[44] Even in France, the most authoritative encyclopedias – the *Grande Encyclopédie* (1885–1902) and the *Encyclopaedia universalis* (1968–75) – were strictly non-lexical. Still, the universal dictionary persisted in less scholarly titles. Above all, it gave rise to the encyclopedic dictionary, which I will cover in the following section.

After triggering the vogue for encyclopedias in the seventeenth century, the historical dictionary went on to co-exist with the modern encyclopedia. In the form of the biographical dictionary, it rivaled nineteenth- and twentieth-century encyclopedias in size and prestige. As history evolved from a field focused on the achievements of the illustrious to one dealing with groups, processes, and continuous narrative, historical encyclopedias lost standing in scholarly circles, but they continued to be published.[45] Many were devoted to specific regions or periods, but some claimed as much generality as Moréri's *Grand Dictionaire* (1674) – for example, the *Diccionario geográfico-histórico de todas las partes del mundo* (*Geographico-Historical Dictionary of All Parts of the World*, 1863–8) and the *Encyclopedia of World History* (2000) by Facts on File. At the same time, one can argue for a lineage from the historical dictionary to the modern encyclopedia, as did a review of the *English Cyclopaedia* (1854–62) in 1863. According to the reviewer, the modern encyclopedia was not to be traced back to Chambers' *Cyclopaedia* but instead to the works of Moréri, Hofmann, Coronelli, and

[43] Yeo, "Encyclopedism," 670; Yeo, *Encyclopaedic Visions*, 13. See also Collison, *Encyclopaedias*, 103–4.
[44] On the *Encyclopédie* in this regard see Leca-Tsiomis, "Langue," 203–14.
[45] Chappey, *Ordres*, 318–25.

Zedler, "the real and direct ancestors of the great cyclopedias of our own day." The basis for the judgment was the importance of historical material to modern encyclopedias such as the *English Cyclopaedia*.[46]

The Encyclopedic Dictionary

Like "universal dictionary," the term "encyclopedic dictionary" has had various meanings. It has always referred to something between an encyclopedia and a dictionary, but different interpretations have been made of the kind of hybridity it embodies. Here, after reviewing the term's different meanings, I will focus on the encyclopedic dictionary that was most often evoked from the early twentieth century onward: an encyclopedia that also dealt with everyday language.

In sub-titling his *Cyclopaedia* a "dictionary," Chambers anticipated the later combination of "encyclopedic" and "dictionary." Likewise, the *Encyclopédie* was sub-titled a "dictionary," and D'Alembert called it an "encyclopedic dictionary."[47] For Chambers as well as for Diderot and D'Alembert, their works were dictionaries in being alphabetical and encyclopedias in connecting knowledge via overviews, cross-references, and other devices.

The *Encyclopédie* inspired the Croatian scholar Julije Bajamonti, who began compiling but never published a *Dizionario enciclopedico* in the late eighteenth century.[48] Around the same time, the expression "encyclopedic dictionary" appeared in the titles of certain volumes of the *Encyclopédie méthodique* (1782–1832) – for example, in the *Dictionnaire encyclopédique des amusemens des sciences, mathématiques et physiques* (*Encyclopedic Dictionary of Amusements of the Mathematical and Physical Sciences*, 1792). For Jacques Lacombe, the compiler, his work was above all a dictionary, but he linked it with encyclopedias by pointing out that it covered knowledge neglected in the *Encyclopédie* and at risk for neglect in the *Encyclopédie méthodique*. It therefore completed the "circle" of the encyclopedia.[49]

Like Chambers's and D'Alembert's, Lacombe's use of the term "encyclopedic dictionary" depended on a fading interpretation of the word "encyclopedia," namely as a connected system of knowledge. As "encyclopedia" came to refer to an alphabetized book, with or without a pretention

[46] Review of *English Cyclopaedia*, 370. For a similar judgment see Schneider, "Europea," 432, 447.
[47] *Encyclopédie; ou, Dictionnaire*, 1: xxxiv.
[48] Gostl, "Five Centuries," 88–9.
[49] *Dictionnaire encyclopédique*, 1: vii.

to connectedness, the meaning of "encyclopedic dictionary" was destined to change, but it did so only slowly. As late as the mid nineteenth century, the encyclopedic dictionary continued to be contrasted with the systematic "encyclopedia." In the *Supplement to the Fourth, Fifth, and Sixth Editions of the Encyclopaedia Britannica* (1824), for example, the editor Macvey Napier portrayed the encyclopedic dictionary as an alphabetized encyclopedia.[50] More elaborately, in the *Complément du Dictionnaire de l'Académie française* (1842) – the Académie's second effort at supplementing its dictionary with an encyclopedia – the philosopher Louis Barré characterized seven kinds of "dictionaries." Here the universal dictionary was a dictionary of ordinary as well as technical language, but with minimal definitions, whereas the similar encyclopedic dictionary had ampler entries. In this schema, again, the encyclopedic dictionary stood opposed to the encyclopedia, which was necessarily systematic.[51]

In the first half of the nineteenth century, "encyclopedic dictionary" was rare as a title. Nor did authors who chose it bother to rationalize it. In the absence of their rationales, all that can be said is that before 1850, works called encyclopedic dictionaries varied greatly in scope, and few bore much resemblance to the modern encyclopedic dictionary.

Most consistently, members of the Pierer family used it in the titles of their German-language encyclopedia. Already, in the hands of the previous publisher, the first edition (1822–36) had been titled the *Enzyklopädisches Wörterbuch der Wissenschaften und Künste* (*Encyclopedic Dictionary of the Sciences and Arts*). Then, after the physician and publisher Johann Friedrich Pierer and his son took possession of it, they reprinted it as the *Universal-Lexikon* (1835–6), reserving "encyclopedic dictionary" for the sub-title, an arrangement maintained through the work's sixth edition (1875–9). Pierer's encyclopedia came close to being an encyclopedic dictionary in the term's modern sense. In particular, thanks in part to its inclusion of so many keywords, it did treat a large amount of ordinary vocabulary. The first edition had entries, for example, on the words "and" (*und*), "through" (*durch*), and "windy" (*windig*). The coverage was incomplete, though, as shown by the absence of entries on such words as "then" (*dann*), "along" (*entlang*), and "calm" (*ruhig*). Indeed, the editor insisted that it was not a lexical dictionary and would not give words' basic meanings except as a prelude to specialized ones.[52]

---

[50] *Supplement to the Fourth, Fifth, and Sixth Editions*, I: iii.
[51] *Complément*, XVIII–XIX.
[52] [*Pierer's Universal-Lexikon*], 1st edn., I: V–VI.

Only in the late nineteenth century did the term "encyclopedic dictionary" become widespread in titles, and only then was it associated with coverage of both words and things. Pierer may have initiated the association early in the century, but it solidified in Spanish toward 1850, a few decades before doing so in English and French. In 1853, a two-volume *Diccionario enciclopédico de la lengua española* (*Encyclopedic Dictionary of the Spanish Language*, 1853–5) began appearing under the leadership of the journalist and naturalist Eduardo Chao Fernández. At this date, he seems to have considered his title self-explanatory. An encyclopedic dictionary, in his view, was a dictionary that allowed keywords of any kind, that is, a dictionary with an encyclopedic range of articles.[53] True to this conception, his *Diccionario* covered the Spanish language – adjectives and prepositions included – as well as geography, biography, and the terms of the arts and sciences. It was a modern encyclopedic dictionary in name and in scope, and it sold well enough to be published in two further editions. Capitalizing on its success, five "encyclopedic dictionaries" were launched in Spain in the 1890s alone. One of them, significantly, was a *Novísimo diccionario enciclopédico de la lengua castellana* (*Newest Encyclopedic Dictionary of the Castilian Language*, 1898), published by José Espasa. Espasa would go on to publish the *Espasa* (1908–30), the world's largest encyclopedic dictionary, though it was only so identified in Volume LXX.[54]

Britain discovered its own passion for the "encyclopedic dictionary" in the late nineteenth century after the Scottish minister and geologist Robert Hunter edited a set with the title (1879–88). A note in Volume I described it as presenting "the ordinary features of a dictionary of the English language and at the same time treat[ing] certain subjects with something of the exhaustiveness adopted in an encyclopedia."[55] Hunter in fact allowed himself a considerable "exhaustiveness." His articles on the steam engine, the sun, and the tortoise, for example, had around 1,000 words each. At the same time, like Chao, but unlike Pierer, he treated ordinary language as an end in itself. Over the next several decades, the *Encyclopaedic Dictionary* was reprinted and adapted numerous times, often under titles that stressed its hybridity – as the *American Encyclopaedic Dictionary* (1894), *Lloyd's Encyclopaedic Dictionary* (1895), the *Imperial Cyclopaedia and Dictionary* (1901), and so on.[56] Apparently because of the vogue for the

[53] See *Diccionario*, I: III, 862.
[54] Castellano, *Enciclopedia*, 98–104, 359n.
[55] *Encyclopaedic Dictionary*, I: [ii].
[56] Walsh, *Anglo-American General Encyclopedias*, 60.

term "encyclopedic dictionary," the *Imperial Dictionary* (1850) was reissued with a new sub-title in 1882 as an "encyclopedic lexicon." Webster's, the brand established by the American writer Noah Webster, was drawn in soon afterward with *Webster's Encyclopedic Dictionary* (1891). Similar titles would appear under Webster's name for more than a century, but the title lost popularity in English in the early twentieth century, only to re-emerge, decades later, as an option for specialized encyclopedias.

In French too, the title "encyclopedic dictionary" rose into prominence in the late nineteenth century. Jules Trousset's *Nouveau Dictionnaire encyclopédique* (1885–91) was an encyclopedic dictionary in the same sense as Chao's or Hunter's, but the title only arrived definitively with the publication of the *Nouveau Larousse illustré: Dictionnaire universel encyclopédique* (1897–1904). From then on, it was used frequently for Larousse's works of reference, indicating the sub-genre in which Larousse specialized: encyclopedias that functioned simultaneously as dictionaries.

Despite the dominance, since around 1900, of Larousse's and others' understanding of the encyclopedic dictionary, alternative interpretations continued to be made. Specialized encyclopedias and bilingual dictionaries were sometimes called encyclopedic dictionaries into the twenty-first century. Even in German, where the expression "encyclopedic dictionary" was rarer than in English or French, editions of the *Muret-Sanders enzyklopädisches englisch–deutsches und deutsch–englisches Wörterbuch* (*Muret-Sanders English–German and German–English Encyclopedic Dictionary*, 1891–1901) were published throughout the twentieth century, along with other bilingual "encyclopedic dictionaries." Such works were perhaps encyclopedic in having scientific and technical keywords, but their entries were shorter and more dictionary-like than those of other encyclopedic dictionaries.

Another lingering view of the encyclopedic dictionary was that it was defined by brief entries and an affiliation with the *Konversations-Lexikon*. This interpretation can be traced back to the early nineteenth century. An advertisement for the *Encyclopaedia Americana* thus identified Friedrich Brockhaus's *Konversations-Lexikon* as an encyclopedic dictionary in spite of the fact that it did not cover ordinary language. The publishers of the *Americana* saw the encyclopedic dictionary as providing, in essence, "a sufficient amount of easily accessible information."[57] Something similar was suggested in the fourteenth edition (1929) of the *Encyclopaedia Britannica*

---

[57] *Encyclopaedia Americana*, 1st edn., 11: [601–2]. I consulted a copy at the University of Wisconsin, Madison.

in an argument against reducing entries to a uniform size: "[We] cannot become an encyclopedic dictionary on the well-known German model ....
Many important articles remain of outstanding massiveness."[58]

As I will examine the *Konversations-Lexikon* in the following section, the remainder of this one will treat the encyclopedic dictionary in the term's main modern meaning, as an encyclopedia expanded to deal with ordinary language. Having traced the rise of the title "encyclopedic dictionary" in the first half of the section, I will now look at the concept, irrespective of titles.

As we have seen, the encyclopedic dictionary was a descendant of the French universal dictionary. Indeed, the two French embodiments of the universal dictionary before 1750 – Furetière's *Dictionaire* and the *Dictionnaire de Trévoux* – both qualify as encyclopedic dictionaries. The main feature distinguishing them from modern encyclopedic dictionaries was their treatment of proper names. These represented a large share of the keywords in modern encyclopedic dictionaries, but they did not in French universal dictionaries. Nor was nineteenth-century France short of encyclopedic dictionaries before the title was used by Trousset and subsequently popularized. With their rich collections of keywords from both technical and everyday language, Paul-Claude-Victor Boiste's *Dictionnaire universel* (1800) and Louis-Nicolas Bescherelle's *Dictionnaire national* (1843) were both encyclopedic dictionaries, though their entries were brief. More expansive examples were Maurice de la Châtre's *Dictionnaire universel* (1853–4) and Pierre Larousse's *Grand Dictionnaire* (1866–76).

In English as well, the genre of the encyclopedic dictionary had arisen before the title became fashionable in the late nineteenth century. Two eighteenth-century English dictionaries with an encyclopedic aspect were Thomas Dyche and William Pardon's *New General English Dictionary* (1735) and Samuel Johnson's *Dictionary* (1755).[59] Better exemplifying the encyclopedic dictionary was Alexander Aitchison's twenty-three-volume *Encyclopaedia Perthensis* (1806). This work followed the *Encyclopaedia Britannica* in mixing "treatises" with other entries. At the same time, relying on materials from Johnson and others, it functioned as a comprehensive dictionary of English.

Without explaining why, Aitchison distinguished lexical entries by marking them with an asterisk, setting them off against unmarked

[58] *Encyclopaedia Britannica*, 14th edn. (1929), 1: xxii. See also Rey, *Miroirs*, 40–1, 208.
[59] Bradshaw, "Thomas Dyche's *New General English Dictionary*," 143–59; Lynch, "Johnson's Encyclopedia," 129–43.

encyclopedic entries. Similarly, in his *Grand Dictionnaire*, building on the precedent of Bescherelle's *Dictionnaire*, Pierre Larousse identified parts of entries as "encyclopedic."[60] These efforts show the difficulty of separating dictionaries and encyclopedias, notwithstanding such simple principles as that of James Murray, one of the editors of the *Oxford English Dictionary* (1884–1928): "The cyclopedia *describes things*; the dictionary *explains words*."[61] The *Perthensis* marked "Abdomen" as a linguistic entry, for example, presumably because it was copied from Johnson's *Dictionary*, but the definition, taken from a medical writer, was a detailed, encyclopedic characterization of more than 100 words.[62] Likewise, the typical article in Larousse's *Grand Dictionnaire* began with lexical information such as a definition, distinctions among meanings, and examples of usage. Thereafter, certain articles included an encyclopedic addition, labeled "Encycl." (see Figure 1.1). Oddly, neither biographical nor geographical articles were marked as encyclopedic. More inconsistently, examples of usage in the lexical parts of articles frequently veered off into encyclopedic digressions.[63]

The separation of encyclopedic from lexical material in the *Perthensis* and Larousse's *Grand Dictionnaire* hints at uneasiness with the hybridity of the encyclopedic dictionary. Other encyclopedia-planners further separated the two kinds of material. One solution was to publish them within the same work but in different alphabetical sequences. Following Boiste, Pierre Larousse chose such an order for his *Nouveau Dictionnaire de la langue française* (1856).[64] Specifically, after the main dictionary of French, he added sections giving pronunciations, encyclopedic notes, and Latin locutions respectively. Separately alphabetized sections remained a feature of the Larousse company's encyclopedic dictionaries into the twenty-first century, though Pierre Larousse soon decided to integrate much of his encyclopedic content into the dictionary proper.[65] In the same spirit, encyclopedic miscellanies such as the *Volume Library* (1911) and the *Reader's Digest Great Encyclopedic Dictionary* (1964) provided dictionaries of English along with detached encyclopedic material, only some of it alphabetized. Finally, among the best examples of sets with a separately alphabetized encyclopedia and dictionary were the eighteenth (1977–81) and nineteenth

---

[60] Grimaldi, "Interactions," 102–5.
[61] Mugglestone, "*Oxford English Dictionary*," 241.
[62] *Encyclopaedia Perthensis*, 1: 16.
[63] On the interpenetration of lexical and encyclopedic information in the *Dictionnaire national* and the *Grand Dictionnaire* see Grimaldi, "Interactions," 105–8.
[64] Pruvost, "De Diderot," 53–4.
[65] Pruvost, "Pierre Larousse," 32–3.

MIROTON s. m. (mi-ro-ton). Art culin. Plat de tranches de bœuf déjà cuit, que l'on accommode avec des oignons : *Ces oignons crus lui rappelaient certaines sauces Robert et certains* MIROTONS *que son cuisinier exécutait d'une façon supérieure.* (Alex. Dum.) ‖ Espèce de compote : *Un* MIROTON *de pommes.*

— **Encycl.** Le *miroton* est la manière la plus simple d'accommoder le bœuf bouilli. Coupez la viande en tranches de l'épaisseur d'un centimètre. rangez ces tranches dans un plat; saupoudrez-les de sel et de poivre.

Dans un plat qui aille au feu, préparez la sauce suivante : des oignons sont coupés en tranches égales ; on les fait cuire jusqu'à ce qu'ils aient une belle couleur blonde ; alors, saupoudrez-les de farine, salez-les et poivrez ; laissez-les encore quelques minutes sur le feu ; retirez du feu ; ajoutez environ un demi-litre de bouillon : mêlez avec la cuiller de bois ; remettez vingt minutes sur le feu en tournant continuellement. Ajoutez un peu de moutarde ; remuez un instant et versez ce ragoût sur le bœuf ; mettez quelques minutes sur les cendres rouges avec feu dessus.

— *Miroton de pommes.* Choisissez huit ou dix pommes bien saines, de préférence des pommes reinettes ; pelez-les, débarrassez-les de leur cœur ; coupez-les en tranches ; faites-les mariner, pendant trois ou quatre heures, dans une terrine avec du sucre et de la cannelle en poudre, un demi-verre d'eau-de-vie, un jus de citron ; égouttez, garnissez un plat qui aille sur le feu de marmelade de pommes et de marmelade d'abricots mêlées ensemble. Rangez vos tranches de pommes sur cette marmelade ; dressez-les en dôme ; mettez au four ou au four de campagne ; veillez à ce que les pommes prennent belle couleur, ce qui demande environ une demi-heure.

Figure 1.1 Separation of an entry into lexical and encyclopedic parts in Larousse's *Grand Dictionnaire*, Vol. XI. Scanned courtesy of Langsam Library, University of Cincinnati.

(1986–94) editions of Brockhaus's encyclopedia, which included a multi-volume German dictionary as an optional supplement.[66]

As this example indicates, one way of handling separate sequences of entries was to publish them as separate titles that could be marketed as complements, perhaps at a discount. On two occasions, we have seen – in 1694 and in 1842 – the Académie Française lent support to an encyclopedic complement to its lexical dictionary, thus creating a kind of encyclopedic dictionary under two titles. So common had the practice become in the United States by the 1950s that consumers were warned that the purchase of an encyclopedia was "lumped in with the 'privilege' of buying ten years' worth of annual supplements at a reduced price, a bookcase, a two-volume

[66] Hingst, *Geschichte*, 172, 175.

dictionary and an atlas."[67] Such deals anticipated the practice of "bundling" software. Indeed, in 1998, Microsoft began selling its electronic encyclopedia *Encarta* (1993) with a previously developed "Bookshelf" that included a dictionary. Meanwhile, the problem of how to join or not join different kinds of material continued to trouble encyclopedia-makers. By amassing more material within a title, they could appeal to a broader readership and increase their profits on every set, but if their price got too high, they risked being undercut by a publisher offering part of the material separately and for less money.

Various reasons have been given for the development of the encyclopedic dictionary, or at least for the development of particular ones. In the *Encyclopaedia Perthensis*, Aitchison wrote that lexical information was essential in an encyclopedia, since knowledge itself was dependent on language.[68] Other writers evoked the practical goals of utility and convenience, inevitably without acknowledging that what was useful to one reader might be useless to another – and push the price up. The linguist Alain Rey associates the French encyclopedic dictionary with aspirations toward teaching and learning.[69] Associations with pedagogy and the dissemination of knowledge were especially strong with Larousse's encyclopedic dictionaries. The example of Larousse also points to a relationship with scholastic institutions, for the company succeeded in linking its encyclopedic dictionaries with France's emerging educational system.[70]

Perhaps the most intriguing correlation with the encyclopedic dictionary is a geographical one. Encyclopedic dictionaries flourished in Britain, France, Spain, and the United States.[71] As we have seen, the German firm Pierer published one of the first works to be called an encyclopedic dictionary, though it corresponded imperfectly to later conceptions of the genre. Pierer's encyclopedias aside, the expression "encyclopedic dictionary" almost never appeared in the titles of encyclopedias in German. Still, the idea of an encyclopedic dictionary was hardly alien to Germans. Living in Paris in the early twentieth century, Hans Brockhaus was impressed with the *Petit Larousse*, and he eventually imitated it.[72] The resulting encyclopedic dictionary, the *Neue Brockhaus: Allbuch in vier Bänden* (*New Brockhaus: All-Book in Four Volumes*, 1936–8), was revised and republished

---

[67] *Changing Times* (July 1955): 18.
[68] *Encyclopaedia Perthensis*, 1: i.
[69] Rey, *Miroirs*, 208.
[70] Boulanger, "Quelques figures," 93–4.
[71] Hupka, *Wort*, 36–7.
[72] Keiderling, *F. A. Brockhaus*, 157.

through the mid 1980s. The term "Allbuch," or "all-book" – probably invented at Brockhaus – became a German equivalent for "encyclopedic dictionary," though it was never much used.[73] For its main encyclopedia too, the Brockhaus firm saw the combination of the dictionary and the encyclopedia as sufficiently attractive to sell them together, though in separate sequences.

The *Konversations-Lexikon*

After 1800, content was too uniform in general encyclopedias to define recognizable genres, except perhaps in the case of the lexically oriented encyclopedic dictionary. Kinds remained identifiable within the genre of the modern encyclopedia, but they were now defined primarily by the related factors of price, size, organization, and audience. In the nineteenth and twentieth centuries, encyclopedias with long entries such as the *Encyclopaedia Britannica* were thus opposed to encyclopedias with more consistently short ones, notably the *Konversations-Lexikon*. The rivalry between the two models turned on the matter of encyclopedias' purposes and readers. Did readers want deep, even instructional, coverage of disciplines, as assumed in the *Britannica*, or did they want readily accessible information, as proponents of the *Konversations-Lexikon* insisted? The organizational aspect of this dilemma will be treated in Chapter 5, and its impact on readers in Chapter 9. Here I present a history of the *Konversations-Lexikon* and an evaluation of the degree to which it counts as a genre.

The origins of the *Konversations-Lexikon* are usually traced back to around 1700. The first works of reference to be called *Konversations-Lexika* were editions and imitations of the *Reales Staats- und Zeitungs-Lexicon* (*Real Lexicon of Politics and Periodicals*, 1704), a one-volume encyclopedia compiled anonymously but associated with Johann Hübner, the respected pedagogue who signed the preface. As of the third edition of 1708, the work's title changed to *Reales Staats- Zeitungs- und Conversations-Lexicon*, making it an encyclopedia for facilitating conversation as well as for understanding periodicals and politics. By the early nineteenth century, the *Reales Staats- Zeitungs- und Conversations-Lexicon* had gone through more than forty editions. It was so successful and popular that it might be considered as forming a genre in its own right. Before the early nineteenth

---

[73] Wiegand, *Wörterbuchforschung*, 55–6.

century, though, it lacked the international appeal of the eighteenth-century proto-encyclopedias treated above. Instead, it remained largely confined to German-speaking Europe, though translations were made into Dutch and Hungarian, and though encyclopedias elsewhere were advertised as aids to conversation.[74]

The *Reales Staats- Zeitungs- und Conversations-Lexicon* was dominated by geographical knowledge, but the genre of the *Konversations-Lexikon* acquired greater generality and a new sense of purpose in the early nineteenth century. A step in this direction came with the *Conversationslexikon* (1796–1808) of Renatus Gotthelf Löbel and Christian Wilhelm Franke, later acquired by Friedrich Brockhaus. In the preface, Löbel criticized the *Reales Staats- Zeitungs- und Conversations-Lexicon* for old-fashioned narrowness, and claimed that his and Franke's work would have a more modern breadth.[75] Accordingly, whereas more than three-quarters of the keywords beginning with "D" in the first edition of the *Reales Staats-Zeitungs- und Conversations-Lexicon* were names of places or geographical features, less than a sixth fell in these categories in Löbel and Franke's *Conversationslexikon*.[76] Among other articles, their *Conversationslexikon* offered biographies of living people, which were still rare in encyclopedias. After Brockhaus took possession of the encyclopedia in 1808, he further advanced Löbel's goal of making the *Konversations-Lexikon* comprehensive and up-to-date, notably by stressing biographies of the living.[77]

As it went from edition to edition in the early nineteenth century, Brockhaus's *Konversations-Lexikon* changed. It grew incrementally, though without approaching the size of such gigantic contemporary works as the *Encyclopédie méthodique* (1782–1832) or Johann Samuel Ersch and Johann Gottfried Gruber's *Allgemeine Encyclopädie der Wissenschaften und Künste* (*General Encyclopedia of the Sciences and Arts*, 1818–89). At the same time, it became more objective and scholarly in tone, shedding the liberal polemics and essay-like articles of its early editions. Increasingly, it was written and overseen by specialized contributors, not just compiled by Brockhaus or a few fellow generalists. Another shift took place between the sixth (1824) and seventh (1827) editions. Beginning with the sixth edition, the Brockhaus firm issued supplements dealing with current events, seeking to turn the

---

[74] See for example Lieshout, "Dictionnaires," 148.
[75] [*Grosse Brockhaus*], 1st edn., I: III–V.
[76] In both works, I checked all the entries under "D," ignoring entries consisting of a cross-reference alone. See also Loveland, "Encyclopaedias," 168.
[77] [*Grosse Brockhaus*], 5th edn., 1st printing, X: V ("Vorrede").

Konversations-Lexikon into a storehouse of stable knowledge to facilitate revisions.[78] The encyclopedia became less topical.

In the meantime, Brockhaus's *Konversations-Lexikon* had grown popular enough to be the target of imitation and piracy. From 1818 onward, it was published in Leipzig in the kingdom of Saxony. Outside the kingdom, it had little protection against copying before the late nineteenth century. Under these circumstances, it was repeatedly counterfeited or adapted by other publishers. Equally serious threats came in the form of merely similar works. The three main ones were associated with the names of their publishers, Pierer, Meyer, and Herder.

The first major rival to Brockhaus's *Konversations-Lexikon* was Pierer's encyclopedia, launched in 1822 according to plans drawn up by Ludwig Hain, a deserter from Brockhaus's team.[79] With its original titles of "encyclopedic dictionary" and "universal dictionary," Pierer's encyclopedia might seem a long way from a *Konversations-Lexikon*. As we have seen, it was different from Brockhaus's work in treating everyday language, albeit incompletely and against its stated policy. Its backers, moreover, sought to set it apart from Brockhaus's encyclopedia, situating it in a middle zone between the *Konversations-Lexikon* and Ersch and Gruber's *Allgemeine Encyclopädie*. As they presented it, it was more affordable and consultable than the *Allgemeine Encyclopädie* but more sober, accurate, and extensive than Brockhaus's work.[80] Pierer's first edition avoided the overt politicizing of Brockhaus's early *Konversations-Lexika*. By the 1860s, however, Brockhaus and other publishers of *Konversations-Lexika* were converging toward Pierer in this respect.[81] Sold by the Pierer family in the mid nineteenth century, Pierer's encyclopedia disappeared after a seventh edition (1888–93).

The Pierer firm's nemesis was the work of the publisher Joseph Meyer. In 1826, he founded the Bibliographisches Institut, which would publish the encyclopedia named after him, among other titles. Like Friedrich Brockhaus, Meyer was a liberal who battled with censorship. In the beginning, his encyclopedia was fiery, but it took on a more neutral posture in the second half of the century, thus charting a trajectory similar to Brockhaus's. Meyer's first encyclopedia, *Das grosse Conversations-Lexicon für die gebildeten Stände* (*The Great Conversational Dictionary for the Cultivated*

---

[78] Hingst, *Geschichte*, 120–2, 190–1.
[79] Spree, *Streben*, 95.
[80] [*Pierer's Universal-Lexikon*], 1st edn., I: XIII–XIV.
[81] Spree, *Streben*, 226.

Classes, 1840–53), nicknamed the *Wunder-Meyer*, was a colossus in forty-six volumes. It was so much larger than the company's next encyclopedia that it is often called the "zeroth" edition, whereas the first edition is considered to be the *Neue Conversations-Lexikon* (*New Conversational Dictionary*) of 1857–60.

Competition was intense between Meyer's and Brockhaus's encyclopedias. Realizing that the size of the *Wunder-Meyer* would prevent it from being revised fast enough to counter editions by Brockhaus, Joseph's son Herrmann Julius Meyer shortened the encyclopedia from forty-six to fifteen volumes, thereby matching Brockhaus's in its extent.[82] Meanwhile, the Bibliographisches Institut benefited from an early advantage over Brockhaus and Pierer in the field of illustration. Already on its first appearance in 1840, the *Wunder-Meyer* was illustrated, whereas Brockhaus's and Pierer's encyclopedias remained unillustrated for years. Belatedly, for the thirteenth edition (1882–87) of its *Konversations-Lexikon*, the Brockhaus firm adjusted to expectations and brought in illustrations.

With these and other moves away from their original models, the encyclopedias of Brockhaus and Meyer came to resemble each other more and more closely. Nevertheless, a political gap opened up between them in World War II. For the most part, Brockhaus kept its distance from the Nazis' ideas, though not in an aborted reworking (1939) of the fifteenth edition of its main encyclopedia, and not in the *Taschen-Brockhaus* (*Pocket Brockhaus*, 1940). Perhaps as a result, the Brockhaus family was accused of being fractionally Jewish, a charge that proved difficult to lay to rest. By contrast, the Bibliographisches Institut was led by Nazis. With support from the government of Germany's Third Reich, the company started but never finished an infamously "Nazified" eighth edition (1936–42) of its encyclopedia.[83]

After the war, Brockhaus and the Bibliographisches Institut were both split into two in the partition of Germany. In East Germany, both were nationalized, and the Bibliographisches Institut purged of Nazis.[84] The latter firm continued to publish general encyclopedias, notably *Meyers neues Lexikon* (*Meyer's New Lexicon*, 1961–4), the first major German encyclopedia to promote the materialism of Karl Marx and his followers. In West Germany, Brockhaus and the Bibliographisches Institut pursued their old rivalry. The Bibliographisches Institut published a final edition of its main

[82] Estermann, "Lexika," 248.
[83] Keiderling, *F. A. Brockhaus*, 164–70; Prodöhl, *Politik*, 76–144, 190.
[84] Prodöhl, *Politik*, 213–36.

encyclopedia as *Meyers enzyklopädisches Lexikon* (1971–9). At twenty-five volumes, it was the biggest German encyclopedia of the twentieth century, but its sales were lackluster. Finally, in 1984, financially troubled by new competition and a market saturated with encyclopedias, Brockhaus and the Bibliographisches Institut merged.[85]

A fourth German *Konversations-Lexikon* remains to be covered, namely that of Herder. When Karl and Benjamin Herder published their five-volume *Herders Conversations-Lexikon* (1854–7), it was less a threat to Brockhaus than the encyclopedias of Pierer and Meyer. In the first place, it was a Catholic work, whereas Germany's dominant encyclopedias were all tacitly Protestant. In the second place, it was a third as long, volume-wise, as Brockhaus's encyclopedia, designed as it was for a less affluent public. Nevertheless, the market for "small" encyclopedias was destined to grow, eliciting new offerings from Brockhaus and other companies. Already, in the same year that the Herders launched their encyclopedia, Brockhaus had published its comparably small *Kleineres Brockhaus'sches Conversations-Lexikon* (*Smaller Brockhaus Conversational Dictionary*, 1854), the first of the company's many attempts at a shorter encyclopedia. Then, in the twentieth century, the Herder firm created an expanded version of its encyclopedia, the twelve-volume *Grosse Herder* (*Great Herder*, 1931–5). Now the two companies were competing head to head.

In varying their encyclopedias' sizes and prices, Herder and Brockhaus were engaged in a practice common among encyclopedia-makers by the mid nineteenth century, one in which Larousse and the Bibliographisches Institut also excelled. Their success in diversifying makes the identity of the *Konversations-Lexikon* all the more problematic. At the minimum, a genre including Herder's early encyclopedias and the forty-six-volume *Wunder-Meyer* – all self-styled *Konversations-Lexika* – was evidently a broad one. More importantly for our purposes, it is unclear what characteristics these *Konversations-Lexika* shared.

Foreign adaptations of the *Konversations-Lexikon* raise similar doubts. From the early nineteenth century onward, Brockhaus's encyclopedias inspired imitations, translations, and adaptations abroad, but such offshoots had a range of relationships to the works they were modeled on.[86] Among foreign offshoots, the *Encyclopaedia Americana* (1829–33), Otto Wigand's Hungarian *Konversations-Lexikon* (1831–4), and the *Popular Encyclopaedia* (1841) – which borrowed from Brockhaus via the *Americana* – all made

---

[85] Keiderling, *F. A. Brockhaus*, 271–8, 325–8; Peche, *Bibliotheca*, 393.
[86] See [Piltz], "Zur Geschichte," xxxii–xxxvi.

substantial use of material assembled by Brockhaus.[87] Likewise, 40 percent of the articles at the start of the *Dictionnaire de la conversation et de la lecture* (*Dictionary of Conversation and Reading*, 1832–9) were translated from Brockhaus's *Konversations-Lexikon*, but rivalry with the *Encyclopédie des gens du monde* (1833–44), another adaptation of Brockhaus's work, pushed both toward less reliance on translated articles.[88] So too the *Enciklopedičeskij slovar'* (*Encyclopedic Dictionary*, 1890–1904), a Russian adaptation undertaken by Brockhaus and the publisher Ilya Efron, was initially criticized for being insufficiently Russian, after which a new editor reduced the role of translation from the *Konversations-Lexikon*.[89]

At the other end of the spectrum, some supposed offshoots of Brockhaus's *Konversations-Lexikon* were mostly independent of it from the beginning. One was *Chambers's Encyclopaedia* (1868), named after its publishers, William and Robert Chambers – and not to be confused with Ephraim Chambers' unrelated *Cyclopaedia*. In 1852, the Chambers brothers bought the right to translate Brockhaus's encyclopedia into English, but borrowing from the German work was never central to the composition of *Chambers's Encyclopaedia*, in part because the British preferred a terser, less deductive, and less digressive approach.[90]

Given the variety of *Konversations-Lexika* and their foreign reworkings, how can we characterize them in a unified way? One possibility is to concentrate on conversation, following the lead of the title. As a goal of eighteenth- and nineteenth-century *Konversations-Lexika*, enabling conversation was an ideal, an ideal drawn from French society and an imagined "public sphere" of sociability among equals. The early *Konversations-Lexika* of Brockhaus and Meyer did have conversational aspects. They were written in an effusive, essay-like style, they were substantive but not so detailed as to pass for pedantic, and they included passages perhaps meant to be learned in order to impress fellow socialites.[91]

Already by the mid nineteenth century, however, the relation between conversation and *Konversations-Lexika* was growing weaker. In part, *Konversations-Lexika* were becoming more scholarly. Readers were now assumed to be members of the social circles to which earlier editions had promised them entry through conversation. At the same time, the

[87] Weiss, "Americanization," 286–7; Lipták, "Sammlung," 191, 194–5; Spree, *Streben*, 289–93, 297.
[88] Loveland, "Two French 'Konversationslexika,'" forthcoming.
[89] Prodöhl, *Politik*, 58–9.
[90] See Cooney, "Die deutschen Wurzeln," 199–207; Spree, *Streben*, 293–310.
[91] Spree, *Streben*, 269–83; Hingst, *Geschichte*, 38–40, 65–73, 189–90.

conversational style of early-nineteenth-century *Konversations-Lexika* gave way to brevity and objectivity.[92] Indeed, for his fourth edition (1817–19), Friedrich Brockhaus abandoned *Konversations-Lexikon* as a title, now calling his work the *Allgemeine Hand-Encyclopädie* (*General Hand-Encyclopedia*), but he soon realized that the title, however archaic, appealed to the public. Thereafter, consequently, *Konversations-Lexikon* returned as a sub-title, only to become the main title again for the twelfth edition (1875–9). Upon its final demise with the fifteenth edition (1928–35), *Konversations-Lexikon* was replaced with the firm's name as a title. The *Konversations-Lexikon* had turned into *Der grosse Brockhaus* (*The Great Brockhaus*).[93]

Alternatively, instead of defining the *Konversations-Lexikon* in terms of conversation, one might cast it as an essentially popular, or non-scholarly, encyclopedia.[94] Certainly it was set off against Ersch and Gruber's *Allgemeine Encyclopädie* for much of the nineteenth century, and not without reason. Yet it did grow more scholarly. Furthermore, while encyclopedias were obviously premised on differing degrees of learning among readers, they were never strictly separated into learned and unlearned – a point I will elaborate on in Chapter 9.

In the end, the *Konversations-Lexikon* was less a fixed genre than an evolving set of tendencies linked with a name. These tendencies were exemplified by Brockhaus's encyclopedias and partially incorporated into a wide range of other ones. Among them was a tendency toward popularization, but this was a matter of degree, not of kind. Indeed, by the mid nineteenth century, Brockhaus and the Bibliographisches Institut were both publishing more accessible alternatives to their established, expanding, and increasingly learned *Konversations-Lexika*, beginning with the *Kleineres Brockhaus'sches Conversations-Lexikon* and *Meyers Hand-Lexicon* (1872). Quick re-editions were also characteristic of Brockhaus's encyclopedias, but editions grew less frequent as the company aged. Finally, *Konversations-Lexika* stressed topicality in the early nineteenth century, and were associated with liberalism and the promise of freedom.[95] By mid-century, however, they had distanced themselves from current affairs and were becoming less opinionated. At this point, a new tendency took hold of *Konversations-Lexika*, that of offering curt, almost definitional

[92] Hingst, *Geschichte*, 54–6, 117, 190–2; Spree, *Streben*, 21, 149–99.
[93] Hingst, *Geschichte*, 150–4.
[94] See for example Meyer, "Konversations-Lexikon," 8–9, 49.
[95] Spree, *Streben*, 64–5, 323; Puschner, "Mobil gemachte Feldbibliotheken," 73–4.

articles that emphasized the certainty and authority of knowledge, a tendency treated further in Chapters 2 and 9.

Children's Encyclopedias

Non-alphabetical encyclopedic works were written for children from the seventeenth century onward. A pioneer in the endeavor was the Czech pedagogue Iohannes Comenius. His *Orbis sensualium pictus* (*The Visible World in Pictures*, 1653) was a theologically organized encyclopedic work designed to instruct children and teach them to read. It was the first book to use illustrations to provide a complete education at an elementary level. A century later, Comenius's ideas were pursued by the preacher and publisher Johann Siegmund Stoy. His three-volume *Bilder-Akademie für die Jugend* (*Picture-Academy for the Young*, 1784) was similar to Comenius's *Orbis*, but he also invited purchasers to cut out the 468 illustrations in the non-textual volume, glue them on cardboard, and place them in a divided box for instruction and play.[96]

Without being identified as works for children, some alphabetical encyclopedias from before 1900 mentioned young people as readers. A smaller number mentioned children, usually as part of a family. One purported goal of the *Encyclopaedia Americana* (1829–33), for example, was "to animate youth to a perseverance in virtue and to the pursuit of true glory."[97] Similarly, Jean-Henri Schnitzler, the editor of the contemporaneous *Dictionnaire de la conversation et de la lecture*, addressed his encyclopedia to five groups of readers, among them the "young initiate seeking to begin a field of study" and parents eager to satisfy their children's curiosity.[98] More generally, by the late nineteenth century, encyclopedias were frequently marketed to families with children.

Many such encyclopedias were poorly designed for the young. As late as the early twentieth century, in fact, it was assumed that a children's encyclopedia could be based on a normal encyclopedia, as Janet Hogarth suggested in describing her efforts to make a "junior Britannica" from the *Encyclopaedia Britannica*: "It was to be made up of shortened, brighter versions of the 'E. B.' articles, with lots of pictures."[99]

---

[96] Heesen, *World*, 3–7.
[97] *Encyclopaedia Americana*, 1st edn., I: viii.
[98] "… le jeune adepte qui cherche à se mettre sur la voie d'un genre d'étude." *Dictionnaire de la conversation*, XXIV: 277.
[99] Boyles, *Everything*, 406. A *Britannica Junior* was finally published in 1934.

Or the children's encyclopedia could be the same as the adults'. To help sell its pirated version of the ninth edition (1875–89) of the *Britannica*, the Werner company published a guide recommending articles in the encyclopedia to different readers. The five-chapter part for "young people" began with a simple and friendly invitation: "Allow me to introduce you, boys and girls, to the *Encyclopaedia Britannica*."[100] Unfortunately, most of the articles recommended for "boys and girls" were dry and sophisticated. "Ichneumon," one of them, started as follows:

> [It is] a genus of small carnivorous mammals belonging to the family *Viverridae*, and resembling the true civets in the elongated weasel-like form of the body and in the shortness of the limbs. There are, according to Gray (*British Museum Catalogue*, 1869), 22 species of ichneumons, the great majority of which are confined to the African continent, the remainder occurring in Persia, India, and the Malay archipelago, and one, the Andalusian ichneumon (*H. Widdringtonii*, Gray), in the Sierra Moreno of Spain.[101]

Werner's guide was more credible in recommending the encyclopedia to students, though the suggested readings point primarily to advanced students.

Encyclopedias for schools and students had appeared in the seventeenth and eighteenth centuries, among them Laurence Echard's *Classical Geographical Dictionary* (1715) and Benjamin Hederich's *Reales Schul-Lexicon* (*Real School Lexicon*, 1717). In the nineteenth century they flourished, buoyed by the expansion of schooling in Europe. A leader in the elaboration of scholastic encyclopedias was Pierre Larousse, a former teacher who found the French educational system overly rigid. Larousse is sometimes credited with writing the first children's encyclopedia, but the work in question was non-alphabetical, his *Petite Encyclopédie du jeune âge* (*Small Encyclopedia for the Young*, 1853).[102] More importantly for our purposes, he created a durable model for a scholastic work of reference with his encyclopedic dictionary, the *Nouveau Dictionnaire de la langue française* (1856), the prototype, ultimately, for the *Petit Larousse* (1905).[103] Despite being politically radical and anti-clerical, Larousse assured readers that his *Nouveau Dictionnaire* was suitable for school-children of either

---

[100] Baldwin, *Guide*, 21.
[101] *Encyclopaedia Britannica*, 9th edn., XII: 629. The text is identical in Werner's "R. S. Peale reprint" of 1893. "Ichneumon" is recommended for children in Baldwin, *Guide*, 24.
[102] Coyne, "Effects," 8.
[103] On the kinship between the titles see Pruvost, "Du *Nouveau Dictionnaire*," 58.

sex, since it withheld information about sexuality. He claimed to have followed the advice of an ecclesiastic on the matter.[104]

In the anglophone world, *World Book* (1917–18) became the leader among children's encyclopedias. From the beginning, it was connected with schooling. The first edition reflected the ideas of its editor-in-chief, the professor and pedagogical theorist Michael O'Shea. Teachers too were involved in the production of *World Book*, notably as consultants and door-to-door salespeople. In the mid twentieth century, the owners of *World Book* also sponsored and took account of pedagogical research, which investigated such topics as layout, readability, and the curriculum in schools.[105] Initially, *World Book* was marketed primarily to teachers, but in the 1920s it began to be marketed to parents as well, a more lucrative market in the long run.[106] This shift in audience suggests the ease with which a scholastic encyclopedia could move outside schools.

In its early editions, *World Book* had many articles written for adults – for example, those on museums and children's literature.[107] Responding to changes in pedagogical theory, however, the encyclopedia focused increasingly on giving children what they needed to learn on their own. In style and language, the set became more suitable for young people as the twentieth century advanced.[108] In 1960, for instance, the article "Electricity" began with a paragraph that was simple enough to be used in an elementary school: "[Electricity] is a form of energy. We know what it is by what it does. Electricity gives us light, heat, and power. It brings us radio, television, motion pictures, and the telephone."[109] Still, *World Book* harmonized best with students' level in secondary school. Tellingly, despite advertising *World Book* as suitable for elementary school, the publisher designed *Childcraft* (1934) for children of this age.[110]

World Book's success was spectacular. By the 1930s, it was outselling all other children's encyclopedias in the anglophone market.[111] By the 1960s, it was being advertised, accurately, as the world's best-selling encyclopedia.[112] Likewise, as of 1971, the publisher Field Enterprises was earning more money from *World Book* than any other publisher was from any

---

[104] Lehmann, "Evolution," 223.
[105] Coyne, "Effects," 9; Murray, *Adventures*, 17–18, 74, 109–11, 199–203.
[106] Murray, *Adventures*, 31, 40, 50, 69.
[107] *Ibid.*, 30; Henry, "Survey," 23–5, 29–31, 35, 52–4.
[108] See Henry, "Survey," iii, 5–6, 26, 54–5, 57–8.
[109] *World Book* (1960), v: 146.
[110] Edgerton, "How Difficult are the Children's Encyclopedias?," 381; Murray, *Adventures*, 18–19, 92–3.
[111] Murray, *Adventures*, 108.
[112] See for example *New York Times*, November 30, 1965: 37.

encyclopedia.[113] Indeed, in the 2010s, *World Book* was one of the few multi-volume encyclopedias to survive as a printed work.

World Book's achievement inspired other American publishers to launch similar works, but expectations were rising for children's encyclopedias. In 1945, the professor Ronald Edgerton criticized three of them – *World Book*, *Compton's Pictured Encyclopedia* (1922), and *Britannica Junior* (1934) – for offering articles that were too complex, linguistically, for students not yet in secondary school.[114] Studies such as Edgerton's, which sought to measure readability as a function of age, were important because schools and libraries were under pressure to buy encyclopedias for specific ranges of age. Gone were the days in which the *Encyclopaedia Britannica* could be represented as satisfying the needs of "boys and girls." Writing in 1978, for example, the professor of librarianship William Katz assumed that a typical library would purchase three kinds of encyclopedias – one for adults, one for "young people," and one for children.[115]

Conversely, by the second half of the twentieth century, the makers of children's encyclopedias were approaching the problem of readability proactively, drawing up guidelines for allowable vocabulary or requiring a certain score on a test for readability.[116] Such methods could not guarantee that articles were understandable conceptually, but they did curb unrealistic views about the likely users of encyclopedias.[117]

Outside the United States, *World Book* faced challenges. Beyond the usual problems of adjusting material to other cultures, plans to adapt and translate *World Book* were hampered by its relationship with the American curriculum. Toward 1960, after the demise of a "British Empire Edition" from before World War II, the owners of *World Book* began designing an anglophone "international" edition (1966) to be marketed in Britain, Australasia, parts of Africa, and India. Among other changes, the encyclopedia had to be detached from the American curriculum and from American geography, culture, and language. To make it more local, two volumes on the targeted region were included with each international set.[118] Decades later, a Spanish edition was also brought out. The thirteen-volume *Enciclopedia estudiantil hallazgos* (*Student's Discovery Encyclopedia*,

---

[113] Coyne, "Effects," 11–12. See also Katz, *Basic Information Sources*, 138.

[114] Edgerton, "How Difficult Are the Children's Encyclopedias?," 460–4.

[115] Katz, *Basic Information Sources*, 139. For a list of anglophone encyclopedias for children, see Zischka, *Index*, 8–9.

[116] See for example Kogan, *Great EB*, 274–5; American Library Association, *Purchasing*, 33.

[117] Edgerton, "How Difficult Are the Children's Encyclopedias?," 381–2.

[118] Murray, *Adventures*, 215–23. See also Delavenay, "Quelques aspects," 836–44. I have only seen such supplements for the British Isles and Australasia.

2001), for example, was a translation of the *World Book Student Discovery Encyclopedia* (2000), a variant designed for elementary school.

In the meantime, non-American companies were producing children's encyclopedias of their own. After World War II, German encyclopedia-makers entered the market.[119] Among Brockhaus's offerings, *Mein erster Brockhaus* (*My First Brockhaus*, 1963) was a brief alphabetical book for children learning to read. A true children's encyclopedia, the four-volume *Kinder-Brockhaus* (*Children's Brockhaus*), appeared in 1992.[120] As we have seen, the French had a tradition of publishing encyclopedic dictionaries for scholastic use, though not for young children until after World War II. By the 1960s, the market had been stratified by Larousse and its rivals, so that different titles were produced for different ages of children.[121] As of the beginning of the twenty-first century, French publishers thus recognized four levels of scholastic or encyclopedic dictionaries, which corresponded to ages four to six, six to eight, seven to twelve, and thirteen and over.[122] Such sub-divisions point to the strength of the market.

Conclusion

Titles are both clues and traps with respect to kinds of encyclopedias. Since the eighteenth century, for example, the words "encyclopedia" and *Konversations-Lexikon* have been common in titles, but their claims to defining genres are different. As a genre, the modern encyclopedia was more porous than most, thanks in part to a blurred boundary with the lexical dictionary. Nevertheless, after the successful merger of the historical dictionary with the universal dictionary and the dictionary of the arts and sciences around 1800, it was solid and stable enough to be a useful interpretative category for consumers and publishers. An encyclopedia, henceforth, was an alphabetical work of reference that explained things and concepts, not just from the arts and sciences but also from history and geography. Germans preferred the title "lexicon" to that of "encyclopedia," but they were not writing essentially dissimilar works.

The *Konversations-Lexikon*, in contrast, may have been a genre in the form of the *Reales Staats- Zeitungs- und Conversations-Lexicon* or in the form of

---

119 Keiderling, "Lexikonverlag," 460. For a list of German encyclopedias for children, see Zischka, *Index*, 5.
120 Keiderling, *F. A. Brockhaus*, 252–3, 360–1.
121 Mollier and Dubot, *Histoire*, 501–2, 572–3, 582–3.
122 Lambrechts, "Conception," 153–4. For a list of French encyclopedias for children see Zischka, *Index*, 8.

early editions of Brockhaus's encyclopedia, but these forms were distinct. Nor was the *Konversations-Lexikon* stable under Brockhaus's stewardship. It started out as a liberal, essay-prone encyclopedia that was republished frequently, but the time between editions gradually lengthened, and it soon became bigger, more scholarly, and more objective. Brockhaus eventually designed smaller *Konversations-Lexika* to complement its original one. Nor do other alleged *Konversations-Lexika* from in- and outside Germany all fit the same mold.

Given this diversity, one might say that the *Konversations-Lexikon* was co-extensive with the encyclopedia in general, but the term's usage suggests otherwise. In practice, it refers to a collection of predominantly German works, a collection that is regularly set off against other encyclopedias, or just the *Encyclopaedia Britannica*. Considered in a limited historical context – the heyday of the *Reales Staats- Zeitungs- und Conversations-Lexicon*, say, or the early years of Brockhaus's and Meyer's encyclopedias – the *Konversations-Lexikon* can be seen as a sub-genre of the encyclopedia. What my analysis does not support is the idea that it was a single kind of encyclopedia throughout its history or one that can be distinguished easily from other encyclopedias.

Neither the encyclopedic dictionary nor the children's encyclopedia was as attached to a title as the *Konversations-Lexikon*. Encyclopedic dictionaries were similar to French universal dictionaries. These, too, mixed encyclopedic with lexical material, but without as many historical or geographical keywords. Perhaps because the encyclopedic dictionary was at an indefinite point between the encyclopedia and the dictionary, it did not have a consistent title, though "encyclopedic dictionary" gained acceptance around 1900.

Encyclopedias for children and scholastic purposes appeared under varied titles as well. Some clearly indicated a public of young people, but others were hard to interpret without the guidance of sub-titles, prefaces, and advertisements. In the latter group, for example, were the titles of the *Petit Larousse* and *World Book*. However identified, children's encyclopedias ended up forming a loosely defined genre as well as sub-genres in the twentieth century. They were characterized, above all, by being directed toward children, by dealing with curricular subjects, and by being approachable.

Beyond their strengths and weaknesses as possible genres of encyclopedias, the encyclopedic dictionary, the *Konversations-Lexikon*, and the children's encyclopedia all had some of the same indeterminacy as the genre of the modern encyclopedia itself. In particular, none of them came in a standardized size, which meant that none of them had a standardized price. It was partly for this reason that nineteenth-century publishers began differentiating their encyclopedias into "great" and "small" works. Using such descriptors along with titles, prefaces, and advertisements – all clues to genre – publishers and purchasers were able to communicate about kinds of encyclopedias and what to expect of them.

CHAPTER 2

The Contents of Encyclopedias

It might seem that a book about encyclopedias should be mostly about their contents. After all, what was an encyclopedia but a collection of contents? One response is that encyclopedias were part of a system, one that included their creators, their users, and their roles in society. Seen from this vantage, their contents were not necessarily of the highest importance, even to a purchaser. He or she might be swayed more by an encyclopedia's appearance or the advertisements promoting it. Still, advertisements and appearance had connections with contents. Furthermore, even if no one but editors appreciated encyclopedias' contents in all their detail, purchasers and readers were at least somewhat aware of them. Studying these contents not only illuminates the production of encyclopedias but also their potential readership and the contours of knowledge as judged fit for the public.

The previous chapter, on genres of encyclopedias, also dealt with their contents, since content contributed to determining genre. Genre, however, did not capture everything about encyclopedias' contents. Despite their similar coverage since around 1800, each had its emphases. Aspects of these emphases will be treated throughout this book. Here I will take an expansive view of encyclopedias' contents, specifically with respect to the qualities of up-to-dateness, practicality, objectivity, and cosmopolitanism. Under various names, all of these qualities were seen as desirable in encyclopedias, but all had their costs, which favored their opposites. Studying these qualities and their realization in encyclopedias sheds light on the struggle to bring ideals to bear on the material of encyclopedias – and in such a way as to maintain a market.

Progress and Its Pressures

Around the time of the Renaissance, educated Europeans began to see knowledge as advancing. This was the perception debated in the seventeenth- and eighteenth-century Quarrel of the Ancients and the Moderns. Later, in the nineteenth century, as news came to be available from day to day, consumers became more demanding in their expectations of the up-to-date. Real or imagined, the progress of knowledge and the quickening pace of events both put pressure on encyclopedias to stay up-to-date.

One way to show up-to-dateness was to feature material so new that it had not yet been published. Like twentieth-century newspapers, encyclopedias were not immune to the charm of a "scoop." Such scoops were often scientific before 1850. John Harris, for example, took pride in offering an unpublished paper by Isaac Newton in his *Lexicon Technicum* (1704).[1] Fortunato De Felice, the editor of a revised version (1770–80) of the *Encyclopédie* published in Yverdon, was so worried that research by Jean-André Deluc would undercut the encyclopedia's coverage of meteorology that he persuaded the author to let him take material from a forthcoming book.[2] A few decades later, David Brewster bragged that his *Edinburgh Encyclopaedia* (1808–30) displayed exceptional "originality" and that two subjects treated there had not even been named when the work was begun. One was the polarization of light, covered by its discoverer, Hans Oersted.[3]

As these examples indicate, encyclopedias depended on specialists for accounts of cutting-edge research. From the mid nineteenth century onward, experts disseminated their research in journals and books, and only thereafter in encyclopedias, if in fact they wished to. In the eighteenth and early nineteenth centuries, though, when fewer options were available for specialized publishing, and when the biggest encyclopedias were seen as central to the scholarly world, some researchers chose encyclopedias to publish their results for the first time. In addition, as a publication not subject to review by one's peers, an encyclopedia could be a comfortable space for exploring ideas, as D'Alembert and Nicolas Desmarest did in their entries on optics and geology in the *Encyclopédie*.[4]

Encyclopedists who sought out the latest news and discoveries to show up-to-dateness could find themselves thwarted by the realities of publishing. In the eighteenth and nineteenth centuries, many encyclopedias were

---

[1] Bradshaw, "John Harris's *Lexicon Technicum*," 110.
[2] Cernuschi, "ABC," 133–5.
[3] Yeo, introduction, xiii–xv; Collison, *Encyclopaedias*, 175–6.
[4] Ferlin, "D'Alembert," 153–71; Taylor, "Peculiarly Personal Encyclopedia," 40.

published over more than a decade. They spanned wars and revolutions among other events, by the end of which entries from the beginning of the alphabet might be obsolete. Obsolescence affected scientific and technological entries too.

By the early twentieth century, publishers were able to release big encyclopedias all at once, or in a matter of months. Still, even quickly published encyclopedias fell foul of time. An editor of Brockhaus's encyclopedia in the early 2000s estimated that only 3 to 4 percent of a big encyclopedia would ever need revising, but revising even that percentage presented a challenge.[5] Alternatively, according to the 1958 edition of the *Encyclopaedia Britannica*, 75 percent of an encyclopedia's contents did not need revision except "at long intervals." At the time, the *Britannica*'s editors were in fact fostering such durability by instructing contributors to avoid mentioning dates, since dates might reveal when an article was written.[6] Regardless, 25 percent of the *Britannica* apparently required updating at less than "long" intervals. In practice, intervals of one or two decades were typical between editions of multi-volume encyclopedias from the eighteenth to the mid twentieth century.

Three procedures slowed the pace of an encyclopedia's obsolescence. First, updates could be inserted at the end of the alphabet under contrived keywords. In Krünitz and others' *Oeconomische Encyclopädie* (1773–1858), for example, the entry "Vis Electrica" ("Force of Electricity") was added to supersede the seventy-eight-year-old entry "Electricität."[7] In the *Encyclopédie méthodique* (1782–1832), the first parts published on medicine, among other fields, had grown so out-of-date by the early 1800s that a decision was made to update them both in an appendix and in articles under related keywords. "Chlorosis," for instance, was updated in an article entitled "Pâles couleurs" ("Pale Colors"), which referred to a symptom of chlorosis, a form of anemia. At this point, the *Méthodique* was following normal practice, but in Volume x of the sub-series on medicine, one of the editors took the unusual step of listing fifty articles that supplied updates, thereby enabling readers to find them despite the odd keywords under which they appeared.[8]

Second, a separately alphabetized appendix could be placed at the end of a volume. This expedient was used in the *Encyclopédie méthodique*,

[5] For the estimate see Keiderling, *F. A. Brockhaus*, 333–4.
[6] Einbinder, *Myth*, 56, 75.
[7] Fröhner, *Technologie*, 38–9, 459–60.
[8] Braunrot and Doig, "*Encyclopédie*," 29; Doig, *From Encyclopédie*, 34n.

and it was frequent in the history of Brockhaus's encyclopedias. A few of Brockhaus's appendices were even planned in advance. In the nineteenth edition (1986–94), for example, the publisher announced at the outset that appendices would be placed at the ends of Volumes VI, XII, XVIII, and XXIV to provide updates.[9] Unlike the preponderantly scientific updates in eighteenth-century encyclopedias, most of the ones in these appendices added to biographies or dealt with unfolding political events.

A third way of avoiding a new edition was to issue a supplement of separate volumes. From the seventeenth century onward, this was a common procedure for extending an encyclopedia's life. Updating, in fact, was just one of the purposes that supplements served. They also allowed encyclopedia-makers to introduce articles on overlooked topics, remind the public of their encyclopedia's existence, and increase the sales of an out-of-date encyclopedia, since the original was usually marketed along with the supplement.

In the mid nineteenth century, several publishers experimented with offering updates in yearbooks and periodicals. Beginning with the sixth edition (1824), the Brockhaus firm moved topical content out of the *Konversations-Lexikon* and into a supplement, in part to lessen revisions to the main encyclopedia. Brockhaus's supplements started out alphabetical, but the ninth edition was supplemented with the non-alphabetical *Gegenwart* (*The Present*, 1848–56), a series that began with a report on the recent uprising in Paris. Other publishers began giving updates in periodicals. The Larousse company, for instance, issued a twenty-four-page monthly from 1907 to 1957, the *Larousse mensuel illustré* (*Illustrated Larousse Monthly*), originally to update the *Nouveau Larousse* (1897–1904) and Larousse's other encyclopedias. Unlike Brockhaus's *Gegenwart*, each issue of *Larousse mensuel* was in alphabetical order. Otherwise – wrote the editor, Claude Augé – it was "a genuine magazine."[10]

A more typical choice for updates was the one-volume yearbook. Yearbooks were first published as free-standing titles. They began to be associated with encyclopedias in the second half of the nineteenth century. Already, from 1865 to 1873, the encyclopedia-maker Pierer had published three volumes of *Pierers Jahrbücher* (*Pierer's Yearbooks*). In the twentieth century, yearbooks became ubiquitous. The *Encyclopaedia Britannica*, the *Encyclopedia Americana*, and the *Espasa*, for example, were all supplemented

9 [*Grosse Brockhaus*], 19th edn., 1: "Vorwort."
10 *Larousse mensuel* 1 (1907–10): "Préface."

with yearbooks, in 1913, 1923, and 1935 respectively. Thanks to regular updates in yearbooks and appendices, the *Espasa* remained in print, largely unchanged, from 1908 to the twentieth-first century.[11]

In the *Espasa*'s first yearbook, a preface explained the choice of a year-book over a monthly, alleging that the latter would be prone to error and shallowness.[12] Yearbooks too were criticized for being journalistic, however. According to the physicist Harvey Einbinder, writing in 1964, the *Britannica*'s yearbook neglected intellectual developments, read like a "digest" of news, and wrongly followed journalists in spurning scholarly references.[13] Nor were yearbooks much connected with the encyclopedias they accompanied. In the second half of the twentieth century, exceptionally, the editors of *World Book* strengthened the connection. To show that an article in the encyclopedia was updated in the yearbook, they mailed purchasers a sticker to affix alongside it (see Figure 2.1).[14]

Larousse discontinued the *Larousse mensuel* in 1957: "Today … re-editions at an accelerated pace allow our dictionaries … to track current events more closely."[15] Already in the eighteenth century, the *Reales Staats-Zeitungs- und Conversations-Lexicon* went into re-editions at intervals of just two or three years, whether through a determination to keep abreast of the times or because of a decision to respond to demand incrementally. In the early nineteenth century, Friedrich Brockhaus saw updating as essential to his project. He insisted that his *Konversations-Lexikon* must never be out of print and ensured that his re-editions were thoroughly revised.

In the late nineteenth century, the editors of *Johnson's New Universal Cyclopaedia* promised to revise and reissue the encyclopedia from "month to month, as the demand may require."[16] Such diligence would have put even Brockhaus to shame, but it is unlikely that demand required monthly reissues or that the editors were as conscientious about revising as they asserted. More seriously, toward 1930, the publishers of *Compton's Pictured Encyclopedia*, the *Encyclopaedia Britannica*, and other anglo-phone encyclopedias adopted a system of "continuous revision."[17] Under

---

[11] See, however, Silva Villar and Silva Villar, "Pérez Hervás," 485–94.

[12] [*Espasa: Suplemento, 1934*], XI.

[13] Einbinder, *Myth*, 304–5.

[14] I would like to thank Patricia Clark Roper for showing me her copy. See also Lih, *Wikipedia Revolution*, 18–19. On renovations to *World Book*'s yearbook for 1962 see Murray, *Adventures*, 229–32.

[15] "Aujourd'hui … des éditions à une cadence accélérée permettent à nos dictionnaires … de suivre l'actualité de plus près." *Larousse mensuel* 14 (December 1957): 369.

[16] *Johnson's New Universal Cyclopaedia*, 1: xiv.

[17] Khan, *Principles*, 281; Coyne, "Effects," 15; Kruse, "Story," 20–1, 390–1.

Figure 2.1 Stickers indicating updates in *World Book*. On the left, there is a sticker below the article on Martin Luther King Jr. in the 1967 edition, which refers to an update in the 1969 yearbook. On the right are a set of stickers and directions for using them from the 1987 yearbook. Scanned by the author from a set owned by Patricia Clark Roper. Images from *The World Book Encyclopedia*, Field Enterprises Educational Corporation © 1967; and *The 1987 World Book Year Book: The Annual Supplement to The World Book Encyclopedia* © 1987. By permission of *World Book*, Inc.

this system, a fraction of an encyclopedia was revised every year, so that its contents changed gradually rather than suddenly with each edition. Continuous revision stabilized publishers' revenue, helped encyclopedias stay current without the expense of a new edition, and allowed editorial staffs to be maintained indefinitely, building their expertise. Another possible outcome could be unwarranted tranquility about recycling old entries, since most would be carried over from year to year. Annual revisions to *World Book* – an encyclopedia revised continuously since 1934 – were thus less significant in the 1960s than the company advertised.[18] Continuous revision was never adopted universally. Among

[18] Coyne, "Effects."

the large encyclopedias untouched by it were those of Brockhaus and *Chambers's Encyclopaedia*.

Long before it was possible to revise encyclopedias electronically via the internet, entrepreneurs created frameworks for replacing old material. The *New International Encyclopaedia* (1902–4) had removable maps.[19] Around 1900, loose-leaf books – binders in which pages could be added or removed – began to grow popular in law and accounting.[20] The trend spread to encyclopedias. In 1909, *Nelson's Encyclopaedia* (1905), previously published with a traditional binding, was advertised in a "perpetual loose-leaf" edition. The publisher, Thomas Nelson, promised subscribers 500 pages of updates per year, which they could insert in place of obsolete pages by loosening a nut on the patented binding (see Figure 2.2). The system remained in place until World War II. Cincinnati's public library bought a set of *Nelson's* in 1912, for example, and took advantages of updates through at least 1931. By then, more than half the pages had been removed and replaced (see Figure 2.3).[21] The loose-leaf format was taken up by other encyclopedia-publishers in the anglophone world. Although enthusiasm had slackened by the start of World War II, loose-leaf supplements were still being issued to *Chambers's Encyclopaedia* in the second half of the century, and *Webster's Encyclopedic Dictionary* was published as a loose-leaf in 1961.[22]

In France, the experiment of the non-alphabetical *Encyclopédie française* (1935–66) points to the limitations of loose-leaf encyclopedias. Designed to be updatable on the model of juridical works, the *Encyclopédie française* allowed for the replacement of pages, constructed as it was of "independent booklets … clamped in the springs of specially designed electric bindings."[23] Eleven volumes appeared in the 1930s. Then, after an interruption due to World War II, work on the encyclopedia resumed in 1952. New volumes were published, and updates with such titles as "La Médecine depuis 1940" ("Medicine since 1940") were issued for insertion in previous volumes. By 1960, however, collaborators were balking at updating what had already been published. Instead,

[19] Collison, *Encyclopaedias*, 200.
[20] Petit, "Loose-Leaf Publications," 1700–1; Wootton and Wolk, "Evolution," 80–98.
[21] A "Publisher's Note" in Volume 1 stated that the loose-leaf edition was first published in 1909.
[22] Walsh, *Anglo-American General Encyclopedias*, 8, 22, 28, 94, 105, 178, 180; Michel and Herren, "Unvorgreifliche Gedanken," 64.
[23] "… cahiers indépendants … pris dans les ressorts de reliures électriques spécialement étudiées." Febvre, "Encyclopédie," cahier 4, 14. The bindings were "electric" in being made with an electrical binding machine. On the inspiration from juridical works see Pruvost, "Dictionnaires," 232.

Kindly mention Illustrated World when writing advertisers.

Figure 2.2   Advertisement showing the releasable binding in *Nelson's Perpetual Loose-Leaf Encyclopaedia* (1909), from *Illustrated World* 24 (October 1915). Scanned courtesy of the Public Library of Cincinnati and Hamilton County.

Figure 2.3   A rebound edition (1911) of *Nelson's Perpetual Loose-Leaf Encyclopaedia*
along with a page of updates ("Airway Map of the United States and Canada") that
was never inserted. Photographed courtesy of the Public Library of Cincinnati
and Hamilton County.

they insisted on rewriting volumes in their entirety, thus making the
innovative binding irrelevant.[24] The dream of creating a permanent
encyclopedia had lapsed.

   In August 1937, shortly after the launch of the *Encyclopédie française*, the
writer H. G. Wells sent the editors his plans for an international encyclopedia, nicknamed the "World Brain" – or so states a note in Wells's book
World Brain (1938). His proposal may have appeared in the *Encyclopédie française*, but it was probably just sent as a token of encouragement.[25] In any

[24] See Berger, introduction, IX–X; Cain, introduction, VI.
[25] I have not found the essay in the *Encyclopédie française*, but because of the updates, copies vary in
      content.

event, inspired by the technology of micro-photography, Wells imagined an encyclopedia containing more information than anything previous but small enough, physically, to be inexpensive and handy. In addition, Wells's "World Brain" would have been updated frequently, seemingly by replacing it in part or in full. Also in the first half of the twentieth century, the Belgian visionary Paul Otlet and the American inventor Vannevar Bush came up with their own plans for portable, updatable encyclopedias. In the end, none of these projects led to anything concrete. Nowadays, they are cited as anticipating the electronic encyclopedias of a half-century later, though their projects can also be related to those of the past.[26]

While the ideas of Wells, Otlet, and Bush may appear pioneering in retrospect, it is too easy to dismiss the period's actually realized schemes for updating encyclopedias as failures.[27] Certainly the *Encyclopédie française* had been largely forgotten by the time of its last volume in 1966, but as shown in Chapters 6, 8, and 9, it had handicaps unrelated to its publication as a loose-leaf or even its interruption by World War II. *Nelson's*, for its part, saw its final edition as a multi-volume encyclopedia in 1940. When the company returned to encyclopedia-making in 1951, it did not bring back the loose-leaf.[28] Nevertheless, *Nelson's* had survived as a loose-leaf for roughly three decades, during which time it was imitated and widely advertised. For all of these reasons, it would be wrong to see the loose-leaf encyclopedia as ill-conceived, as an incorrect solution to the problem of keeping encyclopedias up-to-date. Instead, like preceding solutions, this one was imperfect, but good enough to attract consumers for many years. No more can be said of today's solutions to the same problem – Wikipedia's included.

Practical Knowledge

When not empty boasts, claims that a given work encompassed all knowledge were made with an exclusionary vision of knowledge. The kinds of knowledge it did not cover could be nearly invisible to the compiler or editor. "Holes" only became apparent later as new kinds of knowledge acquired legitimacy. Such was the situation of many practical forms of knowledge. Indeed, even nowadays, knowledge is often seen as

---

[26] See for example Reagle, *Good Faith Collaboration*, 28; Yeo, "Before Memex," 21–44.
[27] For one such judgment see Collison, *Encyclopaedias*, 7.
[28] Walsh, *Anglo-American General Encyclopedias*, 107–8.

synonymous with abstract, theoretical knowledge, while merely factual or practical knowledge is neglected as trivial.[29]

Practical knowledge and useful knowledge are not necessarily the same thing. From the seventeenth century onward, almost all encyclopedias were touted as useful. They could be useful in supplying information or in helping readers toward personal or professional goals. At the minimum, certain encyclopedias were meant to help people in school. In nineteenth- and twentieth-century France, for example, Larousse and other companies designed encyclopedias to fit into the educational system, thus giving their works an intrinsic utility. Like many others, this kind of usefulness tended toward the theoretical and away from the practical. Conversely, much of the practical knowledge recorded in encyclopedias was useless to the majority of those who consulted them. One of the best examples is techno-logical knowledge.[30] Here, in fact, I will focus on encyclopedias' coverage of technology – or the "mechanical arts," in older parlance – as well as their coverage of a potentially more useful kind of practical knowledge, know-ledge related to health and domestic affairs.

From Greek antiquity onward, the mechanical arts, with their utili-tarian goals, were contrasted unfavorably with the liberal arts, worthy of cultivation by the elite. In the seventeenth and eighteenth centuries, attitudes changed. Intellectuals began studying the mechanical arts as they were then being practiced. Governments provided encouragement, eager as they were to capitalize on machines and inventions. Academies and societies were charged with improving the mechanical arts. In 1675, the French minister Jean-Baptiste Colbert thus ordered the Académie Royale des Sciences to draw up descriptions of machines used in the arts, a project that began in 1694 and led to the publication of the *Description des arts et métiers* (*Description of the Arts and Crafts*, 1761–88). The hope was that the mechanical arts would progress under public scrutiny, just as they had stagnated when hidden by guilds.

Among early encyclopedias, the dictionary of the arts and sciences reflected current interest in the mechanical arts, though it did not, at the outset, cover them well.[31] Harris, for instance, mingled with instrument-makers and touted their work in the *Lexicon Technicum* (1704), but he neglected more traditional arts such as brewing and agriculture. By con-trast, in the *Encyclopédie* (1751–72), the mechanical arts were not only

[29] See North, "Encyclopaedias," 193–4; Burke, *Social History*, 13–14.
[30] Hass, *Grosse Lexika*, 21n.
[31] Yeo, *Encyclopaedic Visions*, 63–4, 147.

valorized but were covered in a thorough and reasonably up-to-date way. We now know that a group of Parisian Benedictines was working on an encyclopedia emphasizing the mechanical arts at almost exactly the same time, using many of the same sources as the *Encyclopédie*.[32] Although their encyclopedia went unpublished, it shows that the mechanical arts excited encyclopedists of very different backgrounds.

The *Encyclopédie*'s sub-title was *Dictionnaire des sciences, des arts et des métiers*. The word "métiers" ("crafts") – a late addition – was a way of underscoring its treatment of the practical arts.[33] More explicitly, in the prospectus and introduction, Diderot and D'Alembert signaled their determination to advance and confer dignity on the mechanical arts. They promised visits to workshops to collect information, a task that Diderot initially assumed as his own.[34] Similar research apparently undergirded other encyclopedic works, including Richelet's *Dictionnaire françois* (1680), Jacques Savary des Bruslons and others' *Dictionnaire universel de commerce* (*Universal Dictionary of Business*, 1723–30), and Noël-Antoine Pluche's *Spectacle de la nature* (1732–50).[35] Such research was difficult, as Samuel Johnson noted in introducing his *Dictionary* (1755): "I could not visit caverns to learn the miner's language … nor visit the warehouses of merchants, and shops of artificers, to gain names of wares, tools, and operations."[36] Diderot himself did more research on the mechanical arts in libraries than workshops, though visits to workshops did play a role.[37] His reliance on printed sources led to anachronisms as well as charges of copying from the forthcoming *Description des arts et métiers*, the authors of which had already visited workshops.[38] Still, for all its faults, the *Encyclopédie* covered the mechanical arts better than any previous encyclopedia.

At the same time, the *Encyclopédie*'s achievement hints at limits to encyclopedias' coverage of technology. First, one of the goals of Diderot's technological articles was to make readers understand a machine's operation, ideally to the point that they would be able to reconstruct it if civilization collapsed. Accordingly, he did not shirk from using technical

---

[32] Holmberg, *Maurists' Unfinished Encyclopedia*, 168–88.
[33] Compare the titles of 1746 and 1748 in Luneau de Boisjermain, *Mémoire*, 12–16 ("Pièces justificatives"). See also Holmberg, *Maurists' Unfinished Encyclopedia*, 171.
[34] Proust, *Diderot*, 150–2.
[35] Considine, *Academy Dictionaries*, 43; Proust, *Diderot*, 179–81; Koepp, "Advocating," 246–8, 262.
[36] Yeo, *Encyclopaedic Visions*, 145.
[37] Proust, *Diderot*, 180–1, 194–5; Pinault [Sørensen], "Sur les planches," 355.
[38] Lough, *Encyclopédie*, 86–91; Bléchet, "Précurseur," 401.

vocabulary, though he also simplified and "improved" it.[39] Tellingly, however, René-Antoine Ferchault de Réaumur, an expert on technology and one of the authors of the *Description des arts et métiers*, pronounced the *Encyclopédie* both too long and too short, perhaps thinking of his more detailed research into the mechanical arts.[40] Similarly, a review of the *Complete Dictionary of Arts and Sciences* (1764–6) – which had articles on technology translated from the *Encyclopédie* – criticized it for not recognizing that "in subjects of handicraft, the *general* principles of the art are all that books can be supposed to convey."[41]

Second, the hope that describing the mechanical arts would allow the enlightened to improve them remained unfulfilled in the *Encyclopédie*. The writer Alexandre Deleyre, one of Diderot's co-authors on technological matters, dutifully made proposals for improving the art of pin-making in his article "Epingle," but they were impractical.[42]

Third, and most importantly, Diderot worried about readers' enthusiasm for the mechanical arts. Midway through his article "Bas" – on a device for knitting stockings – he expressed doubt that readers understood what he had written thus far. A half-century later, the entry on the same machine in the *Encyclopédie méthodique* pronounced it too complicated to be described there.[43] In fact, nearly all subsequent general encyclopedias retreated from Diderot's ideal of describing machines comprehensively, concentrating instead on their main parts and overall function. Presaging these sentiments in the late eighteenth century, the publisher Panckoucke eliminated technological plates in a new edition of the *Encyclopédie*.[44]

In German, nonetheless, an even more exhaustive account of the mechanical arts was still being published through the mid nineteenth century, in Krünitz and others' *Oeconomische Encyclopädie* (1773–1858), later retitled the *Oeconomisch-technologische Encyclopädie*. Specialized technological encyclopedias such as Adrian Beier's *Allgemeine Handlungs-Kunst- Berg- und Handwercks-Lexicon* (*General Lexicon of Business, Art, Mining, and Crafts*, 1722) had already appeared. The *Oeconomische Encyclopädie* was more general, though it did exclude biographies and

[39] Proust, *Diderot*, 211–16.
[40] Stalnaker, *Unfinished Enlightenment*, 117–19; Proust, *Diderot*, 202–3.
[41] Review of *Complete Dictionary*, 23. On copying from the *Encyclopédie* into the *Complete Dictionary* see Loveland, "Two Partial English-Language Translations," 182–3.
[42] Benrekassa, "Didactique," 304. See also Proust, *Diderot*, 203–4.
[43] Stalnaker, *Unfinished Enlightenment*, 119–22.
[44] Birn, "Mots," 637–8.

many forms of abstract and non-utilitarian knowledge. Ultimately finished in 242 volumes, it was one of the richest of technologically oriented encyclopedias, devoting dozens, even hundreds, of pages to subjects barely registered elsewhere. The entry on indigo, for example, ran to more than 120 pages, or 36,000 words, covering the indigo plant's world-wide production, the dye's effects on health, and its chemical properties, among other topics. The *Encyclopédie* had devoted just 5 pages to indigo and 26 pages to dyeing in general (roughly 6,000 and 30,000 words respectively).[45]

The *Oeconomische Encyclopädie* elicited admiration and sold well at first, but interest waned as it dragged on. One reviewer warned that certain entries were "too drawn out and almost overly complete."[46] General encyclopedias, for their part, did not seek to match its technological coverage. Even Ersch and Gruber's *Allgemeine Encyclopädie* (1818–89), a bigger encyclopedia, covered waterworks such as dams and harbors in a narrower way, though with more mathematics.[47] Likewise, the *Encyclopaedia Britannica*, while expansive on technology relative to other encyclopedias, devoted 30,000 words to dyeing as of 1940 – less than the *Oeconomische Encyclopädie* had to indigo alone.

Entries on technology were an expected part of encyclopedias by the mid 1800s, but they had more limited goals than those of the *Encyclopédie* or the *Oeconomische Encyclopädie*. As a rule, they presented technology in its broad outlines, and despite its growing role in society, it was limited to a minor portion of entries and pages. The directors of France's *Grande Encyclopédie* (1885–1902) thus agreed to devote 7.5 percent of their space to technology and industry.[48] Similarly, in the ninth edition (1875–89) of the *Britannica*, 12 percent of the entries of ten or more pages were on the "practical arts."[49]

As noted above, encyclopedias' coverage of the mechanical arts may have been practical in dealing with methods of making and doing things, but it was of little use to most people. It is hard to imagine, for instance, who would have used articles on the mechanical arts in

[45] On Krünitz's coverage of indigo see Fröhner, *Technologie*, 182. Compare *Encyclopédie; ou, Dictionnaire*, VIII: 679–83, XVI: 8–33.
[46] "… zu weitläuftig und beinahe übervollständig." Fröhner, *Technologie*, 96. More generally, see Fröhner, *Technologie*, 56, 58–98.
[47] *Ibid.*, 438–55.
[48] *Grande Encyclopédie: Inventaire*, I: XI–XII.
[49] Kruse, "Story," 190.

the *Encyclopédie*, though perhaps they guided entrepreneurs thinking of starting a business.[50]

Potentially more useful to a large public was practical knowledge related to domestic affairs, as communicated, above all, by specialized encyclopedias. Some of these were devoted to the household or rural life, both referred to as "economies" in the language of the time. One of the most influential was Noël Chomel's *Dictionnaire oeconomique* (1709), based on his non-alphabetical *Recueil de plusieurs lettres familières d'un curé* (*Collection of Several Informal Letters from a Priest*, 1697), written for a public of landowners as well as priests. Along with advice on morality, Chomel's *Dictionnaire* provided recipes, remedies for illnesses, and "secrets" for improving agriculture.[51] Somewhat less practical were encyclopedias for women, a genre inaugurated in Britain with the *Ladies Dictionary* (1694) and developed in German as the "dictionary of the ladies' room" (the *Frauenzimmer-Lexikon*). The first of the latter, Gottlieb Siegmund Corvinus's *Nutzbares, galantes und curiöses Frauenzimmer-Lexicon* (*Useful, Gallant and Curious Dictionary of the Ladies' Room*, 1715), included articles on famous women, women's games, and feminine religious orders, alongside information on cooking, dressing, and other domestic activities.[52] Later women's encyclopedias tended to stray less from the topic of women's work in the household – for example, *Every Woman's Enquire Within: A Guide to Household Knowledge* (1940).[53]

Neither encyclopedias for women nor encyclopedias of rural life were particularly general, but general encyclopedias borrowed from both. Together with the equally practical *Dictionnaire universel de commerce*, Chomel's *Dictionnaire* was a source for encyclopedias all through the eighteenth century. Along with other material, the *Encyclopédie* took recipes from it – for which Diderot was criticized, presumably because knowledge of cooking was seen as too lowly and indeterminate for an intellectual monument.[54] Krünitz planned to translate his *Oeconomische Encyclopädie* from an adaptation (1770–1) of Chomel's *Dictionnaire*, though he quickly began incorporating other material.[55] Finally, it is possible that the first edition of

---

[50] Koepp, "Making."

[51] Leca-Tsiomis, "Rhétorique," 116–23.

[52] Brandes, "*Frauenzimmer-Lexicon*," 23–7; Goodman, *Amazons*, 11–39. On the *Ladies Dictionary* see Considine and Brown, introduction, vii–xli.

[53] For a bibliographical sampling see Zischka, *Index*, 5, 253–4.

[54] See *Encyclopédie; ou, Dictionnaire*, v: 646v; Albertan, "Journalistes," 109.

[55] Fröhner, *Technologie*, 25–8.

Brockhaus's *Konversations-Lexikon* was published in parallel as a women's encyclopedia, specifically as a *Frauenzimmer-Lexicon zur Erleichterung der Conversation* (*Lady's Dictionary for Facilitating Conversation*).[56] If so, it was an oddity among *Frauenzimmer-Lexika*, for it emphasized abstract and factual over practical knowledge.

Whether taken from specialized encyclopedias or other sources, information on the household and everyday living was a vital if secondary part of general encyclopedias. German encyclopedias were especially practical this way. The first *Deutsche Encyclopädie* (1778–1807) featured recipes as well as directions for chores such as doing the laundry.[57] In the early nineteenth century, the future founder of psycho-physics, Gustav Theodor Fechner, compiled a *Hauslexikon* (*House-Lexicon*, 1834–8). He conceived it as a practical alternative to Brockhaus's *Konversations-Lexikon*, which emphasized *Bildung*, or cultivation. The *Hauslexikon* covered the sciences better than encyclopedias of the household, but true to its title, it also offered an abundance of practical information. One article, "Auswanderung" ("Emigration"), advised readers on moving to North America, an important option to consider for nineteenth-century Germans.[58] Similar articles appeared in other German encyclopedias. In the *Wunder-Meyer* (1840–53), the article "Auswanderung" was seventy-two pages long. Among other things, it recommended emigration for skilled, strong, hard workers between twenty and forty years old; it provided prices for transport between different American cities; and it detailed a budget for establishing a farm on the American prairie.[59] The *Wunder-Meyer* is rightly considered a learned encyclopedia, but it was also a practical one.

In the early twentieth century, the editors of Herder's *Konversations-Lexikon* devised a typographical method of stressing its practicality. Already in the one-volume *Kleine Herder* (*Small Herder*) of 1925, the firm had experimented with "boxed articles" (*Rahmenartikel*). These were longer, framed articles, often on subjects with a practical aspect – how to set up an aquarium, say. Attention to practical matters was presented as the encyclopedia's strength.[60] Soon afterward, *Rahmenartikel* were used in the *Grosse Herder* (*Great Herder*, 1931–5), the fourth edition of Herder's main encyclopedia, which was

---

[56] Hingst, *Geschichte*, 30.
[57] Goetschel, Macleod, and Snyder, "*Deutsche Encyclopädie*," 273.
[58] Arendt, *Gustav Theodor Fechner*, 33–4, 43–7, 59–60.
[59] [*Meyer's Konversations-Lexikon*], "0th" edn., IV: 890–1, 898–901.
[60] *Kleine Herder*, "Geleitwort."

advertised as more practical than rival *Konversations-Lexika*: "[It] will be not a museum of knowledge but rather the tool of our era."[61] Here, a new means was used to identify "information for practical living": a dotted line in the margin alongside the information (see Figure 2.4).[62] Ironically, since it was marketed on the basis of practicality, the encyclopedia had only a minor proportion of material identified as practical – around 1 percent in the first 200 pages of Volume III, for example.

Herder's marking of practical information reveals assumptions about readers. Why, for instance, was the statement in "Barock Möbel" ("Baroque Furniture") that such furniture remained available identified as practical unless because readers were seen as potential buyers? Likewise, ample "practical" information on the cultivation of flowers points to an audience with the leisure and enthusiasm for gardening as a hobby. So too, in the fourteenth edition (1929) of the *Encyclopaedia Britannica*, the treatment of crosswords was justified as an indulgence in a serious work, but the question of whose indulgence was left unasked.[63] As these examples indicate, useful and practical knowledge could overlap with an imagined readership's entertainment and pastimes.

A second lesson of Herder's experiment with marking the practical is that practicality was a matter of form as well as of content. Practical sections in the encyclopedia used the imperative and even the informal, somewhat intimate pronoun *du* ("you"): "Protect yourself against infection!"[64]

As this directive suggests, medicine was an area where encyclopedias could provide information applicable in the household. The learned printer William Smellie, who compiled the first edition (1771) of the *Encyclopaedia Britannica*, saw it as a vehicle for democratizing knowledge, and borrowed much of his treatise "Medicine" from a work designed to allow people to tend to their own needs.[65] A more cautious attitude toward self-medication emerged in the following century. The editors of the second edition (1840–8) of Pierer's encyclopedia declined to cover illnesses too specifically for fear of encouraging people to try curing themselves.[66] Likewise, the article "Asphyxie" in the *Encyclopédie nouvelle* (1834–42) offered guidelines for treating an asphyxiated person in an emergency, but only after stipulating

---

[61] "[Er] wird kein Museum des Wissens, sondern das Werkzeug unserer Epoche." Keiderling, "Lexikonverlag," 444. See also Keiderling, "Lexikonverlag," 450–1.

[62] "… wichtige Angaben für das praktisches Leben." [*Grosse Herder*], 4th edn., I: "Zeichen."

[63] *Encyclopaedia Britannica*, 14th edn. (1929), I: xxxii.

[64] "Schütze dich vor Ansteckung!" [*Grosse Herder*], 4th edn., I: 689.

[65] Kafker and Loveland, "William Smellie's Edition," 28, 48.

[66] Spree, *Streben*, 40.

Echidna (griech. = Schlange), im griech. Mythus ein räuberisches Ungeheuer, halb Jungfrau, halb Schlange. Wurde von Argos getötet.

Echidna, Gattung der Kloakentiere, die ↗ Ameisenigel.

Echiniten, die fossilen ↗ Seeigel.

Echinocactus, artenreichste Kakteengattung, verbreitet von Nevada bis Patagonien; meist kuglige Pflanzen von der Größe einer Walnuß bis zu der eines Reiters, mit gegliederten Rippen, die zu 4 bis 100 u. mehr auf Höckern ob. Warzen vielgestaltige u. schönfarbige Nadeln tragen („Igelkaktus"); nur wenige Arten, wie E.myriostigma, die ↗ Bischofs-mütze, stachellos. Aus dem Schei-tel der Stachel-polster sprossen die farbenpräch-tigen Trichter-blüten, meist gelb, auch rot ob. weiß. Beliebte, leicht zu kultivie-rende Kakteen fürs Kalthaus u. mäßig warme Zimmer, bes. E. minusculus, klein, rasenför-

Echinocactus minusculus

mig, mit milchweißen Blüten, E. bicolor nebst der Abart tricolor mit 2- bzw. 3farbigen Stacheln, E. corniger mit hakig gekrümmten Nadeln („Hörnerkaktus"), E. ingens, eine der größten Arten, deren Stacheln in der Heimat (Mexiko) als Zahnstocher dienen, E. Grusoni mit bes. seltsamer Bestachelung usw. Die kleine, flachscheibenförm. u. stachellose Erdkaktee E. (Anhalonium, Lophphora) Williamsii (Lewinii), in Nordmexiko Peyotl ob. Pellote, auch Hikuli, in Arizona Mezkal genannt, ist stark giftig, wird aber von den Indianern als Berauschungs- u. Schlafmittel gekaut; die daraus bereitete Droge Anhalonium ist bes. in Nordamerika ein beliebtes Heilmittel gegen Herzkrämpfe, Asthma, Husten u. a.

⦙ Kultur: wie bei allen ↗ Kakteen; wegen des
⦙ langsamen Wachstums bes. für das Zimmer
⦙ geeignet.

Echinocereus, Kakteengattung mit 60 Arten in Mexiko u. den Ver. Staaten, vom Igelkaktus (Echinocactus) durch die walzenförmi. Gestalt (daher „Igelsäulen- ob. -kerzenkaktus") unterschieden, mit eingebuchteten Rippen, kurzen Sta-

Echinocereus dasyacanthus var. cristata

cheln u. kurzröhrigen, meist roten Blüten; bilden durch reiche Grundsprossung oft dichte Rasen. Dankbare Zimmerkakteen, im Sommer am sonnigen Fenster, im Winter im mäßig warmen Zimmer, bef. E. pectinatus var. caespitosa mit starker Sprossung, E. Delaetii, ganz mit weißen Haaren bedeckt, E. Salm Dyckianus, mit langröhr., orangeroten Blüten, E. dasyacanthus mit ovalen, bei der var. cristata gewundenen Sprossen u. a.

Kultur wie bei allen ↗ Kakteen; wegen des
Schleimgehalts bef. widerstandsfähig gegen
Trockenheit.   [schelhäuter.

Echinodermata, Tierklasse, die ↗ Sta-
Echinoidea, Ordnung der↗Stachelhäuter, die ↗ Seeigel.

Echinokokken, Hülsen- ob. Blasenwürmer, in Menschen u. Tieren lebende Entwicklungsstadien des Hunde-↗Bandwurms.

Echinokokkenkrankheit, die ↗ Blasenwurmkrankheit.   [↗ Kugeldisteln.

Echinops, Gattung der Köpfchenblütler, die
Echinopsis, Kakteengattung mit 25 Arten im südl. Südamerika; mehr ob. minder kuglige Gestalten („Seeigelkaktus") mit meist gekerbten u. fast höckerlosen Rippen, stark bestachelten Polstern u. weißen ob. gelben, langröhrigen Trichterblüten („Trompetenkaktus"), die sich gegen Abend öffnen u. meist schon am folgenden Tage wieder schließen. Bekannte u. dankbare Zimmerkakteen, bes. E. tubiflora mit sehr langen, grünlichweißen u. E. Eyriesii mit nach Jasmin duftenden weißen Blüten.

Kultur: im Sommer an sonnigem Fenster ob. im Freien, über den Winter in mäßig war-mem Raum, sonst wie bei al-

Echinopsis tubiflora (¹/₁₅ nat. Gr.)

len ↗ Kakteen; blühen schon als jüngere Pflanzen.

Echinorhynchus, Hauptgattung der ↗ Kratzer (schmarotzender Würmer).   [igel.

Echinus, Gattung der regelmäßigen ↗ See-

Echinus (griech. = Igel), beim Kapitell der dorischen Säule der Wulst, der den Übergang vom Säulenschaft zum Abakus vermittelt.

Echium, Gattung der Borraginaceae; E.vulgare, Heilpflanze, der ↗ Natternkopf.

Echnaton, ägypt. König, ↗ Ägypten, Gesch.

Echo, das, 1) in der ↗ Akustik: der Widerhall von Schallwellen infolge Brechung an akustisch reflektierenden Schichten wie z. B. Felswänden, Gebäudemauern, Waldrand, Wolken (der Donner ist das E. der elektr. Entladungen beim Gewitter).

Da das menschl. Ohr nur 10 Schallempfindungen in der Sek. unterscheiden kann u. der Schall zur Fortpflanzung Zeit (340 m/sec) braucht, muß die Entfernung zwischen der Schallquelle u. der zurückwerfenden Wand mindestens 17 m (17 m Hin- u. 17 m Rückweg

Figure 2.4   Dotted lines indicating practical information in articles on cactus-cultivation in the fourth edition of Herder's *Konversations-Lexikon*. Scanned courtesy of the Klau Library, Cincinnati, Hebrew Union College – Jewish Institute of Religion. With permission from Herder.

that professional treatment should always be sought: "God forbid that we consider ... preaching medicine without a medical doctor."[67] As the twentieth century approached, all that remained of an earlier ambition to disseminate a maximum of medical know-how was scattered information on preserving health, treating minor annoyances, and dealing with emergencies. In the latter capacity, several American encyclopedias of the second half of the century continued to explain in detail how to offer "first aid."[68]

By the mid nineteenth century, the place of practical knowledge in encyclopedias had become strained. Practical knowledge retained appeal as an element of encyclopedism, and encyclopedias were criticized for not including enough of it. As we have seen, Fechner marketed his *Hauslexikon* as being more practical than Brockhaus's *Konversations-Lexikon*. Depicting the encyclopedias of Brockhaus and Meyer as short on practicality came to be easier as they grew more scholarly. The preface to an unfinished *Allgemeines Konversations-Lexikon* (*General Conversational Dictionary*, 1928) thus accused other *Konversations-Lexika* of sacrificing practicality for a vain show of learnedness. By contrast, claimed the preface, the *Allgemeines Konversations-Lexikon* would meet readers' needs and be their "advice-giver and ... friend."[69] Anticipating such criticism, Brockhaus and the Bibliographisches Institut had begun selling less scholarly alternatives to their own *Konversations-Lexika*. Brockhaus, for instance, published a seven-volume *Illustrirtes Haus- und Familien-Lexikon* (*Illustrated House and Family Lexicon*) from 1860 to 1865. It was advertised as less intellectual than Brockhaus's main *Konversations-Lexikon* and as including more practical knowledge related to the family and household.[70]

Other nineteenth- and twentieth-century encyclopedias were marketed as being practical despite their preponderantly non-practical content. Toward 1900, for example, official and unofficial purveyors of the *Encyclopaedia Britannica* promoted it as practical in all walks of life. An advertisement for the tenth edition (1902–3) claimed that it could save money on bills: "The doctor, the carpenter, the lawyer have all gone to the *Encyclopaedia Britannica* to learn. WHY NOT GO DIRECT and save the expense of an intermediary?"[71] More elaborately, the Werner company,

---

[67] "A Dieu ne plaise que nous pensions ... à prêcher la médecine sans médecin." *Encyclopédie nouvelle*, II: 444.
[68] See for example *Merit Students Encyclopedia*, VII: 68–74; *Encyclopedia Americana: International Edition*, XI: 266–73.
[69] "... Ratgeber und ... Freund." Peche, *Bibliotheca*, 20.
[70] See for example [*Grosse Brockhaus*], 11th edn., XV: XXIII.
[71] Einbinder, *Myth*, 46.

having adapted the ninth edition for Americans without authorization, published a *Guide to Systematic Readings in the Encyclopaedia Britannica* (1895), addressing it to a wide range of working people as well as students and children. Many of the readings proposed there were touted as "practical." The *Guide* went through several editions and was imitated by an official look-alike, the *Reader's Guide to the Encyclopaedia Britannica* (1913). Both guides signaled material relevant to different professions and pastimes, some of it practical, despite the ninth edition's reputation as the "scholar's edition." As Werner's *Guide* noted, the article "Angling," for instance, had a section on how to catch fish with a rod.[72] For the most part, however, the guides referred readers to theoretical discussions rather than anything directly applicable.

Revealingly, the editor James Garvin refused an article on etiquette for the fourteenth edition (1929) of the *Britannica* because it risked being "parodied."[73] Articles on etiquette had appeared in other encyclopedias and would continue to do so. *World Book* maintained its article into the twenty-first century. Citing George Washington, the article in the 1918 edition advised against humming in social settings. By 1960, the article was illustrated and signed by Emily Post, a columnist on etiquette. Among other things, it recommended that boys walk to the left side of girls and that everyone "break bread before buttering" (see Figure 2.5). Like any prescriptions, these would have been easy to parody, though Post admitted that politeness varied with culture.[74]

As this example hints, practical knowledge was most plentiful in less scholarly encyclopedic works, notably non-alphabetical ones and children's encyclopedias. Among the former was *Ogilvie's Encyclopaedia of Useful Information* (1891), which supplied advice on marriage, a guide for the conversationalist, tips for removing stains, and much more in the same vein. Children's encyclopedias too were regularly practical. Under "C," for example, the 1957 edition of *Britannica Junior* gave instructions for canoeing, taking care of a canary, playing checkers and chess, cooking, and camping. One piece of advice for campers gives a sense of these articles' informal practicality: "If you think you are lost [in wooded country], sit down and spend half an hour considering your situation, to overcome any feelings of panic."[75]

[72] Baldwin, *Guide*, 46–7, 287; *Encyclopaedia Britannica*, 9th edn., II: 32–44, XXI: 31–2. See also Kogan, *Great EB*, 62–3.
[73] Kogan, *Great EB*, 224.
[74] *World Book* (1918), 3: 2085; *World Book* (1960), V: 297–9.
[75] *Britannica Junior*, IV: 49.

Come to the Dinner Table
with clean hands

"Please" and "Thank You"
are passwords of courtesy.

Use Knife and Fork to
cut large pieces of food

Place Knife and Fork
at side of plate

Break Bread before buttering. Chew with mouth closed.

and friendship, and there are many occasions when it is necessary. People always shake hands with a guest of honor. On all formal occasions, the host and hostess must shake hands with strangers, and naturally shake hands with friends. Guests shake hands with the host and hostess when they leave. Children do not shake hands often, but they all do at times.

Most of the rules of etiquette in relations between men and women are based on good reasons. When women wore long, flowing skirts, its was difficult for them to alight from a carriage. Gentlemen helped them. Today, it is polite for a man to stand ready to give his hand to a woman getting out of a car, in case she needs assistance.

Other rules of etiquette are based on what is called *good taste*. There are things we do not do because they would offend other people. Most of our eating manners are based on good taste. We do not shovel food into our mouths, talk with our mouths full, or eat messy food with our fingers. To do so would be unpleasant for other people to watch. We take frequent baths, brush our teeth, and wear clean clothes, both because it is good for our health and because it makes life more pleasant for the people around us.

Formal and Informal Etiquette. Many rules of etiquette are simply *forms* for performing various social acts. These forms vary from country to country, from period to period, and from group to group. Generally, the simpler people's lives are, the simpler are their social customs. Two or three hundred years ago in Europe, the rich nobles who lived at kings' courts enjoyed a highly developed social life. They did no work, so to pass the time, they added to the ceremonies of the court and made more and more rules of etiquette. They developed rules of behavior for every social function. Often there were no particularly good reasons for the rules.

The ways of formal etiquette remain today. These customs include the proper way to conduct weddings, to set silverware and dishes on a table for a formal dinner party, and to send invitations for a social function. These customs vary with different groups. As a rule, wealthy members of what is called "high society" have more complicated and more rigid forms of etiquette than less well-to-do people. The customs of people who live in cities differ from the customs of those who live in small towns. One example is in visiting customs. In formal city society, women usually pay formal calls on newcomers to their social group. They make calls only at certain hours. Sometimes the visitor does not even see the person on whom she is calling. She merely leaves her card. In small towns, women call immediately on new people. They call informally on all newcomers, regardless of their "social standing." People consider such calls neighborly. There is no real difference in etiquette between the two customs. The formal action among the city group is the proper thing to do, but it would be considered snobbish in small towns.

Conversation is one of the most important aspects of human relations. The way we talk to people largely determines the way they feel about us. Polite speech is the surest mark of good manners. Rudeness to those who serve us marks an impolite person. Etiquette provides rules for both what we say and how we say it. An uneducated man may use bad grammar, but the kindness and tact with which he speaks will mark him as a

Introduce Persons who
have not met before

A Boy Walks at the girl's
left, or nearest the curb.

Sit Quietly in a movie to
avoid disturbing others.

Offer Your Place to older
persons who are standing

Figure 2.5   Advice on etiquette from the 1960 edition of *World Book Encyclopedia*.
From "Etiquette." *The World Book Encyclopedia*, Field Enterprises Educational
Corporation © 1960. By permission of *World Book*, Inc.

Such material was growing rarer in encyclopedias for adults, as indicated, for example, by the evolution of the *Encyclopaedia Britannica* in the twentieth century. Whatever Garvin's scruples about an article on etiquette, the fourteenth edition was more practical than those that preceded it, but the trend was not lasting, for the fifteenth edition, the *New Encyclopaedia Britannica* (1974), was markedly less so.[76] In the opinion of Warren Preece, one of the planners and then the editor, an encyclopedia offering "instructions on building a birdhouse and dipping candles" would be compromised by the effort to make it "all things to all men."[77]

Encyclopedias' retreat from practicality reflected three trends. First, it went hand in hand with an increasing emphasis on objectivity, as characterized below. Knowledge of how to do something is tied to tradition and cannot be made as impersonal as scientific knowledge. Coverage of food, for example, is never objective, motivated as it is by a cultural framework. Second, whereas idealism helped turn the *Encyclopédie* into a technological showcase, and whereas practicality was the founding principle of the *Oeconomische Encyclopädie*, subsequent encyclopedia-makers covered technology like any other subject, calibrating its presence to match the public's interest – which was not seen as passionate. Third, encyclopedias may never have excelled at offering practical information, much of which was transmitted directly from person to person, but they were also, in this area, rivaled by other books, whether cookbooks, medical manuals, or guides to pastimes.

Impartiality and Objectivity

To judge by their prefaces, one might conclude that all encyclopedias were objective. Yet they were regularly denounced as biased, both by contemporaries and later generations. One reason for the discrepancy is that standards varied and changed. Thus, however biased it looked to outsiders, an encyclopedia might seem objective to its authors or editors. Furthermore, the discourse in encyclopedias' prefaces was aspirational and promotional as well as descriptive. So it was, evidently, in the *Schweizer Lexikon* (*Swiss Lexicon*, 1945–8), a Swiss encyclopedia meant for sale in Germany, where self-professed "objectivity" co-existed with an article on Germany that neglected to mention the Nazis' efforts to exterminate the Jews.[78] Much the same can be said of Encyclopaedia Britannica's statement

---

[76] Kruse, "Story," 364; Kogan, *Great EB*, 232; Runte and Steuben, "*Encyclopaedia*," 92.
[77] Preece, "Notes," 19.
[78] Prodöhl, *Politik*, 169–74.

that the Chinese encyclopedia (1986) it co-produced with Encyclopedia of China remained "objective." In fact, controversial material was simply eliminated to accommodate Chinese views.[79] More generally, the contents of encyclopedias almost inevitably fell short of editors' statements about objectivity.

In the seventeenth and eighteenth centuries, many encyclopedists vaunted their "impartiality," often under this name, and often to ward off accusations of religious partiality.[80] In a plea to Louis XIV for permission to publish his encyclopedia, the Protestant Samuel Chappuzeau thus promised not to be "partial," that is, not to favor either Catholics or Protestants.[81] Similarly, in his re-edition (1701) of Furetière's *Dictionaire*, the Protestant Basnage claimed to have made it suitable for use by anyone. In particular, he committed himself to maintaining "all measures of civility on religious matters in giving each party the honorable names it gives itself."[82] One of his purposes was to win over Catholics in France, the biggest market for books in French. Alternatively, in 1737, the Freemason Andrew Michael Ramsay proposed a dictionary of the arts of sciences that would completely steer clear of religion and politics. This route to avoiding partiality was mostly ignored by encyclopedists, though it did have a precedent in Harris's *Lexicon Technicum* (1704) and was implemented, surprisingly, by Parisian Benedictines in an unpublished encyclopedia toward 1750.[83]

Around 1800, encyclopedists' concerns about impartiality broadened. Reacting to controversies in and around modern science, they began to make pronouncements about scientific impartiality. More importantly, politics became a center for debates about partiality. Now joining the ranks of encyclopedias promoting specific religions were unabashedly political encyclopedias. In the German states, the early-nineteenth-century *Konversations-Lexikon* was associated with liberalism, the cause of social liberty and private property. A few politically opposed works were nonetheless published, including the Catholic, anti-liberal *Allgemeine Realencyclopädie oder Conversationslexicon für das katholische Deutschland* (*General Real*

---

[79] *New York Times*, September 11, 1986: C19.

[80] On religious controversy and eighteenth-century encyclopedias see Leca-Tsiomis, "Du *Dictionnaire*"; Sullivan, "Circumscribing Knowledge," 315–16, 321–29.

[81] Jennings and Jones, *Biography*, 188–9.

[82] "… toutes les mesures d'honnêteté sur les matières de religion, en donnant à chaque parti les noms honorables qu'il se donne à lui-même." Furetière and Basnage, *Dictionaire*, 1: *3r.

[83] Holmberg, *Maurists' Unfinished Encyclopedia*, 4, 146–8, 154–5, 232–41. For another precedent see Gasparri, *Etienne Chauvin*, 129, 229.

Encyclopedia or Conversational Dictionary for Catholic Germany, 1846–50).[84] In early-nineteenth-century Britain, encyclopedias were less attached to political movements, but they still had ideologies. The *Encyclopaedia Metropolitana* (1817–45), for instance, represented the "Anglican establishment" against the *Encyclopaedia Britannica*, then marked by the skeptical utilitarianism of Jeremy Bentham.[85] The French saw perhaps the widest range of politicized encyclopedias during the period. Their options ran from the secular, left-leaning *Encyclopédie nouvelle* (1834–42) to the conservative Catholic *Encyclopédie du dix-neuvième siècle* (*Encyclopedia of the Nineteenth Century*, 1838–53).

In the second half of the nineteenth century, encyclopedias became less political even as they fell under the influence of nationalism. One reason was economic. As a preface to Meyer's *Konversations-Lexikon* observed in 1909, only an encyclopedia that rose above the divisions of domestic politics could expect to succeed on a national scale.[86]

The terms used for referring to impartiality and analogous principles evolved over time. "Impartial" was frequent in encyclopedias through the end of the nineteenth century, while "objective" gained ascendance in the twentieth century. France's *Grande Encyclopédie* (1885–1902), for example, still offered "impartiality," not only in the moral and social sciences but also in the natural ones.[87] Similarly, Thomas Baynes' introduction to the ninth edition (1875–89) of the *Britannica* called it "impartial" and insisted that it would present knowledge, not opinions, in science and religion as well as philosophy.[88] If his words were meant to soothe people afraid of "advanced" thinking, they were untrue to the encyclopedia as it developed. In biology, for instance, Baynes recruited Thomas Huxley to write "Evolution," a treatise denounced by two American competitors as contrary to the Bible and religion in general.[89]

In the twentieth century, many encyclopedias promised objectivity – sometimes along with impartiality, as it occurred in the *Enciclopedia italiana* (1929–39), where neither concept, unfortunately, was defined or explained.[90] Already in the middle of the previous century, the prefaces to the tenth edition (1851–5) of Brockhaus's *Konversations-Lexikon* and

[84] Spree, *Streben*, 64.
[85] Schmidt, "Visionary Pedant," 128. See also Spree, *Streben*, 264–5, 323.
[86] Spree, *Streben*, 15–16, 48–50, 226.
[87] *Grande Encyclopédie: Inventaire*, I: I, IX–X.
[88] *Encyclopaedia Britannica*, 9th edn., I: viii.
[89] Einbinder, *Myth*, 38; Kogan, *Great EB*, 53–4, 65–6. See also Phelps, "*Encyclopaedia*," 72–3.
[90] *Enciclopedia italiana*, I: XV.

the third edition (1865–73) of the *Allgemeine Realencyclopädie* evoked the works' objectivity under that name, though the latter also mentioned a Catholic viewpoint.[91] The first reference to objectivity in the preface to an encyclopedia in English was that of Hugh Chisholm in the eleventh edition (1910–11) of the *Britannica*, but his discussion of the "objective view" made it sound like impartiality. Specifically, he stressed the need to give "representation to all parties, sects and sides" and to explain beliefs in the language of those believing them.[92] A presumably different kind of "objectivity" was rejected in the article on Oscar Wilde, because the writer's perceived immorality allegedly prohibited it.[93]

Objectivity was different from impartiality. The word acquired its modern meanings in the nineteenth and twentieth centuries. Unlike impartiality, which hinted at controversy between two or more viewpoints, objectivity could be demanded outside any controversy and in the absence of settled viewpoints. By the late nineteenth century, it was seen as a standard for knowledge, one requiring depersonalization and distance with respect to things studied.[94] Already in the *Encyclopédie* (1751–72), Diderot characterized the ideal encyclopedia-editor as being "truthful, from no country, from no sect, from no state," a characterization that anticipated later notions of objectivity.[95] An advertisement for the ninth edition (1875–89) of the *Britannica* cited other conflicts of interest that its contributors avoided: "No personal or corporate bias has ever been suffered to interfere with the broad honesty of the work."[96] Conversely, critics faulted encyclopedists for insufficient detachment from what they wrote on. At one extreme, a writer for *Johnson's New Universal Cyclopaedia* (1875–7) was accused of being paid by manufacturers to highlight their products in his articles "Carriages," "Clocks," "Hotels," and "Furniture."[97]

In the early twenty-first century, the collaborative online encyclopedia Wikipedia popularized the idea of a "neutral point of view," or "NPOV," as a norm for contributors. Previously Wikipedians had been asked to be "unbiased."[98] Like impartiality, and unlike objectivity, neutrality suggests a

---

[91] Spree, *Streben*, 85; *Allgemeine Realencyklopädie*, I: III–IV. See also Peche, *Bibliotheca*, 13. The preface to the ninth edition (1843–8) of Brockhaus's *Konversations-Lexikon* promised to present things in their "objectivity." See Spree, *Streben*, 42.
[92] *Encyclopaedia Britannica*, 11th edn., I: xxi.
[93] Wright, *Misinforming*, 58–9.
[94] Daston, "Objectivity," 597–614; Daston and Galison, *Objectivity*, 34–5.
[95] "… véridique, d'aucun pays, d'aucune secte, d'aucun état." *Encyclopédie; ou, Dictionnaire*, V: 648v.
[96] Boyles, *Everything*, 354.
[97] "Reply," 30.
[98] Reagle, *Good Faith Collaboration*, 57.

balance between opposed points of view. It suits Wikipedia, where authors nudge articles back and forth as they try to establish consensus. Previous encyclopedists too had laid claim to a middle ground – for example, certain editors of Brockhaus's and Meyer's nineteenth-century *Konversations-Lexika*.[99] As shown below and in Chapter 7, one way of being religiously neutral was to divide articles up, typically into Protestant, Catholic, or secular parts. Despite recourse to the concepts of fairness or balance in the prefaces of encyclopedias, the term "neutral" was rarer than "impartial" or "objective," though it came up occasionally. For the directors of the *Grande Encyclopédie* (1885–1902), impartiality was not the same thing as "passive neutrality," which would mean considering all viewpoints as equally valid.[100] In the *New Encyclopaedia Britannica* (1974), the editors used "neutrality" and "objectivity" as synonyms, both referring to balance in the face of "reasonable differences of opinion."[101]

As these examples indicate, encyclopedias were neither consistent with one another nor philosophically searching in their claims about impartiality, objectivity, and related ideals. Critics analyzed their objectivity with equal casualness. In the late twentieth century, the American Library Association thus chose objectivity as a criterion for evaluating encyclopedias, and made it a matter of giving opposed viewpoints, avoiding societal "biases," and being faithful to "mainstream thinking."[102] Within the main text of encyclopedias, subtler accounts of objectivity appeared in scientific and philosophical articles, but they were even more detached from the realities of encyclopedia-writing than the pronouncements of prefaces – which tended to be too abstract and absolute to help contributors write articles. More useful for understanding the objectivity of encyclopedias are guidelines and practices underpinning the construction of articles. To these I now turn for the remainder of the section.

Guidelines for contributors to encyclopedias almost all touched on objectivity. In his one year as director of the developing *Encyclopédie* (1751–72), for example, the mathematician Jean-Paul De Gua de Malves wrote instructions for potential contributors. Here, among other things, he made two demands related to objectivity: not to dwell on one's own discoveries, and to treat philosophical systems in an "impartial" way.[103] When the publisher Charles Knight decided to allow biographies of living

[99] Spree, *Streben*, 197, 237–8, 252–3.
[100] *Grande Encyclopédie: Inventaire*, I: x.
[101] *New Encyclopaedia Britannica* (1974), *Propaedia*: xv.
[102] American Library Association, *Purchasing*, 12.
[103] Favre and Dürr, "Texte," 63–5; Théré and Charles, "Nouvel élément," 118–19.

people in the *English Cyclopaedia* (1854–62), he probably gave contributors guidelines like the ones proposed in his autobiography, namely to avoid hypotheses and rely on "authentic materials."[104] Vaguer in this regard, the guide for contributors to the *Grande Encyclopédie* (1885–1902) merely announced that the encyclopedia would be impartial, before turning to superficial aspects of article-writing.[105] Indeed, standards for such matters as spelling, abbreviations, bibliographies, and the length of articles routinely dominated guidelines for contributors.

Since formal guidelines were both incomplete and easy to ignore, expectations about objectivity were also communicated on a case-by-case basis. When one of the publishers of the *Encyclopaedia Americana* (1829–33) flagged the article "Jesuits" as unfair to Catholics, the editor Francis Lieber proposed inserting a second article on the Jesuits, this one written by a Jesuit for Brockhaus's *Konversations-Lexikon*.[106] Contributors, moreover, must have had their own standards for objectivity, independent of what editors or publishers told them. Investigating their attitudes is difficult, but we can examine their articles to see how a sense of objectivity was created, or not. This approach to objectivity is all the more valuable in that it matches readers' experiences of using encyclopedias. Here I will review six elements of objectivity as created in texts. These correspond, respectively, to texts' being impersonal, unopinionated, dispassionate, serious, authoritative, and anonymous.

Within entries in encyclopedias, one textual feature that was ruled out by objectivity, but not impartiality, was allusion to the author. Personalization had once been seen as desirable in scientific discourse. In the seventeenth and eighteenth centuries, many researchers used first-person singular pronouns to narrate their scientific observations and experiments. Such pronouns enhanced the credibility of the knowledge being communicated, since they helped conjure up a scene for readers to "witness." The same kinds of pronouns appeared in some of the period's encyclopedias, though most had different purposes. In the *Lexicon Technicum* (1704), for instance, Harris used them to underline his philosophical loyalties ("I wish that … [astrology] may be quite forgotten"), to hedge ("this, I believe, was first done by Descartes"), and to credit his sources ("the following converging series … the late Mr. [Thomas?] Wastell … sent me").[107] Even a century later, Desmarest used them

[104] Knight, *Passages*, II: 226–7.
[105] *Grande Encyclopédie: Instructions*, 6. Compare *Grande Encyclopédie: Inventaire*, I: 1.
[106] De Kay, "Encyclopedia," 209–10.
[107] Loveland, *Alternative Encyclopedia?*, 15.

hundreds of times to report observations in the volumes on geography (1795–1816) in the *Encyclopédie méthodique*.[108]

In other encyclopedias from around 1700 – among them Furetière's *Dictionaire* and Chambers' *Cyclopaedia* – first-person singular pronouns were already rare. Revealingly, when the editor Smellie adapted texts for the first edition (1771) of the *Encyclopaedia Britannica*, he replaced first-person singular pronouns with first-person plural or third-person constructions.[109]

Nor, for the most part, is there personal information about authors in the encyclopedias they worked on. Despite their first-person singular pronouns, Harris's *Lexicon* and Desmarest's volumes on geography tell us little about their authors except as intellects and professionals. Only rarely did encyclopedias feature personal disclosures, but three exceptions are worth considering: Dennis de Coetlogon's *Universal History of Arts and Sciences* (1745), the *Encyclopaedia Americana* (1829–33), and Larousse's *Grand Dictionnaire* (1866–76).

All through the *Universal History*, Coetlogon made personal revelations in the first-person singular. His "impartiality" must not have struck him as requiring impersonalness. In "Apparitions," for example, he remembered dressing up as a ghost to frighten a professor who told stories about ghosts. Like his generous coverage of his own theories, his autobiographical disclosures were an attempt to impose his identity on the *Universal History*, but they had other meanings too. Like Jean-Jacques Rousseau, the inventor of autobiography, Coetlogon took pleasure in evoking his past for the public to appreciate. For both men, it was a way of reimagining themselves. Still, whereas Rousseau sought to represent his innermost being, Coetlogon contented himself with allusions to his involvement in events, adventures, and occasions of state.[110]

Composed as it was of scattered statements, Coetlogon's "autobiography" in the *Universal History* was like that of Lieber in the *Encyclopaedia Americana*, but the latter was sparser, perhaps because Lieber had collaborators writing articles.[111] Indeed, since articles were unsigned, it can be difficult to decide what to attribute to Lieber. As he was not a physician, statements in "Cholera" about cases faced by "the writer" could not have been his.[112] Other self-references are ambiguous, but three kinds can

[108] Taylor, "Peculiarly Personal Encyclopedia," 40–1, 44.
[109] Loveland, *Alternative Encyclopedia?*, 16.
[110] *Ibid.*, 18, 87–8, 180, 215.
[111] See Weiss, "Americanization," 275.
[112] See for example *Encyclopaedia Americana*, 1st edn., XIII: 410, 424.

confidently be attributed to Lieber: first, those in articles known independently to be his work; second, those alluding to "the editor"; and third,
those that mirror what we know of his life – for example, reminiscences
about being a soldier in the Napoleonic wars or about time spent in prison
for political activities.[113] Unlike Coetlogon, Lieber referred to himself in
the third person. As editor, paradoxically, he seems to have banned the
first-person singular, apparently because he saw it as too conspicuously
personal.

Larousse's *Grand Dictionnaire* presented much of its autobiographical
content in formal biographies in the third person. One was in the preface,
while two others were in articles entitled "Larousse" – both posthumous
but probably composed by Larousse.[114] In addition, many entries had
sections in the first-person plural, Larousse's preferred mode for referring
to himself.[115]

Like the *Universal History*, Larousse's *Grand Dictionnaire* was opinionated, but it was also subjective in two ways that the *Universal History*
and the *Encyclopaedia Americana* were not, namely in being passionate
and full of playfulness. In all three of these characteristics, the *Grand
Dictionnaire* had precedents. In the first half of the nineteenth century,
French and German encyclopedias especially were markedly opinionated, in part because of the model of Brockhaus's liberal *Konversations-
Lexikon*. Emotions too were expressed freely in early-nineteenth-century
encyclopedias, as measured, for example, by the number of exclamation
points.[116] Lastly, among encyclopedias, playfulness is associated with
Bayle's *Dictionaire* and the *Encyclopédie*, both sometimes mischievous in
their subversion of dogma. The *Grand Dictionnaire*, as well, featured subversive playfulness, but it also had the merely imaginative playfulness of
certain encyclopedic works for children – some of which went so far as
to make room for fiction.[117] Consider the article "Mansarde," on garrets.
After noting that garrets were romanticized as places of youthful delight,
the author conjured up an imagined scene: "On a nail, one hangs the coat

[113] See for example *ibid.*, I: 616, III: 311, XIII: 500.
[114] For two autobiographies see Larousse, *Grand Dictionnaire*, I: LXXIV–LXXVI, X: 211. For claims that
  Larousse wrote the latter article and much of his biography in the first supplement (1877) see
  Pruvost, "Pierre Larousse," 13; Mollier and Dubot, *Histoire*, 205–6.
[115] Rey, "Lexicographe," 137–8. For examples see Mollier and Ory, *Pierre Larousse*, 85–94.
[116] On opinions and emotions in early-nineteenth-century encyclopedias see Loveland, "Two French
  'Konversationslexika,'" forthcoming.
[117] For examples of fiction in twentieth-century encyclopedic works see Tracy, *World*, 192–7; Walsh,
  Anglo-American General Encyclopedias, 99, 137.

of Lisette, who has come tick-tocking at the door; under-skirts serve as curtains, and it is delightful … in verse. In prose, one is not happy in a garret aged either twenty or thirty."[118]

Well before Larousse's time, encyclopedias were being pushed toward an appearance of objectivity. Coetlogon's *Universal History* was far less successful than the *Lexicon Technicum* or Chambers' *Cyclopaedia*, its more conventional rivals in the 1740s. Even more tellingly, the editors of a revised edition (1759) of Coetlogon's encyclopedia eliminated its most subjective and personal parts.[119] Larousse's *Grand Dictionnaire* sold well, perhaps because its flaunting of norms for objectivity resonated with its republican and anti-clerical ideals.[120] Still, after the launch of the "impartial" *Grande Encyclopédie* (1885–1902), the *Grand Dictionnaire* began to come across as old-fashioned. When the Larousse company returned to the market for big encyclopedias, it did so with a work marking a repudiation of Pierre Larousse's subjectivity, the *Nouveau Larousse illustré* (1897–1904).[121]

By around 1900, then, a consensus had emerged making encyclopedias off-limits to personal disclosures, explicit opinions, passionate language, and playfulness. Two other aspects of encyclopedias' objectivity defied consensus, however, or rather, resulted in different consensuses.

One concerned the manner in which encyclopedists constructed articles to give them authority. Consider Ulrike Spree's comparison of Brockhaus's *Konversations-Lexikon* and the *Encyclopaedia Britannica*. In the course of the nineteenth century, *Konversations-Lexika* in general abandoned the subjective traits of their beginnings, notably polemics. Articles in Brockhaus's *Konversations-Lexikon* started to look like enlarged definitions, becoming concise, impersonal, factual, and neutral in tone.[122] In the early nineteenth century, British encyclopedias had been less journalistic and less explicitly political.[123] For this reason, their evolution toward objectivity was less dramatic. Regardless, the *Britannica* never became objective in the way Brockhaus's *Konversations-Lexikon* did. Instead of centering articles on definitions and presenting information as evident, the *Britannica*

---

[118] "On accroche à un clou le manteau de Lisette, qui vient faire tic-toc à la porte, les jupons servent de rideaux, et c'est charmant … en vers. En prose, on n'est bien dans un grenier ni à vingt ans ni à trente." Larousse, *Grand Dictionnaire*, x: 1096.

[119] Loveland, *Alternative Encyclopedia?*, 60–6, 76–9.

[120] On the work's sales see Ory, "*Grand Dictionnaire*," 229; Mollier and Dubot, *Histoire*, 131, 173–4; Pruvost, "Pierre Larousse," 38–9. On its political and religious positions see Mollier and Dubot, *Histoire*, 123–9.

[121] See Mollier and Dubot, *Histoire*, 193–4, 319.

[122] Hingst, *Geschichte*, 54, 194; Spree, *Streben*, 171, 226, 327; Belgum, "Documenting," 96–8, 101–2.

[123] Spree, *Streben*, 37, 67, 76–7, 316.

tended to re-enact the logic by which knowledge was created. In other words, articles acquired authority in Brockhaus's *Konversations-Lexikon* by avoiding any reference to uncertainty or debate, whereas they did so in the *Britannica* by showing how reason could navigate knowledge.[124]

Another area where encyclopedias had contrasting practices relating to objectivity was the assignment of authorship. As shown below in Chapter 7, motives were variable for identifying or not identifying authors of articles, but one motive for not doing so was to suggest objectivity. In principle, anonymous articles were more objective than signed ones, coming as they seemed to from no one in particular. Indeed, according to Philippe Castellano, the absence of signatures in the *Espasa* (1908–30) was part of a strategy to make it appear more objective.[125] Likewise, the editors of the *Enciclopedia italiana* (1929–39) decided to publish biographies anonymously when they dealt with the living, surely in part because such impersonalness established a protective air of objectivity.[126] Conversely, in the ninth edition (1971–9) of Meyer's encyclopedia, when 100 essays were brought in to supplement the regular, "objective" entries – which were anonymous – they were all signed.[127]

The correlation between objectivity and anonymity was not absolute. Despite its credo of impartiality, the *Grande Encyclopédie* (1885–1902) offered signed entries, which the director Ferdinand-Camille Dreyfus justified as allowing authors to take responsibility for their personal views.[128] Nor did the editors of the *Britannica*, who encouraged contributors to sign, see as persuasive a link between objectivity and anonymity as they did between signatures and intellectual authority.[129] They might have taken comfort in the precedent of modern science, where publications remained signed despite the pressures of objectivity.

Objectivity in encyclopedias was formed over centuries from a disparate collection of attitudes, procedures, and compositional practices. Encyclopedists were ultimately so successful in cultivating it that encyclopedias came to be seen as inherently objective. As a result, they became ideal for convincing people of things that they might have considered skeptically had they encountered them elsewhere.[130] Among these things were ideas about nations and nationality, which are treated below.

---

[124] *Ibid.*, 161–2, 171–6, 191–2, 327. See also Schmitt and Loveland, "Scientific Knowledge," 340–5.

[125] Castellano, *Enciclopedia*, 114, 369–70.

[126] See Cavaterra, *Rivoluzione*, 52–3.

[127] [*Meyer's Konversations-Lexikon*], 9th edn, I: "Vorwort."

[128] *Grande Encyclopédie: Inventaire*, I: XII.

[129] See Spree, *Streben*, 95–6.

[130] Estermann, "Lexika," 249; Spree, *Streben*, 311.

Nationalism

Nationalism is an instance of partiality, or non-objectivity, but it deserves special attention in the context of encyclopedias. On the one hand, encyclopedias could be vehicles for nationalism. Governments, in particular, often supported them, and sometimes played a role in determining their contents, conceiving them as tools for promoting a nation, an empire, or an ideology. On the other hand, nationalism provides an avenue for exploring the broadening of encyclopedias' markets and the exportation of the model of the European encyclopedia.

This section will begin with a look at three aspects of encyclopedias' nationalism: their celebration of specific nations, the national or geographical focus of their content, and their status as national symbols. Then I will analyze nationalism in three "national" encyclopedias: the *Encyclopaedia Britannica*, the *Enciclopedia italiana*, and the *Bolshaia sovetskaia entsiklopediia*. Finally, I will consider the spread of nationalistic encyclopedias on the European model beyond western Europe.

The clearest way in which nationalism manifested itself in encyclopedias was through exaltation of a nation or empire. In the second (1812–19) through the seventh (1827) editions of Brockhaus's *Konversations-Lexikon*, the article on Prussia celebrated the nation's achievements in the Napoleonic wars: "What the nation and the army, what the king and the princes, what the men and women ... have done, suffered, and accomplished with enthusiastic heroism has been consecrated by history to immortality."[131] A century later, the *Espasa* catered to Catalonia, the Spanish nation, and the Spanish-speaking world. Articles on Hispanic American countries were to be written by locals, a policy justified privately as one that "will greatly flatter these countries and contribute to disseminating the work."[132]

Nationalism in encyclopedias could be negative as well as positive. Pejorative national stereotypes were common in eighteenth-century encyclopedias, including those of the drunken German, the proud Spaniard, and the miserly Swiss. Cross-border copying between encyclopedias and other texts, frequent in the years before international copyright, helped spread the stereotypes, but encyclopedists tended to

---

[131] "Was die Nation und das Heer, was der König und die Prinzen, was die Männer und Frauen ... mit begeistertem Heldenmut getan, gelitten und gewirkt haben, das hat die Geschichte der Unsterblichkeit geweiht." [*Grosse Brockhaus*], 5th edn., 1st printing, VII: 810; Meyer, "Konversations-Lexikon," 159.

[132] "... halagará mucho a estos países y contribuirá a la difusión de la obra." Castellano, *Enciclopedia*, 248.

spare their compatriots from the worst defamations. In his *Cyclopaedia* (1728), for example, Chambers listed eight national stereotypes in the article "Nation," including that of the "wicked and unlucky" Englishman. Like the rest of his list – minus the "idle" Irishman – this stereotype seems to have come from a French encyclopedia, the *Dictionnaire de Trévoux*. In the sixth edition (1750) of the *Cyclopaedia*, though, the stereotype was replaced with a less negative one, that of the "serious" Englishman.[133] In the same spirit, the damning portrait of Spain in the *Encyclopédie méthodique* (1782–1832) was accompanied by a rebuttal in the Spanish translation (1788–94), though the Spanish government still ended up stopping it after ten volumes. Similarly, the depiction of Italians in the *Méthodique* was rejected and rectified in a partial French edition (1784–1817) published in Padua.[134]

Around 1800, nationalism in encyclopedias became shriller and more political, partly in reaction to the French Revolution. The third edition of the *Encyclopaedia Britannica* and its *Supplement*, typically, trumpeted British patriotism while disparaging France and the French Revolution.[135] A half-century later, in the heyday of colonialism, it was common for European encyclopedias to express condescension toward indigenous peoples in Europe's colonies. Thus, despite Pierre Larousse's commitment to political equality in France, the article "Nègre" in his *Grand Dictionnaire* (1866–76) expressed support for colonialism and noted the "deficiency" of blacks in Africa. Likewise, even after the liberation of Spain's American colonies, the *Espasa* condemned native Bolivians as lazy and reserved the term "Bolivian" for descendants of Spaniards.[136]

By the middle of the twentieth century, nationalistic discourse had become suspect in Europe and much of the world. It was blamed for having contributed to the twentieth century's wars, and it no longer fit with views of race and colonialism. Besides revising entries on geographical, historical, and sociological topics to bring them into line with current positions, encyclopedia-makers responded in two ways to growing mistrust of nationalism. One of their responses was to enlist foreign contributors. Some such contributors were recruited to act as "insiders" – a role explored further in Chapter 7 – that is, to write as citizens on their own countries. Others

---

[133] Chambers, *Cyclopaedia*, ii: 616; [*Dictionnaire de Trévoux*], 2nd edn., iv: 33; Paul, "Wache auf," 197–217. See also Furetière and Basnage, *Dictionaire* (1701), ii: lllllllr.

[134] Donato, "Writing," 18, 21–5.

[135] Doig *et al.*, "Colin Macfarquhar," 237–40; Doig, Kafker, and Loveland, "George Gleig's *Supplement*," 290–3.

[136] Mollier and Dubot, *Histoire*, 127; Castellano, *Enciclopedia*, 412.

were recruited to guard against parochialism. Already in 1936, for example, the historian Lucien Febvre, the editor of the *Encyclopédie française*, offered just one criticism of the volume on health and physiology, namely that the contributors were almost all French.[137] Second, instead of lauding the nations under which they were published, prefaces to twentieth-century encyclopedias placed an increasing emphasis on cosmopolitanism.

Another way encyclopedias could be nationalistic was through the emphases of their coverage, notably their coverage of people and places. Nationalism in this form, though occasionally denounced, was less contrary to twentieth- and twenty-first-century sensibilities than it was in its other forms. Indeed, an encyclopedia covering all nations equally would have been doomed, for it would have forced potential purchasers to pay for a huge amount of unneeded content. In any event, encyclopedias differed in how much they focused on national affairs. In early-nineteenth-century France, for example, the *Encyclopédie des gens du monde* was less centered on France than the comparably sized *Dictionnaire de la conversation*. It devoted just 121 pages to its series of articles on France, in contrast to 368 in the rival encyclopedia. Based in Strasbourg and sympathetic to Protestantism, the *Encyclopédie des gens du monde* was presumably meant for a more cosmopolitan audience, perhaps even an international one.[138]

In the early twentieth century, the researcher María Calvo measured the space allotted to the articles on nations in the *Grande Encyclopédie* (1885–1902), the fourteenth (1892–5) and fifteenth (1928–35) editions of Brockhaus's encyclopedia, the *Espasa* (1908–30), the second edition (1914–16) of the *New International Encyclopaedia*, and the eleventh (1910–11) and fourteenth (1929) editions of the *Encyclopaedia Britannica*. Her conclusion was that only the *Espasa* treated Spain and Latin America adequately, but her findings also hint at degrees of cosmopolitanism. Above all, the *Espasa*, which devoted a whole volume to Spain, would seem to have been the most centered on its country of origin, followed at a distance by Brockhaus's *Konversations-Lexikon*. The *Britannica*, for its part, emerges from the comparison as being cosmopolitan with respect to England but being as nationalistic as Brockhaus's work when considered with respect to both England and the United States.[139]

Translations and adaptations of encyclopedias are revealing of national biases, for they almost all corresponded with shifts in nationalism. When

---

[137] Febvre, introduction to Vol. VI, cahier 4, 10.
[138] Loveland, "Two French 'Konversationslexika,'" forthcoming. See also Rowe, "Tous le savoirs," 16.
[139] See Calvo, "Enciclopedia," 19, 22, 30–2, 50–1. For a similar analysis of *Chambers's Encyclopaedia* see Kavanagh, *Conjuring*, 81–2.

Moréri's *Grand Dictionaire* (1674) was adapted abroad, it was enhanced with content reflective of its new nationality.[140] The same shifts befell Bayle's *Dictionaire* (1697). In one English-language adaptation, it was supplemented with 900 British biographies.[141] Similarly, the *Encyclopédie* (1751–72) may have disseminated the universalistic philosophy of the Enlightenment, but its contents were seen as too French by the Swiss team who revised it in Yverdon. Among other changes, they strengthened its coverage of non-French geography and attempted to cover law from a perspective transcending both French and Swiss localism.[142] So too, in the nineteenth century, Brockhaus's *Konversations-Lexikon* was adapted for reuse in other countries, but even when adaptations stayed close to the original – as did, for example, the *Encyclopaedia Americana* (1829–33) and Wigand's Hungarian *Konversations-Lexikon* (1831–4) – they boasted better coverage of the countries they appeared in.[143] By the twentieth century, publishers were taking an active role in adapting their encyclopedias for other nations. As we have seen, the owners of *World Book* adapted it for non-American anglophones and then Spanish-speakers. In both cases, the encyclopedia's nationalism had to be recalibrated.

Encyclopedias could also be nationalistic in a symbolic sense. Some were championed as a nation's or a language's first encyclopedia. In the Netherlands, for example, the *Algemeen historisch, geographisch en genealogisch Woordenboek* (*General Historical, Geographical, and Genealogical Dictionary*, 1724–37) was marketed this way, despite being an adaptation of Moréri's *Grand Dictionaire*.[144] National content was not even necessary for symbolic purposes. The Irish *Encyclopaedia Britannica* (1790–98) was nearly identical to its source, right down to a bias against Catholicism, but the publisher James Moore presented it as a triumph for Ireland, presumably because of the sheer work involved in producing the reprint.[145]

Nicknamed "Moore's Dublin edition" to distinguish it from the Scottish one, the Irish *Britannica* illustrates the nationalizing power of names.[146] Indeed, the word "national" eventually became common in the titles of encyclopedias, though less so than references to particular nations. Already

---

[140] Paul, "Enzyklopädien," 30.
[141] Thomas, *Changing Conceptions*, 5.
[142] Donato, "Eighteenth-Century Encyclopedias," 959–63; Cernuschi, "ABC," 129.
[143] On the American and Hungarian adaptations in this regard see Müller-Vollmer, "*Encyclopaedia*," 307, 310–11; Lipták, "Sammlung," 194–5.
[144] Paul, "Dieses Universal-Lexicon," 34–5; Paul, "Enzyklopädien," 30–1.
[145] Kafker and Loveland, "Publisher," 126–31, 138; Archbold, "Most Expensive Literary Publication," 187.
[146] For the nickname see *Encyclopaedia Britannica*, 3rd edn., Irish edn., 1: title page; Kafker and Loveland, "Publisher," 134.

in 1771, the *Dictionnaire de Trévoux* was touted as "national" in its preface, as was the [*New*] *Cyclopaedia* (1819–20) in an advertisement.[147] Soon afterward, titles began making the same claim, as in the *Österreichische National-Enzyklopädie* (*Austrian National Encyclopedia*, 1835–7) and Britain's *National Cyclopaedia of Useful Knowledge* (1847–51). Meanwhile, from the nineteenth century onward, many encyclopedias were given titles that referred to a homeland – for example, the *Encyclopaedia Americana* (1829–33) and the *Enciklopedija Jugoslavije* (*Yugoslavian Encyclopedia*, 1955–71). The word "international," for its part, only entered encyclopedias' titles around 1900, and then sporadically, notably in the *New International Encyclopaedia* (1902–4).

Among the most famous of national encyclopedias were the *Britannica*, the *Enciclopedia italiana*, and the Soviet Union's *Bolshaia sovetskaia entsiklopediia*. To these I now turn as examples of how encyclopedias could be nationalistic.

Ironically, the *Britannica* was first published in Scotland, but its title signaled commitment to a unified Britain. On a pragmatic level, the title was probably also intended to boost sales outside Scotland. In its contents, the early *Britannica* was both Scottish and British: Scottish in its borrowing from Scottish intellectuals, and British in its patriotism and promotion of English relative to the Scottish vernacular.[148] By 1800, though some still saw it as Scottish, it was becoming a symbol of Britain.[149]

In the nineteenth and early twentieth century, British nationalism grew stronger in the *Britannica*, as did the pride it expressed about Britain's colonial empire. Embarrassing as such sentiments may be in retrospect, they were not unusual then. Nor was the *Britannica*'s nationalism ever unambiguous. Indeed, it would have been difficult for the *Britannica* – with hundreds of contributors by the mid nineteenth century, some of them non-anglophones – to speak with just one voice on any subject. Admiration for German scholarship, for instance, constituted a significant undertone to the nationalism of the eleventh edition (1910–11).[150] At the same time, isolated contributors questioned the *Britannica*'s dominant ideologies. The activist Pyotr Kropotkin, for example, wrote an entry on "Anarchism" for the eleventh edition that hardly lent support to British nationalism or colonialism: "The state organization, having

[147] Wionet, "Esprit," 289; Colman, *Vagaries*, [61].
[148] Kafker and Loveland, *Early Britannica*, 6–8.
[149] Doig *et al.*, "Colin Macfarquhar," 249.
[150] Thomas, *Position*, 8–9.

always been ... the instrument for establishing monopolies in favor of the ruling minorities, cannot be made to work for the destruction of these monopolies."[151]

In the early twentieth century, Britain lost much of its hold over the *Britannica*. Americans had acquired partial ownership in 1897, followed by full ownership in 1901. By the time of the eleventh edition, the United States was the encyclopedia's principal market.[152] As of 1929, with the fourteenth edition, nearly half the contributors were Americans.[153] In 1917, the American critic Willard Wright wrote a book denouncing the *Britannica* as unacceptably British in content. Although his book contained some truth, a campaign to strengthen the work's American content had been under way since the start of the century.[154]

In Italy, the publication of the *Enciclopedia italiana* coincided with the height of fascism, an ideology that stressed a collective identity defined by the nation. The editor, Giovanni Gentile, was an enthusiastic fascist. So too was Giovanni Treccani, the industrialist who helped fund the venture. Despite Gentile's assurances that the *Italiana* would tolerate multiple viewpoints, some non-fascists saw it as a tool of fascism and refused to collaborate.[155] The *Italiana* had a signed contribution by the ruler of Italy, Benito Mussolini, in the article "Fascismo," though he was assisted by Gentile, who was also responsible for the rest of the article. Many political articles in the *Italiana* upheld fascism and referred to "Fascismo."[156] Nevertheless, for whatever motives, non-fascists and apolitical scholars – including more than 100 Italian Jews and hundreds of foreigners – chose to collaborate on the *Italiana*. Gentile's apparent tolerance in this regard enraged ultra-fascists.[157] Furthermore, studies of the encyclopedia's contents in different domains have concluded that fascism did not mark it pervasively.[158] It was presumably in part for this reason that the encyclopedia was reprinted after World War II.

Neither the *Italiana* nor the *Britannica* was as nationalistic as the second edition (1949–58) of the *Bolshaia sovetskaia entsiklopediia*. The

---

[151] *Encyclopaedia Britannica*, 11th edn., 1: 914. The editors added a note on violence by anarchists; see 1: 916–17n. On the range of ideologies in the eleventh edition see Boyles, *Everything*, 258.

[152] Kruse, "Story," 231, 240, 284.

[153] Einbinder, *Myth*, 52.

[154] Kruse, "Story," 279–81, 284–5.

[155] Turi, *Mecenate*, 37–44, 51–7.

[156] *Ibid.*, 133–98.

[157] Giordano, *Filologi*, 21–3; Turi, *Mecenate*, 48–51, 57–8, 61–9; Cavaterra, *Rivoluzione*, 15–34, 40–2, 65–73.

[158] See for example Durst, *Gentile*, 18, 84–5, 217; Giordano, *Filologi*, 7, 9, 23–4, 200–2.

article there on World War II, for example, grossly exaggerated the Soviet role in the war. Elsewhere the encyclopedia dwelt on the biologist Trofim Lysenko's officially sanctioned but erroneous theories, and praised a half-fictionalized Russian for flying the world's first airplane – an achievement that went unmentioned in the less ideological third edition (1970–7).[159] With the onset of the Cold War, critical attention to the second edition in the United States and western Europe revealed further instances of nationalism and anti-Americanism. Not surprisingly, the *Bolshaia sovetskaia entsiklopediia* was seen as representing the knowledge of communism, while the *Britannica* was touted as an emblem of democracy or western thinking, a role that the owners gladly took on.[160]

Faced with such models in the nineteenth and twentieth centuries, governments elsewhere welcomed the prospect of having their own national encyclopedias. National rivalry in encyclopedia-making was not new in itself. Already at the beginning of the eighteenth century, Coronelli lamented the fact that Italy, the "mother of science," lacked works of reference comparable to those of other places. He saw his *Biblioteca universale* as an instrument for unifying the Italian language, the Italian people, and the Italian states.[161] Soon afterward, the renown of the British *Cyclopaedia* and then the French *Encyclopédie* provoked jealousy elsewhere. Ironically, in the nineteenth and twentieth centuries, it was France's turn to be envious of other nations' encyclopedias, a situation bemoaned with self-interest in the prefaces to the *Grande Encyclopédie* (1885–1902) and the *Encyclopédie française* (1935–66).[162] Within western Europe, Britain by now enjoyed the greatest complacency on the score of encyclopedias, thanks above all to the *Britannica*.

In a longstanding progression that peaked in the mid twentieth century, the fact of producing a national encyclopedia such as those of Britain, France, and Germany came to be seen as a sign of a country's strength and modernity. Nor were such encyclopedias just signs. In the eyes of supporters, they could influence perceptions, not only domestically but also elsewhere. The first edition (1925–6) of the *Australian Encyclopaedia* thus represented a "conscious effort" to strengthen Australians' identification with their nation and create a positive image of Australia abroad.[163]

[159] Hogg, "*Bolshaia sovetskaia entsiklopediia*," 37–8, 48.
[160] Einbinder, *Myth*, 343–4.
[161] Coronelli, *Biblioteca*, 1: †2v; Fuchs, "Nationality," 208–9.
[162] *Grande Encyclopédie: Inventaire*, 1: 1; Monzie, "Pour une encyclopédie française," cahier 4, 5. See also Robichez, "*Encyclopédie*," 820–1.
[163] Kavanagh, *Conjuring*, 33, 51–5, 105.

Likewise, during World War II, both the Swiss and the German governments hoped that encyclopedias would improve their countries' images. Swiss publishers sought to profit from the turmoil in Germany and cut into the market for German-language books. One element of their challenge was the *Schweizer Lexikon* (1945–8), designed as a substitute for Meyer's and Brockhaus's large encyclopedias, both on hold since 1942. The *Schweizer Lexikon* was backed by the Swiss government as well as private investors. One of their motives was non-commercial: to improve Switzerland's international standing, marred by its neutrality during the war, by depicting it as a place of democracy and culture. Meanwhile, in 1944, while Germany lay ravaged by bombings and shortages, Nazi authorities endorsed plans to produce a new encyclopedia, partly to stop Swiss publishers from taking over the market, but also to give Germany a better reputation abroad. Planning continued among German bureaucrats into 1945, but they could not decide whether the task should be confided to Brockhaus or to the Bibliographisches Institut.[164]

A variant on the national encyclopedia was the kind written in exile to promote a nation-to-be. After World War II, for example, a Ukrainian encyclopedia (1949–52) was initiated in Munich by Ukrainian expatriates. Predictably, it was hostile toward the Soviet Union, which then held Ukraine. In response, the Soviets arranged for the publication of a rival Ukrainian encyclopedia (1959–65) supporting Ukraine's status within the Soviet Union.[165] Here the role of encyclopedias as political instruments is unmistakable.

Whatever their political goals, planners of national encyclopedias had to choose between universal coverage and coverage of merely national topics. An attempt at the former was more prestigious. It showed that a nation had reached a stage where it could ably judge everything. On a practical level, it worked best for encyclopedias in widely read, multi-national languages such as English and Spanish. Such works stood to sell well and could comfortably adopt a trans-national viewpoint, as did, for example, the *Britannica* and the *Espasa*. In contrast, the cost of commissioning coverage of non-national topics could weigh on encyclopedia-publishers in less robust markets. Borrowing from an established encyclopedia was one way of budgeting, and not just for encyclopedias in minor languages.[166] The publisher of the *Australian Encyclopaedia* thus made it a supplement to a

[164] Prodöhl, *Politik*, 145–96.
[165] Ptashnyk, "*Enzyklopädie*," 433–45.
[166] On borrowed content in national encyclopedias see Gluck, "Fine Folly," 244–5.

British encyclopedia, the new edition (1925–7) of the *Illustrated Chambers's Enyclopaedia*, with which it was sold at a discounted price.[167] Regardless, most national encyclopedias published outside Europe and the United States concentrated on their country or region of origin, whether on Canada in the *Canadian Encyclopedia* (1985) or Bangladesh in *Banglapedia* (2003).

Language aside, national encyclopedias from the late nineteenth century onward resembled each another when local in scope and resembled the European encyclopedia when universal. In short, they expressed nationalism within the framework of international templates. Even in Japan and China – countries with a tradition of encyclopedism based on classificatory order and collages of excerpts – the European example was contagious. In nineteenth-century Japan, favor for western knowledge weakened the long dominance of Chinese conceptions of encyclopedism. In 1868, the government commissioned a translation of a Scottish encyclopedic work, William and Robert Chambers' *Information for the People* (1835). In response, alarmed conservatives with support from the government began compiling an encyclopedic work along Chinese lines – Japan's largest ever – but it was one of the last of its kind. Henceforth, Japanese encyclopedias, including the *Nihon hyakka daijiten* (*Great Encyclopedia of Japan*, 1908–19), would be alphabetical and would focus on information rather than extracts.[168] Likewise, after experimenting with a mixed, Sino-European encyclopedism around 1900, the Chinese produced their *Zhōngguó dà bǎikē quánshū* (*Great Encyclopedia of China*, 1980–93), among other works, in a European mold, ordering it first by disciplines and then alphabetically.[169]

Conclusion

The contents of encyclopedias can be studied in different ways. One can look at the structure of articles, uncover their sources, investigate the treatment of particular subjects, or examine the list of keywords to see how it was drawn up. Some of these possibilities are explored elsewhere in this book, and all have been tested by other scholars.

Here I have dealt with a handful of general tensions affecting the contents of the European encyclopedia. On the one hand, encyclopedia-makers

---

[167] Kavanagh, *Conjuring*, 76, 105. The *Illustrated Chambers's Encyclopaedia* was a new title for *Chambers's Encyclopaedia*.
[168] Gluck, "Fine Folly," 233–8.
[169] Amelung, "Zwischen 'Geschäft' und 'Aufklärung' "; Bauer, "Encyclopaedia," 689–91.

were torn between a desire to keep their works up-to-date and a contrary desire to publish and sell them. Up-to-dateness in encyclopedias was all the more crucial in that most were too expensive to replace every few years. On the other hand, encyclopedists had to decide how and in what measure the knowledge they communicated would be practical or theoretical, objective or subjective, or cosmopolitan or national. It was not an easy decision, for all these possible emphases could have value for readers. Further complicating the matter was the fact that there was more than one way of being practical, theoretical, objective, and so on. The same tensions beset other publications focused on knowledge, but they were managed by encyclopedists with a certain distinctiveness. In the world of encyclopedias, objectivity, for example, was at the same time a catchword for marketing and a standard imposed by editors and prescribed to collaborators. The four tensions examined here were managed differently, moreover, from encyclopedia to encyclopedia as well in different historical settings. As a result, European encyclopedias continued to differ in their contents, though less after 1800 than in the previous century.

CHAPTER 3

Size, Price, and the Economics of Encyclopedias

At first glance, the scope, quality, and organization of an encyclopedia might appear far more important than its size or its price. Presumably for this reason, size and price are rarely emphasized in histories of encyclopedism. Yet evaluations of encyclopedias in terms of scope, quality, and organization alone misrepresent how these books appeared to contemporaries. On the one hand, an overpriced encyclopedia was irrelevant to most people, however good it may have been otherwise. On the other hand, an encyclopedia's size could matter as much as its scope, for a large encyclopedia that gave a subject a small proportion of space might cover it better than a small encyclopedia that gave it a large proportion of space. Size, above all, was a limiting factor in the value of encyclopedias as sources of knowledge.

Needless to say, encyclopedias did not always function as they were designed to. As we will see in Chapter 9, their social and cultural functions sometimes overshadowed their intellectual purposes. Like other books, they could be bought for display. Alternatively, they could be marketed to families as guarantees that children would have opportunities. In both of these instances, size and price played significant roles, suggesting the extent of one's culture or wealth, say, or of one's commitment to supporting a family.

The size and price of encyclopedias were in rough correlation. Bigger works used more paper and required more labor, which pushed up costs. Indeed, size and price were two of the most important variables in the economy of encyclopedia-making. Accordingly, this chapter will not only deal with encyclopedias' size and price but also with the economics of their production and sale. In this sense, it constitutes a link between Chapters 1 and 2, on encyclopedias' contents, and Chapters 8 and 9, on encyclopedias' publishers and users respectively.

Specifically, I will argue that the size of the biggest encyclopedias increased from 1680 to 1840. After 1840, one component of encyclopedias continued to grow, namely illustrations. Postponing this topic to Chapter 6, I will concentrate here on quantity of text, partly because it is easier to measure, and partly because encyclopedias were primarily textual. With this exclusion, the size of the biggest encyclopedias stabilized after 1840. By this time, the forces responsible for the earlier growth of encyclopedias were in decline, overwhelmed by a new insistence on commercial accountability and optimal marketing. After my examination of encyclopedias' size, I will turn to their prices, both in relation to the social status of buyers and as the final element of publishers' engagement with the economics of encyclopedias.

The Growth and Shrinkage of Encyclopedias

From the late seventeenth century to around 1840, the size of encyclopedias evolved in two contrary ways.

On the one hand, encyclopedia-makers abandoned the largest formats for printing. A book's format was the number of times a sheet had to be divided to make a page. Format and size were technically unrelated, but for the period before 1800, they were approximately equivalent, so that folios were large books, quartos and octavos intermediate ones, and duodecimos small ones. Most of the best-known encyclopedias before 1750 were published in folio, including Moréri's *Grand Dictionaire*, Furetière's *Dictionaire*, Bayle's *Dictionaire*, Harris's *Lexicon*, Chambers' *Cyclopaedia*, and the *Grosses vollständiges Universal-Lexicon*.

From the seventeenth century onward, quartos, octavos, and even duodecimos co-existed with folios in the world of encyclopedias. Above all, the best-selling *Reales Staats- Zeitungs- und Conversations-Lexicon* was published in octavo through the whole eighteenth century, but it was not the only contemporary encyclopedia not to appear as a folio. François Foppens's *Dictionnaire géographique* (1694) was published in duodecimo, Jablonski's *Allgemeines Lexicon* (1721) in quarto, and the *New and Complete Dictionary of Arts and Sciences* (1754–5) in octavo. In the second half of the eighteenth century, the formats of quarto and octavo became dominant for encyclopedias, displacing folios. Maintaining the tendency, nineteenth- and twentieth-century encyclopedias had pages that were large but not ostentatiously so.

The size and bulk of volumes are worth noticing, for they give us clues about encyclopedias' uses and users. A volume in folio was too big to be held comfortably in the hands or the lap. Rather, it was meant for use on a table or desk. One of the Italian translators of the *Cyclopaedia* thus chose to reformat it, publishing his *Ciclopedia* (1747–54) in eight volumes in quarto instead of two volumes in folio, since quartos were more "convenient" for reading and following cross-references.[1] At the same time, the shrinkage of encyclopedias' formats reflected publishers' efforts to sell to less wealthy people, for folios cost more than quartos, quartos more than octavos, and octavos more than duodecimos. Even the same encyclopedia cost less when it was reduced to a smaller format. The *Encyclopédie* (1751–72), for instance, was published in folio for 574 livres, in quarto for 384 livres, and in octavo for 225 livres. The editions in folio were better illustrated, which partly accounts for their price, but the edition in octavo had almost exactly the same content as the edition in quarto.[2]

On the other hand, despite the dwindling format of volumes, the biggest encyclopedias got longer and longer. Consider the case of historical dictionaries. Thanks to their construction on the models and materials of Moréri's *Grand Dictionaire* and Bayle's *Dictionaire*, these works were relatively homogeneous across western Europe and can be treated transnationally. Measured in words, the largest grew steadily through 1759. French versions of the *Grand Dictionaire* remained slightly larger than their offshoots in Dutch, English, German, and Spanish, though they briefly fell behind an English adaptation of Bayle's *Dictionaire*, the *General Dictionary, Historical and Critical* (1734–41; see Table 3.1).

After the mid eighteenth century, historical dictionaries declined in importance, but their content made its way into the universal dictionary and the dictionary of the arts and sciences, helping them grow for another half-century. Purely biographical dictionaries continued to grow, far exceeding less specialized historical dictionaries in size.

As other kinds of encyclopedias were less international than the historical dictionary, I will examine them language by language. In English and French, the length of the longest encyclopedias – the dictionary of the arts and sciences, and the French universal dictionary – grew from the late seventeenth century to 1840, so that records for size were regularly broken. The milestones for British encyclopedias are shown in Table 3.2. A similar progression took place in France, leading to a record that would not be surpassed (Table 3.3).

In German, by contrast, a lasting record was set in the first half of the eighteenth century (Table 3.4). Large encyclopedias continued to

---

[1] *Ciclopedia*, 1: "Prefazione del traduttore." See also Farinella, "Traduzioni," 108–9.
[2] Darnton, *Business*, 33–6; Doig, "Quarto and Octavo Editions," 121, 135.

Table 3.1   *Textual size of the biggest historical dictionaries, 1674–1759*

Author and title	Edition	Volumes of text (without supplements)	Pages of text	Words
Moréri, *Grand Dictionaire*	1st (1674)	1, in folio	1,300	1,500,000
Moréri, *Grand Dictionaire*	2nd (1681)	2, in folio	2,600	3,000,000
Moréri, *Grand Dictionaire*	8th (Amsterdam, 1698)	4, in folio	2,000	4,000,000
Moréri, *Grand Dictionaire*	new (1712)	5, in folio	4,000	5,000,000
Moréri, *Grand Dictionnaire*	new (1725)	6, in folio	6,000	7,000,000
General Dictionary	1734–41	10, in folio	7,500	9,000,000
Moréri, *Grand Dictionnaire*	1759	10, in folio	9,000	11,000,000

Table 3.2   *Textual size of the biggest British encyclopedias (historical dictionaries excluded), 1704–1820*

Author and title	Edition	Volumes of text (without supplements)	Pages of text	Words
Harris, *Lexicon*[a]	1st (1704)	1, in folio	1,000	1,000,000
Chambers, *Cyclopaedia*	1st (1728)	2, in folio	2,000	3,000,000
Encyclopaedia Britannica	2nd (1778–83)	10, in quarto	10,000	10,000,000
Encyclopaedia Britannica	3rd (1797)	18, in quarto	15,000	15,000,000
Encyclopaedia Britannica	4th (1810)	20, in quarto	16,000	16,000,000
Rees, *[New] Cyclopaedia*	1819–20	39, in quarto	32,000	32,000,000

[a]   I am discounting the second volume (1710) because it was separately alphabetized. Only with the fifth edition (1736) were the two volumes merged.

Table 3.3   *Textual size of the biggest French encyclopedias (historical dictionaries excluded), 1690–1832*

Author and title	Edition	Volumes of text (without supplements)	Pages of text	Words
Furetière, *Dictionaire*	1st (1690)	3, in folio	2,000	2,500,000
Dictionnaire de Trévoux[a]	2nd (1721)	5, in folio	5,000	7,500,000
Dictionnaire de Trévoux	5th (1752)	7, in folio	7,000	10,000,000
Diderot and D'Alembert, *Encyclopédie*	1751–65	17, in folio	16,000	19,000,000
Encyclopédie méthodique	1782–1832	*c.* around 200, in quarto[b]	120,000	120,000,000

[a]   The fourth edition (1740) of the *Dictionnaire de Trévoux* appeared in six volumes but was the same size as the 1721 and 1732 editions.

[b]   Schmitt, "Inventaire," 210.

Table 3.4   *Textual size of the biggest German encyclopedias*
(historical dictionaries excluded), 1721–50

Author and title	Edition	Volumes of text (without supplements)	Pages of text	Words
Jablonski, *Allgemeines Lexicon*	1st (1721)	1, in quarto	1,000	1,000,000
Jablonski, *Allgemeines Lexicon*	2nd (1748)	2, in quarto	1,500	1,500,000
Grosses vollständiges Universal-Lexicon	1732–50	64, in folio	120,000	120,000,000

be published in German. The *Oeconomische Encyclopädie* (1773–1858) extended to 242 volumes in octavo, with some 170,000 pages and 50 million words. Ersch and Gruber's *Allgemeine Encyclopädie* (1818–89) comprised 167 volumes at the time of its abandonment in 1889, with some 80,000 pages and 80 million words. Had it been finished, it might have run to 110 million words. Lastly, the *Wunder-Meyer* (1840–53), the biggest encyclopedia to be completed in nineteenth-century Germany, had 46 volumes with some 50,000 pages and 80 million words. Still, the record of the *Universal-Lexicon* was never broken.[3]

In the late twentieth century, the *Guinness Book of World Records* dubbed Spain's *Espasa* (1908–30) the world's largest encyclopedia. The main text of the *Espasa* comprised 72 volumes with some 105,000 pages and 100 million words, but the editors of the *Guinness Book* added in supplements and updates that appeared from 1930 onward.[4] Counting supplements with an encyclopedia is methodologically dubious, since they were often detached afterthoughts, with different goals. By this logic, the honor of the largest printed encyclopedia should go to the *Universal-Lexicon* (see Figure 3.1) or the *Encyclopédie méthodique*, though both were outdone by an unprinted Chinese encyclopedic collection, the *Siku quanshu* (1773–82) with its 800 million characters, and they were all dwarfed by Wikipedia, which had attained over a billion words in its English-language version by 2009.[5] Nor, within Europe, did previous encyclopedic works come close to the size of the *Universal-Lexicon* or

[3] Hingst, *Geschichte*, 13, 40.
[4] Loveland, "Why Encyclopedias Got Bigger," 237.
[5] Blair, *Too Much*, 29–30; Tammet, *Embracing*, 205. A smaller eighteenth-century Chinese encyclopedic collection, the *Gujin tushu jicheng*, with 100 million characters, was in fact printed. See Drège, "Des ouvrages," 32–3.

Figure 3.1 The *Universal-Lexicon* on a book-case. The set occupies shelves 2 through 5 on the left and shelf 1 on the right. The volumes are 35 centimeters high. Photograph courtesy of the Rare Books and Manuscripts Library of Ohio State University.

the *Encyclopédie méthodique*.[6] Finally, though lexical dictionaries broke their own records for size through the late twentieth century, the largest among them, the Dutch *Woordenboek der nederlandsche taal* (*Dictionary of the Dutch Language*, 1864–1998), was only half as big as Europe's biggest encyclopedias.

In sum, encyclopedias grew enormously in the period from 1680 to 1840, gradually in English and French, and explosively in German. At the same time, some encyclopedias moved in the opposite direction, a tendency less dwelt on in histories of encyclopedism. Abridgments were published, among them a three-volume abridgment of the *Dictionnaire de Trévoux*

[6] See Beyer, "Encyclopédies," 29–30; Blair, *Too Much*, 7.

in 1762 and a five-volume abridgment of the *Encyclopédie* in 1768.[7] In the mid eighteenth century, a fashion developed for "portable" encyclopedias in smaller formats, though they were portable only in a relative way.[8] Typically, Jean-Baptiste Ladvocat's *Dictionnaire historique portatif* (1752), an abridgment of Moréri's *Grand Dictionaire*, comprised two volumes in octavo. From edition to edition, it grew gradually larger, so that it finally had to be abridged in its own right.[9] Another kind of portability was achieved in Edward Augustus Kendall's *Pocket Encyclopedia* (1802), which appeared in six volumes just 14 cm in height. It inspired imitations, including Brockhaus's *Taschen-Encyklopädie* (*Pocket Encyclopedia*, 1816–20). A more durable title for Brockhaus was the *Kleineres Brockhaus'sches Conversations-Lexikon* (1854). This work started a system, among publishers, of issuing both "small" and "great" encyclopedias simultaneously. An extreme case in the history of miniaturization was Daniel Sanders's *Konversations-Lexikon* (1896). Between covers measuring just 24 × 32 mm, it offered some 500 pages of densely printed articles (see Figure 3.2). It was sold in a case containing a magnifier and equipped with a ring so that it could be attached to a necklace or to a watch-chain.[10]

Sanders's *Konversations-Lexikon* was a singularity, but larger one-volume encyclopedias sold abundantly even as the stereotypical encyclopedia grew to encompass multiple volumes. In France, a crisis in publishing from 1780 to 1820 brought the size of nearly all encyclopedias down to just one or two volumes. Among the more successful of the period's encyclopedias was Boiste's one-to-two-volume *Dictionnaire universel* (1800).[11] Capitalizing on French demand for scholastic dictionaries after the enactment (1833) and extension (1882) of mandatory schooling, the Larousse firm became a leader in single-volume encyclopedic diction-aries, beginning with the one-volume *Nouveau Dictionnaire de la langue française* (1856).[12] Another influential example was *Kürschners Taschen-Conversationslexikon* (*Kürschner's Pocket Conversational Dictionary*, 1884), also in one volume, designed to be cheaper and smaller than the "small" encyclopedias of Brockhaus and the Bibliographisches Institut. It spawned offshoots in other languages, including *Cassell's Miniature Cyclopaedia*

---

[7] Miller, "Last Edition," 47; Lough, *Essays*, 43–6.
[8] Rétat, "Age," 186–9; Lieshout, "Dictionnaires," 148–9.
[9] Harvey and Heseltine, *Oxford Companion*, 208.
[10] Peche, *Bibliotheca*, 473; Keiderling, *F. A. Brockhaus*, 25–7.
[11] Pruvost, "De Diderot," 53–4, 56.
[12] Boulanger, "Quelques figures," 93–4; Pruvost, "Pierre Larousse," 32–3.

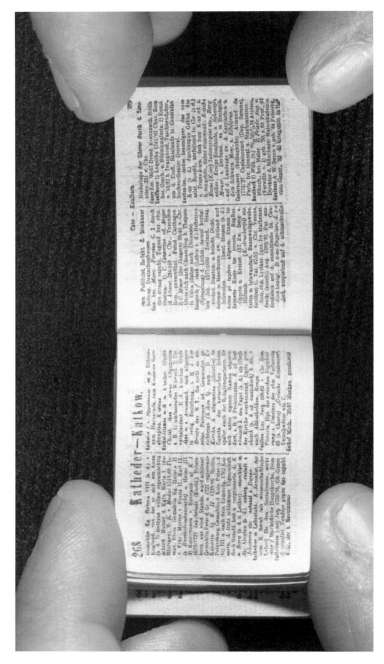

Figure 3.2 Photograph showing the size of Sanders' *Konversations-Lexikon.*
Photograph courtesy of Western Michigan University, Special Collections.

98

(1888), while Larousse's *Nouveau Dictionnaire* was transformed into the best-selling *Petit Larousse* (1905).[13]

The trick for publishers was to advertise their small encyclopedias as preserving all that was worthwhile in a large encyclopedia at a much lower price. Hinting that bigger works were merely plumped up with filler was one common strategy, the converse to advertisements of unprecedented coverage. In 1788, for example, the preface to the *New Royal Cyclopaedia and Encyclopaedia* accused recent editors of Chambers' *Cyclopaedia* of adding "the most tedious details, and unnecessary disquisitions on exploded subjects … in order to spin it out to an unnecessary length." The preface went on to argue, in another typical strategy, that the contents of bigger encyclopedias had been mysteriously distilled into the present encyclopedia.[14] Taking a bleaker tack, the editor of the one-volume *Columbia Encyclopedia* (1935) argued that the progress of knowledge had destroyed any middle ground between specialized libraries and the "first aid" available in a small encyclopedia: "Since first aid is all that a general encyclopedia can now give successfully, it is all that *The Columbia Encyclopedia* attempts to give."[15]

Small encyclopedias, in other words, were as vital a part of the book-trade as big ones. They remain under-represented in histories of encyclopedias because of unwillingness to take them seriously. A few were admittedly written as jokes. One was a *Dictionnaire portatif par ordre alphabétique; ou, pensées libres d'un jeune militaire qui s'amuse les matins à réfléchir, n'ayant rien de mieux à faire* (*Portable Dictionary in Alphabetical Order, or, Free Thoughts of a Young Soldier who Entertains Himself by Thinking in the Morning, Having Nothing Better to Do*, 1756), which featured some two dozen pages of moralizing, witty comments under alphabetized keywords. Other short alphabetical works had the scope of an encyclopedia but verged on being dictionaries through the brevity of their articles. Yet even the many short works that were undeniably encyclopedias are rarely studied by scholars, in part because they represent a less intellectual side of encyclopedism.

Reasons for Growth

Growth and shrinkage in the size of encyclopedias were both part of the same process of diversification, usually the sign of commercial success.

[13] Peche, *Bibliotheca*, 326; Pruvost, *Dent-de-lion*, 44.
[14] Howard *et al.*, *New Royal Cyclopaedia*, 1: iii. See also Yeo, *Encyclopaedic Visions*, 117.
[15] *Columbia Encyclopedia*, 1st edn., "Preface."

Why encyclopedias were successful from 1680 to 1840 is not hard to
imagine. Although the trends were irregular and often gradual, more and
more people were becoming literate, geared toward consumption, and
wealthy enough to spend money on books. In this climate, growth in the
size of the biggest encyclopedias reflected publishers' confidence in the
market for books. Other factors, however, contributed too, as we will see
in the following paragraphs.

Even if no one, toward 1700, had the idea of writing or publishing an
encyclopedia as big as the *Grosses vollständiges Universal-Lexicon* or the
Encyclopédie méthodique, people were aware of the possibility of making
encyclopedias bigger. If nothing else, the fact that encyclopedias were
smaller than libraries argued for their potential expansion as storehouses of
knowledge. In 1691, a review of a new edition of Moréri's *Grand Dictionaire*
noted ironically that some people "only ask for enlarged editions, especially
regarding dictionaries, which, to believe what is said, can never be too
big."[16] More concretely, around 1700, Coronelli planned an encyclopedia
meant to have forty-five volumes in folio, though the volumes were to be
thinner than those of most contemporary encyclopedias.[17] Unfortunately,
he abandoned his *Biblioteca* after only seven volumes. More generally,
when encyclopedists criticized one another for neglecting material or
attempted to rationalize their own exclusions, they were implicitly conjuring up scenarios of growth. Still, the impulse to expand was only gradually acted on.

One hypothesis for explaining the growth of encyclopedias from 1680
through 1840 is that they expanded in response to available funding. Capital
was unquestionably a problem for the period's publishers. Most of what
they had was in the illiquid form of stockpiled books. Loans from banks or
private creditors were hard to obtain on acceptable terms. Nor could booksellers' families offer them as much support as subsequent publishing dynasties – Hachette in France, say, or Brockhaus in Germany. Some projects
foundered – or were never begun – for lack of capital. Funding was a
factor, in particular, in Coronelli's failure to finish his *Biblioteca*.[18]

Yet seventeenth- and eighteenth-century publishers did take on and
finish big, costly projects. Protectors and governments sometimes assisted
with funding. Alternatively, partnerships with colleagues allowed publishers

---

[16] "... ne demandent que des éditions augmentées, surtout en fait de dictionnaires, qui, à ce qu'on dit,
    ne sauraient jamais être trop amples." Review of *Grand Dictionaire*, 118–19.
[17] Fuchs, "Vincenzo Coronelli," 154–5.
[18] *Ibid.*, 317.

to pool their resources. Just as important were the devices of subscription and serial publication, characterized more fully in Chapter 9. Finding people willing to subscribe to a work before publication began reduced publishers' risks and could also raise capital, since payment was usually required in stages. Subscription was used for encyclopedias as early as 1728, with the first edition of the *Cyclopaedia*, and it was used for the two largest encyclopedias printed, the *Grosses vollständiges Universal-Lexicon* and the *Encyclopédie méthodique*, among many others. Another strategy often combined with subscription was serial publication, in which installments were sold cheaply and without bindings over several years. Just as purchasers of serially published encyclopedias were spared the distress of a single huge expenditure, the publishers responsible for them received a steady stream of income to continue their projects.

Under these circumstances, a mere lack of capital would not have ruled out the appearance of an encyclopedia as big as the *Universal-Lexicon* a few decades earlier. A more critical factor was the market and publishers' intuitions about it. In 1700, encyclopedias had yet to be standardized in their contents or functions, and publishers were cautious about exploring and cultivating demand for them. In his preface to the *Curieuses Natur-Kunst- Gewerck- und Handlungs-Lexicon* (1712), Hübner mused that even if a truly comprehensive encyclopedia could be written, it would be too big and expensive to be of much use.[19] Hübner was an educator, but his sentiments were probably shared by the majority of publishers.

Over time, as the public for books and reading expanded, and as encyclopedias acquired roles and value in European society, a few publishers grew bolder, but it is worth pointing out how bankruptcy threatened two of the boldest, Zedler and Panckoucke. Despite his prior experience with multi-volume publications, Zedler went bankrupt just three years into publishing the *Universal-Lexicon*. Only a partnership with a Leipzig businessman allowed him to carry on.[20] Panckoucke, for his part, did not live to see the end of the *Encyclopédie méthodique*, but it still imperiled his finances. In 1788, it came close to collapsing – one of a number of barely averted collapses – because of defections among subscribers unwilling to tolerate its constant expansion. A decree from the government granting Panckoucke immunity from lawsuits by subscribers was a significant element in his recovery.[21] Even so, two of the encyclopedia's sub-series were

[19] Hübner, "Vorrede," [)(4r] (§29). See also Chambers' judgment in Yeo, *Encyclopaedic Visions*, 143.
[20] Carels and Flory, "Johann Heinrich Zedler's *Universal Lexicon*," 165–6, 169–71.
[21] Darnton, *Business*, 473–5.

never finished: a rapidly outdated one on France's National Constituent Assembly, and one on worms. In addition, a few sub-series were promised but never started.[22] These stories suggest that other publishers were justified in being cautious about the size of encyclopedias.

Another factor affecting the size of encyclopedias was the law, or its absence. In 1774, the British House of Lords ruled that no one could hold the rights to a published text forever. The ruling did not end uncertainty or customary assumptions about copying, but it did solidify the fourteen-to-twenty-eight-year terms for copyright established in the Act for the Encouragement of Learning (1710).[23] It also created a more competitive market for books. For the remainder of the century – after which copyright was once again strengthened – new titles proliferated, while prices dropped dramatically for those out of copyright.[24] Intriguingly, British dictionaries of the arts and sciences ballooned after the mid 1770s. Did limitations on copyright favor bigger encyclopedias? Here, leaving the general matter of copyright and encyclopedias for Chapter 4, I will argue that laws governing copyright affected the size of encyclopedias in two distinct ways.

A comparison with French and German encyclopedias is a good place to start. In France, the royal privilege authorizing a book's publication was of indefinite duration, in practice, for much of the eighteenth century. It gave publishers effective monopolies over such works as Moréri's *Grand Dictionaire*, and Savary and others' *Dictionnaire universel de commerce*. Meanwhile, however, presses outside France could reprint French titles with almost no threat of punishment.[25] Thanks to this unwanted competition from foreigners, the situation in France before the French Revolution resembled that in Britain after 1774, and the quick growth of French encyclopedias in the first half of the century – clearly a consequence of the rivalry and copying between Furetière's Dutch-published *Dictionaire* and the Catholic *Dictionnaire de Trévoux* – supports the idea that limitations on copyright encouraged expansion.

In the German states, the multiplicity of governmental and administrative territories meant that anything published there risked being reprinted.[26] Still, the *Universal-Lexicon*'s enormousness did not result from

---

[22] Braunrot and Doig, "*Encyclopédie*," 15, 49, 93–4, 98; Schmitt, "Inventaire," 210.
[23] On ambiguities regarding copyright before and after 1774 see Sher, "Corporatism," 36–82; Sher, *Enlightenment*, 25–30; Raven, *Business*, 230–8, 342–7.
[24] St. Clair, *Reading Nation*, 54, 113–21.
[25] Birn, "Profits," 134–5. On the extended privileges for the encyclopedias of Moréri and Savary see Birn, "Profits," 141, 161.
[26] Saunders, *Authorship*, 106–7; Estermann and Jäger, "Voraussetzungen," 19.

competition stirred up by weak protection of copyright. As Zedler's first and only encyclopedia, it entered and exited from competition at the same time. Furthermore, Zedler was successful in getting privileges from different authorities, and in using them, in particular, to suppress a partial reprint.[27] Yet in another sense, the *Universal-Lexicon* did depend on what were, in retrospect, loose laws concerning copying. The fact that much of it could be copied from other works of reference allowed Zedler to keep his costs low, which was crucial to his completion of a huge encyclopedia.[28]

In Britain, despite the growth of the biggest encyclopedias in the 1770s, the role of limited copyright in the expansion of encyclopedias is less apparent. Long before the legal ruling of 1774, British historical encyclopedias had grown to considerable length. Four adaptations of Bayle's *Dictionaire* were published in English before 1750, the first and shortest (1709) in four volumes, the fourth and longest (1734–41) in ten. This fourth translation, published at the same time as a third one (1734–8), was vaunted as including not only Bayle's *Dictionaire* but also biographies of British and Irish public figures. The additions were meant to give the work prominence in a competitive field, but they also made it bigger. In part, the competition among these reworked translations of Bayle's *Dictionaire* reflected publishers' inability to monopolize foreign titles, which followed from the absence of international copyright. The evolution of copyright, though not the legal watershed of 1774, thus played a role in the growth of these titles. Still, the most direct cause was the tightness of the market, a cause that produced similar effects in France and Germany.

In the end, legal considerations of a different order probably affected British encyclopedias as much as the demise of perpetual copyright in 1774. In particular, a law proposed in Parliament after the launch of the *Cyclopaedia* (1728) would have forced the publisher of a new edition to publish, additionally, a compendium of all the major changes to the previous edition. The law was never enacted, but it seems to have discouraged Chambers from revising the *Cyclopaedia* beyond minor tinkering.[29] He must have wondered if an enlarged edition could survive competition with the combination of the previous edition and a supplement of additions and changes. If so, he may have been justified, though subsequent

---

[27] Carels and Flory, "Johann Heinrich Zedler's *Universal Lexicon*," 167–71.

[28] For examples of copying see Nobre, "Difusión," 116–17; Kossmann, "Deutsche Universallexika," 1579–81. On copying as a strategy for cutting Zedler's costs see Prodöhl, "Aus denen besten Scribenten," 84–8.

[29] Bradshaw, "Ephraim Chambers' *Cyclopaedia*," 125n; Yeo, *Encyclopaedic Visions*, 143–4. For his complaints see Chambers, "Some Considerations," 4.

publishers – among them, later publishers of his own *Cyclopaedia* – sometimes issued such supplements alongside new editions, presumably to earn at least something from those disinclined to replace an older edition.[30] Regardless, if the publishers of the *Encyclopaedia Britannica* had faced the prospect of a similar law in the 1770s, they might have issued a second edition the same size as the first. Instead, they expanded the *Britannica* from three to ten volumes.

Other reasons for the expansion of the biggest encyclopedias through 1840 were intellectual, psychological, and socio-cultural, though inevitably such forces were intertwined with one another and with commercial and legal ones. On an intellectual level, changes to knowledge favored expansion. On the one hand, the fact that encyclopedias grew during a period of "enlightenment" and scientific discovery might seem self-evident. The quantity of knowledge was undoubtedly increasing insofar as producing and recording knowledge were becoming the business of more and more people as well as the object of more and more books.

On the other hand, the goals of encyclopedias were still being adjusted to the modern reality of unbounded knowledge. In Richard Yeo's view, dictionaries of the arts and sciences were deliberately kept short in the early eighteenth century so as to condense knowledge rather than replicate its entire extent.[31] As we have seen, some people were already imagining large encyclopedias by then. A few even began them. Regardless, in the course of the century, encyclopedists amplified their claims to completeness.[32] The idea of encyclopedias as storehouses of indefinite extent was more widespread in 1800 than 1700.

Likewise, in hindsight, nearly all seventeenth- and eighteenth-century encyclopedias had room to grow, for they were specialized relative to their counterparts of the nineteenth and twentieth centuries. As shown in Chapter 1, the three most general kinds of encyclopedias in the period from 1650 to 1750 were the dictionary of the arts and sciences, the French universal dictionary, and the historical dictionary. One of the first attempts to combine them was that of Zedler, in the *Universal-Lexicon*. Its simple scope goes a long way toward explaining its size.

In Britain and France, it took longer to attain the scope of the modern encyclopedia. The more gradual addition of historical material to the

---

[30] See for example *Daily Advertiser*, May 22, 1740: [4]; January 15, 1743: [4]. On Bayle's determination to publish updates to his *Dictionaire* separately see Lieshout, *Making*, 44–6.

[31] Yeo, *Encyclopaedic Visions*, 60–1.

[32] See Rudy, *Literature*, 1, 12–13, 122–6. On the rhetoric of completeness in encyclopedism in general see König and Woolf, *Encyclopaedism*, 7–8.

French universal dictionary and the dictionary of the arts and sciences probably contributed to their more gradual growth. As in the German states, these and other additions relative to previous editions or the works of competitors were advertised as improvements and justified as responding to public demand. One reason for the expansion of the *Encyclopaedia Britannica* from the first (1771) to the second edition (1778–83) was the introduction of biographical articles. Whatever the origins of this reform, the preface to the second edition championed the new biographies as "useful and entertaining" and boasted that they were not to be found in other British encyclopedias.[33] In France, Panckoucke defended the expansion of the *Encyclopédie méthodique* since the time of the prospectus by citing overlooked disciplines that had to be dealt with.[34] At times, he pushed responsibility for his encyclopedia's expansion back onto readers, stating, for instance, that the sub-series on antiquities had grown because of the public's desire for complete coverage.[35]

Despite claims that the public was clamoring for additions, much of the new material that inflated encyclopedias was inserted with little thought for the needs of a readership. Above all, eighteenth- and nineteenth-century encyclopedias grew significantly longer than advertised, a fact that led to anger on the part of subscribers. The *Universal-Lexicon*, for example, was supposed to be finished in twelve volumes in folio, not sixty-eight after two decades of labor.[36] In his prospectus of 1751, Diderot asserted that the *Encyclopédie* would be finished in ten volumes by 1754, not in twenty-eight volumes in 1772, as it finally was. This discrepancy led a subscriber to file a lawsuit.[37] Likewise, Krünitz announced the *Oeconomische Encyclopädie* (1773–1858) as a translation of a reworking of Chomel's *Dictionnaire* (1709), which would have made it an encyclopedia of around sixteen volumes. Instead it expanded to 242 volumes and was only completed posthumously after eighty-six years. Reviewers turned negative after the first thirty volumes, demanding that the encyclopedia be brought to a close.[38]

Blame for such overruns typically fell on the publishers. They, after all, were the ones finally deciding what would be published. In fact, those who reissued encyclopedias deserve much of the responsibility for the growth

---

[33] *Encyclopaedia Britannica*, 2nd edn., 11: vii. On why biographies were brought in see Doig *et al.*, "James Tytler's Edition," 80.
[34] Tucoo-Chala, *Charles-Joseph Panckoucke*, 337–8.
[35] Panckoucke, "Lettre," 15.
[36] Kossmann, "Deutsche Universallexika," 1571.
[37] [Diderot], prospectus, [12]; Lough, *Encyclopédie in Eighteenth-Century England*, 96, 99.
[38] Fröhner, *Technologie*, 25, 36, 89, 97.

of encyclopedias before 1840. They acquired experience and capital with each edition, resources that may have encouraged them to attempt bigger editions. If an encyclopedia was to be marketed in a new edition, moreover, a distinction had to be created with respect to the old one. Increased size was an obvious quality to emphasize, since it suggested the incompleteness of smaller encyclopedias.

Yet contributors and editors played a role, too, in making encyclopedias grow. Many contributors expanded entries in order to earn more, as they were generally paid by how much they wrote, but many others did so because of intellectual idealism. Motives were often mixed. The naturalist Jean-Baptiste de Lamarck thus presented his work on botany for the *Encyclopédie méthodique* as worthy of extra volumes, claiming that no one before had covered the subject so thoroughly, but under Panckoucke's scheme of paying, he stood to earn extra money from expansion as well.[39] At this point, a disciplined editor might have ordered him to stay within prescribed limits, but editors were often reluctant to rein in contributors, some of them eminent, or stifle enthusiasm. Panckoucke himself exhibited both of these shortcomings, so much so that the *Méthodique* grew from a projected forty-two volumes to more than four times as many.[40]

Beyond the mindsets of editors, publishers, and their collaborators, another factor supportive of largeness in encyclopedias was a widely shared culture, one that awakened interest in a community of purchasers. The *Encyclopédie* (1751–72), above all, was underpinned by and devoted to the values of the Enlightenment. Drawing on excitement about the Enlightenment helped it become the largest French encyclopedia to date. Attunement to powerful cultural forces could be an important first step toward commercial viability, which was never a given for a big encyclopedia.

The Established Encyclopedia

Long encyclopedias were not limited to the eighteenth or nineteenth centuries. As we have seen, the *Espasa* (1908–30) was huge, as was China's seventy-four-volume *Zhōngguó dà bǎikē quánshū* (1980–93). Yet after 1840, few large encyclopedias were anything but one-time creations, occasionally updated with supplements or yearbooks. By contrast, encyclopedias premised on re-editions stabilized in size in the nineteenth

---

[39] Darnton, *Business*, 424, 476.
[40] For Panckoucke's original plans see Braunrot and Doig, "*Encyclopédie*," 7.

and twentieth centuries. Even when big, they rarely exceeded thirty volumes or 40 million words.

The *Encyclopaedia Britannica*, for example, had attained 16 million words by 1810. It continued to grow for next hundred years, reaching 38 million words with its eleventh edition (1910–11). Then, after two editions consisting of supplements, the *Britannica* shrank with its fourteenth edition (1929), though it had expanded again, to 43 million words, by the time it resurfaced as the *New Encyclopaedia Britannica* (1974). Before the fourteenth edition, the *Britannica*'s advertising relied heavily on the idea of progress as growth. Accordingly, the preface to the fourteenth edition was forced to present the relationship between knowledge and encyclopedias in a different light. Specifically, the preface argued that however "agreeable" it might be to write an encyclopedia with 100 volumes or even 1,000, such a work would be inappropriate for "ordinary needs."[41] William Cox, the former salesman who became president of Encyclopaedia Britannica in 1923, was more explicit in a letter to the editor Garvin: "Personally I can't understand why anyone should object to making a book for the *many* instead of a book for the *few*."[42] Concerns about profitability were latent in discussions of encyclopedias' size.

Likewise, Brockhaus's *Konversations-Lexikon* began as a six-volume encyclopedia with some 3,000 pages and 1 million words. These numbers increased steadily throughout the nineteenth century. Exasperated over complaints about the things his *Konversations-Lexika* failed to cover, Friedrich Brockhaus promised, sarcastically, to issue a 100-volume edition – a promise fulfilled indirectly by the company's acquisition of Ersch and Gruber's *Allgemeine Encyclopädie* in 1830.[43] Yet the company refused to allow its main encyclopedia to expand out of control. Twice in the twentieth century, its *Konversations-Lexikon* shrank. First, for the sixteenth edition (1952–63), which appeared in the aftermath of World War II, the firm decided that Germans could no longer afford an encyclopedia as big as the fifteenth edition (1928–35) and reduced the number of volumes from twenty-five to twelve. Similarly, the eighteenth edition (1977–81), in twelve volumes, was shorter than the seventeenth edition (1966–74), apparently as part of an effort to target a younger audience.[44] Indeed, like its title, the size of Brockhaus's *Konversations-Lexikon* was regularly adjusted to match

[41] *Encyclopaedia Britannica*, 14th edn. (1929), 1: xiii; see also 1: xviii–xix, xxi–xxii. On this edition's shrinkage see Kruse, "Story," 354.
[42] Kogan, *Great EB*, 221.
[43] See Collison, *Encyclopaedias*, 162.
[44] Hingst, *Geschichte*, 164, 170–1; Iben, review, 69.

what its purchasers were imagined to want, but none of the editions was very long. The last (2005–6) and longest edition had some 25,000 pages and 25 million words.

Perhaps the memory of its involvement with Ersch and Gruber's *Allgemeine Encyclopädie* kept Brockhaus from trying a huge encyclopedia of its own. After purchasing the *Allgemeine Encyclopädie*, the firm made an effort to discipline editors and contributors so that the encyclopedia could finally be finished. Among other reforms, editors were to be paid by the part, not by the page. Yet authors remained late and long-winded with their submissions, and editors unwilling to enforce needed changes. In fact, it was under Brockhaus's leadership that a 3,668-page article on Greece – the longest ever in an encyclopedia – appeared in the *Allgemeine Encyclopädie*. These factors, along with the constant progress of knowledge, convinced Brockhaus to abandon the encyclopedia after 1889. In spite of oversight from the world's most successful encyclopedia-publisher, an encyclopedia proposed to subscribers as a thirty-volume set to be finished in eight years was thus discontinued, still incomplete, after 167 volumes and seventy-one years of work.[45] This was the worst overrun in the history of encyclopedias.

Brockhaus's German rivals learned their own lessons about size. Pierer's encyclopedia (1822–36) started out longer than those of Brockhaus, which prevented it from being revised and reissued as fast. Recognizing the problem, the owners shortened the third edition (1849–52) and retreated to imitating Brockhaus's formula.[46] Likewise, Meyer's *Konversations-Lexikon* began with a colossal edition in forty-six volumes, the so-called *Wunder-Meyer* (1840–53), but the company's next encyclopedia was only half as big, supposedly because Meyer's son, Herrmann Julius, thought revising a longer encyclopedia would be unwieldy.[47]

In France, after the last edition of the *Dictionnaire de Trévoux* in 1771, the biggest encyclopedias were published in a single edition. Such was the case, for example, of the *Encyclopédie méthodique* (1782–1832) and the *Grande Encyclopédie* (1885–1902). After Pierre Larousse's death, the Larousse firm retained its status as one of France's leading providers of encyclopedias and dictionaries, but it did so by abandoning the model of Larousse's *Grand Dictionnaire* (1866–76), notably regarding size. The company's next multi-volume encyclopedia, the *Nouveau Larousse illustré* (1897–1904), was less than half as big. Thereafter, in a strategy like that of Brockhaus and other

---

[45] For the early plans see Rüdiger, "Ersch/Gruber," 22, 37–42, 61–3.
[46] Jäger, "Lexikonverlag," 554–5; Hingst, *Geschichte*, 37–8.
[47] Hingst, *Geschichte*, 46.

firms, the Larousse company sold encyclopedias in multiple sizes and formats to different audiences, but without producing anything as big as the *Grand Dictionnaire*.[48]

In none of the dominant languages of modern encyclopedism did encyclopedias grow much, if at all, after the mid nineteenth century. In the context of the German states, where the size of encyclopedias had peaked by the time of the *Wunder-Meyer* (1840–53), Georg Jäger argues that moderation in sizing resulted from maturity in the market for encyclopedias and from publishers' awareness of how to attract different groups.[49] These explanations are useful but invite elaboration.

At first glance, it might seem that technological progress – by making encyclopedias cheaper to publish – would have encouraged firms to try larger works. Paper, which until then accounted for much of books' cost, fell sharply in price once machines took over production in the early nineteenth century. Overhead excluded, paper represented three-quarters of the cost of reissuing the *Encyclopédie* in quarto (1777–9), for example, whereas it counted for just a sixth of the cost of producing early parts of the *Encyclopaedia Metropolitana* (1817–45).[50] Steam-powered presses proliferated around the same time, making printing quicker and less expensive. Because of the cost-saving implied by such printing, Brockhaus was able to keep the price per volume the same for the seventh (1827) as for previous editions of the *Konversations-Lexikon*, in spite of an increase in the dimensions of volumes.[51]

For large and reprintable books such as encyclopedias, a less familiar technology was valuable: stereotyping. Before the early nineteenth century, if an encyclopedia was to be reprinted, the type had to be reset, since publishers lacked the resources to save and store thousands of frames of type.[52] In stereotyping, a metal copy was made of each frame of type and each plate. The copies could be stored for possible use in a reprint, while the movable type was freed up for other projects. With stereotyping, publishers

---

[48] On the segmentation of the book-market as a nineteenth-century innovation see Weedon, *Victorian Publishing*, 1–2; Estermann and Jäger, "Voraussetzungen," 24–5.

[49] Jäger, "Lexikonverlag," 541–2.

[50] Darnton, *Business*, 186; Collison, *Encyclopaedias*, 234. Unlike reissuers of the *Encyclopédie*, the publishers of the *Metropolitana* had to pay their contributors, but even if we exclude "literary expenses," they spent less on paper as a fraction of cost. On the declining cost of book-making materials see Weedon, *Victorian Publishing*, 57, 85–8.

[51] Hingst, *Geschichte*, 127.

[52] Jean Pruvost states that Pierre Larousse saved all the frames of type for his *Grand Dictionnaire*, but what he saved was probably a collection of stereotypes. Compare Pruvost, "Pierre Larousse," 39; Mollier and Dubot, *Histoire*, 174.

escaped the worry of trying to guess an optimal pressrun. Having made an investment in stereotypes, they could easily print more copies as demand warranted. For revised editions, moreover, they could reuse any stereotypes unaffected by updates – notably plates, which were expensive to make.

One of the first encyclopedias to take advantage of stereotyping was the *Encyclopaedia Americana* in 1829.[53] In 1833, the preface to the *Penny Cyclopaedia* blamed certain "trifling errors" – "the breaking off of a letter, or a stop at the end of a line" – on the process of stereotyping.[54] By contrast, the compiler J. L. Blake mentioned the stereotyping of his *Family Encyclopedia* (1834) as proof of its seriousness, notwithstanding its origins as a "periodical," that is, as an encyclopedia published in installments: "Still it has been the intention of the compiler, to give it a character fitting it for standing use. Accordingly, it has been stereotyped, and will hereafter be furnished to the public in successive editions."[55] The *Encyclopaedia Britannica* began to be stereotyped around the same time. By relying as much as possible on stereotypes of the seventh edition (1842), the publisher Black was able to produce the eighth edition (1853–60) for a lesser amount.[56]

Thanks to technology, then, the cost of the materials in encyclopedias fell, as did the cost of manufacturing their volumes. Capital, too, became more available. Banking and commercial finance improved in the second half of the nineteenth century, moving publishing, overall, into the world of capitalism. Encyclopedia-publishers became less fixated on the short term. One advantage, for example, that the family-owned Espasa company derived from its merger with Calpe in 1925 was access to the better banks of northern Spain. Before, it had depended on revenues from each of the *Espasa*'s installments to carry on publishing.[57] Similarly, after World War II, the Deutsche Bank extended generous credit to the war-ravaged Brockhaus firm to allow it to start work on larger projects.[58]

Under these circumstances, why did encyclopedias not continue to grow after the mid nineteenth century just as they had previously? One way of approaching the question is to review causes for the growth of encyclopedias through 1840. These included the development of a market for encyclopedias, but the market, once established, hardly subsided. On the contrary,

[53] De Kay, "*Encyclopedia*," 207.
[54] *Penny Cyclopaedia*, 1: IV.
[55] Blake, *Family Encyclopedia*, 1: "Preface."
[56] Collison, *Encyclopaedias*, 142–3; Kruse, "Story," 161–2, 166–7.
[57] Castellano, *Enciclopedia*, 93–4, 133–4.
[58] Keiderling, *F. A. Brockhaus*, 230.

encyclopedias – like books in general – were purchased in ever greater quantities. Sales of the *Encyclopaedia Britannica*, for instance, stood at around 120,000 sets annually in the early 1990s, whereas 200 years earlier, fewer than 10,000 sets of the first edition were sold, and far fewer in any one year.[59] The pressrun of the nineteenth edition (1986–94) of Brockhaus's encyclopedia came to 400,000 sets, a record for the company.[60] Likewise, though the *Petit Larousse* sold an impressive 100,000 copies in 1905, it subsequently averaged half a million per year.[61]

Total sales notwithstanding, publishers recognized that big encyclopedias had drawbacks, and small ones advantages. In the late nineteenth century, a testimonial for *Johnson's New Universal Cyclopaedia* highlighted the convenience of its small size:

> It can lie on my table as a dictionary, and I can refer to its contents without rising. But a work in twenty or thirty volumes must be kept on the shelves of a library, and to consult it a writer must lay aside his pen, rise from his seat, and look [seek] out a particular volume. Perhaps in five minutes he has to repeat the same operation.[62]

An illustration at the start of the encyclopedia made the same point (see Figure 3.3). Encyclopedias' volumes, moreover, could sometimes be heavy. One-volume encyclopedias were among the heaviest per volume – witness the 12 lb (5.4 kg) edition of the *Random House Encyclopedia* (1977) from 1990 – but they could be slid around on desks rather than carried from shelves.[63]

Yet a work's smallness, in physical terms, did not in itself rule out an abundance of content. In the crudest of expedients, a publisher could shrink margins and characters to fit more material in. Without necessarily requiring a magnifier, many nineteenth- and twentieth-century encyclopedias came exceedingly close. As editor of the fourteenth edition (1929) of the *Encyclopaedia Britannica*, Garvin expressed pride that "the small type, used to a very large extent in earlier editions, has been abandoned entirely except in bibliographies and extended quotations," but even normal type in the fourteenth edition was far from big.[64]

When resizing type, publishers occasionally fiddled with columns as well. From the beginning, following in a tradition already established

[59] *New York Times*, May 16, 1995: D22; Kafker and Loveland, "William Smellie's Edition," 58–9.
[60] Keiderling, *F. A. Brockhaus*, 366.
[61] Blois, "Dictionnaire," 162.
[62] "Testimonials," 2. See also *Johnson's New Universal Cyclopaedia*, 1: 1.
[63] For the weight of *Random House* see *New York Times*, September 17, 1990: D10.
[64] *Encyclopaedia Britannica*, 14th edn. (1929), 1: xxxi. On sizes of type in the eleventh edition see Boyles, *Everything*, 253.

Figure 3.3   Illustration from Volume 1 of *Johnson's New Universal Cyclopaedia* showing three of the four volumes on a desk. Scanned courtesy of Middlebury College Special Collections and Archives, Middlebury, Vermont.

for dictionaries, most encyclopedias offered two columns per page, but when text was compressed to save on paper or volumes, more columns appeared, as in Larousse's *Grand Dictionnaire* (1866–76), which squeezed in four. Abbreviations were another means of cramming more on a page. The Brockhaus firm began using them in the mid nineteenth century, around the same time it switched from a single column per page to a space-saving two (see Figure 3.4).[65] Although abbreviations were almost always explained in a preface or appendix, they made an encyclopedia harder to use. Tellingly, Brockhaus, among other encyclopedia-makers, trimmed them back in its electronic encyclopedias.[66]

[65] Hingst, *Geschichte*, 192.
[66] Keiderling, "*Brockhaus*," 207.

Figure 3.4   The one-column layout in the ninth edition (1843–8) of Brockhaus's *Konversations-Lexikon* versus the four-column layout in Larousse's *Grand Dictionnaire*. Photograph courtesy of Langsam Library, University of Cincinnati.

In the same spirit, two experiments with the *Britannica* in the early twentieth century proved that big encyclopedias could be cut back in bulk. First, by printing the eleventh edition (1910–11) on thin but tough "India paper," the publishers reduced its weight by three-quarters and its volume by two-thirds. Second, they shrank the pages of the eleventh edition by a factor of two in order to create the "Handy Volume Issue."[67] Neither innovation had much effect on the broader market for encyclopedias. Nor did the space-saving (and cost-saving) idea of printing encyclopedias in paperback – which was sporadically tried in the twentieth century.[68] If the physical size of encyclopedias concerned consumers, it was not a priority.

[67] Kruse, "Story," 303–5, 320.
[68] See for example Keiderling, "*Brockhaus*," 203; Walsh, *Anglo-American General Encyclopedias*, 70, 122, 142, 191. See also Schopflin, "Encyclopaedia," 198–9, 251.

The market for encyclopedias, then, continued to strengthen from 1840 to about 1990, and it was not obviously skewed to exclude larger sets. We are left to consider changes to other factors driving encyclopedias' earlier growth. One was an environment that limited copyright – whether by statute or the absence of statutes – which discouraged monopolies and encouraged competition and textual borrowing. Did stricter copyright after 1840 curb the growth of encyclopedias? As international copyright took decades to negotiate, encyclopedias continued to be pirated by foreigners through the early twentieth century. Above all, the ninth edition (1875–89) of the *Britannica* was counterfeited a dozen times in the United States between 1875 and 1905.[69] Some of the "reprints" expanded the encyclopedia in useful directions, mostly toward American content, though the publisher J. M. Stoddart also expanded the index. Indeed, if legal and political decisions had not put an end to the piracy in the early twentieth century, the *Britannica* and its American imitators might have pushed one another to greater size, just as Furetière's *Dictionaire* and the *Dictionnaire de Trévoux* had in the early eighteenth century.

Instead, laws governing copyright became at the same time more stringent and more international in the course of the twentieth century. Had he lived in our own times, Zedler would have found his *Grosses vollständiges Universal-Lexicon* (1732–50) prohibitively expensive, for he could no longer have copied others' texts with impunity. By the late nineteenth century already, encyclopedia-publishers were buying the rights to works they intended to copy from. Conversely, when they decided to stop revising and republishing an encyclopedia, they could be confident of finding a buyer for the content they owned.

A last set of factors contributing to the growth of encyclopedias before 1840 were cultural, intellectual, and psychological. Movements as inspiring as the Enlightenment may have been rarer in later centuries, but national encyclopedias stepped in and tried to rally citizens. One of the most successful in this respect was actually trans-national, the Spanish *Espasa* (1908–30). While billed as a voice for Hispanic America too, the *Espasa* appealed to the dreams of its places of origin: first, those of Barcelona, desirous of entering into European modernity, and second, those of Spain, in quest of new relations with its former colonial empire after the Spanish–American War (1898).[70] Nationalism may also have

---

[69] Kruse, "Story," 196–8.
[70] [*Espasa*], I: VIII–IX; Castellano, *Enciclopedia*, 12–13, 16–17, 23, 537, 542–3.

helped support the *Enciclopedia italiana* (1929–39) – another big encyclopedia, with thirty-six volumes and some 50 million words – but it did not prevent the *Italiana* from coming close to insolvency and requiring help from the government.[71]

On an intellectual level, much of the expansion of eighteenth-century encyclopedias reflected gains in scope, as the dictionary of the arts and sciences and the universal dictionary took on history and geography. After 1800, gains in scope tended to be minor until the arrival of Wikipedia in the twenty-first century. Large encyclopedias of the nineteenth and twentieth centuries had more depth than small ones, but little more scope – a fact that may have hindered efforts to drum up enthusiasm for further expansion.

In many ways, psychologically, contributors from after 1840 resembled those from before. In aggregate, they were still poor at meeting deadlines, they were eager to earn more, and they were prone to disregarding limits on articles' length. Critically, however, they faced stricter managing editors than earlier contributors had, presumably because the functions of editors, contributors, publishers, and financers were more clearly separated.[72] Overruns became less likely as financers and publishers demanded accountability from editors and contributors, though they still occurred sometimes. As we have seen, Brockhaus was unable to rein in Ersch and Gruber's *Allgemeine Encyclopädie* (1818–89), but failing to do so, the firm chose to abandon it rather than keep wasting money. The Brockhaus-Efron encyclopedia, or *Enciklopedičeskij slovar'* (1890–1904), more than doubled in size with respect to projections, but mainly because it was redesigned as an original Russian encyclopedia, not just a translation of Brockhaus's *Konversations-Lexikon*.[73] Another latter-day instance of a poorly controlled encyclopedia was the *Espasa* (1908–30), but here the inflation was willful. Once the encyclopedia had proved to be profitable, limits on the length of articles were less firmly enforced.[74]

Yet for every instance of overruns from the mid nineteenth century onward, one can find instances of checks on expansion. The *Penny Cyclopaedia* (1833–43), for example, was planned for eight volumes but spent more than two volumes on "A." At this rate, calculated a reviewer,

---

[71] Rovigatti, "Gli anni," 11–12.
[72] See for example Raven, *Business*, 349–50; Parinet and Tesnière, "Entreprise," 136, 147; Jäger, "Lexikonverlag," 542.
[73] Hexelschneider, "Brockhaus," 211–14. See also Prodöhl, *Politik*, 58–9.
[74] Castellano, *Enciclopedia*, 144–5, 160–1, 166.

the encyclopedia would require forty volumes to finish.[75] The organizers responded with an apology in Volume VI and imposed tighter control, so that the set was ultimately finished in twenty-seven volumes. As editor of the *Encyclopaedia Britannica* around the same time, Napier wanted to extend it from twenty volumes to twenty-five. In his arguments to Adam Black, the publisher and owner, he cited the greater length of the encyclopedia's rivals as well as advances in knowledge and the need to include material for all kinds of readers. In the course of negotiation, Napier and Black reached a compromise, and the seventh edition (1842) was published in twenty-two volumes, albeit slightly larger ones than those used before.[76] William Smith, an editor of the ninth edition (1875–89) of the *Britannica*, later characterized his relationship with the Black firm as less constraining. Supposedly, it involved little more than sending and receiving a paycheck. If so, Smith must have internalized an order to keep the encyclopedia from growing, for he insisted on cuts in order to introduce a treatise on "Totemism," for example.[77]

Consider next why established firms sometimes shortened encyclopedias in the nineteenth and twentieth centuries. One reason was the difficulty of revising longer encyclopedias, which led to out-of-date content and delayed new editions beyond those of competitors. Such considerations took on added importance as artistic and intellectual labor became more expensive. After Microsoft bought the rights to use *Funk and Wagnalls New Encyclopedia* (1971) in its electronic encyclopedia *Encarta* (1993), for instance, it estimated needing $7 million to rewrite and update the text.[78] Two centuries earlier, the publishers of the *Britannica* had paid the writer James Tytler around £30 a year over less than a decade to compile the second edition (1778–83) from the much shorter first edition.[79] The comparison is apt in that Tytler's second edition, with 10 million words, was the same size as *Encarta* as of 1994.[80]

We should not exaggerate the burden authors' pay imposed on encyclopedia-publishers. In the late seventeenth century, the academician Thomas Corneille obtained perhaps the best deal in history for the author of an encyclopedia. Not content with a simple payment, he negotiated

[75] Review of *Penny Cyclopaedia*, 75.
[76] Kogan, *Great EB*, 44–6. See also Kruse, "Story," 148–9.
[77] Einbinder, *Myth*, 40–1.
[78] Stross, *Microsoft Way*, 91–2.
[79] Doig *et al.*, "James Tytler's Edition," 71.
[80] Kister, *Kister's Best Encyclopedias*, 285, 298.

with his publisher to get half the profits for his *Dictionnaire des arts et des sciences*.[81] In general, on the contrary, editors and contributors to encyclopedias were paid for their labor with wages or a fixed sum, and their pay was rarely a preponderant cost for encyclopedia-makers. The most prestigious encyclopedias were able to get unpaid submissions from people eager to have their work published there. Pay for other contributors – editors excepted – was typically paltry. Contributors to the *Enciclopedia italiana* (1929–39), for example, received 60–100 lire per column.[82] In the early twentieth century, contributors to the *Britannica* made more, around 2 cents a word. Still, at this rate, even the renowned physicist Albert Einstein earned less $100 for his article "Space-Time" in the thirteenth edition (1926).[83]

The amount spent by encyclopedia-publishers on compilation and revision varied with their standards and schedules for updates, but it seems to have decreased over time as a proportion of cost, even if it increased in absolute terms. The acquisition of "literary property" represented 10–30 percent of the cost of the *Encyclopédie* (1751–72).[84] As of 1827, honoraria for authors and editors came to a quarter of the costs of Ersch and Gruber's *Allgemeine Encyclopädie*.[85] Similarly, almost a third of the costs of the *Encyclopaedia Metropolitana* (1817–45) were "literary expenses."[86] On the low end of the spectrum, an announcement from the Bibliographisches Institut put honoraria at 10 percent of the cost of the *Wunder-Meyer* (1840–53).[87] Also toward mid-century, 20–25 percent of the costs of the seventh and eighth editions of the *Britannica* were payments to editors and contributors.[88]

These percentages seem to have fallen, on the whole, by the twentieth century. In the early twentieth century, pay to collaborators amounted to 15 percent of the costs of the *Enciclopedia italiana*.[89] In the mid twentieth century, revisions to the *Britannica* were covered with just 2–4 percent of income.[90] As income includes profit as well as costs, the proportion of costs

[81] Martin, *Livre*, II: 917.
[82] Cavaterra, *Rivoluzione*, 47–8.
[83] Einbinder, *Myth*, 266.
[84] See Bowen, "*Encyclopédie*," 19–21.
[85] Rüdiger, "Ersch/Gruber," 36.
[86] Collison, *Encyclopaedias*, 234.
[87] Sarkowski, *Bibliographische Institut*, 73.
[88] Kruse, "Story," 167.
[89] Turi, *Mecenate*, 69.
[90] Einbinder, *Myth*, 55.

accounted for by revisions must have been higher, but less so than 100 or 200 years earlier. Likewise, hunting for a partner among encyclopedia-publishers in the late 1980s, Microsoft was struck by how inexpensive it was to maintain an encyclopedia.[91] Yet even if the cost of writing or revising an encyclopedia fell relative to other costs in the twentieth century, it may have remained a deterrent to bigger encyclopedias, as one more cost to double, for example, if a publisher decided to double an encyclopedia in size.

A second reason evoked by publishers for reducing the size of an encyclopedia was to make it appealing to a broad audience. In a way, it would seem that if Zedler could find a market for a 120-million-word encyclopedia in the mid eighteenth century, subsequent publishers should have been able to do so within their more populous and literate societies. Still, the labor required to compile such an encyclopedia would have cost more than it had Zedler, thus pushing up prices and limiting potential purchasers. Publishers continued to print gigantic series into the twentieth century, but with limited pressruns and modest goals for profitability. Indeed, a facsimile of Ersch and Gruber's *Allgemeine Encyclopädie* was published from 1969 to 1992, though the publisher obviously did not have to pay authors for articles.[92] Regardless, in the absence of governmental patronage of the sort that shored up the *Enciclopedia italiana* (1929–39), few twentieth-century publishers were inclined to relinquish the large, proven audiences for stereotypical encyclopedias in favor of less established ones for much bigger works. Advised by their accountants, investors and owners preferred financial prudence.

Pricing and Purchasers

Pricing, like sizing, was central to the economics of encyclopedia-making. Price was the final element decided by publishers in a commercial calculation meant to generate profits. It was also a limiting factor in making a sale. Furthermore, it correlated with an encyclopedia's size, though reputation and quality mattered as well. Indeed, size was often taken as determining price. In 1779, the former Jesuit Alessandro Zorzi thus vowed to keep his *Nuova enciclopedia italiana* short – specifically, less bulky than the *Encyclopédie* – to make it affordable to more potential purchasers.[93]

---

[91] Stross, *Microsoft Way*, 82.
[92] Rüdiger, "Ersch/Gruber," 61.
[93] Zorzi, *Prodromo*, xxi.

Publishers and editors found ways, nonetheless, to pack more into encyclopedias without raising prices. Any of the space-saving procedures mentioned above could result in lower prices: reducing the format, cutting back on the margins, choosing a smaller typeface, and using abbreviations. So could critical editing. With this assumption, the editors of the second edition (1840–8) of Pierer's encyclopedia promised to remove what was obsolete in the previous edition and edit the rest for concision to reduce the encyclopedia's size and therefore its price.[94] As it turned out – in this case and others – additions more than compensated for any cuts, thereby frustrating the editors' strategy. Some campaigns to control prices were successful, however. Brockhaus, for example, followed through with its plan to set the same price for the tenth (1851–5) as for the ninth (1843–8) edition of its *Konversations-Lexikon*, despite adding pages and increasing their size.[95]

Conversely, a small encyclopedia might cost as much as a large one, since price, in the abstract, reflected the interplay of supply and demand. In practice, prices for encyclopedias were first set by publishers and then adjusted by retailers. Publishers controlled the supply of their own encyclopedias by choosing a pressrun, but they had imperfect knowledge of their competitors' supplies. Nor, before the invention of stereotyping, did they have an easy way of adding to an initially determined pressrun. Worse still, before the twentieth century, they had few tools for gauging the public's demand for encyclopedias. Besides intuition, the best means of estimating it was, for a long time, extrapolating from how a comparable work sold, but markets could be saturated by competitors' offerings or even the success of one's previous edition. A more sophisticated instrument for predicting demand was demographic analysis. In the early twentieth century, Albert Brockhaus observed that his firm and the Bibliographisches Institut were selling 30,000–40,000 sets per edition of their large *Konversations-Lexika*, but he sensed that they ought to be doing far better. Working from suppositions about the age and gender of Europe's German-speakers, he calculated the potential market at roughly a million.[96]

Lacking certainty about demand, publishers struggled to set optimal prices. Hans Brockhaus, for instance, disagreed with his father Albert's thoughts on pricing the fifteenth edition (1928–35) of the

[94] [*Pierer's Universal-Lexikon*], 2nd edn., 1: xxxiv–xxxix.
[95] Hingst, *Geschichte*, 137; Peche, *Bibliotheca*, 90–1.
[96] Keiderling, *F. A. Brockhaus*, 68.

Konversations-Lexikon. His arguments were qualitative. Specifically, in his view, the price should be 12 marks per volume instead of just 10 because the public would be willing to pay more for a modernized work.[97] Under these circumstances, prices were frequently changed. When it failed to sell, the price of the first edition (1822–36) of Pierer's encyclopedia was thus substantially reduced, which led to a five-fold increase in sales.[98] For its first edition (1917–18), the price of *World Book* went the opposite way, rising during publication from $32 to $48.50 as the publisher attempted to make a profit.[99]

Beyond supply and demand, encyclopedia-makers were obliged to respond to the prices of rivals. In the early nineteenth century, for instance, Friedrich Brockhaus put pressure on A. F. Macklot, who was counterfeiting the *Konversations-Lexikon*, by keeping prices low.[100] Similarly, faced with American piracy of the ninth edition (1875–89) of the *Encyclopaedia Britannica*, the British publishers, the Blacks, authorized a new printing on cheaper paper so that it could be sold at the same price as the first of the counterfeits.[101]

As this last example shows, the same encyclopedia, content-wise, could be sold at different prices. Already in 1690, Furetière's *Dictionaire* was published in folio as well as in quarto, undoubtedly with a corresponding difference in price.[102] Seventeenth- and eighteenth-century encyclopedias were usually bound by purchasers to suit their budgets and tastes, but publishers often advertised different grades of paper, thus creating a range of prices for the same work. From the nineteenth century onward, they offered different bindings as well. In an example of a minimum of diversification, the *Petit Larousse* was sold in two forms from 1905 to 1968. As of 1905, the cloth-bound edition cost 5 francs, whereas the leather-bound edition cost 7.5 francs.[103] At the other end of the spectrum, the fifth edition (1819–20) of Brockhaus's *Konversations-Lexikon* was available in five options, ranging in price from 12.5 to 45 taler.[104] In the late twentieth century, while Brockhaus maintained more affordable options for luxury, wealthy book-lovers could pay more than 10,000 marks – enough for a

97 *Ibid.*, 69.
98 Meyer, "Konversations-Lexikon," 63.
99 Murray, *Adventures*, 32.
100 Hingst, *Geschichte*, 115, 118.
101 Kruse, "Piracy," 315.
102 Behnke, *Furetière*, 27–41.
103 Blois, "Dictionnaire," 164–5.
104 [*Grosse Brockhaus*], 5th edn., 1st printing, 1: "Anzeige."

new car! – for special issues of Brockhaus's *Konversations-Lexikon* designed by famous artists.[105] A pioneer in the analysis of the encyclopedias as luxuries had been Herrmann Julius Meyer, the head of the Bibliographisches Institut in the second half of the nineteenth century. In particular, he laid out strategies for selling deluxe sets of Meyer's *Konversations-Lexikon* to three different groups: tasteful connoisseurs, the socially privileged, and the rich.[106]

How much one paid for an encyclopedia also depended on how and when it was bought. Traveling salespeople sold encyclopedias for less than stores. Many were given a free hand to negotiate with customers. Publishers themselves cut their prices for early purchasers, whether through subscription or a temporary offer, though some of their discounts were only discounts in relation to prices that almost nobody paid. In twentieth-century America especially, the same encyclopedia was sometimes marketed under different titles for different prices. The *World Scope Encyclopedia* (1945), for example, was reissued in 1953 under two different titles: the *New World Family Encyclopedia* and the *Standard International Encyclopedia*. In the latter two forms, it was meant to be sold in supermarkets for a much cheaper price. Since the 1920s, however, the United States' Federal Trade Commission had frowned on the publication of an encyclopedia under different titles, and it charged the publisher of the *World Scope Encyclopedia* with "deceptive selling practices" in 1954.[107]

For those looking for bargains, prices were lower for used or dated encyclopedias. In a typical instance, a five-year-old set of the *Merit Students Encyclopedia* (1967) sold for less than half the price of a new one in 1981.[108] In nineteenth-century Germany, enough used sets were in circulation to depress prices for new sets. Some sets were repossessed when consumers fell behind in their payments, but publishers such as the Bibliographisches Institut were also responsible, since they bought or gave credit for old encyclopedias.[109] The incentive was widespread and sometimes mentioned in advertising. In the early twentieth century, for example, the publisher of *Nelson's Perpetual Loose-Leaf Encyclopaedia* offered to mail potential purchasers a list of "allowance[s]" given for "old encyclopedias."[110]

---

105 Keiderling, *F. A. Brockhaus*, 342–3, 369–70; Hingst, *Geschichte*, 184–7.
106 Sarkowski, *Bibliographische Institut*, 104; Hingst, *Geschichte*, 47–8.
107 Walsh, *Anglo-American General Encyclopedias*, 110, 189–90.
108 Kister, *Encyclopedia Buying Guide*, 3rd edn., 37.
109 Spree, *Streben*, 140; Jäger, "Lexikonverlag," 552.
110 *New York Times*, May 1, 1909: 5; *Southwestern Law Review* 1 (June 1916): VII.

Finally, encyclopedias could be consulted for free. As noted in Chapter 8, they were occasionally offered as prizes for buying something else. More importantly, they were available in libraries. Before 1800, almost no libraries were free and open to everyone, but some commercial "lending libraries" did stock encyclopedias. The *Grosses vollständiges Universal-Lexicon* was apparently available in a few such institutions, as were the *Encyclopédie* and the second edition (1778–83) of the *Encyclopaedia Britannica*.[111] Non-commercial, or "public," libraries, which only became common toward 1900, were considerably more likely to have encyclopedias.[112]

When encyclopedias were in libraries, users of encyclopedias did not have to be purchasers. Still, enough users were purchasers to warrant analysis of their identity. Here price was crucial despite its variability, for many people could simply not afford an encyclopedia. Books in general were expensive before the nineteenth century, and encyclopedias were among the largest and most expensive. An unbound first edition of Bayle's *Dictionaire*, for example, comprised two volumes in folio and sold for 34 guilders – a sum that a skilled worker would have taken a month to amass.[113] The three-volume 1701 edition of Furetière's *Dictionaire* cost 60 guilders.[114] In early-eighteenth-century Britain, the first volume of the *Lexicon Technicum* sold for 25 shillings, and the first edition of the *Cyclopaedia* for 42 shillings. As the latter sum was the monthly income of a "modest middle-class family,"[115] buying either encyclopedia would have been extravagant within this group. Despite the presence there of artisans, the works' lists of subscribers confirm the impression that purchasers were predominantly from the upper middle class and above.

The trend toward bigger encyclopedias raised prices further. Coronelli, for example, planned to charge 16 lire per volume for his *Biblioteca* (1701–6), only about a third of the cost of the *Lexicon Technicum*.[116] Had the work been completed in the forty-five volumes projected – instead of abandoned – it would nonetheless have cost 720 lire, fifteen times as much. While the first, one-volume edition of Moréri's *Grand Dictionaire* probably cost around 20 livres, a five-volume edition cost 75 livres in 1711,

[111] Spree, *Streben*, 109; Benhamou, "Diffusion," 267–8; Doig *et al.*, "James Tytler's Edition," 147.
[112] Spree, *Streben*, 133.
[113] Lieshout, *Making*, 35; Lucassen, "Wage Payments," 261.
[114] Lieshout and Lankhorst, *Eleven Catalogues*, 187–8, 304.
[115] Yeo, *Encyclopaedic Visions*, 50–1.
[116] Fuchs, "Vincenzo Coronelli," 154–5.

an eighth of the annual salary of a professor at the Collège de France.[117] Similarly, the price per volume of Zedler's *Universal-Lexicon* may have been low, but the total price came to more than 100 taler. Thanks to its high price, it was acquired mainly by libraries.[118] Finally, the *Encyclopédie méthodique* was initially promised for 672 livres, but its price grew with its size, rising to 3,000 francs by the time of its termination in 1832. As of 1831, in comparison, the average annual salaries of a worker and a civil servant were 580 and 685 francs respectively.[119]

As we have seen, Panckoucke reissued the *Encyclopédie* in smaller formats to attract the less wealthy. As published in quarto (1777–9), it would have been a "manageable luxury" for a provincial magistrat or a prosperous priest. Even when printed in octavo (1778–82), however, it remained beyond the budget of artisans such as locksmiths and carpenters, costing as it would have more than a year of their work.[120] So too, the final edition of the *Dictionnaire de Trévoux*, comprising eight volumes in folio, cost 208 livres in 1771, roughly the same as the *Encyclopédie* in octavo.[121] More affordable encyclopedias – smaller in format or the number of volumes – cropped up sporadically in eighteenth-century France, but none acquired the stability of Moréri's *Grand Dictionaire*, Bayle's *Dictionaire*, the *Dictionnaire de Trévoux*, or the *Encyclopédie*, all of which were large and expensive by the second half of the century.

Encyclopedias were somewhat more affordable in eighteenth-century Britain. Indeed, one of the century's best-sellers among works of reference sold for 6 shillings, less than a quarter of the price of the *Lexicon Technicum*. This was Dyche and Pardon's *New General English Dictionary* (1735), printed in one volume in octavo, a lexical dictionary with encyclopedic content.[122] Alongside such expensive works as the *Universal-Lexicon* and the first *Deutsche Encyclopädie*, the eighteenth-century German states boasted a strong current of inexpensive encyclopedias. Above all, the *Reales Staats- Zeitungs- und Conversations-Lexicon* was published in octavo throughout its more than century-long existence. As of 1704, it was complete in one volume and sold for one taler, less than a hundredth

[117] "Catalogue," 1 [309]; Sgard, "Echelle," 426. My estimate for the price of the first edition is based on the price of Bayle's *Dictionaire* as given above.
[118] Spree, *Streben*, 108–9.
[119] Darnton, *Business*, 456–7; Baczko, "Trois temps," 796n; Morrisson and Snyder, "Inégalités," 142.
[120] Darnton, *Business*, 274–7.
[121] *Esprit des journaux* 6 (June 1778): 418–19.
[122] See for example *Daily Advertiser*, May 22, 1740, [4]. On editions of the title see Bradshaw, "Thomas Dyche's *New General English Dictionary*," 160–1.

the price of the *Universal-Lexicon*. Like other encyclopedias, the *Reales Staats- Zeitungs- und Conversations-Lexicon* expanded. By the time of its last edition in 1824–8, it extended to four volumes but still cost just 6 talers.[123] Such prices put it within the budget of a broad middle class, as did the prices of other small encyclopedias in German.

After 1800, Germans continued to enjoy relatively affordable encyclopedias, notwithstanding the counter-examples of the *Wunder-Meyer* (1840–53) and the *Allgemeine Encyclopädie* (1818–89).[124] One reason for the low prices of German encyclopedias was their frugality with images, which remained a disproportionate contributor to cost. Herder spurned them completely in the first two editions (1854–7, 1875–9) of its *Konversations-Lexikon* to keep the price down.[125] Remarkably, the five-volume first edition cost just 8 talers, around twenty days' work for a teacher in a rural school.[126] Brockhaus too managed to keep prices low, in part by publishing *Konversations-Lexika* without illustrations through the late nineteenth century.[127]

While affordable to many, the large *Konversations-Lexika* of Brockhaus and Meyer remained out of reach for the poor. Typically, the seventeen-volume fifth edition (1893–7) of Meyer's *Konversations-Lexikon* was sold overwhelmingly to the middle and upper classes. Of the work's buyers, 38 percent were governmental and administrative officials, 17 percent merchants, 15 percent from the military, 13 percent teachers, and 5 percent landholders.[128] Happily for those unable to purchase a large encyclopedia, there were smaller, less expensive ones, including the eight-volume *Allgemeines deutsches Volks-Conversations-Lexikon* (*General German People's Conversational Dictionary*, 1845–9), priced at 10 talers or less; the four-volume *Kleineres Brockhaus'sches Conversations-Lexikon* (1854), priced at 7 talers; and early editions of Herder's *Konversations-Lexikon*.[129] By the late twentieth century, while only 5–8 percent of German households owned a large encyclopedia, a majority owned works of reference of some size and form.[130]

In Britain, the *Penny Cyclopaedia* (1833–43) was conceived as a medium for educating the working class. As the title announced, the price was

---

[123] Peche, *Bibliotheca*, 262, 293.
[124] On pricing for these works see Spree, *Streben*, 125–6; Rüdiger, "Ersch/Gruber," 51–2.
[125] Meyer, "Konversations-Lexikon," 57.
[126] Keiderling, *F. A. Brockhaus*, 85. For the salary of a contemporary teacher see Spree, *Streben*, 125.
[127] For prices for Brockhaus's *Konversations-Lexika* see Keiderling, "*Brockhaus*," 198.
[128] Sarkowski, *Bibliographische Institut*, 118. See also Spree, *Streben*, 125–6.
[129] Spree, *Streben*, 118; Peche, *Bibliotheca*, 19, 124; Hingst, *Geschichte*, 51–3.
[130] Hingst, *Geschichte*, 171–2.

initially a penny per weekly installment. Since it was planned for eight volumes, the first of which appeared in sixty-six installments, the price for the set would have been £2 4s.[131] At this price, it would have cost a carpenter – one of the highest paid artisans – around two weeks of wages. By comparison, each volume of Rees's [*New*] *Cyclopaedia* (1819–20) and the *Encyclopaedia Metropolitana* (1817–45) cost roughly £2, and the sets ran to forty-five and thirty volumes respectively.[132] Serialization, furthermore, made the *Penny* more affordable, since the cost was to be distributed over a decade. As it turned out, though, the publication of installments accelerated, which raised weekly charges. Worse still, the number of volumes rose to twenty-seven, increasing the final price from around £2 to £10.[133]

Among the period's large encyclopedias, the *Penny* remained the cheapest, cheaper than the [*New*] *Cyclopaedia* or the *Metropolitana*, but it was not within the budget of many carpenters. Only at the end of the century did a large British encyclopedia sell for little enough to draw in such purchasers. Specifically, the first edition of *Chambers's Encyclopaedia* (1868) was published in 520 weekly numbers costing 1½d. apiece, for a total cost of £3 5s.[134] Eighty thousand sets were sold through 1880. Most undoubtedly went to the middle class – as did most sets of Meyer's *Konversations-Lexikon*, which was selling more than 200,000 sets by the late nineteenth century – but *Chambers's* was accessible to the lower class too.[135]

In France, the *Encyclopédie nouvelle* (1834–42), like the *Penny Cyclopaedia*, was designed to be sold cheaply and to the masses. In keeping with the original title of *Encyclopédie pittoresque à deux sous* (*Two-Sou Pictorial Encyclopedia*), the work's backers planned to sell installments for only 2 sous. With fifty-two installments in each of eight volumes, the set would have cost about 41 francs.[136] An average worker earning 580 francs a year could perhaps have afforded it over the course of eight years, but it went up in price. By 1839, the price per volume had risen, so that the total expected price was 128 francs. In 1847, the encyclopedia was advertised for sale, still incomplete, for 130 francs.[137]

[131] For the number of volumes planned see Knight, *Passages*, 1: 200–1.

[132] Schmidt, "Visionary Pedant," 13.

[133] Knight, *Passages*, 1: 202; *Political Dictionary*, 1: [883].

[134] *Chambers's Encyclopaedia*, new rev. edn., 1: vii.

[135] Cooney, "Die deutschen Wurzeln," 207; Sarkowski, *Bibliographische Institut*, 118; Roberto, "Democratising," 100–6, 225–7, 231, 267–8. See also Spree, *Streben*, 124–6, 144–5. I would like to thank Rose Roberto for sending me material concerning the sales of *Chambers's*.

[136] Griffiths, *Jean Reynaud*, 124, 132–3.

[137] *Bibliographie de la France*, July 6, 1839: 316; *Appleton's Library Manual*, 128.

French workers had another option, for nineteenth-century France had encyclopedic dictionaries, many of them compact and inexpensive. Above all, in 1856, Pierre Larousse published his one-volume *Nouveau Dictionnaire de la langue française* for just 2¼ francs. This was the direct ancestor to the *Petit Larousse* (1905), which sold for 5 francs at the start of the twentieth century and came to be owned by 80 percent of French households.[138]

Even in the twentieth century, lower-class consumers were a tiny minority of those buying large encyclopedias. Indeed, the middle class was the leading consumer of small encyclopedias too. In part, many encyclopedia-producing countries had become middle-class societies. Still, by the early twentieth century, encyclopedias were in a "mass-market" in two different senses. First, they were sold in mass, sometimes in more than 100,000 sets. Second, in their smaller forms, they were within reach of most people in the countries they appeared in. They were affordable to the lower class as well as the broadening middle class.

While encyclopedias were gradually democratized from the eighteenth century onward, they did not go down in price in a consistent trajectory. Larousse, for example, had a near monopoly on French encyclopedias for much of the twentieth century, a situation that allowed it to keep prices high.[139] Even outside situations of monopoly, consumers had to pay more for encyclopedias with prestigious names such as Larousse. Conversely, the publishers of such encyclopedias had an interest in maintaining high prices, since anything less might discredit the brand. In the late twentieth century, typically, the difference in price between the *Encyclopaedia Britannica* and other large encyclopedias on the anglophone market followed in part from their quality and size, but it also reflected their symbolic stature. In 1977, for example, the *Britannica* retailed for $699, the *Encyclopedia Americana* for $480, *World Book* for $273, and *Funk and Wagnalls New Encyclopedia* for just $65, though even the latter work won praise from critics.[140]

Conclusion

The economic side of encyclopedias remains understudied. Information on pricing is hard to find for encyclopedias from before the mid eighteenth century, and measuring size can be tedious. More importantly,

---

[138] *Ecole normale*, December 15, 1858: 64; Blois, "Dictionnaire," 162.

[139] Mollier and Dubot, *Histoire*, 361–2, 666–7.

[140] For the prices see Katz, *Basic Information Sources*, 149. For positive comments about *Funk and Wagnalls* see for example Katz, *Basic Information Sources*, 138n; Kister, *Encyclopedia Buying Guide*, 2nd edn., 124–33.

scholars rarely emphasize encyclopedias' sizes and prices because they see encyclopedias primarily as intellectual projects. This tendency is unfortunate, for it prevents us from appreciating encyclopedias in all their breadth.

Growth was not constant among encyclopedias from 1680 to 1840, but from decade to decade over much of the period, the biggest encyclopedias set records for the size of their texts. Attention to records lends itself to a scattered and unenlightening perspective, since records – being exceptions – fit poorly in a framework of large-scale explanation. Viewed from this vantage, this chapter would be superficial if its only contribution were to establish the *Grosses vollständiges Universal-Lexicon* and the *Encyclopédie méthodique* as the biggest printed encyclopedias. Like all records, however, the records set by encyclopedias are meaningful in aggregate and as progressions. Two trends stand out: the quick growth of the biggest encyclopedias from 1680 to 1840, and their lack of growth afterward.

As noted above, these trends are not the only ones imaginable or worthy of study. To measure size, I counted words – and nothing else. A focus on illustrations would point to ongoing growth after the mid nineteenth century. Words are nonetheless easily quantified, and an encyclopedia's word-count is a useful measure of size, one correlated with both informational richness and physical bulk. By whatever means the size of encyclopedias is measured, it can be studied as something that went down instead of up, for example in "portable" or abridged encyclopedias. My choice to concentrate on expansion and multi-volume encyclopedias was motivated by their scholarly and cultural prominence, but small encyclopedias too have a story to tell.

In any event, the fact that encyclopedias set records for size through the mid nineteenth century but not afterward deserves explanation. Causes for their growth included the rise of the genre as a recognizable commodity, competition between rival works, an abundance of borrowable material unprotected by copyright, and idealism and profiteering on the part of contributors. After the mid nineteenth century, factors that inhibited their growth included the establishment of a settled market for selling them; the increasing cost of compiling and revising; and the financial conservatism of the larger, more compartmentalized companies that came to publish them. Although the quantity of knowledge and of book-buying readers both continued to increase, encyclopedias were now oriented less toward charting ways of encompassing knowledge than to serving accustomed roles with respect to the public. Only with the triumph of Wikipedia in the early 2000s would these roles be redefined as comprehensively as they were in the 1700s.

Pricing, for its part, does not match size perfectly in the case of encyclopedias. As the production of volumes represented much of an encyclopedia's cost through the mid nineteenth century, economies of scale were less important before then in allowing for lower prices as a result of high sales. Still, as the example of the *Encyclopédie* shows, a reduction in format could go a long way toward cutting prices. By the second half of the nineteenth century, material costs had fallen enough to make economies of scale significant, and the middle class had expanded. In this context, for the first time, a few large encyclopedias such as Meyer's *Konversations-Lexikon* and *Chambers's Encyclopaedia* were sold in quantities approaching or exceeding 100,000, and at prices accessible to at least some in the lower class. In the meantime, costs diminished for small encyclopedias too, bringing them within range of the vast majority of households in western Europe, the United States, and other places. High prices for encyclopedias persisted selectively in the twentieth century, notably for deluxe editions and prestigious titles. Overall, though, by this time, the eighteenth-century ideal of spreading knowledge throughout society had been realized in the form of the encyclopedia.

CHAPTER 4

Preparing an Encyclopedia

Like the three previous chapters, this one deals with encyclopedias as vehicles for content, but it deals with content not in its finished form but instead through the processes by which it took shape. In focusing on preparation in relation to content, I will disregard the physical processes of putting together an encyclopedia – for example, printing and binding. These were essential to preparing an encyclopedia, but they were little different from the processes of putting together other books.

Specifically, I will examine four tasks involved in the preparation of encyclopedias, all intellectual, administrative, or managerial. These were the tasks of planning, arranging for contributors, managing information, and compiling articles. Editing, a fifth task, will be dealt with in passing, but I will treat it more fully in Chapter 7 as part of my discussion of the figure of the editor. Not every encyclopedia demanded attention to every one of these tasks, and the tasks varied in importance from work to work. Nor were they unique to encyclopedias. Indeed, much of the chapter can be read as applying to other books. Still, the fact that encyclopedias were alphabetical imposed a certain distinctiveness on planning and information-management, if not other tasks. It was not the same thing, moreover, to recruit a contributor for an encyclopedia as it was to recruit an author for a review or a textbook. Lastly, since encyclopedia-compilers often borrowed from elsewhere, the final section of the chapter examines juridical and other means of protecting texts against copying.

Planning an Encyclopedia

Many encyclopedias from before the mid nineteenth century were not carefully planned. One indication is the irregularity with which they covered the alphabet. Time after time, the number of pages devoted to "A" was disproportionately large, thanks both to longer, more patiently written articles and to articles on minute subjects, whereas articles at the end of the alphabet showed signs of negligence. The *Encyclopédie nouvelle* (1834–42), for example, gave well over a volume to "A" before disposing of "S" through "Z" in a single last volume. Rarer, but still testifying to a lack of rigor in planning, were the encyclopedias that expanded in the course of the alphabet, among them the *Grosses vollständiges Universal-Lexicon* (1732–50) and the first *Deutsche Encyclopädie* (1778–1807), though the latter was abandoned at "K."[1]

Another indication of poor planning is the discrepancy between encyclopedists' plans and the works that they published. As shown in Chapter 3, publishers repeatedly promised smaller encyclopedias than the ones they brought out. More generally, prospectuses and advertisements from before publication erred in their claims about encyclopedias' contents. Some of the inaccuracy was promotional bluster, but some arose from bad planning. On a different level, plans for multi-volume encyclopedias can be extrapolated from cross-references to entries in later installments or volumes, which may not have been drafted when the cross-reference was put in. Cross-references to entries not providing the content they were supposed to suggest imperfect planning, as do cross-references to missing entries. In his *Dictionaire* (1697), for example, Bayle referred to some fifty articles that he never got around to writing.[2]

Regardless of planning, many encyclopedias from before the mid nineteenth century took shape as a function of available material, not through decisions about how space should be allocated. Symptomatic of the tendency is disproportion in the length of articles. We cannot say how long a given article ought to have been, but some stand out as disproportionate. In the *Universal-Lexicon*, for example, the entry on Leipzig – the encyclopedia's hometown – was considerably shorter than the entry on Wurzen, a neighboring town of just 2,000 people. The best explanation is that Wurzen had a diligent historian – perhaps Gotthelf Becker, a local principal – one who accepted the publisher's invitation to send in material.[3] Similarly, the longest article in the *Universal-Lexicon* was on Christian Wolff's philosophy. At 175 pages, it was much longer, for example, than the articles on Leibniz (20 pages) or Plato's philosophy (8 pages). Wolff was a significant presence in the early eighteenth century, but the main reason

---

[1] Kossmann, "Deutsche Universallexika," 1571; Goetschel, Macleod, and Snyder, "*Deutsche Encyclopädie*," 258.

[2] Lieshout, *Making*, 94–7.

[3] Löffler, "Wer schrieb den Zedler?," 278–9.

for the article's length is that the editor Ludovici – the probable author – was an expert on Wolff.[4]

Still, no encyclopedia was wholly unplanned. A common short-cut in planning was to draw on the keywords of another work of reference or a previous edition of the same encyclopedia. In the late seventeenth century, Furetière mocked the dictionary-writers of the Académie Française for spending their time listing words from other dictionaries.[5] For his *Nuova enciclopedia* a century later, Zorzi planned to mix keywords from two Italian dictionaries and the French *Encyclopédie*.[6] Krünitz, for his part, took most of the keywords for the *Oeconomische Encyclopädie* (1773–1858) from a dictionary by Johann Christoph Adelung, only adding some technical terms – which Adelung later incorporated into his dictionary.[7] Likewise, to begin work on the *Enciclopedia italiana* (1929–39), editors in charge of disciplines were sent lists of articles in the eleventh edition (1910–11) of the *Encyclopaedia Britannica* to review as a basis for the new encyclopedia's keywords.[8]

Copying from other dictionaries and encyclopedias was not the only way of establishing keywords. John Dunton, the compiler of the *Ladies Dictionary* (1694), got ideas for keywords from letters to his periodical, the *Athenian Mercury*.[9] In the 1950s, working on *Collier's Encyclopedia* (1949), the librarian Louis Shores extended the approach. He proposed determining the encyclopedia's keywords mathematically, through a numerical survey of indexes to periodicals – but his idea went unheeded.[10] By the early twenty-first century, Brockhaus was having computers monitor databases and searches on its website to help generate keywords.[11] In any event, however well chosen, pre-defined lists of keywords had to be modified as an encyclopedia developed.

In itself, borrowing keywords provided just a sketch of a plan, but many encyclopedists went further in modeling their encyclopedias on an already published one, perhaps the previous edition of their own encyclopedia. From the seventeenth century onward, building on the foundation of another encyclopedia was in fact the normal backdrop for preparing

[4] Schneider, *Erfindung*, 175–6.
[5] Quemada, *Dictionnaires*, 177.
[6] Zorzi, *Prodromo*, xiv–xvii.
[7] Fröhner, *Technologie*, 454–5.
[8] Turi, *Mecenate*, 109–10. On the role of other encyclopedias in the establishment of the *Italiana*'s nomenclature see Cavaterra, *Rivoluzione*, 42.
[9] Paul, "Dieses Universal-Lexicon," 29–30.
[10] Shiflett, *Louis Shores*, 153, 185.
[11] Keiderling, *F. A. Brockhaus*, 332–3.

an encyclopedia. In such a scenario, planning was reduced to specifying changes with respect to a model. These included updates, corrections, improved coverage of certain subjects, and adjustments to local religious and political views. When an encyclopedia was based on an extra-territorial model, its planners usually promised more on the nation being adapted to.

Diderot and D'Alembert's *Encyclopédie* (1751–72) was one of hundreds of encyclopedias to be based on another, but it was also defined by creative planning and unplanned mutations. The interplay of these factors in its development gives a sense of the fluidity with which encyclopedias could form. As pitched to the publisher André Le Breton, the *Encyclopédie* was supposed to be a five-volume translation and expansion of Chambers' *Cyclopaedia*. In 1746, Le Breton identified a second source, Harris's *Lexicon Technicum*.[12] His first appointee as editor, the mathematician De Gua, decided to involve specialists and drew up a plan for their work, providing guidelines on such matters as articles' length, the order of sub-articles, and the work's coverage. As editor, he stipulated, he would take responsibility for making articles stylistically uniform.[13]

We do not know if Diderot and D'Alembert, the new editors after De Gua's resignation in 1747, were aware of his plan. Regardless, they took the *Encyclopédie* in a different direction. Like De Gua, they saw the value of stressing technology and bringing in specialists, but unlike him, they saw no reason to respect Catholic orthodoxy, and they did not trouble themselves with limiting articles' length.[14] As Diderot's prospectus shows, some of the *Encyclopédie*'s features were planned: its emphasis on technology; its visual lavishness; its inclusion of articles of varying lengths; and its dependence on a team of specialists, their contributions to be free from any meddling by the editors. This latter policy, evidently, ran counter to De Gua's goal of making articles uniform.

The prospectus may have hinted at the *Encyclopédie*'s subversive agenda, announcing as it did that the work would destroy errors and prejudice.[15] Perhaps, too, the placement of religion next to divination and black magic in the attached tree of knowledge, the "Système figuré" ("Figural System"), heralded an anti-religious agenda.[16] Still, Diderot characterized these practices as abuses of religion, and even the work's critics seem to have

[12] Holmberg, *Maurists' Unfinished Encyclopedia*, 107–9; Lough, "Le Breton," 267–87.
[13] Favre and Dürr, "Texte," 51–68; Théré and Charles, "Nouvel élément," 105–23.
[14] Kafker and Loveland, "Vie," 200–3.
[15] [Diderot], prospectus, 1–6.
[16] Darnton, *Great Cat Massacre*, 199–200.

been little concerned with this detail from the "Système figuré."[17] It is true that the offending categories of black magic and divination were removed from the tree of knowledge in two contemporary encyclopedias less critical of religion: John Barrow's *Supplement to the New and Universal Dictionary of Arts and Sciences* (1754) and the Yverdon *Encyclopédie* (1770–80) – but so too were other categories.[18] Furthermore, while promising more orthodoxy than the *Encyclopédie*, Zorzi, an abbot, maintained the juxtaposition in the revised map of knowledge (1779) for his *Nuova enciclopedia*.[19] In short, if the famous radicalism of the *Encyclopédie* was planned from the start, Diderot muffled his intentions in the prospectus.

Whatever the editors' forethought regarding its subversiveness, the *Encyclopédie* was planned badly in some respects. Neither Diderot nor D'Alembert had planned for biographies, but their most prolific contributor, Louis de Jaucourt, began inserting them in Volume VI, albeit under individuals' places of birth.[20] Scholars have pointed out other about-faces in the course of publication. Above all, the editors' plans to create systematic order alongside the work's alphabetical order were unrealistic. D'Alembert argued that the *Encyclopédie* had three mechanisms that, working together, made it systematically coherent: cross-references, the "Système figuré," and parenthetical rubrics in articles referring to disciplines in the "Système figuré" – "Géog." for geography, "Hist. nat." for natural history, and so on. Alarmingly, he admitted that cross-references and rubrics might be missing from some articles, in which case he advised the reader to imagine what they ought to be.[21] In the end, the claim that cross-references and rubrics would create a unified system was in conflict with Diderot's policy of not tinkering with articles. As shown in Chapter 5, contributors used rubrics and cross-references in different ways – and the editors balked at imposing a standard.

More rigorous planning for encyclopedias began around 1800. In the prospectus for the *Encyclopédie méthodique* (1782–1832), Panckoucke specified the number of volumes for each of his twenty-six subjects. As it turned out, the encyclopedia was quite different from what it was originally planned as. Still, Panckoucke was one of the first encyclopedia-editors to set the relative weights of subjects before publication began. The

---

[17] Loveland, "*Laissez-Faire* Encyclopedia?," 209.
[18] Loveland, "Two Partial English-Language Translations," 173n. Notice, for example, the suppression of categories relating to "monsters" in De Felice, *Encyclopédie*, 1: "Système figuré."
[19] Zorzi, *Prodromo*, XIV, XVI, "Divisione della metafisica" (fold-out diagram after p. 38).
[20] Perla, "Unsigned Articles," 190–1.
[21] *Encyclopédie; ou, Dictionnaire*, 1: xviii–xix. See also [Diderot], prospectus, 11.

organization of the *Méthodique* – by disciplines, not the alphabet – probably favored such planning. Indeed, Coleridge put together a similar plan for the non-alphabetical *Encyclopaedia Metropolitana* (1817–45). Despite his resignation as editor, the published encyclopedia remained close to what he had outlined. Coleridge considered himself the first person to "methodize" an encyclopedia. One work he saw as unmethodized was the *Supplement to the Fourth, Fifth, and Sixth Editions of the Encyclopaedia Britannica* (1824), which was vague about the "method" by which it was organized.[22] Among other signs of disorder, over half the alphabet was relegated to Volume VI, a disparity for which the editor offered an unconvincing excuse.[23]

In the second half of the nineteenth century, alphabetical encyclopedias too began to have their balance of subjects planned in advance. A pioneer was the *Grande Encyclopédie* (1885–1902). According to the director, Dreyfus, the encyclopedia was prepared in stages. The number of volumes was set at twenty-five, the main divisions of knowledge were decided on, a set of keywords was drawn up, and the keywords were sent to contributors, who reviewed past works of reference before beginning their entries.

At this point, it became necessary to decide the length of specific entries. Planning from top to bottom, the directors gave each division of knowledge a certain number of columns, which editors then distributed among their keywords. The division on history and geography was given the most space (9,000 columns), followed by literature (6,000 columns), miscellaneous material (5,400 columns), physics and chemistry (4,500 columns), the natural sciences (4,500 columns), politics, economics, administration, and finance (4,500 columns), law (4,500 columns), art and archeology (4,500 columns), and other domains. Reviewing his plans for the allocation of space, Dreyfus acknowledged the need to be flexible.[24] Nevertheless, thanks in part to such planning, the *Grande Encyclopédie* managed to avoid expanding much. It ended up being just 20 percent longer than planned.

In enduring, family-owned companies such as Larousse and Brockhaus, planning could be for the long term, but it was also more limited, since the previous edition formed a basis on which to plan. A company's experience with planning could be helpful as well. Albert Brockhaus, who led the company around 1900, expressed pride in its accumulated wisdom: "If it were so easy to publish a big encyclopedia, then every donkey would

[22] Schmidt, "Visionary Pedant," 84–5, 120; Collison, *Encyclopaedias*, 238.
[23] *Supplement to the Fourth, Fifth, and Sixth Editions*, I: xxxiii.
[24] *Grande Encyclopédie: Inventaire*, I: XI–XII.

do it."[25] From 1912 to 1913, fearful that time and war would disperse or destroy the company's collective intelligence, he wrote a confidential, 200-page "Lexikon-Testament" explaining how to prepare the fifteenth edition when a good time arrived, as it finally did in the late 1920s. The "Lexikon-Testament" illustrates a different kind of planning from that described above for the *Grande Encyclopédie*, one oriented toward business and practicalities. One of its concerns was to find a viable position for Brockhaus's next encyclopedia with respect to the offerings of the Bibliographisches Institut. Among other aspects of planning, Albert made recommendations for the new edition's price, size, and layout, the purchasers to be targeted, the understandability of articles, and advertisements. A century later, in the early 2000s, Brockhaus continued to insist on the pragmatic dimension of planning, though the duration of planning, formerly four to six years, had dropped to only a year.[26]

Though never owned by the same people for more than a handful of editions, the *Britannica* was another work whose planning was simplified by the existence of a previous edition. Before the twentieth century, though, it took years, even decades, to see an edition to completion, a fact that made departures from planning almost inevitable. The same problem afflicted other encyclopedias until publication began to be speeded up in the early twentieth century. After the drawn-out publication of the ninth edition (1875–89) of the *Britannica*, the tenth edition (1902–3), a supplement, was published in only nine months. Around the same time, the sixteen-volume *Encyclopedia Americana* was brought out over the course of 1903–4. The eleventh edition of the *Britannica* was then vaunted as embodying the ideal of "simultaneous production," though the twenty-nine volumes were actually published at intervals in 1910–11. The ideal of simultaneity was more properly realized with the fourteenth edition (1929). All editorial work on the set was completed before any of the volumes was sent to the press.[27] Under these circumstances, a closer match could be imposed between plans and realities.

In the second half of the twentieth century, planning for the *Britannica* was taken to a more abstract level. Already in 1947, a board of directors was appointed to conduct long-term planning, but it did not, for a time, advocate significant change. One factor that impelled it to was the

[25] "Wenn es so leicht wäre, ein grosses Lexikon herauszugeben, würde es jeder Esel machen." Keiderling, *F. A. Brockhaus*, 329.
[26] *Ibid.*, 67–70, 329.
[27] *Encyclopaedia Britannica*, 11th edn., 1: xii; Kogan, *Great EB*, 94; Kruse, "Story," 169, 180, 276, 300, 348.

publication of Harvey Einbinder's critique, *The Myth of the Britannica* (1964). At some point, the board concluded that the encyclopedia worked for reference but not education. In response, between 1965 and 1968, the philosopher Mortimer Adler devised and gained approval for a secret plan for strengthening the work's educational aspect. His plan was to divide the *New Encyclopaedia Britannica* into three sub-series: the *Micropaedia*, offering short entries; the *Macropaedia*, offering long ones; and a one-volume *Propaedia*, providing an overview of knowledge.[28] Only after settling on this overall plan did the editors begin normal planning, defining areas of knowledge, reflecting on their balance, and distributing space among them.

For enthusiasts, the resulting fifteenth edition (1974) may have represented a "revolution in encyclopedia-making," as one of its prefaces claimed.[29] Still, despite years of planning, the *New Encyclopaedia Britannica* – as it was titled – ended up being similar to other encyclopedias, including two in which the work's owners had a financial stake. First, from the 1930s onward, *Britannica Junior* (1934) had been split into two sub-series that resembled the *Micropaedia* and *Macropaedia*.[30] Second, the *Encyclopaedia universalis* (1968–75), a French work co-published with Encyclopaedia Britannica through an agreement dated 1966, was divided into three sub-series strongly reminiscent of the *Micropaedia*, the *Macropaedia*, and the *Propaedia*.[31] Did the *New Encyclopaedia Britannica* draw inspiration from the *Encyclopaedia universalis*, or did the *Universalis* simply take advantage of Adler's planning?[32] Whatever the answer, the effort to redesign the *Britannica* did not lead to a break from precedent among encyclopedias.

By and large, publishers and editors planned encyclopedias better with each passing century. To a degree, better planning resulted from the standardization of encyclopedias and the professionalization of the people and processes behind them. In addition, the development of controls on the business of encyclopedia-making – independent financial officers, boards of directors, shareholders, and so on – favored encyclopedias grounded on planning. Lastly, it may be true that surprises and heterogeneity appealed to a certain sensibility in the seventeenth and eighteenth centuries, so that

[28] Stockwell, *History*, 117–18; *New Encyclopaedia Britannica* (1974), *Propaedia*: ix–x; Preece, "Notes," 144. For a suggestion that plans were still fluid in 1968 see Preece, "Notes," 22.
[29] *New Encyclopaedia Britannica* (1974), *Propaedia*: ix.
[30] Walsh, *Anglo-American General Encyclopedias*, 15; *New York Times*, December 1, 1935: BR40.
[31] On the agreement with *Encyclopaedia Britannica* see *Yearbook: Commercial Arbitration* 30 (2005): 1136–37; Vanche-Roby, "Nomenclature," 177.
[32] For the former argument see Seckel and Tesnière, "De Panckoucke," 437.

editors of the period had little incentive to remove them through better planning.[33] Conversely, however, when Bayle attributed his *Dictionaire*'s disorder to the public's need for "variety," it is hard not to wonder if he was imagining a public to suit his own habits as an "associative" encyclopedist rather than a carefully planning one.[34]

Managing Contributors and Information

Once a plan for an encyclopedia was made – or not made – it was time to engage writers and assemble their articles. Both tasks could be simple or complicated. At one extreme, the composition of an encyclopedia could be undertaken by a single person, whether self-selected or recruited by a publisher. Publishers in search of such a compiler often set their sights low, intending to make the work anonymous and calculating that they could reduce costs by hiring someone obscure, young, disreputable, or otherwise unable to command a high salary. For the second edition (1778–83) of the *Britannica*, the publishers thus picked Tytler, an unstable, alcoholic, perennially indigent man of letters.[35]

Even one of the publishers of Ersch and Gruber's *Allgemeine Encyclopädie* (1818–89) – a collaborative work – wondered if he should hire less prestigious but more obedient editors.[36] Still, when publishers sought what were later called managing editors, they looked for more respectable candidates, not only for the purposes of advertisement, but also because such editors were better at recruiting collaborators. For the *Supplement to the Fourth, Fifth, and Sixth Editions of the Encyclopaedia Britannica* (1824), for example, the publisher Archibald Constable chose Napier as editor. A young solicitor and librarian, Napier did not have high standing in the intellectual world. Indeed, he had to rely on others to put him in touch with some of his best prospects for contributing. He nonetheless moved in better circles than the *Britannica*'s earliest editors, and by the time of the seventh edition (1842), he had developed his own network of possible contributors.[37]

Once chosen, the editor of a collaborative encyclopedia faced the task of enlisting contributors. Although most contributors were recruited – that is, sought out by an encyclopedia's publisher or editor – some were

---

[33] Schneider, *Erfindung*, 118–19.
[34] Lieshout, *Making*, 65–6.
[35] Doig *et al.*, "James Tytler's Edition," 71–5.
[36] Rüdiger, "Ersch/Gruber," 36–7.
[37] Yeo, *Encyclopaedic Visions*, 255–60; Kogan, *Great EB*, 35–7; Kruse, "Story," 150.

volunteers. It is well known how important volunteers were to the *Oxford English Dictionary* (1884–1928), collecting quotations to document words' history and usage, but volunteers made their mark on encyclopedias too. Once an encyclopedia was published, readers found errors and oversights, and sent in corrections. One such reader, the magistrate Louis Lautour du Châtel, uncovered 1,300 omissions in the first edition (1704) of the *Dictionnaire de Trévoux* and mailed in material to remedy them for the second edition. He was rewarded for his effort with two complimentary copies.[38]

More generally, encyclopedia-editors received unsolicited material on a regular basis. In some cases, we lack certainty about what was solicited and what was not. Regardless, editors had reasons for considering unsolicited material, even when it was weak. First, it saved them work. Second, the author of an accepted submission might become a subscriber or help promote the encyclopedia. Lastly, ties of friendship and benevolence probably sealed the acceptance of many a proposed article. As a lecturer on mathematical subjects, Harris, for example, could have written the entries on mathematics in the *Lexicon Technicum* (1704) without assistance, but he nonetheless included a handful by Humphry Ditton, whom he praised as a mathematician and patronized in other ways.[39]

Between the late seventeenth and the early nineteenth century, moreover, it was common for encyclopedia-makers to invite volunteers to participate. Sometimes the invitation concerned only the learned, as in the preface to the *Encyclopédie moderne* (1823–32).[40] Alternatively, it could be limited to correcting mistakes, as it was in the *Curieuses Natur- Kunst- Gewerck- und Handlungs-Lexicon* (1712) and Volume 1 of the *Grosses vollständiges Universal-Lexicon* (1732–50).[41] At times, it was broader. Mixing a rhetorical platitude with the developing notion of the public as judge, certain encyclopedists admitted that they might have made errors or left things out but invited readers to help out by suggesting changes for later. In his *Dictionnaire* (1694), for example, Corneille issued such an invitation because "only the public knows everything quite perfectly."[42] After the *Cyclopaedia* (1728) was published, Chambers urged the public to mail in material for a second edition: "Not a college, a chapter, a mercantile

[38] Leca-Tsiomis, *Ecrire*, 121.
[39] Loveland, "Varieties," 94.
[40] *Encyclopédie moderne*, 1: xii.
[41] Hübner, "Vorrede," [](5v) (§XLVIII); *Grosses vollständiges Universal-Lexicon*, 1: 16.
[42] "Il n'y a que le public qui sache tout bien parfaitement." Corneille, *Dictionnaire*, 1: áiiir. See also Proust, *Diderot*, 179.

company, a ship, scarce a house, or even a man, but may contribute his quota to the public instruction."[43]

Many such invitations were made for rhetorical as much as practical purposes. Inviting the public to participate was a tactic, among other things, for marketing books.[44] Yet some readers responded, and editors in turn incorporated some submitted materials. From the first edition onward, the preface to Moréri's *Grand Dictionaire* (1674) thus invited submissions from readers, notably on their forebears, and scattered remarks in the published work prove that such submissions were in fact used: "We present this article as it was sent in by the family."[45] For his *Biblioteca* (1701–6), Coronelli solicited contributions from readers all over Europe, not only to flatter them and make them subscribers, but to get local information for the encyclopedia. Toward the latter end, he mailed out hundreds of questionnaires. It is impossible to know how many were returned and made use of, but combined with his correspondence, the richness of the *Biblioteca* suggests the initiative paid off.[46] Likewise, after taking over as editor of the *Universal-Lexicon*, Ludovici appealed to the public for biographical and geographical material. The appeal was plainly successful. Some of the work's biographies had information that only the subject, or an intimate, was likely to know. Furthermore, the encyclopedia covered living professors from its hometown of Leipzig disproportionately – a case where volunteers probably wrote on themselves.[47]

Thanks to a growing commitment to the authority of expertise, few editors invited contributions from the public at large between the mid nineteenth century and the arrival of Wikipedia around 2000. In 1868, the editors of the eleventh edition (1864–8) of Brockhaus's *Konversations-Lexikon* acknowledged receiving "a lot of contributions and corrections from volunteers," which they claimed, diplomatically, to have used "as much as possible."[48] Around a century later, an American observer of the encyclopedia-industry wrote that volunteers were disallowed: "Manuscripts of encyclopedia articles are not submitted on the authors' initiative to acquisitions editors, but instead are commissioned by the encyclopedia

[43] Chambers, "Some Considerations," 4.
[44] See Ferdinand, "Constructing," 168–9.
[45] "On donne cet article tel qu'il a été remis par la famille." Moréri, *Grand Dictionaire*, new edn., III: 874. For an invitation to submit material see Moréri, *Grand Dictionaire*, 1st edn., a4r. See also Chappey, *Ordres*, 101–2.
[46] Fuchs, "Vincenzo Coronelli," 121–3, 147–53, 187–8.
[47] Löffler, "Wer schrieb den Zedler?," 273–6; Schneider, *Erfindung*, 104, 107–8.
[48] "… eine Menge freiwilliger Beiträge und Berichtigungen … soweit es möglich war." [*Grosse Brockhaus*], 11th edn., XV: XXI.

itself."[49] In any event, whatever the period, the articles that volunteers succeeded in placing in encyclopedias were mostly biographical and geographical, whereas articles on the arts and sciences were typically solicited or compiled by an editor. While alien to Wikipedia, where volunteers compose all articles, this division of labor is reminiscent of the *Oxford English Dictionary*'s reliance on volunteers to collect data and on experts to analyze it and formulate entries.

As important as volunteers were, recruited authors were the mainstay of encyclopedia-compilation. How they were recruited is not always clear, but before the twentieth century, personal and local relations were undoubtedly critical. Diderot, for example, recruited his landlord, his friend Rousseau, and an ironmaster from his hometown to write for the *Encyclopédie* (1751–72).[50] Institutions were another channel for recruiting contributors. One conjecture regarding the anonymous authors of the *Grosses vollständiges Universal-Lexicon* (1732–50) is that many were recruited from the University of Leipzig.[51] Among other institutions, contributors to the twentieth-century *Espasa* were recruited from the Catalan Institute for the Art of the Book and the University of Barcelona, both having connections with the publisher Espasa.[52] Institutional recruiting could be seen in a negative light. In 1949, the librarian Shores attempted to establish the *National Encyclopedia* (1932) at Florida State University, where he was a dean, but his colleagues expressed outrage, fearing he would exploit students and faculty in the production of articles.[53]

When recruitment was personal or institutional, it tended to operate in a limited area, thus making encyclopedias in a certain sense local. When contributors lived nearby, communication was simpler, especially before the invention of the telegraph. Here French encyclopedias had an edge on those from less centralized countries or linguistic regions, since they could take advantage of Paris's wealth of population and talent. By contrast, the editor of the eighteenth-century *Deutsche Encyclopädie* (1778–1807) suffered from the difficulty of coordinating his team, though it was concentrated in the region of Hesse-Darmstadt and otherwise restricted to German-speaking Europe.[54]

[49] O'Sullivan, "Acquisition," 28.
[50] Kafker, *Encyclopedists*, 38–40.
[51] Schneider, "Zedlers *Universal-Lexicon*," 200.
[52] Castellano, *Enciclopedia*, 42, 65, 541.
[53] Shiflett, *Louis Shores*, 113–14.
[54] Decker, "*Deutsche Encyclopädie*," 150.

However convenient it was for editors to work with local contributors, they found themselves faced with a growing dispersion and internationalism. Over a dozen contributors to the *Encyclopédie* were foreigners, for example.[55] From the late eighteenth century onward, more and more editors solicited articles from specialists, who could live anywhere. International recruiting could give a work prestige and authority, but it had other purposes too. Already by the early twentieth century, a desire to appear cosmopolitan or enable trans-national marketing encouraged some editors to recruit from abroad. Americans were added as contributors to the *Encyclopaedia Britannica* to make the ninth edition (1875–89) more inviting to the American public, just as the preface to the *Espasa* (1908–30) highlighted the work's Latin American contributors as giving it a unique pertinence to "countries overseas" ("países de ultramar").[56] Thinking politically, the editor Gentile noted the internationalism of contributors to the *Enciclopedia italiana* (1929–39) to dampen accusations that the encyclopedia was fascist or intolerant of dissidence.[57] In the late twentieth century, the goal of recruiting contributors globally – now linked to concerns about nationalism and Eurocentrism – led to odd schemes. For the *New Encyclopaedia Britannica* (1974), for instance, senior editors were told to propose three people who could write on a given subject, one of whom had to live outside the United States. In the end, fully half the contributors were foreigners, which presumably helped the encyclopedia avoid being "parochially Western."[58]

After recruiting contributors, editors turned to the long-term endeavor of retaining and managing them, that is, keeping them on time and on target with what they wrote. Many contributors were tardy in submitting materials. Editors were thus forced to act as coaches or counselors. They also had to be tactful when reacting to over-long or otherwise faulty submissions, since a brusque response might induce a contributor to quit. These problems were all the worse when contributors were celebrities. In the *Supplement to the Fourth, Fifth, and Sixth Editions of the Encyclopaedia Britannica* (1824), for example, the editor Napier observed: "If an encyclopedia is to be composed of original articles, written by men of eminence … it will always be found difficult, if not impossible, to limit each contribution to the space required by the general plan."[59] As we saw in Chapter 3,

---

[55] Kafker, *Encyclopedists*, 20–1.
[56] Kruse, "Story," 186n; Castellano, *Enciclopedia*, 245–6.
[57] *Enciclopedia italiana*, 1: XIII.
[58] *New Encyclopaedia Britannica* (1974), *Propaedia*: xiv, xvi.
[59] *Supplement to the Fourth, Fifth, and Sixth Editions*, 1: xxxii.

failures to enforce limits on article's length were a factor in overruns in the size of encyclopedias. Yet throughout the nineteenth century, despite Napier's pessimism, the *Britannica*'s editors were successful in controlling contributors' wordiness.[60] Editors, evidently, were approaching the ideal evoked by Hogarth, a member of the staff of the *Britannica* in the early twentieth century: "[The editor] should be able to withstand the verbose and conceited contributor. But it is difficult to keep an expert, or an enthusiast, within his appointed limits, though a due sense of proportion and firmness in maintaining it is the whole duty of an editor."[61]

For collaborative encyclopedias, another aspect of management was balancing tensions between contributors or among disciplines. At a minimum, two or more contributors might want to treat the same topic. At worst, they might contradict one another. On the one hand, redundancy and contradictions could be dealt with editorially. According to De Felice, for instance, eliminating repetition was one of his duties as the editor of the Yverdon *Encyclopédie*.[62] On the other hand, editors could deal with such problems before they arose. To facilitate work on the *Enciclopedia italiana*, for example, the editor arranged meetings among the teams responsible for disciplines to settle on boundaries. The human stakes were high. The sub-editor in charge of physical geography resigned after his article on atolls was replaced with one by a naturalist. The team working on military affairs grew discouraged, for its part, about encroachments on its territory by other teams and their disciplines.[63]

At some point, the editor of a collaborative encyclopedia had to organize submissions, a task not so different from the one faced by lone compilers with regard to their own notes. Well into the twentieth century, the process depended on pieces of paper. An editor could arrange bits of paper by attaching them with pins, binding or otherwise affixing them in books, or putting them in a possibly divided or "pigeonholed" compartment. In the preparation of encyclopedias as well as of dictionaries, slips or packets of paper corresponding to articles could be arranged alphabetically as they arrived – and moved to new locations if they needed retitling. Only exceptionally have traces of the papers survived, but we have testimonials about their use. For a proposed re-edition of Savary and others' *Dictionnaire universel de commerce* in the mid eighteenth century, the writer André

[60] Loveland, "Unifying," 75–7.
[61] Boyles, *Everything*, 262.
[62] Cernuschi, "ABC," 139.
[63] Cavaterra, *Rivoluzione*, 39, 130, 151–2, 168–9.

Morellet thus signaled material to be copied or paraphrased, had secretaries copy it onto standardized cards, and filed the cards in the 800 slots of a specially designed cabinet.[64]

Cabinets for filing had become common in offices by the early twentieth century, but as late as 1917, the editor Arthur Jose was grateful to have "a table, two chairs, and a cupboard with shelves above it" for his work on the *Australian Encyclopaedia*. Earlier, in fact, he had pleaded with the publisher for shelving where he could "arrange the articles in separate piles."[65] By contrast, enormous files of cards underlay the production of the *Enciclopedia italiana* (1929–39) and the encyclopedias of Brockhaus and the Bibliographisches Institut in the first half of the twentieth century. In 1945, with the blessing of the Americans who were conquering Leipzig at the end of World War II, Brockhaus's files were loaded onto a truck and taken to American-occupied Wiesbaden. At Brockhaus's new headquarters, they occupied a whole wall and served as the basis for the firm's sixteenth edition (1952–63). The Bibliographisches Institut, less fortunate, saw its files destroyed in the war and was unable to return to making large encyclopedias for more than two decades.[66]

Before the invention of the typewriter and the computer, submissions to an editor were ordinarily handwritten, whether by the author or by a secretary, but another option was to cut out a printed text for use as an article, with or without annotations. In general, the procedure required two copies of a source, since cutting out text on one side of a page would make the text on the other side unavailable for use.[67]

Compilation by cutting was ideal for re-editions and encyclopedias premised on copying. The academician Jean-Henri-Samuel Formey, for example, had been making suggestions for articles in the Yverdon *Encyclopédie* when the editor, De Felice, urged him to send in material cut out of books: "You could even spare the trouble of writing by cutting up the book that you take the articles from, and by covering each article with a sheet of white paper, with the heading of the article, always beginning with the definition." De Felice's white papers were an aid to filing, intended to separate bits of detached text and indicate the keywords where they would fit in the encyclopedia.[68] Similarly, Smellie, the editor of the

---

[64] Perrot, "Dictionnaires," 55. On slips of paper in the period's information-management see Considine, "Cutting," 487–99.

[65] Kavanagh, *Conjuring*, 58.

[66] Cavaterra, *Rivoluzione*, 43–4; Keiderling, *F. A. Brockhaus*, 224, 244, 378.

[67] Blair, *Too Much*, 96, 205.

[68] "Vous pourriez même épargner la peine d'écrire, en coupant le livre d'où vous enlèveriez les articles, et en couvrant chaque article d'une feuille de papier blanc, avec l'étiquette de l'article, commencé

first edition (1771) of the *Encyclopaedia Britannica*, reportedly "used to say jocularly, that he had made a dictionary of arts and sciences with a pair of scissors, clipping out from various books a 'quantum sufficit' of matter for the printer."[69]

Alternatively, just as scholars took notes in the margins of books, an encyclopedia could be prepared as a series of annotations within a copy of an already published encyclopedia. The resemblance between editions of Furetière's *Dictionaire* (1690) is sufficiently close, for example, that revisers must have submitted the previous edition in its entirety, with few suggestions for cuts, along with annotations or inserted papers. This hypothesis fits with the style of the editing, in which articles were rarely recast but instead simply supplemented. In his article "Arteil" ("Toe"), for example, Furetière wrote that "the people wrongly say 'orteil,'" to which a later reviser added a counter-correction: "And that is how it should be said."[70] Whatever the methods of those who reworked Furetière's *Dictionaire*, we know that Bayle revised his *Dictionaire* (1697) by annotating the first edition and attaching sheets of paper for longer additions. In part for this reason, he too was prone to purely additive editing, detrimental though it was to the work's coherence and consistency.[71]

After the editor of a collaborative encyclopedia received materials for articles, he or she might revise them, whether alone or with the author. In the direst scenario, an article could be rejected. As shown in Chapter 7, censors sometimes thrust themselves into the process, pressuring editors to revise or reject articles. Negotiations were usually necessary to modify an article that was to appear under its author's name, and they could be fraught. Sometimes the best solution was to run an article anonymously. This was another area where editors had to be shrewd about managing people. Nor was negotiation always productive or possible. Failing to win reassurance from the editor Gentile that he would have control over his contribution to the *Enciclopedia italiana* (1929–39), the historian Adolfo Omodeo declined to write and went on to resign.[72] Jose, the editor of the *Australian Encyclopaedia*, summarized the problem from an editor's perspective in 1919: "When a man has been engaged to do an article, and some

toujours par la définition." I would like to thank Alain Cernuschi for correcting the quotation and helping me understand the "papier blanc." For the unrectified quotation see Häseler, "Extraits," 285.

[69] Kerr, *Memoirs*, 1: 362–3. More generally, on cutting up books for scholarly purposes, see Blair, "Reading Strategies," 25–8.

[70] Loveland, "Varieties," 95. On "additive" revisions to the encyclopedia see Behnke, *Furetière*, 50–2, 108.

[71] Lieshout, *Making*, 55–62.

[72] Turi, *Mecenate*, 211–12.

of his work is obviously and irrefutably wrong, what is my duty? Do I put it straight, and have the article published as his? Or do I leave it wrong and let his signature take the blame? Or do we delete the signature and do what we like with the article?"[73]

Once they were revised to the satisfaction of editors, articles were normally recopied for easier filing and typesetting. The typewriter, invented around 1870, helped with the task. So did computers, which were already handling accounting for *World Book* and Larousse's works in the early 1950s.[74] Around 1970, Encyclopaedia Britannica began using computers to edit and set type, a practice that quickly became universal.[75] As individual contributors came to own typewriters and then computers, they too began to use them, encouraged by editors. Still, neither the typewriter nor the computer put an end to hand-written submissions or the disorder of files, whether in cabinets or computers' memories. Even a sub-editor for the *Espasa*, for instance, wrote out articles long-hand on scraps of paper such as bills and envelopes.[76]

At some point, ordered material corresponding to an installment or volume was sent to the compositor, and printed proofs were returned to the editor or contributor. If corrections were numerous, every page of the encyclopedia might end up being reset and printed again, as Adam Black, the publisher of the *Britannica*, complained in the late nineteenth century.[77] Regardless, the long journey to publication was now nearly complete.

Compilation and Copying

In the early twentieth century, Hogarth, a member of the editorial staff for the *Encyclopaedia Britannica*, described what she saw as the hypocrisy of encyclopedia-making: "Every encyclopedia cribs from its predecessors as much as it dares, keeping one eye on the laws of copyright … To assume airs of omniscience whilst really ransacking the reference books of the habitable world … is a pose which naturally deceives no one inside the office."[78] Corroborating her point, Martin Gierl has studied the entries "A" and "Aa" in encyclopedias from the seventeenth to the twentieth century

[73] Kavanagh, *Conjuring*, 3.
[74] Murray, *Adventures*, 238–40; Mollier and Dubot, *Histoire*, 537.
[75] Stockwell, *History*, 118.
[76] Castellano, *Enciclopedia*, 310.
[77] Boyles, *Everything*, 240.
[78] *Ibid.*, 334–5.

and demonstrated the recurrence of certain assertions, some of them incorrect – evidence of copying on a grand scale.[79]

By Hogarth's time, copyright had become strict enough to make editors and contributors wary of borrowing. Before, they had borrowed with less circumspection, and they had borrowed whole passages rather than phrases or facts. Indeed, from the seventeenth century through the mid nineteenth century, encyclopedias were in large measure compiled – that is, pieced together from texts taken from elsewhere. Even Bayle's *Dictionaire* (1697), long admired for its original arguments, was qualified by its author as a "work of compilation" because it was so full of quotations.[80]

Bayle himself was scrupulous about crediting sources, but many encyclopedists were not. Authors' reasons for not citing sources were various. In the *Encyclopédie* (1751–72), contributors sometimes avoided citing illegal works, and they sometimes left out citations to avoid the appearance of pedantry.[81] Often, however, non-citation was a matter of hiding one's copying. Nor was it limited to menial writers. Desmarest, a respected geographer who wrote for the *Encyclopédie méthodique*, copied more than 8 percent of his material there without naming a source.[82] In the early nineteenth century, the French author Charles Nodier went so far as to characterize dictionaries and encyclopedias as "plagiarism in alphabetical order."[83]

Admittedly, the boundaries between compiling and other means of producing texts are hard to define. Within encyclopedias, one can usefully distinguish word-for-word copying, abridgment, paraphrasing, and the composition of comparatively original material. On another level, we can differentiate among encyclopedias' sources. These ranged from works of reference to what we would now call primary sources. One widespread practice, hardly reprehensible, was that of "self-plagiarism," in which contributors borrowed from their own publications. Regardless of such nuances, copying was rampant in the history of encyclopedias, and it was frequently undertaken without acknowledgment. In this sense, encyclopedia-writing had a certain distinctiveness, albeit one shared by other kinds of compiling.

Instances of copying are sometimes amusing, just as they could be to contemporaries. Around half the article "Plagiaire" in the *Encyclopédie*, a

[79] Gierl, "Compilation," 90–3.
[80] Bayle, *Dictionaire*, 1: 5–6 ("Préface"). See also Lieshout, *Making*, 89.
[81] Edelstein, Morrissey, and Roe, "To Quote," 214–15, 220–32.
[82] Taylor, "Peculiarly Personal Encyclopedia," 43.
[83] Randall, *Pragmatic Plagiarism*, 110.

defense of textual borrowing in dictionaries of the arts and sciences, was copied from "Plagiary" in Chambers' *Cyclopaedia*. Chambers, for his part, seems to have copied half of his own article from the article "Plagiaire" in the 1721 edition of the *Dictionnaire de Trévoux*, which was copied in turn from Furetière's *Dictionaire*.[84] After its appearance in the *Encyclopédie*, the same text went on to appear in Rees's [*New*] *Cyclopaedia* (1819–20). In none of these articles did the compilers acknowledge their sources. Even more curious is the article "Nachdruck derer Bücher" ("Reprinting of Books") in Zedler's *Grosses vollständiges Universal-Lexicon* (1732–50). On the one hand, it condemned the reprinting of books, while on the other hand, it was copied from a book accusing the *Universal-Lexicon* of just such reprinting.[85]

When done inattentively, copying could lead to inaccuracy, anachronism, or simple nonsense. Compilers of encyclopedias sometimes copied texts without essential images or removed articles from other contextualizing elements.[86] The German theologian Johann Franz Buddeus, who should have known better, copied misinformation about Berlin into an adaptation (1709) of Moréri's *Grand Dictionaire* – a mistake that disappointed the king of Prussia.[87] Another case of unwise copying involved fictive biographies that were mysteriously inserted into *Appleton's Cyclopaedia of American Biography* (1887–9) and subsequently appeared in other historical and biographical encyclopedias.[88] Indeed, a few works of reference were deliberately prepared with a small number of fictitious entries – for example, the biography of "Lillian Virginia Mountweazel" in the *New Columbia Encyclopedia* (1975) – which could be used to confirm copying if it took place.[89] Less underhandedly, critics embarrassed the publishers of reissued encyclopedias by seizing on dated articles copied from previous editions – for instance, one on feathers in the 1963 printing of the *Encyclopaedia Britannica*, which evoked the importance of feathers for making pens.[90]

The digitization of books has made copying easier to track. Searching for a passage from an encyclopedia throughout the internet may quickly prove that it was printed somewhere beforehand. Nevertheless, caution is

[84] Loveland, *Alternative Encyclopedia?*, 82.
[85] Kaminski, "Musen," 680–5.
[86] See for example Schmitt, "Voyages," 33; Loveland, "Louis-Jean-Marie Daubenton," 191–3; Dorn, Oetjens, and Schneider, "Sachliche Erschliessung," 114–16.
[87] Paul, "Dieses Universal-Lexicon," 32.
[88] Dobson, "Spurious Articles," 400–1.
[89] Lynch, *You Could Look It Up*, 153–4; Katz, *Basic Information Sources*, 267.
[90] Einbinder, *Myth*, 297. On the age of the passage see Stockwell, *History*, 117.

needed in this kind of research, for the fact that a passage is identical in two different books does not necessarily mean that one was the source for the other. The copying could have taken place through an intermediate text, or both could have been copied from an earlier source. So argued the seventeenth-century encyclopedist Chappuzeau, for example, after the privilege for his *Bibliothèque universelle* (*Universal Library*) was revoked for alleged plagiarism (as well as inappropriate content).[91] Likewise, according to one study in which computers gauged copying by finding "similar passages," some 5 percent of the text in the *Encyclopédie* came from the *Dictionnaire de Trévoux*. Or did it? In fact, since the *Encyclopédie* was based on Chambers' *Cyclopaedia*, which was indebted in turn to the 1721 edition of the *Dictionnaire de Trévoux*, some of the similar passages came from the *Cyclopaedia* after being translated from French to English and then back again.[92]

Copying may have been routine among encyclopedists, but they did it in different ways and to different extents. Before the twentieth century, some copied nearly everything in another encyclopedia, taking advantage of the weakness of protections for texts. Like many successful books of the time, Furetière's Dutch-published *Dictionaire* (1690) was counterfeited on several occasions. A first unauthorized reprint was probably done in Lyon.[93] Then in 1704, a retitled, slightly altered version of the 1701 edition was published without any acknowledgment of where it came from. Instead, the compilers attributed the idea of the *Dictionnaire de Trévoux* to Louis-Auguste de Bourbon, the prince of Dombes, the principality where the town of Trévoux was located. The theft was all the more embittering because it involved a Catholic take-over of a Protestant encyclopedia. Basnage, the current editor of Furetière's *Dictionaire*, protested that he and Furetière at least deserved to be credited, but the *Dictionnaire de Trévoux* went on to prosper and become, for a time, France's foremost encyclopedia.[94] As of 1732, publication of the encyclopedia had moved from Trévoux to Paris. Predictably and perhaps deservedly, the *Dictionnaire de Trévoux* was now counterfeited, in the semi-independent duchy of Lorraine. One effect of the reprinting was to push France and Lorraine to negotiate protection against cross-border copying in the 1740s.[95]

---

[91] Caullery, "Notes," 142–4.
[92] Leca-Tsiomis, "Use," 468–9.
[93] Behnke, *Furetière*, 38–41.
[94] Leca-Tsiomis, *Ecrire*, 51, 91–102; Behnke, *Furetière*, 98–120; Eick, "Defining," 169–70, 177–82.
[95] Ronsin, "Editions," 156–7.

Another strong seller of the early eighteenth century, the Leipzig-based *Reales Staats- Zeitungs- und Conversations-Lexicon*, was reprinted by competitors in Regensburg starting in 1735, in Vienna starting in 1780, and in Graz starting in 1805. The *Encyclopédie* too was pirated in French editions published in the Italian cities of Lucca and Livorno. The *Konversations-Lexikon* as well had barely begun to take off under Friedrich Brockhaus's leadership when, in 1817, he faced a counterfeit printed by Macklot in separately governed Stuttgart – and this was only the start of his battles against copying.[96] Finally, after beginning with liberal copying from Owen's *New and Complete Dictionary of Arts and Sciences* (1754–5), the *Encyclopaedia Britannica* became a victim of international piracy.[97] Already in the late eighteenth century, the publishers Thomas Dobson and James Moore reprinted it in their American (1789–98) and Irish (1790–8) editions.[98] Piracy of the *Britannica* then exploded in the United States at the end of the nineteenth century, and it went on for decades before being halted by agreements on international copyright.

Pirated encyclopedias posed a grave threat to publishers when they appeared in the same language and the same market. Of less concern to publishers were translated versions, generally unauthorized before the late nineteenth century. All the best-selling encyclopedias of the seventeenth and eighteenth centuries were in fact translated: Moréri's *Grand Dictionaire* into Dutch, English, German, and Spanish; Bayle's *Dictionaire* into English and German; the *Reales Staats- Zeitungs- und Conversations-Lexicon* into Dutch and Hungarian; Chomel's *Dictionnaire oeconomique* into Dutch, English, and German; and Chambers' *Cyclopaedia* into Italian, not to mention into French as the point of departure for the *Encyclopédie*. In the early nineteenth century, Brockhaus's *Konversations-Lexikon* set records for foreign-language adaptations, appearing in Danish, Dutch, English, French, and Swedish.[99] Much of the original *Encyclopaedia Americana* (1829–33), for instance, was translated by Lieber and his associates, without permission or payment, from the seventh edition (1827) of Brockhaus's *Konversations-Lexikon*. The Brockhaus firm does not seem to have born ill will toward Lieber. Already in his lifetime, the biography in Brockhaus's *Konversations-Lexikon* praised him and noted how respected the *Americana* was.[100]

[96] Collison, *Encyclopaedias*, 164.
[97] On copying from Owen's encyclopedia see Kafker and Loveland, "William Smellie's Edition," 20.
[98] Arner, *Dobson's Encyclopaedia*; Kafker and Loveland, "Publisher," 115–39.
[99] Müller-Vollmer, "Encyclopaedia," 1: 306.
[100] [*Grosse Brockhaus*], 10th edn., IX: 588.

While some encyclopedias were just counterfeits or unauthorized revisions of others, many depended on copying of less objectionable kinds. The most defensible was compiling from one's previous edition. In the eighteenth century already, the *Dictionnaire de Trévoux*, the *Reales Staats-Zeitungs- und Conversations-Lexicon*, and the *Encyclopaedia Britannica* were all functioning this way. In subsequent centuries, more and more encyclopedias went into multiple editions and thus accrued the benefits of having an established text. As we have seen, the risk of such recycling was keeping dated material, but the benefit was saving on intellectual labor. On a more general level, publishers could legitimately use content from any book they owned the rights to. As the editor and publisher of the *Encyclopédie méthodique*, Panckoucke thus used material not only from the *Encyclopédie*, which he had been licensed to publish since 1768, but also from non-encyclopedias under his ownership, among them Georges-Louis Leclerc de Buffon and others' *Histoire naturelle* (1749–89).[101]

Another option for encyclopedia-publishers aiming to publish inexpensively was to recycle their content in a different encyclopedia – a shorter one, say, or one directed toward a different audience. The journalist William Duckett, the owner and planner of the *Dictionnaire de la conversation et de la lecture* (1832–9), was a pioneer in adapting content to different formats and purposes.[102] In addition to being continued with a sixteen-volume supplement (1844–51), his encyclopedia was reissued – abridged and revised – as a ten-volume encyclopedia for women and children, the *Dictionnaire de conversation à l'usage des dames et des jeunes personnes* (*Dictionary of Conversation for the Use of Ladies and Young People*, 1841). Then, from 1852 to 1858, a second edition appeared, followed by reprints through the late 1870s.

Not all copying came from previous editions or titles owned by the publisher. Even when it did not, though, encyclopedists had four ways of justifying their borrowing.

First, copying could be rationalized as something indulged in by all encyclopedists and therefore not realistically to be avoided. "We all pillage each other," wrote Chappuzeau in the late seventeenth century, defending his borrowing for an unpublished *Bibliothèque*.[103]

Second, copying served the public by opening up access to knowledge. In court, the publishers of the second edition (1778–83) of the *Britannica*

---

[101] Doig, *From Encyclopédie*; Duris, "Entre Buffon et Linné," 581–3.
[102] Mollier, "Encyclopédie," 295, 301–2.
[103] "Nous nous pillons tous les uns les autres." Caullery, "Notes," 144.

took the argument to an extreme. Charged with unauthorized copying from books by the historian and journalist Gilbert Stuart, they maintained that their copying had stimulated interest in Stuart's books and thus paradoxically benefited him.[104]

Third, like abridgers and translators, encyclopedists could add value to sources by reworking or structuring them. Chambers, for example, insisted that he had acted originally in creating a unified encyclopedia from borrowed materials – the *Cyclopaedia*.[105] Other encyclopedists shared his pretensions, though few were as innovative in ordering their works.

Fourth, intellectuals increasingly recognized the existence of a collection of texts from which authors could borrow unapologetically – a public domain, in modern terms. In part because art was premised on imitation – not so different from copying – numerous writers from the late seventeenth century onward considered copying from the Ancients legitimate, though not from the Moderns. Foreigners and obscure writers were also judged fair game for copying. In the eighteenth century, moreover, certain art-theorists saw originality of expression as a precondition for owning the rights to one's handiwork.[106] This view turned merely informational texts into everyone's property.

In practice, encyclopedists did treat informational texts differently. In the *Encyclopédie*, for example, contributors cited sources more consistently when borrowing "passages that expressed an authoritative judgment or contained a particularly elegant turn of phrase" than when copying anecdotes, historical descriptions, and other "trivial" information.[107] A similar attitude may have underlain Chambers's statement in "Plagiary" that dictionaries of the arts and sciences, if not of all subjects, were entitled to borrow from other works. Even courts grew receptive to the distinction between informational texts and texts that could be counted as private property. In the early nineteenth century, for instance, a French court rejected a suit against Louis-Gabriel and Joseph-François Michaud for unauthorized copying. According to the plaintiff, the Michaud brothers had copied articles from a recent edition (1810–12) of Louis-Mayeul Chaudon's *Nouveau Dictionnaire historique* (1766) into their own biographical encyclopedia, the *Biographie universelle* (1812–28). In the view of the court, though, the articles in the two works were bound to be about

[104] Doig *et al.*, "James Tytler's Edition," 144–5.
[105] Chambers, *Cyclopaedia*, 1: i. See also Yeo, *Encyclopaedic Visions*, 207–13.
[106] Loveland, *Alternative Encyclopedia?*, 86.
[107] Edelstein, Morrissey, and Roe, "To Quote," 227.

the same, regardless of borrowing, since the facts of people's lives did not allow for much variance.[108]

While copying could be defended, it was mainly in private that editors and publishers encouraged contributors to copy, whether explicitly or by implication. De Felice, the editor of the Yverdon *Encyclopédie* (1770– 80), recommended copying straightforwardly in a letter to a contributor, pointing out that "a dictionary-maker is not asked to create new material."[109] More generally, publishers of encyclopedias from at least the *Encyclopédie* (1751–72) onward provided libraries for editors and contributors to use. Here dictionaries and encyclopedias were inevitably present, inviting contributors to some form of borrowing.[110] Indeed, editors sometimes stipulated that contributors begin their research by consulting articles on the subject in other encyclopedias and dictionaries. This was the protocol for the *Grande Encyclopédie* (1885–1902) and the *Espasa* (1908–30), for example.[111] The result was extensive paraphrasing if not outright copying.

Even when the whole of an encyclopedia was not taken from another one, some encyclopedists copied extensively from particular sources, especially dictionaries, encyclopedias, and periodicals. As late as the early twentieth century, the entire dictionary of the Real Academia Española was merged into the *Espasa*, albeit lightly camouflaged with changes of wording.[112] Such camouflaging was unnecessary in the time of the *Grosses vollständiges Universal-Lexicon* (1732–50), which incorporated much of eleven smaller encyclopedias, including the *Reales Staats- Zeitungs- und Conversations-Lexicon* and Corvinus's *Nutzbares, galantes und curiöses Frauenzimmer-Lexicon*.[113]

At the same time, acting within the bounds of the strictest legality, the publisher Zedler arranged for someone to comb through the issues of a periodical he had purchased, with the goal of turning it into material for the *Universal-Lexicon*.[114] This was the operation of making "extracts," which was frequently conducted by anonymous assistants. Pervasive in encyclopedia-making before the mid nineteenth century, it was crucial to the composition of the *Oeconomische Encyclopädie* (1773–1858), for example.[115] In the Yverdon *Encyclopédie* too (1770–80), it played a

---

[108] Chappey, *Ordres*, 65–6.

[109] "Un faiseur de dictionnaire n'est pas appelé à faire du neuf." Cernuschi, "Travail," 293.

[110] For allusions to books supplied to the authors of the *Encyclopédie* see May, "Documents," 31–98.

[111] *Grande Encyclopédie: Inventaire*, 1: xi; Castellano, *Enciclopedia*, 164–5.

[112] Castellano, *Enciclopedia*, 205–6.

[113] Schneider, *Erfindung*, 81–2.

[114] Dorn, Oetjens, and Schneider, "Sachliche Erschliessung," 109.

[115] Fröhner, *Technologie*, 356–8.

significant role. There, contributors borrowed at least 280 pages from the journal of Berlin's Académie Royale des Sciences et Belles-Lettres, around 5 percent of the articles in Johann Georg Sulzer's *Allgemeine Theorie der schönen Künste* (*General Theory of the Fine Arts*, 1771–4), and almost a third of Jean-Etienne Montucla's *Histoire des mathématiques* (1758) – all indications of systematic extracting.[116]

Copying could also be unsystematic, an occasional practice by wayward contributors. In 1930, for instance, Encyclopaedia Britannica, now owned by Americans, sued William Quarrie, the owner of *World Book*, for copying articles. The plaintiff sought an injunction to stop the publication of *World Book* and a half-million dollars in damages. From among the seventy-seven articles cited as examples of copying, Quarrie's researchers discounted half as being based on a source common to the *Britannica* and *World Book*, but they also found a contributor who admitted to copying from the *Britannica*. Luckily for Quarrie, it turned out that the plaintiff had falsified articles to make the copying look worse. Its case having weakened, Encyclopaedia Britannica settled out of court for $50,000.[117]

As a result of the skirmish, editors at *World Book* set up a system in which contributors had to name their sources for every article and confirm that they had not copied.[118] It remained hard, nonetheless, for the publisher of a collaborative encyclopedia to guard against the risk that a contributor might copy. The risk was ever present, moreover, for copying could facilitate the work of the lazy or harried. All that an editor could do was establish guidelines and controls for encouraging responsibility. Editorial laxness, by contrast, made copying likelier. Responding to complaints from Gentile about articles on art for the *Enciclopedia italiana* (1929–39), the sub-editor Ugo Ojetti explained that his younger contributors tended to "plagiarize" from other encyclopedias – thus demonstrating his awareness of an abuse he had seemingly done nothing to stop.[119]

Encyclopedists under the influence a stern or lax editor were in some ways like schoolchildren under the care of their teachers. From the early twentieth century onward, educators were ambivalent about the growing presence of encyclopedias in students' homes. Children, in their view, should not simply copy what was in an encyclopedia but should rather,

[116] Cernuschi, "*Encyclopédie*," 107; Burnand and Cernuschi, "Circulation," 256; Cernuschi, "Travail," 295.
[117] Murray, *Adventures*, 84–8.
[118] *Ibid.*, 87.
[119] Bernabò and Tarasconi, "Epistolario," 158.

presumably, draw on a variety of sources and use their own words.[120] However intimidating it appeared to the young, the same course of action had been taken by most encyclopedists since the mid nineteenth century. When they did not merely inherit texts from a previous edition, they typically consulted a range of works, including encyclopedias, and then made an effort to ensure that what they wrote was recognizably different.

Controlling Copying and Plagiarism

Plagiarism developed into a pressing concern after 1500 as books became marketable, as authors proliferated and fought to assert status, and as originality replaced imitation as the key to esthetic value.[121] Well before the advent of effective laws governing copyright, uncredited copying was regularly treated as wrong, notably by critics who dealt with encyclopedias. Before the twentieth century, accusations of plagiarism were rampant in discourse about encyclopedias. Zedler's *Grosses vollständiges Universal-Lexicon* (1732–50), for example, was persistently taxed with plagiarism, becoming the "Universal-Plagiat" in one satirical view.[122] Similarly, in the early nineteenth century, the *Penny Cyclopaedia* was condemned for publishing "portions" of extant encyclopedias along with extracts from "all the new works on geology, astronomy, physics, geography, and the other sciences, as well as the arts."[123] Likewise, after the American publisher Funk and Wagnalls reprinted the ninth edition (1875–89) of the *Encyclopaedia Britannica*, the *New York Evening Post* denounced it for engaging in "theft" and "piracy," even though no statute prohibited the copying.[124]

One reason for the vehemence of accusations of plagiarism was that laws regarding copying were often too weak to be of service before the twentieth century. Recognizing the unlikeliness of legal action, critics took their complaints to the public, partly to discourage sales of the works they were targeting. Friedrich Brockhaus did so, for instance, when faced with Macklot's reprint of his *Konversations-Lexikon* in 1817. Perhaps sensing, correctly, that his legal actions against Macklot would be ineffective, he did all he could to make the public aware that Macklot was a plagiarist. In 1818, he published a leaflet condemning Macklot's reprint. He went on

---

[120] See for example Freeland, *Improvement*, 267; Brown, *Putting*, 3; Giacobbe, "Learning," 134.
[121] Kewes, *Plagiarism*, 14–18; Hayes, "Plagiarism," 117–18.
[122] Kaminski, "Musen," 679–80. On copying as fundamental to Zedler's project see Prodöhl, "Aus denen besten Scribenten," 82–94.
[123] "Chartered Booksellers," 73.
[124] Cook, "Reshaping," 237.

to air his grievances in prefaces, advertisements, and releases to the press and to the main institution of the German Confederation, the Bundestag. Lastly, on the title page of the fifth edition (1819–20) of his *Konversations-Lexikon*, he printed a verse condemning plagiarism by the Spanish poet Pedro Calderón. He doubted that Macklot would dare to reprint it.

To have invested so much in his crusade against Macklot, Brockhaus must have believed it would limit the spread of the reprint. Indeed, while he was unable to stop it by legal or political means, the reprint struggled, commercially, and was soon given up.[125] Still, it is unclear, overall, how much effect negative publicity had on encyclopedias accused of plagiarism, for purchasers had little reason to care where a work's content came from. Wars between encyclopedias tended to be fought over other issues such as bias, scope, and accuracy – issues in which the public had a more direct interest.

Another non-juridical strategy for dealing with plagiarism was to publish new editions to overwhelm a reprint or render it dated. The owners of the *Cyclopaedia* thus published a new "edition" – actually a reprint – to lure buyers back from Coetlogon's *Universal History* (1745), a third of which was copied from their *Cyclopaedia*.[126] Similarly, when Macklot began counterfeiting Brockhaus's *Konversations-Lexikon*, he was copying from the third edition (1814–19). Brockhaus responded by launching a fourth edition (1817–19) before finishing the third. He hoped that the fourth edition would be granted a license in Württemberg, where Macklot was based, but the new edition itself probably reduced Macklot's sales, if also the sales of Brockhaus's previous editions.[127]

Whatever the animosity between a publisher and a reprinter, negotiation was possible, and it sometimes bore fruit. In the best of all outcomes, a pirate might abandon a reprint if given an incentive. In 1752, for example, the printer Pierre Antoine, from Lorraine, asked the Parisian booksellers behind the *Dictionnaire de Trévoux* to include him in a partnership, and the parties agreed to a deal. Antoine was allowed to sell 2,000 copies with his name on the title page, but he could sell no closer to Paris than 36 leagues, or 150 km. Given his history as a counterfeiter of the *Dictionnaire de Trévoux*, the Parisians must have been seeking, above all, to neutralize him as a possible threat to their business.[128]

---

[125] Peche, *Bibliotheca*, 70, 350–55; Hingst, *Geschichte*, 118–19.
[126] Loveland, *Alternative Encyclopedia?*, 65–6, 106.
[127] Hingst, *Geschichte*, 106, 118; Collison, *Encyclopaedias*, 158–9.
[128] Ronsin, "Editions," 157–8.

Somewhere on the scale between negotiation and legal action was recourse to a guild or fellow publishers to handle an instance of copying. Booksellers, printers, and others involved in the book-trade were organized into guilds in the seventeenth and eighteenth centuries. Guilds were legally chartered, with responsibilities toward governments and control over members. Booksellers' guilds helped regulate literary property, and they sometimes settled disputes over copied material. In England, registration of titles with London's Company of Stationers, the main guild for book-sellers, allowed owners to pursue copiers in the guild's separate courts.[129]

In addition to guilds, partnerships among booksellers were a means of protecting literary property. In eighteenth-century Britain, publishing was often undertaken by congers, which divided up ownership. Such sharing had various purposes, but one effect was to unite publishers in the struggle against piracy. The conger responsible for the first edition (1728) of Chambers's *Cyclopaedia* had eighteen members, and the work's owner-ship was later split into shares as small as one sixty-fourth.[130] Involvement with the *Cyclopaedia* was so pervasive among London's booksellers that Coetlogon, who copied from it, seems to have had trouble finding periodicals willing to advertise his *Universal History*.[131] In Paris as well, though partnerships usually extended to just a handful of publishers, relationships between licensed booksellers were close, reinforced by bonds of kinship and marriage. Such relationships promoted cooperative behavior, pushing literary piracy toward the provinces and foreign locations. Many publishers also had international allies, from whom they could request aid in discouraging pirates abroad.

In short, self-policing and cooperation in a community of publishers could be deterrents to copying, in many cases more potent ones than legal barriers.[132] Nevertheless, when less formal means failed, publishers could turn to courts or the government. In the seventeenth and eighteenth cen-turies, licenses and privileges issued by governments gave owners a mon-opoly over a work. The most expansive was the "imperial privilege," for the Holy Roman Empire, but its value was limited relative to competing local privileges.[133] Nearly all privileges and licenses were designed to expire, though owners could renew them, sometimes indefinitely. In 1674, in an

[129] Johns, *Nature*, 213–30.
[130] Bradshaw, "Ephraim Chambers' *Cyclopaedia*," 138; Yeo, *Encyclopaedic Visions*, 198–9.
[131] Loveland, *Alternative Encyclopedia?*, 64, 76–8.
[132] See Sher, *Enlightenment*, 26, 353–7.
[133] Wittmann, "Soziale und ökonomische Voraussetzungen," 10; Juntke, *Johann Heinrich Zedler's Grosses vollständiges Universallexikon*, 20–1.

extraordinary triumph, the Académie Française secured a permanent mon-
opoly over dictionaries of French. As a result, Furetière had to publish
his *Dictionaire* (1690) outside of France, though once it was published, it
was disseminated in France, perhaps with complicity from French authorities.[134] The Dutch government, for its part, gave the Leers brothers a license
to publish Furetière's *Dictionaire*. Accordingly, Reinier Leers was able to
seize 200 copies of *Dictionnaire de Trévoux* (1704) – a near-reprint – upon
their arrival in Holland, an action that was subsequently upheld in court.[135]
Unfortunately, France was the biggest market for Furetière's *Dictionaire*,
and there the Leers had little power.

It is true that, occasionally, foreigners could persuade a government to
crack down on plagiarism. Louix XIV, the king of France, told his agent
in Geneva to encourage the town's government to block publication of an
encyclopedia by Chappuzeau, since it allegedly borrowed from Moréri's
Grand Dictionaire, published in France. The intervention was successful.[136]
But what worked for France against a town near its border was unlikely to
work in less disproportionate circumstances.

Literary property could also be protected by laws. One was Britain's Act
for the Encouragement of Learning (1710). In theory, it supplanted earlier
rules governing copying, whether based on licenses, guilds, or a traditionally recognized copyright derived from English common law. New works,
when registered with the Company of Stationers, were protected for fourteen years, with a possible extension for another fourteen.[137] The notion
of a common-law copyright did not disappear, but it proved ineffective at
protecting encyclopedias. So it did, in particular, in a suit (1743–8) by the
Cyclopaedia's London owners against a Scottish reprint.[138]

Controlling copying via statute was not easy either. In this sense, legal
action was often just a prelude to negotiation and settlement. In Britain,
the Act for the Encouragement of Learning focused on illegal reprints,
not the more limited copying characteristic of encyclopedias. For this
reason, apparently, prosecutions of encyclopedia-publishers for violating
copyright seem to have been rare – and then inconclusive.[139] In the case
against the publishers of the *Encyclopaedia Britannica* for copying from

---

[134] Rey, "Antoine Furetière," 70–1; Behnke, *Furetière*, 27n.
[135] Behnke, *Furetière*, 129.
[136] Jennings and Jones, *Biography*, 130–2.
[137] Feather, *Publishing*, 58–63; Saunders, *Authorship*, 54–5.
[138] Feather, *Publishing*, 81; Feather, "Publishers," 17.
[139] See Yeo, *Encyclopaedic Visions*, 204–6. More generally, on the inconclusiveness of cases concerning
     abridgment, see Stern, "Copyright," 77–8.

Stuart's books, for example, litigation ran from 1783 until at least 1786, and the plaintiffs finally settled for copies of the *Britannica* worth £300.[140] Similarly, after filing a suit for piracy against the owner of the *London Encyclopaedia* (1829), the owners of the *Encyclopaedia Metropolitana* (1817–45) ultimately settled out of court for a "considerable sum of money." The suit had been going badly. While working as editor of the *London Encyclopaedia*, Thomas Curtis had felt entitled to borrow from the *Metropolitana*, on which he had collaborated. The judge, for his part, had refused to place an injunction on the *London Encyclopaedia* until "the extent of the alleged piracy" could be precisely determined.[141]

Britain was precocious in its elaboration of copyright, but by the early nineteenth century, laws defining copyright were in effect all over Europe. Their principal defect was that they applied within borders, outside of which reprinters could operate freely. This defect was felt acutely in the German and Italian states, where governments remained numerous and poorly coordinated, but even large, relatively centralized states such as Britain and France found themselves put upon by foreign reprinters.

Once Irish and Scottish reprinting had been regulated or eliminated, the worst offender again British copyright was the United States. There British titles were counterfeited as a matter of course. British publishers resented the piracy all the more bitterly as the United States became the biggest market for anglophone books. In the case of encyclopedias, American piracy lasted a century, beginning and ending with the *Britannica*, from Dobson's version (1789–98) to reprints of the ninth edition (1875–89). In between, it is unlikely that rights were paid for such American re-editions as the *New and Complete American Encyclopaedia* (1805–11) or the *Library of Universal Knowledge* (1880–1), adapted from the *Encyclopaedia Perthensis* (1806) and *Chambers's Encyclopaedia* (1868) respectively.[142]

In the eighteenth century, France had struggled with literary piracy in Switzerland and the Low Countries, but in the first half of the nineteenth century, the biggest problem was Belgium. Unlike American reprinters, Belgians were publishing not just for fellow citizens but also for France. Among their reprints and revisions of encyclopedias published in France were an edition (1827–32) of the *Encyclopédie moderne* (1823–32) and two encyclopedias indebted to the *Encyclopédie des gens du monde* (1833–44): the *Nouvelle Encyclopédie des gens du monde* (*New Encyclopedia of People of*

---

[140] Zachs, *First John Murray*, 189–91; Doig *et al.*, "James Tytler's Edition," 144–5.
[141] *Revised Reports* 26 (1896): 114, 123–5.
[142] Walsh, *Anglo-American General Encyclopedias*, 59, 95.

the World, 1842) and the *Nouveau Dictionnaire de la conversation* (*New Dictionary of Conversation*, 1842–5).[143]

Over the course of the nineteenth century, states and jurisdictions negotiated successfully for cross-border copyright. As a result, piracy declined in the German book-trade after 1850, for instance.[144] France and Switzerland signed an agreement on copyright in 1864, though Switzerland, by that date, was no longer the source that it had once been of pirated reprints. In 1852, France went so far as to promise, unilaterally, that it would honor and protect copyrights issued anywhere else. That same year, it came to an understanding with Belgium.

In the meantime, the idea of an international form of copyright was gaining momentum. It drew support from such writers as Victor Hugo, the first president of the Association Littéraire Internationale (1878). It also fed on growing awareness of internationalism, emblematized and amplified by universal expositions and fairs.[145] In 1887, the Berne Convention for the Protection of Literary and Artistic Works was approved by Belgium, France, Germany, France, Italy, the United Kingdom, Spain, and Switzerland, among other countries. By the terms of the convention, signatories had to enforce copyright for both foreign and domestic titles. It was because of the Berne Convention, for instance, that Brockhaus was able to sue the Swiss publisher of the *Schweizer Lexikon* (1945–8) for copying from the second edition (1943) of the *Neue Brockhaus*.[146]

Americans attended the meetings leading up to the Berne Convention, but the United States did not become a signatory until more than a century later, in 1989. From the mid nineteenth century onward, many Americans espoused international copyright, but the country was well served by the current state of affairs. Publishers paid nothing to acquire most foreign titles, and they shared their savings with purchasers. Americans, furthermore, tended to see the book-trade as a commercial activity, one focused on publishers and readers rather than authors or artwork. Nor was the United States willing to accept copyrights without any requirement that titles be registered – a position incompatible with the Berne Convention. Accordingly, Congress adopted the narrower Chace Act in 1891, which led to agreements on copyright with other countries, including the United

---

[143] On the latter two titles see Loveland, "Two French 'Konversationslexika,'" forthcoming.
[144] Spree, *Streben*, 287–8.
[145] Saunders, *Authorship*, 169–70.
[146] Keiderling, *F. A. Brockhaus*, 248.

Kingdom. To qualify as protected under the Chace Act, a work had to be naturalized in two respects. Not only did the owner have to register it for copyright in the United States, but the type it was printed from had to be set there as well.

The Chace Act came too late for the Black firm of Edinburgh, the owner of the ninth edition of the *Britannica*. When the ninth edition was started, no one registered it for American copyright, and the type was set in Britain. Black recruited American publishers to distribute it in the United States, but the approved sets sold poorly, in part because American counterfeits were cheaper, and in part because some of them featured improvements. Black sued repeatedly in American courts, albeit with fewer successes than failures. American judges ruled predictably that Americans were entitled to reissue foreign works. Black responded by enlisting more American contributors and having them get copyrights on individual articles. A note in Volume IX announced that certain entries had been copyrighted in the United States. The wilier reprinters simply avoided these articles, but even one who reprinted them was cleared of wrongdoing, for the judge found that the warning had been given too late.[147] Later, Black and its successors began to triumph, winning injunctions against reprints in 1893, 1903, and 1904. In part, the firm's restructuring as an American company – Encyclopaedia Britannica of Illinois, founded in 1903 – improved its position in legal proceedings. The company's readiness to litigate also pushed reprinters to negotiate or settle. Ultimately, though, the *Britannica* was only secured against American piracy by compliance with the Chace Act. American sets of the eleventh edition (1910–11) were typeset and manufactured in the United States.[148]

The *Britannica* was never again as much plagiarized as it had been from 1875 to 1905, but copying remained a concern for its owners. Even in the second half of the twentieth century, they were still struggling with piracy. Specifically, they now faced reprinted editions exported from Taiwan, a nation long reluctant to sign treaties protecting copyright.[149] Still, combined with the Chace Act, the company's campaigns against American reprints had led to a climate in which counterfeiters of encyclopedias were commercially marginalized.

---

[147] Kruse, "Story," 199–200. See also Kruse, "Piracy," 313–28.
[148] Kruse, "Story," 205–25.
[149] Walsh, *Anglo-American General Encyclopedias*, 52. For examples see *New York Times*, July 6, 1963: 3; September 27, 1988: D24.

Despite the decline of reprinting and verbatim copying as laws governing copyright strengthened in the nineteenth and twentieth centuries, paraphrasing remained common in the composition of encyclopedias. As we have seen, the editors of the *Espasa* (1908–30) paraphrased the entire dictionary of the Real Academia Española. So did other contemporary Spanish encyclopedias, few of them bothering to ask for permission. The Academia complained about the *Espasa* but did not pursue the infringement, perhaps because it had members who wrote for the work. Indeed, when consulted by the government in 1910, the Academia recommended the *Espasa* for purchase by Spain's public libraries.[150]

Nor was the *Espasa*'s borrowing just a matter of paraphrasing. Starting in 1934, José Pérez Hervás, the main artistic editor since 1919, began publicizing its "thefts" to get revenge for his severance. In particular, he asserted, just 10 percent of the illustrations had been properly acquired and paid for. As he described it, the *Espasa*'s unauthorized copying – of both texts and images – involved hundreds of sources, notably such encyclopedias as the *Grande Encyclopédie*, the *Britannica*, and Herder's *Konversations-Lexikon*. Besides publishing a book denouncing the *Espasa*'s copying, Pérez Hervás notified the Union Internationale Littéraire et Artistique, the organization responsible for enforcing the Berne Convention. The Union responded that a plaintiff was needed and that legal proceedings would have to be started in Spain, since the Berne Convention was not meant to undermine national sovereignty. Fratelli Alinari, an Italian company, duly stepped forward to demand compensation for the use of some of it photographs, but the publisher, Espasa-Calpe, took a conciliatory stance and probably settled out of court.

Pérez Hervás also arranged for the *Espasa*'s copying to be discussed at a meeting of Barcelona's Cámara del Libro (Chamber of Books). Yet when the meeting was finally held in 1935, none of the publishers identified as victims voiced accusations against Espasa-Calpe. Perhaps they had already reached settlements, perhaps they too saw themselves as vulnerable to charges of copying, or perhaps they feared reprisals from a powerful publisher controlling much of Spain's paper.[151] In any event, the advent of the Spanish Civil War a year later relegated concern with *Espasa*'s copying to the faraway background of Spaniards' thoughts.

The amount of unauthorized copying behind the *Espasa* might be interpreted as a sign of Spain's marginality within a Europe more committed

---

[150] Castellano, *Enciclopedia*, 204–6, 326–9.
[151] *Ibid.*, 206–17.

to copyright. It is important to remember, though, that José Espasa paid Brockhaus and the Bibliographisches Institut for the right to use material.[152] It is true that the contracts concerned illustrations, first and foremost. Here reliance on the Germans' expertise and already prepared plates seemed destined to save the Spanish publisher money. Still, Espasa's payment for content was a change relative to precedent, and one representative of a trend throughout Europe since around 1850.

Fees for using another encyclopedia's content started out small, especially when the borrowing required translation. For just £400, William and Robert Chambers bought the right to make use of Brockhaus's content in Britain. They hoped the arrangement would help with *Chambers's Encyclopaedia* (1868), though it did so only slightly.[153] Prices for encyclopedias' content nonetheless rose over time. They were highest when the content did not need to be translated, since the contract, in this case, was practically a buy-out. In 1933, for example, *Encyclopaedia Britannica* paid $150,000 for the rights to *Weedon's Modern Encyclopedia* (1931–2), which then served as the foundation for *Britannica Junior*.[154] As these examples indicate, content continued to travel from encyclopedia to encyclopedia, just as it always had, but financial compensation was becoming expected.

Conclusion

Making an encyclopedia involved different kinds of work, even in the intellectual stages focused on here. The work could be coordinated by one or several people, including authors or publishers, but the people most often responsible from the nineteenth century onward were encyclopedias' editors. Editors usually planned an encyclopedia. For less ambitious encyclopedias, planning could mean little more than identifying changes with respect to a prototype or a previous edition. At the bare minimum, a pirate or owner could reprint an encyclopedia with next to no planning. On the other end of the spectrum, the best planning involved reflection on the work as a whole as well as on the distribution of space among disciplines and then within them. Next the editor had to find contributors and organize submissions. Both tasks grew more onerous as articles came to be solicited from hundreds of authors, not just a handful. Contributors

---

[152] According to the *Espasa's* preface, the publisher had acquired rights to Herder's *Konversations-Lexikon* too, but perhaps not to the illustrations, for Hervás denounced their reuse as plagiarism. See Castellano, *Enciclopedia*, 116–22, 176, 208; [*Espasa*], 1: VII.

[153] Cooney, "Catalogue," 17; Spree, *Streben*, 294–6.

[154] Kruse, "Story," 368.

needed guidance, if not coaching or cajoling, and whatever the technology for organization – sorted cards or computers – an editor had to impose procedures for keeping track of material.

Eventually, much of the labor of making an encyclopedia was passed on to contributors. Before writing an article, they were generally directed to consult the best sources, and sometimes instructed to copy or paraphrase. By the mid nineteenth century, though, their assignment had become a delicate one, namely to write an "original" article after examining how others had treated the subject. Copying, once flagrant in the work of encyclopedists, was now merely diluted or camouflaged in many instances.

Conversely, encyclopedia-publishers, like publishers in general, found ways of protecting their works against copying. Laws protecting copyright grew increasingly important as ideals and instruments for discouraging plagiarism, but disputes over literary property tended to be settled outside the court-room, even if legal action was a common opening gambit. In the twentieth century, with the establishment of copyright as international, the content of encyclopedias became a routinely buyable and sellable commodity. While paraphrasing persisted as a mode of compiling, unauthorized reprints were mostly a thing of the past.

CHAPTER 5

The Organization of Encyclopedias

By the fact of being bound, books have an order. They advance from beginning to end as pages are flipped. Pages of text are also ordered, as lines and columns in sequence. In most books, these orders mirror the order of content, so that a biography or a novel, say, can be read in its intended order by simply "following" the book. Works of reference, by contrast, were printed as books and could, in extreme cases, be read cover to cover, but they were designed to allow multiple points of entry and exit. Many encyclopedias, moreover, were meant to show how knowledge connected as a non-linear network. Achieving these goals required organizational tools going beyond the book's intrinsic structure of sequential pages and lines. To ensure ease of access, the most powerful organizational tool was alphabetical order, but it had the effect of dispersing even as it organized, thus necessitating other tools to register links among entries.

Encyclopedias, as conceived here, were alphabetical works, but they were not always so different from non-alphabetical ones. Furthermore, the two types of works remained mutual influences from the seventeenth century to the twentieth century. Accordingly, I start the chapter by examining the opposition between alphabetical and non-alphabetical order in European encyclopedism. Then I turn to other orders, for even within an alphabetical framework, encyclopedias were ordered differently. Specifically, in addition to alphabetical order, this chapter will focus on four components of order: overviews of knowledge, the length of entries, cross-references, and indexes. All four coexisted with alphabetical order. Indeed, the rise of electronic encyclopedias at the end of the twentieth century shows that indexes and cross-references, far from being mere accessories to alphabetical order, can effectively supplant it and bear the organizational weight of encyclopedism alone.

Alphabetical versus Non-Alphabetical Order

From Roman antiquity onward, portions of non-alphabetical encyclopedic works were ordered alphabetically, usually as a last resort, when no other order was suitable. In his first-century *Naturalis historia*, for instance, Pliny put gems in alphabetical order when they did not fit his other orders.[1] Over time, an increasing number of medieval encyclopedic works were ordered alphabetically, especially after 1100. Their authors justified the arrangement as making it easier to find things.[2] As top-level orders, though, thematic, systematic, and miscellaneous arrangements continued to dominate encyclopedic works through the Middle Ages and beyond. Characterizations of alphabetical order as imperfect, arbitrary, or merely convenient suggest that it was seen as inappropriate for presenting all knowledge, but by the sixteenth century already it was widely used in other contexts, notably in dictionaries in the broad sense of the time. As we have seen, such dictionaries were among the ancestors of the European encyclopedia. By the mid eighteenth century, an "age of dictionaries" was under way as western Europe was flooded with dictionaries of language, history, arts and sciences, and other subjects.[3] In the *Curieuses Natur-Kunst- Gewerck- und Handlungs-Lexicon* (1712), Hübner observed wistfully that public favor had turned toward alphabetical arrangement.[4] Though still considered a dictionary, the European encyclopedia had begun to take shape in its modern, alphabetical form.

Why did the authority of encyclopedism pass from non-alphabetical to alphabetical works in the seventeenth century? One explanation is that knowledge was expanding outside traditional disciplines and categories. Alsted, for example, included so many new disciplines in his non-alphabetical *Encyclopaedia* (1630) that some of them contradicted his methodology. The fact that his *Encyclopaedia* was "bursting out" of its seams may have pushed later writers to order encyclopedias alphabetically.[5] Still, if any one way of ordering material non-alphabetically appeared moribund to contemporaries, they were free to invent a new one, and so some did through the end of the twentieth century. It was not obvious to Coleridge, for instance, that systematic encyclopedism was doomed, or he would not have proposed what he did for the *Encyclopaedia Metropolitana* (1817–45).

Another explanation for the rise of alphabetical order relates to religion. By the mid seventeenth century – in this schema – the Christian

---

[1] Doody, *Pliny's Encyclopedia*, 114–15; Pliny, *Natural History*, 160–7.
[2] Meier, "On the Connection," 94, 107–10. More generally, see Daly, *Contributions*, 93–6.
[3] See for example Lieshout, "Dictionnaires," 131; Rétat, "Age," 186. For statistics see Headrick, *When Information Came of Age*, 167–72.
[4] Hübner, "Vorrede,")(3r–)(3v (§§17–27).
[5] Blair, "Organizations," 292–3.

theology that had structured encyclopedic works for the previous millennium was no longer adequate for guaranteeing the unity of knowledge.[6] If so, it is curious that the first great success among encyclopedias, Moréri's *Grand Dictionaire* (1674), was compiled by a priest. It defended Catholic orthodoxy so staunchly that Bayle accused Moréri of having borrowed from a "crusader's sermon."[7] Later centuries too produced zealously religious encyclopedias, and the majority of modern encyclopedias remained respectful of Christianity. It may be true, nonetheless, that religion had lost credibility as a framework for ordering knowledge.

Other explanations for the modern encyclopedia's alphabetical order are more broadly epistemological, that is, dependent on changing conceptions of knowledge. Charles Porset argues that alphabetical order could only become dominant in a world in which knowledge had been fragmented by the breakdown of medieval systems. In such a world, knowledge was no longer seen as something to be recovered or reflected, as it generally had been around 1600, but rather as something to be indefinitely created.[8] In a similar spirit, Keith Baker claims that the *Encyclopédie* (1751–72) had to be an alphabetical work because of its authors' – and the Enlightenment's – philosophical humility and refusal of rationalism.[9]

One problem with such views is that they suggest an inevitability to alphabetical order, one belied by the persistence of non-alphabetical encyclopedism. Nor did alphabetical order always imply a rejection of dogmatism. Consider, for example, the decree that called the second edition of the Soviet *Bolshaia sovetskaia entsiklopediia* (1949–58) into existence: "[It] should elucidate broadly the world-historical victories of socialism in our country … It must show the superiority of socialist culture over the culture of the capitalist world."[10]

The idea that alphabetical order represented freedom from systems and hierarchies is sometimes extended to the political realm. There is something egalitarian about presenting people's names, say, alphabetically. Whether in an encyclopedia or a biographical dictionary, alphabetical order brought together people of different social ranks. In the eighteenth and nineteenth centuries, as more and more non-nobles entered biographical collections, critics grumbled about the consequences of allowing the alphabet to mix people up. The writer and countess Stéphanie-Félicité de

[6] Schmidt-Biggemann, "Enzyklopädie," 1–2, 15–18.
[7] "… sermon de croisade." Miller, "Louis Moréri's *Grand Dictionnaire*," 27.
[8] Porset, "Encyclopédie," 253–64. See also Vasoli, *Enciclopedismo*, 89–91.
[9] Baker, "Epistémologie," 51–4.
[10] Hogg, "*Bolshaia sovetskaia entsiklopediia*," 31.

Genlis denounced Louis-Gabriel Michaud's *Biographie universelle* (1812–28) in these terms, for instance: "Here, alphabetical order, the enemy of all distinction, mixes up positions and ranks bizarrely … Leaders and soldiers are not always where they should be."[11]

At the same time, authors with no interest in social leveling wrote alphabetical works, apparently unconvinced that they were upending society. At times they made a perfunctory nod to hierarchies. In cases in which his biographical subjects shared the same name, for example, Moréri announced that his *Dictionaire* would first cover popes, kings of France, and other princes. Only thereafter would it turn to intellectuals.[12] Still, in the end, alphabetical order could be enrolled in the service of different ideologies and conceptions of knowledge. It was not necessarily a step toward liberation from anything.[13]

In any event, political and philosophical explanations for the development of alphabetical encyclopedias miss other factors. One was commercial. To say that Diderot and D'Alembert's *Encyclopédie* had to be alphabetical because of its editors' or authors' beliefs is to ignore the reality of how it took shape. Once engaged as editors in 1747, Diderot and D'Alembert steered it toward content representative of the Enlightenment, but nothing suggests that they ever had a say about how it was organized. Rather, the printer Le Breton, a figure only weakly associated with the Enlightenment, embraced a proposal for an updated translation of Chambers' *Cyclopaedia*.[14] Far from being political or philosophical, his motives were financial. Aware of the alphabetical *Cyclopaedia*'s success, he gambled on the success of an enlarged French translation. In this case, as in others, it was an encyclopedia-publisher who opted for alphabetical order, not an intellectual who had lost faith in traditional systems and hierarchies.

Pointing out publishers' roles in making encyclopedias alphabetical is, in some measure, begging the question, for publishers such as Le Breton were merely trying to guess what the public would pay for. The reading public, for its part, grew and changed in the decades around 1700. Symptomatic of its growth – and reinforcing it – was the multiplication of periodicals. To understand them, readers were encouraged to buy encyclopedias. In the

---

[11] "L'ordre alphabétique, ennemi de toute distinction, y confond étrangement les places et les rangs … Les chefs et les soldats n'y sont pas toujours à leur place." Chappey, *Ordres*, 48, 123, 175.

[12] Walters, "Juigné Broissinière's Contribution," 169; Moréri, *Grand Dictionaire*, 1st edn., á3v.

[13] Yeo, *Encyclopaedic Visions*, 25–6; Eick, "Violence," 102n.

[14] On Le Breton and the Enlightenment see Merland and Reyniers, "Fortune," 72, 86, 90; Kafker and Loveland, "André-François Le Breton," 122–3.

German states, works titled *Zeitungs-Lexika*, or "periodical-dictionaries," flourished for a century after 1700. Another factor that boosted demand for encyclopedias – and easily consultable ones – was the emerging idea of the "public sphere," where anyone could contribute to discourse. To do so effectively, one might need to prepare by consulting an encyclopedia – as publishers of *Konversations-Lexika* were quick to propose. A further inspiration for participating in the public sphere was the example of "critical" works such as Bayle's *Dictionaire*, where received truths were subjected to skeptical scrutiny. These works demonstrated the freedom from intellectual authority to which speakers in the public sphere were supposed to aspire.[15]

Meanwhile, as the market for encyclopedic works spread outward from scholars, non-alphabetical organization began to appear inconvenient and mysterious. In his preface to the *Curieuses Natur- Kunst- Gewerck- und Handlungs-Lexicon*, for example, Hübner wrote that systematically ordered knowledge would disappear only if true learning did, but he recognized the attractiveness of alphabetical order. In his view, it was a response to the expansion of knowledge and a concession to a public unwilling to learn how to approach knowledge systematically.[16] In fact, even intellectuals such as Hübner were growing accustomed to and reliant on alphabetical works of reference.

Whatever the reasons for their proliferation, alphabetical encyclopedias did not put an end to non-alphabetical encyclopedic works, which kept on appearing. Some were conceived for novelty or strategic advantage. Having saturated the market for the *Encyclopédie*, Panckoucke seized on a proposal for a more coherent encyclopedia and came up with the *Encyclopédie méthodique* (1782–1832), an encyclopedia organized first around subjects and only then by the alphabet and other means. Sensing a niche for a systematic encyclopedic work, the creator of the *Neue Encyklopädie der Wissenschaften und Künste* (*New Encyclopedia of the Sciences and Arts*, 1858) also abandoned alphabetical order and criticized it as leading to fragmentation.[17] Larousse, for its part, published the *Grand Mémento encyclopédique* (1937), which was non-alphabetical, as a complement to its encyclopedias. One goal was to lure purchasers away from the encyclopedias of Aristide Quillet, which were designed like the *Mémento* for self-education. A second benefit was

[15] Michel and Herren, "Unvorgreifliche Gedanken," 19. On *Zeitungs-Lexika* see Lehmann, *Geschichte*, 29–33; Meyer, "Konversations-Lexikon," 36.
[16] Hübner, "Vorrede,")(2r–)(3v (§§4–27).
[17] Peche, *Bibliotheca*, 414.

to undermine the newly begun *Encyclopédie française* (1935–66), which was also non-alphabetical.[18]

Other encyclopedic works were non-alphabetical because of intellectual idealism. Their creators shared Hübner's view that true knowledge demanded systematic arrangement. Such was the conviction of Coleridge in planning the *Encyclopaedia Metropolitana* (1817–45). His publishers were pleased with his proposal for a non-alphabetical work, since they wanted something distinctive to compete with the *Encyclopaedia Britannica* and Rees's [*New*] *Cyclopaedia* (1819–20).[19] Likewise, two unfinished encyclopedic works of the twentieth century, the *International Encyclopedia of Unified Science* (1938–69) and the *Encyclopédie française*, were both non-alphabetical, having been planned by idealists determined to make knowledge something more than information.

In becoming the *New Encyclopaedia Britannica* in 1974, even the *Britannica* retreated from alphabetical order. It now had three sub-series. Two were alphabetical – the *Macropaedia* consisting of general articles, the *Micropaedia* of narrower ones – while the third, the *Propaedia*, was a non-alphabetical overview. Already in 1826, the French statesman François Guizot had recommended two linked encyclopedias, one with short, superficial entries, the other with more elaborate ones suitable for study.[20] As we have seen, similar sub-series had been tried in *Britannica Junior* (1934) and the *Encyclopaedia universalis* (1968–75). The latter work was meant to promote understanding and not give "raw information" unless it was necessary for some higher purpose.[21] So too, in the recollection of the editor, Preece, the planners of the *New Encyclopaedia Britannica* decided it was no longer worthwhile publishing a twenty-four-volume encyclopedia just to allow readers to "look it up." Instead, education had to be the primary goal.[22]

The *Méthodique*, the *Metropolitana*, and the *New Encyclopaedia Britannica* were all large and well known, but all through the heyday of the modern encyclopedia there were humbler encyclopedic works that were ordered non-alphabetically. Their existence has been neglected in histories of encyclopedism, in part because of a bias toward prestigious works. In *Anglo-American General Encyclopedias* (1968), S. Padraig Walsh wrote that

---

[18] On the didactic purpose of the *Grand Mémento* see *Grand Mémento*, I: VII–VIII. On rivalry with the works of Quillet and the *Encyclopédie française* see Mollier and Dubot, *Histoire*, 10–11, 424–36.
[19] Schmidt, "Visionary Pedant," 56.
[20] *Encyclopédie progressive*, 28–30.
[21] *Encyclopaedia universalis*, I: XIV–XVI.
[22] Preece, "Notes," 16, 22.

"few non-alphabetical works are still in existence."[23] His bibliography of encyclopedic works does not support the claim, though, for the proportion of non-alphabetical works listed is neither negligible nor in decline as a function of time. What seems to have motivated his judgment is his sense that they were failures. Among recent examples, he found little to praise except in the American *Book of Knowledge* (1912), the *Lincoln Library of Essential Information* (1924), the *Oxford Junior Encyclopaedia* (1948–54), and *Our Wonderful World* (1955–7). Tellingly, only one of these titles, the *Book of Knowledge*, was out of print when he pronounced non-alphabetical order almost extinct.[24] In contrast, he condemned the majority of non-alphabetical encyclopedic works, sometimes for representing random accumulations of knowledge, but more often for lacking proper indexes and thus being poor instruments for consultation. So perhaps they were, but in laying such emphasis on consultation, he blinded himself to their other uses, notably by children.

Indeed, from the seventeenth century onward, many non-alphabetical encyclopedic works were aimed at non-scholars, often young people or gentlemen with practical interests.[25] Consider some examples from the seventeenth and eighteenth centuries. Published in London, Richard Blome's *Gentleman's Recreation* (1686) consisted of two parts, the first characterized on the title page as "an encyclopedia of the arts and sciences," the second focusing on hunting, related sports, and agriculture. In France, Chevigny's *Science des personnes de la cour, d'épée et de robe* (*The Science of People of the Court, the Sword and the Robe*, 1706) was published in two volumes in duodecimo and covered a select group of disciplines, explaining them through a series of answers to questions. Gradually revised and enlarged, it went through numerous editions in the 1750s, appearing in Italian, Spanish, and even partially in Russian as well as in rival Catholic and Protestant French-language versions.[26] Also aimed at young people – and more comprehensive than its title suggests – was Pluche's thematically organized *Spectacle de la nature* (1732–50), one of the century's best-sellers in France and Britain.

In the nineteenth and twentieth centuries, non-alphabetical encyclopedic works continued to flourish and continued to target young people,

---

[23] Walsh, *Anglo-American General Encyclopedias*, xvi.
[24] See *ibid.*, 14, 95–6, 138–9, 254–5.
[25] See Dierse, *Enzyklopädie*, 64–5.
[26] See review of *Science*, 234–5; Collison, *Encyclopaedias*, 100–1. A Spanish translation was published in 1729–30.

self-educators, and the practically minded. *Enquire Within upon Everything* (1856) had sold more than 1.5 million copies by the early twentieth century and gone through 126 editions by 1976.[27] Filled with advice about food, manners, ceremonies, the law, and other subjects, it was designed for middle-class people seeking self-improvement and guidance. Quite different in nature were a series of non-alphabetical encyclopedic works designed by Quillet, beginning with *Mon professeur: Grande Encyclopédie autodidactique moderne illustrée* (1907). These works stressed academic knowledge, presented for a readership of self-educators and students. Alternatively, *Richards Cyclopedia* (1933), a thematically arranged set published in several editions through 1962, was written for a primarily juvenile audience.

As we have seen, non-alphabetical encyclopedic works could be gigantic, as the *Encyclopédie méthodique* (1782–1832) was. Yet after 1650, most were not. Indeed, at their smallest, it is hard to distinguish them from almanacs, miscellanies, and guidebooks dispensing lessons and tables of data. Into this ambiguous category fall such titles as *Whitaker's Almanack* (1868) and *Schlag auf, sieh nach! Ein praktisches Nachschlagbuch* (*Flip It Open, Have a Look! A Practical Work of Reference*, 1953).

Non-alphabetical encyclopedic works were thus plentiful during the period of the modern encyclopedia. With a handful of exceptions, they were also low in status – which is one reason for their poor showing in histories of encyclopedism. Another is over-emphasis on the fact that some were republished in alphabetical order.[28] Chomel's *Dictionnaire oeconomique* (1709), for example, can be seen as the alphabetical "modernization" of an earlier, thematic work by the same author.[29] In a more limited conversion, the *Kleine Beckmann* (1927) started off as two separately alphabetized volumes, one on the humanities and one on the sciences, but the volumes were integrated in response to complaints, thereby forming *Beckmanns Welt-Lexikon und Weltatlas* (*Beckmann's World Lexicon and World Atlas*, 1931).[30] And despite re-editions and a certain success, the American *Book of Knowledge* (1912) was recast as the alphabetical *New Book of Knowledge* in 1966 – an indication, for Walsh, that

---

27 For the first claim see the title page of the 130th edition (1923).
28 See for example Rétat, "Age," 190.
29 Donato, "Übersetzung," 543–5, 552–6.
30 Peche, *Bibliotheca*, 31–2.

the alphabetical encyclopedia had by then "almost completely ousted the systematically arranged work."[31]

On the other hand, the conversion could go in either direction. Augustin Roux, for example, used materials from the *Encyclopédie* and other works in his thematically organized *Nouvelle Encyclopédie portative* (1766).[32] As we have seen, Panckoucke cited unhappiness with the fragmentation of knowledge to justify a new "edition" of the *Encyclopédie*, the non-alphabetical *Encyclopédie méthodique*.[33] Similarly, the *Penny Cyclopaedia* (1833–43) was reorganized as the *English Cyclopaedia* (1854–62), where alphabetical order was subordinated to four divisions of knowledge.[34] A century later, the *New Encyclopaedia Britannica* too broke with the longstanding alphabetical order of the *Britannica*.

Why dwell on the survival of non-alphabetical encyclopedic works in a book on encyclopedias? As encyclopedic works could be reordered, going from non-alphabetical to alphabetical as well as vice versa, they were part of intersecting systems of textual production. Some encyclopedia-makers, moreover, published works of both kinds, recycling content from one to the other. More generally, alphabetical and non-alphabetical encyclopedic works were mutual influences. They borrowed content from one another, and they were regularly rivals in the field of reference. Lastly, encyclopedias themselves were ambiguous with respect to alphabetical order. Many included short, separately alphabetized sections along with a main body of alphabetical articles. In Larousse's encyclopedic dictionaries, for instance, separate sections treated such material as foreign phrases and proper names. Other encyclopedias had separately organized appendices, indexes, atlases, or guides for study. Further stretching the notion of an alphabetical structure were encyclopedic works divided into largely alphabetical sub-series. In short, books were alphabetized to different degrees, which created a gray zone between alphabetical and non-alphabetical works.

Overviews and Trees of Knowledge

In a sense, non-alphabetical encyclopedic works constituted overviews in their own right, since their contents were supposed to mirror the structure of knowledge or things. From Roman antiquity onward, some of

[31] Walsh, *Anglo-American General Encyclopedias*, xvi, 14.
[32] Kafker and Kafker, *Encyclopedists*, 345. For a contemporary Italian proposal to reissue the *Encyclopédie* as a non-alphabetical work see Abbattista, "Folie," 428–30.
[33] Braunrot and Doig, "*Encyclopédie*," 6–8, 128; Kafker, "Epilogue," 300.
[34] Brake, *Print*, 34–5; Knight, *Passages*, iii: 272–3.

them nonetheless offered more manageable overviews, whether tables of contents or diagrams of knowledge.[35] The latter peaked in the seventeenth century under the influence of the logician and pedagogue Petrus Ramus. Alsted's *Encyclopaedia* (1630) in particular drew on Ramus's protocol of definitions and divisions to generate a common structure for its treatment of knowledge. Consistent with the visual aspect of Ramus's pedagogy, Alsted's *Encyclopaedia* started with twenty-six pages of diagrams showing the configuration of knowledge and disciplines.[36]

The earliest alphabetical encyclopedias did not bother with overviews. As we have seen, Moréri's *Grand Dictionaire*, a historical dictionary, had no entry on history. In his *Lexicon Technicum*, Harris treated disciplines more thoroughly than Furetière or Corneille had, but with the exception of a thematic index in the volume of 1710, he made no attempt to deal with knowledge in general.

Then, in 1728, Chambers set a new trend with his *Cyclopaedia*. Determined to avoid making a "confused heap of incongruous parts," he inserted a preface on the nature of knowledge, language, and dictionaries. There, among other things, he provided a diagram of knowledge, which led to the enumeration of forty-seven arts and sciences, each followed by sub-topics corresponding to articles and "indicating the order they are most advantageously read in" (see Figure 5.1).[37]

Two decades later, Diderot and D'Alembert reworked Chambers' overviews for the *Encyclopédie*. D'Alembert's introduction, the "Discours préliminaire," narrated both the rise of knowledge and the way it ought to have arisen in a more reasonable world. Like Chambers' preface, the "Discours préliminaire" was widely admired. In 1779, Zorzi wrote that leaving it out of his own encyclopedia would be sacrilegious, no less so than removing one of Raphael's masterpieces from an old room.[38] While acknowledging the arbitrariness of any tree of knowledge, D'Alembert and Diderot supplied one, perhaps feeling obligated by Chambers' example. Theirs, inspired by Francis Bacon, organized knowledge around human thinking – specifically, around the faculties of reason, memory, and imagination (see Figure 5.2). As many scholars have noted, the arrangement and divisions of this tree of knowledge are at odds with the contents of the

---

[35] On diagrams of knowledge through the time of the Renaissance see Shackleton, "Encyclopaedic Spirit," 384; Yeo, *Encyclopaedic Visions*, 23–5, 132–3; Rey, *Miroirs*, 76–7.
[36] Hotson, *Johann Heinrich Alsted*, 15.
[37] Chambers, *Cyclopaedia*, I: i–vi.
[38] Zorzi, *Prodromo*, xi.

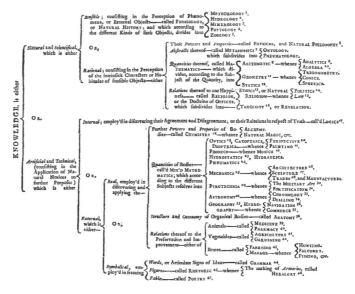

² **HYDROLOGY**, or the History of W A T E R; including that of *Springs, Rivers, Acidula,* &c. of *Lake, Sea, Ocean,* &c. of *Tides, Deluge,* and the like.

³ **MINEROLOGY**, or the History of E A R T H; I°, Its Parts, as *Mountain, Mine, Mofs, Bog, Grotto*; and their Phænomena, as *Earth, quake, Volcano, Conflagration,* &c. Its Strata, as *Clay, Bole, Sand-* &c. 2°, Foffils or Minerals, as *Metals, Gold, Silver, Mercury,* &c. with Operations relating to 'em, as *Fufion, Refining, Purifying, Parting, Effaying,* &c. *Litharge, Lavatory, Pinea,* &c. Salts, as *Nitre, Na-tron, Gemma, Allum, Armoniac, Borax,* &c. Sulphurs, as *Arfenic, Amber, Ambergreafe, Coal, Bitumen, Naphtha, Petrol,* &c. Semi-metals, as *Antimony, Cinnabar, Marcafite, Magnet, Bifmuth, Calamine, Cobalt,* &c. Stones, as *Marble, Porphyry, Slate, Asbeftos,* &c. Gems, as *Diamond, Ruby, Emerald, Opal, Turcoife,* &c. *Emery, Lapis,* &c. whence *Ultramarine, Azure,* &c. Petrifactions, as *Cryftal, Spar, Stalactites, Trochites, Cornu Ammonis,* and the like.

⁴ **PHYTOLOGY**, or the History of P L A N T S; their Origin, in the *Seed, Fruit,* &c. Their Kinds, as *Tree, Herb,* &c. extraordinary Species, as *Tea, Coffee, Paraguay, Vine, Ginfeng, Cotton, Tobacco,* &c. *Coral, Mufhroom, Truffle, Parafite, Miffelto, Mofs,* &c. Parts, as *Root, Stone, Flower*; *Wood,* as *Guaiacum, Saffafras, Ebeny, Aloes,* &c. Leaf, as *Foliation, Roll,* &c. Bark, *Quinquina,* &c. *Piftil, Farina, Stamina,* &c. Operations thereof, as *Vegetation, Germination, Cir-culation,* &c. Circumftances, as *Perpendicularity, Parallelifm, Fer-tility,* &c. Productions, as *Honey, Wax, Balm, Sugar, Manna,* &c. *Gum, Refin, Camphor,* &c. *Indigo, Opium, Galls,* and the like.

Figure 5.1 The diagram of knowledge in the *Cyclopaedia*, along with recommendations for reading about three of the forty-seven disciplines. Scanned courtesy of the Department of Special Collections, Memorial Library, University of Wisconsin, Madison.

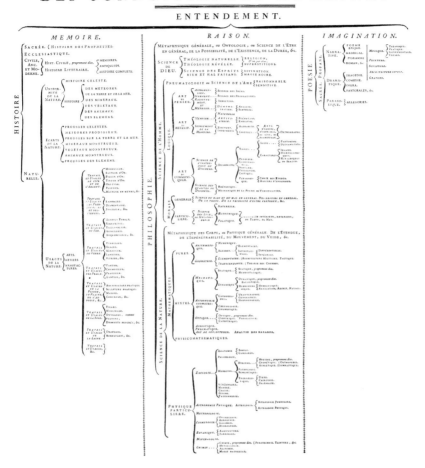

Figure 5.2   The "tree of knowledge" in the *Encyclopédie*. Photographed by the author from his printed facsimile (Pergamon Press, 1969), Vol. 1. With permission from Elsevier.

Encyclopédie.[39] Yet along with the "Discours préliminaire," it remains one of the encyclopedia's most studied parts, often with the assumption that it was a fundamental and carefully meditated key to the work.

[39] See for example Ehrard, "Arbre," 233–9; Cernuschi, "Arbre," 377–82; Leca-Tsiomis, "Système," 85–97.

In Britain, thanks to the *Cyclopaedia* and the *Encyclopédie*, overviews of knowledge were a predictable feature of dictionaries of the arts and sciences for the rest of the century. Barrow's introduction to the *New and Universal Dictionary of Arts and Sciences* (1751) even attempted a synthesis of the two encyclopedias' overviews.[40] Soon afterward, the *New and Complete Dictionary of Arts and Sciences* (1754–5) criticized the trees of knowledge in the *Cyclopaedia* and the *Encyclopédie* – the former "scholastic," the latter too complicated – and went on to give its own.[41] Other contemporary British encyclopedias offered overviews as well, most of them unoriginal and indebted to the *Cyclopaedia*. Even as late as 1819, a prospectus for the *Encyclopaedia Edinensis* (1827) promised an overview still recalling those of the *Cyclopaedia* and the *Encyclopédie*, "a preliminary dissertation, tracing the progress of human knowledge from its origin to its present state of improvement, marking its various mutual relations, and pointing out the manner of reading and studying this work as a connected and systematic whole."[42]

Unlike British encyclopedias, eighteenth- and nineteenth-century German encyclopedias tended not to offer overviews, with the notable exception of Ersch and Gruber's *Allgemeine Encyclopädie* (1818–89).[43] No overview ever appeared in the *Reales Staats- Zeitungs- und Conversations-Lexicon* (1704), for example, though Hübner presented a minimal one in another encyclopedia he patronized, the *Curieuses Natur- Kunst- Gewerck- und Handlungs-Lexicon* (1712).[44] In 1739, Ludovici, newly appointed as editor, announced that the *Grosses vollständiges Universal-Lexicon* (1732–50) would end with an overview. It was supposed to be massive, occupying one or two volumes, but it never materialized.[45] Compiling the *Oeconomische Encyclopädie* (1773–1858) in the second half of the century, Krünitz made no effort to indicate the structure of knowledge, a decision respected by the following editors.[46]

Representative of a broad trend in German encyclopedism, makers of nineteenth- and twentieth-century *Konversations-Lexika* were largely indifferent to the idea of overviews.[47] Through the mid twentieth century,

---

40 Loveland, "Two Partial English-Language Translations," 172–3.
41 *New and Complete Dictionary*, 1: iv–v.
42 Millar, prospectus, 2.
43 On the outlines of knowledge in the latter work see Rüdiger, "Ersch/Gruber," 19–20.
44 Spree, *Streben*, 31; Hübner, "Vorrede," [)(4r]–[)(5r] (§§32–43).
45 Kossmann, "Deutsche Universallexika," 1575.
46 Reinstein, "*Oeconomische Encyclopädie*," 67, 69–70, 80–1.
47 Spree, *Streben*, 83–4.

prefaces and afterwords in Brockhaus's *Konversations-Lexika* avoided giving overviews or analyzing knowledge. Rather, they concentrated on the encyclopedia, presenting its history and noteworthy contents. An afterword in the eleventh edition (1864–8) argued that, contrary to received views, short articles were better than long articles at communicating overviews, since they characterized their subjects with respect to broad swathes of knowledge and did not get bogged down in details.[48] By this criterion, the *Konversations-Lexikon* may have had overviews, but they were narrower and less ambitious than those in the *Cyclopaedia* or the *Encyclopédie*.

French encyclopedias were intermediate between British and German ones in their attention to overviews. Some left them out – the *Dictionnaire de la conversation* (1832–9) and the *Encyclopédie des gens du monde* (1833–44), for example – while others included them. As we have seen, the *Encyclopédie* offered overviews, and they carried through into re-editions and adaptations. So did several encyclopedias of the early nineteenth century. The *Encyclopédie moderne* (1823–32) had a tree of knowledge and essays on three major departments of knowledge. These materials appeared in the final volume of text, though, while the preface in Volume I argued that trees of knowledge were less necessary than in Diderot and D'Alembert's time, since readers were already familiar with knowledge's breadth.[49] Similarly, in their last volume and first volume respectively, the *Encyclopédie du dix-neuvième siècle* (*Encyclopedia of the Nineteenth Century*, 1838–53) and the *Encyclopédie catholique* (1840–8) both featured a tree of knowledge as well as a narrative account of it.

Panckoucke, for his part, was committed to offering overviews in the *Encyclopédie méthodique* (1782–1832). Indeed, his rationale for ordering the work non-alphabetically was to foster coherence where the *Encyclopédie* had supposedly fragmented knowledge. Overviews were to take two forms: introductions to sub-series, and tables indicating the place of entries within a discipline and the order they could be read in to form a "didactic treatise."[50] Many of the specialists responsible for sub-series fulfilled Panckoucke's wishes, but others did not, often through negligence or unforeseen circumstances but sometimes because they doubted that overviews were useful or possible. The author of the sub-series *Finances* (1784–7), on a politically sensitive topic, seems to have avoided offering

[48] [*Grosse Brockhaus*], 11th edn., XVI: VIII–IX.
[49] *Encyclopédie moderne*, I: xiv. For the overviews see *Encyclopédie moderne*, XXIV: 273–578.
[50] Panckoucke, *Prospectus*, I: 54–5.

overviews to stay out of trouble.[51] Beyond his successes and failures in securing overviews of disciplines, Panckoucke never attempted an overview of knowledge. The prospectus itself – a preliminary overview – was divided up by disciplines. Even his *Vocabulaire universel*, promised and probably started but finally abandoned after 1814, was conceived as an index, though it would have indicated the disciplines in which concepts were covered. As a result, the *Encyclopédie méthodique* became a collection of dictionaries of disciplines, all available for separate purchase after 1789. Significantly, in a notice from around 1825, Panckoucke's daughter and successor, Pauline Agasse, changed the sub-title of the encyclopedia, calling it a "universal library" – an expression that highlighted the separateness of sub-series.[52]

At roughly the same time as certain contributors to the *Encyclopédie méthodique*, other encyclopedists too began to express disenchantment with trees of knowledge and overviews, in part because specialization was weakening the conception of knowledge as unified. The editors of the *Encyclopaedia Britannica* exemplified the progression. The first edition (1771) of the *Britannica* did not have an overview. The omission may have been deliberate, but the lack of any commentary suggests that it was an oversight. In any event, skepticism about trees of knowledge became a point of pride for the *Britannica*. The preface to the third edition (1797) cited the philosopher Thomas Reid on the futility of classifying knowledge. Likewise, in the opening pages of the *Supplement to the Fourth, Fifth, and Sixth Editions* (1824), the philosopher Dugald Stewart criticized the overview of knowledge in the *Encyclopédie* and cast doubt on the value of any large-scale overview.[53] Consistent with his argument, the *Supplement* started with "dissertations" on areas of knowledge, but none of them dealt with knowledge in general. The dissertations lingered through the eighth edition (1853–60) of the *Britannica* and inspired similar partial overviews in the *Popular Encyclopaedia* (1841).[54]

Taking a lighter tone than Stewart, the editor of the first *Deutsche Encyclopädie* (1778–1807) dismissed trees of knowledge as beyond human ability and deferred the "honor" of connecting things that were barely

---

[51] Doig, "*Encyclopédie*," 62–4.
[52] Baczko, "Trois temps," 782–5; Braunrot and Doig, "*Encyclopédie*," 14–15; Porret, "Savoir," 49–50. Volumes of the *Méthodique* continued to be published with the old sub-title. On the *Vocabulaire* see Doig, *From Encyclopédie*, 107, 269n; Panckoucke, *Prospectus*, II: 383; Baczko, "Trois temps," 782–5.
[53] Kafker and Loveland, "William Smellie's Edition," 25; Doig *et al.*, "Colin Macfarquhar," 168–9; Yeo, *Encyclopaedic Visions*, 177–80, 191–2, 253–5.
[54] Kruse, "History," 152–4, 163, 191; Spree, *Streben*, 44–5; Walsh, *Anglo-American General Encyclopedias*, 146.

connected to the *Encyclopédie*.[55] So too, in the unfinished *Encyclopédie progressive* (1826), Guizot stressed the divergence between the *Encyclopédie* and its overview of knowledge. More generally, he mocked the idea of forcing a system onto the "chaos" of a collaborative encyclopedia and rejected non-alphabetical classification as worthless except within disciplines.[56]

Reflecting such skepticism, overviews had declined in encyclopedias by the early nineteenth century, though without disappearing. Indeed, a rebirth of sorts occurred in the twentieth century as concerns grew about over-specialization and the value of traditional education.[57] In this context, admitting that encyclopedias fragmented knowledge, the fifth edition (1952–6) of Herder's *Konversations-Lexikon* included a systematically organized final volume entitled *Der Mensch in seiner Welt* (*People in Their World*).[58] Even Brockhaus's *Konversations-Lexikon*, long indifferent to overviews, briefly changed course. In the sixteenth edition (1952–63), the last volume thus offered both a diagram of knowledge and a series of essays on broad fields of knowledge. The editor justified the overviews as useful for study, as complementing the insights of specialized disciplines, and as inherently interesting for "quiet hours of reading."[59] Regardless, the overviews never returned. Likewise, the publisher's preface to the *Enciclopedia* [*Einaudi*] (1977–84) bemoaned the "terrorism of disciplines" and promised to communicate not a summary of facts but an examination of concepts and their inter-connections.[60] Accordingly, Volumes XV and XVI were devoted to diagrams and interdisciplinary studies of knowledge, albeit on a "local" rather than all-encompassing scale.

In spite of the upswing, overviews remained rarer in the twentieth century than they had been in the eighteenth – unless we count those with more modest goals than displaying the contours of knowledge.[61] Two of these amended goals will be considered in the following paragraphs: offering the studious an educational tool, and promoting understanding of a given encyclopedia.

Overviews imagined as maps of knowledge were different from those imagined as educational tools. First, the latter tended to appear in a

[55] Goetschel, Macleod, and Snyder, "*Deutsche Encyclopädie*," 268–9.
[56] *Encyclopédie progressive*, 4–8.
[57] See for example Burke, *Social History … II*, 262; Geiger, *Research*, 233–5.
[58] [*Grosse Herder*], 5th edn., X: v.
[59] [*Grosse Brockhaus*], 16th edn., XIII: 1.
[60] *Enciclopedia* [*Einaudi*], I: XIII–XV. A similar contemporary encyclopedia was the *Enciclopedia del novecento* (1975–84). See Rovigatti, "Gli anni," 20, 22.
[61] See Spree, *Streben*, 54, 315.

less prominent place than the head of Volume I, since they were meant for the studious, not everyone else. Second, unlike maps of knowledge, overviews imagined as educational tools were geared toward practicality, not philosophical truth. In fairness, the editors of the *Encyclopédie* (1751–72) recognized that their tree of knowledge was an arbitrary device, but D'Alembert belabored the philosophical and historical relations among disciplines in his preceding narrative. By contrast, when overviews finally appeared in the *Encyclopaedia Britannica* in the nineteenth and twentieth centuries, they did so in an unphilosophical framework.

The resuscitation of overviews in the *Britannica* began inadvertently and on a small scale. In acknowledging contributors and announcing new entries, prefaces to the *Britannica* from the third edition (1797) onward gave something like overviews of the works' contents. These overviews were finally identified as such – the one in the seventh edition as an "outline ... of its contents" and the one in the eighth edition as a "list of the leading articles in the principal departments."[62] Then, in the final pages of the eleventh edition (1910–11), the editors inserted what they thought was "the first attempt in any general work of reference at a systematic subject catalogue or analysis of the material contained in it." Their goal was to allow "students" to research whole subjects.[63] Finally, in keeping with the planners' goal of creating an "educational instrument" as well as a work of reference, a full volume of the *New Encyclopaedia Britannica* (1974), entitled the *Propaedia*, was devoted to surveying knowledge. It did so not only with essays and diagrams but with courses of reading.[64]

In fact, officially designated "study-guides" had been produced for many American encyclopedias throughout the century, including editions of *World Book, Funk and Wagnalls New Standard Encyclopedia* (1931), *Collier's Encyclopedia* (1949), and the *Encyclopedia International* (1963–4).[65] The study-guide could be an option or an integral part of a set. In the latter case, ordinarily, it was consigned to the last volume. Among the first of these guides was the one issued by the Werner Company in 1895 to accompany its pirated version of the *Encyclopaedia Britannica*. The owners of *Britannica* then responded with their own *Reader's Guide* in 1913. In both instances, the publishers were promoting specialized courses of study, for groups such as

---

[62] *Encyclopaedia Britannica*, 7th edn., I: xix; *Encyclopaedia Britannica*, 8th edn., I: xx–xxvi.
[63] *Encyclopaedia Britannica*, 11th edn., XXIX: 879.
[64] *New Encyclopaedia Britannica* (1974), *Propaedia*: ix, 8.
[65] Murray, *Adventures*, 74–5; Henry, "Survey," 33–4, 39–40, 42; Walsh, *Anglo-American General Encyclopedias*, 55–6, 67; Shiflett, *Louis Shores*, 160–1, 186.

farmers, soldiers, and students. The overviews provided were thus largely within fields, not of all knowledge. The same was true of *Propaedia* and other encyclopedias' study-guides.

Alternatively, overviews could help people understand an encyclopedia, whether readers or planners. The planners of the *Grande Encyclopédie* (1885–1902) claimed to have drawn inspiration from the philosopher Auguste Comte's classification of knowledge, but the effects of the inspiration were left unspecified. More importantly, during planning, space was allotted among nine fields of knowledge with no obvious relation to those highlighted by Comte.[66] This division of knowledge – a kind of editor's overview – was an early element of planning. Its publication in the foreword was probably meant above all to show the editors' discipline and forethought, though it functioned secondarily as a survey of knowledge as the encyclopedia presented it. Similarly, the overview of knowledge in the sixteenth edition (1952–63) of Brockhaus's *Konversations-Lexikon* included a circular diagram used to plan the encyclopedia.[67] Finally, the *Propaedia* was allegedly written before the rest of the *New Encyclopaedia Britannica*, to facilitate planning.[68]

As these examples show, besides helping editors, overviews could give readers a sense of an encyclopedia and what to expect of it, if not of all knowledge. Elements of such pragmatism crept into even philosophical overviews, but some overviews were largely about a given work's contents. Consider, for example, Pierer's encyclopedias in the mid nineteenth century. Already in the first edition (1822–36), the preface offered an overview of the work's coverage, with tips on what information and keywords could be looked up, or not. The amount of guidance increased with the second edition (1840–8). While the editors advised reading the entire forty-four-page preface, they also put in a short guide to using the encyclopedia, printed in red ink for visual salience.[69] In fact, like the guide, much of the preface was about the encyclopedia's contents and how to use them. Pierer dropped its lengthy preface with the fourth edition (1857–65), settling instead for a curt one typical of contemporary German encyclopedias. Regardless, pragmatic overviews were gaining ground on philosophical ones in the prefaces of encyclopedias – and not just in German.

---

[66] *Grande Encyclopédie: Inventaire*, I: VII–VIII, XI.
[67] [*Grosse Brockhaus*], 16th edn., XIII: 1–2.
[68] *New Encyclopaedia Britannica* (1974), *Propaedia*: 7.
[69] For the advice see [*Pierer's Universal-Lexikon*], 2nd edn., I: VI.

To the extent that they were abstract and philosophical, overviews of knowledge had peaked in the mid eighteenth century, especially in Britain, with a mild resurgence in the mid twentieth century. On a philosophical level, the project of constructing a system of knowledge was being treated with skepticism by 1800. In addition, encyclopedias had shifted from being near the forefront of intellectual culture before 1850 to being closer to popularization from that time forward. Pedagogical overviews, for their part, became popular in the twentieth century, above all in the form of study-guides. Still, the majority of nineteenth- and twentieth-century encyclopedias offered neither kind of overview.

Length of Entries

In the seventeenth century, entries in encyclopedias were almost all short. The point of alphabetical order, after all, was to make information accessible. Consequently, encyclopedists such as Bayle who pushed the length of their entries beyond a few pages – and up to around twenty pages in the case of his article "Spinoza" – risked turning alphabetical order into a joke.[70] When entries were short, encyclopedias had little need for sub-titles, marginal summaries, or other indications of structure, but as entries lengthened, the need for internal organization intensified. Already in the first edition of his *Grand Dictionaire* (1674), Moréri divided his article on America, which comprised 1,500 words, into sections with sub-titles.[71] As the last editor of the *Grosses vollständiges Universal-Lexicon* (1732–50) – where entries grew longer in the second half of the alphabet – Ludovici introduced sub-titles in most articles on countries.[72] Similarly, the *Encyclopaedia Britannica* had its "treatises," which were ordinarily long. From the first edition (1771) onward, many were split into parts. To guide reading further, the editor Tytler put summaries of sections and paragraphs in the margins of certain treatises in the second edition (1778–83).

Encyclopedias also used sub-articles to organize material. Sub-articles were entries with the same keyword that gave a term's meanings in different domains. A lack of logic in their order could lead to frustration,

---

[70] "Spinoza" grew from eighteen pages in the first edition to twenty-one in the second. It was apparently the longest article in the *Dictionaire*. See Popkin, *History*, 252n.
[71] Moréri, *Grand Dictionaire*, 1st edn., 101–2. See also Schneider, "Des transferts," forthcoming.
[72] Schneider, *Erfindung*, 40, 119–20, 130–2.

as expressed in a review of the first edition of *The New International Encyclopaedia* (1902–4): "There are nearly forty … [articles entitled 'Albert'], beginning with the husband of Lotte in Goethe's 'Sorrows of Werther,' and ending with Albertus Magnus. Between these two extremes there surges a host of emperors, dukes, musicians, and geographical names, arranged neither by dates, by rank, nor the alphabet."[73] Although sub-articles could have been alphabetized by the words after a keyword, they were normally not. In the *Universal-Lexicon*, for example, keywords representing things were placed before identical keywords referring to people, while articles on people with the same last name were alphabetized by their first names.[74] By contrast, the editors of the *New Encyclopaedia Britannica* (1974) stipulated that "where the same name may denote a person, place, or thing, the articles will be found in that order."[75] More philosophically, in the *Encyclopédie* (1751–72), Diderot suggested ordering sub-articles by a progression of ideas, a principle that left room for improvisation.[76] In Pierer's encyclopedia, a term's meanings were presented as a logical hierarchy. Numbers indicated its primary meanings, Roman letters its secondary meanings, and Greek letters its tertiary meanings.[77]

Whether or not they were ultimately split into sub-entries, long entries grew longer through the mid nineteenth century, forcing authors and editors to confront the problem of order within them. Just as encyclopedias could grow beyond their projected length through the interaction of lax editors with wordy contributors, the same combination could inflate individual articles. Diderot, for example, who vowed not to alter submissions to the *Encyclopédie*, accepted articles of more than forty pages on a handful of subjects, and not necessarily the most important ones.[78] When editors were contributors, they sometimes allowed themselves exceptionally long entries. Ludovici, we have seen, unbalanced the *Universal-Lexicon* with a 175-page article on Wolff's philosophy. Similarly, the editors Pierre Leroux and Jean Reynaud gradually lengthened their articles for the *Encyclopédie nouvelle* (1834–42) in order to publicize their theoretical views. At the beginning of his 77-page article "Eclectisme," Leroux warned his readers that the article would be as long as a book, and indeed, like many long

---

[73] *New York Times*, November 15, 1902: BR8.
[74] Kossmann, "Deutsche Universallexika," 1583–4.
[75] *New Encyclopaedia Britannica: Micropaedia* (2005), 1: 153. The same note can be found scattered throughout the *Micropaedia*.
[76] See for example Coleman, "Figure," 69–74.
[77] Spree, *Streben*, 224–5.
[78] See Loveland, "Unifying," 63.

articles written for encyclopedias, it was also published separately, as a book in its own right.[79]

For the most part, long articles appeared in encyclopedias erratically, with no explanation for how long they were. Leroux thought they would give his encyclopedia substance, but he did not say so publicly.[80] Nor would a subscriber to Ersch and Gruber's *Allgemeine Encyclopädie* (1818–89) have had any reason to anticipate an article on Greece that ran to 3,668 pages. Whether because of abundant material or because of interest or nationalism on the part of the public, geographical articles were among the longest in encyclopedias from the nineteenth century onward, but why would there be so much on Greece in a German encyclopedia? Far easier to rationalize was the volume-long article on Spain in the *Espasa* (1908–30), since the encyclopedia was premised on remedying neglect of the Hispanic world in other works of reference.[81]

In some encyclopedias, long articles acquired a rationale and a name – specifically, the name "treatise." A treatise, in theory, was a formal or systematic view of a subject, but in the context of encyclopedias, the word's meaning shifted away from considerations of structure and content, and toward one of length. The idea of putting treatises in encyclopedias may have occurred to several people independently before 1800, but it was most firmly rooted in a British tradition.[82]

The British experiment with treatises began with Harris's *Lexicon* (1704), the first encyclopedia to include treatises under that name. As his sub-title indicated, Harris's goal was to explain disciplines as well as their terms. For trigonometry, surveying, and other subjects, he therefore provided "entire treatises." The two longest in his first volume, at twenty-two pages apiece, were "Hydrostaticks" and "Trigonometry."[83] Like other long entries on disciplines, these were laid out as sequences of results to be mastered. At the price of imbalance in the length of his entries, Harris offered readers the possibility of learning the substance of certain disciplines.

The next encyclopedia to have treatises was Coetlogon's *Universal History* (1745). Like Harris, Coetlogon justified his treatises on pedagogical grounds, arguing that entries in the *Cyclopaedia* and other encyclopedias were too short to teach readers the arts and sciences. To remedy the problem,

---

[79] *Encyclopédie nouvelle*, IV: 462; Griffiths, *Jean Reynaud*, 168–9, 174n, 206.

[80] Griffiths, *Jean Reyaud*, 173.

[81] [*Espasa*], I: XIII.

[82] For a possible instance of independent invention see *Encyclopédie méthodique: Manufactures*, I: xxvii. See also Doig, *From Encyclopédie*, 265.

[83] Harris, *Lexicon*, I: a3r.

he constructed the *Universal History* entirely of treatises. Specifically, it consisted of 169 treatises averaging 15 pages in length but varying between the extremes of "Cosmography" (14 lines) and "Geography" (113 pages).

Typographically, Harris had not differentiated between treatises and other entries. As in the majority of contemporary encyclopedias, titles of entries in the *Lexicon Technicum* were printed in capital letters along the columns' left margins, while running titles were printed as three-letter abbreviations on the top of each column. In the *Universal History*, by contrast, treatises were printed with a distinctive typography. Each began with a large title placed across the two columns. Running titles as well were centered across the page, not the column, and almost all of them provided the treatise's full name (see Figure 5.3). The same protocol for titles and running titles would be observed in the treatises in the *Encyclopaedia Britannica* – and many of its imitators – through the early twentieth century.

After Coetlogon died, the *Universal History* was revised as the *New Universal History of Arts and Sciences* (1759). In neither form was it praised much, whether for its organization or anything else, but it seems to have had an influence on the *Britannica*. There, in the first edition (1771), the editor, Smellie, vaunted the novelty by which the *Britannica* would distinguish itself from the other encyclopedias: "Instead of dismembering the sciences … they [the 'editors'] have digested the principles of every science in the form of systems or distinct treatises, and explained the terms as they occur in the order of the alphabet." Disciplines, in other words, were to be covered in treatises, whereas "terms" would be the object of traditionally short articles. Both would be alphabetized in the same sequence. By this means, declared Smellie – a proponent of spreading knowledge throughout society – "any man of ordinary parts, may … learn the principles of agriculture, of astronomy, of botany, of chemistry, etc. etc. from the *Encyclopaedia Britannica*."[84]

The preface to the first edition announced the work's organizational scheme as wholly original, but editors of the *Britannica* from the nineteenth century onward suggested it was adapted from the *Universal History*. In fact, the *New Universal History* was the likely inspiration. Smellie was familiar with the re-edition of Coetlogon's encyclopedia, he borrowed from its contents in the *Britannica*, and he cited it in the bibliography there.[85] Taken together, these observations support the claim that

[84] *Encyclopaedia Britannica*, 1st edn., 1: v; Loveland, *Alternative Encyclopedia?*, 144.
[85] Loveland, *Alternative Encyclopedia?*, 141–2.

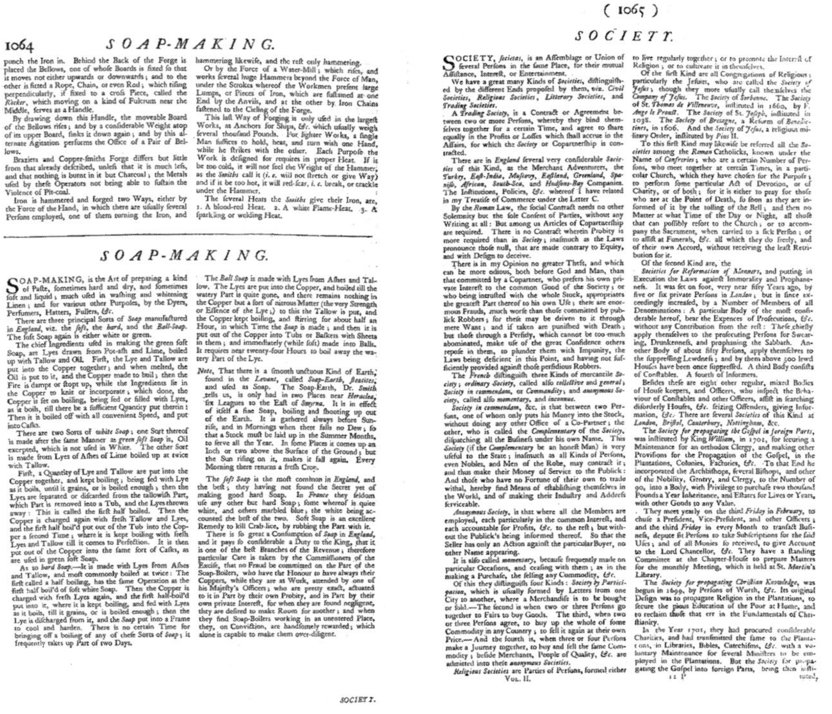

Figure 5.3   Running titles and cross-titles in Coetlogon's *Universal History*.
Scanned courtesy of Indiana State University Special Collections,
Cordell Collection of Dictionaries.

Coetlogon had an influence on the *Britannica*. Furthermore, they point to Smellie – and not to the work's publishers, as some accounts have it – as primarily responsible for the *Britannica*'s organization.[86]

Smellie's decision to organize the *Britannica* as an alphabetical sequence of treatises and articles came with enduring consequences. Subsequent editors of the *Britannica* maintained the arrangement for over a century. Soon they attracted imitators. Already in 1788, two nearly identically titled encyclopedias highlighted their own use of treatises: George Selby Howard and others' *New Royal Cyclopaedia* and William Henry Hall's *New Royal Encyclopaedia*.[87] The *Britannica*'s once distinctive structure became even

[86] For further evidence see *ibid.*, 142n.
[87] Doig *et al.*, "James Tytler's Edition," 49–50.

more popular in early-nineteenth-century Britain. By 1817, the publishers of the fifth edition could claim realistically that a mix of articles and treatises was customary for encyclopedias "in this country at least."[88] For many planners of encyclopedias, the question was no longer whether but how far they should go in respecting the trend. At one end of the spectrum, the *Encyclopaedia Edinensis* (1827) was advertised as combining articles and treatises to better advantage than any previous encyclopedia.[89] At the other end, even Rees, who criticized treatises as out of place in an encyclopedia, covered disciplines amply in his revised *Cyclopaedia* (1778–88) and expanded articles to "enormous length" in the [*New*] *Cyclopaedia* (1819–20).[90]

Indeed, in the *Britannica* and other works, the distinction between articles and treatises gradually faded. From the first edition onward, certain articles in the *Britannica* were longer than treatises, but the fact that treatises were on disciplines justified their special typographical treatment. With the passage of time, though, articles grew longer, especially geographical ones. Evidently uninterested in maintaining the theoretical distinction between articles and treatises, or perhaps unaware of it, editors began to elevate all kinds of long articles – many of them not on disciplines – to the status of treatises.[91]

Prefaces in the *Britannica* dwelt on the virtues of its mix of articles and treatises through the time of the ninth edition (1875–89), but the eleventh edition (1910–11) repudiated the "tendency in previous editions ... to make inclusive treatises of the longer articles," calling it "cumbrous" and inconvenient for readers.[92] Accordingly, though variability persisted in entries' length, the last of the typographical cues used by Coetlogon and Smellie to distinguish treatises from articles – large cross-heads for titles – disappeared in the eleventh edition. All entries were now articles. When the encyclopedia returned to distinguishing short and long entries with the separate sub-series of the *New Encyclopaedia Britannica* (1974), inspiration seems to have come from other twentieth-century encyclopedias and not, ironically, from the *Britannica*'s own eighteenth- and nineteenth-century history.

Why, after the experiments of Harris, Coetlogon, and Smellie – all pedagogically motivated – did treatises become popular in encyclopedias

---

[88] *Encyclopaedia Britannica*, 5th edn., 1: vii.
[89] Millar, prospectus, 1–2.
[90] Yeo, *Encyclopaedic Visions*, 185; Upton, "Some Landmarks," 51; review of *Edinburgh Encyclopaedia*, 186. Notice Rees's repudiation of treatises in Rees, [*New*] *Cyclopaedia*, 1: vi.
[91] Loveland, "Unifying," 73–6.
[92] *Encyclopaedia Britannica*, 9th edn., 1: v; *Encyclopaedia Britannica*, 11th edn., 1: xviii.

around 1800? Certainly the *Britannica*'s prestige from the third edition onward encouraged their spread.[93] Editors of encyclopedias, moreover, could use the prospect of writing treatises to recruit distinguished experts. Conversely, early-nineteenth-century scientists sometimes had trouble finding places to publish. In Britain, the problem was particularly acute, a fact that helps account for the institutionalization of treatises there.[94] On a more abstract level, treatises fit not only with reliance on specialists but also with the narrower scientific disciplines emerging from broad groupings such as natural philosophy and natural history.[95] Another factor favoring treatises was the diminishing status of facts and observations. Both were highly valued in eighteenth-century views of knowledge, and short entries were ideal for presenting them as such, without forcing readers into a definite judgment on how they should be ordered or made into knowledge. In physics, for example, one reviewer insisted that the compiler of an encyclopedia should not "be of any opinion; at least not so far as to prevent a fair stating of arguments in justification of different hypotheses, which the reader has a right to have laid before him for his own judgment."[96] By the early nineteenth century, in contrast, the public's judgment counted for little in many disciplines, and long entries reflected the ascendancy of theories over observations and facts.[97]

The *Britannica* was admired, but outside of English, its organization went almost unimitated. Only the second *Deutsche Encyklopädie* (*German Encyclopedia*, 1886–90), to my knowledge, adopted its mix of formally distinguished articles and treatises.[98] In part, publishers recognized that extensive coverage of any subject had limited appeal. In the *Encyclopédie progressive* (1826), the minister Guizot endorsed treatises for scholarly encyclopedias, but he admitted that elementary encyclopedias, with their brief, numerous entries, were better suited to the times.[99]

Another reason for the *Britannica*'s weakness as an international model was mounting enthusiasm for an alternative, the *Konversations-Lexikon*. In the fifth edition (1819–20) of Brockhaus's *Konversations-Lexikon*, an

[93] Loveland, *Alternative Encyclopedia?*, 146.
[94] Einbinder, *Myth*, 33–4; Hughes, "Science," 347.
[95] Yeo, *Encyclopaedic Visions*, 184–7, 246–83; Yeo, "Reading," 39–49. On similar developments in France see Darnton, *Business*, 447–54.
[96] Review of *Complete Dictionary*, 18.
[97] On these connections see Yeo, *Encyclopaedic Visions*, 187–91; Loveland, "Unifying," 68–9; Anderson, *Between the Library and the Laboratory*, 42–69; Pickstone, *Ways*, 10–12, 71. See also Schubring, "Mathematische Wörterbücher," 114–28.
[98] Jäger, "Lexikonverlag," 554.
[99] *Encyclopédie progressive*, 13–36.

afterword linked short articles with the work's mission of providing a maximum of people with the minimum of information needed for conversation and reading. The editors, stated the afterword, had been vigilant about articles' length, rejecting or shortening the "treatises" ("Abhandlungen") that some contributors submitted.[100] Similarly, Brockhaus's eleventh edition (1864–8) drew a contrast between popular and learned encyclopedias, stipulating that the former must not present original research or be long-winded.[101] Comparison with the *Britannica* was merely latent.

Whatever its editors claimed on the matter, Brockhaus's commitment to short articles should not be exaggerated. The supplement (1810–11) to the first edition featured a thirty-page article on Napoleon Bonaparte.[102] The fifth edition (1819–20) had several articles of twenty pages or more, mostly on countries. In the course of the century, moreover, the longest entries in Brockhaus's encyclopedia tended to lengthen, just as they did in other German *Konversations-Lexika*. Articles on European countries were regularly the longest, but other subjects gave rise to long articles too. Scientific entries, by contrast – originally the longest in the *Britannica*, though geographical entries eventually outstripped them – rarely went beyond five pages in Brockhaus's work.[103] Variations in entries' length remained smaller than in the *Britannica*, though they gradually increased until the twentieth century.

Regardless, the contrast between the models of Brockhaus and the *Britannica* was often overdrawn. In *Chambers's Encyclopaedia* (1868), for instance, the Chambers wrote that the *Konversations-Lexikon* had been created to steer encyclopedias back to their "original purpose," namely by eliminating "long and formal treatises" in favor of shorter entries suitable for consulting.[104] Not only was the assertion false in historical terms, but it exaggerated the contemporary reality of the *Konversations-Lexikon*.

In the twentieth century, the opposition between the *Britannica* and the *Konversations-Lexikon* became even less clear with regard to the length of entries. As we have seen, the *Britannica* dropped treatises with its eleventh edition. While long entries remained, none were as long as the longest of the previous century.

[100] [*Grosse Brockhaus*], 5th edn., 1st printing, X: III, VI, XIII–XIV ("Vorrede").
[101] [*Große Brockhaus*], 11th edn., XV: V–VIII.
[102] Hingst, *Geschichte*, 105.
[103] On scientific versus geographical entries see for example Loveland, "Unifying," 77; *Encyclopaedia Britannica*, 14th edn. (1929), I: XXX.
[104] *Chambers's Encyclopaedia*, 1st edn., I: "Notice."

Meanwhile, the makers of *Konversations-Lexika* experimented with special entries of more than average length. As we have seen, Herder introduced boxed articles alongside its normal articles, first in the *Kleine Herder* of 1925 and then in the *Grosse Herder* of 1931–5. Boxed articles were originally meant to cover practical topics.[105] In the *Grosse Herder* of 1952–6, though, their function changed. They were now supposed to treat scattered subjects from a Catholic perspective, in keeping with Herder's religious stand.[106]

Likewise, the ninth edition (1971–9) of Meyer's *Konversations-Lexikon* had 100 "special contributions" ("Sonderbeiträge") interspersed among articles by their thematic relevance. These essays were meant to supply "a living picture of the scientific and social developments of our time."[107] Among others, the encyclopedia featured such speculative, polemical pieces as "Why Am I a Christian?" and "The Parliamentary System – How Much Longer?" Then, probably in imitation of Meyer's "Sonderbeiträge," Brockhaus put some 240 articles on "contemporary critical concepts" in its nineteenth edition (1986–94). Outlined in blue, these were unusually long articles on topical, at times controversial, subjects, including aggression, waste-disposal, and noise.[108]

The resemblance between the *Britannica*'s treatises and the essays that cropped up in twentieth-century *Konversations-Lexika* did not reflect an underlying continuity of aims. Above all, the distinctive German entries were not surveys of subjects or pedagogical units. Longer entries, in sum, could serve different ends, though in all cases they allowed material to be presented at length.

Cross-References and Indexes

In a perfect world, an encyclopedia would have had no need for cross-references or for an index, since people would have found what they wanted in the first entry consulted. Advertisements imagined encyclopedias in just such a world. Consider this one for the *New International Encyclopaedia* in 1928: "Nearly 75,000 separate articles are placed alphabetically, eliminating the need for a cumbersome index – and making it possible to find any

---

[105]   *Kleine Herder*, "Geleitwort."
[106]   Peche, *Bibliotheca*, 235–6.
[107]   "… ein lebendiges Bild von den wissenschaftlichen und gesellschaftlichen Entwicklungen unserer Zeit." [*Meyers Konversations-Lexikon*], 9th edn., 1: "Vorwort." See also Peche, *Bibliotheca*, 393; Sarkowski, *Bibliographische Institut*, 186.
[108]   [*Grosse Brockhaus*], 19th edn., 1: "Vorwort." See also Peche, *Bibliotheca*, 116.

article within 12 seconds."[109] In reality, no one could guess all the keywords under which users might search for material, and an encyclopedia where every search led straight to the right article would be too filled with repetition to be published on paper.

Both cross-references and indexes served to remedy the insufficiency of a given selection of keywords, but by different means. Cross-references directed readers to articles from within other articles, while indexes did so from an expanded list of keywords, separately alphabetized and normally placed at the end of an encyclopedia. Indexing became a profession in the twentieth century, with accepted procedures and standards, whereas cross-referencing remained an idiosyncratic activity, tied to the methods of each encyclopedia.[110] In spite of these differences, encyclopedists came to see cross-referencing and indexing as complements. The common belief that an index could replace cross-references, or cross-references an index, argues for their treatment as close relations.

In the seventeenth and early eighteenth centuries, dictionaries and encyclopedias had cross-references, but they were mainly for dealing with synonyms and variants in spelling. Among encyclopedias, two works from around 1700 may have played a role in introducing substantial cross-references – that is, cross-references connecting concepts or suggesting avenues for research. The first was Bayle's *Dictionaire*. Although Bayle did not make many references from entry to entry – that is, true cross-references – his entries referred to footnotes again and again. If nothing else, he showed encyclopedists how their texts could be linked with a structure that went beyond the order of exposition within entries. A second model for encyclopedists' use of cross-references was Harris's *Lexicon*. Harris boasted that his readers could get a complete course in geometry "by the help of very easy references from one place to another."[111] He rarely made explicit cross-references such as "see 'Geometry,'" but he did italicize technical terms – among other words – in many articles, just as he did the names of articles in explicit cross-references. Italicizing, it would seem, was his way of guiding readers from article to article. As an infrequent alternative to the explicit cross-reference, the same means of cross-referencing was used in the *Encyclopédie*.[112]

The *Cyclopaedia* (1728) was the first encyclopedia to have a network of explicit cross-references. Chambers may have drawn inspiration for his

[109] *New York Times*, October 7, 1928: BR13.
[110] On indexing as a profession see Wellisch, "Indexing," 269.
[111] Harris, *Lexicon*, I: a2v.
[112] See for example *Encyclopédie; ou, Dictionnaire*, VIII: 266, 267, 270, 599, 600, 610, 611, 615.

cross-references from the *Lexicon Technicum* and other works of reference as well as the tradition of the commonplace book, in which ideas were organized under interlinked headings.[113] As he designed it, the *Cyclopaedia* was teeming with cross-references. Consider a sample consisting of the articles – not the sub-articles – in the first twenty pages under "D." Here, in the first edition, 65 percent of the articles had cross-references.[114] The article "Anatomy," typical of many on disciplines, had around fifty cross-references in a little more than a column.[115] Furthermore, the number of cross-references increased significantly in the second edition (1738). There, more than three-quarters of the articles had cross-references in the first twenty pages under "D." Likewise, within the sample, the total number of cross-references went from 227 in the first edition to 359 in the second. The number of cross-references in the *Cyclopaedia* then remained stable through the 1740s, only to decline after 1750.[116] Thanks to Chambers' example, though, they had become an expected component of the modern encyclopedia.

One encyclopedia that imitated the *Cyclopaedia*'s system of cross-references was the *Encyclopédie*. Its cross-references have a reputation for being systematic and subversive, which derives from statements by the editors as well as a tendency to reduce it to extracts related to the Enlightenment.[117] In fact, the *Encyclopédie*'s cross-references were not part of a system. It is true that they were deployed systematically by some individuals. The naturalist Louis-Jean-Marie Daubenton, for example, included a cross-reference to "Plante" in nearly all his articles on plants, whereas Diderot and Jaucourt almost never referred to "Plante" in their own articles on plants. In any event, many of the cross-references in the *Encyclopédie* were simply copied from the *Cyclopaedia*. It is likely that Diderot added cross-references to others' articles occasionally. Still, he did not edit submitted cross-references to a significant extent. In this respect, he differed from modern encyclopedia-editors as well as a few contemporary ones, among them Ludovici in the *Grosses vollständiges Universal-Lexicon*,

[113] Werner, "Modernité," 164–5; Yeo, *Encyclopaedic Visions*, 104–19. See also Goyet, "Encyclopédie," 493–4.

[114] Similar estimates can be found in Yeo, *Encyclopaedic Visions*, 132; Bradshaw, "Ephraim Chambers' *Cyclopaedia*," 125–6.

[115] Ten of these cross-references were in the sub-article "Anatomy of Plants." The number of cross-references in "Anatomy" stayed the same through the fifth edition.

[116] Loveland, *Alternative Encyclopedia?*, 62–3.

[117] For the editors' assertions see [Diderot], prospectus, 11; *Encyclopédie; ou, Dictionnaire*, 1: xviii–ix, v: 642v–644r.

De Felice in the Yverdon *Encyclopédie*, and Zorzi in his projected *Nuova enciclopedia*.[118]

In "Encyclopédie" – an article that, paradoxically, lacked any cross-references – Diderot offered the most methodical account of the *Encyclopédie*'s cross-references, though some of his comments concerned an ideal encyclopedia more than the one he was editing. In his article, he identified several kinds of cross-references. One was the heuristic cross-reference, crafted by a genius to facilitate the discovery of truths or inventions. Two centuries later, the *Encyclopaedia universalis* (1968–75) proposed something similar with a category of cross-references characterized as unexpected, fortuitous, and intellectually stimulating.[119] Neither encyclopedia provided examples. As a result, intriguing as the notion is to scholars studying Diderot, it is not clear if heuristic cross-references were ever used.

The most famous of the cross-references mentioned in Diderot's article were defined as those that "will secretly attack, shake, overthrow certain ridiculous opinions that one would not dare insult overtly."[120] Already in Diderot's time, readers discovered and led one another to a certain number of such cross-references. Enemies of the *Encyclopédie* were particularly enthusiastic about tracking them down. In 1769, building on Diderot's association of subversive cross-references with secrecy, the Benedictine biographer Chaudon declared them the key to the *Encyclopédie*'s "system, the secret of a mysterious philosophy."[121]

In truth, the idea that subversive cross-references were a central, systematic, and clandestine element of the *Encyclopédie*'s propaganda is a matter of fantasy – Diderot's of a better, more cleverly executed encyclopedia, and Chaudon's and others' of a hidden conspiracy. In the first place, the cross-references could hardly have been secret after Diderot announced them in "Encyclopédie." In the second place, they were rare. None of the first 150 cross-references under "D," for example, appears to be subversive in any way. Again and again, historians of the *Encyclopédie* return to the same examples of subversive cross-references. Ironically, at least one of them is grossly misleading. This is in "Anthropophages," which refers to "Eucharistie" after evoking pagans' interpretation of the Eucharist as

---

[118] Loveland, "*Laissez-Faire* Encyclopedia?," 216–17.
[119] *Encyclopaedia universalis*, I: XVI, XVIII: V.
[120] "… attaqueront, ébranleront, renverseront secrètement quelques opinions ridicules qu'on n'oserait insulter ouvertement." *Encyclopédie; ou, Dictionnaire*, V: 642v–643r. In the *Grand Dictionnaire* (1866–76), Pierre Larousse allegedly used cross-references to outwit his censors. See Mollier and Dubot, *Histoire*, 123–4.
[121] Chaudon, *Dictionnaire*, I: 145–6. See also Leca-Tsiomis, "Capuchon," 349.

cannibalism. At first glance, the cross-reference might seem subversive, a slur on Catholicism stuck in an otherwise dreary article. Unfortunately for the clarity of this analysis, the article was copied, along with the cross-reference, from Chambers' *Cyclopaedia*.[122] Despite being copied, it was signed by the Catholic theologian Edme-François Mallet. As Mallet was still living when the article appeared, he would surely have protested if his signature had been put on an article considered injurious to Catholicism.

Although very few were subversive, the *Encyclopédie* was not short of cross-references. Once again counting in the first twenty pages under "D," I found that a third of the articles had cross-references while the total number of cross-references – necessarily approximate because of imprecise references such as "see these words in their articles"[123] – was around eighty, or a third of the number in the 1728 *Cyclopaedia*.[124] For all their abundance, cross-references in the *Encyclopédie* were thus less densely deployed than they were in the *Cyclopaedia*.

Thanks to the *Cyclopaedia* and the *Encyclopédie*, cross-references became common in the European encyclopedia, but almost always at lower densities than in either model.[125] Even encyclopedias advertised as having numerous cross-references rarely had as many. Two such encyclopedias from the following century were the *Encyclopédie des gens du monde* (1833–44) and *Chambers's Encyclopaedia* (1868). If we judge by the first twenty pages of "D," once again, the former had an average of a cross-reference per article – roughly as many as the *Encyclopédie*, but fewer than the *Cyclopaedia*. *Chambers's Encyclopaedia*, for its part, had fewer than either model, with an average of one cross-reference for every three articles.[126]

One reason for the falling density of cross-references in encyclopedias was the rising proportion of historical and geographical articles once they were added to dictionaries of the arts and sciences and universal dictionaries toward 1750. For the most part, such articles did not have any cross-references, since they dealt with simple facts without a systematic component.[127] Alternatively, restrictions on cross-references could be a

---

[122] Leca-Tsiomis, "Capuchon," 350.
[123] "Voyez ces mots à leurs articles." *Encyclopédie; ou, Dictionnaire*, IV: 613.
[124] See also Blanchard and Olsen, "Système," 45, 47.
[125] For a similar judgment see Hüe, "Structures," 313. On French encyclopedists' enthusiasm for cross-references around 1800 see Rétat, "Age," 192–3.
[126] For statements about cross-references see *Encyclopédie des gens*, I: viii; *Chambers's Encyclopaedia*, 1st edn., I: "Notice".
[127] Michaud nonetheless endorsed cross-references for his *Biographie universelle* (1812–28). See Rétat, "Encyclopédies," 509.

matter of policy. Panckoucke, for instance, pledged not to overdo them in the *Encyclopédie méthodique* (1782–1832).[128]

Indeed, as Panckoucke realized, cross-references were potentially an inconvenience for readers. The fact was not lost on Chambers' rivals in Britain. The *Supplement* (1744) to Harris's *Lexicon* declared that Chambers had trapped the reader "in so intricate a maze [of cross-references], that it is almost impossible that he should extricate himself."[129] Similarly, reducing the need to follow cross-references was one of the rationales for treatises in the early *Encyclopaedia Britannica*.[130] Even Chambers acknowledged that readers would not want to "go a long circuit and be bandied from one part of the book to another."[131] In a variation on this logic, an Italian translator of the *Cyclopaedia* deemed cross-references incompatible with the format of most encyclopedias, since folios were too unwieldy for switching between articles.[132] Of the few encyclopedias that outdid the *Cyclopaedia* in cross-referencing, it is no accident that the majority appeared in a single volume. One was the *New Columbia Encyclopedia* (1975). As of 1978, it was advertised as containing 66,000 cross-references, or some 20 per page.

The role of such material considerations in limiting reliance on cross-references is also substantiated by the abundance of cross-references in electronic encyclopedias, including Wikipedia. Instead of being hunted down over volumes and pages, cross-references can now be pursued with the tap of a finger. In today's context, Chambers's invention seems even more prescient than it did at the time.[133]

A final factor that lessened dependence on cross-references was the improvement of indexes, since these provided a systematic means of finding information. Readers, increasingly, could pursue "cross-references" of their choosing simply by looking a word up in the index. Detailed alphabetical indexes appeared in the Middle Ages and then proliferated in the era of print.[134] Non-alphabetical encyclopedic works were often published with indexes, including Alsted's *Encyclopaedia* (1630).

[128] Panckoucke, *Prospectus*, 1: 55. See also Watts, "*Encyclopédie*," 349.
[129] *Supplement to Dr. Harris's Dictionary*, 4.
[130] Yeo, *Encyclopaedic Visions*, 179; *Encyclopaedia Britannica*, 2nd edn., 1: vi.
[131] Chambers, *Cyclopaedia*, 1: ii.
[132] Farinella, "Traduzioni," 108–9. For additional eighteenth-century criticism of cross-references see Burke, *Social History*, 186–7; Garofalo, *Enciclopedismo*, 34; *Encyclopédie; ou, Dictionnaire*, v: 644r; Chaumeix, *Préjugés*, 1: 36–8.
[133] On relations between cross-references and hyperlinks see Zimmer, "*Renvois*," 95–110.
[134] Rouse and Rouse, "Naissance," 77–85; Weijers, "Funktionen," 22–4, 29–31; Eisenstein, *Printing Press*, 90–4; Blair, "Annotating," 75–85.

Some early encyclopedias were indexed as well, including Hofmann's *Lexicon universale* (1677), Bayle's *Dictionaire* (1697), and Coronelli's *Biblioteca* (1701–6).[135] Still, most were not, perhaps for want of resources on the part of authors or publishers, but above all because they were composed of short entries, which made them into something like indexes themselves.[136] Neither Furetière's *Dictionaire* (1690) nor the first edition of the *Cyclopaedia* had an index, for example. The *Encyclopédie* too appeared without any index, though it acquired one, belatedly, in 1780.[137] France's biggest encyclopedias of the following century – Larousse's *Grand Dictionnaire* (1866–76) and the *Grande Encyclopédie* (1885–1902) – both lacked an index. Large encyclopedias continued to appear without indexes into the twentieth century, among them the *Espasa* (1908–30), and *Chambers's Enyclopaedia* from 1858 to 1948.[138]

Before the mid nineteenth century, in any case, indexes in encyclopedias were often ineffective at helping readers find details. Some just allowed access through an alternative language. Early editions of the *Reales Staats-Zeitungs- und Conversations-Lexicon* (1704) thus featured two indexes, one for terms in Latin, the other for terms in modern non-German languages. Both indicated articles where information could be found on a given non-German term.

Other indexes might more properly be called tables of contents. Harris, for instance, placed a fifty-page "index" at the end of the second volume (1710) of the *Lexicon Technicum*, but it was organized around disciplines, under each of which articles were listed alphabetically. Topics not corresponding to keywords were not in the list. Many encyclopedias had tables of contents through the mid nineteenth century, though most, unlike Harris's, were purely alphabetical. Favor for such tables was reinforced by Brockhaus's *Konversations-Lexikon*.[139] Löbel had planned to index the first edition (1796–1808) but did not live to do so.[140] The second edition (1812–19) provided a table of contents – that is, a list of articles – at the end of each volume. This practice endured through the time of the twelfth edition

[135] Lehmann, *Geschichte*, 13; Fuchs, "Vincenzo Coronelli," 203; Burrell, "Pierre Bayle's *Dictionnaire*," 89.
[136] On relations between indexes and financing see Kafker, "Encyclopedias," 1: 398. See also Harris, *Lexicon*, 1: biv.
[137] Kafker, "Role," 21.
[138] Law, "Indexing," 13; Castellano, *Enciclopedia*, 356.
[139] See for example Loveland, "Two French 'Konversationslexika,'" forthcoming.
[140] [*Grosse Brockhaus*], 1st edn., 1: ix.

(1875–9), but for the eighth edition (1833–7) Brockhaus offered a true index too (1839).[141] As a way of opening up encyclopedias, the table of contents had outlived its prime, but it continued to crop up as an easily compiled alternative to a true index – for example, in the first edition of the *Bolshaia sovetskaia entsiklopediia* (1926–47).[142]

Even when not merely tables of contents, indexes in encyclopedias could be partial or provisional. A few treatises in the early *Encyclopaedia Britannica* were indexed individually, for instance.[143] It made less sense to index volumes in a multi-volume encyclopedia, since readers would have to check through a series of indexes – unless the publisher issued a final general index. Volume-based indexes were nonetheless taken up by several American encyclopedia-makers with the resources to publish their whole sets at once, including, at some point, the makers of *Compton's Encyclopedia* (1968) and *The New Book of Knowledge* (1966). Two rationales were set forth. First, a volume's index could briefly identify keywords not included in the encyclopedia. Second, in a school or a library, they allowed more than one student to use an index – albeit an incomplete one – at the same time.[144]

Indexes improved in the nineteenth century and became widespread in encyclopedias. The *Britannica* acquired its first with the seventh edition (1842), a 187-page one.[145] In the German states, Brockhaus offered a first encyclopedia-index in 1839. It took the form of a 283-page volume. Soon afterward, in 1855, the Bibliographisches Institut issued an index of around 1,000 pages for the *Wunder-Meyer* (1840–53).[146] The indexes were even larger in the first (1857–60) and second (1861–7) editions of Meyer's *Konversations-Lexikon*, though mainly because they were now used for updates as well.

Compared with British and French works, nineteenth-century German encyclopedias focused more on indexes and other tools for finding material while paying less attention to overviews and relationships within knowledge.[147] In the twentieth century, however, both Brockhaus and the Bibliographisches Institut let their indexes lapse, or replaced them with narrower tools such as indexes of names. Shortly before the appearance of the index-less seventeenth edition (1966–74) of Brockhaus's encyclopedia,

---

[141] Peche, *Bibliotheca*, 58–60; Hingst, *Geschichte*, 130.
[142] Hogg, "*Bolshaia sovetskaia entsiklopediia*," 22, 24.
[143] Doig *et al.*, "James Tytler's Edition," 78; Doig *et al.*, "Colin Macfarquhar," 165.
[144] See Katz, *Basic Information Sources*, 160; American Library Association, *Purchasing*, 25–6, 33–4.
[145] Kruse, "Story," 148.
[146] Peche, *Bibliotheca*, 84; Sarkowski, *Bibliographische Institut*, 72.
[147] For the comparison between British and German encyclopedias see Spree, *Streben*, 83–4, 314.

the editor Karl Pfannkuch expressed frustration that Germans considered the *Encyclopaedia Britannica* – with its index and long articles – the model for encyclopedias.[148] For him and his colleagues, the place of the index in an encyclopedia based on relatively short articles was far from secure.

Another reason advanced for not compiling an index was the adequacy of cross-references. The development of the *Cyclopaedia* from 1728 to the early nineteenth century illustrates the relationship between indexes and cross-references. The *Cyclopaedia*'s first index, a meager nine-page one, was added in the second edition of 1738. When Rees took over as editor in the late eighteenth century, he charted a different course, reducing the number of cross-references and introducing a partly alphabetical eighty-page index. In his judgment, the index would conduct readers "from one subject to another, much better than any number of references incorporated in the work itself."[149] By the time he began work on his [*New*] *Cyclopaedia* (1819–20), Rees apparently had second thoughts, or was daunted by the prospect of indexing this much larger encyclopedia, for he chose to do without one. Now he wrote that cross-references "will serve, like the index of a book, but much more effectually, to conduct the reader from one subject to another."[150]

Valid or not, the notion that an index could replace a system of cross-references, or cross-references an index, took root among encyclopedists, especially in twentieth-century America.[151] The index to *World Book* (1917–18), for instance, was dropped in the 1920s in favor of numerous cross-references and a volume-long study-guide. Librarians and educators allegedly suggested the change, deeming the index "superfluous," perhaps thinking that students would be reluctant to use it.[152] In 1972, the index returned – at the request of librarians, ironically – despite the company's protest that the cross-references were adequate.[153] In the *New Encyclopaedia Britannica* (1974), the sub-series *Micropaedia* was sub-titled and to some degree accepted as an index.[154] In effect, many entries there referred to the *Macropaedia*, and there was no other index – a source of outrage to some. Still, as the addition of a true index in 1985 showed, the *Micropaedia* was

[148] Keiderling, "*Brockhaus*," 201–202n. On the intermittence of indexes at Brockhaus and the Bibliographisches Institut in the twentieth century see Peche, *Bibliotheca*, 104–18, 379–95.
[149] Werner, "Abraham Rees's Eighteenth-Century *Cyclopaedia*," 195; Rees, *Cyclopaedia*, 1: iv.
[150] Rees, [*New*] *Cyclopaedia*, 1: vi–vii.
[151] See for example Katz, *Basic Information Sources*, 148; American Library Association, *Purchasing*, 28.
[152] Collison, *Encyclopaedias*, 202–4; Henry, "Survey," 33–4; Murray, *Adventures*, 74. On the latter possibility see American Library Association, *Purchasing*, 41.
[153] Coyne, "Effects," 12, 58.
[154] See for example *New York Times*, March 9, 1975: BR7.

simply a collection of brief, heavily cross-referenced articles doing some of the work of an index. Here in the pre-1985 *New Encyclopaedia Britannica* – as in the index-less *Encyclopaedia universalis* (1968–75) – cross-references were as dense as they had been in the *Cyclopaedia*. With the addition of the index to the *New Encyclopaedia Britannica*, cross-references in the main sub-series were, predictably, scaled back.[155]

In the world of encyclopedias, the balance between cross-references and indexes had shifted toward the latter by the mid nineteenth century. One factor was the logic of specialization. While the work of creating cross-references was usually spread out among contributors and editors, indexing was done independently from other editing. Indexes, consequently, could be more homogeneous than cross-references. Indeed, through the late nineteenth century, indexes were still being credited to individuals. The indexes to the seventh (1842), eighth (1853–61), and ninth (1875–89) editions of the *Britannica*, for example, were all compiled single-handedly. Remarkably, the indexer for the eighth edition was paid just £25.[156] For the eleventh edition (1910–11), by contrast, the index was drawn up by "a staff of ladies" under the supervision of Hogarth, a graduate of the University of Oxford with years of experience supervising clerical work.[157] Later indexes were prepared with a changing assortment of systems for data-management, but they continued to be collaborative.[158] In any event, indexing for the *Britannica* and the majority of twentieth-century encyclopedias was now done professionally, in isolation from the composition of the encyclopedia.

For the eleventh edition of the *Britannica*, Hogarth and her team tried to create the first index that did not just record every mention of a term but rather referred readers to "substantial" information.[159] Likewise, in the *Encyclopaedia universalis* (1968–75), the editor, Claude Grégory, poked fun at nineteenth-century indexes for being indiscriminate. In the *Universalis*, he insisted, anything indexed in the somewhat index-like sub-series *Thesaurus* would have a minimum of "intelligibility."[160]

---

[155] Runte and Steuben, "*Encyclopaedia*," 86, 92–4. On cross-references in the *Universalis* see Vanche-Roby, "Nomenclature," 180–2. I counted 284 cross-references in the first 20 pages under "D" in the 1974 *Micropaedia* (versus 62 in the 2005 *Micropaedia*) and 586 in the 1990 *Thesaurus*, also without an index.

[156] Kruse, "Story," 150, 159, 192. The index to the ninth edition was "compiled" by William Cairns but "revised and arranged" by three other people. See *Encyclopaedia Britannica*, 9th edn., xxv: v.

[157] Thomas, *Position*, 22–5.

[158] On systems for indexing see for example Kruse, "Story," 402, 405; Kogan, *Great EB*, 289.

[159] Thomas, *Position*, 24–5.

[160] *Encyclopaedia universalis*, XVIII: v.

In practice, it was difficult to say what constituted a substantial or intelligible mention. Consider the ninth edition (1875–89) of the *Britannica*, where the Hawaiian (or Sandwich) Islands were evoked in a single sentence in "Knighthood": "There are innumerable grand crosses, commanders, and companions of a formidable assortment of orders in almost every part of the world, from that of the Golden Fleece of Spain and Austria to those of St. Charles of Monaco and of King Kamehameha of the Sandwich Islands."[161] "Ichthyology" too referred to Hawaii in a single sentence, as the only place in the world to have a siluroid fish.[162] Neither of these mentions appeared in the index published in Edinburgh, which referred to only four items under the heading "Hawaiian Islands," but both were included – along with twenty more – in the bigger index published by Stoddart for his American counterfeit. Did Stoddart plump up his index with trivial mentions, as the comments of Hogarth and Grégory might lead us to believe? In fact, librarians allegedly favored Stoddart's reprint because of the index.[163] This example points to the complexity of setting the bounds for an index. Indeed, the evolution of "engines" for searching the internet since the late twentieth century shows that the relevance of items can be judged in different ways.

By the end of the twentieth century, the editors of the *Encyclopedia Americana* were telling their readers to consult the index first, before seeking out articles in the main text.[164] Such idealism recalls Chambers' in inviting readers of the *Cyclopaedia* to use cross-references to build a "treatise" from myriad short articles.[165] It is unlikely that many people chose to bypass the essential convenience of any encyclopedia – the alphabetical entries – in favor of an indirect route, but indexes, like cross-references, remained important complements to the alphabetical order of entries.

Conclusion

Breaking with the thematic and other orders of earlier encyclopedic works, the European encyclopedia was organized as an alphabetical sequence of entries. This order was not in itself incompatible with systems, hierarchies,

---

[161] *Encyclopaedia Britannica*, 9th edn., XIV: 121.
[162] *Ibid.*, XII: 675.
[163] Phelps, "*Encyclopaedia*," 80–1; Kruse, "Piracy," 316–17. Compare also the indexes in *Encyclopaedia Britannica*, 9th edn., XXV: 202; *Encyclopaedia Britannica*, 9th edn., American reprint, [XXV]: 416.
[164] See for example *Encyclopedia Americana: International Edition*, I: v. For a similar suggestion see *New Encyclopaedia Britannica: Micropaedia* (2005), I: 14.
[165] Chambers, *Cyclopaedia*, II: 975.

or traditional orthodoxy. It was never, moreover, a single, all-determining framework, but rather a first step toward organizing materials. In any event, a yearning for coherence haunted encyclopedists intermittently throughout the era of alphabetical order, partly in response to criticism that encyclopedias fragmented knowledge and thwarted learning. One expression of this yearning was the overview of knowledge, modeled in the *Cyclopaedia* and the *Encyclopédie*. Such overviews met with skepticism in the early nineteenth century, but rather than disappearing, they took on new functions within encyclopedism, notably the more humble ones of helping students to study and familiarizing users with how an encyclopedia worked.

Long entries and cross-references were two additional means of making encyclopedias coherent. While the opposition between the treatises of the *Encyclopaedia Britannica* and the short, supposedly uniform entries of the *Konversations-Lexikon* was regularly exaggerated, encyclopedists had real choices about how long to make entries and how to structure them. Cross-references, for their part, are frequently associated with the Enlightenment and the *Encyclopédie*, though they were rarely subversive in any encyclopedia, and were more densely deployed in Chambers' *Cyclopaedia*. Thanks to Chambers' innovation, cross-references became a fixture in subsequent encyclopedias, usually in a minor role but occasionally as a pre-meditated replacement for an index. Unlike long entries and cross-references, indexes were not intended to make encyclopedias cohere, but they did organize the works' contents against a richer selection of keywords, thus helping users to locate material. Indexing was neglected, overall, in encyclopedias published before the mid nineteenth century, but it spread quickly thereafter and became more comprehensive.

CHAPTER 6

Illustrations in Encyclopedias

Though encyclopedias were abundantly illustrated from the mid nine-teenth century onward, illustrations play a minor role in histories of encyclopedias.[1] This weak point in scholarship reflects the marginalization of the visual within intellectual history, if not from intellectual culture in general. Illustration is seen as ornamental rather than as a vehicle for com-municating knowledge. Since it is hard to say what, exactly, a picture can teach us, it is easy to dismiss it as a superfluous touch. Illustrated books are also associated with childhood and an inability to read well. If a work of fiction is illustrated, for example, it was probably written for children. These are associations that the makers of illustrated encyclopedias have been at pains to dispel.

Illustrators, moreover, have been written out of encyclopedias over the years. In the era of copperplates – that is, above all, the seventeenth and eighteenth centuries – most plates had signatures identifying the artist as well as the engraver. As illustrations became smaller and cheaper in the nineteenth century, signatures grew rarer and almost disappeared. Even encyclopedias committed to identifying their article-writers did not usu-ally bother to identify their illustrators. Consider, for example, the *Grande Encyclopédie* (1885–1902). It had a list of contributors in every volume, and a substantial proportion of entries were signed, supposedly to allow authors to air personal interpretations and give the public a guarantee of authority.[2] Yet the names of illustrators went unpublished, and almost none of the illustrations had any signature. The assumption was that images did not allow for interpretation, and that they did not need a signature to be authoritative. The assumption was wrong, though. While the illustrations in encyclopedias may not have "lied" – consistent with the truism that

[1] Hupka, *Wort*, 2–4, 67.
[2] *Grande Encyclopédie: Inventaire*, 1: XII. Nearly half of the first 100 articles in Volume XV were signed. I did not count the articles consisting of only a cross-reference.

202

pictures do not – the sections following show that interpretation was at their essence, whether it came from the artist or someone else.

However ornamental they may have been in some cases, and however hidden their creators may be, illustrations in encyclopedias are worthy of study. To a degree, their development merely mirrors the development of book-illustrations in general, responding to the same mix of techno-logical, commercial, and cultural shifts. Yet the story of illustrations in encyclopedias is also a specific one. First, worries about images as possibly frivolous were more acute for encyclopedias than they were for other books, since encyclopedias were seen as being among the most serious of books. Second, editors of encyclopedias chose to illustrate a distinctive collection of subjects, though it varied over time and from title to title. Third, and lastly, relations between texts and images were particularly complicated in the case of encyclopedias, in part because of the works' size, and in part because images could relate to multiple articles.

Technical Innovation and the Proliferation of Illustrations

From the Renaissance onward, a variety of books had frontispieces, typo-graphical ornaments, and decorative "vignettes" – visual embellishments separating sections of text (see Figure 6.1). Diagrams became established in books about knowledge, encouraged by Ramus's doctrines, among other factors. Ramistic diagrams of relations within knowledge were for the most part rendered crudely with straight lines and brackets, but the humanist Christofle de Savigny's *Tableaux accomplis de tous les arts libéraux* (*Complete Tables of All the Liberal Arts*, 1587) offered elegance and a certain naturalism in its pictorial overviews of knowledge and disciplines. Savigny's diagram of music, for example, included images of musical instruments arranged around a chart showing relationships among musical concepts, terms, and notation (see Figure 6.2).

By this time, the techniques used to illustrate encyclopedias through the early nineteenth century had already been brought into partnership with print. The two most important were printing with woodblocks and printing with etched or engraved plates of metal.

Woodblocks – blocks of wood on which images were carved in relief – were applied to printing things such as playing cards in the early fifteenth century. Printers, artists, and writers were soon joining forces to produce books illustrated with "woodcuts" – as the images made with woodblocks were called. Such images lacked subtlety, but since diagrams were oriented toward utility anyway, they were usually printed as woodcuts in

Figure 6.1　Page with vignettes from the *Supplément* (1752) to the *Dictionnaire de Trévoux*.
Scanned courtesy of the Archives and Rare Books Library, University of Cincinnati.

seventeenth- and eighteenth-century encyclopedias. Woodcuts were used for the geometrical diagrams in Harris's *Lexicon* (1704), for example (see Figure 6.3). Remarkably, they were still being considered for Brockhaus's *Konversations-Lexikon* in the early twentieth century.[3]

A second set of techniques for making reproducible images involved engraving or etching, typically on a plate of copper, which created a "copperplate." Copperplates allowed for finer, more precise lines than woodcuts. In the *Lexicon Technicum*, this technique was reserved for subjects needing more detail – for example, anatomy and architecture (see Figure 6.4). It had two disadvantages. First, it was more expensive than illustrating with woodcuts, as it required more labor from artists as well as special paper, which raised costs for binding. Second, unlike woodblocks,

[3] Keiderling, *F. A. Brockhaus*, 68.

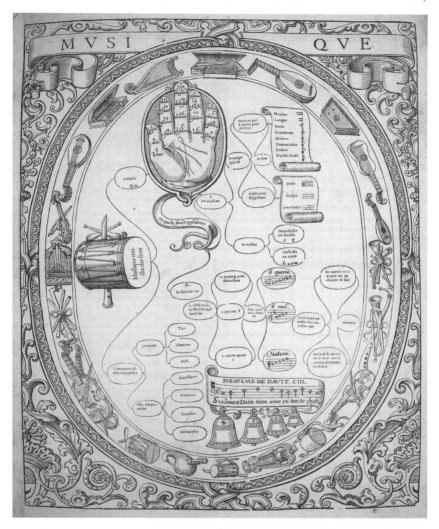

Figure 6.2   Diagrammatic overview of music in Savigny's *Tableaux accomplis*.
Scanned courtesy of the Newberry Library, Chicago.

engravings and etchings were prepared as intaglios – that is, with the areas
to be printed recessed on the plate instead of raised up. As a result, while
a woodcut could be set in the midst of a frame of type and then inked
and printed along with the text, a copperplate could not. For this reason,

Figure 6.3　Examples of woodcuts in the third edition (1716) of Harris's *Lexicon Technicum*. Scanned courtesy of the Public Library of Cincinnati and Hamilton County.

copperplates were printed on separate pages, often placed at the end of a volume or set.

Whether made as woodcuts or copperplates, illustrations had appeared in many books before 1700, but with the exception of diagrams, they were scarce in encyclopedias.[4] In particular, beyond frontispieces, decorations, and a small number of diagrams – some genealogical, some mathematical – Moréri's *Grand Dictionaire* (1674), Furetière's *Dictionaire* (1690), Corneille's *Dictionaire* (1694), and Bayle's *Dictionaire* (1697) were all devoid of pictures. In part, seventeenth-century encyclopedism was strongly influenced by lexical tradition, an influence that encouraged authors to think of their projects as verbal.[5] The value of illustrations in

[4] Hupka, *Wort*, 76–7.
[5] For a similar argument see Siegel, "Orte," 171.

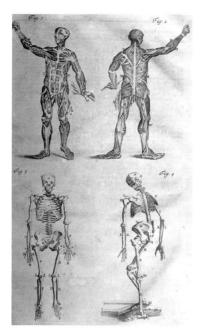

Figure 6.4   Example of a copperplate, on anatomy, in the third edition (1716) of Harris's *Lexicon Technicum*. Scanned courtesy of the Archives and Rare Books Library, University of Cincinnati.

encyclopedias was still unproven, moreover. Financial considerations too could convince an encyclopedia-publisher to do without illustrations. Woodcuts were inexpensive, but they were starting to be seen as crude and old-fashioned by around 1700.[6] As noted earlier, it was costly to prepare copperplates. Before copyright was secured for images in the eighteenth and nineteenth centuries, the designs tended to be copied, which saved on honoraria.[7] Still, making an engraving was demanding in itself. Among other things, the image had to be flipped right-to-left to appear correctly when printed. Perhaps inadvertently, but perhaps to save time and money, the engraver for the *Complete Dictionary of Arts and Sciences* (1764–6) did not flip technological plates – some of them evidently taken from the *Encyclopédie* – which resulted in a large number of left-handed workers.[8]

[6] Hupka, *Wort*, 110; Smith, "Woodcut Illustration," 1265.
[7] On the development of copyright for images see for example Rose, "Technology," 63–6.
[8] Review of *Complete Dictionary*, 5–6; Loveland, "Two Partial English-Language Translations," 175, 182–3.

Cost notwithstanding, many encyclopedias were illustrated from the eighteenth century onward. Some were specialized encyclopedias, among them two dictionaries of practical living, the *Dictionarium Rusticum et Urbanicum* (1704) and the first edition of Chomel's *Dictionnaire* (1709). Others were dictionaries of the arts and sciences. Indeed, in the *Lexicon Technicum*, Harris criticized Corneille's *Dictionnaire* for having "no cuts nor figures at all," hinting that coverage of the arts and sciences required them.[9] Along with Etienne Chauvin's more philosophical *Lexicon rationale* (1692), published in Latin, the *Lexicon Technicum* excelled in its scientific illustrations. Both works featured woodcuts as well as copperplates, but in different proportions. The *Lexicon rationale* had thirty copperplates but no woodcuts, whereas the first, one-volume edition of the *Lexicon Technicum* had around 600 fields of woodcuts and 7 copperplates, plus the frontispiece.[10] Two other dictionaries of arts and sciences of the early eighteenth century were Jablonski's *Allgemeines Lexicon* and Chambers' *Cyclopaedia*. Opposite in this regard to the *Lexicon rationale*, the *Allgemeines Lexicon* had more than 100 fields of woodcuts but only a handful of copperplates, whereas Chambers pursued a more balanced strategy, with 20 copperplates and some 100 woodcuts.[11]

Before the 1760s, few dictionaries or encyclopedias from outside Britain were heavily illustrated.[12] One reason for the discrepancy was the mathematical character of the dictionary of the arts and sciences as it developed in Britain, which pushed British encyclopedias toward geometrical diagrams. Two more possible influences, the philosophy of John Locke and a certain empirical spirit, are treated in the following section.

France had almost no illustrated encyclopedias before the *Encyclopédie* (1751–72), a fact partly accounted for by the lexical inclination of French encyclopedias under the influence of the Académie Française. The German states, for their part, had Europe's most literate middle class – which made for a competitive market in books – but lacked wealthy book-buyers of the sort who supported the lavish encyclopedias of Britain, France, and the Italian states. These factors conspired to keep the price of books low and to limit the use of copperplates. German encyclopedias, accordingly,

[9] Harris, *Lexicon*, 1: a2r.
[10] For the purposes of this paragraph, a field of diagrams is a collection of one of more diagrams not separated by text.
[11] On the *Cyclopaedia*'s plates see Werner, "Planches"; Stewart, "Illustrations," 70–81. On illustrations in the *Allgemeines Lexicon* see Hupka, *Wort*, 90. The only plates I found are the frontispiece and two on heraldry.
[12] Hupka, *Wort*, 91.

were apt to skimp on illustrations or use woodcuts through the nineteenth century and beyond.

Around 1750, two encyclopedias from outside Britain set a new standard for the illustrated encyclopedias of the nineteenth and twentieth centuries. The first was Pivati's *Nuovo dizionario* (1746–51), which had almost 600 copperplates scattered throughout its ten volumes in folio. We do not know why it was so well illustrated. In the early 1740s, Pivati had begun compiling a *Dizionario universal*, which ended up foundering. There were thirteen plates in Volume 1. Undeterred by the failure, Pivati went on to propose the *Nuovo dizionario*, the first volume of which had forty-nine plates. Perhaps the sharp increase in the number of plates merely corresponded with the decision to set the price high and cater to the taste for luxury among Venice's elite. Perhaps, too, the illustrations were a way of countering a translation (1748–9) of the *Cyclopaedia* into Italian, a project announced six months before the *Nuovo dizionario* began appearing. As it turned out, the translation was published with just eighty-nine plates, and in the smaller format of quarto. These features allowed it to be sold for less than a third as much money as the *Nuovo dizionario*, and they were surely a factor in its enrollment of far more subscribers.[13] Pivati may have reconsidered his enthusiasm for illustrations after the experience, for he used them only sparingly in his unfinished *Dizionario poligrafico* (*Polymathic Dictionary*, 1761–7).[14]

A few years after the start of Pivati's *Nuovo dizionario*, illustrations arrived in French encyclopedias. For their dictionary of the arts and sciences – ultimately abandoned – a group of Parisian Benedictines prepared some 200 illustrations around 1750. The editor, Antoine-Joseph Pernety, an artist, took images from elsewhere and adapted them himself. Intriguingly, like many of the artists behind the *Encyclopédie*, he simplified images of tools and machines, demonstrating a similar commitment to technological rationalism. The Benedictines' decision to use illustrations represented a shift toward a focus on things, and a rejection of the lexical focus of previous French encyclopedias.[15]

Where the Benedictines failed, the *Encyclopédie* succeeded – and it did so with around 2,900 copperplates, thereby becoming the best-illustrated encyclopedia to date. It is futile to try to quantify the amount of information in images, but one could argue that the *Encyclopédie* was a bigger

---

[13] Infelise, "Enciclopedie," 163–9, 179–80.
[14] *Ibid.*, 185–9.
[15] Holmberg, *Maurists' Unfinished Encyclopedia*, 10–11, 132–7, 175–81, 187–8, 213–14, 243–5.

encyclopedia, with its thousands of pictures, than the *Grosses vollständiges Universal-Lexicon* (1732–50), which was textually much longer but barely illustrated.[16]

To a degree, the pictorial aspect of the *Encyclopédie* simply grew with the rest of the work. As of 1745, the publisher Le Breton was planning a five-volume work, the final volume to be taken up with 120 copperplates. By 1751, the prospectus was promising eight volumes of text and two of plates, thus maintaining the balance between text and plates. Thereafter, however, the number of plates grew out of proportion to the quantity of text. In part, publishing plates was a means of generating income and placating subscribers while publication of the textual volumes was being held up by the government. In part, as well, accusations of plagiarism from the forthcoming *Description des arts et métiers* (1761–88) – hardly without merit – pushed Diderot to demonstrate the originality and superiority of the *Encyclopédie*'s plates.[17]

In any event, the *Encyclopédie*'s collection of plates was dwarfed by that of the *Encyclopédie méthodique* (1782–1832), which ended up including around 6,500.[18] This total was the consequence of a gradual expansion, one that paralleled the expansion of the encyclopedia in general, so that, proportionally, the *Méthodique* was less amply illustrated than the *Encyclopédie*. By this criterion, in fact, the *Encyclopédie* was not only better illustrated than any of its predecessors but was also better illustrated than almost any of its successors. Admittedly, its eleven volumes of plates included captions and explanations as well as illustrations, but even on a conservative estimate, roughly a sixth of the *Encyclopédie* was devoted to images.[19] So-called pictorial encyclopedias such as Brockhaus's *Bilder-Atlas zum Conversations-Lexikon* (*Picture Atlas for the Conversational Dictionary*, 1841–4), *I See All* (1928–30), and the *Duden Pictorial Encyclopedia* (1935) obviously had a higher proportion of images, but few other encyclopedias did.

One encyclopedia that came close was Brockhaus's *Konversations-Lexikon* at the start of the twenty-first century, where illustrations were allotted between an eighth and a sixth of the space.[20] Yet, among major encyclopedias, only the *Enciclopedia italiana* (1929–39) seems to have

[16] On the rarity of illustrations in the *Universal-Lexicon* see Siegel, "Orte," 171–9.
[17] Schwab, Rex, and Lough, *Inventory*, VII: 6.
[18] Watts, "*Encyclopédie*," 359.
[19] There were around 17,500 pages of text in the main series and the volumes of plates. The plates were spread over 3,000 leaves, or 6,000 pages, but they were printed on just one side of the page. See Schwab, Rex, and Lough, *Inventory*, I: 45, VII: 40.
[20] Keiderling, "*Brockhaus*," 208.

outdone the *Encyclopédie* in this regard. So suggests, anyway, a sampling of the first 200 pages of Volume XVIII, where illustrations took up more than a third of the space. Here, evidently, the work was taking shape just as the editor, Gentile, had hoped: "In keeping with Italy's heritage, we wanted the encyclopedia to be richly illustrated and speak to the eyes and the imagination as well as the mind, and to reproduce as many as possible of the images described or mentioned."[21]

The *Encyclopédie* may have been better illustrated than almost any subsequent encyclopedia, but it did not end the evolution of illustrated encyclopedias. One of the most visible developments after 1800 was the tendency to place illustrations right in the text instead of on separate pages. Woodcuts had permitted such placement for centuries, but new technologies achieved the same effect with less sacrifice of subtlety. In particular, line-cuts – or wood engravings – were produced with engravers' tools applied at right angles to the grain in extremely hard wood, which allowed details to be rendered more precisely than they had been in woodcuts. Unlike copperplates, significantly, line-cuts were produced in relief and could be printed with text. Along with the *Encyclopédie nouvelle* (1834–42) and the *Nuova enciclopedia popolare* (1841–9), the *Penny Cyclopaedia* (1833–43) was one of the first encyclopedias to benefit.[22] Using line-cuts, the editors were able to put illustrations on a large proportion of pages – on roughly half of the first 100 pages of Volume I, for example, though the proportion had dropped to a quarter by Volume XIII (see Figure 6.5).

Line-cuts and woodcuts retained a significant role in encyclopedias through the end of the century. As late as 1861, for example, the editors of the eighth edition (1853–60) of the *Encyclopaedia Britannica* apologized for the "predominance of woodcuts over engravings" – a necessary imperfection, they asserted, in a work that aspired to be fully illustrated.[23] The *Britannica*'s ninth edition (1875–89) also mixed woodcuts and line-cuts with other kinds of images.[24] Around 1900, however, line-cuts gave way to images produced by photo-mechanical processes. These too could be placed on the same page as texts, though for better effect they were

---

[21] "Secondo il genio italiano abbiamo voluto que l'enciclopedia fosse riccamente illustrata, e parlasse agli occhi e alla fantasia oltre che al pensiero, e presentasse il maggior numero possibile delle immagini che descrive o ricorda." Rovigatti, "Gli anni," 5. I measured images on pp. 1–100 in Volume XVIII, including those on unnumbered sheets.

[22] On line-cuts in the two former works see Hupka, *Wort*, 113.

[23] *Encyclopaedia Britannica*, 8th edition, [xx] (index): "Preface," xxviii.

[24] See Phelps, "*Encyclopaedia*," 58–9; Kruse, "Story," 191.

days, when the species was of common occurrence, it was a practice to run the young birds (before they were able to fly) with greyhounds. So far from this possibility existing with the present remnant of the breed, the young birds, upon being alarmed, constantly squat close to the ground, in the same manner as the young of the lapwing, golden plover, &c., and in that position are frequently taken by hand; indeed this is even the habit of the female during incubation.' Selby's remarks on its powers of flying are corroborated by the 'Booke of Falconrie or Hawking' (1611), where under the head of 'Other flights to the field called great flights,' at p. 83, we find it thus written:—' There is yet another kind of flight to the fielde, called the great flight, as to the cranes, wild geese, bustard, bird of paradise, bittors, shovelars, hearons, and many other such like, and these you may flee from the fist, which is properly tearmed the source. Neverthelesse, in this kind of hawking, which is called the Great Flight, the falcons or other hawks cannot well accomplish their flight at the cranes, bustard, or such like, unlesse they have the helpe of some spaniell, or such dogge, wel inured and taught for that purpose with your hawke. Forasmuch as great flights require pleasant ayde and assistance, yea and that with great diligence.' As an article of food the flesh of the bustard is held in great estimation. It is dark in colour, short in fibre, but sweet and well flavoured. In the last edition of Montagu's Dictionary it is stated, that in 1804 one was shot and taken to Plymouth market, where a publican purchased for a shilling what would have fetched two or three guineas where its value was known. It was however rejected at the second table as improper food, in consequence of the pectoral muscles differing in colour from the other parts of the breast, as in some of the grouse. There were country gentlemen supping at the inn on the following evening, and hearing of the circumstance, they desired that they might be introduced to the princely bird, and partook of it cold at their repast. The bustard seems, with accidental exceptions, to have always brought high prices. We do not indeed find it at the feast given at the 'intronzation' of George Nevell, Archbishop of York, in the reign of Edward IV.; but, if the Earl of Northumberland's household book, it appears among the birds appropriated to his lordship's table; it has no price placed opposite to it, as in the case of all the other birds with one other exception.

[Otis Tarda. Female.]

ASIATIC SPECIES.

We select *Otis nigriceps* as an example. The specimen from which the figure in Mr. Gould's magnificent work ('Century of Birds from the Himalaya Mountains') was taken, was brought from the highlands of the Himalaya; but it is by no means confined to that locality. Col. Sykes observed it in the wide and open country of the Mahrattas, where it lives in large flocks, and where it is considered one of the greatest delicacies as an article of food. It is indeed so abundant in the Deccan, that Col. Sykes records, in the

[Otis Tarda. Male.]

[Otis Nigriceps. Male.]

Figure 6.5   Line-cuts of bustards from the *Penny Cyclopaedia*, Vol. VI. Scanned courtesy of the Louis Round Wilson Special Collections Library of the University of North Carolina at Chapel Hill.

sometimes placed separately on heavier paper – a topic I return to at the end of the section.

In the German states, the Bibliographisches Institut took the lead in bringing illustrations to the *Konversations-Lexikon*. Traveling in England, the Institut's founder, Joseph Meyer, had familiarized himself with the recent American technology of steel engraving. Before trying it in an encyclopedia in 1840, he used it in atlases and an illustrated magazine.[25] By that time, steel plates had already appeared in the *Pfennig Encyclopädie* (*Penny Encyclopedia*, 1834–7), but Meyer did better, setting a record for illustrations in a German encyclopedia with the 1,800 plates in his *Wunder-Meyer* (1840–53).[26] Sensing the public's enthusiasm, the Bibliographisches Institut continued to emphasize the visual in its encyclopedias, though steel plates soon gave way to line-cuts and other types of images.[27] Even after it began delegating the production of images to specialized firms in the late 1800s, the Bibliographisches Institut maintained its reputation as a leader in illustration. The colored plates for the *Espasa* (1908–30), for example, were printed by the Bibliographisches Institut and shipped to Barcelona, until rising costs pushed the Spaniards to take over after World War I.[28]

Brockhaus began experimenting with illustrations in the mid nineteenth century, but its first impulse was to publish pictorial works separately. First came the *Bilder-Conversations-Lexikon* (*Pictorial Conversational Dictionary*, 1837–41) – a small *Konversations-Lexikon* with images in the midst of articles – and then the thematically arranged *Bilder-Atlas* (1841–4). Despite the success of the *Bilder-Atlas*, Brockhaus went on publishing its main encyclopedia without illustrations, in large part to save money. Tellingly, one of the company's first moves after acquiring Ersch and Gruber's *Allgemeine Encyclopädie* in 1831 was to drop illustrations or replace copperplates with images made with lithography – a less expensive new technology in which images were printed from a stone surface after being created there in an oily substance from a drawing or photograph.[29]

Brockhaus's skepticism about illustrations proved to be untenable. Toward the end of the nineteenth century, Meyer's *Konversations-Lexikon* was outselling Brockhaus's by a factor of three to one. Facing decline,

---

[25] Sarkowski, *Bibliographische Institut*, 36–40, 44–50.
[26] On steel plates in the *Pfennig* see Hupka, *Wort*, 115.
[27] Sarkowski, *Bibliographische Institut*, 40.
[28] Castellano, *Enciclopedia*, 118–22, 130, 195–9. On the Institut's delegation of image-production see Jäger, "Lexikonverlag," 545, 563.
[29] Rüdiger, "Ersch/Gruber," 47, 62.

Brockhaus relented and brought in images for its thirteenth edition (1882–7), though they remained separated from articles for the time being.[30] By the early twentieth century, the company had recovered from its visual deficit and was exporting illustrations all over Europe. Indeed, it was able to compensate for lowered demand for encyclopedias during World War I by making maps, just as the Bibliographisches Institut did in World War II.[31]

Delay though it did, Brockhaus was not the last encyclopedia-publisher to adopt illustrations. Another German *Konversations-Lexikon*, Herder's encyclopedia, only took them up in the early twentieth century.[32] José Espasa as well published an unillustrated encyclopedia in 1898, the *Novísimo diccionario enciclopédico*, but he followed it with the *Espasa*, now imitating the model of Meyer and Brockhaus, and reaching out to a public used to illustrated magazines. By this time, illustrations had become a selling point for Spanish encyclopedias in general, though the *Espasa* could boast more than any of its competitors.[33] In any event, while many dictionaries remain unillustrated even today, almost all encyclopedias were illustrated by the early twentieth century. A significant influence in this direction was the *Petit Larousse*. Upon its first appearance in 1905, the *Petit Larousse* offered 5,800 images in a single small volume with 45,000 articles. As a best-seller among works of reference, it demonstrated the potential for an encyclopedia that was illustrated richly and with esthetic charm.[34]

From the beginning, the *Petit Larousse* had illustrations in color – one element of its formula for winning over readers. It was not, however, the first encyclopedia to take up color. In the seventeenth and eighteenth centuries, illustrations were occasionally colored by hand,[35] presumably as gifts for patrons or at the request of the owners. Exceptionally, hand-colored plates were supplied systematically in *Pantologia: A New Cyclopaedia* (1813), in a special edition of the *Encyclopaedia Londinensis* (1810–29), and in a partial edition (1782–1813) of the *Oeconomische Encyclopädie*.[36] Indeed, through the mid nineteenth century, water-colorists were on the payroll of the Bibliographisches Institut. Their job was to highlight borders on maps

---

[30] Hingst, *Geschichte*, 144–5.
[31] Prodöhl, *Politik*, 62–3, 134–42; Jäger, "Lexikonverlag," 562.
[32] Hupka, *Wort*, 116–17.
[33] Castellano, *Enciclopedia*, 106–8, 112, 200, 545–6.
[34] See Mollier and Dubot, *Histoire*, 305–7.
[35] See for example Loveland, "Two Partial English-Language Translations," 173n; Doig, *From Encyclopédie*, 122.
[36] "Dictionaries," 549–50; Fröhner, *Technologie*, 72–3.

in the *Konversations-Lexikon*. Only for the third edition (1874–8) was their labor replaced with a mechanical procedure based on lithography.[37]

More generally, images in encyclopedias began to be colored mechanically in the mid nineteenth century. One of color's main applications, initially, was indicating borders on maps, as in Meyer's *Konversations-Lexikon* and the *Grande Encyclopédie* (1885–1902).[38] Maps were also colored in the ninth edition (1875–89) of the *Encyclopaedia Britannica*, as were a few other plates, but despite being a specialist in illustrations in color, the encyclopedia's publisher, A. and C. Black, did not use them much in the late-nineteenth-century *Britannica*.[39]

In the late nineteenth century, lithography was the normal option for colored images in encyclopedias.[40] In the twentieth century, it was supplanted by "offset" printing, in which the image was printed not from the coated face of a piece of metal or stone but instead from an intermediate one, ordinarily of rubber. Presses designed for offset could make sharper images, and make them faster. The *Grosse Herder* (1931–5), for instance, featured colored plates produced with offset, along with plates made with other techniques, colored and not.

Most of the colored plates in the *Grosse Herder* were tagged with the number of colors used, whether four, five, or "many." As this notation indicates, printing in color required separating an image into constituent colors, usually with a series of optical filters, and printing them separately. The printing, in turn, could be done over continuous areas or as small dots. The latter, "half-tone," procedure, which allowed gray to be simulated with tiny black dots, was important in making printed images affordable in the late nineteenth century. It was thanks to such savings that the illustrations in many encyclopedias were predominantly in color by 1950 – fully 80 percent, for example, in the eighteenth edition (1977–81) of Brockhaus's encyclopedia.[41] Half-tone printing required four colors to create a full spectrum, but encyclopedists sometimes opted for two-color printing for its cheapness and clarity. Through the 1990s, for instance, there were still two-color maps and pictures in *Compton's Encyclopedia* – to the dismay of the American Library Association.[42]

---

[37] Sarkowski, *Bibliographische Institut*, 50, 103.
[38] Hupka, *Wort*, 117; Jacquet-Pfau, "Lexicographie," 37.
[39] Phelps, "*Encyclopaedia*," 59. Volume 1 of the ninth edition had no colored plates that were not also maps.
[40] Keiderling, *F. A. Brockhaus*, 37.
[41] *Ibid.*, 270. On the half-tone process and its inexpensiveness see also Roberto, "Democratising," 72–3.
[42] American Library Association, *Purchasing*, 26–7.

Like printing in color, photography revolutionized the commercial production of images. By the 1860s, illustrators were imitating the style of photographs, as they did, for example, in *Chambers's Encyclopaedia*.[43] A few reproductions of photographs – printed in black and white with the half-tone procedure – appeared in the Italian *Enciclopedia popolare illustrata* (1887–90), but photographs were rare in encyclopedias until around 1900.[44] Thereafter they proliferated, threatening to squeeze out all other images. They were already abundant in the *Espasa* (1908–30), for example.[45] In Herder's *Konversations-Lexikon*, which was only illustrated for the first time with the third edition of 1902–7, photography had become the dominant mode of illustrating by the time of the fourth edition (1931–5).

Color and photography might appeal to the public, but no illustration could be satisfying without the right paper. Better illustrations demanded thicker, glossier paper, partly to keep the image from showing through on the back, partly because printing could create indentations, and partly because glossy paper kept ink on its surface and made it more vivid. Through the early twentieth century, as an accessory to good paper, a protective tissue was sometimes bound next to images to keep them from sticking to the pages that faced them.[46] With or without the tissue, thick paper was expensive, and too much glossiness could create glare and impede the reading of texts.[47] As long as texts and the best-quality images were kept separate in encyclopedias – a typical solution into the twentieth century – each could be printed on its own kind of paper, but efforts were also made to develop a compromise. By the second half of the twentieth century, many encyclopedias were printed, texts and images alike, on just one kind of paper. One reviewer thus credited offset printing with allowing the *American People's Encyclopedia* (1967–74) to "include relatively fine-screen half-tones on dull finish paper."[48]

Paper was not the only surface on which encyclopedias were printed. Cardboard was used for the colored "models" of a dynamo, a horse, a rose, and a steam-turbine in *Nelson's Perpetual Loose-Leaf Encyclopedia* (1909), since they had to survive repeated unfolding to reveal layers of structure. Plastic and other materials were used in transparent "overlays," which became common in encyclopedias in the second half of the century.[49] Like

---

[43] Roberto, "Democratising," 61, 214–17.
[44] Hupka, *Wort*, 20–1, 116–17.
[45] Castellano, *Enciclopedia*, 421.
[46] Sarkowski, *Bibliographische Institut*, 118.
[47] Nault, "Evaluating," 265.
[48] Peche, *Bibliotheca*, 23.
[49] See for example Shiflett, *Louis Shores*, 153; Murray, *Adventures*, 190.

the models in *Nelson's*, overlays allowed viewers to see hidden layers, in this case by turning pages on which the same object was represented at different depths, with some space left transparent so that deeper layers could be seen across shallower ones. Overlays were especially popular in illustrations of human anatomy.

Despite advances in printing and paper-production, quality often suffered as the number of illustrations rose in encyclopedias.[50] Neither line-cuts nor half-tones were designed to be admired in the way that eighteenth-century copperplates or nineteenth-century lithographs were – though cheap illustrations were appreciated by far more people. A great many of the illustrations in the *Espasa*, for example, were mediocre.[51] Similarly, illustrations tended to shrink as they went up in number, particularly in the confines of shorter encyclopedias. The quality of illustrations was limited by other factors as well. Before the mid twentieth century, many editors and publishers saw them as peripheral to encyclopedia-making and therefore unworthy of significant thought or expense. Thus, for the seventh edition (1842) of the *Encyclopaedia Britannica*, the editor, Napier, left decisions about illustrations "almost wholly" to the publishers.[52] Even for *World Book* (1917–18), conceived from the beginning as an illustrated encyclopedia, illustrations were so underbudgeted through the 1950s that they regularly had to be sought out for free.[53]

A few twentieth-century encyclopedias nonetheless won acclaim for their illustrations. Foremost among them was the *Enciclopedia italiana* (1929–39). In the words of one reviewer from 1938, it was "incomparably the most attractively produced and lavishly illustrated of the encyclopedias on the market."[54] On a strictly numerical level, the *Italiana* was less "lavishly" illustrated than some later encyclopedias. All told, it offered around 30,000 illustrations, versus 40,000, for instance, in the twenty-first edition (2005–6) of Brockhaus's *Konversations-Lexikon*.[55] Still, the illustrations in the *Italiana* were much bigger, on the average, than the ones in any edition of Brockhaus's encyclopedia. In addition, many of them were printed on thick, glossy paper and with good resolution.

The *Italiana* had illustrations of various kinds, but by far the most space was allotted to black-and-white photographs. In this sense, it was already

[50] Hupka, *Wort*, 118.
[51] Castellano, *Enciclopedia*, 202–3.
[52] *Encyclopaedia Britannica*, 7th edn., 1: xlii–xliii.
[53] Murray, *Adventures*, 194–7.
[54] Foligno, review, 446.
[55] Schafroth, "*Enciclopedia*," 410.

old-fashioned within a decade of being completed, for color was by then taking encyclopedias over. As this observation indicates, encyclopedia-publishers issuing multiple editions had to redo their illustrations at regular intervals because of new technologies for capturing the visual.[56] In other words, just as entries in encyclopedias had to be updated in light of advances in knowledge, illustrations had to be updated for the same reason, but they also required updating for technical reasons. Wear, too, made it necessary to replace illustrations, notably woodcuts.[57] Illustrations, in short, were at risk of being dated on several grounds. Consumers, consequently, could use them as a proxy for an encyclopedia's up-to-dateness.[58] Conversely, encyclopedia-makers that kept abreast of means of illustrating played up their know-how. In 1906, an advertisement for *Nelson's Encyclopaedia* thus included the following, representative statement: "The illustrations are especially attractive, every branch of the engraver's art having been brought into use: colored plates, half-tones, maps in black and white and in color, zinc etchings, wood cuts, etc."[59]

To a large extent, illustration-making was technologically driven, like printing in general. As a result, its story in encyclopedism is one that fits well into a narrative of progress. On the one hand, in a progression that stretched into the twentieth century, more encyclopedias were illustrated from decade to decade, and they were more abundantly illustrated, while on the other hand, they incorporated color and acquired the capacity to reproduce photographs. Not all encyclopedias, however, were committed to illustration or able to invest in it. Furthermore, technological progress was not without drawbacks. Early enthusiasm for photography, in particular, ended up being tempered in the second half of the twentieth century. Already at mid-century, the editor of *Collier's Encyclopedia* announced that despite a policy of giving preference to photographs, paintings had been commissioned to represent animals, and only "schematic ... line drawings" were clear enough for some scientific fields.[60] Likewise, in the *Petit Larousse*, photographs were substituted for drawings in the mid twentieth century, but many photographs had been replaced by drawings and diagrams as of 1981, apparently to make the illustrations more pedagogical.[61]

---

[56] See for example Keiderling, "Lexikonverlag," 446–7; Peche, *Bibliotheca*, 435.
[57] See for example the criticism in Doig *et al.*, "James Tytler's Edition," 145; "Cyclopaedia Illustrations," 10–11.
[58] Katz, *Basic Information Sources*, 145.
[59] *New York Times*, June 4, 1906: 4.
[60] *Collier's Encyclopedia* (1950), 1: vi.
[61] Pruvost, "Illustration," 749–50. See also Lamoureux, "Médium," 187–92.

Reasons for Illustration

Some encyclopedists wanted their works to be illustrated but could not persuade publishers. The *Lexicon Technicum* (1704) had illustrations, for example, but not as many as Harris had hoped for.[62] Indeed, all through the history of the European encyclopedia, irrespective of progress in their production and printing, illustrations cost publishers more than comparably sized texts.[63] A determination to expand texts without expanding an encyclopedia could also put illustrations in danger of cutbacks. The editors of the one-volume *Columbia Encyclopedia* (1935) thus dispensed with all illustrations to save space and money, though they ended up publishing a separate pictorial encyclopedia for the second edition (1950), the *Columbia Encyclopedia Supplement of Illustrations* (1956).[64]

The ambivalence of the *Columbia* raises a question. Given space and a budget, were illustrations worth including rather than, say, more, larger, articles? One answer – albeit a more and more marginal one – was that they were not, or not for the most part. Just as Harris mocked French encyclopedists for telling readers what a dog, a cat, a horse, and a sheep were, Pierre Larousse mocked fellow encyclopedist Jean-François Dupiney de Vorepierre for depicting a donkey in his *Dictionnaire français illustré* (1863). More generally, Larousse made fun of Dupiney's whole project of illustrating an encyclopedia: "The encyclopedic part … strikes the eye with the wealth it lays out: engravings! engravings!"[65] Larousse considered images costly and cumbersome.[66] Accordingly, he published his *Grand Dictionnaire* (1866–76) with few of them except for headpieces at the start of the sections for "A," "B," and so on. Most of the non-decorative illustrations were diagrams, but two portraits of Napoleon, exceptionally, appeared in the article "Bonaparte."[67] Ironically, a picture of the donkey appeared in the *Petit Larousse* (1905), thirty years after Pierre's death.[68] By then, the Larousse company had become famous for its illustrations.

A more typical attitude was that encyclopedias should be illustrated, but only for instructional purposes, not entertainment. Some of those responsible

---

[62] Harris, *Lexicon*, I: b1v.
[63] See for example Nault, "Evaluating," 262–3.
[64] For the rationale for cutting illustrations see *Columbia Encyclopedia*, 1st edn., "Preface."
[65] "La partie encyclopédique … frappe l'oeil par le luxe qu'elle étale: des gravures! des gravures!" Larousse, *Grand Dictionnaire*, I: xlv. For Harris's mockery see Harris, *Lexicon*, I: a2r.
[66] Mollier and Dubot, *Histoire*, 324–5.
[67] Larousse, ed., *Grand Dictionnaire*, II: 925, 929.
[68] Pruvost, "Illustration," 743.

for alphabetical encyclopedias were fervent believers in the educational power of images – Knight, for example, who published the richly illustrated *Penny Magazine* and *Penny Cyclopaedia* (1833–43).[69]

For the pedagogically inclined, one rationale for illustration was the difficulty of characterizing objects or concepts without it. According to Locke's *Essay Concerning Humane Understanding* (1690), certain ideas were beyond definition, whether because of their simplicity, their susceptibility to different analyses, or human ignorance.[70] Along with a more general tendency toward empirical thinking, Locke's ideas may have been a factor in the early adoption of illustrations in British encyclopedias and dictionaries.[71] Certainly Locke saw the advantages of a dictionary with "little drafts or prints," insisting that "the shape of a horse or cassowary will be but rudely and imperfectly imprinted on the mind by words; the sight of the animals does it a thousand times better."[72] As examples of things that a dictionary should illustrate, Locke cited not only animals but also plants, musical instruments, and articles of clothing.[73] These were all kinds of things that encyclopedias would soon devote images to. Without naming Locke, encyclopedists such as Diderot and Larousse echoed his complaints about definitions. For Diderot, if not Larousse, this was an argument for illustrations.[74]

In 1996, the historian Randall Stross mourned the rise of multimedia in electronic encyclopedias as "one small, and late, chapter" in the establishment of an impatient, visually preoccupied Age of Entertainment.[75] Whether or not they bred impatience, illustrations in encyclopedias had long served esthetic as well as pedagogical goals. One of the anatomical plates in the *Encyclopédie* (1751–72) thus pictured a skeleton holding a shovel (see Figure 6.6), in imitation of Andreas Vesalius's famous design, and in conformity with the artistic genre of the *memento mori* ("remember that you have to die").[76] Indeed, in his prospectus of 1751, besides insisting on the need for images to avoid vagueness and obscurity, Diderot stressed the capacity of the *Encyclopédie*'s plates to arouse curiosity, and bragged that they were more beautiful than Chambers' plates.[77]

[69] Gray, *Charles Knight*, 8, 30–5, 56–7, 62–3.
[70] McLaverty, "From Definition," 384–6.
[71] Hupka, *Wort*, 92–4.
[72] Locke, *Essay*, ii: 159, 163 (Book iii, Chapter 11, §§21, 25).
[73] *Ibid.*, ii: 163–4 (Book iii, Chapter 11, §25).
[74] [Diderot], prospectus, 5; Pruvost, "Illustration," 747–8.
[75] Stross, *Microsoft Way*, 92–3.
[76] Stewart, "Illustrations," 73–5, 91–3.
[77] [Diderot], prospectus, 5–6.

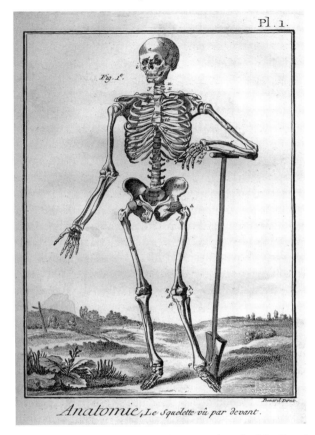

Figure 6.6   Image of a skeleton from the "new edition" of the *Encyclopédie*
published by Pellet in 1777–80. Scanned courtesy of the Archives and Rare
Books Library, University of Cincinnati.

Many subsequent encyclopedia-makers treated beauty as something
aspired to in their own illustrations. In his preface and article "Enciclopedia"
for the *Enciclopedia italiana* (1929–39), for instance, Gentile stated that
illustrations were chosen for esthetic as well as documentary reasons.[78] The
sixth edition (1902–8) of Meyer's *Konversations-Lexikon* expressed a nearly
identical policy.[79] More coyly, the preface to Spain's *Gran enciclopedia*

[78] Rovigatti, "Gli anni," 5.
[79] [*Meyer's Konversations-Lexikon*], 6th edn., 1: VII.

Rialp (1971) stated that the illustrations were not included for decorative purposes alone.[80]

Reviewers, for their part, often praised encyclopedias' illustrations for their esthetic value – or decried them as unappealing. Indeed, by the mid nineteenth century, as encyclopedias began to be marketed to less privileged readers, critics' admiration for images could turn into suspicion or scorn, for one person's beautiful image was another person's tasteless or titillating one. Associated with periodicals, mechanically produced images were seen by some as symptomatic of cultural decline.

One man convinced of the sensationalism and irrelevance of most illustrations was Febvre, the original editor of the *Encyclopédie française* (1935–66). Here he promised purely instructional illustrations, notably diagrams and black-and-white pictures. He also planned to steer clear of "these marvelous images in color" – perhaps an allusion to Larousse's encyclopedias.[81] More generally, he encouraged mistrust of the visual, which in his view "invades everything nowadays and … misleads the simple, bedazzles the weak, and diverts from their normal path even minds capable of a sound response."[82] In the end, while the *Encyclopédie française* was somberly illustrated, it did contain color, and it did feature images that might be judged decorative – for example, a picture of a mask from the Ivory Coast at the start of Volume vii, before the main text began.

The opposition between decorative and explanatory images was a truism of discourse about encyclopedias. On the one hand, encyclopedists claimed that their own illustrations explained things. Sometimes they went farther, insisting that their illustrations had no other function. Meanwhile, on the other hand, they accused rivals or forebears of offering illustrations that were merely ornamental. Both kinds of judgments were evidently exaggerated.

Just as importantly, the opposition neglects other ways illustrations could function. In particular, two of their other functions in medieval Christian manuscripts are relevant to encyclopedias.[83] First, they could have a localizing function, helping readers recognize pages and situate their reading. Second, illustrations in an encyclopedia could have a dignifying function. Seen in this light, the ornate letters and headpieces separating the sections of encyclopedias were not just decorations but also ceremonial

---

[80] *Gran enciclopedia*, i: viii.
[81] Febvre, "Encyclopédie," cahier 4, 13; Febvre, introduction to Vol. vi, cahier 4, 9–10.
[82] "… envahit tout aujourd'hui et … égare les simples, hallucine les faibles et détourne même de leur voie normale des esprits capables d'une saine réplique." Febvre, introduction to Vol. vi, cahier 4, 9.
[83] See Illich, *In the Vineyard*, 107–10.

markers. In addition, as a study of the *Petit Larousse* (1905) has concluded, illustrations could function as appeals to emotion or as devices for "lightening" the page.[84]

This last function – creating a pleasing layout – is attested by how illustrations were distributed, as well as by comments from editors and publishers. In many encyclopedias, illustrations were distributed more regularly than if they had been inserted at random, as if editors were under orders to avoid too many pictureless pages. So they were in some cases. In the 1960 edition of *World Book*, for example, every "major article running a page or longer" was to have a full-page illustration. Illustrations were in fact provided in 79 percent of all articles.[85] However unfair, a critique of *Johnson's New Universal Cyclopaedia* (1875–7) is suggestive of readers' expectations by the late nineteenth century: "Nowhere does the tired eye light on a relieving and helpful illustration."[86]

The emotional function of images is borne out, for its part, by a pamphlet touting the illustrations in the *American Cyclopaedia* (1873–6) against those in *Johnson's*. In an era in which images enjoyed the allure of scarcity, the pamphlet pointed out that one could get textual information from friends or a "post-office directory," but not illustrations. More importantly, it argued, most people cared less about an encyclopedia's articles than they did about its pictures. This claim was speculative, but as shown in Chapter 9, it finds support in stories about how people used encyclopedias. So does the pamphlet's suggestion that illustrations in encyclopedias helped awaken curiosity.[87] The backers of *Johnson's*, on the contrary, cast scorn on curiosity aroused by the visual: "Bird's-eye views of cities and meager and inaccurate maps … are of no other use than to amuse children, and they cannot have been put into a cyclopedia for any other purpose than to catch the eye and form a bait for the ignorant."[88]

Subjects and Styles

Whatever their functions, illustrations in encyclopedias can be categorized by their subjects. The most important of these categories will be covered in the following paragraphs, in roughly the order of their appearance in encyclopedias.

[84] Lamoureux, "Médium," 181–2, 196–8.
[85] Murray, *Adventures*, 196; Coyne, "Effects," 36, 49.
[86] "Cyclopaedia Illustrations," 3. See also the analysis in Rivalan Guégo *et al.*, *Gran enciclopedia*, 78.
[87] "Cyclopaedia Illustrations," 2.
[88] "Reply," 19.

Among the earliest illustrations in encyclopedias were frontispieces, vignettes, and diagrams. Frontispieces appeared in many encyclopedias through the early nineteenth century. They were often allegorical. Even the eminently practical *Curieuses Natur- Kunst- Gewerck- und Handlungs-Lexicon* (1712) included a frontispiece featuring Minerva and Mercury, the latter symbolizing trade and perhaps also the trade in knowledge in which encyclopedists were involved.[89] For the frontispiece of the *Cyclopaedia* (1728), Chambers and his publishers adapted an etching (1698) by Sébastien Le Clerc depicting ancient scholars engaged in learned activities. With alterations – notably the addition of a hot-air balloon late in the century – the same frontispiece appeared in several eighteenth-century encyclopedias: Coetlogon's *Universal History* (1745), Rees's revised *Cyclopaedia* (1778–88), Howard and others' *New Royal Cyclopaedia* (1788), Hall's *New Royal Encyclopaedia* (1788), and the third edition (1797) of the *Encyclopaedia Britannica* (see Figure 6.7).[90]

Alternatively, a frontispiece could be a portrait, typically of a deceased or venerable author. The frontispiece to Coronelli's *Biblioteca* (1701–6) showed him presenting the encyclopedia to Pope Clement XI, to whom it was dedicated. Furetière's *Dictionaire* (1690) – which was posthumous – depicted its author in a frontispiece, as did the [*New*] *Cyclopaedia* (1819–20), though Rees was still living. The *Oeconomische Encyclopädie* (1773–1858) had frontispieces in the first 187 volumes as well as the last one, Volume CCXLII. All of them were portraits, and most were of Prussian aristocrats known for practical achievements – an apt set of patrons for a utilitarian encyclopedia. Krünitz put in his own portrait in Volume XIII.[91]

Opening portraits and other frontispieces were in decline by the early nineteenth century. In the *Britannica*, for instance, the third edition's frontispiece lingered for the next several editions, but the publishers of the seventh edition (1842) neither reused nor replaced it, and no further frontispieces ever appeared. Allegory was less appreciated than it had been before, patronage mattered less to encyclopedias' success, and the authors and editors of encyclopedias were becoming less recognizable and less worthy of portraits.

At the same time, the retreat of illustrations from the front matter of encyclopedias represented a new seriousness. In dispensing with a

[89] Schneider, *Erfindung*, 207–16.
[90] Loveland, *Alternative Encyclopedia?*, 55; Doig *et al.*, "Colin Macfarquhar," 166–8; Yeo, *Encyclopaedic Visions*, 236. For an analysis of the frontispieces in several eighteenth-century encyclopedias see Yeo, *Encyclopaedic Visions*, xiv, 120–1, 138–9, 236–8.
[91] Fröhner, *Technologie*, 99–106.

Figure 6.7   Frontispiece for the third edition of the *Encyclopaedia Britannica*.
Scanned by the author from his copy.

frontispiece or decoration at the start of the *Espasa* (1908–30), for example, the editors were following their German models, but they were also trying to make the *Espasa* look sober and rigorous.[92] Such sobriety was the rule

[92] Castellano, *Enciclopedia*, 138, 416, 464.

Figure 6.8　The title page of the *Nouveau Larousse illustré* (1897–1904).
Photographed by the author from his copy.

among twentieth-century encyclopedias, though decoration persisted in
the form of discreet symbols, later protected as trademarks. In 1890, the
Larousse firm acquired its famous image of a woman blowing dandelion-
seeds, which was meant to represent the dissemination of language and
knowledge (see Figure 6.8).[93] For its logo, the *Espasa* used an image of
Athena, the Greek goddess of wisdom and war. The choice seems to
have reflected the dream of turning Barcelona into a modern-day Athens
that could lead the Hispanic world in the fight against ignorance.[94] The
Britannica began using a stylized thistle, an emblem of Scotland, as an
element of decoration in 1929.[95]

[93] Lamoureux, "Médium," 178.
[94] Castellano, *Enciclopedia*, 129, 136–7.
[95] *Changing Times* 22 (November 1968): 24.

Besides vignettes and frontispieces, there was another kind of illustration that lacked any relationship with particular articles: the ornamental letter, used for introducing the keywords that began with a given letter. An ornamental letter could be little more than an oversized letter in an unusual font, but it could also depict objects whose names began with that letter. In the *Encyclopédie*, for the example, the decorative "C" preceding the keywords starting with "C" had a chemist inside it. Elaborating on the idea, certain headpieces, or introductory images, presented a collection of objects whose names began with the letter that was being introduced. Such decoration was widespread in nineteenth- and twentieth-century France, notably in Larousse's encyclopedias (see Figure 6.9).[96] In the period from 1925 to 1947, the headpiece for the letter "C" in the *Petit Larousse* included sixty-odd objects whose names began with "C." Nor were such puzzles confined to popular encyclopedias. Even the self-consciously serious *Grande Encyclopédie* (1885–1902) incorporated them into headpieces.[97]

In some encyclopedias, the illustrations went little beyond frontispieces, vignettes, and decorative letters, but such encyclopedias grew rare after the mid nineteenth century. By then, the dominant illustrations were the ones explicitly connected with one or more articles. These are my subject for the rest of the section.

The most common illustrations in seventeenth- and eighteenth-century encyclopedias were diagrams. Distinguishing diagrams from other illustrations is in some cases difficult, but diagrams represent things from a more abstract viewpoint. Examples of diagrams in the period's encyclopedias include trees of knowledge, genealogical and geometrical diagrams, fragmented representations of devices and processes, and diagrams of formations such as that of the Reichs-Tag ("Imperial Assembly") in Jablonski's *Allgemeines Lexicon* (1721) and the *Grosses vollständiges Universal-Lexicon* (1732–50) (see Figure 6.10).[98]

Geometrical diagrams were among the most frequent. They dominated the plates in Chauvin's *Lexicon* (1692) and Chambers' *Cyclopaedia*, as well as the woodcuts in Harris's *Lexicon* (1704) and the *Allgemeines Lexicon*. Geometrical reasoning was fundamental to contemporary mathematics. Only late in the eighteenth century did Joseph-Louis Lagrange announce, famously, that he had written a mathematical book without any diagrams.[99]

---

[96] Male, "Ornamental Illustrations." On France's unique cultivation of such decoration see *ibid.*, 78.
[97] See *ibid.*, 41n, 52–3.
[98] On this last diagram see [Jablonski], *Allgemeines Lexicon*, 611; Siegel, "Orte," 172–3.
[99] Hankins, *Science*, 29.

Figure 6.9   Headpiece from the 1923 edition of the *Petit Larousse illustré*. Photographed by the author from his copy. With permission from Larousse. © Larousse.

Under these circumstances, diagrams were critical for communicating mathematical knowledge. Geometrical images were sometimes mixed with representations of non-mathematical objects – for example, with views of the eye and other organs, or with depictions of mechanical devices. Indeed, the boundary between geometrical and technological diagrams was fluid, and all four of the encyclopedias mentioned above featured diagrams of experimental instruments, designed to draw attention to their operation and structure.

In addition to geometrical and technological diagrams, which made up nearly all of Chauvin's illustrations, Harris, Jablonski, and Chambers offered heraldic images, mostly coats of arms. In some encyclopedias, such images had a strategic function. In the *Universal-Lexicon*, for example, coats of arms – along with opening portraits and genealogical trees – were included as a way of engaging or expressing gratitude to patrons. Indeed, the editor, Ludovici, invited nobles to send in copperplates displaying their families' genealogical trees – along with payment, he stipulated, to cover the extra cost of printing the plates in the encyclopedia. In the

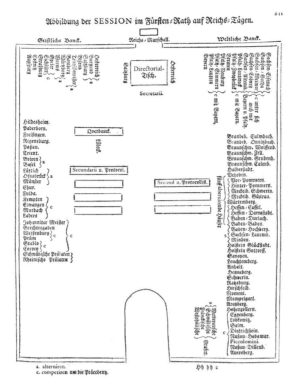

Figure 6.10   Diagram of seating for rulers of the Holy Roman Empire, from Jablonski's *Allgemeines Lexicon*. Scanned courtesy of the Louis Round Wilson Special Collections Library of the University of North Carolina at Chapel Hill.

end, the *Universal-Lexicon* had five fold-out genealogical trees, as well as representations of two coats of arms.[100]

Unlike the *Universal-Lexicon*, dictionaries of the arts and sciences did not have biographical articles, but at times they mentioned specific nobles and depicted their imagery in articles on the elements of coats of arms. The article "Clarion" in the *Lexicon Technicum* was thus illustrated with a coat of arms identified as belonging to the "earl of Bath, by the name of

---

[100]   Siegel, "Orte," 174–6; Schneider, *Erfindung*, 108; Löffler, "Wer schrieb den Zedler?," 276–7.

Greenvile."[101] Many heraldic images in dictionaries of the arts and sciences were generic, however. Nor did the accompanying articles usually refer to families or individuals. In fact, the primary reason for the images of heraldry in seventeenth- and eighteenth-century encyclopedias was the works' upper-class readership, a group with a strong interest in the trappings of nobility. Lastly, the fact that Harris illustrated heraldry in the *Lexicon Technicum* probably encouraged his successors to do so.

Technology was another subject that gained an early foothold in encyclopedias' imagery. Whereas previous encyclopedias had focused on technologies of use to the experimenter, the *Encyclopédie* devoted more than half its plates to the mechanical arts in general, displaying the operations of book-binding, tanning, sugar-refining, and pin-making, among many others. Indeed, the main discussion of illustrations in the prospectus came in the context of the mechanical arts. Here Diderot argued that illustrations were needed to make the mechanical arts understandable. Certain movements performed by workers in the course of their labors were hard to explain, for example, but easy to show.[102]

In keeping with the *Encyclopédie*'s goal of making the mechanical arts transparent and thereby improvable, Diderot and his artists chose an analytical style of illustrating. In a typical technological plate, the tools of an art appeared neatly arranged against a blank background, while one or more accompanying images showed workers engaged in different steps of the art (see Figure 6.11). Skeptics of the idea of covering technology in encyclopedias were harsh in their judgments. Commenting on plates in the *Complete Dictionary of Arts and Sciences* (1764–6) taken from the *Encyclopédie*, one reviewer observed, "They give not only common tools, as files, hammers, and shears, but a perspective view of tradesmen's shops, where perhaps you see the maker trying a pair of shoes on the feet of the wearer, or a boy turning a wheel for grinding razors; all [of] which may do very well to amuse children."[103]

Compared to most preceding and subsequent ones, the *Encyclopédie*'s illustrations of the mechanical arts were utopian. Not only were workers depicted as self-absorbed and almost dispossessed of individual identity, but their workplaces were unrealistically spacious and clean.[104] In addition

---

[101] Harris, *Lexicon*, I: s3v.
[102] [Diderot], prospectus, 5–6.
[103] Review of *Complete Dictionary*, 5.
[104] Sewell, "Visions." See also Proust, *Marges*.

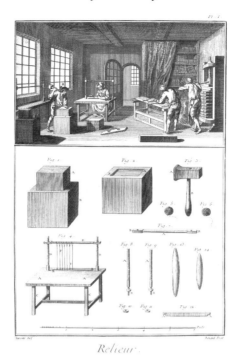

Figure 6.11   Plate showing book-binders and their tools, from the *Encyclopédie*.
Scanned courtesy of the Archives and Rare Books Library, University of Cincinnati.

to promoting an analytical perspective, these distortions had ideological value. In the interpretation of William Sewell, they anticipated a later world in which workers, removed from guilds and interpersonal companionship, were subordinated to the ends of science-based industry.[105]

Besides encouraging images of the mechanical arts, henceforth widespread in the European encyclopedia, the *Encyclopédie* participated in a movement among contemporary encyclopedias to introduce illustrations of plants and animals. Such illustrations were rare before the 1740s. Plants and animals were already covered amply in French and German encyclopedias, but without illustrations. By contrast, British dictionaries of the arts and sciences were pictorially rich but barely touched on plants

---

[105] Sewell, "Visions," 276–9.

or animals, perhaps because natural history seemed more like a kind of history – unsystematic and fact-filled – than a true art or science. Harris, for example, insisted that "the bare names of animals and vegetables" were not technical terms and thus did not belong in his *Lexicon Technicum*.[106] The first encyclopedia to depict plants and animals abundantly was Pivati's *Nuovo dizionario* (1746–51). Soon afterward, British encyclopedists began doing so too, thanks to the example of the *Supplement to Mr. Chambers's Cyclopaedia* (1753), where thousands of articles and ten of twelve plates were devoted to plants and animals.[107] In France, the *Encyclopédie* and then the *Encyclopédie méthodique* (1782–1832) shattered all records for the illustration of living beings. The former had more than 150 plates depicting plants and animals, and the latter more than 2,400.[108]

Plants and animals continued to be profusely illustrated, especially in popular encyclopedias and those meant for the young. In the *Penny Cyclopaedia* (1833–43) and *Chambers's Encyclopaedia* (1868), they were the object of between a third and half of the illustrations.[109] Likewise, they were frequently pictured in the *Petit Larousse*. In the fifth edition (1906), a third of the illustrations were thus of whole plants or animals, and another tenth of plants and animals in partial or schematic views. The proportions were similar in 2007.[110] In encyclopedias focused on knowledge unique to a nation, plants and animals could go farther in dominating imagery. They were the object of more than 50 percent of the illustrations in the *Australian Encyclopaedia* (1925–6), for instance.[111]

In Volume xv of the *Grande Encyclopédie* (1885–1902), only an eighth of the illustrations in the first 100 pages were devoted to whole plants and animals, but another sixth showed them in partial views. The bee, for example, was not represented naturalistically in the article on the subject, as it was in the *Penny Cyclopaedia* and in numerous editions of the *Petit Larousse*. Instead, the article in the *Grande Encyclopédie* offered images of the bee's head, among other parts, and diagrams of its circulatory and respiratory systems (see Figure 6.12). This approach to living beings as

---

[106] Harris, *Lexicon*, 1: a2r.
[107] Plates 2–11 dealt wholly with plants and animals, while Plate 1 did in part. See also Loveland, "Animals," 514–15.
[108] Schwab, Rex, and Lough, *Inventory*, vii: 145–60; Doig, *From Encyclopédie*, 72–73, 85.
[109] Roberto, "Democratising," 123–5. Many of the "medical" images concerned animals.
[110] In both editions, I sampled pp. 700–99.
[111] Kavanagh, *Conjuring*, 142.

Figure 6.12   Diagrammatic and partial views of the bee in the *Grande Encyclopédie*. Photographed by the author courtesy of Langsam Library, University of Cincinnati.

subjects for imagery mirrored the encyclopedia's intellectual ambitions, while the pictures of whole plants and animals in the *Penny Cyclopaedia* and the *Petit Larousse* were designed to satisfy curiosity and communicate less specialized knowledge.

Regardless of their purposes, images of plants and animals were abundant in encyclopedias from the mid eighteenth century onward – a fact that invites explanation. Why not lavish as much attention on images of towns, say, or mountains? Much of the emphasis was inherited. The European encyclopedia grew up in a world where people lived with and depended on plants and animals, where they gardened and went to zoos, where they craved the exotic, and where Europe's artists had already consecrated plants and animals as worth depicting. Encyclopedists, moreover, were quick to take advantage of available material, and images of living beings were there for the taking. Finally, it may be that plants and animals are inherently salient in our perception.[112] In a similar vein, humans' attraction to faces helps explain the success of portraits once they entered encyclopedias in the early nineteenth century. By contrast, Brockhaus's experiment with hand-written signatures by noteworthy people proved to be short-lived, confined to the fifteenth edition (1928–35) of its *Konversations-Lexikon*, where they were reproduced alongside biographies.[113] A signature, like a portrait, offered a visual suggestion of an individual's personality, but on a cognitive level it was much less appealing.

In the 1700s already, encyclopedias offered portraits, but almost never for articles on individuals. In this respect, they were behind certain biographical collections – notably Paulus Freher's illustrated *Theatrum virorum eruditione singulari clarorum* (*Theater of Famous Men of Great Learning*, 1688) – though it is worth noting that even the *Dictionary of National Biography* (1885–1900) and the *Allgemeine deutsche Biographie* (*General German Biography*, 1875–1912) appeared without illustrations. Before the mid nineteenth century, many of the portraits in encyclopedias were in fact presented as antiquities or objects of art. Like other articles on cities in Pivati's *Nuovo dizionario*, for instance, the article "Venezia" provided illustrations of the city's architectural monuments, including statues and reliefs representing famous Venetians. The article "Cardinale," for its part, included illustrations of generic and specific ancient cardinals, reproduced from medals and other antiquities, while the article "Religione" included an image of Confucius (see Figure 6.13).

The association of portraits with art and antiquities meant that they tended to depict people from long-ago epochs. In encyclopedias, the correlation held through the early nineteenth century. In the *Encyclopédie méthodique*, for example, the volume of plates on antiquities (1804) featured numerous portraits of ancient notables, whereas the encyclopedia's main stock of biographies, in the sub-series *Histoire* (1784–1804), had no illustrations. One factor was availability. While portraits of public figures

---

[112] Corbin, "Image-outil," 261.

[113] For examples see [*Grosse Brockhaus*], 15th edn., xviii: 130, 133, 135. Neither the fourteenth (1892–5) nor the sixteenth (1952–7) edition featured such signatures. On the Brockhaus family's collection of autographs see Keiderling, *F. A. Brockhaus*, 258.

J Dei dei Cinesi cavati dalla Cina d.l Chirchero.

Figure 6.13   Image of Chinese "gods," including Confucius, in Pivati's *Nuovo dizionario*,
Vol. VIII. Scanned courtesy of the Houghton Library, Harvard University.

from classical antiquity were widely available and could often be copied from medals or coins, portraits of more recent notables were rarer until around 1850. For the *Biographie universelle* (1812–28), a biographical encyclopedia, the publishers made a deal to supply subscribers willing to pay extra with 900 portraits adapted from the collection of the painter Charles-Paul Landon.[114] In his quest to include artwork in the *Penny Cyclopaedia* (1833–43) and other works, the publisher Knight also arranged for support from collectors, who allowed his artists to access their private galleries. By this means, he became the first to reproduce certain portraits, though he used them infrequently in the *Penny Cyclopaedia*, preferring instead to emphasize other kinds of images.[115]

Even when portraits appeared in encyclopedias' biographical articles, ancient relics and masterpieces maintained their priority as sources for many years, presumably once again for reasons of cost. Volume XXIV of the *Grande Encyclopédie* (1885–1902), for example, had a thirty-page article on Napoleon Bonaparte, but the volume's only illustrated biography was the much shorter one on the Roman emperor Nero, which included a sketch from a bust in the Louvre.[116] Ironically, just a few decades earlier, the *Wunder-Meyer* (1840–53) had provided more than fifty illustrations of the "hero of modern times" intermixed with the text of the article "Bonaparte" – a rare departure from the work's usual practice of confining images to separate pages.[117]

In its opening volumes, the *Encyclopédie nouvelle* (1834–42) took a more consistent approach to biographical portraits. The work's original title was *Encyclopédie pittoresque*, which signaled an emphasis on the pictorial in general. The *Pittoresque* offered illustrations in dozens of biographical articles, many on people deceased after 1700. Volume I, for example, featured eleven portraits of such people, including one of Tsar Alexander I of Russia, who had only died in 1825. The encyclopedia soon changed direction, however. At the end of the installments for Volume II, the editors Leroux and Reynaud changed the title to *Encyclopédie nouvelle*, no longer wishing to associate with popular enthusiasm for images, and aspiring toward a grander, more philosophical encyclopedism.[118] Illustrations dwindled in subsequent volumes, and had all but disappeared by the start of Volume V.

---

[114] Chappey, *Ordres*, 71.
[115] On Knight's reproduction of portraits see Gray, *Charles Knight*, 62–3.
[116] *Grande Encyclopédie: Inventaire*, XXIV: 960.
[117] "… Heros der neuen Zeit." [*Meyer's Konversations-Lexikon*], "0th" edn., V: 1.
[118] Griffiths, *Jean Reynaud*, 124, 134, 153–4.

In the *Wunder-Meyer* (1840–53) as well, portraits were advertised on the title page and devoted to such recent figures as the celebrities of the revolutions of 1848.[119] Meyer's ownership of an illustrated magazine and an album of portraits helped him come up with affordable pictures. Having examined the first 12 of the 800 plates in the *Wunder-Meyer*, Meyer's rival Heinrich Pierer wrote that most of them were merely decorative images of people, places, and "the like," and that most had been reproduced from Meyer's previous publications.[120]

Just as it took encyclopedias other than historical dictionaries decades to take in biographies, despite the early lead of the *Grosses vollständiges Universal-Lexicon* (1732–50), many nineteenth-century encyclopedists ignored the example of the *Encyclopédie nouvelle* and the *Wunder-Meyer* in the matter of portraits. Instead, they reserved illustrations for non-biographical subjects or allowed them for just a tiny number of biographical articles. In the early twentieth century, at last, encyclopedias began to offer illustrated biographies as a matter of course. One influence in this direction was the *Petit Larousse*. Already in the first edition of 1905, it had 700 portraits among its 6,000 images. Conversely, despite the example of the unauthorized *New American Supplement to … the Encyclopaedia Britannica* (1897), which offered hundreds of portraits, the *Britannica* was a laggard in this respect, disdaining illustrated biographies through the early 1920s and only fitfully providing them in the fourteenth edition (1929).[121] If the days were gone in which Pierer could dismiss portraits as decoration, their presence in encyclopedias remained hard to rationalize, as suggested by this statement in the twentieth-century *Encyclopedia Americana*: "Photographs reveal … the personalities of people."[122]

Related to portraits were encyclopedias' images of places, often cities or landscapes. Such illustrations had a long history in other books, but they came late to encyclopedias. Here again, Pivati's *Nuovo dizionario* (1746–51) was an innovator, boasting as it did dozens of views of cities and their monuments, views that only became common in encyclopedias after 1800.

---

[119] Peche, *Bibliotheca*, 366.

[120] [*Pierer's Universal-Lexikon*], 2nd edn., 1: XLV. See also Sarkowski, *Bibliographische Institut*, 72.

[121] I found no illustrated biographies in Volume XII of the ninth edition (1875–89), Volume X of the eleventh edition (1910), or Volume II of the twelfth edition (1921–2).

[122] *Encyclopedia Americana: International Edition*, 1: vi.

Another approach to geographical representation was through maps and diagrams. Concrete in its geographical imagery, the *Nuovo dizionario* did not take this approach, but the *Encyclopédie* did. Specifically, it offered ten maps of Asia, the Arctic, and North America, thereby becoming the first encyclopedia to be furnished with maps. It also provided naturalistic depictions of places, notably mines and remarkable landscapes, but it was illustrated more abstractly than the *Nuovo dizionario*.

Unlike Pivati's panoramas of cities, the *Encyclopédie*'s maps initiated an immediate trend. Within a decade, maps were appearing in other encyclopedias. Already in the first edition (1771) of the *Britannica*, there was a reasonably comprehensive collection of maps, namely of five continents. More dramatically, in 1771, a prospectus was published in Monaco for a new edition of the *Encyclopédie*, which would have been provided with some 400 maps.[123] In the nineteenth century, encyclopedists began to use color for maps, adding to their clarity and readability. In the second half of the century, their maps came to represent features other than cities and rivers, whether vegetation, population, or religious beliefs.[124] Meanwhile, the number of maps in the average encyclopedia increased. The one-volume *Petit Larousse* had 120 maps when it started in 1905, while the gigantic *Enciclopedia italiana* (1929–39) had 14 of Argentina alone. More generally, the *Italiana* boasted excellent maps, thanks to the collaboration of the map-oriented Italian Touring Club.[125]

Images of cities, for their part, lapsed for several decades after the *Nuovo dizionario* but entered encyclopedias more durably around 1800. Their presence remained more precarious than that of portraits. As we have seen, supporters of *Johnson's New Universal Cyclopaedia* derided the maps and cityscapes in the *American Cyclopaedia* (1873–6) as childish. In response, a proponent of the *American Cyclopaedia* faulted *Johnson's* for not portraying the monuments of Mecca, Paris, or other great cities, and asserted that "those 'old ruins' and 'public buildings' are just the illustrations intelligent readers demand and prize."[126] Cities were depicted especially abundantly in the *Enciclopedia italiana*. There, for example, the articles "Buenos Aires" and "Vienna" offered, respectively, fifteen and twenty-seven views of the cities' attractions, among them streets and monuments. Such views remained rarer in other encyclopedias, perhaps because they risked seeming

[123] Lough, "Prospectus," 113.
[124] See for example Roberto, "Democratising," 113, 130–1.
[125] Calvo, "*Enciclopedia*," 35; Cavaterra, *Rivoluzione*, 128–9. For a rumor that the government forced the Touring Club into an unfair relationship with the *Italiana* see Turi, *Mecenate*, 72–3.
[126] "Cyclopaedia Illustrations," 2–3, 11.

touristy and unobjective. At times, urban maps and aerial photographs replaced them. So useful and informative were maps of cities in World War I that the Bibliographisches Institut was forbidden to publish them.[127]

As the above examination of portraits and city-views shows, the tradition of depicting art in encyclopedias was a longstanding one, but it was initially focused on sculpture, stamped medals, and architectural features. Despite the prestige of painting, and despite encyclopedias' coverage of the subject in texts, paintings were rarely reproduced in encyclopedias before the mid nineteenth century. Doomed to lack subtlety and authenticity if not also color, and requiring significant investment in the era of engraving, such reproductions had little to commend them to publishers. They finally came into their own in encyclopedias in the early twentieth century, when it became feasible to print from photographs. Here the *Enciclopedia italiana* outdid all its predecessors, devoting a large portion of its illustrations to works of art, notably paintings. The article on Michelangelo, for instance, had more than 100 black-and-white photographs – many of paintings – including a large, fold-out image of the ceiling of the Sistine Chapel (see Figure 6.14). Elsewhere in the encyclopedia, a small but stunning minority of paintings were printed in color.

Connections between Texts and Images

Certain images in encyclopedias were cut off from the text, not only vignettes and frontispieces but others as well. As noted above, the illustrations for the second edition (1950) of the *Columbia Encyclopedia* were placed in a supplement. They were not referred to in articles and did not refer back to articles. Similarly, some eighty pages of special images were introduced in the 2000 edition of the *Petit Larousse*. Although the images represented things covered in articles, no links were established between the images and articles, and the images were clustered in thematic groups, not placed by entries.

Even beyond such unusual cases, the connection between texts and images was often problematic in encyclopedias. Three impediments threatened it: technological limitations, a prolonged schedule of publication, and the general difficulty of drawing texts and images into a constructive relationship. Let us review each impediment in turn.

On the level of technology, one barrier to close relations between texts and images has already been alluded to: the need to put some illustrations

[127] Jäger, "Lexikonverlag," 566.

Figure 6.14   A fold-out photograph of the ceiling of the Sistine Chapel in the article on Michelangelo in the *Enciclopedia italiana*, Vol. xxiii. Photographed by the author courtesy of Langsam Library, University of Cincinnati. By kind permission of the Istituto della Enciclopedia Italiana Treccani.

on their own sheets of paper. This barrier shrank in the nineteenth and twentieth centuries as techniques for printing and making paper evolved, but it did not disappear.

Before 1800, moreover, the separation of high-quality plates from encyclopedias' articles was worse than it had to be, because in order to cut costs, publishers created "miscellaneous" plates combining images made for different articles. Almost inevitably, miscellaneous plates were bound at a distance from some of the articles they illustrated. In part for this reason, and also because illustrations could relate to multiple articles, the plates in encyclopedias from before the mid nineteenth century were regularly bound together at the ends of volumes or at the end of a set. One encyclopedia thus organized was Chauvin's *Lexicon rationale* (1692), where thirty mostly miscellaneous plates appeared after the main text. Notes next to articles referred to numbered illustrations, which the reader could locate by going through the plates at the end of the book. Searching for an illustration would have been harder in the first edition (1771) of the *Encyclopaedia Britannica*, where plates were scattered throughout the three volumes. Worse still, many of the plates treated miscellaneous subjects, only one of which was normally covered in an article on the facing page. To find an illustration referred to in an article, the reader could thus choose, inconveniently, between flipping through pages in the vicinity or consulting the "Directions to the Binder" in Volume III, which specified the location of every plate.[128]

Serialization further complicated the placement of plates. Subscribers to serially published encyclopedias received plates as well as articles in their installments. The two did not always harmonize. In the *Encyclopédie méthodique* (1782–1832), for example, most installments brought together unrelated materials. The fortieth installment, typically, juxtaposed texts on antiquities and surgery with plates depicting birds and mammals.[129] Likewise, in the [*New*] *Cyclopaedia* (1819–20), the plates and texts in a given installment "bore no relation" to one another.[130] In the installments of other encyclopedias, efforts were made to match texts and images. The publishers of the *Encyclopaedia Metropolitana* (1817–45), for instance, committed to ensuring "that the plates and the correspondent text are published as much as possible together."[131] Temporarily, then, texts and

---

[128] *Encyclopaedia Britannica*, 1st edn., III: [954].
[129] Evenhuis, "Dating," 43. The plates of birds and mammals had explanations, but the encyclopedia's sub-series on birds and mammals appeared in different installments.
[130] Pestana, "Rees's *Cyclopaedia*," 353, 357.
[131] *Monthly Review* 87 (1818): 4 [612].

relevant images could be close to each other, even if the images were to be bound as a separate collection, as they were in the *Metropolitana*, among other works.

In any event, while publishers provided guidelines for the placement of plates, we know from surviving sets that not all purchasers respected them. Putting the plates all together at the end of a set made it cumbersome to refer to them from earlier volumes, but spreading them out in a set lessened their value as a collection. At least one publisher combined the two systems for the placement of plates. For a surcharge, James Moore offered some sets of his Irish edition (1790–8) of the *Britannica* with two copies of every plate, one bound at an appropriate place in the main text, the other bound with all the other plates in two final volumes.[132]

In encyclopedias in which illustrations were bundled together, whether at the end of the set or at the end of each volume, the question arose of how to order them. One response was to place them in the order in which they were referred to. Another was to organize them alphabetically or systematically by their general topic. Hybrid orders were common. In the *Encyclopédie* (1751–72), plates appeared in an order defined by three factors: the alphabetical order of the subjects they pertained to, relations of affinity among these subjects, and the fortuitous circumstances of their production.[133] For his revised version (1770–80) of the *Encyclopédie*, the editor De Felice considered ordering the illustrations alphabetically by title, but he finally chose not to, preferring instead to keep related images together.[134] His and other encyclopedists' wariness of ordering illustrations alphabetically probably reflected awareness that the titles of illustrations, unlike those of articles, would be too indeterminate to allow for effective searching. In addition, thematic order made encyclopedias' illustrations into visual surveys or albums.

With the development of line-cuts in the early nineteenth century, publishers were no longer forced to choose between crude, well-placed woodcuts and detailed copperplates set at a distance from articles. As we have seen, the *Penny Cyclopaedia* was a pioneer in embracing the technology, and its approach to illustration gradually spread. It was in the third edition (1874–78) of Meyer's *Konversations-Lexikon*, for example, that the Bibliographisches

[132] Kafker and Loveland, "Publisher," 115–16, 130–1.
[133] Schwab, Rex, and Lough, *Inventory*, VII: 7, 13–15.
[134] Hupka, *Wort*, 98.

Institut began placing illustrations on the same page as texts – 1,460 of them, as it turned out.[135] Then, in the early twentieth century, Brockhaus developed a technique for putting high-quality colored images in the middle of texts, though it required added labor. Specifically, the images were printed on plates and then snipped out and affixed next to relevant articles. To the envy of the Bibliographisches Institut, this procedure was used for *Der kleine Brockhaus* (*The Small Brockhaus*, 1925) and the fifteenth edition (1928–35) of the company's main encyclopedia.[136] Lithography provided another means of placing colored images in among texts, but doing so meant using paper appropriate for both texts and images.

By the mid twentieth century, the practice of placing illustrations on faraway pages had almost disappeared from encyclopedia-making, only persisting in exceptional cases and for the highest-quality images. What remained was the less serious problem of locating illustrations to best advantage on pages or in articles. To facilitate design and updating, some publishers confined illustrations to the margins of pages, or to other fixed slots.[137] In 1958, for example, the traditionally two-columned *Petit Larousse* was given a third column to accommodate images, though images were also allowed in the other two columns. Ten years later, however, the third column had largely been taken over by text.[138]

Whatever the protocol for locating illustrations on an encyclopedia's pages, short articles, by this time, were almost always on the same page as images solely devoted to them. Only in long articles did images risk being pages away from passages referring to them, a problem that lacked any perfect solution. An analogous but more general problem was the placement of illustrations pertinent to multiple articles. The customary solution was to place them with the article most specifically pertinent, but it was not always followed. To the pride of its editors, the sixth edition (1902–8) of Meyer's *Konversations-Lexikon* offered images bringing together interconnected individuals, for example researchers on Africa in the article "Afrika."[139] In practice, these groupings meant that articles on the individuals were less often illustrated. Nor did unillustrated biographies refer to the portraits of groups.

[135] Sarkowski, *Bibliographische Institut*, 221.
[136] Keiderling, "Lexikonverlag," 447–4. See for example *Kleine Brockhaus*, 77, 347, 705; [*Grosse Brockhaus*], 15th edn., XVIII: 281, 417, 465.
[137] See for example Hupka, *Wort*, 185, 194–6.
[138] Blois, "Dictionnaire," 198–9.
[139] [*Meyer's Konversations-Lexikon*], 6th edn., I: VIII.

More common than the decision to place portraits together was the decision to place an encyclopedia's maps all together. As we have seen, maps appeared in encyclopedias from the mid eighteenth century onward, but the first encyclopedias with atlases taking up a whole volume were the *Encyclopédie méthodique* in 1787 and Rees's *[New] Cyclopaedia* in 1820.[140] Separating maps from the rest of the encyclopedia had its advantages. Articles referring to the same region could rely on the same map, readers could find maps in the absence of references, and the atlas could be marketed as an independent production. Unless maps were repeated, though, an encyclopedia with an atlas made its users consult two volumes to get all the information available on a geographical subject. Accordingly, though many encyclopedias had atlases from the nineteenth century onward, many did not, among them the *Penny Cyclopaedia* (1833–43), the *Grande Encyclopédie* (1885–1902), the *Espasa* (1908–30), and the *Enciclopedia italiana* (1929–39).

Nor was Brockhaus's *Konversations-Lexikon* or the *Encyclopaedia Britannica* consistently provided with a separate atlas. While it did include maps, Brockhaus's *Bilder-Atlas* offered images of all kinds. Much later, the publisher planned but did not follow through on an atlas for the fifteenth edition (1928–35) of its *Konversations-Lexikon*. Instead, a first atlas appeared with the sixteenth edition (1952–63). The volume was neither numbered nor marked as belonging to the encyclopedia, undoubtedly because Brockhaus counted on selling it separately. The *Britannica*, for its part, first acquired an atlas in its tenth edition (1902–3), only to lose it in the eleventh edition (1910–11) and then reinstate it.[141] Finally, perhaps in response to such critics as Harvey Einbinder, who pointed out that the atlas was getting out of date, the company abandoned it again with the fifteenth edition (1974), though an independently sold atlas continued to appear under the company's name.[142]

Compounding the problems of simple physical separation, another impediment to close relations between texts and images was their production at different times. Before the twentieth century, few publishers had the resources to prepare and print all the volumes of a large work at once. Consequently, they issued multi-volume encyclopedias over years or even decades, so that any illustration not published alongside a referring article risked being altered or forgotten by the time it was finally scheduled for publication.

[140] See Braunrot and Doig, "*Encyclopédie,*" 64; Collison, *Encyclopaedias*, 109–10.
[141] Kruse, "Story," 248.
[142] For Einbinder's criticism see Einbinder, *Myth*, 306.

The *Encyclopédie* was profoundly affected by this impediment. A small number of woodcuts were published on the same page as articles – for example, the diagrams for damask-weaving in the article "Damas" – but most illustrations were saved up for the volumes of copperplates. Seven volumes of articles had already been published when the first volume of plates appeared in 1762, and the volumes of articles had all been finished for seven years when the last volume of plates appeared in 1772. Under these circumstances, it would have required a more careful editor than Diderot to ensure that the plates corresponded to what was written in articles. The correspondence was so poor, in fact, that new texts had to be written to explain what was in the plates. Some of these texts were mere captions, but others took up pages because of advances in knowledge or changes to the plates since the publication of the articles they were originally meant for. As the plates were ordered inconsistently and did not have an index, they were also hard to find on the basis of references in articles.[143]

Problems with illustrations of the sort faced by the *Encyclopédie* became rarer and less acute as fewer images were separated from articles referring to them and as the time required to publish a large encyclopedia ultimately diminished. An advertisement for *Collier's Encyclopedia* (1949) suggests, nonetheless, that the problem of physical separation had not yet been fully resolved by the mid twentieth century: "[The illustrations in *Collier's*] are integrated with the text, like a magazine. Not grouped in sections. As you read, you see."[144]

As barriers to connecting texts and images gradually shrank, the question remained of how to relate them – on a same page, conceivably – in the most useful way. Links could be established through textual references to images, captions identifying images, and letters or numbers associating textual details with details in images. All these devices grew less explicit as the distance went down between texts and their images. Regardless, neither captions nor other formal links between texts and images determined the character of their relationship. In the abstract, this relationship could take one of three forms. In the first, the image did no more than illustrate and corroborate information in an article. In principle, mathematical diagrams fell into this category, though readers may have found the accompanying texts hard to follow without diagrams. Second, a text could do little more than supply names for the elements of what was pictured. Such was the role of captions and even, occasionally, of entire entries, notably in

---

[143] Pinault [Sørensen], "Rôle," 141–3; Schwab, Rex, and Lough, *Inventory*, VII: 12, 15–16.
[144] *Saturday Review*, March 19, 1960: 24.

pictorial encyclopedias and dictionaries. Third, the text and image could have equal standing, both providing information that the other did not, even if they overlapped in some of their content.

Evidently encompassing a range of possibilities, this latter relationship was the most frequent in encyclopedias. Consider, for example, the connection between biographical articles and the portraits that went with them. In purely textual encyclopedias such as Wigand's *Konversations-Lexikon* (1831–4), biographical articles sometimes noted their subjects' appearance, but few encyclopedias bothered when the biography was illustrated.[145] Nor could illustrations vie with articles in covering a subject's life or accomplishments.

Similarly, pictures of plants and animals conveyed a better idea of proportions, shapes, and so on than any text. In the 2000 edition of the *Petit Larousse*, the article on the wild sheep, typical of many on animals, left almost the whole task of describing the animal physically to the accompanying image, only identifying it as a "wild ruminant … akin to the sheep, with powerful, coiled horns."[146] More anomalously, the image of the razorbill in the *Petit Larousse* showed the bird flying. Despite confusion in French between the razorbill (*pingouin*) and the penguin (*manchot*), the article itself did not even allude to the razorbill's ability to fly.[147]

In depicting living beings, illustrations communicated information concisely and appealingly, but they were also more ambiguous than textual descriptions. Readers could reasonably ask themselves what in an image was meant to be essential, typical, or accidental. This concern was all the more serious for photographs and colored images, since the organism photographed might be unusual, and since colors and markings could vary among things of one kind. It is not surprising, in this light, that after an initial vogue in encyclopedias through the mid twentieth century, photographs seem to have stagnated with respect to other images. For plants and animals especially, drawings enjoyed a revival, offering readers images in which extraneous information was limited.

Conclusion

Today's encyclopedias – which is to say, electronic encyclopedias – have moved beyond illustration to "multi-media," integrating sound and visual

---

[145] See Lipták, "Sammlung," 195–6.
[146] "… ruminant sauvage … voisin du mouton, aux puissantes cornes enroulées." *Petit Larousse*, 674. See also Corbin, "Image-outil," 259–60.
[147] Corbin, "Image-outil," 262; *Petit Larousse*, 784.

movement into their articles. In so doing, they have enhanced the experience of using an encyclopedia. Without recordings of sound, how could an article – or even a musical score – represent the sound of a magpie or an orchestral arrangement? Without clips of film, how could an article represent an actor's style of acting? Whatever the answers to these kinds of questions, encyclopedias were nonetheless useful before the possibility arose of recording sound and movement.

Much the same can be said of encyclopedias without illustrations, or without charming or well-placed ones. In hindsight, looking backward from such works as a twenty-first-century *World Book* or the *Enciclopedia italiana*, encyclopedias were all, in their own ways, inadequately illustrated before the mid nineteenth century, but readers still flocked to them, confident of encountering something of value. Encyclopedias without pictures persisted into the twentieth century – proof that illustrations were never essential – and however few, detached, or crude the earliest images in encyclopedias were, they opened up possibilities.

Besides displaying objects that were difficult to characterize in words – among them machines, geographical regions, and living beings – illustrations marked encyclopedias in less obvious ways. For one thing, they brought encyclopedias into contact with nineteenth- and twentieth-century popular culture – for example, with the culture of postcards and magazines – a development linked with the popularization of knowledge. At the same time, they accentuated the status of encyclopedias as esthetic objects. So appealing were their best plates, whether copperplates or lithographs, that some were cut out and sold for collecting or framing. On a different level, illustrations added to the wonder that encyclopedias aroused, complementing the wonder aroused by descriptions of the exotic or the sublime, say, with a distinctively visual wonder. Once encyclopedias acquired illustrations, children in particular could browse through encyclopedias without needing to read, thereby both satisfying and whetting their curiosity.

CHAPTER 7

Authorship in Encyclopedias

This chapter examines a broad group of people involved in the making of encyclopedias, namely their authors. Authorship is understood here as involving compilers, editors, and revisers of articles alongside those authors considered as responsible for original articles. One reason for the breadth of my conception of authorship is that, historically, editors of encyclopedias were also their authors, and both were compilers. Furthermore, articles in encyclopedias were often collaborative, depending as they did on borrowed material as well as on revisions by editorial staffs. A final complication to the notion of authorship is that of censorship. Although a censor's duties could be limited to approving or disapproving an article, many offered advice for rewriting or even did it themselves.

While one point of the chapter is to expand the notion of authorship in the context of encyclopedias, another is to differentiate among kinds of authors. In the first section, I look at the identities of encyclopedists, including their social status, background, and gender, as well as means of crediting them for what they wrote. Thereafter I embark on a typology of authorship. First, I examine the role of the encyclopedia's "editor," who was usually a contributor through the mid nineteenth century. Then I consider other kinds of authors, notably specialists, showing how they participated in the writing of encyclopedias and how notions of authorship varied with context.

Who Wrote Encyclopedias?

Within encyclopedias, contributors were identified in various ways. An author claiming responsibility for one or more volumes of a whole encyclopedia was typically named on the title page, as were, occasionally, small groups of authors. Prefaces, for their part, frequently gave the names of contributing authors, sometimes with lists of specific articles written, but more often with an indication of the subjects they wrote on. Prefaces were ordinarily issued when an encyclopedia was finished. As a result, if authors were identified there, entries could be anonymous at the time of their appearance, though contributors' names sometimes cropped up in advertising.[1] In the course of the nineteenth century, lists of contributors at the beginnings or ends of encyclopedias gradually replaced acknowledgments within the preface. Finally, instead of, or in addition to, these kinds of lists, many encyclopedias adopted a means of crediting authors that had been used in the *Encyclopédie* (1751–72). Under this system, entries were marked with "signatures," which ranged from authors' full names to letters or numbers linked with their names in a key.[2] The use of coded signatures could lead to inadvertent or deliberate obscurity. In the first *Deutsche Encyclopädie* (1778–1807), for example, the key to the signatures appeared only in 1790, a lag that created twelve years of anonymity.[3] The identity of "X," who wrote for the eleventh edition (1910–11) of the *Encyclopaedia Britannica*, is still a mystery.[4]

Signatures had a range of meanings. On a most basic level, they assigned responsibility for what an article said. Thus, when the *Encyclopédie* was condemned by the government in 1759, it was condemned as a whole, but contributors must have feared punishment for entries marked as their own, for many ended their participation or went anonymous. Indeed, legal problems forced even the authors of the *Dictionnaire de Trévoux* (1704) – whose situation I will return to – to compromise their carefully constructed anonymity.[5]

While signatures assigned responsibility, they did not tell the whole story. Some were erroneous, and some were placed in articles copied from elsewhere. Contributors who signed in the latter case may have been trying to exaggerate their labor, but the signature might simply mean that a contributor had verified and approved the material copied.[6]

Besides identifying authors, signatures had symbolic value. Jaucourt, a respected nobleman with links to the minister Guillaume-Chrétien de Malesherbes, continued to sign articles for the *Encyclopédie* even after it was suspended – a powerful expression of support for the project.[7] Likewise, in

---

[1] See Schmidt, "Visionary Pedant," 172–3.
[2] On the *Encyclopédie*'s innovation see Loveland, "*Laissez-Faire* Encyclopedia?," 215–16. The *General Dictionary, Historical and Critical* (1734–41) had used signatures in a limited way. See Rivers, "Biographical Dictionaries," 149.
[3] Zelle, "Auf dem Spielfeld," 32.
[4] Boyles, *Everything*, 312, 419.
[5] Leca-Tsiomis, *Ecrire*, 140–1.
[6] Cernuschi, "*Encyclopédie*," 109; Cernuschi, "ABC," 132.
[7] Leca-Tsiomis, "*Encyclopédie*," 74–5.

1845, a supplement (1844–51) to the *Dictionnaire de la conversation* included an article on cannons ("Canon") signed by Louis-Napoléon Bonaparte, the future emperor Napoléon III. Irrespective of its content, the article was a statement of political dissidence, since Bonaparte was then in prison for trying to overthrow the government. Once Bonaparte was elected president in 1848, Duckett, the *Dictionnaire*'s initiator, sought to capitalize on his early support for the former prisoner, notably in his publication of the article "Canon."[8]

Signatures also encouraged a sense of ownership even before the law recognized it. D'Alembert, for example, sold some of his articles from the *Encyclopédie* to a Dutch publisher for inclusion in his *Mélanges* (*Miscellanies*, 1759). Diderot and the publishers of the *Encyclopédie* reacted with dismay, considering his actions contrary to the rules for literary property.[9] Just a few years before, in fact, D'Alembert himself had tried to stop a proposed revision of the *Encyclopédie*, Formey's *Encyclopédie réduite* (1767) – to prevent competition, no doubt, but perhaps too because the revision would not have been based on Formey's articles alone and could not, therefore, be justified in terms of authorial ownership.[10]

Just as identifications of authors were meaningful, so was anonymity – for not all contributors to encyclopedias were named in the work. Harris and Chambers, for example, both relied on anonymous helpers to prepare the *Lexicon Technicum* (1704) and the *Cyclopaedia* (1728) respectively.[11] Many encyclopedias went further, not naming any authors, whether on the title page or anywhere else. Among the motives for such silence could be the lack of a clear author or reluctance to identify an author short on prestige. In the eighteenth-century German states, it was common for encyclopedia-compilers to be anonymous, hidden behind the names of better-known patrons. In particular, neither the *Reales Staats- Zeitungs- und Conversations-Lexicon* (1704) nor the *Curieuses Natur- Kunst- Gewerck- und Handlungs-Lexicon* (1712) divulged the names of its author. Instead, both works highlighted the involvement of Hübner – a respected teacher, writer, and scholastic administrator – who wrote the prefaces and nothing else. Hübner came to be treated as the author of the *Reales Staats- Zeitungs- und Conversations-Lexicon*, not only in common parlance but even on title

[8] Loveland, "Two French 'Konversationslexika,'" forthcoming.
[9] Diderot, *Correspondance*, II: 274.
[10] See Kafker and Loveland, "Antoine-Claude Briasson," 134–5.
[11] Harris, *Lexicon*, I: a2v; Bradshaw, "Ephraim Chambers' *Cyclopaedia*," 124.

pages from the 1740s onward. Likewise, the *Dictionary of Arts and Sciences* (1807) and the *British Encyclopaedia* (1809) were presented as being edited by the clergyman George Gregory and the chemist William Nicholson respectively, but both were actually edited by a far less esteemed man, the Unitarian radical Jeremiah Joyce, once charged with treason.[12] The publishers had good reason to keep his participation secret.

The role of anonymous encyclopedists came to light in the rivalry between the *American Cyclopaedia* (1873–6) and *Johnson's New Universal Cyclopaedia* (1875–7). In the *American Cyclopaedia*, the front matter of Volume XI identified the astronomer Richard Proctor as the author of "Moon" and other articles, but he admitted under pressure that he could not take responsibility for the material there. At first, he claimed that additions had been made after he checked the proofs. Later, he changed his excuse, thereby strengthening suspicions that he was not the real author. Conversely, the owners of the *American Cyclopaedia* argued that their former editor, having changed sides, was responsible for "most" of *Johnson's*, despite the many signatures.[13] Similar accusations were a constant in the history of the European encyclopedia.

Anonymity did not have to be absolute. Failing to pinpoint specific authors, some encyclopedias credited their creation to groups, usually a society of scholars or gentlemen, as did the title pages of the *Supplement to Dr. Harris's Dictionary of Arts and Sciences* (1744), the first *Deutsche Encyclopädie* (1778–1807), and the *Allgemeines deutsches Conversations-Lexicon* (1833–7). Such attributions were sometimes accurate, but we know that the ones in the first (1771) and second (1778–83) editions of the *Encyclopaedia Britannica* were not, since both were compiled not by any "society of gentlemen" but instead, overwhelmingly, by lone compilers of low social standing.[14]

Anonymity could have strategic value that went beyond the identity of particular authors. In the mid twentieth century, for example, editors removed signatures from aging entries in the *Britannica*. The goal was to hide the fact that the entries had their origins in much earlier editions.[15] The authors of the eighteenth-century *Dictionnaire de Trévoux* had more elaborate reasons for remaining anonymous. The first edition (1704) was slightly adapted from the 1701 edition of Furetière's *Dictionaire*. According

---

[12] Issitt, "From Gregory's *Dictionary*," 5, 10.
[13] "Cyclopaedia War," 9–11; "Reply," 24–6, 30.
[14] Kafker and Loveland, "William Smellie's Edition," 10–67; Doig *et al.*, "James Tytler's Edition," 68–155.
[15] Einbinder, *Myth*, 7.

to Marie Leca-Tsiomis, the adaptation was undertaken by Parisian Jesuits and their allies, who hid their identities to avoid being called plagiarists, to shirk responsibility for any remaining traces of Protestantism, and to create a fictive independence from explicitly Jesuit institutions such as the *Mémoires de Trévoux*, a periodical. Still, despite repeated denials, the *Dictionnaire de Trévoux* was widely assumed to be by Jesuits in all its editions through the mid eighteenth century.[16]

Another rationale for anonymity developed in nineteenth-century encyclopedias, especially German *Konversations-Lexika*. From the early nineteenth century onward, editors of *Konversations-Lexika* reserved the right to edit submissions as they saw fit – which they could do all the more easily in that few contributors were celebrities. Articles, accordingly, were rarely identified as the work of individuals. Instead, largely spurning the signatures pioneered in the *Encyclopédie*, German *Konversations-Lexika* relied on an older system for acknowledging authorship: presenting a list of contributors with their areas of responsibility. Before 1850, a significant minority of articles in Brockhaus's *Konversations-Lexika* ended with symbols identifying their authors, but the public was not always supplied with a key.[17] In any event, such signatures had disappeared by the second half of the century, leaving behind just anonymous articles and lists of contributors not specifically credited with any one article.[18]

Dispensing with signatures in articles had two main advantages. First, it gave editors greater freedom to modify articles in the name of creating a homogeneous work. When, on the contrary, an editor altered articles that were to be published with signatures, problems ensued. Certain contributors to the *Enciclopedia italiana* (1929–39), for example, were so unhappy with editorial meddling that they requested the deletion of their planned signatures.[19] To pre-empt such problems, the editor De Felice made at least one contributor to the Yverdon *Encyclopédie* (1770–80) sign a contract allowing changes to any article submitted.[20] Second, unsigned articles were associated with objectivity. Not only did signatures threaten the ideal of knowledge as impersonal, but named contributors might try to justify their signatures with a personal touch.[21] Proponents of signatures

---

[16] Leca-Tsiomis, *Ecrire*, 70–90, 115–26, 132–3.
[17] Loveland, "Two French 'Konversationslexika,'" forthcoming. On Brockhaus's reluctance to disclose authors' names see Prodöhl, *Politik*, 43–5.
[18] I found no signatures, for example, in the first 100 pages of the tenth edition (1851–5).
[19] Cavaterra, *Rivoluzione*, 40, 54.
[20] Cernuschi, "ABC," 139.
[21] See Castellano, *Enciclopedia*, 369–70.

could argue, moreover – as did the foreword to the *Grande Encyclopédie* (1885–1902) – that only by signing entries could authors responsibly disseminate their personal views and thus avoid merely compiling what had already been written.[22]

Whether identified or not, authors of encyclopedias were of all different kinds. Among them were pre-eminent artists, philosophers, inventors, and scientists, including the novelist Walter Scott, a contributor to the *Edinburgh Encyclopaedia* (1808–30); the revolutionary Vladimir Lenin, a contributor to the seventh edition (1910–48) of the *Enciklopedičeskij slovar'*; and the physicist Einstein and the industrialist Henry Ford, both contributors to the thirteenth edition (1926) of the *Encyclopaedia Britannica*. From the nineteenth to the early twentieth century, editors of prestigious encyclopedias in English especially sought out famous intellectuals to write and sign articles. The names of these celebrities bolstered encyclopedias' authority, and their attractiveness to both buyers and other potential contributors.[23] Thus, in his [*New*] *Cyclopaedia* (1819–20), which included articles by the musicologist Charles Burney and the chemist Humphry Davy, Rees wrote that "persons, eminently distinguished in those branches of science to which they had devoted their talents … not only consented to be co-adjutors, but to give celebrity to the work by allowing their names to be annexed to it."[24] More cynically, De Felice, the editor of the Yverdon *Encyclopédie*, complained that what sold encyclopedias was not excellent content but rather the "big names" ("grands noms") of certain contributors.[25]

In France, intellectual celebrities were never again as predominant among an encyclopedia's contributors as they had been for the *Encyclopédie méthodique* (1782–1832). Among other authorities, the publisher Panckoucke was able to enlist the leading members of the Académie Royale des Sciences and the Académie Française. So exalted were expectations regarding contributors that one of the sub-editors felt obliged to defend a collaborator's competence because his name was not famous or even very well known.[26]

By the second half of the nineteenth century, editors of French and German encyclopedias were moving away from reliance on intellectual celebrities. Even Ersch and Gruber's *Allgemeine Encyclopädie* (1818–89),

[22] *Grande Encyclopédie: Inventaire*, 1: xii.
[23] Yeo, *Encyclopaedic Visions*, 257–9; Yeo, introduction, 1: xi–xiv.
[24] Rees, [*New*] *Cyclopaedia*, 1: iii.
[25] Donato, "Jean Henri Samuel Formey's Contribution," 97.
[26] Doig, *From Encyclopédie*, 78. See also Darnton, *Business*, 430–7.

the most scholarly encyclopedia in German, was faulted by one critic for having been written by "common copyists" ("ordinärer Tagschreiber") rather than celebrities, though the editors expressed pride in their team of contributors.[27] Conversely, Herrmann Julius Meyer, the head of the encyclopedia-making Bibliographisches Institut in the mid nineteenth century, complained of his experience with famous authorities who, in his view, were paid more for what they did not write than for what they did.[28]

In any event, the majority of encyclopedists were strangers to fame. They came to encyclopedia-writing for a variety of reasons. A few considered it a calling. Jaucourt was so passionate about it that he joined the team behind the *Encyclopédie* (1751–72) after losing his first encyclopedia because of a shipwreck. Then, after compiling 17,000 articles for the *Encyclopédie*, he apparently went to on work on another encyclopedia. For him, as a wealthy nobleman, contributing to the *Encyclopédie* was not about money, though he did receive some, along with some books.[29] Beyond any financial considerations, contributing to an encyclopedia could be a way of establishing a reputation, making a statement, or showing patriotism.

Most encyclopedists, however, expected a stipend or even a career, whether as researchers or paid compilers. An encyclopedia's main author or editor typically made a respectable living, but the careers of lower-ranked encyclopedists were almost all humble. Consider, for example, the account of a junior encyclopedist in Emile Zola's novel *Le Voeu d'une morte* (*A Dead Woman's Wish*, 1866), which may have reflected a stint by the young Zola as an anonymous writer for Larousse's *Grand Dictionnaire*: "Georges introduced Daniel to a sort of author-publisher ... and got him accepted as a collaborator on an encyclopedic dictionary that occupied around thirty young people ... They compiled, they collated for ten hours and they earned eighty to a hundred francs per month ... [The boss] did not even read the manuscripts, and he signed the whole work."[30]

Outside fiction, a similar picture emerges of the ill-used encyclopedist. Midway through the preparation of the *American Cyclopaedia* (1873–6), for instance, the publisher Appleton decided to replace specialized

[27] Rüdiger, "Ersch/Gruber," 54–7; Spree, *Streben*, 95. On the decline of insistence on famous contributors toward 1900 see Spree, *Streben*, 101.

[28] Estermann, "Lexika," 249.

[29] Haechler, *Encyclopédie*, 159–66, 506; Leca-Tsiomis, "*Encyclopédie*," 71, 76; Kafker and Loveland, "André-François Le Breton," 123–4.

[30] "Georges présentait Daniel à une sorte d'auteur-éditeur ... et le faisait admettre comme collaborateur à un dictionnaire encyclopédique qui occupait une trentaine de jeunes gens ... On compilait, on collationnait pendant dix heures et on touchait quatre-vingts à cent francs par mois ... [Le patron] ne lisait même pas les manuscrits, et il signait le tout." Mitterand, "Zola," 115–16.

contributors with "young men" earning "moderate wages."[31] Likewise, while certain contributors to the *Espasa* (1908–30) earned 20 pesetas per page, almost enough to buy a volume of the encyclopedia, members of the anonymous staff took in just 30 pesetas per week for compiling two pages a day. Indeed, they were nicknamed the "starved-to-death from upstairs," a combined reference to their poorness and their work on the top floor of the editorial office.[32]

In addition to their general lack of prestige, a few patterns stand out regarding encyclopedists' identities, and specifically regarding their backgrounds and gender.

Three kinds of professional backgrounds were common among encyclopedia-writers, though none was preponderant. First, many encyclopedists were ecclesiastics, in part because ecclesiastics had the education and leisure to pursue literary activities. Into this category, for example, fell Coronelli, the author of the *Biblioteca universale* (1701–6) and a Franciscan official; Harris, the author of the *Lexicon Technicum* (1704) and an Anglican clergyman; and a fifth of the known contributors to the first *Deutsche Encyclopädie* (1778–1807).[33] The eighteenth century's best-known encyclopedia may have been the anti-religious *Encyclopédie*, but France's longest-running encyclopedia before the arrival of Larousse – the *Dictionnaire de Trévoux* – was compiled mainly by Jesuits for most of its history. As we have seen, eighteenth-century French Benedictines cultivated encyclopedism too. A group of them, headquartered in the abbey of Saint-Germain-des-Prés, worked for over than a decade on their own dictionary of the arts and sciences, though it ended up going unpublished.[34]

Long after 1800, ecclesiastics continued to play a role in the production of encyclopedias and of knowledge in general.[35] As contributors to encyclopedias, they were particularly active in Catholic countries. They made up around a quarter of the contributors to the *Espasa*, for example.[36] As editor of the *Enciclopedia italiana* (1929–39), Gentile gave them control of articles on religious subjects. Altogether, they amounted to just 4 percent of contributors, but after the Lateran Treaty between Italy's government and the Vatican in 1929, their influence over the encyclopedia grew.[37]

---

[31] "Reply," 29–30.
[32] "… los muertos de hambre de arriba." Castellano, *Enciclopedia*, 160–1, 167, 475.
[33] For the last fact see Goetschel, Macleod, and Snyder, "*Deutsche Encyclopädie*," 325–32.
[34] Holmberg, *Maurists' Unfinished Encyclopedia*.
[35] Burke, *Social History … II*, 233–4.
[36] Castellano, *Enciclopedia*, 347, 447.
[37] Durst, *Gentile*, 43–4, 54–7; Turi, *Mecenate*, 93.

Second, many encyclopedists were journalists. In the twentieth century, Harvey Einbinder lamented a trend he saw in the development of the *Encyclopaedia Britannica*: "The editors of the ninth edition were scholars, and the eleventh edition was directed by a journalist with scholarly ambitions. Subsequent editors have been journalists."[38] Accurate as it was in a limited context, his statement is at odds with the broader history of the *Britannica* and other encyclopedias. The first two editions (1771, 1778–83) of the *Britannica* were edited by writers with a substantial experience of journalism, as were such encyclopedias as the 1701 and 1708 editions of Furetière's *Dictionaire*, the *Universal History* (1745), and the Yverdon *Encyclopédie* (1770–80).[39] In the late nineteenth century, the owners of *Johnson's New Universal Cyclopaedia* (1875–7) boasted that "in the department of American geography alone, nearly 2,000 editors of newspapers" had contributed on their own towns.[40] A half-century later, only 13 of 700 contributors to the *Espasa* were identified as journalists, but far more, undoubtedly, hid their affiliation with journalism behind a more impressive professional title.[41] Around the same time, the eleventh edition (1910–11) of the *Britannica* was criticized in the United States because the editor chose to rely on journalists rather than academic specialists.[42]

The reasons for the presence of journalists among encyclopedists are not hard to fathom. Writing for periodicals and compiling encyclopedias were both unprestigious, so that writers forced to engage in one activity often found themselves forced to engage in the other. More positively, journalism and encyclopedia-making required some of the same skills. In both activities, writers had to synthesize and summarize information for the public. Both activities, moreover, subjected writers to deadlines – which could be almost identical for, say, a weekly periodical and an encyclopedia published in weekly installments.

Third, many encyclopedists were teachers or other employees of schools, including Chauvin, the author of the *Lexicon rationale* (1692) and a professor as well as a Protestant pastor; Jablonski, the author of the *Allgemeines Lexicon* (1721) and a tutor to the future king of Prussia, Friedrich Wilhelm I; and around a fifth of the contributors to the third edition (1797) of

---

[38] Einbinder, *Myth*, 268–9.
[39] Kafker and Loveland, "William Smellie's Edition," 14, 64; Brown, "James Tytler's Misadventures," 47–8; Leca-Tsiomis, *Ecrire*, 38; Loveland, *Alternative Encyclopedia?*, 36–40; Häseler, "Extraits," 282–3.
[40] "Fishing," 14.
[41] Castellano, *Enciclopedia*, 222, 224, 229, 250.
[42] Thomas, *Position*, 16–17.

the *Britannica*.[43] Probably the most famous of teacher-encyclopedists was Pierre Larousse, who edited the *Nouveau Dictionnaire* (1856) and the *Grand Dictionnaire* (1866–76), among other works of reference. To design and market such works, he drew on both his experiences and his connections as a former teacher.

In the course of the nineteenth century, teachers at schools and universities came to dominate lists of encyclopedias' contributors. Almost half of the 379 contributors initially listed for Ersch and Gruber's *Allgemeine Encyclopädie* (1818–89) were professors at universities.[44] Likewise, almost 30 percent of the 243 contributors listed in Volume 1 of the *Grande Encyclopédie* (1885–1902) were identified as teachers at universities or elsewhere. Similarly, as of 1925, most of those invited to contribute to the *Enciclopedia italiana* were teachers at universities.[45] As we have seen, the eleventh edition of the *Encyclopaedia Britannica* was criticized in the United States for being too journalistic. Thereafter, however, the *Britannica* aligned itself with academia. Some three-quarters of the contributors to the 2002 edition of the *New Encyclopaedia Britannica* thus held positions in universities, while many of the remaining quarter held positions in museums, academies, and other institutions of learning.[46]

In the twentieth century, librarians and archivists, often employees of universities, began contributing to encyclopedias in considerable numbers, probably in part because of their access to books and records, and probably in part because they were active in criticizing and selecting encyclopedias. Epitomizing the period's deference toward librarians was *Collier's Encyclopedia* (1949). In 1946, the president of the Collier Company asked for help from the American Library Association in designing an encyclopedia. The result was *Collier's*, the second edition (1962) of which was edited by the librarian Louis Shores. The publisher may have recruited him to help sell the encyclopedia to other librarians, but Shores, as an editor, was not just a figurehead.[47]

In addition to these three professional backgrounds, another identity shared by encyclopedists was that of their gender. Before 1800, almost no women were credited with having contributed to an encyclopedia. Symptomatically, we know of only one woman who wrote articles – most likely Jaucourt's sister-in-law, Suzanne-Marie de Vivans – and two who

---

[43] On the contributors to the latter work see Doig *et al.*, "Colin Macfarquhar," 169–71.

[44] Rüdiger, "Ersch/Gruber," 20.

[45] Cavaterra, *Rivoluzione*, 39–40.

[46] These generalizations reflect extrapolation from *New Encyclopaedia Britannica* (2002), *Propaedia*: 531–34.

[47] Collison, *Encyclopaedias*, 212–13; Shiflett, *Louis Shores*, 101, 152, 180.

worked on illustrations for the *Encyclopédie*.[48] In the case of the *Encyclopédie* and other encyclopedias, more women may have contributed in informal roles, whether as researchers, secretaries, or uncredited writers, just as they did to other intellectual projects. Exemplifying such unacknowledged work was the writer Agnes Hall, who contributed anonymously to the *British Encyclopaedia* (1809).[49]

By Hall's time, women were beginning to be mentioned as contributing encyclopedists, for example in the *Dictionary of Arts and Sciences* (1807), the *Encyclopédie des gens du monde* (1833–44), and the *Encyclopédie nouvelle* (1834–42).[50] In a departure from the tendency for women's encyclopedias, the author of the *Female's Encyclopaedia* (1830) claimed to be a woman.[51] In the second half of the nineteenth century, the *Britannica* acquired its first woman contributor, with the eighth edition (1853–60).[52] In part because of its beginnings as a translation, *Chambers's Encyclopaedia* (1868) depended on the labors of a number of women. Meanwhile, in German encyclopedias, women lagged as a presence, despite the writer Therese Huber's contribution to Brockhaus's *Konversations-Lexikon* in the early nineteenth century.[53]

Even in the first half of the twentieth century, women's role in the composition and editing of encyclopedias remained a minor and subordinate one. Only in 1916, for example, did a first woman join the editorial staff at Larousse. The company's leadership was exclusively masculine and remained so for years.[54] Acknowledging a woman assistant editor in 1935, the editor of the *Columbia Encyclopedia* wrote: "The traditional rule for preparing a reference work is, find the right woman and do what she says."[55] He was mostly joking, evidently – and drawing on a condescending platitude for praising a woman subordinate. Hiring women in the bindery was a way of cutting costs for the publisher of the *Espasa* (1908–30), but of more than 500 named contributors to the Spanish encyclopedia, just 4 were women.[56] Likewise, women made up only 2 percent of named contributors to the eleventh edition (1910–11) of the *Encyclopaedia Britannica* despite

---

[48] Lough, *Encyclopédie in Eighteenth-Century England*, 44–5; Haechler, *Encyclopédie*, 101; Kafker and Pinault Sørensen, "Notices," 211–12, 226.
[49] Schmidt, "Visionary Pedant," 179.
[50] Issitt, "From Gregory's *Dictionary*," 19; Rowe, "Upwardly Mobile Footnotes," 436; Griffiths, *Jean Reynaud*, 143–4; *Encyclopédie nouvelle*, 11: 825–8.
[51] Lynch, *You Could Look It Up*, 183.
[52] Kruse, "Story," 282n.
[53] Spree, *Streben*, 100, 278; [*Grosse Brockhaus*], 5th edn., 1st printing, x: xv ("Vorrede").
[54] Mollier and Dubot, *Histoire*, 260, 544, 674–5.
[55] *Columbia Encyclopedia*, 1st edn., "Preface."
[56] Castellano, *Enciclopedia*, 93, 224, 244.

their greater presence on the editorial staff, where they worked on articles anonymously.[57]

Women's participation in encyclopedia-making grew during World War II as men left their positions to serve in the military. So it went, for example, at Brockhaus and the Bibliographisches Institut.[58] Around the same time, woman began to accede to positions of editorial leadership. In the 1920s already, the future economist Persia Campbell had been an assistant to the editors of the *Australian Encyclopaedia*, but in the 1940s and 1950s women became editors in their own right – of *Chambers's Encyclopaedia*, the *Encyclopedia Americana*, and the *Grolier Encyclopedia*.[59]

Authors versus Compilers and Editors

As noted in Chapter 4, nearly all encyclopedias included large quantities of borrowed material, sometimes from other works, sometimes from a previous edition of the same encyclopedia. Regardless, certain encyclopedists claimed to be authors even if others regarded them as compilers, or, worse still, as plagiarists. At stake in such claims was more than just pride, for authorship could be tantamount to ownership from a moral if not necessarily a legal perspective.[60]

Title pages often implied a more limited role for encyclopedists than that of author. In the seventeenth and eighteenth centuries, they frequently specified one or more writers, but in a manner more suggestive of compiling than authorship. On its title pages, for example, the *Allgemeines Lexicon* (1721) was said to be "drawn up in proper order and diligently brought together" by an anonymous member of the Royal Academy of Prussia, namely Jablonski.[61] Taking this logic to an extreme, the title page of the last edition (1727) of Furetière's *Dictionaire* announced that the work had been "gathered and first compiled" by Furetière, "corrected and augmented" by Basnage, and "revised, corrected, and considerably augmented" by Jean-Baptiste Brutel de la Rivière.[62]

By contrast, the *Lexicon Technicum* (1704) was announced on its title page as being "by" Harris, the *Nuovo dizionario* (1746–51) as "by"

[57] Thomas, *Position*, viii, 18–21.
[58] Prodöhl, *Politik*, 96, 182.
[59] Kavanagh, *Conjuring*, 75–6; Walsh, *Anglo-American General Encyclopedias*, 22, 44, 72.
[60] Stern, "Copyright," 69–70, 77–84.
[61] "… in gehöriger Ordnung verfasst und mit Fleiss zusammen getragen."
[62] "… recueilli et compilé premièrement … corrigé et augmenté … revu, corrigé, et considérablement augmenté."

("di") Pivati, and the *Supplement to the Third Edition of the Encyclopaedia Britannica* (1801) as "by" George Gleig. Authorship, in these cases, was being proclaimed with as much force as it was on the title pages of plays and novels. Such attributions were not necessarily indicative of any difference in originality. Harris, for example, avowed in his preface that "much the greater part" of the *Lexicon Technicum* was taken from other books.[63] Similarly, in a revealing turnaround, Jablonski presented the first edition (1721) of his *Allgemeines Lexicon* as the work of an anonymous compiler, but in the second, posthumous, edition (1748), his name was printed in red letters at the top of the title page.

As collaborative encyclopedias multiplied, title pages began to display the names of editors. The word "editor" and its cognates were not much applied to encyclopedia-editors before 1800. Exceptionally, in the publishers' records and in the *Encyclopédie* itself, Diderot and D'Alembert were referred to as "éditeurs," along with their predecessor in the position, De Gua.[64] At times, though, they were referred to in other ways, occasionally with alternative nominal forms – for example, as the "heads" ("chefs") of the *Encyclopédie* – but more often with verbs that spelled out their duties, as on the title page: "arranged and published [by Diderot and D'Alembert]."[65] The century's favor for this latter way of identifying editors suggests that the concept of editorship had not yet solidified in the context of encyclopedias. Even as late as the early nineteenth century, it was not obvious to everyone that encyclopedias were "edited." The title page of the *Edinburgh Encyclopaedia* (1808–30), for example, announced that it had been "conducted" by Brewster, whom we now call the editor.

In his article "Editeur" in the *Encyclopédie*, Diderot proposed the following definition of "editor": "This name is given to a man of letters willing to take up the task of publishing the works of another."[66] By this definition, Diderot and D'Alembert were indeed editors, at least early on, entrusted as they were with publishing an enlarged French translation of Chambers' *Cyclopaedia*. Still, if they or their publishers had realized how far the *Encyclopédie* would stray from being a mere edition or adaptation of the *Cyclopaedia*, they might not have opted to call themselves "editors." Or perhaps they were moving toward another conception of the editor, namely as someone overseeing a collaborative text.

---

[63] Harris, *Lexicon*, 1: a2v.
[64] See for example May, "Documents," 18, 21; *Encyclopédie; ou, Dictionnaire*, 1: i, 11: 846.
[65] "… mis en ordre et publié." For a reference to "chefs" see [Chaudon], *Religion* 11 (1760): 363.
[66] "On donne ce nom à un homme de lettres qui veut bien prendre le soin de publier les ouvrages d'un autre." *Encyclopédie; ou, Dictionnaire*, v: 396.

In "Editeur," at any rate, Diderot insisted that the *Encyclopédie*'s collaborative character meant that neither editor was responsible for its contents. Conversely, as pointed out in Chapter 4, he and D'Alembert were committed to publishing submissions exactly as written. Modern encyclopedia-editors were less fastidious about intervention.

Another eighteenth-century encyclopedist who took up the title of "editor" was Zorzi, in his proposal (1779) for a *Nuova enciclopedia italiana*. His conception of his editorship was different from that of Diderot and D'Alembert, though he too assured contributors that their submissions would be published unaltered. First, he set himself at the head of eight specialized sub-editors, thereby anticipating the editorial hierarchies of the following centuries. Second, whereas Diderot and D'Alembert were vague about their editorial duties, Zorzi assigned himself two specific ones: removing redundancy and coordinating cross-references.[67] Except in rare instances, Diderot had left even the latter task to individual contributors.[68]

In German, encyclopedias' intellectual leaders were not referred to as "editors," or with any cognate. As we have seen, eighteenth-century German encyclopedias were often secretive about authorship. When authors were mentioned, their duties were usually spelled out with verbs, though the designation "Verfasser" ("compiler") was sometimes used. Then, in the early nineteenth century, the title "Redakteur" became common, along with the more impersonal "Redaktion" ("editorial staff"). According to the definition in the *Oeconomische Encyclopädie* (1773–1858), a "Redakteur" was a person who put together a collaborative work to make it uniform.[69] An alternative to "Redakteur" for naming the editor was "Herausgeber." The editor Löbel, for example, referred to himself this way in the first edition (1796–1808) of Brockhaus's *Konversations-Lexikon*.[70] So did Ersch and Gruber on the title page of the *Allgemeine Encyclopädie* (1818–89). As synonyms for "editor," "Redakteur" and "Herausgeber" were not always distinguished.[71] Unlike a "Redakteur," though, a "Herausgeber" could be involved in the commercial side of encyclopedia-making. Accordingly, certain encyclopedia-publishers, Joseph Meyer included, considered themselves "Herausgeber," in contrast to the "Redakteure" who worked on their

---

[67] Zorzi, *Prodromo*, XVII–XIX.

[68] Loveland, "*Laissez-Faire* Encyclopedia?," 216–17, 220.

[69] Krünitz *et al.*, *Oeconomische Encyclopädie*, CXXI: 377.

[70] [*Grosse Brockhaus*], 1st edn., I: x.

[71] Karl Espe, for instance, became the "Redakteur" when he took over the "Herausgabe" of the eighth edition (1833–7) of Brockhaus's encyclopedia. See Peche, *Bibliotheca*, 84–5.

orders.[72] Over time, "Redakteur" and variants such as "Chefredakteur" ended up dominating as titles for the editors of encyclopedias.

Bypassing the words "editor" and "Redakteur," we can learn about editorship from the history of those in charge of preparing the content of encyclopedias, whatever the contemporary terminology for denoting their functions. Before the mid eighteenth century, most encyclopedias were ascribed to individuals, though they were inevitably collaborative to a degree. It was only with the arrival of substantially collaborative encyclopedias in the mid eighteenth century that the modern concept of editorship began to emerge. Even then, the tasks of recruiting contributors and revising their submissions were long seen as secondary to an editor's main task, which was writing articles. The publishers of the *Encyclopédie*, for example, named De Gua editor, but they left him the option of finding collaborators or compiling the encyclopedia himself.[73] Similarly, Diderot and D'Alembert, the subsequent editors, wrote thousands of articles alongside the many more they solicited from others. A few decades later, Smellie compiled the first edition (1771) of the *Encyclopaedia Britannica* almost single-handedly, but he was nonetheless named its "editor" on his tombstone around 1795. His relatives may have been thinking of contemporary usage rather than the usage of 1771, for by the late eighteenth century, the *Britannica*'s intellectual leaders were calling themselves editors.[74] They now saw recruiting specialists as a significant part of their job.

Along with finding contributors, imposing homogeneity was an aspect of encyclopedia-editing that gained importance with time. Already in 1686, Chappuzeau argued that a single person – in fact, he himself – should compile the supplement to Moréri's *Grand Dictionaire* so as to make the style uniform. Likewise, in the preface to his revised editions (1701, 1708) of Furetière's *Dictionaire*, the editor, Basnage, apologized for leaving transitional "scars" within articles and for not, overall, making the text more homogeneous. Conversely, Chambers declared that the second edition (1738) of his *Cyclopaedia* had been "rendered more uniform, its parts in many places better disposed, as well as more conformable to each other, and the references reformed throughout."[75] Nevertheless, as we have seen, the editors of the *Encyclopédie* refrained from inhibiting the diversity of

[72] See for example Sarkowski, *Bibliographische Institut*, 71.
[73] May, "Documents," 19–20.
[74] See *Encyclopaedia Britannica*, 3rd edn., 1: xii–xiii. Notice in contrast the reference to "compilers" in *Encyclopaedia Britannica*, 2nd edn., 1: vii.
[75] Loveland, "*Laissez-Faire* Encyclopedia?," 213.

articles submitted, and they were not, for the time being, the only editors disinclined to.

Friedrich Brockhaus and his associates played a big role in making homogeneity an encyclopedia-editor's concern. Writing in the fifth edition (1819–20) of the *Konversations-Lexikon*, Brockhaus and Hain explained the division of labor within their editorial partnership. Whereas Brockhaus's duties were managerial, Hain was responsible for revising submitted articles and putting in cross-references to create a kind of harmony.[76] From this period onward, revising and homogenizing were regularly among the duties of an encyclopedia's editors.[77]

Further complicating the notion of editorship, eighteenth- and nineteenth-century publishers sometimes took on duties we now assign to editors. Zedler, for example, apparently picked the contributors to his *Grosses vollständiges Universal-Lexicon* (1732–50), though he later gave Ludovici the encyclopedia's "directorship" ("Direction").[78] Similarly, the publisher Panckoucke became a kind of editor for the *Encyclopédie méthodique* (1782–1832), defining its organization, writing the preface, and recruiting contributors to handle particular subjects.[79] Pierre Larousse took on even more roles for his *Grand Dictionnaire* (1866–76), specifically those of the publisher, the printer, a leading contributor, and the editor. Although he did have collaborators, the title page stated, grandiosely, that the encyclopedia was "by" ("par") Larousse. Such sweeping ascriptions of authorship had all but vanished from encyclopedias by then.

In the course of the nineteenth century, encyclopedia-editors distanced themselves from the composition of articles and devoted more attention to managing collaborators and their contributions. In the judgment of the editor Napier, writing in the seventh edition (1842) of the *Encyclopaedia Britannica*, the editor of an encyclopedia "is the sole director and fashioner of the fabric … but he may not himself have furnished any of the materials … His duties lie in judging of those materials, in selecting the workmen, and directing their operations."[80]

---

[76] [*Grosse Brockhaus*], 5th edn., 1st printing, x: IX–XI ("Vorrede").

[77] See for example Kruse, "Story," 165; Castellano, *Enciclopedia*, 167–9; Sarkowski, *Bibliographische Institut*, 188; Keiderling, *F. A. Brockhaus*, 331. On the persistence of heterogeneousness see for example Spree, *Streben*, 284–6.

[78] Kossmann, "Deutsche Universallexika," 1569–70; *Grosses vollständiges Universal-Lexicon*, XIX:)(IV–)(2r. Jacob August Franckenstein and Paul Daniel Longolius probably acted as editors before Ludovici.

[79] Braunrot and Doig, "*Encyclopédie*," 8–9.

[80] *Encyclopaedia Britannica*, 7th edn., I: xix.

At the same time, the facets of editing began to be separated, and editing took on a hierarchical aspect, as "general," "managing," and "senior" editors came to direct specialized sub-editors. As we have seen, both Zedler and Panckoucke acted as managing editors, leaving the textual side of editing to their subordinates. The process was more explicit in the development of Brockhaus's *Konversations-Lexikon*. After recruiting contributors for the second edition (1812–19) himself, Friedrich Brockhaus appointed a second editor in 1812 and became the chief editor. Then, for the fifth edition (1819–20), he relied on reviewing by specialized sub-editors.[81] Although he remained involved with contributors – more so than senior editors of the following decades – he prefigured such editors in supervising a hierarchy.[82] By the 1820s, Pierer's *Konversations-Lexikon* was being produced the same way. In this case, the hierarchy ran from an editor-in-chief (representing the "Hauptredaktion," or main editorial team) to specialized sub-editors ("Subredaktoren") and ultimately contributors ("Mitarbeiter").[83]

By the mid twentieth century, the editors responsible for an encyclopedia were myriad, as were their titles. In general, a senior editor dealt with administration and planning, a managing editor coordinated the work of sub-editors, and lower-ranked editors occupied themselves with the details of revising texts. Thus, the ninth edition (1971–9) of Meyer's *Konversations-Lexikon* distinguished editors-in-chief, managing editors ("leitende Redakteure"), and other editors ("Redakteure").[84] In large anglophone encyclopedias especially, the roster of editors could extend even further. In the 1998 edition of the *Encyclopedia Americana*, for instance, there was a list of more than fifty members of editorial staff, which included an editor-in-chief, an executive editor, a managing editor, artistic editors, regular editors, associate editors, editorial assistants, copy-editors, a "production editor," and proofreaders.[85]

Informants, Proofreaders, and Censors of Encyclopedias

Unlike a contributor, an informant for an encyclopedia provided information, but not in the form of a text to be published. Rather, the information

---

[81] Hingst, *Geschichte*, 105, 111–12.
[82] For Brockhaus's and Hain's duties see *ibid.*, 112–13. On Brockhaus's tendency to direct his contributors' work see Spree, *Streben*, 94.
[83] [*Pierer's Universal-Lexikon*], 1st edn., i: xiv–xv.
[84] [*Meyer's Konversations-Lexikon*], 9th edn., xxv: 866.
[85] *Encyclopedia Americana: International Edition*, i: vii.

provided had to be written up by the person it was provided to. In this light, references to informants were not so different from citations of printed works. Indeed, in the absence of other evidence, it can be hard to interpret certain statements about encyclopedias' sources. When the preface to Corneille's *Dictionnaire* (1694) asserted, for example, that Michael Ettmüller "supplied extensive comments [on medicine]," it meant that Corneille had consulted Ettmüller's books, since the physician had been dead since 1683, whereas the statement in the *Encyclopédie* (1751–72) that "M. Allard … supplied us with the models of several machines" referred to an informant, since it was placed in a list of people – not publications – who had provided assistance.[86]

Some informants were published scholars, for example the chemist Joseph Black and the physician-naturalists John Latham and William Wright, all thanked in the third edition (1797) of the *Encyclopaedia Britannica*.[87] Others held privileged social positions. Exceptionally, King Edward VII agreed to assist with the coverage of knightly orders in the eleventh edition (1910–11) of the *Britannica*.[88] Likewise, in the mid twentieth century, writers for *World Book* apparently contacted such celebrities as John Fitzgerald Kennedy, Charles de Gaulle, Wernher von Braun, and John Steinbeck to get information for articles.[89] Crediting distinguished figures as informants was a polite form of tribute – and a sly form of advertising – as much as an avowal of indebtedness.

By contrast, many of the informants mentioned in encyclopedias were little known. They tended to live on the periphery of the Republic of Letters, if even that, since book-writers could be "consulted" through what they published. Harris, for example, got information for his *Lexicon Technicum* (1704) from instrument-makers, including a barometer-maker.[90] Likewise, one of the goals of the *Encyclopédie* was to coax information out of people experienced in the mechanical arts so that their techniques could be publicized. The plan was for encyclopedists to interview such people and then write articles. So it often occurred, but a greater number of artisans were able to write than expected. When they submitted their own texts, Diderot had to differentiate between authors and informants. If a text required reworking, he might deem the source an informant and

[86] Corneille, *Dictionnaire*, I: aiiiv; *Encyclopédie; ou, Dictionnaire*, III: xv.
[87] *Encyclopaedia Britannica*, 3rd edn., I: xvi.
[88] Kogan, *Great EB*, 167–8.
[89] Murray, *Adventures*, 193.
[90] Harris, *Lexicon*, I: L2v, L3v.

himself the author, whereas if it did not, the artisan might be credited as a true author.[91]

Akin to informants were proofreaders of encyclopedias, or at least some among them. Publishers had long employed menial proofreaders, namely correctors, and editorial staffs came to rely on the services of copy-editors, but some proofreaders worked on a more intellectual level. Harris, for example, wrote in the *Lexicon Technicum* that the entries on law had been "carefully examined and corrected by a gentleman of known ability in that profession."[92] True or not, evocations of proofreading functioned strategically as assurances of quality. It is no accident that they often appeared in prospectuses and prefaces, both prime sites for advertising.

Whatever the reality of Harris's legal expert, it is unlikely, in general, that authorities did as much proofreading as encyclopedias' prefaces suggested. Consider the case of the botanist Antoine de Jussieu. He is sometimes considered the first expert to have collaborated on an encyclopedia, namely the second edition (1721) of the *Dictionnaire de Trévoux*, but the preface merely credited him with criticizing botanical entries. Indeed, the preface admitted that his collaboration had ended prematurely, supposedly because he had to travel. In fact, Jussieu almost certainly withdrew for lack of interest.[93] Even in the opening volumes, his influence was slight. The only trace I have found of it occurs some twenty pages into the encyclopedia, in the article on the apricot. Here the opinion of "one of the most skilled botanists in France" was cited to cast doubt on a claim inherited, like most of the article, from Furetière's *Dictionaire*.[94] The article on the coffee-tree, for its part, was based on Jussieu's "Histoire du café" (1716) or a derivative text. Jussieu was the first to study the plant scientifically, but he was neither mentioned in the article nor cited as a source – odd treatment if the author expected him to proofread it.[95]

By the mid nineteenth century, encyclopedias were being set up under the supervision of committees and boards of directors. The members of such groups, inevitably distinguished, were usually listed at the front of an encyclopedia, as if to suggest they had reviewed and approved it, but as critics observed, nothing proved that they were acquainted with what was in it. The *Penny Cyclopaedia* (1833–43), for example, was one of the first encyclopedias to benefit from a body of oversight. Its members

[91] *Encyclopédie; ou, Dictionnaire*, 1: xxxix–xl; Proust, *Diderot*, 191–5, 513–14.
[92] Harris, *Lexicon*, 1: blr.
[93] Loveland, "Varieties," 91.
[94] [*Dictionnaire de Trévoux*], 2nd edn., 1: 42.
[95] Loveland, "Varieties," 91. For a similar argument about Jussieu see Leca-Tsiomis, *Ecrire*, 118–21.

were listed in volumes as well as on wrappers enclosing installments, but repeated errors in their names and titles made one reviewer doubt that "the committee … troubles itself about" the encyclopedia.[96]

The boards behind encyclopedias included politicians. In 1961, the former American president Dwight Eisenhower became the chairman of the advisory board of the *Encyclopedia Americana*, for instance. It is difficult in such instances to believe that the board had much of a role beyond symbolism. Indeed, for legal and other purposes, some associates of encyclopedias took pains to stress limitations on their involvement. Although the University of Chicago derived income from the *Britannica* from 1943 to 1996, for example, and although the encyclopedia was advertised with the university's coat of arms and as benefiting from advice from the university's professors, the University of Chicago was always insistent that it did not guarantee the encyclopedia's content or quality.[97]

In censorship, the tasks of proofreading and providing information assumed a more ominous form. Proofreading could be solicited as a matter of prudence or courtesy, as when Brockhaus sent the statesman Otto von Bismarck a proposed article about him to review before it was published in the twelfth edition (1875–9) of the *Konversations-Lexikon*.[98] Alternatively, censorship could be imposed, usually with the consequence that authors and publishers censored themselves ahead of time as a precaution.

The *Encyclopédie* was one of numerous censored encyclopedias. Theologians were to censor all articles from Volume III onward. Then there was the government. In one of the most dramatic instances, it was probably the minister Malesherbes who ordered the elimination of the article "Constitution," a long article on the controversial papal bull Unigenitus (1713). Since the volume had been printed but not yet distributed, the publishers had the offending pages cut out and replaced. The only remaining traces were a stub of cut paper next to the binding and an asterisk at the bottom of the page marking a "cancellation." In other instances, the publishers may have sent subscribers new pages along with instructions to have them substituted for pages now censored.[99]

In addition to such external censorship, the *Encyclopédie* fell victim to internal censorship. In the 1760s, concerned that Diderot's and others' articles would endanger the enterprise, the publisher Le Breton and his

[96] Review of *Penny Cyclopaedia*, 79. For a similar judgment – and for a reference to the committee's name on wrappers – see "Chartered Booksellers," 73.
[97] Einbinder, *Myth*, 331–2, 341; Kruse, "Story," 383–5.
[98] Meyer, "Konversations-Lexikon," 82–3; Estermann, "Lexika," 255.
[99] Weil, "*Encyclopédie*," 415–18; Schwab, Rex, and Lough, *Inventory*, 1: 127–9, 149–50.

compositor began revising or removing provocative passages. They did so in secret, after the proofs had been turned in. When Diderot discovered the subterfuge in 1764, he was enraged.[100] Traumatic as it was for Diderot, the episode illustrates a mundane reality of contemporary encyclopedism: the vulnerability of texts to revision by censors. Nor was Le Breton the only publisher to alter an encyclopedia behind authors' backs. In the 1720s, the editor Brutel tried to cleanse Furetière's *Dictionaire* of what he deemed lascivious material, but his publisher reintroduced it in an attempt to please readers.[101]

Well after the time of the *Encyclopédie*, censorship remained a threat and a reality for encyclopedias' authors and publishers. One point of the ironic, questioning style of Brockhaus's early *Konversations-Lexikon* was thus to thwart censors.[102] Similarly, Pierre Larousse's whole approach to producing his *Grand Dictionnaire* (1866–76) was conditioned by fear of censorship. In particular, he was determined to do his own printing to avoid allowing an intermediary to alter his work, and he refused to consider revenue from subscribers as truly belonging to him, since he felt obliged to return it if the work ended up being prohibited.[103] The ideal for a publisher was to get an exemption from censorship, as Joachim Pauli did for the *Oeconomische Encyclopädie* (1773–1858). To win the concession – an exceptional one – he argued that the encyclopedia was uncontroversial, that the manuscript was written too untidily and in too many hands to be easily readable, and that censorship would raise the cost of the project and prevent the insertion of material at the last minute.[104]

Censorship continued to affect encyclopedias throughout the twentieth century. The *Enciclopedia italiana* was doubly censored. First, political articles were censored to reflect fascist ideology and the government's viewpoint. In 1933, for example, the editor, Gentile, assured Mussolini that nothing anti-fascist would appear in the encyclopedia.[105] Second, the Catholic Church was involved in censorship. To a degree, Gentile was obliged to submit. The encyclopedia was funded by Treccani, a fervent Catholic, and it had to avoid being condemned by the Vatican to sell well in Italy. Even Mussolini had to defer to the Church. When the pope reacted negatively to rumors about the article on fascism – ghost-written

[100] Gordon and Torrey, *Censoring*, 22–39.
[101] Furetière, Basnage, and Brutel, *Dictionaire*, 1: ****2r; Leca-Tsiomis, *Ecrire*, 106–7.
[102] Spree, *Streben*, 277.
[103] Pruvost, "Pierre Larousse," 36–9.
[104] Fröhner, *Technologie*, 61–3.
[105] Turi, *Mecenate*, 77–8. For examples of political censorship see *ibid.*, 157, 161n, 175.

by Gentile on behalf of Mussolini – the presses were stopped so that the two men could revise it.[106] Early on, Gentile resigned himself to working with Catholic censors under the supervision of the Jesuit Pietro Tacchi Venturi. Despite an evolving friendship between Gentile and Venturi, they battled for years over the extent of the Church's censorship. One of Gentile's strategies was to parcel out knowledge and contributors' assignments in changing patterns so that the Church's share remained narrow. Contested articles were divided into religious and secular parts – for example, an article on the origins of humankind.[107]

Whereas nineteenth-century censorship pushed encyclopedias toward traditional doctrines, twentieth-century censorship could be designed to impose new ideologies. During Germany's Third Reich, for example, the encyclopedias of Brockhaus and Meyer were censored to conform to Nazi ideas. Because encyclopedia-making was too costly to take a risk on, both publishers worked with censors before publication to ensure the acceptability of what was published. As it turned out, much of the censorship involved paying censors to write articles themselves. The publishers were paying, in effect, for protection from the Nazis. As in nearly all censorship, self-censorship played a substantial role too.[108]

Nor did censorship of the two encyclopedias end with the war. Leipzig, home to both Brockhaus and the Bibliographisches Institut, was occupied by the Soviets and then became part of East Germany. At the invitation of American authorities, part of the Brockhaus firm was relocated to Wiesbaden – in what would shortly be West Germany – but the remainder of the firm, along with the Bibliographisches Institut, was now subject to new rules governing censorship. In the late 1940s, the branch of Brockhaus in Leipzig set to work on the first German encyclopedia since the conclusion of the war, a new edition of the *Volks-Brockhaus* (1931). Denied permission to publish, the company turned to its proven strategy of hiring censors as authors, but to no avail. The *Volks-Brockhaus* was banned just days after the first volume appeared in 1950. In the aftermath of the crackdown, Brockhaus was nationalized and the process of censorship modified. Regardless, East German censorship remained too unpredictable for either company to publish a large encyclopedia until around 1960.[109]

[106] Durst, *Gentile*, 30–1, 49; Turi, *Mecenate*, 135; Cavaterra, *Rivoluzione*, 51.
[107] Durst, *Gentile*, 42–61, 85–99, 110; Turi, *Mecenate*, 80–98, 199–240.
[108] Prodöhl, *Politik*, 27–8, 67–120, 142–4.
[109] Keiderling, *F. A. Brockhaus*, 222–5, 296–302; Prodöhl, *Politik*, 197–9, 226–36.

Soviet encyclopedias were even more tightly controlled than those of totalitarian Italy and Germany. The process culminated in the second edition (1949–58) of the *Bolshaia sovetskaia entsiklopediia*. Two years after the first edition (1926–47) was finally finished, the government called for a new one, in large part because the first edition had become ideologically dated. Published at the height of the Cold War, the second edition was the most doctrinaire of the encyclopedia's editions, thick with propaganda and fanciful history – which occasionally necessitated altering photographs. The work's ideology reflected a mindset, but it also reflected fear and the pressures of censorship. Tellingly, after his death, the cult of Joseph Stalin began to ebb in the encyclopedia's pages. Furthermore, the proportion of biographies was just half what it had been in the previous edition, partly because so many people – now purged or blacklisted – could no longer be covered. After Stalin's death, thousands of missing biographies were restored in a supplement. Censorship continued, though. In 1954, for example, subscribers were told to remove pages 21–4 of Volume v and replace them with supplied pages. The point was to eliminate the biography of Lavrentiy Beria, Stalin's chief of security, recently executed and cast out of favor. In compensation, subscribers were given more material on the Bering Sea.[110]

Besides inviting denunciations from foreign observers, censored encyclopedias could sell badly at home. In particular, the "Nazi edition" (1936–42) of Meyer's *Konversations-Lexikon* was aborted at "S" as a commercial disappointment, while the second edition of the *Bolshaia sovetskaia entsiklopediia* had to be marketed with a counter-balancing supplement. By the mid 1950s, it was considered so backward, ideologically and otherwise, that the Soviets reined in an East German attempt at translation.[111]

Specialists and Insiders

Collaborative authorship was not necessarily tantamount to specialization. For its dictionary (1694), for example, the Académie Française worked collectively, but with little impetus toward specialization. Indeed, one of the reasons for its slowness in assembling the *Dictionnaire* was its decision to have the work done in large, unfocused committees.[112] So too, when the Spanish diplomat Álvaro Navia Osorio proposed a *Diccionario universal* in

---

[110] Hogg, "*Bolshaia sovetskaia entsiklopediia*," 31–46; Prodöhl, *Politik*, 236–41.
[111] Prodöhl, *Politik*, 114, 241–54.
[112] Considine, *Academy Dictionaries*, 33–4, 37–8.

1727, he called for the labor to be distributed among contributors letter by letter.[113] Here the goal of collaboration was simply to spread out the work.

A better reason for making encyclopedias collaborative, as Navia Osorio ultimately realized, was to take advantage of authors' specialties. By his time, the ideal of the polymath was losing credibility.[114] Already in 1656, the dictionary-writer Thomas Blount declared that a good dictionary would require "the concurrence of many learned heads" – a criterion that Edward Phillips claimed to have satisfied by consulting specialists for his *New World of English Words* (1658).[115] Likewise, in 1689, the future encyclopedist Jean Le Clerc argued that because a single person could not know enough – or know enough languages – to compile an encyclopedia, the perfection of a work such as Moréri's *Grand Dictionaire* should be entrusted to "several people skilled in history, and in geography, and of various nations."[116] Similarly, in 1702, the French biblical scholar Richard Simon asserted that a great encyclopedia would need to have numerous contributing specialists, since no one could competently deal with everything. Although he was briefly among the leaders of the *Dictionnaire de Trévoux* (1704), Simon was unable to make it correspond to his vision.[117] Failing to believe in a broadly collaborative encyclopedia or see it as feasible, other encyclopedists of the early eighteenth century continued to labor as largely solitary compilers.

Not long after Simon made his proposal, Coronelli recruited an unknown number of collaborators for his *Biblioteca* (1701–6). Two of his goals were to reduce his work-load and gain subscribers, since he calculated that contributors might decide to subscribe. In addition, he expected contributors to act as specialists, since they were instructed to report on local knowledge among other matters, whether of language, geography, or public figures. Unfortunately, we know little about who his contributors were or what they contributed.[118]

The situation is different for the collaboration behind the 1701 edition of Furetière's *Dictionaire*. Basnage had two collaborators, the Dutch physician Pierre Regis and the Protestant minister Gédéon Huët. Huët's role was probably that of an advisor and editor, but Regis was announced as writing on algebra, medicine, botany, and other fields of which Basnage

---

[113] Alvarez de Miranda, "Projets," 108.
[114] See Yeo, "Lost Encyclopedias," 51–3; Burke, *Social History*, 84–5.
[115] Considine, "In Praise," 215. Notice also Locke's position in Yeo, *Encyclopaedic Visions*, 158–9.
[116] "… plusieurs personnes habiles dans l'histoire, et dans la géographie, et de diverses nations." [Le Clerc], review of *Supplément*, 75–6.
[117] Leca-Tsiomis, *Ecrire*, 64–6, 83–4.
[118] Fuchs, "Vincenzo Coronelli," 121–38, 147–53, 187–8.

admitted to ignorance. According to Basnage, Furetière too had been scientifically inept, so much so that Regis had started almost from scratch. This was an exaggeration. In botany, Regis rewrote old articles and introduced thousands of new ones, mostly on exotic plants. In his other fields, he added fewer articles and incorporated Furetière's articles in his revisions.[119]

Robert Collison has called Harris the "original precursor of the modern system of inviting contributions from specialists" because of "advice and help" Harris allegedly received from Isaac Newton and John Ray for the *Lexicon Technicum* (1704).[120] Ray, a naturalist, was the leading authority for the encyclopedia's zoological articles, but nothing suggests that Harris did anything but use Ray's books as sources. Likewise, Harris somehow got a copy of an unpublished paper by Newton – "De natura acidorum" ("On Acids") – and placed it at the start of Volume II (1710) of his encyclopedia, but he may not have had the author's approval.[121] Harris did name a few collaborators in particular entries, but his *Lexicon* was collaborative on a small scale only.

The most explicitly collaborative encyclopedia before the *Encyclopédie* was a Dutch work, the ten-volume *Groot algemeen historisch, geographisch, genealogisch, en oordeelkundig woorden-boek* (*Great General Historical, Geographical, Genealogical, and Legal Dictionary*, 1725–33). Presented as an expanded synthesis of Moréri's *Grand Dictionaire*, the German adaptation (1709) by Buddeus, and Bayle's *Dictionaire*, the *Groot ... woorden-boek* was compiled under the supervision of three successive editors. In addition, the preface credited other scholars for help with the project. Articles under "B," in particular, were apparently contributed by six men, assisted by translators. The preface hinted at specialization among the contributors, but only faintly.[122]

A more credible candidate for an encyclopedia by specialists was the *Grosses vollständiges Universal-Lexicon* (1732–50). According to the preface by Ludewig, Zedler had the *Universal-Lexicon* written by nine "learned people," their number being determined by the number of classical muses. Among these anonymous "muses," as Ludewig called them, a theologian was to cover theological articles; an expert on law, legal articles; a physician, medical articles; and a mathematician, mathematical articles.[123] So

[119] Loveland, "Varieties," 95.
[120] Collison, *Encyclopaedias*, 99.
[121] Loveland, "Varieties," 95. For Harris's claim to have had Newton's "leave" see Harris, *Lexicon*, II: bIV.
[122] *Groot algemeen historisch, geographisch, genealogisch, en oordeelkundig woorden-boek*, I: ***3r. See also Paul, "Enzyklopädien," 31–2.
[123] *Grosses vollständiges Universal-Lexicon*, I: 6, 15.

presented, the *Universal-Lexicon* would seem to have been written by specialists and thus constitute the first realization of Simon's vision. But Ludewig's arguments for dividing the work up were alien to Simon's. Above all, Ludewig spent much of the preface highlighting the difficulty of finishing gigantic texts. On the one hand, individuals who tried rarely lived to complete them, while on the other hand, teams that tried created confusion and contradiction. Ludewig's conclusion was that an encyclopedia required some but not too many contributors, and that each contributor should be given a well-defined specialty, not so much to make the best use of areas of competence as to avoid contradictions between infringing domains.[124]

Regardless of Ludewig's arguments, we do not know how collaborative the *Universal-Lexicon* was. A commitment to reveal the contributors' identities when the work was concluded was never honored. From Zedler's perspective, attributing the work to "muses" rather than specific individuals may have made sense as a way of muddling allegations of plagiarism, but it is unclear why contributors would have accepted anonymity. Most were presumably intellectuals who had not yet established themselves, ready to work for modest wages and go without recognition. Only five have been identified, three of them successive editors, and two others contributors on particular disciplines: the musicologist Lorenz Mizler, on mathematics, and the physician Heinrich Winckler (related to Zedler by marriage), on medicine.[125] Were there actually numerous contributors, or "many Leipzig muses," as a dedication in Volume XXVI stated? Ines Prodöhl has expressed doubt, citing the encyclopedia's low price – which would have pinched salaries – its reliance on copying, and the fact that almost no contributors have been discovered. Katrin Löffler takes the opposite position. In her estimation, the encyclopedia was compiled too quickly – and its copying too tempered with subtle revisions – for it to have been the work of a few people only.[126] The mode of authorship of the *Universal-Lexicon* remains a mystery.

As far as we know, then, the *Encyclopédie* was the first encyclopedia to involve many contributing specialists. Together with the publishers, the first editor, De Gua, recruited a few of the contributors who would become the work's mainstays.[127] Still, it remained for Diderot and D'Alembert, the

[124] *Ibid.*, 1: 7, 9, 13. For evidence that disciplines were covered by more than one person see Dorn, Oetjens, and Schneider, "Sachliche Erschliessung," 120–1.

[125] Loveland, "Varieties," 96–7; Lohsträter, "Periodische Presse," 60, 67–8; Löffler, "Wer schrieb den Zedler?," 272–3.

[126] Prodöhl, "Aus denen besten Scribenten," 88–9; Löffler, "Wer schrieb den Zedler?," 265–71.

[127] Kafker, *Encyclopedists*, 36–7. On De Gua's specific role see Kafker and Loveland, "Vie," 199.

new editors after De Gua left, to muster the vast team that wrote the *Encyclopédie*. All told, we know of some 140 contributors to articles and some 66 to the artwork.[128]

The publication of the *Encyclopédie* did not put an end to minimally collaborative encyclopedias. Remarkably, the 242-volume *Oeconomische Encyclopädie* (1773–1858) was largely the work of four successively appointed compilers.[129] Nevertheless, from the mid eighteenth century onward – and despite this example – the less teamwork an encyclopedia depended on, the more likely it was to be unprestigious and small.

Nor did the *Encyclopédie* clinch the place of the expert among encyclopedia-contributors. As late as the early nineteenth century, Friedrich Brockhaus was using collaborators not for their specialties but instead to cover arbitrary sequences of letters.[130] Furthermore, though most collaborative encyclopedias were premised on specialization, specialties were broad, for the most part, before 1850. In early-nineteenth-century Britain, for instance, the polymath Thomas Young wrote on a wide range of topics for the *Supplement to the Fourth, Fifth, and Sixth Editions of the Encyclopaedia Britannica* (1824) – a range partly justified by the scope of natural philosophy. Attitudes toward unspecialized learning were nonetheless changing, for even Young understood that his contribution might arouse skepticism on account of its breadth.[131]

However loosely specialized their contributors were, collaboratively authored encyclopedias flourished in the second half of the eighteenth century. In Germany, the unfinished *Deutsche Encyclopädie* (1778–1807) had more than sixty contributors, each one supposedly limited to just one discipline. Substantially collaborative encyclopedias were slower to come forth in Britain. A handful of specialized collaborators were advertised on the title pages of a 1755 re-edition of Bailey's *Universal Etymological English Dictionary* and the *Complete Dictionary of Arts and Sciences* (1764–6). It is unclear how collaborative these works actually were, but several encyclopedias of the 1770s and 1780s followed them in indicating contributors on the title page. The first British encyclopedia to have many contributors was the third edition (1797) of the *Encyclopaedia Britannica*. Its team of around 25 authors of articles would

---

[128] Kafker and Kafker, *Encyclopedists*; Kafker and Pinault Sørensen, "Notices."
[129] Fröhner, *Technologie*, 40–57.
[130] Hingst, *Geschichte*, 105, 111–12.
[131] Yeo, *Encyclopaedic Visions*, 267–71.

shortly be dwarfed by the more than 150 collaborating on the *Edinburgh Encyclopaedia* (1808–30).[132]

Through the mid twentieth century, the number of contributors claimed for encyclopedias continued to break records on a regular basis. In the late nineteenth century, the *Grande Encyclopédie* (1885–1902) and the ninth edition (1875–89) of the *Britannica* advertised 450 and 1,100 respectively, while the *Enciclopedia italiana* boasted 3,000 in the early twentieth century.[133] As in the race to recruit intellectual celebrities, encyclopedias in German lagged behind those in English in the number of contributors. Thus, while around 1,300 specialists contributed to the eighteenth edition (1977–81) of Brockhaus's *Konversations-Lexikon*, the contemporaneous *New Encyclopaedia Britannica* (1974) claimed 4,000 contributors.[134] By this time, however, lists of contributors in encyclopedias had already shrunk from their maximum early on in the Cold War between the United States and the Soviet Union. In 1958, the foreword to Volume LI of the second edition of the Soviet *Bolshaia sovetskaia entsiklopediia* announced the participation of more than 9,000 authors.[135] Similarly, around 1970, the *Britannica* was advertising an astonishing 10,400 contributors, more than twice as many as the *New Encyclopaedia Britannica* within less than five years.[136]

Useful as they were in advertising, such numbers were deceptive, for they failed to specify contributors' roles. In the case of the ninth edition (1875–89) of the *Britannica*, it may be that eminent contributors were more prolific than others, but the correlation probably went the other way in many encyclopedias.[137] In the *Grande Encyclopédie* (1885–1902), for example, the young brothers André and Philippe Berthelot were obliged to write hundreds if not thousands of pages on all kinds of subjects when money was unavailable to pay specialized authors.[138] Some encyclopedias, moreover, claimed past contributors as present ones when articles were adapted from previous editions. The 1960 *Britannica* was thus advertised as having forty contributors who had won Nobel Prizes, but many of them had written their articles decades before.[139]

132 Loveland, "Varieties," 98.
133 On the *Italiana* see Cavaterra, *Rivoluzione*, 40n.
134 Keiderling, *F. A. Brockhaus*, 270; *New Encyclopaedia Britannica* (1974), *Propaedia*: xviii.
135 Prodöhl, *Politik*, 237.
136 See for example *Life* 71 (December 31, 1971): 17.
137 On the situation in the ninth edition see Kruse, "Story," 183.
138 Jacquet-Pfau, "Naissance," 102–3, 108.
139 Einbinder, *Myth*, 239.

The development of encyclopedias written by specialists has usually been written as a story of progress, but the progress was not without costs, or independent of the individuals recruited. Specialized contributors could be uninspired compilers. Nor did they always address themselves to the people likely to consult an encyclopedia. In the *Encyclopédie*, despite a promise to stick to generalities in advanced mathematics, D'Alembert used the article "Gravitation" to criticize a paper by a rival, the mathematician Leonhard Euler. Afterward, he noted apologetically that "we assume that readers have in front of them the piece printed in 1749 by M. Euler" – a peculiar assumption.[140] Finally, it could be costly to work with experts, not only because of the honoraria they commanded but also because an editor had to devote time and energy to contacting a different one for each field.[141] Accordingly, even in encyclopedias premised on the involvement of experts – among them, the eleventh edition (1910–11) of the *Britannica* – editors typically assigned short articles to the anonymous staff to ensure that they were on time and did not need further editing.[142]

Up till now, I have considered academic specialists, that is, intellectuals who secured their authority through education or research. Other specialists acquired authority and were picked to write for encyclopedias because of their experiences or their identities. These I call insiders in the following paragraphs, since they saw their subjects from the inside, if also the outside.

Insiders played a big role in encyclopedias' biographies, many of which were contributed by the subject's family or friends. Searching for biographical information for his *Dictionaire*, for example, Bayle got in touch with the families of subjects and occasionally entrusted them with writing whole articles.[143] Expectations about sources for biographical articles gradually changed, but as late as 1812, the writer Genlis excoriated the *Biographie universelle* because its writers lacked first-hand knowledge: "Where do they get the material for these wilting notices? They certainly do not get it from the only ones capable of giving truthful material, that is, from relatives and friends."[144] Even in the early twentieth century, the editor of the eleventh

---

[140] "Nous supposons qu'on ait ici sous les yeux la pièce de M. Euler imprimée en 1749." Loveland, "Varieties," 99–100.

[141] See Yeo, *Encyclopaedic Visions*, 264–6.

[142] Boyles, *Everything*, 253.

[143] Lieshout, *Making*, 86–7, 131.

[144] "Où prend-on les matériaux de ces notices flétrissantes? On ne les tient certainement pas de ceux qui pourraient seuls en donner de véridiques, c'est-à-dire des parents et des amis." Chappey, *Ordres*, 51.

edition of the *Britannica* assigned articles on the living to people who knew them.[145]

Almost as common were articles on places by travelers or residents. In 1686, hoping to write a supplement to Moréri's *Grand Dictionaire*, Chappuzeau told the publisher he had first-hand experience of nearly every country in Europe. Consequently, he argued, his geographical articles would be better than articles compiled from published texts.[146] Chappuzeau was turned down, but a century later, Dobson's American version (1789–98) of the *Britannica* had several geographical articles written by locals.[147] In an era in which scholarship could not always be counted on for information that was recent or concerned the exotic, reliance on insiders was not a bad option for biographical or geographical articles, though it created opportunities for tributes by admirers and patriots.

Encyclopedia-editors recruited another kind of insider for a more basic identity such as sex, ethnicity, race, or religion.

As we have seen, only one woman is known to have written for an eighteenth-century encyclopedia. This was the anonymous author – probably Vivans – of the articles "Falbala" (on a ruffle), "Fontange" (on a headdress), and possibly others in the *Encyclopédie*.[148] It is likely that she chose her subjects – or had them assigned to her – because being a woman gave her authority on fashion.

Women were not picked, ironically, to write articles about women for encyclopedias before the twentieth century, since they almost never had training in medicine, law, or theology, the disciplines that traditionally undergirded such articles. Even in the left-leaning *Encyclopédie nouvelle* (1834–42), the article on women was given not to any of the women contributors but instead to a man, albeit one eager to explore the conflicted position of women in society.[149] In the *Britannica*, the first article on women to be signed by a woman was the one in the tenth edition (1902–3), composed by the writer and socialite Mary Jeune. In the eleventh edition, "Women" was anonymous but probably overseen by the editor, Chisholm. In a toast, he suggested that his women contributors were largely picked for their identities, namely as specialists on "social and purely feminine

[145] Boyles, *Everything*, 255.
[146] Caullery, "Notes," 148.
[147] Loveland, "Varieties," 100–1.
[148] *Encyclopédie; ou, Dictionnaire*, VI: vi.
[149] Griffiths, *Jean Reynaud*, 227; Spree, "Verhinderte 'Bürgerin'?," 296–8. On articles on women in nineteenth-century encyclopedias see Spree, "Verhinderte 'Bürgerin'?," 288–91.

matters," but in fact, in the eleventh edition, women did not tend to contribute on stereotypically feminine topics.[150]

Some insiders were selected to represent racial and ethnic groups. Well into the twentieth century, nearly all encyclopedias had insulting characterizations of races and peoples. The *Britannica*, for example, is often faulted for its depiction of blacks through the mid twentieth century. As late as 1960, for example, the article "Negro" asserted that although the "mental inferiority" of blacks had been exaggerated, it was nonetheless real.[151] The encyclopedia was also demeaning of Romani, among other peoples: "The mental age of the average adult gypsy is thought to be about that of a child of ten. Gypsies have never accomplished anything of great significance in writing, painting, musical composition, science or social organization."[152]

By the mid twentieth century, encyclopedia-editors in the anglophone world were starting to assign articles on racial and ethnic minorities to representatives. At the end of the 1950s, for instance, all the contributors writing on American blacks for the *Encyclopedia Americana*, the *Britannica*, *Collier's Encyclopedia*, and the *American Peoples Encyclopedia* were "well-known negroes."[153] Preference for such insiders had become systematic by the end of the century. In the majority of cases, it was easy to reconcile identity and academic expertise, since professors teaching Latin American or African studies, say, were frequently of Latin American or African ancestry. Explaining the selection of authors for "Negro," the editor of the 1958 edition of the *American Peoples Encyclopedia* made the same argument: "Both authors are Negro Americans who have distinguished themselves in studies of their own race." Yet at times, identity trumped intellectual training. Thus, when Joan Bunche was selected to write "Negro, American" for the 1958 yearbook for the *American Peoples Encyclopedia*, her racial identity – and no doubt her identity as the daughter of a Nobel Peace Prize winner – must have been determinant, not her work as an "editorial researcher for *Look* magazine."[154]

In a similar development, from the late eighteenth century onward, some encyclopedias incorporated contributions from religious minorities as part of an effort to avoid or make amends for misrepresentation. Already

[150] Thomas, *Position*, 26, 37–8. On the authorship of "Woman" in the eleventh edition see Boyles, *Everything*, 312–13; Thomas, *Position*, 38.
[151] *Encyclopaedia Britannica*, 14th edn. (1960), XIX: 344–5.
[152] *Ibid.*, XI: 43.
[153] Hannah, "Comparison," 139.
[154] *Ibid.*, 85, 131–2, 149.

in 1701, Basnage, the new editor of Furetière's *Dictionaire*, assured readers that he would be respectful of religious belief, "giving each camp the honorable names it gives itself."[155] Likewise, a new edition (1743–9) of Moréri's *Grand Dictionaire*, published in France, supplemented its article on the religious reformer John Calvin with a second article on Calvin taken from Bayle's Protestant *Dictionaire*, supposedly out of a sentiment of "natural fairness."[156] More directly, the editors of the first *Deutsche Encyclopädie* (1778–1807) had Catholics and Moravian Brethren write the articles on their faiths; Dobson inserted a Quaker's "Vindication of … George Fox" in his American *Encyclopaedia* (1789–98) as a way of apologizing for the article "Quaker"; and Gleig persuaded John Geddes, a Catholic bishop, to write articles on Catholicism for the third edition (1797) of the *Britannica*. In none of these cases were the insiders unqualified for the tasks that they assumed, but their identities were crucial.[157]

From the nineteenth century onward, it was common to recruit religious insiders to write for encyclopedias. In the early 1820s, Friedrich Brockhaus devised a plan to make his *Konversations-Lexikon* attractive to the minority of Catholics among speakers of German. Henceforth, he announced, it would have articles by Catholics dealing with Catholicism from a Catholic perspective. This commitment apparently continued into the twentieth century, though the company's insistence on anonymous articles prevented the public from ascertaining contributors' religious identities.[158] Among the many other nineteenth- and twentieth-century encyclopedias with a policy of relying on religious insiders were Ersch and Gruber's *Allgemeine Encyclopädie* (1818–89) and the *Encyclopedia Americana* in the mid twentieth century. Citing such examples, Martin Gierl wrote in 1999 that "to engage the best international experts of the day for all subjects, and for controversial positions, the relevant representatives, is the contemporary production ideal of the encyclopedia."[159]

Qualification is needed on this last point, however. Editors of encyclopedias regularly stopped shorted of calling for "representatives" to write on religion. Rather, they promised that articles on religious beliefs

---

[155] "… donnant à chaque parti les noms honorables qu'il se donne à lui-même." Furetière and Basnage, *Dictionaire*, 1: *3r.

[156] Schneider, "Des transferts," forthcoming.

[157] Loveland, "Varieties," 101. See also Spree, *Streben*, 317.

[158] [*Grosse Brockhaus*], 5th edition, 3rd printing, 1: x; Hingst, *Geschichte*, 123; Keiderling, "Lexikonverlag," 443.

[159] Gierl, "Compilation," 95.

would be written from the viewpoint of an insider or be reviewed by one.[160] In fact, the recruitment of insiders to cover religion risked triggering charges of partiality or favoritism.

Ire over religious bias dates back to the beginnings of the European encyclopedia, when Protestants such as Bayle took offense at the militant Catholicism of Moréri's *Grand Dictionaire*, but before 1800, it usually resulted from negative depictions. Then, as encyclopedias embraced the ideal of letting minorities and other groups speak for themselves, overly positive accounts of religious topics became controversial as well – and all the more so when written by insiders.

The issue was particularly divisive in the United States, where encyclopedia-makers were under pressure from different religions. In a bitter struggle between *Johnson's New Universal Cyclopaedia* (1875–7) and Appleton's *American Cyclopaedia* (1873–6), for example, the publisher Alvin Johnson aired rumors that Appleton had given the former Jesuit Bernard O'Reilly the right of "supervision" over articles on Catholicism. In short, argued Johnson, Appleton had "Jesuitized" its encyclopedia (see Figure 7.1).[161] Indeed, fifteen years earlier, Appleton's *New American Cyclopaedia* (1858–63), the precursor to its *American Cyclopaedia*, had pledged that ecclesiastical history and doctrine would be covered by "theologians of the different Christian denominations," a policy that necessitated engaging Catholic contributors.[162] For the *American Cyclopaedia*, Appleton allowed O'Reilly to advertise the acceptability of the encyclopedia to Catholics. O'Reilly hinted, moreover, that articles on Catholic topics lay under the "authority" of the archbishop of New York. Still, the editors denied letting O'Reilly or anyone misrepresent Catholicism or take control of what appeared in the encyclopedia.[163]

Similarly, along with being anti-Catholic, the *Encyclopaedia Britannica* was charged with being pro-Catholic, and with other forms of whitewashing connected with its recourse to religious insiders. In the eleventh edition (1910–11), the editor, Chisholm, wrote that, on delicate subjects, art-icles had been solicited from people of "all shades of opinion."[164] Later, however, in response to complaints about anti-Catholicism, he insisted that it was not the *Britannica's* policy to reserve entries on Catholic

---

[160] See for example *Encyclopaedia Americana*, 1st edn., 1: vii; Thomas, *Position*, 7–8; *Columbia Encyclopedia*, 2nd edn., "Preface"; *Collier's Encyclopedia* (1997), 1: "Preface."
[161] "Fishing," 2, 17.
[162] *New American Cyclopaedia*, 1: vi; "Fishing," 14.
[163] "Fishing," 2, 14–15.
[164] *Encyclopaedia Britannica*, 11th edn., 1: xxi.

Figure 7.1   Drawing denouncing the supposed favor for Catholics in Appleton's *American Cyclopaedia*, from a booklet promoting *Johnson's New Universal Cyclopaedia*. Scanned courtesy of the Library Company of Philadelphia.

subjects for Catholics alone: "Such a course ... would be impracticable with any attempt to write history from an impartial but critical standpoint ... We did, however ... take every reasonable precaution by the cooperation of men of all sorts of religious belief."[165]

In the mid twentieth century, the *Encyclopedia Americana* began advertising that, unlike the allegedly anti-Catholic *Britannica*, it depended on "loyal Catholics to write on Catholic subjects," but the advertisement was disallowed by the Federal Trade Commission. In any event, the *Britannica* was already assigning many Catholic topics to Catholic contributors. The entry on the Jesuits, for example, was rewritten in 1936 by the editor of a Catholic weekly, who made it more positive.[166] Insiders handled entries on other religions as well. An entry on the founder of Christian Science by an adherent remained in the *Britannica* from 1929 to around 1960, despite being condemned for its scholarly weakness.[167] Still, even Harvey Einbinder, a critic of the practice of using religious insiders, concluded that a "policy of appeasing ... religious groups" – by means of insiders, among other things – did not undermine the *Britannica* as much as a tendency to keep old material.[168]

Not all insiders were recruited for identities as deep-seated as sex, ethnicity, race, or religion. The *Enciclopedia italiana*, for example, was one of a number of twentieth-century encyclopedias in which famous athletes wrote about sports.[169] In the early twentieth century, the *Britannica* too began including entries by celebrities whose fame was not intellectual – or not for the most part. According to advertising, the eleventh edition was written by "men of action" as well as "men of learning" and "practical experts," though in practice Chisholm opted for hybrids such as the anarchist and philosopher Kropotkin (the author of "Anarchism") and the explorer and scientist Fridtjof Nansen (the author of "Polar Regions").[170] The thirteenth edition (1926) then had articles by an imposing assembly of men and women of action, among them the industrialist Henry Ford, the magician Harry Houdini, the tennis champion Suzanne Lenglen, the American secretary of state Elihu Root, and the Bolshevik revolutionary Leon Trotsky.

---

[165] Kogan, *Great EB*, 176. Similarly, as of 1958, the *Britannica*'s policy was "to ask leaders of religious faiths to advise and verify factual points." See *ibid.*, 294.

[166] Einbinder, *Myth*, 67–8, 189–92, 287. For similar examples of pro-Catholic entries by Catholics see *ibid.*, 67.

[167] *Ibid.*, 64–6, 287.

[168] *Ibid.*, 193.

[169] Cavaterra, *Rivoluzione*, 173–4.

[170] Kogan, *Great EB*, 168; Thomas, *Position*, 7.

Reflecting on the many political figures who wrote for the thirteenth edition, one reviewer questioned their impartiality.[171] Similarly, in response to the announcement that the boxer Gene Tunney would cover his sport for the fourteenth edition (1929), an anonymous journalist claimed that Tunney's article would be inferior to one by a "detached expert who never set foot in the professional ring." More generally – continued the journalist – people with practical experience, however successful, were not the best suited to writing about the fields they were active in.[172] In assessing available encyclopedias in the second half of the century, the professor of librarianship William Katz expressed agreement, arguing that it was no longer appropriate for someone in an organization such as the Federal Bureau of Investigation to write on that organization for an encyclopedia.[173]

Not only did celebrity retain its allure, however, but sensitivity intensified, from the mid twentieth century onward, to issues of identity, whether religious, racial, ethnic, or sexual. For both of these reasons, it would have been unrealistic for encyclopedias to give up on insiders as potential contributors. While potentially controversial as sources of bias and favoritism, they possessed their own forms of knowledge, and they provided a means of "[not] antagonizing any well-established political, religious, or social organization," a goal of the early *World Book* (1917–18) and surely other encyclopedias.[174]

Conclusion

Encyclopedias were collaborative on an intellectual level, frequently more so than their front matter implied. Even when attributed to a single author-editor, they were almost always collaborative, dependent as they were on the work of assistants, advisors, censors, and others. As this enumeration indicates, authorship was multi-faceted in the case of encyclopedias. The familiar categories of the author, the editor, the contributor, and the compiler do not always fit, especially in the period before 1800, not only because encyclopedia-making evolved over time, but also because encyclopedists used these categories strategically to make claims about ownership, authority, and originality. Authors and contributors,

---

[171] *New York Times*, September 19, 1926: BR2.
[172] *New York Times*, December 1, 1928: [10]. On celebrities who contributed to the fourteenth edition see also Einbinder, *Myth*, 52–3.
[173] Katz, *Basic Information Sources*, 142. J. Edgar Hoover, the head of the Federal Bureau of Investigation, had previously contributed to *World Book*. See Murray, *Adventures*, 136.
[174] Murray, *Adventures*, 20.

in particular, were often little different from compilers, and censors were sometimes responsible for writing whole articles.

Authorship in encyclopedias became complex in a different way as contributors proliferated and editorial offices grew. For reasons of authority as well as expertise, specialists, including insiders, were entrusted with more and more articles. Within this multiplicity, the question of how to credit an encyclopedia's contributors took on added importance. Highlighting prestigious names might enhance a work's status and stimulate sales, but putting signatures in articles made editing delicate and could be seen as detrimental to their objectivity. Under these circumstances, editors developed a range of practices for identifying contributors or leaving them anonymous. Hierarchies emerged too, beginning with differentiation between contributors and editors, and continuing to differentiation among kinds of editors. Besides being defined by their place in the editorial office or the broader intellectual world, authors of encyclopedias were of all different sorts, but they were predominantly men, many of them journalists or ecclesiastics in the eighteenth and nineteenth centuries, and most of them academics by the twentieth century.

CHAPTER 8

Publishing an Encyclopedia

Not all encyclopedias were published. Many were planned but not finished, quite a few were advertised but never finished or published, and some were completed but still never published. Publication was neither a given, nor a process so simple that an ambitious author could necessarily undertake it alone. In fact, behind the great majority of published encyclopedias, usually inconspicuous, was a professional publisher. The publisher could be the person who initiated the encyclopedia, or even occasionally someone who edited or wrote for it, but most publishers played a minor if any role in these activities, concentrating instead on producing the encyclopedia and putting it on the market.

As noted in Chapter 3, the commercial side of encyclopedia-making – where publishing was central – has received less attention than the intellectual side. It needs to be studied, though, if encyclopedias are to be understood in relation to society. With *The Business of Enlightenment* (1979), Robert Darnton made the case for the *Encyclopédie* (1751–72), showing how a work often seen as a collection of ideas was taken up by publishers and then adapted, advertised, printed, and sold. As Darnton emphasized, publishers were critical intermediaries between authors and the public, responsible for establishing a correspondence between them. The only encyclopedias that consumers had the opportunity to buy or consult were profoundly affected by the decisions of publishers.

Here in this chapter I will examine the publishers of encyclopedias as a developing group, especially in relation to specialization, ownership, and the founding of dynasties. Thereafter I turn to their three main responsibilities: advertising, issuing, and selling encyclopedias. All three were fundamental to forming links with the public and thereby making encyclopedias profitable.

Publishers and Owners of Encyclopedias

In the context of encyclopedias, publishing became more specialized with the passage of time. Indeed, the term "publisher" is anachronistic for the period before 1800, since the people who published books had other roles too, whether as printers, as booksellers, or as distributors. Here I will nonetheless use "publisher" for a variety of proto-publishers. Conversely, from the nineteenth century onward, publishers delegated aspects of publishing to specialists – printing to printers, selling to bookstores and salespeople, advertising to marketers, and so on. While all of these activities come up in this chapter, I will focus on publishers as those who guided the process of making works available to the public.

Encyclopedias' owners, for their part, were nearly always the publishers, sometimes as proxies for groups of shareholders, and sometimes under the auspices of larger companies, but it is worth considering two alternatives.

First, planners and authors of encyclopedias occasionally retained ownership, and contracted with a publisher for printing and other work. In eighteenth-century Britain, Temple Henry Croker and others' *Complete Dictionary* and Percival Proctor and William Castieau's *Modern Dictionary* were both published "for the authors," as their title pages attest. In the early nineteenth century as well, Duckett came up with the idea for his *Dictionnaire de la conversation*, appointed the journalist Edme-Joachim Héreau editor, and entrusted publication to Belin-Mandar while still remaining the owner.[1] In general, self-publishing correlated with lackluster commercial results, but Duckett saw his encyclopedia through several editions.

Second, states or governments could be the owners of encyclopedias, or hold a stake. Indeed, from the seventeenth century onward, idealists argued that encyclopedias should be financed by states or run non-commercially. In a review of the *Supplément* (1689) to Moréri's *Grand Dictionaire*, the future encyclopedist Le Clerc argued that only a "prince" could muster the resources to revise a work like Moreri's.[2] Conversely, however, as Diderot pointed out in the *Encyclopédie*, an encyclopedia run by the government risked being finished behind schedule or not at all.[3]

Whatever the truth of the matter, many encyclopedias were subsidized, if not owned, by states. Ostensibly national encyclopedias especially were often thus subsidized, including the *Enciclopedia italiana* (1929–39) and the Yugoslavian *Enciklopedija Jugoslavije* (1955–71).[4] Support came in

---

[1] Loveland, "Two French 'Konversationslexika,'" forthcoming.
[2] Le Clerc, review of *Supplément*, 76.
[3] *Encyclopédie; ou, Dictionnaire*, v: 636.
[4] Turi, *Mecenate*, 69–73; Gostl, "Five Centuries," 120–2.

various forms. In some cases, when a government endorsed an encyclopedia, it could be bought for institutions or officials with public funding, as were the *Oeconomische Encyclopädie* (1773–1858) and the *Espasa* (1908–30).[5] In communist countries, encyclopedia-publishers were owned by the state, or rather the people, and so were encyclopedias. In East Germany, for example, both Brockhaus and the Bibliographisches Institut were nationalized after World War II and transformed into "people's companies."[6]

Leaving aside such complications of ownership, let us turn now to publishers of encyclopedias, the usual owners and providers of capital. Publishers got involved with encyclopedias for different reasons. Some were so ambitious that publishing an encyclopedia was a natural goal, whether because of its potential profitability or because of its symbolic, intellectual, or social value. The publishers of Europe's largest encyclopedias, Zedler and Panckoucke, both fit this description. So does Pierre Larousse. Two decades before the first volume of his *Grand Dictionnaire* (1866–76) appeared, he was already preparing himself to write an encyclopedia along the same lines, namely one promoting the secular and republican ideals of the French Revolution. It is true that he thought about becoming a winemaker when his parents left him a vineyard, but perhaps with the thought of building up capital for publishing.[7]

Most publishers came to encyclopedism more serendipitously. Le Breton, the main publisher of the *Encyclopédie*, was working on a medical encyclopedia when he received a proposal for a French adaptation of Chambers' *Cyclopaedia* and decided to pursue it. In his case, and that of the publishers who joined him, embarking on the project was a defining event. All four continued to publish other books, but the *Encyclopédie* was at the center of their professional life – and of their income.

For other publishers, the decision to take on an encyclopedia was not so momentous. Consider, for example, the Leers brothers of Rotterdam, Arnoud and Reinier. Together or separately, they published several editions of Furetière's *Dictionaire* (1690) as well as Bayle's *Dictionaire* (1697), but they also published hundreds of non-encyclopedias. Likewise, Charles Gosselin agreed to publish the *Encyclopédie nouvelle* (1834–42), but as the publisher of such Romantic authors as Balzac

[5] Fröhner, *Technologie*, 60–2; Castellano, *Enciclopedia*, 328–9, 498–502, 548.
[6] Keiderling, *F. A. Brockhaus*, 293–302; Sarkowski, *Bibliographische Institut*, 168.
[7] Mollier and Dubot, *Histoire*, 33–7.

and Hugo he had bigger investments, and he never returned to the encyclopedia-business.[8] So, too, the publishers of the *Encyclopaedia Americana* (1829–33) gave up on publishing it within a decade. Instead, they devoted themselves to medical works, though profits from the encyclopedia continued to accumulate thanks to their licensing of the stereotypes to others.[9]

However they made their way into the field, some publishers acquired a specialty in encyclopedias and dictionaries. Two families controlled the French market in the early eighteenth century. The Ganeau family held the rights to Bayle's *Dictionaire*, the *Dictionnaire de Trévoux*, and Chomel's *Dictionnaire*, while the Coignard family held the rights to Moréri's *Grand Dictionaire*, the *Dictionnaire de l'Académie françoise*, and Corneille's *Dictionnaire*. In 1743, they joined together to publish a new edition of the *Dictionnaire de Trévoux*.[10] Still, their involvement in encyclopedias was counter-balanced by their involvement in other branches of literature. Toward the end of the century, Panckoucke came closer to being a single-minded encyclopedia-maker as he progressively rid himself of other titles so as to concentrate on publishing journals and the *Encyclopédie méthodique*.[11]

In eighteenth-century Britain, ownership of encyclopedias was more dispersed than it was elsewhere, since most were published by congers until late in the century. Publishing in congers had advantages for publishers. First, they could share risks and resources. Such an arrangement was perfect for projects combining uncertainty with the need for investment, as projects for publishing encyclopedias did. Second, as pointed out in Chapter 3, creating a community of publishers with a stake in the same work helped control piracy. Publishing in congers limited profits, however. At the end of the century, anticipating the future of encyclopedia-publishing, Andrew Bell and Colin Macfarquhar did not mount a conger to publish the *Encyclopaedia Britannica*, the second edition (1778–83) excepted. In part for this reason, they profited handsomely from the encyclopedia, their biggest venture.[12]

Of all eighteenth-century publishers, the one most committed to encyclopedias was the Gleditsch family of Leipzig. In 1741 alone, the firm published twenty encyclopedias, general or specialized.[13] Among other

[8] On Gosselin's involvement with the *Nouvelle* see Griffiths, *Jean Reynaud*, 154.
[9] De Kay, "*Encyclopedia*," 212.
[10] Leca-Tsiomis, *Ecrire*, 131; Eick, "Defining," 186.
[11] Darnton, *Business*, 484.
[12] Doig *et al.*, "James Tytler's Edition," 70–1; Doig *et al.*, "Colin Macfarquhar," 241–2.
[13] Döring, "Leipzig," 126.

titles, Gleditsch was responsible for the century's most reprinted encyclopedia, the *Reales Staats- Zeitungs- und Conversations-Lexicon*, published by the family for over a century, as well as the *Curieuses Natur- Kunst-Gewerck- und Handlungs-Lexicon* and Corvinus's *Frauenzimmer-Lexicon*. As these examples indicate, Gleditsch published short encyclopedias in smaller formats. Along with Fritsch, another local encyclopedia-publisher, Gleditsch saw Zedler's *Grosses vollständiges Universal-Lexicon* (1732–50) as a terrible threat, rightly judging that it would plagiarize from other encyclopedias, but the firm managed to keep publishing its own encyclopedias alongside and after the *Universal-Lexicon*.[14]

A benefit for companies that made encyclopedias a specialty was their growing experience. Publishers themselves acquired experience, as did any editor who kept at the job. Increasingly in the course of the twentieth century, encyclopedia-publishers retained their whole editorial staff from one edition to the next. Here too experience accumulated and mattered. Between editions, moreover, the staff could be put to work on miscellaneous publications. Furthermore, some publishers had the staff answer purchasers' questions when the encyclopedia proved unable to. Advertising such a service was a way of guaranteeing complete, up-to-date knowledge, though not necessarily in the encyclopedia itself.

One of the earliest of these services was a bonus to purchasers of *Nelson's Encyclopaedia* (1905). Subscribers to the encyclopedia received free access to its staff whenever they wanted "a special report on any subject, large or small, old or new … with the positive assurance that … [they] will promptly receive the latest obtainable and most dependable information."[15] In 1936, Encyclopaedia Britannica opened its Library Research Service. Purchasers were entitled to ask as many questions as they wished for a period of ten years, though the number of questions was soon limited to fifty.[16] A similar service offered by Brockhaus was fielding 20,000 questions a year as of 1995.[17]

These and other expedients for making use of editorial staffs took on more importance as encyclopedia-making became less a business in which publishers could dabble. Already by the end of the nineteenth century, it had become harder for newcomers to publish encyclopedias. To do so, by this time, they needed to have the means to advertise, and they needed to

[14] On Fritsch and Gleditsch's fears see Kossmann, "Deutsche Universallexika," 1566.
[15] *New York Times*, May 1, 1909: 5; *Southwestern Law Review* 1 (June 1916): VII.
[16] Kogan, *Great EB*, 243–4.
[17] Keiderling, *F. A. Brockhaus*, 344.

have a network for distributing books. These conditions could be costly.[18] Two additional barriers to entering the market were a lack of experience and not having copyrighted material on which to build. Another problem was the crushing presence of established encyclopedia-publishers with their wide range of offerings. None of these impediments was insurmountable. One notable outsider that broke into the market was A. and F. Pears, a British soap-making company, with *Pears' Cyclopedia* (1897), though it had already entered publishing with a successful periodical, *Pears' Annual* (1891). Another interloper was Tchibo Holding, a German company focused on food and beverages, which turned to encyclopedias in 1976.[19] These were exceptions, though. Among large encyclopedias in English, the only new title to appear in the late twentieth century was the *Academic American Encyclopedia* (1980), published by the American subsidiary (Arête) of the Dutch publisher VNU. Tellingly, in 1982, after two years of poor sales, the *Academic American* began to be published by Grolier, a proven encyclopedia-publisher, and Grolier purchased it outright in 1985.[20]

In the footsteps of Gleditsch, dynastic companies devoted to encyclopedia-making began to dominate the German market in the early nineteenth century. In 1808, Friedrich Brockhaus acquired Löbel and Franke's *Konversations-Lexikon*, which was struggling commercially. In subsequent years, he placed it at the center of his company's business. There it remained, along with books on travel, for much of the nineteenth and twentieth centuries.

Like most nineteenth-century dynasties in the world of publishing, the Brockhaus firm was designed to remain in the family. Friedrich passed the company on to his sons, one of whom passed it on to his own sons, and so on. The pattern continued for over a century. In the mid twentieth century, when Brockhaus's male descendants finally failed to have sons, a son of close relatives became a successor, though he felt obliged to have his name changed to Brockhaus. Besides being led by a family, the Brockhaus firm was run like a family. Its paternalism implied generosity – as when it provided for the families of workers while they were off fighting in World War I – but it came with the expectation that workers would not promote conflict or launch a strike.[21]

---

[18] See Spree, *Streben*, 147.
[19] Collison, *Encyclopaedias*, 196; Keiderling, *F. A. Brockhaus*, 271.
[20] *New York Times*, May 30, 1980: D1; *New York Times*, March 11, 1981: D5; American Library Association, *Purchasing*, 18; *Globe and Mail*, February 7, 1985: B2.
[21] Keiderling, *F. A. Brockhaus*, 66, 91–2, 267–8, 281.

Brockhaus's competitors set up dynasties too. The Pierer family got into encyclopedia-publishing in 1822 when it took control of a *Konversations-Lexikon* begun by a defector from Brockhaus. Only in 1872, midway through the fifth edition (1867–73), did the family sell out to a different publisher.[22] Joseph Meyer, the founder of the Bibliographisches Institut and Meyer's *Konversations-Lexikon*, was too ambitious to limit himself to publishing alone. By the end of his life, he had squandered much of his earnings on investments in railroads and mining.[23] Nevertheless, the Bibliographisches Institut survived. Until around 1970, it was led by members of the family, though sometimes in partnership with leaders recruited externally.[24] The Herder family, finally, was behind Herder's *Konversations-Lexikon* throughout its century-long history – that is, from 1854 to 1968.

In France, Pierre Larousse instituted a dynasty. Neither Larousse nor his partner, Augustin Boyer, had children, but the firm went to relatives after their deaths. Once again, it was important to have the right name, so much so that Pierre's nephew Jules Hollier had his name changed to Hollier-Larousse when he came into leadership. From the mid nineteenth century onward, the Larousse company's specialties were scholastic manuals and works of reference. In the market for encyclopedias and dictionaries, Larousse aimed at domination, which it achieved through a mix of excellence and ruthless competition. By chance, it acquired control over two of its rivals – first the *Grande Encyclopédie* (1885–1902) and then the *Encyclopédie française* (1935–66) – and was able to sabotage them. When other competitors presented themselves – for example, Quillet – Larousse fought back fiercely.[25] For a long time, the company was in a struggle with Hachette, the world's biggest publisher in the late nineteenth century. An agreement signed between the two companies in 1933 limited their competition, however, assigning books related to travel to Hachette, and encyclopedias and dictionaries to Larousse. Through all of these struggles, Larousse continued to be led by descendants of Boyer and Pierre Larousse, though the families relinquished control in the late twentieth century.[26]

In Britain and the United States, enduring encyclopedias were less tied to families and often switched publishers. Among the few works to stay in a family for a half-century or more were *Chambers's Encyclopaedia* (1868)

[22] Peche, *Bibliotheca*, 461.
[23] Sarkowski, *Bibliographische Institut*, 58–60.
[24] On the family's withdrawal from leadership see Keiderling, *F. A. Brockhaus*, 283.
[25] Mollier and Dubot, *Histoire*, 98, 193, 310–12, 424–7, 432–6; Jacquet-Pfau, "Naissance," 100.
[26] Mollier, "Editer," 784; Mollier and Dubot, *Histoire*, 423–4, 610–22, 674–7.

and the *Encyclopaedia Britannica*. After the death of the publishers William and Robert Chambers, the founders of *Chambers's*, control of the company passed to Robert's son, who passed it on to his own son, but it was sold to George Newnes in 1944.[27] The *Britannica*, for its part, was owned and published by the Black firm from 1827 to 1901 – the only extended period in which a family owned it.

More generally, while companies run by families remain competitive in our time, those in the encyclopedia-business faltered and restructured in the early twentieth century. Like Hachette and Larousse, Barcelona's Espasa – responsible for the *Espasa* (1908–30) – started out as a family business with ties to the university. In 1920, following a trend among Spanish businesses, it merged with Calpe to become an "anonymous society," a company owned by an indefinite group of shareholders with limited liability.[28] In the eighteenth century already, shares in British encyclopedias had been traded among publishers, but without any involvement on the part of the public. One motive for letting investors join in owning a company was the lack of a successor within a family. Another, more common one was the need to raise money. The Bibliographisches Institut was made into a publicly traded company in 1915, pushed by financial pressure and the withdrawal of two members of the Meyer family.[29]

Becoming publicly traded was not without costs. After turning Brockhaus into a limited partnership in 1948, Hans Brockhaus considered going farther and making it a corporation with shareholders. In the end, he decided not to, fearing a loss of flexibility.[30] Likewise, when Larousse was restructured as a limited-liability company in 1931, the family would not allow the shares to be freely transferable, since it prized independence over the prospect of new capital. In the early 1970s, however, faced with competition from the *Encyclopaedia universalis* (1968–75) and the works of Quillet and the lexicographer Paul Robert, Larousse reconsidered. To innovate and compete, it needed capital, which a bank agreed to lend, but only if Larousse became a publicly traded company. With few other options, the firm changed its status in 1972.[31]

In the second half of the twentieth century, the businesses responsible for publishing encyclopedias consolidated or were absorbed by

[27] Walsh, *Anglo-American General Encyclopedias*, 22.
[28] Castellano, *Enciclopedia*, 48–51, 65.
[29] Sarkowski, *Bibliographische Institut*, 134.
[30] Keiderling, *F. A. Brockhaus*, 230.
[31] Mollier and Dubot, *Histoire*, 447–8, 574–5.

conglomerates. As of 1978, four firms controlled 95 percent of the American market for encyclopedias, the world's biggest: Encyclopaedia Britannica, which complemented its basic encyclopedia with *Compton's Encyclopedia*, acquired in 1961; Grolier, the owner of the *Encyclopedia Americana*, among other titles; Macmillan, the owner of *Collier's Encyclopedia* and the *Merit Students Encyclopedia*; and Field Enterprises, the owner of *World Book*.[32] In 1978, Field Enterprises sold *World Book* to Scott Fetzer, a diversified company known for its sales of vacuum-cleaners. In the 1980s, a period of profitability for American encyclopedias, Scott Fetzer was acquired by Berkshire Hathaway, while Grolier was purchased by the French giant Hachette.[33]

Hachette, for its part, had been bought by Lagardère, a multi-national company specializing in media, in 1980. Its rival Larousse was taken over by CEP Communications and then rolled into the mega-company Vivendi in 1998. For Vivendi, which sought to rival such media-titans as AOL Time Warner, Larousse was of little importance. Accordingly, after a financial crisis in 2002, it sold Larousse to Lagardère despite concerns about the end of competition between Larousse and Hachette.[34]

Similar acquisitions and mergers took place in Germany. In 1984, impelled by financial weakness, Brockhaus merged with its old rival, the Bibliographisches Institut. Still, the market for German encyclopedias remained divided, for the publisher Bertelsmann, which only began with encyclopedias in 1953, commanded around half of all sales by the time of the merger. Four years later, the newly founded Bibliographisches Institut and F. A. Brockhaus (BIFAB) faced the prospect of a take-over by the British media-magnate Robert Maxwell. Skeptical of its prospects in a huge foreign company, BIFAB arranged instead to become a subsidiary of Langenscheidt, a publisher of bilingual dictionaries. Further complicating the existence of the West German BIFAB was the persistence in Leipzig of East German firms calling themselves, respectively, F. A. Brockhaus and the Bibliographisches Institut. Both were ultimately brought into BIFAB after Germany's reunification.[35] Lastly, in 2009, BIFAB sold Brockhaus to its one-time competitor Bertelsmann.[36]

[32] Katz, *Basic Information Sources*, 137–8.
[33] *New York Times*, May 28, 1989: F15.
[34] Mollier and Dubot, *Histoire*, 621–53.
[35] Keiderling, *F. A. Brockhaus*, 247, 271–8, 283–8, 345–51.
[36] Keiderling, "*Brockhaus*," 196.

Advertising

Advertising was crucial to an encyclopedia's success, and it came to be more so with the passage of time. Already in 1806, the publisher John Murray wrote to Constable, who was then advertising the fifth edition (1817) of the *Encyclopaedia Britannica*: "It is inconceivable how effectually the continued advertisement of a book long previous to publication operates upon people in the country."[37] To some extent, advertising could be supplanted by a sales-force. In the early twentieth century, for example, the publisher of *World Book* could afford to skimp on advertising because of the size and effectiveness of its network of salespeople. In 1945, Field Enterprises took over *World Book* and set up a program for advertising, but policy still stipulated that advertisements should be more "for the benefit of our own salespeople than the consumer."[38] Still, whether it reached the public directly, or indirectly via a salesperson, advertising was by then seen as essential to selling.

In the course of the twentieth century, advertising and marketing became major, even predominant, expenses for encyclopedia-makers. The success of the *Petit Larousse* (1905), for example, was not just a matter of its exceptional quality but also the effect of a generous budget for advertising.[39] By the middle of the century, the owners of the *Britannica* were spending some $4 million per year on advertising, more than any of their competitors, and much more than they were spending on revisions and editorial work.[40] Likewise, in the financial year 1966–7, Brockhaus spent a million marks advertising the seventeenth edition (1966–74) of its *Konversations-Lexikon*, while the title brought in revenue of 10 million marks.[41]

Advertising for encyclopedias took various forms. Publishers brought their publications to book-fairs and broader events. In the seventeenth and eighteenth centuries, the book-fairs held annually in Frankfurt and Leipzig were vital occasions for publishers, both to exchange books and to publicize their offerings. Leipzig's fair had eclipsed Frankfurt's by 1700, and it too faced decline by the end of the century, but other gatherings provided opportunities for the inventive book-advertiser.[42] Around 1900, eager to make itself familiar to the public, the Larousse firm participated

---

[37] Kruse, "Story," 108.
[38] Murray, *Adventures*, 63–4, 116, 143, 218.
[39] Mollier and Dubot, *Histoire*, 308–10.
[40] Einbinder, *Myth*, 55, 269, 326.
[41] Keiderling, *F. A. Brockhaus*, 263.
[42] On the German book-fairs see Wittmann, "Soziale und ökonomische Voraussetzungen," 6–7, 13.

in universal fairs, for example, and a new edition of *World Book* was timed to coincide with the Century of Progress Exhibition in Chicago in 1933.[43] Encyclopedia-makers with a heritage created events of their own to commemorate centennials and other anniversaries. Even the completion of an edition could be cause for festivity. To generate publicity, a series of banquets was thus organized for those involved in the eleventh edition (1910–11) of the *Britannica*.[44] By means of such events, a publisher could impress not just the visitors and journalists attending but also those they communicated with in the following weeks.

On a more general level, making brands familiar and shaping conversation or news were fundamental to advertising. Encyclopedias with poor reputations were often retitled, but encyclopedia-makers at the top of the market were careful to nurture their titles and brands. At the close of the nineteenth century, for instance, Larousse made an effort to convince the public that "Larousse" was a synonym for "dictionary." Later, in the two decades following World War II, the company approached branding in a different way, flooding book-stores with banners, posters, mobiles, and other displays, and putting its name on such mundane objects as lighters, ashtrays, and keychains.[45] Similarly, at the beginning of the century, Albert Brockhaus had suggested advertising on the packaging of perfume and cigars.[46] The public's awareness of an encyclopedia could also be heightened by drama. Indeed, controversy and scandal were apt to fuel sales. If nothing else, Furetière's long battle with the Académie Française brought his *Dictionaire* (1690) to the attention of much of France's educated populace. Other dramas were calculated. In 1960, for example, the owners of *World Book* sponsored an expedition in the Himalayas by Edmund Hillary to search for the Yeti, the "Abominable Snowman." The trip generated publicity, and its findings were recorded in the encyclopedia's yearbook.[47]

In the twentieth century, new media were enlisted to advertise encyclopedias. Early on, there was radio. In the 1920s, it was the medium for a regular, five-minute show demonstrating the value of *World Book*. Specifically, "World-Book Man" would ask and answer such questions as "Why does a barbershop have a red-and-white striped pole in front of it?" Researching trivia in *World Book* became one of the bases for the

---

[43] Mollier and Dubot, *Histoire*, 274; Murray, *Adventures*, 91. See also Castellano, *Enciclopedia*, 430–3.
[44] Kruse, "Story," 309–10; Thomas, *Position*, 18–19, 84–7.
[45] Mollier and Dubot, *Histoire*, 311, 442, 542–3.
[46] Keiderling, *F. A. Brockhaus*, 69.
[47] Murray, *Adventures*, 232–3.

Look-It-Up Club, designed to involve children as well as their teachers.[48] Larousse too was on the radio. In the 1960s, its encyclopedic dictionaries starred in two rival programs. Every weekday, the station Europe 1 offered a program on language and dictionaries featuring "Monsieur Larousse," while Radio Luxembourg had a "Minute Larousse."

In the 1960s, Larousse was also advertising on television.[49] On an international level, the popularity of televised quiz-shows such as *Jeopardy* and *Who Wants to Be a Millionaire?* may have boosted the sales of encyclopedias indirectly. The host of *Jeopardy* was in fact hired to advertise the *American Spectrum Encyclopedia* (1991) on both television and the radio.[50] Overall, though, it remained rare for an encyclopedia to be advertised on television.

Film, finally, was a medium that a few encyclopedia-makers used for publicity. In the 1920s, for example, Brockhaus made a short film promoting its encyclopedia-business. Larousse too commissioned a documentary before World War II. More ambitiously, for its centennial, it spent some 3.6 million francs on a short film, *Je sème à tout vent* (*I Sow to the Winds*, 1952), in which extraterrestrials tried to figure out the story of earth and its inhabitants from one of Larousse's encyclopedic dictionaries. Then – worried, apparently, that the film might be too comic or surreal for its commemorative function – the firm withdrew it abruptly the same year it appeared.[51]

Despite the advantages of other media, advertisements on paper were the main means of promoting encyclopedias throughout their history. Many of these advertisements appeared in periodicals and newspapers. Already in the seventeenth century, British periodicals had advertisements for books, and encyclopedias were heavily advertised there by the early eighteenth century. Only toward 1800, by contrast, did French and German periodicals start to carry advertisements on a comparable scale. On the French side, Panckoucke was an important transitional figure. Unlike earlier publishers, he appreciated the need to stoke demand for books – in his case, for the *Encyclopédie* and the *Encyclopédie méthodique* – by diversifying their formats and advertising them heavily, mostly in periodicals.[52]

In addition to, or instead of, putting notices in periodicals, publishers had other means of using paper to advertise. To publicize all of their

[48] *Ibid.*, 68–9.
[49] Mollier and Dubot, *Histoire*, 543.
[50] Keiderling, *F. A. Brockhaus*, 368; *New York Times*, May 17, 1991: 37.
[51] Keiderling, *F. A. Brockhaus*, 100; Mollier and Dubot, *Histoire*, 443–5, 508–9.
[52] Mollier, "Contexte," 23–5; Mollier, "Editer," 772–5. On advertisements in British periodicals see Ferdinand, "Constructing," 157–73.

offerings, they distributed catalogs or flyers with lists of titles, including encyclopedias. With regard to specific works, they issued prospectuses or leaflets to stimulate interest. Such materials were usually free. Indeed, by the early nineteenth century, people could receive them without even wanting to. Supporters of the *Encyclopédie des gens du monde* (1833–44) thus allegedly threw circulars defaming the *Dictionnaire de la conversation* (1832–9) "into all the carriage-porches" in Paris.[53]

Title pages themselves were a form of advertising. In the seventeenth and eighteenth centuries, they were hung in the windows of book-stores or on the walls. At the time, most encyclopedias' titles pages were printed with alternating sections of red and black ink, which made them more striking as advertisements.

Prefaces and afterwords were also advertisements, whether boastful or modest. They often restated what had already been printed elsewhere – in the prospectus, say, or another advertisement. Conversely, since few purchasers would have read them attentively before making a decision to buy an encyclopedia, prefaces and afterwords were often abridged in more accessible advertisements. In part through this logic, the once extensive prefaces and postfaces in Brockhaus's *Konversations-Lexikon* disappeared in the late nineteenth century, replaced with similar promotional material in periodicals and brochures.[54]

Some advertisements were effective in appearing to be something else. Reviews of books could be little more than disguised advertisements, particularly when the books' publishers owned the journal reviewing them. Likewise, the common practice of sending complimentary copies to journalists, dignitaries, and other people of influence amounted to an effort to curry their favor.[55] Many of the testimonials from readers that came up in advertising were prompted by a free copy – if not from additional conflicts of interest. The owners of *Johnson's New Universal Cyclopaedia* (1875–7) took the strategy of cultivating testimonials to an extreme. Not only did they have contributors pen sugary tributes, but they somehow wrung endorsements out of such celebrities as the former American president Ulysses Grant and the current head of the Supreme Court, Morrison Waite.[56] Hundreds of the resulting testimonials were then published in advertisements and the encyclopedia itself.

[53] "… sous toutes les portes cochères." *Feuilleton* 19 (June 22, 1833): 1; Loveland, "Two French 'Konversationslexika,'" forthcoming.
[54] Hingst, *Geschichte*, 143.
[55] See for example Castellano, *Enciclopedia*, 479, 518–19.
[56] "Testimonials," 7.

Abandoning their forms, let us turn now to the contents of advertisements. Advertisements for encyclopedias touched on both their physical and intellectual aspects. Physical attributes such as size and appearance were regularly shown or described. At times, as I noted in Chapter 3, publishers sold the same encyclopedia in different degrees of luxuriousness, in which case they advertised options for paper or covers. Even in the absence of options, paper and type could be presented as strengths. Prospectuses could be set up to provide a sample of both. Alternatively, to highlight the thin but tough paper used in the eleventh edition (1910–11) of the *Encyclopaedia Britannica*, one advertisement showed a man carrying all twenty-nine volumes.[57]

Somewhere between a physical and an intellectual feature, illustration became a prominent theme in advertisements for encyclopedias. Besides the number of illustrations, publishers advertised their size and variety, their use of color, and the technologies behind them. To judge by some advertisements, one might conclude that encyclopedias were primarily about illustrations. Thus, roughly half the four-page preface to the sixth edition (1902–8) of Meyer's *Konversations-Lexikon* was devoted to illustrations, and an advertisement for the *Espasa* from around 1910 dealt exclusively with the images in "the world's best illustrated work."[58] Publicists, evidently, considered the public fascinated with illustrations. Swept along with the trend, advertisements themselves were becoming visual by the twentieth century. Those for encyclopedias typically offered a view of the set, but also, increasingly, images of users and other things.

Among the intellectual qualities most advertised in encyclopedias were three principal clusters. One was centered on newness, modernity, and up-to-dateness. Titles and sub-titles testified to qualities similar to newness, as in the *Modern Dictionary of Arts and Sciences* (1774), the *Encyclopédie progressive* (1826), and the *Neues Welt-Lexikon* (*New World-Lexicon*, 1948), while up-to-dateness was often advertised through allusion to recent happenings that older encyclopedias missed. Newness, moreover, could be interpreted as involving a broad shift in goals, as when Herder contrasted "old" encyclopedias offering raw information with the practical "new" encyclopedia that was the *Grosse Herder* (1931–5).[59]

Second were the qualities of scope and comprehensiveness. Titles, once again, were at the forefront of advertising. Consider for example

[57] Kogan, *Great EB*, 169–70.
[58] [*Meyer's Konversations-Lexikon*], 6th edn., i: VII–VIII; Castellano, *Enciclopedia*, 295.
[59] Keiderling, "Lexikonverlag," 444.

the adjectives in such titles as the *Grosses vollständiges Universal-Lexicon* (1732–50), the *Complete Dictionary of Arts and Sciences* (1764–6), the *Grande Encyclopédie* (1885–1902), and the *Grosse Brockhaus* – a title first applied to the fifteenth edition (1928–35) of Brockhaus's *Konversations-Lexikon*. Statistics too were marshaled to connote comprehensiveness, as in the statement that the mid-twentieth-century *Encyclopedia Americana* had 59,000 articles.[60] Samples of obscure information to be found in an encyclopedia could also be brought up to suggest comprehensiveness. "Why do snakes always sleep with their eyes open?" asked an advertisement for *World Book* in 1949.[61] Similarly, in the early twentieth century, editions of *World Book* were loaded with entries on small American towns so that traveling salespeople could point them out to potential customers who happened to live there.[62]

A final set of qualities commonly advertised for encyclopedias concerned accuracy, trustworthiness, and objectivity. These qualities were latent in allusions to the authorities behind an encyclopedia. Advertisements frequently identified contributors, whether as individuals or as belonging to groups such as "Nobel prize men."[63] In the eighteenth-century German states, the names of distinguished preface-writers such as Hübner and Christian Wolff were displayed in the front matter to indicate their involvement and support for the project.[64] Elsewhere, the names advertised were those of the compiler, the editor, or other contributors. As noted in Chapter 7, cynics saw the recruitment of well-known contributors as a matter of advertising, not of improving an encyclopedia's content. Regardless, from the nineteenth century onward, encyclopedias were regularly advertised with the names of famous contributors. Among the many thus advertised were Ersch and Gruber's *Allgemeine Encyclopädie* (1818–89), the *Dictionnaire de la conversation* (1832–9), the *Encyclopaedia Metropolitana* (1817–45), the *Grande Encyclopédie* (1885–1902), *Nelson's Encyclopaedia* (1905), and numerous editions of the *Encyclopaedia Britannica*.[65]

[60] *New York Times*, February 10, 1959: 68.
[61] *Life* 27 (November 28, 1949): 12.
[62] Murray, *Adventures*, 73. On the *Encyclopaedia Britannica* in this regard see Boyles, *Everything*, 252.
[63] For the reference to "Nobel prize men" behind the *Encyclopaedia Britannica* see Kogan, *Great EB*, 234.
[64] On Wolff's prefaces see Herren and Prodöhl, "Kapern," 47–8.
[65] See for example Rüdiger, "Ersch/Gruber," 19–20, 54; Loveland, "Two French 'Konversationslexika,'" forthcoming; Schmidt, "Visionary Pedant," 172; *Revue bibliographique belge* 11 (September 30, 1899): VIII; *New York Times*, May 23, 1906: 7. On the *Britannica* see for example Kruse, "Story," 126; Brake, *Print*, 38; Kogan, *Great EB*, 83, 163; Thomas, *Position*, 7, 11; Einbinder, *Myth*, 52.

Besides being implied by the names of contributors, encyclopedias' accuracy and trustworthiness were the subject of more direct claims. In the twentieth century, Brockhaus sometimes hinted that its encyclopedia was infallible, and publicized such slogans as "Brockhaus reports, but never passes judgment: Brockhaus is without prejudice."[66] Meanwhile, in the 1950s, the *Britannica* was widely and misleadingly advertised as "so universally accepted as an authority that courts of law admit … [it] as evidence."[67]

In the end, encyclopedias' intellectual merits were difficult to characterize in the space of an advertisement. As a result, many of the features advertised ended up being exhibited with superficial meticulousness. In the seventeenth and eighteenth centuries, advertisements indicated the scope of an encyclopedia with a long list of subjects or disciplines covered. A later technique for evoking scope was equally mechanical, namely signaling a range of knowledge from an entry under "A" to one under "Z." This was the basis for a slogan by Brockhaus in the late twentieth century: "From 'Amadeus' to 'Zabaglione' – the new *Brockhaus Enzyklopädie* provides knowledge in tune with the times."[68] With similar shallowness, advertisements for encyclopedias from the nineteenth century onward trumpeted numbers – the number of keywords, the number of contributors, the number of maps, and the number of images.

Two truisms came up repeatedly in advertisements for encyclopedias. First was the claim that an encyclopedia could replace a library. This claim was widespread from the seventeenth century onward.[69] Bayle, for example, rationalized the many quotations printed at length in his *Dictionaire* (1697) as giving readers access to other texts and thus an alternative to owning a library. He did not mention the fact that the quotations made his encyclopedia bigger and perhaps too expensive for readers unable to buy a library.[70] Two centuries later, readers were informed that to get everything available in the *Espasa* (1908–30), they would have to acquire a library costing twenty times as much. Ironically, by 1933, with the publication of an "appendix," the *Espasa* had expanded to seventy-two volumes

---

[66] "Brockhaus berichtet, aber richtet nicht: Brockhaus kennt keine Vorurteile." Hingst, *Geschichte*, 63, 168.

[67] Einbinder, *Myth*, 314–16.

[68] "Von 'Amadeus' bis 'Zabaglione' – die neue *Brockhaus Enzyklopädie* liefert das Wissen im Zeichen der Zeit." Hingst, *Geschichte*, 182.

[69] See for example Rochefort, *Dictionaire*, "Au lecteur"; Yeo, "Solution," 64; [Diderot], prospectus, 6; [*Pierer's Universal-Lexikon*], 2nd edn., 1: xxviii; Larousse, *Grand Dictionnaire*, 1: lxiv; Boyles, *Everything*, 352; *Popular Mechanics* (March 1908): 113; *ABC Sevilla*, January 1, 1956: 54. More generally, see Didier, *Alphabet*, 41; Spree, *Streben*, 130.

[70] Bayle, *Dictionaire*, 1: 6; Lieshout, *Making*, 138.

with a total price of more than 3,000 pesetas, thereby approaching a personal library in size and cost.[71] In any event, the value of encyclopedias as substitutes for libraries was lessened by their references to other titles, which readers would have needed a library to explore.[72] Nevertheless, in some circumstances, an encyclopedia might be the closest thing available to a library. It was for this reason that encyclopedias were sometimes brought aboard ships, say, and displayed in hotels.[73]

A second truism in the advertising for encyclopedias was that they could benefit nearly everyone. Moréri, for example, pronounced his *Grand Dictionaire* (1674) useful to all kinds of people, including – he specified – intellectuals.[74] Indeed, before 1800, encyclopedists tended to divide society into two classes, both susceptible to profiting from an encyclopedia. Almost by definition, the unlearned had everything to learn from an encyclopedia, provided it was written at an appropriate level. Meanwhile, the learned were told that, outside their specialties, they too could gain from making use of an encyclopedia.[75]

The claim that encyclopedias served the learned and the unlearned – or the generalist and the specialist, in later terminology – continued to appear in the nineteenth century and afterward, albeit less often and with the proviso that the generalist's interests would be given priority.[76] Increasingly, however, encyclopedias targeted non-intellectuals. A few eighteenth-century encyclopedias were marketed to women or the unlearned, notably Corvinus's *Nutzbares, galantes und curiöses Frauenzimmer-Lexicon* (1715), Dyche and Pardon's *New General English Dictionary* (1735), Carl Christoffer Gjörwell's unfinished Swedish *Encyclopedie* (1777–8), and Johann Ferdinand Roth's *Gemeinnütziges Lexikon für Leser aller Klassen, besonders für Unstudierte* (*Generally Useful Encyclopedia for Readers of All Classes, especially the Unlearned*, 1788).[77] Still, before 1800, it made little sense, economically, to aim an encyclopedia exclusively at the learned or the

---

[71] Castellano, *Enciclopedia*, 482–4, 511–12.

[72] See Maître, "Langue," 324.

[73] On these possibilities see for example Yeo, *Encyclopaedic Visions*, 242; Peche, *Bibliotheca*, 382; [*Meyer's Konversations-Lexikon*], 6th edn., 1: v.

[74] "… gens de lettres." Moréri, *Grand Dictionaire*, 1st edn., 1: á1v, á3v.

[75] For examples of encyclopedias' welcoming the learned and unlearned see [Marperger], *Curieuses Natur- Kunst- Gewerck- und Handlungs-Lexicon*, title page; Chambers, "Some Considerations," 2; Prodöhl, "Aus denen besten Scribenten," 87; *Encyclopédie; ou, Dictionnaire*, 1: xli; [*Grosse Brockhaus*], 1st edn., 1: iv.

[76] See for example [*Meyer's Konversations-Lexikon*], "0th" edn., 1: x; *Century Dictionary*, 1: xii. On the decline of the opposition and of references to readers' social class see Spree, *Streben*, 130–1.

[77] Goodman, *Amazons*, 15–16; Spree, *Streben*, 105; Buller, "Allgemeines Licht," 39–40; Albrecht, "Aufklärerische Selbstreflexion," 235–6.

unlearned. The situation changed in the nineteenth century as the market for encyclopedias expanded. Publishers took to advertising encyclopedias as meant for the "people," since intellectuals were dwindling as a share of the market. Besides adopting the sub-title *A Dictionary ... for the People*, the Chambers brothers admitted that their *Chambers's Encyclopaedia* (1868) was not for the specialist.[78]

After around 1800, while they abandoned the opposition between the learned and unlearned, advertisements maintained the suggestion that encyclopedias had universal appeal, insisting that the works could satisfy every profession. The long list of occupations in an advertisement for the sixth edition (1902–8) of Meyer's *Konversations-Lexikon* was a typical bit of fanfare for making the point: "Officer or official, businessman or tradesman, scholar or technician, forester or farmer, whoever else he may be or whatever professional class he may belong to, every day he is left with questions that he would like information about."[79] Britain's *Nuttall Encyclopaedia* (1900) was recommended, for its part, "to the careful newspaper reader; to heads of families, with children at school, whose persistent questions have often to go without an answer; to the schoolmaster and tutor; to the student with a shallow purse; to the busy man and man of business."[80]

An encyclopedia's imagined readership affected the tone of its advertising, and its advertising in turn affected who bought it. By and large, encyclopedias were advertised soberly, as befitted their status as expensive books of knowledge. In a memorandum, for example, the publisher of the *Espasa* (1908–30) noted the desirability of advertising tactfully to suggest the work's importance.[81] Still, too much discretion might mean that potential markets were being left unexploited. Such was the insight of the Americans who took control of the *Encyclopaedia Britannica* around 1900 and came up with a formula for reviving the sales of the ninth edition (1875–89). Their major initiatives were better advertising; temporary discounts, to pressure consumers to buy; and provisions to allow for buying on credit.[82] One advertisement, hardly isolated in its extravagance, warned of the consequences of not taking advantage of a discount: "You

---

[78] *Chambers's Encyclopaedia*, 1st edn., 1: "Notice."
[79] "Offizier oder Beamter, Kaufmann oder Gewerbetreibender, Gelehrter oder Techniker, Forstmann oder Landwirt, wer es auch immer sei oder welcher Berufsklasse er auch immer angehöre, alltäglich drängen sich ihm Fragen auf, über die er Aufschluss haben möchte." Jäger, "Lexikonverlag," 551. For further examples see [Coetlogon], prospectus; Spree, *Streben*, 4; Castellano, *Enciclopedia*, 509–10.
[80] *Nuttall Encyclopaedia*, vi.
[81] Castellano, *Enciclopedia*, 504.
[82] Kruse, "Story," 226–38.

are asked to choose … [between being among] the actors in the world's drama who have succeeded because they have been prompt, and those who have failed because they have let the moment that never comes back slip past them beyond recall."[83] The Americans' strategy succeeded, stimulating sales of the ninth edition and then selling the tenth, but it put some people off. "You have made a damnable hubbub, sir, and an assault upon my privacy with your American tactics," complained a retired member of Parliament.[84] Accordingly, when the University of Cambridge became a sponsor of the *Britannica* in 1910, it mandated less aggressive advertising, at least within Britain.[85]

An encyclopedia's price was something that could be advertised subtly or insistently. At their most subtle, advertisements could simply avoid mentioning price, leaving potential purchasers to discover it later, or inviting them to send in a request for information. Alternatively, the price or initial payment could be noted in fine print or with genteel vagueness, as in the claim that the *World Wide Illustrated Encyclopedia* (1935) cost "less than the price of three novels."[86] At the opposite extreme, the price of installments figured in the titles of certain nineteenth-century encyclopedias, notably the *Penny Cyclopaedia* (1833–43), the *Pfennig Encyclopädie* (1834–7), and the *Encyclopédie pittoresque à deux sous* (later the *Encyclopédie nouvelle*, 1834–42). Pricing was most conspicuous in advertisements for popular encyclopedias, for serially published encyclopedias, and for American ones. Even elsewhere, however, it could rise to prominence in advertising when encyclopedias faced off in intense competition.

Indeed, competition acted as a spur to comparative advertising in general. So did the choice of newcomers to set themselves up against established encyclopedia-publishers. In the early-nineteenth-century German states, for example, Brockhaus's *Konversations-Lexikon* was regularly the target of comparative advertising. Pierer and Meyer both advertised against it, as did the publisher of the *Allgemeine Realencyklopädie oder Conversationslexikon für das katholische Deutschland* (1846–50). While the latter work borrowed from Brockhaus's encyclopedia, it was advertised as superior in being six guldens cheaper, in opening with a copperplate in every volume, and in featuring typography that made it the "most beautiful" of all encyclopedias.[87] As might be predicted, the publishers of dominant encyclopedias were the

---

[83] Kogan, *Great EB*, 100–1.
[84] *Ibid.*, 105; Boyles, *Everything*, 154. On the success of the strategy see Kruse, "Story," 252–3.
[85] Kogan, *Great EB*, 156–63, 178–9; Einbinder, *Myth*, 50.
[86] *New York Times*, September 22, 1935: BR40.
[87] Peche, *Bibliotheca*, 11–12.

least enthusiastic about advertising comparatively, since doing so meant acknowledging their weaker rivals.

Besides vaunting encyclopedias as intellectual and material entities, advertisements conjured up visions of their users and purchasers. Through the end of the nineteenth century, advertisements referred to potential purchasers in two primary ways. First, as we have seen, they presented encyclopedias as suitable for different classes of readers. Second, they posited effects that possessing an encyclopedia would have on a reader, usually conceived of as an adult man. Readers of a few eighteenth-century British encyclopedias were thus assured that they could get an education by studying treatises, while readers of the nineteenth-century *Konversations-Lexikon* were promised that it would help them to acquire cultivation (*Bildung*), enter the right social circles, understand their reading, or be intellectually "emancipated."[88] The nineteenth century, generally, was the golden age for the notion that encyclopedias could advance people socially as well as professionally.[89] Still, before 1900, advertisements for encyclopedias were mainly about encyclopedias, not the possible reasons for which people might buy them.

In the twentieth century, increasingly, advertisements played to emotions. Consumers continued to be told that they needed encyclopedias in order to do well at work, improve themselves, and keep up with the times, but airier reasons were also suggested. Advertisers encouraged readers to savor vicarious experiences, as in this advertisement from 1930: "Tonight – with the new *World Book Encyclopedia* for your guide and transported only by imagination, why not start on a world tour! Explore the mysterious headwaters of the Amazon – take an around-the-world trip on the Graf Zeppelin – trek over the African field with [David] Livingston[e]."[90] More idiosyncratically, the eleventh edition of the *Britannica* was promoted as a remedy for loneliness as well as ignorance, while the fifth edition (1911) of Brockhaus's small *Konversations-Lexikon* was touted as a means of "dumbfounding" without being "dumfbounded": "I do not let myself be dumbfounded, I look it up."[91] In a subtler spirit, Brockhaus played on its reputation and consumers' supposed impatience and loyalty when

---

[88] See for example Loveland, *Alternative Encyclopedia?*, 129, 144; [*Grosse Brockhaus*], 1st edn., 1: III–IV; [*Meyer's Konversations-Lexikon*], "0th" edn., 1: XI–XII.

[89] See Gluck, "Fine Folly," 228.

[90] *New York Times*, September 28, 1930: BR19.

[91] "Ich lasse mich nicht verblüffen, ich schlage nach." Spree, *Streben*, 4. On the advertisement for the *Britannica* see Einbinder, *Myth*, 51.

it advertised the mid-twentieth-century *Volks-Brockhaus* (1931) with the slogan "back at last."[92]

In the late nineteenth century, the human focus of encyclopedia-advertising began to shift away from the adult man and toward the family, though the focus on individuals was never relinquished.[93] Women were occasionally represented alone with encyclopedias, but the suggestion was not always of intellectual seriousness. Larousse, for example, had the actress Emmanuelle Béart pose with the 2004 edition of the *Petit Larousse* under the statement "Curiosity will always be the prettiest defect."[94] A light-hearted reversal of stereotypical roles was also possible. In one illustrated advertisement from the early twentieth century, a surprised husband asked his wife how she happened to know everything, to which she answered that Brockhaus was responsible (see Figure 8.1).[95] A few decades later, a childless couple was pictured in one of Brockhaus's advertisements, this time on a couch in front of a partly empty bookcase: "Now all that is still missing is the *Grosse Brockhaus*."[96]

More and more, nonetheless, encyclopedias were advertised as part of a household including one or both parents along with their children. The usual message was that an encyclopedia ensured children's success. An advertisement for the *Encyclopedia Americana* in the mid twentieth century thus began with the question, "Why does success come so frequently to young people from homes like these?" Photographs of nine families were set out below, with testimonials about the children's educational achievements: "The families above ... credit the *Americana* with playing a vital role in their children's success."[97]

Subscription, Serialization, and Selling on Credit

As encyclopedias were costly, they created problems of funding for both publishers and purchasers. In the course of the nineteenth century, banking evolved to the point where publishers could borrow enough money to finance an encyclopedia, but the problem of affordability remained for consumers. In this section I will survey three methods of making encyclopedias affordable.

[92] "… endlich wieder da." Keiderling, *F. A. Brockhaus*, 264.
[93] See Spree, *Streben*, 131.
[94] "La curiosité sera toujours le plus joli défaut." *Livres hebdo* 522 (August 22, 2003): 67.
[95] "Woher weisst du das nur alles?" Hingst, *Geschichte*, 146.
[96] "Nun fehlt nur noch der *Grosse Brockhaus*." Keiderling, *F. A. Brockhaus*, 107.
[97] *New York Times*, October 14, 1962: 109.

Figure 8.1   Advertisement for Brockhaus's *Konversations-Lexikon* from around 1900.
Scanned courtesy of Duden from Manfred Limmroth, *Die Kunst, Wissen zu vermitteln*
(Wiesbaden: Brockhaus, 1977).

    One was subscription, in which consumers committed to buying a work before it was published. Subscribers to books that were published all at once paid a portion of the price at the time of subscription and the rest upon delivery, but in the case of books published serially – a practice characterized below – subscribers paid for installments as they appeared. As of 1750, for example, subscribers to the *Encyclopédie* were to pay 60 livres to subscribe, after which they would pay 36 livres for Volume I, 24 livres apiece for Volumes II to VII, and 40 livres altogether for Volumes VIII to X.[98] For encyclopedias published in weekly or monthly installments, subscribers did not typically make a deposit.[99] Thus, subscribers to the

98 [Diderot], prospectus, [12].
99 Wiles, *Serial Publication*, 238–9.

fifth edition (1741–3) of Chambers' *Cyclopaedia* were to pay 6d. a week for twelve pages in folio – but no deposit.[100] Normally, subscription allowed for a discount, especially when it mandated money up front. The price per installment of the *Encyclopédie des gens du monde* (1833–44), for example, was set at 5 francs for subscribers and 6 francs for non-subscribers, but subscribers had to deposit an additional 5 francs when they received the first installment.[101]

Since subscription did not necessitate a large expenditure immediately, skillful "subscription-hunters" were able to convince people to subscribe to works they might not have bought outright.[102] At the same time, the search for subscribers allowed authors and editors to prove the viability of their projects beforehand. Publishers too resorted to subscription to gauge public interest and diminish their risks. At least one of them, Pauli, the original publisher of the *Oeconomische Encyclopädie* (1773–1858), encouraged the public to help, announcing that anyone willing to seek out subscriptions would get a free copy for every ten of them sold.[103]

Though probably always a minor form of publishing, subscription was widespread in the world of encyclopedias from the early eighteenth century onward, and it correlated strongly with the size of a project.[104] The first encyclopedia to be subscribed to was Chambers' *Cyclopaedia* (1728). For the first edition, the publishers garnered 300 subscriptions.[105] Soon afterward the *Grosses vollständiges Universal-Lexicon* (1732–50), the *Nuovo dizionario* (1746–51), and the *Encyclopédie* (1751–72) were sold by subscription, their subscribers totaling around 1,500, 250, and 4,000 respectively.[106] The number of sets subscribed to was less than that sold, since some purchases were made after the deadline for subscribing. Still, the number of subscriptions is a good indicator of an encyclopedia's sales.

Subscription continued through the early twentieth century. Knight, the publisher of the *Penny Cyclopaedia* (1833–43), claimed to have reinvigorated it in the mid nineteenth century after it had declined because of disreputable practices.[107] From its beginnings, subscription had awakened mistrust. Certain titles that subscribers were solicited for failed to appear.

[100] Loveland, *Alternative Encyclopedia?*, 51, 65–6.
[101] Prospectus to *Encyclopédie des gens du monde*, 4. On the possibility of paying extra for serialization see Spree, *Streben*, 126–7.
[102] For the expression "subscription-hunter" see Lockwood, "Subscription-Hunters," 126.
[103] Fröhner, *Technologie*, 94.
[104] On the overall incidence of subscription see Raven, *Business*, 316.
[105] Walters, "Tools," 5–6, 32.
[106] Kossmann, "Deutsche Universallexika," 1567; Garofalo, *Enciclopedismo*, 32; Lough, *Encyclopédie*, 57.
[107] Knight, *Passages*, III: 271–2.

Another cause for suspicion was the pushiness of subscription-hunters. Still, Knight's claim notwithstanding, numerous British encyclopedias were sold by subscription in the early nineteenth century, including the *Britannica*, the [*New*] *Cyclopaedia*, the *Edinburgh Encyclopaedia*, and the *Encyclopaedia Metropolitana*. In addition, among the many nineteenth- and twentieth-century encyclopedias subscribed to were Larousse's *Grand Dictionnaire* (1866–76), the *Grande Encyclopédie* (1885–1902), the *Espasa* (1908–30), and the *Enciclopedia italiana* (1929–39). Brockhaus, remarkably, sold encyclopedias by subscription through the end of the twentieth century.[108]

Early on, especially in Britain but occasionally elsewhere, the names of subscribers appeared in the encyclopedia itself.[109] The goal of such listing was to attract people eager to have their names so memorialized, possibly in proximity to the name of someone famous. By the mid nineteenth century, it was no longer feasible to publish the names of subscribers, since they numbered in the thousands, if not tens of thousands. Subscription, moreover, had lost its suggestion of signifying entrance into a community, one united in its favor for what a book represented. Another implication of subscription, the guarantee of a copy in case they ran out, lost much of its force in the nineteenth and twentieth centuries as it became easier to reprint, notably because of stereotyping, and as encyclopedias converted to continuous revision. Encyclopedias' yearbooks could still be subscribed to in the manner of periodicals, but for encyclopedias themselves, all that remained of the practice was the promise of gradual payment and a discounted price. In both these respects, subscription could be supplanted by purchase on credit, examined later in the chapter. Not coincidentally, subscription disappeared from the marketing of the *Britannica* around 1900, just when the option of buying on credit appeared.

A second strategy for solving consumers' and publishers' problems with funding was serial publication, in which portions of a book – temporarily stitched together and clad in a disposable wrapper – were published at weekly or other intervals over several years. Purchasers collected and then bound the installments in volumes. As encyclopedias took years to compile, an extended schedule of publication might simply mirror their growth as texts. More importantly, with this system, publishers were spared

---

[108] Keiderling, *F. A. Brockhaus*, 263, 271, 370.

[109] Subscribers' names appeared in the *Groot algemeen historisch, geographisch, genealogisch, en oordeelkundig woorden-boek* (1725–33), Pivati's *Nuovo dizionario* (1746–51), and the first *Deutsche Encyclopädie* (1778–1807), for example.

from having to make a huge expenditure all at once, and so too were purchasers, since they paid for installments as they came out. Advertisements thus trumpeted the affordability of serially published encyclopedias, as in the claim that the seventh edition (1842) of the *Britannica* – priced at 3s. per installment – was "within the reach of all classes of the community."[110]

In a sense, any encyclopedia published volume by volume was a serial publication. Among the earliest such works were Coronelli's *Biblioteca* (1701–6) and the *Grosses vollständiges Universal-Lexicon*. Still, the category of serial publications is usually restricted to works with installments of less than a volume. Though not unknown before, serial publication became common in Britain around 1730. Weekly-to-monthly serialization of encyclopedias began in the 1730s as well – specifically, with translations of Bayle's *Dictionaire*. Installments of the *Dictionary, Historical and Critical* (1734–8) contained thirty-two pages and appeared every two weeks, whereas installments of the *General Dictionary, Historical and Critical* (1734–41) contained eighty pages and appeared monthly.[111] Then, in early 1741, Coetlogon launched his *Universal History* as a weekly serial. Within months, his initiative provoked competing serial editions from the owners of Harris's *Lexicon* and Chambers' *Cyclopaedia*. Serial publication was soon widespread for British encyclopedias.[112]

In France and the German states, it was almost a century before encyclopedias were serialized in a comparable way – that is, in installments of significantly less than a volume. In France, the *Encyclopédie méthodique* (1782–1832) was issued in parts, but the parts were large and irregularly published. The *Encyclopédie progressive* (1826), for its part, was advertised as having installments of some 250 pages, but in the end, only a handful of installments appeared. Then, starting in 1832, the *Dictionnaire de la conversation* was serialized into half-volumes of 250 pages in octavo. These installments had fewer pages than those of the *Méthodique*, and they were promised on a schedule of two per month. A year later, the *Encyclopédie pittoresque*, soon to be retitled the *Encyclopédie nouvelle*, was launched on the premise of thinner installments appearing two to three times per week, but it fell behind schedule and was ultimately abandoned.

Meanwhile, in the German states, Pierer's first *Konversations-Lexikon* was published in half-volume installments from 1822 onward. Fechner's

[110] *Spectator* 7 (July 12, 1834): 667.
[111] Wiles, *Serial Publication*, 4–5, 114–16, 287–8.
[112] Loveland, *Alternative Encyclopedia?*, 50, 64–6, 212. The first installment of the *Universal History* was advertised for sale on April 15, 1741. See *Daily Advertiser* (April 15, 1741): [4].

Hauslexikon (1834–8) was serialized in forty-eight smaller installments that came out at intervals of several weeks. Similarly, the *Wunder-Meyer* (1840–53) was advertised as appearing over four years in 252 installments of 60 to 80 pages each, though it ended up requiring a greater number of years and installments. Soon afterward, the ninth edition (1843–8) of Brockhaus's *Konversations-Lexikon* began appearing in 240 weekly numbers.[113]

Why did the serialization of encyclopedias begin later in France and the German states than it did in Britain? Serial publication in general was precocious in Britain. The book-trade there was less regulated, a situation that permitted publishers to experiment. Likewise, France's requirement of pre-publication censorship made serialization impractical, though the Académie Française had once considered it for publishing France's officially sanctioned dictionary (1694).[114] Furthermore, advertising was more developed in Britain than elsewhere, as were networks for distributing books and periodicals. These factors mattered, since the buyers of serial works had to be notified when installments appeared and had to be able to receive them at book-stores, by mail, or through newspaper-deliverers or traveling booksellers. Attitudes among consumers may have been different as well. Acting as his own publisher, the German composer Johann Gottfried Walther began issuing his one-volume *Musicalisches Lexikon* (1732) in installments, for example. Poor sales led him to entrust the project to a publisher, Wolfgang Deer, who insisted on abandoning serial publication, claiming that the small installments would be too hard to deal with. Instead, he told Walther, the encyclopedia should be published traditionally so that it could be displayed in its finished form on book-cases and elsewhere.[115]

In any event, by the mid nineteenth century, serial publication had become the norm for large encyclopedias all over Europe and elsewhere. In the twentieth century, however, the serially published encyclopedia declined. Leading the trend was the *Britannica*. Published in installments of less than a volume from its eighteenth-century beginnings through 1842, the encyclopedia was then issued volume by volume for its eighth (1853–60) and ninth (1875–89) editions before transitioning to simultaneous or near-simultaneous production.[116]

Simultaneous production aimed to remedy the biggest problems with serialization. First, the deadlines necessitated by scheduled installments

[113] Loveland, "How Serialisation Changed the Meanings," 88–9.
[114] Considine, *Academy Dictionaries*, 40.
[115] Loveland, "How Serialisation Changed the Meanings," 89–90.
[116] For an announcement of the upcoming serial publication of the seventh edition see *Spectator* 7 (July 12, 1834): 667.

could result in inaccuracy, whereas the publication of a simultaneously produced encyclopedia could be put off indefinitely until everything was satisfactory. Second, as the editor of the first *Deutsche Encyclopädie* (1778–1807) observed, only an encyclopedia prepared for publication all at once – as his work was not – could be reviewed and adjusted to make sense as a whole.[117] Still, simultaneous production came with its own challenges. One was financial, since the expense of publishing all the volumes was temporarily uncompensated by any revenue. Another was the need to bring an entire encyclopedia into a state of coherence in a short burst of time. Otherwise, if revisions were done gradually, some material would be dated by the time they were finished. In fact, since the eleventh edition of the *Britannica* had been seven years in the making by the time it was published, parts of it were probably already dated when it appeared, even parts not taken over from previous editions.[118] Pessimistically speaking, one could say that anachronisms were scattered through the alphabet with simultaneous publication rather than concentrated in early volumes in a drawn-out encyclopedia.

Soon after its realization in the *Britannica*, simultaneous publication was adopted by other encyclopedia-makers, especially in the United States, but also elsewhere. The publisher Quillet issued the six volumes of the *Dicrionnaire encyclopédique Quillet* (1934) simultaneously, for example – to the bewilderment of his rival Larousse.[119] On the one hand, many publishers now had enough access to capital to print thousands of complete sets at the same time, while on the other hand, less affluent consumers could buy a complete encyclopedia on credit. Although extending credit was risky, it spared publishers the difficulty of coordinating delivery – which could be a challenge in the case of works offered in installments of differing lengths and frequencies.[120]

Serially published encyclopedias did not disappear, though. In the first decade of the twentieth century, three of them were in progress in Barcelona alone, including the *Espasa*.[121] In France, the Larousse company's two biggest encyclopedias of the twentieth century, the *Larousse du XXe siècle* (*Twentieth-Century Larousse*, 1928–33) and the *Grand Larousse encyclopédique* (1960–4), were both published in installments of less than

[117] Goetschel, Macleod, and Snyder, "*Deutsche Encyclopädie*," 272. For similar sentiments see Zorzi, *Prodromo*, xxi–xxii; *Encyclopédie; ou, Dictionnaire*, 5: 643v.
[118] See Boyles, *Everything*, 243.
[119] Mollier and Dubot, *Histoire*, 432–3.
[120] See for example Gove, "Notes," 309.
[121] Castellano, *Enciclopedia*, 132–3.

a volume. Later still, weekly installments of the German *Enzyklopädie 2000: Die aktuelle farbige Lexikonzeitschrift* (*Encyclopedia 2000: The Topical Lexicon-Magazine in Color*, 1969–73) were sold in kiosks. Brockhaus, for its part, published its *Konversations-Lexikon* volume by volume over two or more years until it stopped printing encyclopedias in the early twenty-first century.[122]

A late innovation compared to subscription and serializing, selling on credit was a third means of coping with consumers' lack of funding. When an encyclopedia was serialized, people paid it off gradually, but publishers were careful to deliver only as much as had been paid for. In this sense, the system differed from purchase on credit, in which payments were made after the receipt of all volumes. Expensive goods such as furniture were being purchased on credit by the mid nineteenth century, and the option developed for encyclopedias around the same time.

Ironically, the first offers to sell encyclopedias on credit cropped up in France, a country mistrustful of credit and borrowing. One of the earliest concerned the *Encyclopédie du dix-neuvième siècle*. As of 1852, twenty-four of the encyclopedia's twenty-six volumes had already appeared, and the publisher offered to send them to purchasers for just 64 francs and a promise to pay 50 francs every six months until the total price of around 400 francs had been reached.[123] Shortly thereafter, the publisher Abel Pilon conceived a similar initiative. In 1865, he founded a company to sell books on credit. Then, in 1872, he affiliated himself with Pierre Larousse and began selling the *Grand Dictionnaire* on credit. As of 1873, consumers were to pay 10 francs a month, up to the total price of 200 francs, in exchange for "immediate delivery" of sixteen volumes of the encyclopedia, though in fact only ten volumes had then been published. Larousse's decision to join with Pilon and sell on credit helped ensure his company's success in the long term.[124]

By the end of the nineteenth century, the Bibliographisches Institut too was delivering complete encyclopedias after receiving a deposit. Credit in other forms was so scarce in Germany that people allegedly bought the

---

122 Loveland, "How Serialisation Changed the Meanings," 91.
123 See the advertisement in *Almanach*, [1128].
124 Mollier, "Encyclopédie," 305; Mollier and Dubot, *Histoire*, 16, 23, 135–7, 144; Mollier, *Argent*, 270–4. For the terms of sale by credit in 1873 see *Journal de l'Ain*, March 7, 1873: 4. The *Grand Dictionnaire* is referred to here as the *Dictionnaire de la conversation, universel et encyclopédique*, but its identity as the *Grand Dictionnaire* is corroborated in the advertisement in *Courrier des Alpes*, March 27, 1873: 4.

encyclopedias on credit and then immediately sold them, thereby making the purchase a loan.[125] Brockhaus offered similar terms for the fourteenth edition (1892–5) of its *Konversations-Lexikon*. By the second half of the twentieth century, even the one-volume *Volks-Brockhaus* (1931) could be purchased on credit. Instead of paying 18 marks to buy the encyclopedia outright, financially strapped customers could pay 20 marks incrementally, in monthly payments of 3 marks or more.[126]

In the United States, the ten-volume *Century Dictionary* [*and Cyclopedia*] (1889–91) was sold on credit from the outset. In a typical contract, customers committed to paying $63 for it at a rate of $3 a month. The encyclopedia was to be shipped immediately, but it would remain on loan until the payments were finished in a little less than two years.[127] So successful was the marketing of the *Century Dictionary* that several of the people involved in it were convinced that they could boost the sales of the contemporary *Encyclopaedia Britannica*. Their take-over of the encyclopedia has been narrated earlier, but it is worth repeating here that the introduction of credit was one of their main innovations. This was the first time, in particular, that books had been sold on credit in England.[128]

Publishers' acceptance of selling on credit turned them into something akin to a bank, with all the attendant responsibilities and risks. In 1899, for example, the Bibliographisches Institut was weighed down with $6 million marks in outstanding credit, an amount almost double its annual revenue.[129] From the 1920s to the 1940s, financial services for the *Britannica* were provided by Sears, Roebuck, and Company, the owner of the encyclopedia during the period. As a retailing giant with a specialty in sales by catalog and through the mail, Sears excelled in such tasks as checking customers' credit, sending out bills, processing payments, and collecting debts. These tasks were critical, since four-fifths of customers were buying the *Britannica* on credit by the mid twentieth century. Conversely, when Sears withdrew from the *Britannica* in 1947, even its generous offer to "send my people over to train your people" turned out to be inadequate, and chaos ensued at Encyclopaedia Britannica.[130]

---

[125] Sarkowski, *Bibliographische Institut*, 120.
[126] Keiderling, *F. A. Brockhaus*, 124, 265.
[127] This information derives from the contract attached to a set at the University of Nevada, Las Vegas. See also Kogan, *Great EB*, 69.
[128] Kruse, "Story," 226–9, 232; Kogan, *Great EB*, 82.
[129] Sarkowski, *Bibliographische Institut*, 120.
[130] Kogan, *Great EB*, 204, 212, 228, 253–9, 269–72.

Selling and Salespeople

Occasionally, encyclopedias were not sold at all. On the one hand, certain publishers gave away installments or entire sets of an encyclopedia to attract attention and advertise. To familiarize the public with the *Wunder-Meyer* (1840–53), for example, Joseph Meyer included installments in his magazine *Universum*. Similarly, around 1940, several hundred sets of the fourteenth edition of the *Britannica* were given to listeners who could stump the experts on "Information, Please," an American radio show.[131] On the other hand, a few encyclopedias were created expressly to be given away. *Funk and Wagnalls New Standard Encyclopedia* (1931), for instance, was for many years not available for separate sale, since it was designed as a bonus for those who subscribed to the *Literary Digest*.[132]

Still, the vast majority of encyclopedias were intended for sale. Before the second half of the nineteenth century, encyclopedias were purchased through a subscription-seller or from a book-store. Indeed, through the end of the twentieth century, encyclopedias of one or a few volumes were regularly sold in book-stores, as were, less frequently, large encyclopedias. Over the course of the twentieth century, for example, the proportion of sets of Brockhaus's large encyclopedia that were purchased in book-stores grew from a sixth to more than half.[133] At one extreme, the *Academic American Encyclopedia* (1980) was designed to be sold in book-stores and other stores so that the publisher Arête could dispense with paying salespeople. To promote sales in stores, the company spent freely on advertising, even arranging for commercials on television. Unlike other publishers, Arête did not allow stores to return unsold copies, though its discount to book-stores was generous: 50 percent. As noted earlier, Arête ended up missing its target for sales, and the *Academic American* was taken over by Grolier.[134]

In fact, however appealing the model of selling through book-stores, publishers of large encyclopedias generally spurned it. First, book-stores took a passive approach to selling books. While occasionally promoted with advertising, the books in a book-store just sat on the shelves until a customer found them and decided to buy them. As a result, book-stores were poor channels for tapping hidden demand or for creating demand.

---

[131] Sarkowski, *Bibliographische Institut*, 56; Spree, *Streben*, 231; Kogan, *Great EB*, 244.
[132] Walsh, *Anglo-American General Encyclopedias*, 66.
[133] Keiderling, *F. A. Brockhaus*, 124–5, 267, 355.
[134] *New York Times*, May 30, 1980: D1, D9; *New York Times*, March 11, 1981: D5.

Second, book-stores required a discount from publishers, often a big one, to earn a profit on sales. As encyclopedias were expensive, it was tempting for publishers to sell them independently and bypass the discount. Accordingly, some publishers launched their own book-stores. Calpe, one of the publishers of the *Espasa* (1908–30), set up a book-store in Madrid, where 13 percent of sales were sets of the encyclopedia.[135] Yet neither Calpe nor other publishers were prepared to establish book-stores throughout their markets.

How, then, did encyclopedia-publishers circumvent book-stores and sell their works? As noted above, they sometimes used influence to persuade a government or institution to subsidize purchases. To be successful, such an effort required lobbyists or specialized representatives – for example, those entrusted with arranging sales to universities. Beyond such institutional sales, encyclopedia-makers had three options for selling their products: selling in businesses other than book-stores; selling directly through the mail or catalogs; and, most importantly, selling through traveling salespeople.

Consider first sales in stores other than book-stores. *Nelson's Encyclopedia: Unabridged* (1940) and the *Academic American* were planned to be sold in drug-stores and department-stores, respectively, as well as book-stores, while installments of *Enzyklopädie 2000* (1969–73) were to be sold in kiosks and other shops.[136] None of these settings proved popular for selling encyclopedias, though.

After the book-store, the store that most attracted encyclopedia-publishers was the American supermarket from the mid twentieth century onward, in part because supermarkets were used to low mark-ups, and in part because they drew in more customers than other stores. All told, more than a dozen American encyclopedias were retailed in supermarkets, including the *New World Family Encyclopedia* (1953) and *Webster's Unified Encyclopedia and Dictionary* (1955).[137] Encyclopedias sold in supermarkets were inexpensive – much more so, in some cases, than the same works sold elsewhere. They were published in thin volumes and at times bound as paperbacks. People typically acquired the volumes one at a time, the first at a reduced price.[138] As these characteristics suggest, encyclopedias sold

---

[135] Castellano, *Enciclopedia*, 488–90.
[136] *New York Times*, May 30, 1980: D1; Walsh, *Anglo-American General Encyclopedias*, 107–8; Peche, *Bibliotheca*, 182.
[137] Walsh, *Anglo-American General Encyclopedias*, 6, 56, 67–8, 70, 83, 96, 100–1, 103, 108, 110–11, 122–3, 147, 149, 158, 173, 178, 189.
[138] See for example Williat, "Lucrative Learning," 5–6.

in supermarkets were low in prestige, though critics made an exception for those published by Funk and Wagnalls, judging them respectable and good value.[139] When Encyclopaedia Britannica was exploring the possibility of selling an encyclopedia in supermarkets in 1976, the notion was thus premised on "a discreet distance … between this kind of product and the encyclopedia as a separate entity sold door-to-door."[140]

A second means of selling encyclopedias was through the mail, normally by catalog. Encyclopedias were in publishers' catalogs from their beginnings, and they were sometimes distributed through various early forms of mail. Still, it was only in the nineteenth century, with the development of national postal services, that direct sales by mail came into their own. By the end of the century, selling by mail was one of three ways of marketing Meyer's *Konversations-Lexikon*, for example, along with selling in book-stores and door-to-door.[141] Numerous encyclopedias were sold by mail in the twentieth century, including works by such leading publishers as Brockhaus and Larousse.[142]

In the United States, Chicago became the center of the mail-order business and also a center for encyclopedia-publishing. One significant partnership within the city was between the publishers of *Encyclopaedia Britannica* and Sears, Roebuck, and Company, America's leader in selling by mail. In the 1910s, Sears took charge of selling the miniaturized "Handy Volume Issue" of the eleventh edition, initially offered for just $55. Marketing it in Sears's catalog introduced the *Britannica* to a broader, less wealthy, and more rural readership. As noted above, Sears eventually purchased the *Britannica* and maintained its ownership for around twenty years. Then Sears bought the rights to sell the *American Peoples Encyclopedia* (1948), which it did both by mail and in its network of stores, but poor sales and a governmental reprimand for dishonest marketing led the company to leave the encyclopedia-business in 1959.[143]

A third means of selling encyclopedias was through traveling salespeople. From the mid nineteenth century through the second half of the twentieth, nearly all publishers of large encyclopedias relied on this strategy. The ideas behind it were old ones. Traveling merchants and

---

[139] See for example Katz, *Basic Information Sources*, 63; Walsh, *Anglo-American General Encyclopedias*, 68.
[140] Katz, *Basic Information Sources*, 136n.
[141] Jäger, "Lexikonverlag," 564. See also Hingst, *Geschichte*, 48–9.
[142] See for example Hingst, *Geschichte*, 175; Keiderling, *F. A. Brockhaus*, 354–5; Mollier and Dubot, *Histoire*, 614; Walsh, *Anglo-American General Encyclopedias*, 84, 191.
[143] Kruse, "History," 322; *New York Times*, May 30, 1980: D9; Walsh, *Anglo-American General Encyclopedias*, 7.

book-peddlers had crossed Europe for centuries, while eighteenth-century subscription-hunters paid visits to homes. Unlike the latter, the travelling encyclopedia-vendors of the nineteenth and twentieth centuries were selling already-started encyclopedias or even completed ones, and they were usually more specialized than earlier book-peddlers, often handling a single title or the works of one publisher.

Earning a salary, a commission, or a mix of the two, salespeople were expensive, but the rationale for involving them was nonetheless strong. Demand for encyclopedias – reasoned their publishers – had to be stoked. In the first half of the nineteenth century, for instance, demand for books in general was weak in the German states, while publishers held a more than adequate supply. In this climate, spending more on marketing could boost sales substantially, as Friedrich Brockhaus and Joseph Meyer discovered.[144] Conversely, poor marketing was a factor in the lesser success of Pierer's encyclopedia.[145] And among innovations for marketing encyclopedias, perhaps the most effective was hiring traveling salespeople. Indeed, almost no form of literature was as closely connected with salespeople as the modern encyclopedia.

Teams of traveling salespeople working for specific encyclopedia-publishers appeared in the German states and the United States in the second half of the nineteenth century. They were hired by, among other firms, the Bibliographisches Institut; Brockhaus; and Alvin Johnson, the publisher of *Johnson's New Universal Cyclopaedia*.[146] A shortage of bookstores favored the emergence of such salespeople – as in the Spain of the early-twentieth-century *Espasa* – but they became a significant means of selling encyclopedias in much of the world. A bonus of having them was that they could handle deliveries as well as sales, thus saving money on postal charges.[147]

Only late in the twentieth century did encyclopedia-publishers get rid of their salespeople. Among other causes, more women started working outside the home, leaving no one to answer a salesperson's knocks; legal challenges were mounted to door-to-door selling; and printed encyclopedias ultimately fell into crisis.[148] The number of salespeople at Encyclopaedia Britannica peaked at 2,000 in 1970 and had declined to 1,000 by 1996.[149]

---

[144] See Estermann and Jäger, "Voraussetzungen," 30–1; Spree, *Streben*, 123–4.
[145] Peche, *Bibliotheca*, 456–7.
[146] Spree, *Streben*, 139; Kogan, *Great EB*, 65–6.
[147] Spree, *Streben*, 135. See also Castellano, *Enciclopedia*, 476–8.
[148] On the first two of these causes see for example *Publishers Weekly* 259 (July 23, 2012): 15; Murray, *Adventures*, 104, 169–72; Keiderling, *F. A. Brockhaus*, 354–5.
[149] *New York Times*, March 16, 2008: WK3.

When the company laid off its 70 remaining salespeople in 1998, *The Times* of London interpreted it as the "death of the [encyclopedia-]salesman."[150]

This was a death that next-to-no-one lamented. Complaints about traveling encyclopedia-salespeople were frequent in the nineteenth and twentieth centuries. They may have been exaggerated, but legal intervention shows that they were not without basis.[151] In twentieth-century America, few if any encyclopedia-publishers avoided being admonished by the Federal Trade Commission or convicted in court because of deception by salespeople. In the 1920s, for example, an official guide to selling *World Book* characterized the first step as follows: "What you say at the door to gain an audience … [should be] brief, snappy, but not explaining the exact nature of your business."[152] Fifty years later, the Federal Trade Commission prohibited the tactic, ruling that salespeople must present a card at the door stating their purpose.[153] Another ruse was to make consumers think an encyclopedia was free. In 1971, in a typical instance, representatives of Grolier, the publisher of the *Encyclopedia Americana*, brought 100 students to a motel on the pretext of selling them membership to a club providing discounts. Students who agreed to pay $500 for a decade-long membership were offered "free" encyclopedias, among other titles, not realizing that the fee had been puffed up by Grolier to include the price of the books.[154]

Ill will toward encyclopedia-sellers was rampant. The publisher Arête sought to capitalize on it when promoting the store-sold *Academic American Encyclopedia* (1980). One advertisement showed a woman trying to stop an insistent encyclopedia-salesman from opening her door: "This is no way to buy an encyclopedia." The advertisement went on to state that the *Academic American* cost half as much as the *Britannica*, in part because "we don't pay fat commissions to a door-to-door sales syndicate."[155]

Meanwhile, the pushy, dishonest encyclopedia-seller turned into a stereotype, drawn on for comedy. It appeared on television, for instance, in an episode of *Monty Python's Flying Circus* from 1969. In the sketch, a man rings a doorbell and announces himself as a burglar. At first, the woman inside refuses to let him in, worrying that he is really an encyclopedia-salesman. Finally, convinced that he is just a burglar, she lets him in, and

[150] *The Times*, January 13, 1998: 10.
[151] On the nineteenth-century German situation in this regard see Spree, *Streben*, 137–8.
[152] Murray, *Adventures*, 49.
[153] Kister, *Encyclopedia Buying Guide*, 2nd edn., 18–19.
[154] *Changing Times* 28 (August 1974): 22; *New York Times*, September 12, 1973: 50.
[155] *Texas Monthly* 9 (October 1981): 254.

he begins a pitch to sell an encyclopedia.[156] Most encyclopedia-sellers were undoubtedly less skillful in getting into houses. As the early twentieth-century encyclopedia-salesmen in John Updike's novel *In the Beauty of the Lilies* (2000) discovers, theirs was a world of "doors quickly shut," if not of worse threats such as a "disposition to make of him the morning's entertainment."[157]

Beyond the stereotypes, encyclopedia-sellers varied in their honesty and forcefulness, just as they did in their other characteristics. Nineteenth-century salespeople were almost all men, but in the twentieth century, women increasingly moved into the field, partly because it allowed for a flexible schedule. Of the 80,000 people selling *World Book* in the early 1970s, a majority worked part-time, and two-thirds were women.[158] Indeed, the top-ranked seller of *World Book* in the late 1980s was a woman, Joyce Fishman, responsible for selling an average of 200 sets a year. She earned an 18 percent commission on every sale – slightly more than other salespeople working for *World Book* – thus earning an annual income of $30,000 or so – less than an experienced schoolteacher, but more than a beginning one.[159]

For those as skilled and industrious as Fishman, selling encyclopedias could be a reasonably lucrative career. Furthermore, it was open to those without much education. Publishers generally provided some form of training. In 1924, for example, the publisher of the *Espasa* set up a school for its salespeople to teach them politeness and to help them adjust pitches to the customer's profession, psychology, and cultural background.[160] Many people, however, turned to encyclopedia-selling as a temporary or part-time activity, notably the young. In the mid twentieth century, the publisher of *World Book* recruited schoolteachers as salespeople during the summer, recognizing that they had the time and motivation to take a seasonal job, and would be persuasive as sellers to the families in their area.[161]

Conclusion

In the nineteenth and twentieth centuries, a few publishers rose to eminence because of encyclopedias. Some of their names were consecrated

---

[156] Wirth, "Discursive Stupidity," 281–2.
[157] Updike, *In the Beauty*, 90.
[158] Coyne, "Effects," 11.
[159] *Boston Globe*, August 21, 1989: 10. For schoolteachers' salaries see for example *New York Times*, November 26, 1989: LI10.
[160] Castellano, *Enciclopedia*, 479.
[161] Stockwell, *History*, 137; Murray, *Adventures*, 81, 160.

in titles. Indeed, the names of Larousse and Brockhaus became quasi-synonymous with "encyclopedia." Yet research on the publishers and publication of encyclopedias remains outweighed by research on encyclopedias' contents. To a degree, the imbalance reflects disregard for the practical side of encyclopedism. It also reflects the reality that an encyclopedia's contents are lasting, whereas clues to how it was published are widely dispersed, when not simply destroyed. Advertisements in particular are hard to recover, especially posters, circulars, and wrappers for the installments of serially published encyclopedias. It is challenging, likewise, to reconstruct the details of how an encyclopedia was sold, since a completed set shows little trace of how it was issued and paid for. Even door-to-door sales-people, long a near necessity for selling large encyclopedias, only vaguely endure as a memory and caricature. All these elements of publishing must nonetheless be attended to if we wish to understand encyclopedias in their cultural contexts.

Two factors distinguished the publication of encyclopedias from that of other books. First, encyclopedias were bigger, and sometimes much bigger. The risk associated with publishing them, before 1800 especially, deterred all but the most determined and daring of publishers. Others banded together to lessen their risk – and to pool capital – or resorted to the innovations of subscription and serializing. In the nineteenth and twentieth centuries, the size of encyclopedias continued to matter even as capital became more available and as forecasts for sales grew more reliable. In particular, the fact that encyclopedias were regularly big enough to command a high price made it advantageous for publishers to circumvent book-stores and engage their own salespeople.

Second, encyclopedias were not only expensive but also educational books. Advertisements, consequently, tended toward staidness. Before the mid nineteenth century, they were often little more than descriptions of contents. Thereafter, increasingly, they connected encyclopedias with aspirations and feelings. Advertising for encyclopedias occasionally featured humor, whimsy, and nastiness, but it was owing to the conduct of their salespeople – which could be aggressive, not to mention deceptive – that publishers endured the most scolding for behavior deemed unsuited to purveyors of truth.

CHAPTER 9

Readers and Users of Encyclopedias

Writing a history of reading is challenging.[1] Records can be found of those who borrowed or bought books, but people's interactions with books remain otherwise hard to determine. Above all, exceptional forms of reading are the most likely to leave a discoverable trace. Reviewers and critics compose accounts of their reading, authors and scholars scatter clues about their reading in what they publish, and readers who are struck by a text may refer to the experience of reading it in a letter or diary. Meanwhile, the vast majority of people neither publish nor write about how or what they have read. Unfortunately, these are precisely the readers whose experiences should count most in any history of reading not confined to elites. The problem is analogous to the one, in anthropology, of finding an informant who is both representative and willing to talk for hours with an inquisitive stranger – the anthropologist. Yet the problem is aggravated for the historian of reading by the fact that many book-readers are already long dead and thus inaccessible.

It is especially hard to study how works of reference were used. Scholars declined to cite them, thinking them embarrassing or not worth the bother. Some were marked in or annotated, including institutional copies, notwithstanding the threat of punishment by a watchful librarian, but most owners judged them too valuable to be defaced with writing.[2] One critic of *Johnson's New Universal Cyclopaedia* (1875–7) objected, for example, to a plan by the editor to have owners pen in corrections from a printed list of mistakes: "The plan of making alterations in the margin of the page will not be satisfactory to those who, like myself, prefer see a volume not marred by manuscript annotations."[3] Even in the twentieth century, in an era of polling and behavioral analysis, few data were collected on how

---

[1] On the history of reading and its sources see for example Lyons, *History*, 2–8.
[2] See Blair, *Too Much*, 230.
[3] "*Johnson's New Universal Cyclopaedia*: A Dictionary," 6.

people used encyclopedias. Robert McHenry, an editor-in-chief for the *Encyclopaedia Britannica* late in the century, was only exaggerating a little when he wrote that the "secret of the encyclopedia industry is that we don't know whether or not people read what we publish."[4]

Here, nonetheless, I will venture some conclusions about the uses of encyclopedias and those who used them, drawing on evidence from memoirs and other sources, as well as on extrapolation from encyclopedias' contents. My first section examines some broad ways encyclopedias were used. Then, because many encyclopedias were published in installments, I turn to the question of how they differed from periodicals, notably for readers. In the last two sections, finally, I analyze encyclopedias with respect to education. On the one hand, they were cast as having the power to educate, while on their other hand, their articles were premised on previously acquired knowledge.

Non-Users, Browsers, Readers, Consulters

Alphabetical order made encyclopedias good for consulting, and authors shaped material into the form of an encyclopedia to make it consultable. Consultation, in this light, was what encyclopedias were made for. Here, all the same, I will consider three other ways encyclopedias were used. All three ran counter to the ideal of the encyclopedia as a work to be consulted, but in practice, the first two – non-use and browsing – were probably common, and possibly as common as consultation.

Almost every owner of an encyclopedia left much of it unread. Indeed, a study from the second half of the twentieth century found that only 2 percent of owners looked up material in their large *Konversations-Lexikon* "often or regularly."[5] The other 98 percent were the "non-users" evoked in this section. Their existence, and the existence of overlooked articles, can be inferred indirectly. First, there are older encyclopedias in near-perfect condition – a few with "uncut" pages, that is, with sequences of pages still attached along the edges and thus plainly unread. Second, though many errors were corrected in subsequent editions or pointed out in errata, many others were perpetuated through multiple editions, apparently unnoticed or disregarded by all.

Evidence for the non-use of encyclopedias comes from owners as well. Recalling his upbringing in the mid twentieth century, the journalist

[4] Stross, *Microsoft Way*, 93.
[5] Keiderling, *F. A. Brockhaus*, 343.

Howard Reich wrote that his parents bought him the *Encyclopaedia Britannica* but ordered him not to put his "greasy hands" on it until he became a university student.[6] So too, the story-teller Kambri Crews remembered consulting books on sexuality during her childhood in the 1970s and 1980s while a set of *World Book* "gathered dust."[7] Anecdotes about the neglect of encyclopedias are comparatively rare, presumably because not using an encyclopedia was less remarkable than using one. Still, the possibility was widely appreciated, as indicated, for example, by an advertisement for *Collier's Encyclopedia* in 1960: "The new 20-volume *Collier's* is one encyclopedia that won't gather dust on a bookshelf."[8] In fiction, not surprisingly, an unused encyclopedia signaled a character's pretentiousness or lack of curiosity.

Stories about rarely or never consulted encyclopedias are all the more credible in that encyclopedias had functions that were not intellectual. Some of these functions were concrete and serendipitous. Like other books, encyclopedias could be used to press flowers or to store money, as in Isaac Singer's story "The Key."[9] A late-eighteenth-century enthusiast of the naturalist Jacques-Henri Bernardin de Saint-Pierre advised his son to use the *Encyclopédie* as a chair, while reading, instead, one of Bernardin's books.[10] Similarly, in Colette's novels of the early twentieth century, encyclopedias provided shelter for a cat in one instance and a child in another.[11]

No encyclopedia, obviously, was bought for such purposes, but people did buy them for display. Before the mid eighteenth century, an encyclopedia did little to dress up a room, since it typically extended to just two or three volumes, if even that. In his second edition (1738), Chambers thus boasted that his two-volume *Cyclopaedia* would "answer all the purposes of a library, except parade and encumbrance."[12] As encyclopedias grew, they became more central to private libraries and domestic décor. Wishful thinking played a role, as Coleridge noted in 1803: "Great works are nowadays bought – not for curiosity … but under the notion that they contain all the *knowledge* a man may ever want, and if he has it on his *shelf*, why there it is, as snug as if it were in his *brain*."[13]

---

[6] Reich, *First and Final Nightmare*, 30.
[7] Crews, *Burn*, 45.
[8] *Saturday Review* 43 (March 19, 1960): 24.
[9] *New Yorker*, December 6, 1969: 65.
[10] Llana, "Natural History," 24n.
[11] Pruvost, "De Diderot," 62.
[12] Yeo, "Solution," 64.
[13] Coleridge, *Collected Letters*, II: 962.

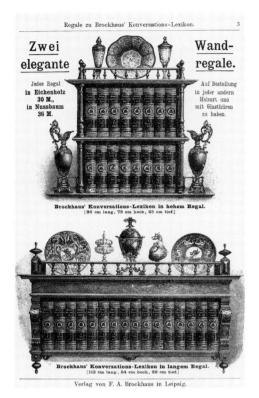

Figure 9.1   Image of a book-shelf for Brockhaus's *Konversations-Lexikon*,
as advertised in the fourteenth edition, Vol. xv. Scan courtesy of the Collections
of the University of Toronto Libraries.

From around 1850 to 1950, encyclopedia-publishers sold custom-made book-shelves and book-cases – to display, for example, the ninth edition (1875–89) of the *Britannica*, the fifth edition (1893–7) of Meyer's *Konversations-Lexikon*, the *New International Encyclopaedia* (1902–4), and the *Espasa* (1908–30).[14] Between 1894 and 1913, Brockhaus sold almost 20,000 sets of its *Konversations-Lexikon*, or 5 percent of the total, along with a book-shelf (see Figure 9.1).[15] The encyclopedia became a visible

---

[14] Kogan, *Great EB*, 83–4; Estermann, "Lexika," 252; *New York Times*, October 20, 1929: BR25; Castellano, *Enciclopedia*, 140, 488–9.
[15] Keiderling, *F. A. Brockhaus*, 28.

fixture in middle-class homes. Already in 1809, a British reviewer imagined that "our children will be as puzzled to find a house unprovided with a general dictionary [encyclopedia], as [to find one] destitute of a window or a hearth."[16] Likewise, in 1907, an article giving a design for a book-case for encyclopedias claimed that they were "rapidly becoming an essential part of the furnishings, not only of the home library but of the sitting-room."[17] Doctors and lawyers were also putting encyclopedias in their offices, perhaps to consult, but also as a sign of learning. In the novel *Madame Bovary* (1856), the hapless medical practitioner Charles Bovary has an "uncut" and thus never-used copy of the sixty-volume *Dictionnaire des sciences médicales* (1812–22) on the shelves in his office.[18]

As this example indicates, encyclopedias had symbolic functions. Above all, they signified learning, or an aspiration to learning, but they had other meanings too. As shown in Chapter 2, they could announce a nation's status and reveal a buyer's patriotism, and they could valorize fields of knowledge merely by covering them, as the *Encyclopédie* did with the mechanical arts. For many in Europe, acquiring the *Encyclopédie* was, more importantly, a sign of solidarity with the Enlightenment. Encyclopedias could also be gifts, notably in rites of passage. In twentieth-century France, certain villages gave children the *Petit Larousse* to solemnize their completion of elementary school.[19] In the late twentieth century, some Germans gave teenagers a set of Brockhaus's *Konversations-Lexikon* or another encyclopedia at the time of their confirmation in a Christian church.[20] Lastly, encyclopedias could represent dreams of success or of relief from insecurities about one's place in society.[21] While sensitivity to such symbolism did not rule out reading or consulting an encyclopedia, neither did it necessitate opening the volumes at all.

Numerous though they may have been, non-users of encyclopedias were not the only owners. Another kind – and not necessarily an owner – was the curious reader, someone looking for stimulation or entertainment rather than anything specific. Within Christianity, curiosity had long been considered a vice, but it was partially rehabilitated in the sixteenth

[16] "Dictionaries," 541.
[17] *Craftsman* 11 (February 1907): 620. See also Jäger, "Lexikonverlag," 541; Michel and Herren, "Unvorgreifliche Gedanken," 51.
[18] Flaubert, *Madame Bovary*, 30. More generally, see Keiderling, "Lexikonverlag," 460.
[19] Pruvost, *Dent-de-lion*, 31–4.
[20] I would like to thank Hans-Jürgen Lüsebrink and Ina Paul for sharing their experiences in this regard.
[21] On encyclopedias' functions, including symbolic ones, see Michel and Herren, "Unvorgreifliche Gedanken," 42–54.

and seventeenth centuries, as it was, for example, in Furetière's *Dictionaire* (1690).[22] References to "curious" content – presumably content that curious readers would delight in – appeared in the titles of encyclopedias and dictionaries through the mid eighteenth century. Among other such titles were those of Moréri's *Grand Dictionaire historique; ou, Le mélange curieux de l'histoire sainte et profane* (*Great Historical Dictionary; or, Curious Miscellany of Sacred and Secular History*, 1674), the *Curieuses Natur- Kunst- Gewerck- und Handlungs-Lexicon* (*Curious Dictionary of Nature, Art, Trades, and Business*, 1712), and Pivati's *Nuovo dizionario scientifico e curioso* (*New Scientific and Curious Dictionary*, 1746–51). The selection of articles in the *Esprit de l'Encyclopédie* (1768) was likewise announced on the title page as containing what was most "curious" and "stimulating" in the *Encyclopédie*.

Encyclopedias were all the more likely to arouse curiosity because of alphabetical order, which brought together articles on disparate topics. Such juxtapositions – Chambers argued in his *Cyclopaedia* (1728) – could help the intelligent discover new truths.[23] For those less ambitious, alphabetical order could be a source of delight in itself.[24] At the minimum, a curious reader could flit from one article to an unrelated one nearby.

Beyond the curiosity-inspiring potential of alphabetical order, seventeenth- and eighteenth-century encyclopedias offered specific curiosities.[25] According to Furetière's *Dictionaire*, a curiosity was something rare, unique, or secret.[26] Such things came up repeatedly in contemporary encyclopedias, in part because curiosities were inherently interesting, but also because the period's intellectuals had a veneration for facts, many of them so extraordinary as to qualify as curious.[27] Chomel thus offered "secrets" in his *Dictionnaire oeconomique* (1709), notably for improving harvests, while Chambers' *Cyclopaedia* had entries on mermaids and tarantulas but not on more mundane animals such as the bear or the cat.[28] In addition, curious readers were courted with humor, surprises, and vicarious thrills. Furetière, who expressed pride in his encyclopedia's curiosities, not only evoked marvels but attempted to amuse or shock readers

[22] Blair, "*Curieux*," 101–7.
[23] Yeo, *Encyclopaedic Visions*, 140–1.
[24] Rauch, *Useful Knowledge*, 32.
[25] Spree, *Streben*, 26; Quemada, *Dictionnaires*, 85–7.
[26] Furetière, *Dictionaire*, 1: zzz2r.
[27] See Daston and Park, *Wonders*, 218, 236–40.
[28] Leca-Tsiomis, "Rhétorique," 121–3; Loveland, "Animals," 513. See also Ross, "Thomas Corneille's *Dictionnaire*," 74.

with incongruous comparisons – for example, between a strawberry and a wet-nurse's nipple, or between the virtues of women and horses.[29] Likewise, in "Russland," on Russia, the *Grosses vollständiges Universal-Lexicon* (1732–50) alternated between apparently objective material and melodramatic recreations of critical events.[30] As Marie Leca-Tsiomis observes, browsers in the period's encyclopedia could expect the unexpected.[31]

In the *Encyclopédie*, marvels such as "monstrous" or deformed living beings continued to be attended to, while subversive messages appeared in odd forms and places, gratifying or outraging those who encountered them. Still, unlike many preceding encyclopedists, neither Diderot nor D'Alembert dwelt on curiosities or advertised the work's appeal to curious readers. It might be inferred, on this basis, that the culture of curiosity was being distanced from encyclopedias. Scientific and philosophical interest in curiosities was certainly waning by 1800, as simple facts came to matter less than theory and analysis.[32] Meanwhile, a growing emphasis on objectivity and homogeneity as ideals for encyclopedias put curiosities in an uncertain position. For proponents of these ideals, oddities, freaks, and secrets did not belong to knowledge, and surprises and drama did not belong in an encyclopedia. By the early nineteenth century, moreover, owners of encyclopedias may have had less time for curiosity than the wealthier, more aristocratic owners of previous centuries.

Regardless, encyclopedias went on serving the curious. One that conspicuously did so was Pierre Larousse's *Grand Dictionnaire* (1866–76). Out of tune with the majority of encyclopedists of his time, Larousse not only flouted the conventions of homogeneity and impersonalness but also included jokes, digressions, and idiosyncratic judgments, all of which favored browsing through his encyclopedia for pleasure. Furthermore, he was skeptical of historical interpretation and continuity in history. Consequently, to make sense of things, he relied heavily on anecdotes – singular curiosities by definition. In the article "Anecdote," he supplied twenty columns of anecdotes, beginning with the following: "Not many days before her death, the young Mme [Louise] d'Houdetot looked very pensive. 'What are you thinking about?' she was asked. 'I am mourning myself.'" Afterward, using a large font for emphasis, Larousse defended anecdotes as appropriate for his encyclopedia. Among other arguments, he

---

[29] Parmentier, "Abondance," 68–9, 74–6; Loveland, "Animals," 511.
[30] Schneider, *Erfindung*, 138–42.
[31] Leca-Tsiomis, *Ecrire*, 50–1.
[32] See Pickstone, *Ways*, 10–12, 60–1, 73.

characterized them as "oases" where readers could take a break from their serious consultations.[33]

Larousse's *Grand Dictionnaire* was exceptional, but encyclopedias for children encouraged curiosity through the twentieth century and beyond. Advertisements highlighted their appeal to the curious, as did this one for *World Book* in 1956: "It excites curiosity, stimulates the desire to learn, [and] opens broad new horizons."[34] Children's encyclopedias did in fact arouse curiosity. One did so, for example, in the future writer Nelly Fouillet in the early twentieth century: "In the evening … I leafed through the Larousse dictionary on the kitchen table. Never, even today, have I tired of turning its pages."[35]

In the end, nonetheless, the type of encyclopedia mattered less than the child who was curious about it. Thus, Robert Chambers – in later life an encyclopedia-maker – satisfied his youthful curiosity with the fourth edition (1810) of the *Encyclopaedia Britannica*: "What the gift of a whole toy-shop would have been to most children, this book was to me. I plunged into it. I roamed through it like a bee. I hardly could be patient enough to read any one article, while so many others remained to be looked into."[36] Likewise, growing up in a Hungarian village before World War II, the future engineer Joseph Molitorisz found himself interested in one title alone, the *Révai nagy lexikona* (*Great Révai Lexicon*, 1911–35), a twenty-one-volume encyclopedia that was only moderately illustrated and not intended for children: "On the rare occasions I was allowed to stay in [my] father's study I sat on the floor paging through the marvelous books. When I was sick and had to stay in bed, my mother brought me one volume at a time, and with that I was well occupied."[37]

At the same time, as texts in encyclopedias grew more to-the-point, homogeneous, unemotional, and predictable, illustrations became sanctuaries for the alluring and wondrous, arousing curiosity and inspiring users to browse. Typically, in his memoirs, the critic Georges Solovieff remembered looking at the illustrations in the *Petit Larousse* while growing up in Berlin in the early twentieth century.[38] Likewise, Horace Porter, a literary scholar, emphasized illustrations in his remembrances of *World*

[33] "Peu de jours avant sa mort, la jeune Mme d'Houdetot avait l'air très pensif. 'A quoi rêvez-vous?' lui dit-on. 'Je me regrette.'" Larousse, *Grand Dictionnaire*, 1: 345, 350. See also Moyal, "Lexiques," 29.
[34] *Life* 41 (November 19, 1956): 105.
[35] "Le soir … je feuilletais le dictionnaire Larousse sur la table de la cuisine. Jamais, même aujourd'hui, je ne me suis lassée d'en tourner les pages." Sainte-Soline, *Années*, 27.
[36] Chambers, *Memoir*, 60.
[37] Molitorisz, *Memoirs*, 30.
[38] Solovieff, *Enfance*, 57.

Book in the mid 1950s: "Those green and white volumes were a godsend. I looked at the colorful pictures of various animals. I studied the marvelous illustrations of human anatomy. I read about electricity."[39]

In keeping with Porter's memory of anatomical images, sexuality was an area where encyclopedias both satisfied and stimulated curiosity. In the absence of other resources, young people turned to encyclopedias for information on the topic, whether visual or textual. William Yeats, the future poet, confirmed his developing knowledge of sexuality in a multi-volume encyclopedia from the late eighteenth century.[40] So too, purportedly, the early-twentieth-century artist George Grosz discovered the facts of sexuality in the article on copulation ("Begattung") in Brockhaus's *Konversations-Lexikon*.[41] More generally, Sigmund Freud, the founder of psychoanalysis, claimed that neurotics satisfied their youthful curiosity about sexual matters by looking things up in a *Konversations-Lexikon*.[42]

As adults – not adolescents – bought encyclopedias, publishers in the nineteenth and early twentieth centuries proclaimed their discretion on sexual topics and accused their rivals of "indelicacy." This latter charge was leveled against *Johnson's New Universal Cyclopaedia* (1875–7), for instance.[43] Conversely, in 1858, Pierre Larousse stressed the suitability of his *Nouveau Dictionnaire* (1856) for use in schools by noting that he had left out "[a]ny words which are the object of indiscreet investigations or questions by students." The *Nouveau Dictionnaire* was the ancestor of the *Petit Larousse* (1905). Indeed, through a combination of omissions and vagueness, the founder's commitment to primness was upheld through the 1959 edition of the *Petit Larousse*. Even thereafter, technical explanations for sexual terms kept children from understanding them.[44] Still, in mid-twentieth-century Quebec, where the stock of books in a household rarely went far beyond the *Petit Larousse*, children were resourceful, not only seeking out definitions of prohibited words but also studying the human bodies in the encyclopedia's reproductions of artworks.[45]

Notwithstanding the popularity of sexual material, curious readers of encyclopedias all pursued their own interests. According to the writer Heinrich Heine, residents of Berlin were eager to receive a supplement to

---

[39] Porter, *Making*, 10.
[40] Yeats, *Reveries*, 26–8.
[41] Sahl, *Memoiren*, 163.
[42] Freud, *Traumdeutung*, 355n.
[43] "Reply," 6.
[44] "Tous les mots qui sont, de la part des élèves, l'objet de recherches ou de questions indiscrètes." Lehmann, "Evolution," 223–37.
[45] Boulanger, "Epopée," 255–6.

Brockhaus's *Konversations-Lexikon* in 1822, knowing it would have articles on much-talked-about contemporaries. Upon receiving the first installment, Heine himself eagerly examined such articles.[46] As a youth in the early twentieth century, the future philosopher Jean-Paul Sartre "reveled" in the summaries of literary works in the *Nouveau Larousse* (1897–1904).[47] And around a century earlier, the young Charles Boner, later a poet, found himself attracted to so many of his encyclopedia's subjects that he stands as a paragon of the curious reader:

> Another work which afforded me endless amusement … was an encyclopedia (the London, or Edinburgh, I don't remember which) in eight folio volumes, belonging to my father. Here, then, I could read at my will on any subjects I chose. One thing led me to another, and one volume was seldom enough to have by me. With this book I could occupy myself a whole day, for if I found one subject a little too dry or tedious, it was easy to turn to another less deep, or to look over the plates of skeletons, of the planets, of flowers, animals, machines, instruments, in fact, all that was therein.[48]

Browsing in an encyclopedia could lead to sustained reading. In the *Encyclopédie*, D'Alembert maintained that "dictionaries by their very form are only appropriate for consulting, and disallow continuous reading."[49] Other encyclopedists, by contrast, insisted that their own encyclopedias were designed to be read. Harris, for example, wrote in the preface to the *Lexicon Technicum* (1704) that "it is a book useful to be *read carefully over*, as well as to be consulted like other dictionaries."[50] Likewise, the publisher Joseph Meyer characterized his *Wunder-Meyer* (1840–53) as a book for reading ("Lesebuch") as well as reference ("Nachschlagewerk").[51]

Such claims invite skepticism, for they doubled as advertisements, but some people clearly read from encyclopedias at length. On more than twenty days between 1812 and 1833, for example, the American minister Thomas Robbins noted in his diary that he had "read encyclopedia," a reference to the *Edinburgh Encyclopaedia* (1808–30), which he was receiving in parts.[52] Only twice did he indicate what his reading concerned: the

[46] Heine, *Sämmtliche Werke*, v: 203–4.
[47] Sartre, *Words*, 71.
[48] Boner, *Memoirs*, 9.
[49] "Les dictionnaires par leur forme même ne sont propres qu'à être consultés, et se refusent à toute lecture suivie." *Encyclopédie; ou, Dictionnaire*, 1: xxxiv.
[50] Harris, *Lexicon*, 1: b1r.
[51] Peche, *Bibliotheca*, 366.
[52] See Robbins, *Diary*, 1: 518, 527, 534, 540, 603, 621, 648, 650, 664, 698, 699, 703, 733, 849, 1014, 11: 102, 103, 170, 304. On his acquisition and binding of the encyclopedia see *ibid.*, 1: 515, 520, 527, 540, 549, 582, 600, 648, 733, 802, 848, 882, 11: 188, 198, 275, 303. Robbins was "pleased" with the *Edinburgh Encyclopaedia* and later acquired the *Encyclopédie*. See *ibid.*, 1: 518, 11: 957.

"subject of my numbers for the newspaper" on August 2, 1828, and "canals" a few days later.[53] Yet his reading was clearly extensive at times, for on two occasions, in 1818 and in 1830, he wrote that he had read from his encyclopedia for "most of the day."[54]

More extraordinarily, throughout the history of the modern encyclopedia, there were anecdotes about people who read whole encyclopedias. Andrew Kippis, who edited the second edition (1778–93) of the *Biographia Britannica* (1747–66), supposedly read a ten-volume translation of Bayle's *Dictionaire* when he was young, while the future empress of Russia, Catherine II, supposedly read a French edition of Bayle's *Dictionaire* over the course of two years.[55] In the case of the *Encyclopédie*, we know of a few instances of comprehensive reading. Pierre Mouchon, the indexer, obviously read it all carefully, while Jaucourt, the main contributor, knew his way around it if nothing else.[56] Collaborators aside, the writer Genlis declared that she had read the *Encyclopédie* twice, a boast she could back up with two volumes of notes.[57] In the next generation, the physicist André-Marie Ampère claimed to have read it all too.[58]

According to legend, the American inventor Thomas Edison read the *Penny Cyclopaedia* (1833–43) "before he was twelve."[59] In the second half of the nineteenth century, a regular at New York's Astor Library was reported to have read the whole "*American Encyclopaedia*" – probably an edition of Appleton's *American Cyclopaedia* (1873–6) – and then started it over from Volume 1.[60] Around 1865, the businessman William Jackson, a member of the British Parliament, gave an autobiographical speech meant to demonstrate the possibility of getting ahead in society. Among other things, he highlighted his youthful reading of the *Britannica*: "It was his education … His subsequent career had been one of uninterrupted success. But he wondered where he should have been had he not read" the *Britannica*.[61] As an adolescent in the 1960s, Margaret Downey, a future activist for atheism, received a set of *World Book* and "made a vow to read … [the volumes] from 'A' to 'Z,'" which she apparently did.[62] Finally, as a stunt, the journalist

---

[53] *Ibid.*, II: 102, 103. Robbins contributed to a newspaper.
[54] *Ibid.*, I: 733, II: 170.
[55] Tankard, "Reference Point," 46; Rétat, *Dictionaire*, 129.
[56] See Baczko, "Trois temps," 763–5. See also *Encyclopédie; ou, Dictionnaire*, V: 648; Groult, *Encyclopédie*, 300; Haechler, *Encyclopédie*, 169.
[57] Genlis, *Mémoires*, VII: 81n.
[58] Hofmann, *André-Marie Ampère*, 13–14.
[59] See for example *Popular Science Monthly* 13 (August 1878): 487.
[60] *Deseret Weekly* 39 (September 28, 1889): 440.
[61] *Christian Miscellany*, second series 12 (1866): 205. See also Boyles, *Everything*, 360.
[62] Downey, "My 'Bye Bull' Story," 11.

A. J. Jacobs read the *New Encyclopaedia Britannica* and chronicled the experience in a book, *The Know-It-All* (2004).[63]

Faced with such feats of reading, it is easy to be doubtful. Genlis, for example, admitted to skipping "geometry" and "astronomy" in the *Encyclopédie*.[64] In other words, she neglected a broad range of mathematical and scientific articles. Jacobs, for his part, confessed to "skimming" certain articles in the *New Encyclopaedia Britannica* or reading them distractedly: "Sometimes, yes, I zone out and merely sweep my eyes swiftly from left to right across the lines as I think about whether we need to get some more Tropicana orange juice or that I forgot to call my sister back."[65] Claims about encyclopedia-reading had strategic goals too, which presumably pushed them toward overstatement. The anecdotes above about Ampère and Edison thus served to bolster their status as precocious geniuses, just as authors of fiction evoked a character's encyclopedia-reading to indicate curiosity, intelligence, or a methodical manner.

Finally, it is worth pointing out that stories about encyclopedia-reading were often matter for humor, a sign of their incongruousness relative to experience. In P. G. Wodehouse's story "The Man with Two Left Feet" (1916), for example, the main character's practice of reading the eleventh edition (1910–11) of the *Britannica* volume by volume is described in these terms: "The ordinary man who is paying installments on the *Encyclopaedia Britannica* is apt to get over-excited and to skip impatiently to volume XXVIII (VET–ZYM) to see how it all comes out in the end. Not so Henry." Later, when Henry discovers that his new acquaintance Minnie dances, he regrets not having arrived yet at the article on dancing, but since he has already finished the volume covering ballet, he is able to impress her with his knowledge of that.[66]

The reviewer of a supplement (1749) to Moréri's *Grand Dictionaire* wrote that "journalists must be the only ones who read a dictionary in its entirety."[67] Indeed, real though it may have been in a tiny fraction of instances, comprehensive encyclopedia-reading was never widespread. Anecdotes about it were exaggerated, whether to embellish a story or make a point about someone's character. The exaggeration derived its force,

[63] For further anecdotes about reading encyclopedias see Lynch, *You Could Look It Up*, 290–3; Jacobs, *Know-It-All*, 269–71.

[64] Genlis, *Mémoires*, VII: 81n.

[65] Jacobs, *Know-It-All*, 63, 276.

[66] Wodehouse, *Man*, 203–6.

[67] "Il ne doit y avoir que des journalistes qui lisent un dictionnaire tout entier." *Mémoires*, February 1750: 227; Lieshout, "Dictionnaires," 143–4.

paradoxically, from the common assumption that encyclopedias were for browsing or consulting in fragments.

In fact, much of the use people made of encyclopedias took the form of consultation, or looking up information on a particular topic. Stories about consulting encyclopedias pale before stories about reading them completely or browsing through them. They are also less numerous, since consultation was rarely experienced as being thrilling, impressive, or worthy of note.

Nevertheless, references to the act of consulting an encyclopedia are not hard to find. Having decided that one of her stories would take place in Lincolnshire, the nineteenth-century writer Harriet Martineau consulted the *Penny Cyclopaedia* for information on the county and an area within it.[68] Similarly, besides "devouring" the *Nouveau Larousse* as a curious child, Sartre consulted and copied from it to develop the background for youthful novels.[69] More generally, the nineteenth-century German author Theodor Fontane used the *Konversations-Lexikon* for his novels as well as his lectures.[70] Likewise, in 1917, desirous of information to make sense of his reading, the traveling French writer Valéry Larbaud visited the public library in Alicante to look up a scientist in the *Espasa* (1908–30).[71] On a less intellectual level, the diarist Anne Frank wrote that "Mr. van Daan," one of her companions in hiding during World War II, "looks up many things in" *Knaurs Konversations-Lexikon* (1932).[72] At times, consultation took on a social dimension, notably in disputes. Thus, when the future president Franklin Roosevelt's family tested his knowledge by asking questions, they "went to an encyclopedia" to check his answers.[73]

Encyclopedias as Periodicals

One way of investigating the reception of encyclopedias is to compare it with that of another form of literature. At first glance, encyclopedias and periodicals may not seem much alike, but they had common features – above all, when encyclopedias appeared in installments. Here I will draw on similarities and differences between the two forms of literature to home in on aspects of the reception of encyclopedias.

---

[68] Martineau, *Autobiography*, II: 159–60.
[69] Sartre, *Words*, 50–1, 71, 143–4.
[70] Hingst, *Geschichte*, 62.
[71] Larbaud, *Journal*, 342.
[72] "… zoekt veel op in Knaur." Frank, *Achterhuis*, 263.
[73] Roosevelt, *Autobiography*, 77.

Boundaries between encyclopedias and periodicals have always been clouded. Encyclopedists were often journalists, as shown in Chapter 7. Many encyclopedias, moreover, dealt with current affairs, and many appeared in installments. From the eighteenth century onward, certain periodicals incorporated a word related to "encyclopedia" into their titles, as did, for instance, the *Journal encyclopédique* (1756–93), the *Cyclopaedian Magazine and Dublin Monthly Register* (1807–9), and *Isis: Encyclopädische Zeitschrift* (*Isis: Encyclopedic Magazine*, 1817–48). Other periodicals were advertised as encyclopedic. In its first issue, for instance, the *Universal Magazine of Knowledge and Pleasure* (1747–1803) promised "a whole body of arts and sciences" in the course of publication.[74] Similarly, in 1845, a reprint of the *Penny Magazine* (1832–45) was advertised as containing "a vast amount of valuable information" and being "consult[able]" by children.[75]

In practice, it was difficult to make a periodical encyclopedic. Consider the instrument-maker Benjamin Martin's *General Magazine of Arts and Sciences* (1755–65). Like the *Universal Magazine*, Martin's *General Magazine* was premised on offering complete coverage of arts and sciences in a gradual manner. Besides offering such miscellaneous items as poems and notes on the weather, each issue added to the ongoing treatment of specific arts and sciences. Martin's plan was for readers to rebind their issues at some point in the future so as to integrate the material on each art or science. What emerged after ten years was a set of complete treatises but hardly an encyclopedia, though it allowed consultation through tables of contents and indexes.[76] The outcome was similar, in the end, to what resulted from series that were published progressively in thematic volumes to form an "encyclopedia" in the indefinite future – for example, *Rowohlts deutsche Enzyklopädie* (1955–84) and the *Encyclopédie de la Pléiade* (1956–91).

One of the most authentically hybrid of encyclopedic periodicals was a short-lived American monthly called the *Current Encyclopedia* (1901–2). It was billed as a solution to the problem of keeping encyclopedias up to date and as a work combining "the features of the periodical and the reference work." Each issue was to be "complete in itself, with the subjects arranged alphabetically." After the issue of April 1902, though, the *Current Encyclopedia* was retitled *The World Today* and endowed with a non-alphabetical opening section on "Events of the Month." The editors explained that the old title had created the erroneous impression that the

[74] Yeo, *Encyclopaedic Visions*, 72.
[75] Loveland, "How Serialisation Changed the Meanings," 98.
[76] Rudy, *Literature*, 116–21.

Current Encyclopedia "was a book and not a periodical." Then, in the second half of 1903, *The World Today* abandoned alphabetical order entirely, thus converting from a hybrid back into a magazine.[77]

Encyclopedia-makers themselves compounded the confusion by issuing periodicals alongside their encyclopedias. As we have seen, Brockhaus published the periodical *Gegenwart* (1848–56) as a complement to its encyclopedia. Larousse did the same with the *Larousse mensuel illustré* (1907–57). Led by *Pierer's Jahrbücher* (1865–73) – a series of supplements to the fourth edition (1857–65) of Pierer's *Konversations-Lexikon* – many such periodicals turned into "yearbooks" and "annuals." These became ordinary accompaniments for large twentieth-century encyclopedias.

In other instances, periodicals were crucial to the marketing of encyclopedias. The second edition (1785–7) of the *Svensk encyclopedie* (*Swedish Encyclopedia*, 1781) was published in installments inserted into a weekly periodical. After readers expressed dissatisfaction with the arrangement, the publisher argued that a serially published encyclopedia was less intimidating than a full set and that periodicals were the future of the Enlightenment.[78] Similarly, American newspapers played a role in distributing pirated versions of the ninth edition (1875–89) of the *Encyclopaedia Britannica*. According to Denis Boyles, "virtually every major newspaper had an 'edition' of the ninth edition." "The Kansas City Star Edition," for instance, was sold by the *Wichita Eagle*. Then, around 1900, American businessmen brokered a deal in which the London *Times* became the main vehicle for marketing the *Britannica*. Among other bits of advertising, *The Times* printed articles from the *Britannica* next to related news-articles.[79]

Beyond the reality of hybrids and partnerships between encyclopedias and periodicals, it is hard to distinguish their content with absoluteness. Both forms were variable and indeed inter-dependent, for encyclopedists and journalists borrowed from one another. On the side of encyclopedists, Krünitz, for instance, gathered much of his material for the *Oeconomische Encyclopädie* (1773–1858) from periodicals, which he valued as sources for their up-to-dateness.[80] Likewise, as a writer for the *Penny Cyclopaedia* (1833–43), the Bible scholar John Kitto was told to keep his "attention

[77] Loveland, "How Serialisation Changed the Meanings," 98–9.
[78] Buller, "Allgemeines Licht," 31–2.
[79] Boyles, *Everything*, 71–2; Kogan, *Great EB*, 75–84.
[80] Fröhner, *Technologie*, 356–8, 413–18.

constantly directed towards the periodical literature of France, and, if possible, Germany, in order to suggest corrections and additions."[81]

Despite commonalities in their material, it is worth considering some ways in which most periodicals differed from most encyclopedias. First, articles in encyclopedias were shorter, in general. There were twelve articles in the first eight-page number of Knight's *Penny Magazine*, for example, whereas the first eight pages of his *Penny Cyclopaedia* had double that number. Not unusual for a *Konversations-Lexikon* in the brevity of its articles, the fifth edition (1893–7) of Meyer's encyclopedia had around a 100,000 articles in its 19,000 pages, so that articles averaged just 200 words each.[82] Periodicals of the time had much longer units. Ironically, Reynaud and Leroux left the monthly *Revue encyclopédique* (1819–35) for a serially published encyclopedia, the *Encyclopédie nouvelle* (1834–42), because they considered periodical literature fragmented.[83] True to this motive, they went on to write long articles for their encyclopedia – some longer than any of the articles in the *Revue encyclopédique* – but they found themselves frustrated by the need to offer brief articles too.[84]

Second, the stereotypical opposition between books and periodicals – the former polished and permanent, the latter slapdash and short-lived – is relevant to the contrast between encyclopedias and periodicals.[85] No doubt encyclopedias had their share of poor articles, just as periodicals had their share of great ones. Nor were the processes of writing an article for an encyclopedia or a periodical necessarily so different. Reynaud, for instance, assured the historian Edgar Quinet – perhaps disingenuously – that articles for the *Nouvelle* could be jotted off quickly and did not need to be as well written as academic publications. In a more casual context, the philosopher Ludwig Feuerbach referred to an overview of a physiological theory as "probably written for an encyclopedia or a periodical," as if the two had the same standards.[86] Yet encyclopedias were more often advertised and regarded as lasting. In a caricature of the literary scene of early-nineteenth-century France, for example, writers were imagined fleeing journalism to devote themselves to encyclopedism, their "only passport to immortality."[87] In one sense, it was true that encyclopedias were enduring, though

[81] Kitto, *Memoirs*, 170.
[82] See Peche, *Bibliotheca*, 377–8. Pages of the encyclopedia had around 1,000 words each.
[83] Griffiths, *Jean Reynaud*, 118, 122–3.
[84] Loveland, "How Serialisation Changed the Meanings," 100.
[85] For the stereotypes see Wald, "Periodicals," 421–2.
[86] Loveland, "How Serialisation Changed the Meanings," 101.
[87] Madrolle, *Tableau*, 284.

this was hardly the sense advertisements suggested. Specifically, they were reprinted or published in new editions, a practice with little analogy in the world of periodicals.

Third, serially published encyclopedias were designed to avoid highlighting their origins as quasi-periodicals. Whereas issues of periodicals were dated and remained so when bound, installments of encyclopedias were overwhelmingly not, except perhaps on the temporary covers with which they were wrapped. Exceptionally, in most of the third edition of (1874–8) of Meyer's *Konversations-Lexikon*, exact dates were printed at the start of installments, there to remain for the encyclopedia's lifetime, but the dating was discontinued in the following edition (1885–90). In other encyclopedias, an installment's first page had symbols – at most – giving the order of its publication relative to other installments (see Figure 9.2). Readers could therefore consult articles without much awareness of how old they were. Likewise, whereas articles in periodicals that went beyond an issue were broken off at a natural point, and sometimes with such phrases as "to be continued," articles in encyclopedias that went beyond an installment were broken off arbitrarily, without any reference to the continuation. This practice gave rise to a peculiar transition in the *Encyclopédie nouvelle*. The editor Leroux needed a small part of "Scolastique" to round out an installment, but having not yet received the article from the historian Jean-Barthélemy Hauréau, he himself wrote the start. Afterward, Hauréau's article was fused onto the editor's lead-in.[88]

Likewise, except in advertisements and prefaces, the authors of serially published encyclopedias avoided alluding to installments in what they wrote, though some of their methods amounted to admission of a work's seriality. One such method was using an entry from later in the alphabet to update an earlier one. As we will see in the following section, contributors to the *Penny Cyclopaedia* also drew attention to its serial publication by setting it up as a course of instruction.

Fourth, and most importantly for my purposes here, the reception of encyclopedias differed from the reception of periodicals, similar though they could be when encyclopedias appeared in installments. Consider first how serial publication affected an encyclopedia's reception. Nothing prevented the buyer of a complete encyclopedia from engaging in browsing or sustained reading, but such uses were encouraged by serial publication. Unlike a finished encyclopedia, a typical installment could be flipped through in less than an hour, or even substantially read over the course of

---

[88] Griffiths, *Jean Reynaud*, 183, 188.

(a) Of all the letters, *A* is obſerved to be that which dumb per-
ſons are ſooneſt taught to pronounce. The reaſon is, that it
does not depend on the muſcles, and other organs of the
mouth, and tongue, which are generally wanting in mutes ;
but on thoſe of the throat and noſe, which they commonly
have. See MUTE.

This firſt, ſimpleſt ſound, ſerves us to expreſs moſt of the ve-
hement movements of the ſoul. It is ſo much the language
of nature, that upon all ſudden and extraordinary occaſions
we are neceſſarily led to it, as the inſtrument readjeſt at hand.
With this we ſpeak our admiration, joy, anguiſh, averſion, ap-
prehenſion of danger, *&c.*—Where the paſſion is very ſtrong,
we frequently inforce the *A*, by adding an aſpirate, as, *Ah.*
See INTERJECTION.

It is obſerved of the Engliſh pronunciation, that we ſpeak the
A with a ſlenderer, and more puny ſound than any of our
neighbours : ordinarily, it is ſcarce broad enough for a French
e neuter ; and comes far ſhort of the groſs *A* of the Germans,
which would make our au, or aw, or o.—In ſome words
however, as talk, wall, ſtall, *&c.* the *A* is broad, and deep
enough. But this, it is obſerved, may not be the mere ſound
of *A* ; but the effect of the ancient orthography, which, as
low as queen Elizabeth, frequently added an u to the *A*, and
wrote taulk, *&c.*

The Romans laid a mighty ſtreſs on their *A* ; and diſtin-

VOL. I. N° I.

(b) unter 52° 33′ nördl. Br. und 13° 22′ öſtl. L. v. Gr.,
in der Provinz Brandenburg, 30 — 48 Meter
über dem Spiegel der Oſtſee, an beiden Ufern der
Spree, welche die Stadt von SO. nach NW. durch=
fließt, ſich gabelt und die Panke in ſich aufnimmt.
Links der Spree geht oberhalb Berlins der neue
Schiffahrtskanal ab, welcher, ungefähr 10,54 Kilom.
lang, durch den 20,34 Kilom. langen Luiſenſtädtiſchen
Kanal mit der Spree innerhalb der Stadt verbunden
iſt; rechts der Spree geht unterhalb der Stadt der
Spandauer Schiffahrtskanal in einer Länge von 12,05
Kilom. zu dem Ausgang des Tegeler Sees in die
Havel. Außerdem iſt der alte Feſtungsgraben zu
erwähnen, welcher um die Spreegabelung herum
einen mit dieſer nicht ganz koncentriſchen Kreis bildet.
Durch dieſe natürlichen Grenzen der Waſſerläufe
ſind die hiſtoriſchen Stadttheile von einander ge=
ſchiede ‥ zwar Alt=Kölln, als Centrum der
Stadt . .n königlichen Schloß auf der Spree=
inſel, Alt=Berlin, von gleichem Alter, mit dem
Rathhaus, nördlich davon gelegen und von dem
hier »Königs= oder Friedrichsgraben« benannten
Feſtungsgraben umſchloſſen, Friedrichswerder
und Neu=Kölln, mit dem Zeughaus und der königl.
Bank, durch den »Kupfer= und Grünen Graben« ab=

Meyers Konv.=Lexikon, 3. Aufl., III. Bd. (6. Mai 1874.)

Figure 9.2   Contrasting conventions for indicating installments. (a) First serially
published edition (1741–3) of Chambers' *Cyclopaedia*, Vol. 1, installment 80; scanned
courtesy of the Public Library of Cincinnati and Hamilton County. (b) Third edition
of Meyer's *Konversations-Lexikon*, start of an installment dated May 6, 1874; scanned
courtesy of the Morris Library, Southern Illinois University, Carbondale.

a week or a month – just in time for receipt of the following installment. Furthermore, while purchasers of serially published encyclopedias must have understood that they were investing in a complete work of reference, they may have felt obligated to make use of installments as they came in, if only to feel comfortable with the ongoing expense.

Certainly reviewers of encyclopedias covered articles more thoroughly when they were treating installments and not a whole set. One reviewer of Larousse's *Grand Dictionnaire* (1866–76) highlighted more than a dozen articles in a forty-page installment running from "Artillerie" to "Assassin." Comparable recommendations appeared in advertising. An advertisement for installments 630–40 of the *Grande Encyclopédie* (1885–1902) thus played up more than twenty articles from within the installments.[89] Acting on the suggestions of advertisements and reviews, people acquiring an encyclopedia serially may have decided to look at articles they would have ignored in a full set.

Testimony from readers is hard to find, but at least some of them approached serially published encyclopedias as they might a periodical, reading from installments and browsing within them. In part because of their personal and political ties with the editors, the composer Frédéric Chopin, the historian Jules Michelet, and the novelist George Sand all read from the *Encyclopédie nouvelle* as it appeared, often in response to recommendations from others. So confident were Leroux and Reynaud that their encyclopedia would be read from installment to installment that they apologized for the starkness of the opening installment: "In our language, at the beginning of the letter 'A,' an encyclopedia always runs into a barrier of heavy words that are difficult to get through."[90]

Regardless of such similarities in their reception, contemporaries had little difficulty distinguishing encyclopedias from periodicals. It is true that the vocabulary of periodicals could be applied to encyclopedias. One eighteenth-century biography alluded to material in "Zedler's [*Grosses vollständiges*] *Universal-Lexicon* and other journals."[91] Some anglophones, likewise, called serially published encyclopedias "periodical productions" or even "periodicals."[92] Others, however, reserved the expressions for true

[89] Loveland, "How Serialisation Changed the Meanings," 96.

[90] "Dans notre langue, au début de la lettre 'A,' une encyclopédie heurte toujours contre une barrière de mots graves et difficiles à franchir." Griffiths, *Jean Reynaud*, 133, 162–3, 173n, 176–7, 210, 240n.

[91] "... im Zedlerschen Universal Lexico und in andern Tagebüchern." Löhstrater, "Periodische Presse," 62.

[92] See for example Schmidt, "Visionary Pedant," 8, 118–19; review of *Penny Cyclopaedia* and other works, 338.

periodicals. In a typical instance, when summarizing his career in a request for a pension, the mathematician William Wallace separated his articles for "periodical works" from those he had written for serially published encyclopedias.[93] More generally, when classifying printed works, contemporaries put encyclopedias that were still being serialized in the same category as finished ones. Consumers, moreover, expressed irritation when encyclopedias dragged on for longer than planned.[94] They would have had no reason for doing so if they had seen encyclopedias and periodicals as roughly equivalent.

Education through Encyclopedias

Encyclopedism and education had longstanding ties. The Greek term at the origin of the word "encyclopedia" referred to an education. As a one-word invention, scholars made "encyclopedia" the equivalent of the Latin *orbis doctrinae* (the circle of learning) during the Renaissance. Ancient and medieval works later classified as encyclopedias functioned as pedagogical manuals and were sometimes used in schools.[95] Organizationally, encyclopedic works shared frameworks with the curriculum of universities, notably the framework of the seven liberal arts. Finally, the concept of encyclopedism was central to German universities from the late eighteenth century through the second half of the nineteenth, though it had little to do with encyclopedias as books.[96]

Alphabetical encyclopedias, for their part, were regularly marketed as aids to learning. Coetlogon, for instance, vaunted his coverage of surgery in the *Universal History* (1745) in the following terms: "The little care master surgeons take, at present, to instruct their pupils in their profession, made me think myself obliged to give them a complete treatise … With the help of this treatise, and some practice, which they may acquire in frequenting hospitals, they may soon become perfect surgeons."[97] Similarly, an advertisement from 1928 announced that the "courses of learning" in the *New International Encyclopaedia* (1902–4) "will give anyone a well-rounded education comparable to that of a university."[98] More realistically, encyclopedias

[93] Craik, "Calculus," 262–3.
[94] See for example Watts, "*Encyclopédie*," 359; Rüdiger, "Ersch/Gruber," 51, 60; Gray, *Charles Knight*, 52.
[95] Codoñer, "De l'Antiquité," 19–22; Meier, "Organisation," 114–15; Twomey, "Towards a Reception History," 332–46.
[96] Schneider, *Erfindung*, 83–8. See also Wellmon, *Organizing*, 91–101; Dierse, *Enzyklopädie*, 41–6, 73–89, 217–18.
[97] Loveland, *Alternative Encyclopedia?*, 129.
[98] *New York Times*, October 7, 1928: BR13.

were recommended to students by teachers and others: Chambers' *Cyclopaedia* (1728) to students at eighteenth-century Cambridge, Moréri's *Grand Dictionaire* (1674) to young nobles in the mid eighteenth century, and the *Petit Larousse* (1905) to twentieth-century school-children.[99]

If nothing else, encyclopedias were a predictable part of libraries at schools and universities from the nineteenth century onward, as suggested by this judgment from the late nineteenth century: "A college, an academy, or a public school deprived of this prolific source of knowledge [a 'good encyclopedia'] must ever remain in the rear of those thus properly equipped."[100] Whether at home or in a library, encyclopedias supplied children with material for homework and reports. In a memory of her childhood in the mid twentieth century, the American professor of literature Alice Kaplan recalled being "allowed to sit at the desk … and do my homework. The *World Book Encyclopedia* was on the first left shelf, so I could look up facts."[101] Growing up in the United States around the same time, the future critic Michael Dirda had to write his reports on subjects beginning with "A," since his mother refused to buy more than the first, discounted, volume of *Funk and Wagnalls Standard Encyclopedia* (1912) and "half-a-dozen other reference sets."[102]

At worst, students simply copied their reports from encyclopedias – a tendency lamented among educators, as noted in Chapter 4. Encyclopedias were in fact blamed for debasing learning. Thus, the eighteenth-century critic Elie-Catherine Fréron argued that "dictionaries" – in which class he put the *Encyclopédie*, then being published – were less instructive than their proponents believed. In using them, he wrote, "one grasps but the shadow and the surface of things, and one considers oneself profoundly educated."[103] In part, such thinking represented intellectual snobbery, resistance to the spread of knowledge throughout society, and fear that non-scholars might rival scholars. At the same time, testimonials confirm that encyclopedias could be superficial instructors. In his autobiography, for example, the writer Edmund Gosse recalled a period of his youth in which the *Penny Cyclopaedia* (1833–43) was "my daily, and for a long time almost my sole study," but all that he retained was an assortment of "stray useless" facts.[104] Likewise, a century later, the writer John Sheirer credited

---

[99] Yeo, *Encyclopaedic Visions*, 166–7; Lieshout, "Dictionnaires," 144; Pruvost, *Dent-de-lion*, 151, 167–73.
[100] "Testimonials," 4.
[101] Kaplan, *French Lessons*, 29.
[102] Dirda, *Readings*, 36.
[103] "On ne saisit que l'ombre et la superficie des choses, et l'on se croit profondément instruit." Lieshout, "Dictionnaires," 146.
[104] Spree, *Streben*, 2–3.

World Book, which he read as a youth, for his acquisition of "half the useless trivia in my head today."[105] Indeed, by this time – as if to aggravate concerns that encyclopedias were thinning down knowledge – it had become common to market them with questions on trivia.

Encyclopedists responded to such concerns in a variety of ways. Some maintained that encyclopedias were not meant to educate, at least not on their own. In the *Encyclopédie*, for example, D'Alembert declared that encyclopedias "will never take the place of books for those seeking to learn."[106] Alternatively, one way of defending encyclopedias as pedagogically useful was to point out that all knowledge had to start superficially. The preface to the *Nuttall Encyclopaedia* (1900) thus asserted that "a little knowledge is not dangerous to those who recognize it to be little."[107] A few decades earlier, as mentioned in Chapter 5, Brockhaus claimed that short articles were better than long ones at presenting their subjects relative to knowledge in general. If so, a beginner or generalist might be better served by an article in a typical encyclopedia than by a treatise or a book on the subject. It is worth noting that anecdotes about learning from encyclopedias tended to focus on initiations rather than later stages of study, as when the future geologist James Hutton reportedly got his start in chemistry from Harris's *Lexicon Technicum* (1704).[108]

Regardless of such arguments, some encyclopedists chose not to defend the encyclopedia but instead to transform it, partly to make it a better tool for instruction. One approach was to link articles, either with cross-references or by listing groups of articles to be read all together. Chambers used both means in the *Cyclopaedia* (1728), a work advertised on its title page as "a course of ancient and modern learning." By following cross-references or working through the list of articles on a particular discipline, the reader stood to gain the "advantages of a continued discourse."[109] For hydrology, the subject of a very short course of reading, the preface advised reading the articles on water, springs, rivers, medicinal springs, lakes, seas, oceans, tides, deluges, "and the like."[110] As this last phrase reveals, the recommendation was open-ended, like all the others in Chambers' preface. Whatever education the *Cyclopaedia* promised, it was evidently exploratory.

---

[105] Sheirer, *Growing*, 70.
[106] "… ne tiendront jamais lieu de livres à ceux qui chercheront à s'instruire." *Encyclopédie; ou, Dictionnaire*, I: xxxiv.
[107] *Nuttall Encyclopaedia*, v.
[108] Hughes, "Science," 342.
[109] Chambers, *Cyclopaedia*, I: i–iii, II: 975.
[110] *Ibid.*, I: iiin.

Thanks to the *Cyclopaedia*, proposed courses of reading became a familiar feature in English-language encyclopedias. Sometimes they appeared in prefaces, but a more lasting solution was to put them at the end of an encyclopedia. Often, in fact, they were put in a separate volume only loosely if at all connected with the rest of the series, as in the *New International Encyclopaedia* as of 1922, *World Book* as of 1925, and *Funk and Wagnalls New Standard Encyclopedia* as of 1935.[111] I examined "study-guides" as sites for overviews in Chapter 5, but they were also sites for experiments in pedagogical idealism. In the *New Encyclopaedia Britannica* (1974), for example, the one-volume *Propaedia* sought to enable "the reader to carry out an orderly plan of reading in any field of knowledge."[112] While promoted by the publisher as "an educational implement like no other encyclopedia had ever had," the *Propaedia* met with criticism, much of it from people doubtful that encyclopedias had an educational mission beyond simple reference. One skeptic denounced the *Propaedia* as a "taxonomic extravaganza" more likely to confuse than enlighten a student.[113]

Whatever benefits he expected from linking the *Cyclopaedia*'s articles, Chambers restricted his work's role as a pedagogical instrument, denying that a dictionary should relate experiments leading to knowledge or "demonstrate everything."[114] From Chambers' perspective, a dictionary-writer should present knowledge from a "historical" perspective rather than trying to construct it on a "scientific" foundation. His allusion to competitors unaware of this truth targeted Harris, whose *Lexicon* featured mathematical proofs and narrations of experiments. In his articles on the hypotenuse and the triangle, for example, Chambers merely stated the Pythagorean theorem without offering proof. Harris, by contrast, proved the theorem three ways and offered proofs for a host of more advanced propositions.[115] In subsequent centuries, as mathematics and science became less approachable, encyclopedists increasingly sided with Chambers, summarizing results without detailing reasons.

A second means of making encyclopedias more pedagogically promising was to stock them with treatises. As shown in Chapter 5, one of the main purposes of treatises, when they first appeared in encyclopedias, was to promote education. All the eighteenth-century pioneers in bringing

---

[111] Collison, *Encyclopaedias*, 200, 203; Walsh, *Anglo-American General Encyclopedias*, 67.
[112] *New Encyclopaedia Britannica* (1974), *Propaedia*: 8.
[113] *New Scientist* 64 (October 3, 1974): 50. For the quotation from the publisher see Shores and Krzys, "Reference Books," 166.
[114] Chambers, *Cyclopaedia*, I: xxiii. See also Schubring, "Mathematische Wörterbücher," 119–20, 124–5.
[115] Compare Chambers, *Cyclopaedia*, I: 281, II: 243; Harris, *Lexicon*, I: uuuiv, 7B1r–v.

treatises to encyclopedias – the *Lexicon Technicum*, the *Universal History*, and the first edition of the *Encyclopaedia Britannica* – were premised on the idea that encyclopedias could teach. This conception of encyclopedias survived into the twenty-first century, but it was always dominated by a rival conception in which encyclopedias merely supplemented traditional education.

The development of the *Britannica*, the archetypal encyclopedia with treatises, confirms the persistence of pedagogical thinking in planning and editing. Many of the treatises in the first edition were adapted from textbooks and introductions to the sciences.[116] One reviewer nonetheless condemned it for mistaking "the proper use of works of this kind, which can never answer the purpose of teaching the arts and sciences; but can only serve … to refresh the memories of those who are already well-grounded in fundamentals."[117] Still, from the late eighteenth century to the middle of the twentieth, prefaces to the *Britannica* mentioned the possibility of studying treatises. A high point in this current was James Baldwin's *Guide to Systematic Readings in the Encyclopaedia Britannica* (1895). It presented "courses of study," or trajectories among entries, "which may be pursued independent of schools," though it expressed doubt that mathematics could be learned from an encyclopedia.[118] By contrast, the preface to the fourteenth edition (1929) downplayed the *Britannica*'s educational value, asserting that no one could learn a science from an encyclopedia.[119] Then, in another turnaround, optimism about encyclopedias as teaching tools resurfaced with the *New Encyclopaedia Britannica*.

Testimonials from readers confirm that the *Britannica* could be educational. In the early nineteenth century, the future geologist Hugh Miller discovered the *Britannica*'s treatises. Impressed with their readability, he "read all of the work that would read [*sic*] – some of it oftener than once."[120] In a more specific recollection, the scientist Michael Faraday – a specialist on electrochemistry and electromagnetism – reported getting his first ideas on electricity from the treatise "Electricity" in the third edition (1797) of the *Britannica*.[121] He chose his source well, for according to a review of the seventh edition (1842), encyclopedias were the best place to look for an up-to-date treatise on an "exact science."[122]

---

[116] Loveland, "Unifying," 67–8; Kafker and Loveland, "William Smellie's Edition," 28.
[117] [Bewley], review, 305. For similar judgments see Loveland, *Alternative Encyclopedia?*, 120n.
[118] Baldwin, *Guide*, 4, 106. See also Kogan, *Great EB*, 191–2.
[119] *Encyclopaedia Britannica*, 14th edn. (1929), 1: xxi.
[120] Yeo, *Encyclopaedic Visions*, 187.
[121] Doig *et al.*, "Colin Macfarquhar," 202.
[122] Hughes, "Science," 347.

Another method of making an encyclopedia pedagogically credible was briefly explored in the *Penny Cyclopaedia* (1833–43). It hinged on the encyclopedia's serial publication, for each installment was to lay the groundwork for subsequent ones. In the first installment, for example, the article "Aardvark" included two additions to prepare readers for "later" articles on natural history. First, a footnote contrasted species' scientific and popular names, and indicated how scientific names would be presented. Second, a page-long digression in the main text of the article explained the terms "Mammalia," "Edentata," "class," "order," "genus," and "species," which would "otherwise be obscure or unintelligible to an ordinary reader." More generally, "Aardvark" stated, since the *Penny Cyclopaedia* would use terms before they came up in their own articles, "it is proposed ... to give a brief explanation of such terms as they occur; so that the general reader may be enabled to comprehend their meaning ... without the trouble of referring to other sources."[123] Unfortunately for the "ordinary reader," contributors to the *Penny Cyclopaedia* quickly gave up on making installments accessible upon their appearance.[124]

No amount of tinkering with the form and content of encyclopedias could satisfy everyone wishing to make them educational. As a result, some of the most pedagogically determined of would-be encyclopedists simply abandoned alphabetical order. The *Encyclopédie française* (1935–66), for instance, was originally conceived by Anatole de Monzie, France's minister of education, as an alphabetical work, one that would rival the national encyclopedias of England, Greece, Italy, and the Soviet Union.[125] Instead, the future editor, Febvre, imposed his own plan on the work, making it iconoclastic and non-alphabetical. In Febvre's view, a traditional encyclopedia would have offered information but not what counted: a path to understanding and appreciating creative thinking. To achieve this goal, he centered volumes on thematic "problems" such as matter, life, or human society.[126] Volume 1, for example, was devoted to "mental tools" and composed of three parts, on thought, language, and mathematics respectively. The parts were then further divided into sections and other units.

The *Encyclopédie française* was a commercial disaster, in part because of its interruption by World War II; in part because it was sabotaged by

---

[123] *Penny Cyclopaedia*, 1: 1n, 2. See also *ibid.*, 6: "London Advertisement."
[124] Loveland, "How Serialisation Changed the Meanings," 97–8.
[125] Robichez, "Encyclopédie," 820–1. The encyclopedias to be rivaled were the *Encyclopaedia Britannica*, the *Megale hellenike enkyklopaideia* (*Great Greek Encyclopedia*, 1926–34), the *Enciclopedia italiana*, and the *Bolshaia sovetskaia entsiklopediia*.
[126] Robichez, "Encyclopédie," 821–4.

the rival Larousse company; and in part because it was written for a tiny elite, despite Monzie's claim that it was meant for "all comers" ("tout venant").[127] In other hands, the idea of a thematically ordered encyclopedic work emphasizing instruction proved to be fruitful. The publisher Quillet, above all, had been producing such works successfully since the early twentieth century, beginning with the six-volume *Mon professeur: Grande Encyclopédie autodidactique* (1907) and proceeding to the *Nouvelle Encyclopédie autodidactique* (*New Autodidactic Encyclopedia*, 1922). Quillet targeted readers of modest means who hoped to study their way to an improved education.[128] Unlike the *Encyclopédie française*, which overshot the capacities of any commercially viable readership, Quillet showed sensitivity in matching its material to the needs of an audience.[129]

Significantly, in S. Padraig Walsh's bibliography of anglophone encyclopedic works from the eighteenth century onward, many of the titles stressing education were non-alphabetical, among them *Peale's Popular Educator* (1883) and *Practical Knowledge for All: Comprising Easy Courses in Literature, Language, History, Geography, the Arts and Sciences* (1934). Likewise, encyclopedic works for children, which were almost all oriented toward education, remained a preserve of non-alphabetical order through the end of the twentieth century.[130]

Encyclopedias, then, could be adapted or abandoned in the name of creating an educational work of reference. Even when not conceived by pedagogical reformers, however, they could be educational. According to the editor of the sub-series *Mathématiques* in the *Encyclopédie méthodique* (1782–1832), all it would take to learn mathematics from the encyclopedia was reading the articles twice.[131] This was questionable guidance. Still, with enough effort, a reader could learn something from the coverage in any encyclopedia. In this sense, the claim that encyclopedias served education – a claim advanced in the *Encyclopédie des gens du monde* (1833–44), the eleventh edition (1864–8) of Brockhaus's *Konversations-Lexikon*, and *Collier's Encyclopedia* (1949), among other encyclopedias – was far from empty.[132]

It is important to remember, moreover, that education meant different things to different people and that individuals used encyclopedias in

---

[127] Pruvost, "Dictionnaires," 233; Mollier and Dubot, *Histoire*, 425–7; Robichez, "*Encyclopédie*," 828–9.
[128] Mollier and Dubot, *Histoire*, 320, 424–5, 429.
[129] See for example Mazière, "Cellule," 74.
[130] Walsh, *Anglo-American General Encyclopedias*, xvi.
[131] Costabel, "Mécanique," 65.
[132] See *Encyclopédie des gens*, i: i; [*Grosse Brockhaus*], 11th edn., xv: v–vi; *Collier's Encyclopedia* (1997), i: "Preface."

different ways. Browsing through one of Larousse's large encyclopedias around 1930, the young Frenchman François Minghetti saw himself as furthering his education, and he surely was to a degree, even if he was not attaining educational mastery.[133] Likewise, in the mid nineteenth century, Louis Fontane, the writer Theodor's father, purportedly got all his knowledge from Brockhaus's *Konversations-Lexikon*. This achievement elicited derision from his wife Emilie, but he himself expressed satisfaction with whatever education he had gotten this way.[134] Nor were encyclopedias cut off from interaction with other avenues for learning. Toward the end of his life, the twentieth-century physicist Richard Feynman remembered having his father read to him from the *Britannica*, an experience all the more educational in that his father went on to show him, imaginatively, what articles meant.[135] Encyclopedias, in short, could be as educational as people made them.

Intellectual Elitism versus Popularization

The learnedness of encyclopedias can be gauged in different ways. First, drawing on surveys or lists of subscribers, one can look at the educational and professional backgrounds of those who bought them. Only 5 percent of subscribers to the Irish edition (1790–8) of the *Encyclopaedia Britannica* were identified as having degrees, for example, but 10 percent had the title "Reverend," which also implied a certain educational attainment.[136] The publisher Brockhaus, for its part, did a study of its customers' professions in the mid twentieth century. According to its findings, professions requiring less education increased among purchasers from the fifteenth (1928–35) to the sixteenth edition (1952–63) of the *Konversations-Lexikon*. By this criterion, the encyclopedia was becoming less learned, though school-teachers were the most frequent buyers of the sixteenth edition.[137]

Second, publishers and editors of encyclopedias made decisions about which readers to aim for. Many of these decisions were announced to the public. Whether in advertisements, prefaces, or even titles, nearly all encyclopedias had something to say about who their targeted readers were. Two typical strategies in this regard were to include almost everyone in the

---

[133] See Minghetti, *Vas-y*, 59. The encyclopedia was presumably the *Nouveau Larousse* (1897–1904) or the *Larousse du XXᵉ siècle* (1928–33).
[134] Peche, *Bibliotheca*, 85.
[135] Feynman, *Perfectly Reasonable Deviations*, 332–3.
[136] Kafker and Loveland, "Publisher," 136.
[137] Keiderling, *F. A. Brockhaus*, 246–7.

plausible readership or to issue the same material for different audiences. More credible than such announcements – though still sometimes fanciful – were companies' internal decisions about desired readerships. In a document drawn up before World War I, for example, Albert Brockhaus stressed the need to make the company's encyclopedia accessible to graduates of an average secondary school, a "Realschule," and not just to graduates of the most academically advanced ones, the "Gymnasien."[138]

Third, just as the prices of encyclopedias limited who could buy them, their contents limited who could use them. Choices regarding such matters as mathematical symbolism, technical vocabulary, bibliographies, allusions, and linguistic complexity placed bounds on the likely readership for articles in an encyclopedia. At one extreme, an encyclopedia in Latin was of no use to anyone unable to read in that language. Even after the waning of wholly Latin encyclopedias, Latin keywords and quotations persisted in encyclopedias. Dyche and Pardon's *New General English Dictionary* (1735) was thus advertised as suitable for those "unacquainted with the learned languages."[139] Reasoning similarly, the editor Reynaud reminded a contributor to the *Encyclopédie nouvelle* (1834–42) to try to avoid Latin "as the encyclopedia is read by lots of women."[140] Likewise, in the *British Encyclopaedia* (1809), meant for the less learned, the compiler Joyce used vernacular names as keywords for living beings that were treated under their Latin names in his *Dictionary of Arts and Sciences* (1807), meant for the learned.[141]

All three of these methods for measuring learnedness have their deficiencies, but they are the best tools available for analyzing how learned an encyclopedia was. Accordingly, these are the methods – especially the last two – that underpin my analysis of encyclopedias' learnedness here.

My first observation regarding learnedness is that it is too often presented in absolute terms, dividing encyclopedias neatly into learned and unlearned. In this vein, a truism in the history of German encyclopedism is that encyclopedias were learned – and thus used by the learned – before 1800 but that the learned encyclopedia died in the following century. Ersch and Gruber's *Allgemeine Encyclopädie* (1818–89) looms large in this schema as the last learned encyclopedia, belatedly published and duly a failure.[142] In the German context as in others, though, this schema is faulty.

[138] *Ibid.*, 68.
[139] *Daily Advertiser*, May 22, 1740: [4].
[140] "… comme l'encyclopédie est lue par beaucoup de femmes." Griffiths, *Jean Reynaud*, 228–9.
[141] Issitt, "From Gregory's *Dictionary*," 27. More generally, see Schmitt and Loveland, "Scientific Knowledge," 329–30.
[142] Hass, *Grosse Lexika*, 10; Meyer, "Konversations-Lexikon," 9; Wendt, *Idee*, 40.

As we have seen, advertisements for encyclopedias stressed their value to learned audiences through the late eighteenth century, but they did so far less thereafter – a development that might seem to prove that learned readers, once foremost, no longer counted. Still, even before 1800, the learned were not the only group targeted by encyclopedias. The sub-title to the *Curieuses Natur- Kunst- Gewerck- und Handlungs-Lexicon* (1712) was typical in this respect, mentioning both the learned and the unlearned as standing to benefit.[143] Nor were encyclopedias of the late seventeenth century meant for the learned alone. As Bayle wrote in his *Dictionaire* (1697), defending the work's raciness, a big book that that failed to interest non-scholars risked losing money.[144] He himself steered his encyclopedia slightly away from his scholarly interests and toward entertainment to make it appealing to a broad audience.[145] More generally, the very point of encyclopedias in the vernacular was to enlarge the potential market. Finally, criticism of encyclopedias for debasing learning was already widespread by the early eighteenth century. If the period's encyclopedias had been for learned readers alone, it is unlikely that such criticism would have resonated so powerfully.

For all of these reasons, it would be wrong to characterize seventeenth- and eighteenth-century encyclopedias or their users as simply "learned." Yet such characterizations are frequent, undoubtedly because they give differences a comforting sharpness. Despite an assertion to the contrary by the publisher Zedler, for example, the *Grosses vollständiges Universal-Lexicon* (1732–50) has long been seen primarily as a work for the learned.[146] Against this received view, Ulrich Schneider has argued that it favored use by the unlearned, notably through its practicality, its reliance on German, and its accessible treatment of scientific and medical topics.[147] Still, it was hardly a work of popularization, one to be pitted against a largely imaginary tradition of wholly learned encyclopedias. Although it was overwhelmingly in German, it had an abundance of keywords in other languages, including hundreds in Hebrew and ancient Greek.[148] This fact alone shows its involvement with learned culture. So does its 175-page

---

[143] More generally, see Spree, *Streben*, 105.
[144] Bayle, *Dictionaire*, 1: 7.
[145] Lieshout, *Making*, 105, 196.
[146] See for example Kossmann, "Deutsche Universallexika," 1575; Meyer, "Konversations-Lexikon," 9. For Zedler's claim see Prodöhl, "Aus denen besten Scribenten," 87.
[147] Schneider, *Erfindung*, 41–2, 98, 164.
[148] *Ibid.*, 164–5.

article on Wolff's philosophy, which was mostly a "chronological presentation of 425 … polemical writings for and against Wolff."[149]

Conversely, the idea that the learned encyclopedia died after 1800 is dubious. Focusing on the German tradition, supporters cite the breakdown of Ersch and Gruber's *Allgemeine Encyclopädie* and the concomitant rise of the *Konversations-Lexikon*. In the nineteenth century – they argue – learned knowledge migrated away from the general encyclopedia and into "Fachlexika," or specialized dictionaries.[150] Such works certainly proliferated in the nineteenth and twentieth centuries, and they were usually more scholarly than general encyclopedias, but it remains debatable how dead the learned general encyclopedia was. On the one hand, as noted in Chapter 1, Brockhaus's *Konversations-Lexikon* grew more learned in the second half of the nineteenth century while still avoiding the depth of the *Allgemeine Encyclopädie*. On the other hand, the latter work may have been among the most learned of nineteenth-century encyclopedias, but it was not without tendencies toward popularization. Like the *Konversations-Lexikon*, in particular, it emphasized cultivation (*Bildung*) and practicality.[151]

In any event, a nineteenth-century demise of the learned encyclopedia is even harder to establish in English or French. For several decades around 1800, France had its own gigantic, drawn-out encyclopedia, the *Encyclopédie méthodique*. Like Ersch and Gruber's *Allgemeine Encyclopädie*, it was both tremendously learned and in some ways accessible. It included, for instance, a volume of trivia and anecdotes, the *Encyclopédiana* (1791), as well as volumes on scientific, mathematical, and other games. In mathematics, less frivolously, it encouraged beginners by improving on the coverage of basics in the *Encyclopédie*.[152] Nor did it signal an end to great learnedness in French encyclopedias. In their own ways, two subsequent ones – the *Grande Encyclopédie* (1885–1902) and the *Encyclopaedia universalis* (1968–75) – were equally learned.

Anglophones, for their part, had the *Encyclopaedia Britannica*, but its learnedness peaked later and less conclusively than the story of the death of the learned encyclopedia would imply. As noted in Chapter 5, the first edition (1771) of the *Britannica* was founded on the principle of transmitting knowledge to "ordinary" people even if certain treatises were written

---

[149] Carels and Flory, "Johann Heinrich Zedler's *Universal Lexicon*," 194.
[150] See for example Lehmann, *Geschichte*, 59; Meyer, "Konversations-Lexikon," 9; Hingst, *Geschichte*, 188.
[151] Fröhner, *Technologie*, 438–55; Spree, *Streben*, 35, 155–6.
[152] Doig, *From Encyclopédie*, 13, 16–17; Coste and Crépel, "Prospectus," 493, 499–500, 506, 512–13.

for specialists.[153] By the time of its third edition (1797), the encyclopedia was evolving to serve a more educated readership.[154] In the seventh edition (1842), the editor, Napier, announced that the *Britannica* was not "suited, chiefly, to the wants of the unlearned; it must now be considered as one of the most dignified and efficient expedients for the diffusion of matured knowledge."[155] For many enthusiasts, the ninth edition (1875–89) of the *Britannica*, nicknamed the "scholar's edition," represented the high point of the work's learnedness, but others situated this high point either earlier or later.[156] Regardless, if the *Britannica* became less learned in the twentieth century, the transformation was a slow one. In the tenth edition (1902–3), for example, the article "Algebraic Forms," by the British mathematician Percy MacMahon, was allegedly understandable to only one person in the United States.[157] However exaggerated the anecdote, the article was technical and mathematically demanding. Similarly, despite an ongoing tendency toward popularization, much of the eleventh edition (1910–11) was written for an educated elite, as were scientific entries in later editions.[158]

Generalizations about the fate of the learned encyclopedia suffer, above all, from the fact that such works can be conceived in more than one way, as can the popularizing encyclopedias that supposedly replaced them. One conception was presented by Guizot in the *Encyclopédie progressive* (1826). Guizot thought that eighteenth-century encyclopedists had wrongly imagined their readers as a homogeneous group, whereas nineteenth-century encyclopedists were making peace with the idea that different readers might be best served by different encyclopedias. In his view, the ideal was to offer two kinds. An elementary encyclopedia would have short articles on every word in a language. For those wanting more, it would refer to an encyclopedia offering treatises for study – a learned encyclopedia in Guizot's conception.[159]

Schnitzler, the editor of the *Encyclopédie des gens du monde* (1833–44), agreed with Guizot's premise of different encyclopedias for different readers, but he took issue with Guizot's proposal for two opposed encyclopedias,

---

[153] *Encyclopaedia Britannica*, 1st edn., 1: v. "Midwifery," for example, was written for a medical professional. See Kafker and Loveland, "William Smellie's Edition," 50.

[154] Kafker and Loveland, *Early Britannica*, 6.

[155] *Encyclopaedia Britannica*, 7th edn., 1: v–vi. See also Yeo, *Encyclopaedic Visions*, 275–8.

[156] Einbinder, *Myth*, 41–2, 58–9, 159–60.

[157] Kruse, "Story," 246–7.

[158] See for example Einbinder, *Myth*, 151–4, 242; Katz, *Basic Information Sources*, 143. On popularization in the eleventh edition see Kruse, "Story," 286–8; Kogan, *Great EB*, 171.

[159] *Encyclopédie progressive*, 24–37.

arguing that one would be too elementary and the other too learned to be of use. Instead, he asserted, an encyclopedia should aim for a middle ground appropriate for a specific social group. In the case of his own work, the group in question was the fashionable upper classes (the "gens du monde").[160]

In practice, more generally, it is hard to match real encyclopedias with Guizot's two types. Indeed, though he praised Brockhaus's *Konversations-Lexikon* and the *Edinburgh Encyclopaedia* (1808–30) as the most successful of elementary and learned encyclopedias respectively, neither one fit his typology.[161] Brockhaus's *Konversations-Lexikon* was never intended to offer entries on every word in German, and not all the entries were minimalistic. The *Edinburgh Encyclopaedia*, for its part, had numerous brief entries along with its treatises. Furthermore, many of the treatises began with fundamentals before going on to more sophisticated material. In other words, even an encyclopedia with detailed and ultimately scholarly treatises could have an element of popularization.

Consider, in this light, the coverage of calculus in encyclopedias. Some treated it in just a few sentences as something beyond readers' abilities or interests. This was the approach taken in Dyche and Pardon's *New General English Dictionary* (1735) and Roth's *Gemeinnütziges Lexikon für Leser aller Klassen* (1788), among other works. In addition to giving a sentence-long characterization of calculus, the early *World Book* (1917–18) observed that it was taught "only in colleges and universities after a thorough preparation," and mentioned two problems it could be drawn on to solve.[162]

In the case of encyclopedias' treatment of calculus, brevity correlated with vagueness and recourse to unexplained technical terms. The latter possibility is illustrated by the early *Petit Larousse* (1905). With no further detail, it defined calculus as the "combination of differential and integral calculus, designed to study the variation of functions with infinitely small variations in variables."[163] This definition illustrates the principle that the shorter the article, the more previous knowledge it took for granted.[164] Longer articles could cover calculus just as inscrutably, but some started

[160] *Encyclopédie des gens*, 1: vi–vii, 9: 490; Rowe, "Tous les savoirs," 13–15.

[161] See *Encyclopédie progressive*, 22–4.

[162] [*World Book*], 11: 1049. Michael O'Shea, the first editor of *World Book*, questioned the educational value of mathematics and Latin. See Murray, *Adventures*, 9.

[163] "… ensemble du calcul différentiel et du calcul intégral ayant pour but d'étudier la variation des fonctions pour des variations infiniment petites des variables." *Petit Larousse* (1923), 141. The same definition appeared in 1905.

[164] See Spree, *Streben*, 198.

slowly, from basic mathematics, and offered the possibility of mastering material. Two such articles were by the mathematician William Wallace, a contributor to encyclopedias in the early nineteenth century. Up till then, the *Britannica* had covered calculus in a dense, succinct article cluttered with misprints. Abandoning this relic, Wallace wrote a new article for the fourth edition (1810), introducing the subject over eighty-two pages, and then wrote an even longer account for the *Edinburgh Encyclopaedia*. The latter entry was praised by the astronomer John Herschel as an "elementary treatise."[165] Other encyclopedias followed with similar offerings, including *World Book* after its initial refusal to delve into calculus.[166]

At the same time, it was not just encyclopedias' content that gave them an aura of learnedness. An article's structure and style were also important, and here again there were different ways of establishing learnedness. As Ulrike Spree has shown in her comparison of Brockhaus's *Konversations-Lexikon* with the *Britannica* at the end of the nineteenth century, the two encyclopedias were both scholarly in their own manner. Brockhaus's *Konversations-Lexikon* provided definition-like entries and presented knowledge as authoritative and absolute, almost never referring to doubts or disputes. The *Britannica*, by contrast, thrust readers into a re-enactment of scholarly discourse and reasoning, demonstrating how knowledge was formed and defended. This approach was not only learned but was calculated to awaken popular interest in the production of knowledge.[167]

To a degree, the *Britannica*'s learned style was a luxury permitted by its adoption of treatises, whereas the curt, commanding style of Brockhaus's *Konversations-Lexikon* followed from the decision to favor short entries. Still, even the long articles in Brockhaus's *Konversations-Lexikon* offered little more than collections of facts, while a number of short entries in the *Britannica* also sketched out lines of interpretation and reasoning. In any case, the *Britannica* was not alone among encyclopedias in displaying the arguments behind knowledge. Another encyclopedia that did so was Rees's [*New*] *Cyclopaedia* (1819–20), and not just in long articles. Consider this passage from the half-page article "Absorption," on the lymphatic system:

> The only opportunity which anatomists have hitherto met with of observing the orifices of these [absorbent] vessels, is upon the villous coat of the intestines. The accounts which have been given of them in that situation

[165] Doig *et al.*, "Colin Macfarquhar" 250; Craik, "Calculus," 247–9.
[166] See for example *World Book* (2001), III: 21–5.
[167] Spree, *Streben*, 155–80, 185–6, 191–4.

are so various … as not to warrant the insertion of any description … The evident reluctance with which the absorbents admit noxious matter has led to the general belief, that their mouths are irritable … Various theories have been formed to account for the admission of matter into the orifices of the absorbing vessels; but whichsoever theory be adopted, it is previously necessary to admit a corresponding aptitude in the vessel to receive, and in the matter to be received. This being granted, some physiologists have imagined that the absorbent attracted matter into its mouth, in the same manner that capillary tubes imbibe fluids. A little reflection is sufficient to show that the absorbing vessels are not circumstanced like capillary tubes … immersed in a fluid.[168]

Comparable meta-discourse on the production of knowledge can be found in earlier encyclopedias. Indeed, the point of the "critical" encyclopedias of the seventeenth and eighteenth centuries was to open up knowledge to doubt and uncertainty. In Bayle's *Dictionaire historique et critique* (1697), for example, articles presented knowledge in a confident narrative, while the footnotes exposed arguments for and against what was said. Even outside the contested domain of religion, critical thinking was valued in contemporary encyclopedias. The editor De Felice thus approved articles on almost completely unknown animals for the Yverdon *Encyclopédie* (1770–80) as long as contributors made them "critical, by showing how little confidence one should have in what others … have said."[169] This was a way of making learnedness compatible with ignorance.

All in all, in encyclopedias, learnedness and unlearnedness were not so much opposed poles as moderate inclinations on a variety of scales. What made them into opposites was promotional discourse. Some encyclopedists presented their works as learned or as meant for the unlearned. More often, however, advertisements cast encyclopedias as representing a happy medium between excessively learned and unlearned works. In a typical instance, the publisher Heinrich Pierer positioned the first edition (1822–36) of his encyclopedia as avoiding the extremes of the *Allgemeine Encyclopädie* and the *Konversations-Lexikon*. Similarly, in the late twentieth century, the *Academic American Encyclopedia* was advertised as occupying a middle ground between the *Britannica* and *World Book*, the former supposedly written for scholars, the latter supposedly inadequate for a "bright" adolescent.[170] In reality, encyclopedias were neither as

---

[168] Rees, [*New*] *Cyclopaedia*, 1: 13v.
[169] "… critiques, en faisant sentir le peu de cas qu'on doit faire de ce que les autres … ont dit." Cernuschi, "ABC," 128.
[170] [*Pierer's Universal-Lexikon*], 1st edn., 1: XIII–XIV; *New York Times*, November 12, 1978: NJ14.

extreme nor as focused in their targeting of readers as competitors claimed, though they did differ.

Indeed, different articles in an encyclopedia were frequently written for different readers. On the one hand, the discrepancy reflected subjects' accessibility. In particular, scientific and mathematical subjects became less accessible with the passage of time, demanding an increasing amount of prior knowledge or training. Concepts in these areas could sometimes be explained without jargon or symbols, but the results risked being vague or misleading. On the other hand, variation in the approachability of articles could be caused by careless editing. In this regard, encyclopedia-editors grew ever more stringent in the nineteenth and twentieth centuries. The Brockhaus firm was a pioneer in establishing uniformity in articles' demandingness, in part because Friedrich Brockhaus and subsequent editors insisted on the prerogative of rewriting submissions, and in part because the original criterion for treating a subject was its conversational value, not its value as knowledge.

In the twentieth century, procedures were set up to standardize the peda-gogical level of articles. For the first edition (1917–18), the leaders of *World Book* tested material on school-children to make sure it was understand-able. Later they commissioned research to quantify readability. Beginning in the 1950s, Edgar Dale, a professor of education and a consultant for *World Book*, developed a way of measuring how readable words were in their various meanings. In 1976, in collaboration with Joseph O'Rourke, he published *The Living Word Vocabulary*, a list of 44,000 words considered in a specific word-meaning, each graded by its familiarity to people of different ages and educational backgrounds. Thus, the word "eon" was marked as familiar to 62 percent of students just starting at a university. Editors at *World Book* made systematic use of the list. Their goal was not to make the encyclopedia entirely homogeneous, but to match articles to the education of the people most likely to read them.[171] Likewise, in scientific and mathematical articles, the editors of *World Book* arranged material to create a progression of difficulty, so that readers of different abilities could all take away something from the resulting "pyramid."[172]

Despite the trend toward homogeneity in the level of articles, encyclopedias continued to overshoot their targeted readerships. As we have seen, the *Penny Cyclopaedia* (1833–43) became too expensive for most

---

[171] Murray, *Adventures*, 17–18, 109–10, 136; Dale and O'Rourke, *Living Word Vocabulary*, 1, VII–VIII, 262.
[172] On "pyramidal" articles see Kister, *Encyclopedia Buying Guide*, 2nd edn., 34.

of the lower class. Just as significantly, its publisher, Knight, struggled to get authors to write for the less educated.[173] Much the same happened with the *Encyclopédie nouvelle* (1834–42), originally intended for a popular audience, but increasingly a platform for the editors and their friends to publish long-winded essays on their own theories.[174] In the twentieth century, the failure of the *Encyclopédie française* to reach its imagined audience of everyone was even more flagrant. In part, the work's failure was that of contributors unwilling or unable to popularize knowledge, but it also followed from an initial decision to break knowledge up in unfamiliar patterns and force readers to study.[175] Finally, a persistent theme in reviews of American encyclopedias in the twentieth century was that despite being advertised as suitable for students, many were not, or at least not for students of the advertised level. Encyclopedias for adults were susceptible to the same criticism. For knowledge of science, one reviewer argued, most adults would be better served by a children's encyclopedia.[176]

Conclusion

How encyclopedias were used remains largely hidden from view, since most instances of using them left no written trace. Inferences can be drawn, though, from testimony by users, from the contents of encyclopedias, and from other sources. Encyclopedias were not meant to be read from beginning to end, and overwhelmingly they were not. Still, consultation was not the only use people found for encyclopedias. Many saw little need to open their encyclopedia, since the work's point was in display or as a symbolic presence. Many others, especially young people, engaged with encyclopedias through a process of browsing. Such browsing was favored by serialization, a widespread means of issuing encyclopedias for over a century. When published serially, encyclopedias shared features with periodicals, but they were also quite different. The public, above all, expected encyclopedias to be finished and to present knowledge in a more stable form than periodicals did.

Encyclopedias were clearly educational in a limited sense, since they supplied information to those who engaged with them. Yet all through the history of the European encyclopedia, there were editors and publishers who sought something deeper. Specifically, they wanted their encyclopedias

---

[173] Gray, *Charles Knight*, 5, 66–7; Spree, *Streben*, 128–9.
[174] See Griffiths, *Jean Reynaud*, 127, 168–9, 173–4, 206–7, 227.
[175] Robichez, "*Encyclopédie*," 828–9.
[176] Katz, *Basic Information Sources*, 143.

to be just as educational as a course or a textbook. Not everyone thought it possible. Debates about encyclopedias' role as pedagogical instruments were all the more strident in being proxies for debates about how to structure society and communicate knowledge within it. These debates never ended, but the goal of making encyclopedias more broadly educational led to such innovations as treatises and study-guides. Furthermore, at the minimum, we know that certain individuals studied parts of encyclopedias, thus proving that they could be educational for some.

On a practical level, encyclopedia-editors had to match their materials to the educational background of a targeted reader. Such a reader is hard to extrapolate from an encyclopedia's contents, since he or she seems to vary from article to article – though editors grew more vigilant about making articles about the same in their intellectual demands. In any event, the targeted reader evolved. From the seventeenth to the twentieth century, the learned declined as a proportion of encyclopedias' readership. Still, the opposition between the eras of learned and popular encyclopedias – with one replacing the other around the early nineteenth century – should not be overdrawn. The "learned" encyclopedias of the seventeenth and eighteenth centuries had to humor the less learned to be commercially feasible, and difficult material cropped up in encyclopedias through the end of the twentieth century. Encyclopedia-users, for their part, were divided by their learnedness, but they were also divided, just as importantly, by the purposes that brought them to encyclopedias.

CHAPTER 10

Encyclopedias after Print

Printed encyclopedias continue to exist, notably in libraries, but in the age of the internet they appear ponderous, expensive, and prone to obsolescence. As a result, though printed books in general are nowhere near gone, the printed encyclopedia is dying if not already dead. Large encyclopedias, above all, have almost vanished from the market.

The last printed edition of Brockhaus's encyclopedia – the twenty-first – appeared from 2005 to 2006, and the editorial staff was dismissed in 2008.[1] The *Encyclopaedia Britannica*, for its part, was suspended as a printed work in 2012. Although the announcement led to a run on available sets, no further editions will be printed.[2] Soon afterward, France's *Encyclopaedia universalis* was retired from print, and its publisher forced into financial restructuring.[3] For now, the only encyclopedias that are still being printed are either small, like the *Petit Larousse*, or meant for the young, as *World Book* is.

In the meantime, new forms of encyclopedism have developed, bringing change to the ways knowledge is organized and communicated. With the advantage of hindsight, it is easy to overlook the first electronic encyclopedias, those published on disks from the mid 1980s onward. Yet they transformed encyclopedia-publishing by driving down prices and introducing "multi-media" – moving images and sounds. My first section is thus devoted to encyclopedias on disks, along with other electronic encyclopedias of the same era. Thereafter I turn to encyclopedias on the internet, covering not only electronic versions of printed encyclopedias, but also Wikipedia. With the rise of this last work especially, a genre that has been stable since around 1800 has been refashioned. Still, not everything about Wikipedia is new, and the same holds for electronic encyclopedism

---

[1] *Tageszeitung*, June 13, 2013: 14.
[2] See *New York Times*, April 2, 2012: B4.
[3] *Monde*, November 15, 2012: 26; November 23, 2014: 5.

in general. Accordingly, I will make repeated comparisons with printed encyclopedias to show how they resembled and differed from their electronic successors.

Encyclopedias on Disks

Encyclopedias on disks were not the first electronic encyclopedias. An "electronic Larousse," for example, was exhibited at the 1958 World's Fair, where it answered queries from visitors. It ran on a Control Data 3600 computer using magnetic-core memory.[4] Electronic encyclopedias were not widely available, though, before they were published on disks.

The disks on which encyclopedias appeared were made of stiff plastic coated with metal, and etched with tiny pits that could be read with a laser. The largest was the laser-disk, while the most successful were the compact disk (CD) and the digital video-disk (DVD). The former was devised in the late 1970s for recording and playing music. In the mid 1980s, drives for reading CDs, or CD-ROMs (CDs with "read-only memory"), began appearing on personal computers. The earliest CDs had a capacity of around 700 Mb. This was too little to accommodate the biggest encyclopedias, but the DVD, invented in 1995, had a capacity more than six times as large. A disk's capacity, moreover, was not absolute, since data were susceptible to being "compressed." Microsoft's expertise in compressing graphics and audio would thus prove an advantage in the race to fit multi-media onto encyclopedias on disks.[5]

In the 1970s, Larousse had helped design and manufacture a disk for data-storage, but it did not attempt to put any of its encyclopedias on disks, presumably because consumers had no means of reading them.[6] Then, in the 1980s, just as personal computers were appearing with appropriate drives, several companies began selling encyclopedias on CDs. A major reason for the publisher Grolier's interest in the *Academic American Encyclopedia* (1980) was the fact that it had been prepared in machine-readable form, a characteristic that made its electronic publication easier. In the early 1980s, having acquired the *Academic American*, Grolier tried a system of downloading articles by telephone. Then, in 1985, it published an unillustrated version of the *Academic American* on

---

[4] Mollier and Dubot, *Histoire*, 537–8.
[5] Kister, *Kister's Best Encyclopedias*, 286.
[6] Mollier and Dubot, *Histoire*, 612–13.

a non-compact laser-disk, promising that audio and video were soon to follow, as was an edition on CD when the technology spread.[7] By contrast, *Compton's Multi-Media Encyclopedia* (1989) – another disk-published title, based on the printed *Compton's* and aimed at children – did offer multi-media. Among other things, the electronic version of *Compton's* included sixty minutes of music, speeches, and other audio, as well as an on-screen terrestrial globe that could be rotated and magnified.[8] Soon afterward, Grolier too began offering multi-media, including segments of video, with its *New Grolier Multi-Media Encyclopedia* (1992).[9]

Beside its reduced price, the laser-disk version of the *Academic American* had a functional advantage over the printed edition: giving users the power to search the full text of the encyclopedia as well as its keywords. As searches of full texts are now taken for granted, it is worth dwelling on their novelty in the context of encyclopedias. In printed encyclopedias, indexes allowed readers to search for material not represented in keywords, but even the best printed indexes showed fewer results than full-text searches of electronic encyclopedias. To early reviewers, the abundance of results produced by full-text searches could be perplexing, since many of them turned out to be misleading or trivial – more, in particular, than in the "noisiest" printed index. Readers had to filter them in accordance with their needs. In addition, for those skilled enough, some electronic encyclopedias allowed searches to be conducted with logical and other operators, so that one could search, for example, for two words in proximity. Provisions for searching electronic encyclopedias became less important as the works moved off disks and onto the internet, where searching could be entrusted to specialized "engines" such as Alta Vista and Google.

More generally, electronic encyclopedias came with an "interface" and product-specific methods for accessing information. Their effectiveness, convenience, and "user-friendliness" were all of concern to possible buyers. In the early 1990s, for example, *Compton's Multi-Media Encyclopedia* had eight modes of entry: "Idea/Picture Search," "Title Finder," "Topic Tree," "US History Timeline," "World Atlas," "Researcher's Assistant," "Science Feature Articles," and "Picture Explorer." Critics nonetheless found the interface difficult to navigate, more so than those of other electronic

[7] Kister, *Kister's Best Encyclopedias*, 257; *Wall Street Journal*, July 15, 1985: 1; *Philadelphia Daily News*, November 5, 1985: 49.
[8] *Chicago Tribune*, September 21, 1989: 6.
[9] *Information Today* 9 (June 1992): 23.

encyclopedias.[10] Like tools for searching, interfaces declined in importance as encyclopedias moved to the internet.

Thanks to savings on material and manufacturing, electronic encyclopedias could be sold for much less than their printed equivalents. Whereas the printed version of the *Academic American* cost $650 in 1985, for example, the disk cost only $90.[11] Other publishers balked at pricing electronic encyclopedias in proportion to their physical cost, sensing that doing so would jeopardize their printed encyclopedias. Indeed, Encyclopaedia Britannica, the owner of *Compton's Multi-Media Encyclopedia* when it came out, set its price higher than that of the printed *Compton's*.[12] Like other publishers, however, Encyclopaedia Britannica was also selling its electronic encyclopedia as part of a package of software.[13] In this form, the price was effectively lower. Furthermore, a CD of *Compton's Multi-Media* was offered as a bonus to those who bought *Compton's* as a printed set.

Encyclopaedia Britannica showed foresight in getting *Compton's Multi-Media* to the market in 1989, but it was unwilling to venture deeply into electronic encyclopedism, whether by pricing *Compton's Multi-Media* competitively or by launching an electronic version of the *Encyclopaedia Britannica*. Its hesitation on the latter score was partly a consequence of the *Britannica*'s size. In fact, when the *Britannica* was finally published electronically in 1993, it occupied two disks even without any of the illustrations that had been in the printed set.[14] In this case and others, switching between disks could be as cumbersome as switching between the volumes of a printed encyclopedia. Indeed, a test done in 2000 suggested that finding an article in the printed version of Brockhaus's encyclopedia took less time than finding it in one of the company's electronic versions, whether on CD, on DVD, or on the internet.[15] The results of the test were colored by questionable assumptions. Above all, the test assumed that a printed encyclopedia would be located nearby – and not, for example, on another floor of a house – and that networks, disks, and computers would never improve in performance. In particular, as more computers were made with "hard drives" for storing data, the number of disks required

[10] See for example Kister, *Kister's Best Encyclopedias*, 273–4.
[11] *Philadelphia Daily News*, November 5, 1985: 49. The CD was forecast to sell for $199.
[12] *Chicago Tribune*, September 21, 1989: 6. As of 1994, *Compton's* was listed at $569 for libraries, versus $795 for *Compton's Multi-Media*. See Nichols, *Handbook*, 10.
[13] See for example *Popular Science* 240 (May 1992): 38.
[14] *New York Times*, September 29, 1993: D12.
[15] Keiderling, *F. A. Brockhaus*, 375.

for an encyclopedia became less important, since their contents could be transferred to the computer itself. Still, splitting the *Britannica* between two CDs – and splitting other encyclopedias among even more disks – was hardly ideal, especially early on in the evolution of the personal computer.

A second factor that discouraged Encyclopaedia Britannica from selling its main encyclopedia electronically was its reliance on salespeople. Having a multitude of salespeople only made sense, economically, when encyclopedias were expensive. Salespeople, for their part, could not make a living from commissions on inexpensive CDs. For both of these reasons, the company was reluctant to sell its electronic encyclopedias for much less than its printed ones. In 1995, for example, the price of the *Britannica* was $995 on CD versus $1,500 on paper.[16] Such pricing was meant to preserve a commercial model with more than a century of success, the model of a printed encyclopedia sold mostly by salespeople.

Unfortunately for Encyclopaedia Britannica and other established encyclopedia-makers, the trend toward low prices for electronic encyclopedias became irresistible as ownership of computers rose to high levels. As of 1993, just 23 percent of American households owned a computer, but along with the many households then thinking of buying one, these were households predisposed to acquiring an electronic encyclopedia.[17] Nor was owning a computer a necessity for those wishing to buy an electronic encyclopedia. Several publishers partnered with manufacturers to offer electronic encyclopedias on other devices, all of them simpler – and cheaper – than a computer. In early 1991, the *Columbia Electronic Encyclopedia*, based on the printed *Concise Columbia Encyclopedia* (1983), was advertised as "the world's first hand-held electronic encyclopedia." Physically, it was battery-powered, with a screen allowing the display of up to eight lines of text. Also in 1991, *Compton's Concise Encyclopedia*, on CD, was sold with a portable CD-player developed by Sony, the Data Discman (see Figure 10.1).[18] Such device-specific encyclopedias dwindled as more consumers acquired computers.

By the early 1990s, sales of printed encyclopedias were already declining. Whereas 117,000 sets of the *Encyclopaedia Britannica* were sold in 1990, for instance, only 51,000 were sold in 1994. As of 1992, Encyclopaedia Britannica had negative income. Likewise, sales of *World Book* fell from

---

[16] *New York Times* (May 16, 1995): D1.
[17] See US Census Bureau, *Population Profile*, 40.
[18] Kister, *Kister's Best Encyclopedias*, 264–7.

Figure 10.1 Sony's Data Discman displaying material from *Compton's Concise Encyclopedia*. When folded, the Discman measured around thirteen by ten by three centimeters. The disc on the right is for the *New Grolier Electronic Encyclopedia*. Photograph courtesy of Nate Hoffelder, *The Digital Reader* (www.the-digital-reader.com).

330,000 in 1988 to around half as many in 1992.[19] The American economic recession of 1990–1 was a contributing cause, but so too was competition with electronic encyclopedias, real or anticipated. By the end of the decade, Kenneth Kister, an evaluator of encyclopedias, wrote that "no consumer today in his right mind would buy a printed encyclopedia."[20]

The emerging catastrophe for printed encyclopedias was compounded by the arrival of *Microsoft Encarta*. To encourage consumers to purchase computers for homes, Microsoft was eager to create good electronic content, including an encyclopedia. In 1985, it tried to buy non-exclusive rights to the *Britannica*. Rebuffed, the corporation made advances to the publisher of *World Book*, again unsuccessfully. Then, in the late 1980s, Microsoft acquired the right to use *Funk and Wagnalls New Encyclopedia*

[19] *New York Times*, May 16, 1995: D1; Stross, *Microsoft Way*, 91.
[20] *New York Times*, February 26, 1998: G12. Kister was less categorical in 1994. See Kister, *Kister's Best Encyclopedias*, 19, 253–6.

Figure 10.2 The package for Microsoft *Encarta* in 1993.
Photograph scanned courtesy of Microsoft Corporation.

(1971) and planned to invest $7 million to make its adaptation competi-
tive. After years of delays caused by doubts about profits and feasibility,
Microsoft recruited Peter Mollman, the retired president of World Book,
who had been frustrated with his company's slowness to start publishing
electronically. Thanks to Mollman's expertise and a decision to put *Encarta*
onto an extant "platform" for content – Microsoft's "Bookshelf" – the
encyclopedia was finally published in 1993 (see Figure 10.2).[21]

Encarta was initially sold in stores for $395, the same price as *Compton's
Multi-Media*. To Microsoft's surprise, sales were lackluster. In part, *Funk
and Wagnalls* had a poor reputation. Rivals in the market for electronic
encyclopedias made fun of *Encarta* for developing out of a "supermarket encyclopedia." In part, as well, people were disappointed with the
encyclopedia's multi-media, which had been limited by the need to put
the work on one disk. The designers had in fact focused on audio, which
took less space than video. Even among encyclopedias being published
on CD, *Encarta* controlled just 3 percent of the market in 1993. Then,
responding to a discount on *Compton's Multi-Media*, Microsoft lowered its
own price even further – to $99 – for the holidays at the end of the year.
Now sales increased by a factor of twenty-four. *Encarta*, suddenly, had
half the market for encyclopedias on disk. Price, it turned out, had been a
determining factor, though the number of computers able to play multi-
media was also rising.[22]

[21] Stross, *Microsoft Way*, 70–92, 99–101.
[22] *Ibid.*, 101–5.

Like other products developed by Microsoft, *Encarta* was soon adapted for other countries. Heading abroad, it enjoyed three advantages. First, it was generally considered the best encyclopedia on disk.[23] Second, it was written in English, the most international of the world's languages. Third, since the United States was a leader in the number of computers in homes, *Encarta* was launched earlier than most of its foreign competitors. As a result, even after the delays that translation entailed, it appeared in Europe's main languages – and other languages as well – before competition solidified.

Consider, for example, the situation in the Netherlands. The country's most distinguished encyclopedia was the so-called *Winkler Prins*, named after its original editor, the clergyman Anthony Winkler Prins. The first edition was published from 1870 to 1882 as the *Geïllustreerde encyclopaedie* (*Illustrated Encyclopedia*), and new editions were then published for over a century. Elsevier, the publisher, declined to put the final edition (1990–3) onto CD, however, judging the Dutch-language market too limited for the investment to pay.[24] Instead, Elsevier opted for collaboration with Microsoft, providing content for *Encarta 98 encyclopedie: Winkler Prins editie* (*Encarta 98 Encyclopedia: Winkler Prins Edition*, 1997).

A French edition of *Encarta* began selling in 1996 and quickly ascended to commercial dominance.[25] No French encyclopedia-maker was able to beat it to the market. As we have seen, the French publisher Hachette had acquired Grolier in 1988, thus availing itself of Grolier's work on electronic encyclopedias. By 1995, Hachette was planning an electronic encyclopedia in French, but the *Encyclopédie Hachette multimédia* did not appear until 1998. Around the same time, the publisher joined with Apple to sell encyclopedias pre-installed on new Apple computers – an example of the widespread practice of "bundling." Like Hachette, Larousse responded belatedly to the arrival of *Encarta*, putting the *Petit Larousse* on a CD in 1997 and issuing the *Grand Larousse* with an accompanying CD in 2005.[26]

Germans took to personal computers faster than other Europeans, thus giving German publishers time to experiment before Microsoft disembarked. Already in 1989, Bertelsmann had published the *Bertelsmann*

[23] See for example Kister, *Kister's Best Encyclopedias*, 285–7; Stockwell, *History*, 179.
[24] *Wall Street Journal: Europe*, June 12, 1995: 8.
[25] Viera, *Edition*, 173–4.
[26] *Wall Street Journal: Europe*, June 12, 1995: 8; Mollier and Dubot, *Histoire*, 613, 655–6. For a slightly different chronology see Pruvost, *Dent-de-lion*, 159–60.

Lexikodisc (*Bertelsmann Disk-Lexicon*) – a textual version of the company's multi-volume encyclopedia – though without much success. By the time *Encarta* arrived in Germany in 1996, Bertelsmann had pre-empted it with *Bertelsmann Discovery: Das grosse Universallexikon auf CD-ROM* (*Bertelsmann Discovery: The Great Universal Lexicon on CD-ROM*, 1995), a product meant to compete with *Encarta* for the European market in general.[27] The amalgamation of Brockhaus and the Bibliographisches Institut – BIFAB – was slower to take up electronic publishing than the much larger Bertelsmann. BIFAB allowed Microsoft to draw on one of its smaller encyclopedias for "LexiROM" (1995), a collection of works of reference that was similar to "Bookshelf." It was only in 1998, though, that a large encyclopedia owned by BIFAB, the *Brockhaus in fünfzehn Bänden* (*Brockhaus in Fifteen Volumes*, 1997–9), was sold on CD, as *Brockhaus multimedial*. Within a short time, Brockhaus was the leading producer of German encyclopedias with multi-media.[28]

In the business of Brockhaus and other established encyclopedia-makers, disks did not immediately supplant printed books. Some publishers marketed disks as accessories or complements. In 1992, the year before putting its main encyclopedia on disk, Encyclopaedia Britannica thus published an index on CD to accompany the printed set.[29] Alternatively, even when an entire encyclopedia was issued on disk, it could be helpful to own both the printed and electronic versions. While the printed set could be displayed and consulted or leafed through, the disk could be used for searches, if nothing else. Thanks to the example of *Encarta*, however, the connection between printed encyclopedias and their electronic equivalents grew ever frailer. As prices for encyclopedias on disks plummeted, moreover, the purchase of a printed encyclopedia began to seem like an extravagance. Already in decline since the early 1990s, the sales of such encyclopedias had dropped to a pittance by the end of the decade. Sales of the printed *Encyclopaedia Britannica*, typically, dropped 85 percent in the course of the 1990s.[30]

Even as they were putting their encyclopedias on disks, publishers were predicting the demise of the disk, forecasting its replacement by files and services on the internet. Disks had in fact become irrelevant

[27] *Wall Street Journal: Europe*, June 12, 1995: 8.
[28] Keiderling, *F. A. Brockhaus*, 373–4.
[29] American Library Association, *Purchasing*, 38–9.
[30] *The Times*, January 13, 1998: 10.

to encyclopedism by 2005. The period of disk-based encyclopedias was therefore a short one, but it transformed the encyclopedia. For the first time, encyclopedias could offer multi-media. While multi-media was limited in early electronic encyclopedias, its promise was clear, as was its attractiveness to the consumer. Skeptics might denounce it as "bells and whistles," but who could deny the educational value of the more-than-a-thousand clips of music on the original *Encarta*, for instance?[31] Giving readers a sense of a musical work using language alone was even more difficult than giving them a sense of a machine or a painting. Publishers, consequently, invested further in multi-media, so that as DVDs and the internet superseded CDs, multi-media in encyclopedias continued to grow. From 1993 to 2001, for example, *Encarta* doubled its selection of videos and increased its audio even more.[32] In quest of something similar, World Book turned to a technological giant – Microsoft's rival, IBM (International Business Machines) – for help with its own *World Book Multi-Media Encyclopedia* (1995).[33]

As encyclopedias went digital, some of their features passed away almost unnoticed. Alphabetical order, in particular, all but disappeared as a principle of consultation and order. So did separately alphabetized sequences of keywords. The version of the *Britannica* on DVD, for example, abandoned the distinction between the short entries in *Micropaedia* and the long ones in *Macropaedia*.[34] Instead of following the alphabet to find desired keywords, users of electronic encyclopedias could just type them in. Doing so was convenient as long as a computer was handy and already running, but a few critics felt nostalgia for alphabetical order's distractions. No longer, they lamented, would readers be drawn to an unrelated entry that just happened to be placed next to the entry being searched for.[35] In their own ways, however, electronic encyclopedias encouraged curiosity. Full-text searches could turn up unexpected results. Likewise, the fact that it was easy to look things up and follow hyper-links – links to other texts, whether inside or outside a given encyclopedia – probably promoted exploring. Some encyclopedias on disks also included peripheral features designed to be

---

[31] Kister, *Kister's Best Encyclopedias*, 286.
[32] *Technology and Learning* 14 (1993): 33; Stross, *Microsoft Way*, 89–91; *Press*, November 23, 2000: 33.
[33] *World Book* (2001), VI: 270.
[34] Runte and Steuben, "*Encyclopaedia*," 99.
[35] See for example Lynch, *You Could Look It Up*, 227; Bulliet, "Of Encyclopedias," 53–4. On vestiges of alphabetical order in electronic encyclopedias see Schopflin, "Encyclopaedia," 264, 281.

played with. *Brockhaus multimedial* (1998) offered quizzes, for example, while *Compton's Encyclopedia Deluxe* (1998) – a retitled electronic version of *Compton's Encyclopedia* – had a virtual planetarium.[36]

Texts, in the end, were the least innovative aspect of encyclopedias on disks. The amount of text that they offered tended to increase, but for the most part, they showed conservatism if not negligence in this domain.[37] As we have seen, *Funk and Wagnalls* supplied the foundation for the text of *Encarta*. Indeed, by 1998, the content of *Funk and Wagnalls* was being published electronically by eight different license-holders.[38] Microsoft started out doing little editing on what it had inherited from *Funk and Wagnalls*. Instead, it focused the energy of *Encarta*'s staff on illustrations and multi-media. In subsequent years, the text of *Encarta* improved, partly because of the hiring of editors from Grolier, World Book, and Encyclopaedia Britannica.[39] Yet in 1998, hoping to strengthen the encyclopedia's text in response to new competition, Microsoft again turned to the strategy of purchasing content, this time from *Collier's Encyclopedia*.[40] Nor did Encyclopaedia Britannica invest heavily in textual improvements. In the 2009 edition on DVD, for example, many entries were shorter than the corresponding ones in the printed edition, though the DVD had enough space to accommodate several works of reference alongside the encyclopedia.[41] Texts were not a pressing concern in a period in which competitiveness hinged on multi-media and in which low prices for disks were compelling encyclopedia-publishers to lay off employees.

From Encyclopedias on the Internet to Wikipedia

Meanwhile, another revolution in technology and society was preparing its own sequel to the story of encyclopedias. Around 1993, networking among personal computers began to enter the mainstream in the United States and elsewhere, fueled by the protocols of the World Wide Web. From the public's perspective, the internet had been born. Encyclopedias appeared on the internet at roughly the same time as they did on disks.

---

[36] On these features see Keiderling, *F. A. Brockhaus*, 373; Stockwell, *History*, 178.
[37] See for example the statistics on *Brockhaus multimedial* in Keiderling, *F. A. Brockhaus*, 374.
[38] *Library Journal* 123 (November 15, 1998): S6.
[39] Stross, *Microsoft Way*, 89–92.
[40] *Los Angeles Times*, February 9, 1998: 1.
[41] Runte and Steuben, "*Encyclopaedia*," 98–101.

Indeed, an encyclopedia could be on the market in both forms simultaneously. Furthermore, encyclopedias on disks provided links to the internet, whether for updates or more information. Still, the two kinds of encyclopedia were different enough to justify treating them separately. In particular, encyclopedias on the internet were ultimately less hampered by limits on space, and they came into their own in the early twenty-first century, just as encyclopedias on disks began fading.

The first company to put an encyclopedia online was Encyclopaedia Britannica. In 1981, it licensed the text of its encyclopedia for use on LexisNexis, a closed, subscription-based network that that allowed legal professionals, among others, to research documents electronically.[42] The following year, users of CompuServe, a less professionally oriented network, were able to access an electronic edition of *World Book*.[43] But it was the *Academic American Encyclopedia* that soon rose to the forefront of encyclopedias online. In 1982, it appeared on Dow Jones News and Retrieval, an electronic service covering business and finance.[44] The next year, Grolier let another firm, Bibliographic Research Services (BRS), make the *Academic American* available to its subscribers. BRS was used primarily for professional purposes, but its arrangement with Grolier was meant to draw in people using computers from home. A decade later, the *Academic American* was being offered by "almost all of the commercial dial-up information services," including CompuServe, Delphi, and Prodigy.[45]

Unlike these services, the internet was an open network. Here too Encyclopaedia Britannica took the lead among encyclopedia-publishers. Clearly the company's decline in the age of electronic encyclopedias was not due to a simple unwillingness to innovate. When the *Encyclopaedia Britannica* first appeared on the internet in 1994, it was offered to colleges and universities only. The price was $1 per year for every full-time enrollment. Soon afterward, individuals were allowed to subscribe for $150 per year.[46] With prices like these, the company – and its salespeople – had little to lose.

At the time of its launch, *Britannica Online* included all the articles but not all the images in the printed edition. Nor was it as rich in multi-media

[42] Flagg, "Online Encyclopedias," 134.
[43] *InfoWorld* 5 (June 13, 1983): 34.
[44] *PC* 1 (November 1982): 34.
[45] Flagg, "Online Encyclopedias," 134; Kister, *Kister's Best Encyclopedias*, 256.
[46] *Database* 18 (February/March 1995): 16; *Chicago Sun-Times*, October 12, 1995: 53.

as the contemporary disk-based edition of the *Britannica*. This was a general weakness of early online encyclopedias, since connections to the internet were still too slow to play multi-media without bothersome pauses.[47] Over time, *Britannica Online* was split into different versions for different publics and contexts. All of them diverged from the printed edition, adding entries and multi-media, though the printed edition remained, as of 2012, the most abundantly illustrated.[48]

Many encyclopedias appeared on the internet in the second half of the 1990s. Grolier published the *Encyclopedia Americana* there in 1997, adding numerous links to the internet, partly to compensate for a shortage of illustrations.[49] That same year, Grolier offered its *Grolier Multi-Media Encyclopedia* online. The next year, it followed with an online edition of the *New Book of Knowledge* (1966). Both in print and online, Grolier's encyclopedias were meant for different audiences and thereby fit into a coherent strategy.[50] Just behind its rivals, *World Book* went online in 1998–9, first for schools and libraries and then for individuals.[51] *Encarta*, for its part, appeared on the Microsoft Network in 1995, in abridged form on the internet as the *Encarta Concise Encyclopedia* (1997), and on the internet in its entirety in 1998.[52]

Outside the United States, the shift from disks to the internet occurred several years later. In France, Havas, the owner of Larousse, published an electronic encyclopedia in 1999, the *Kléio-Larousse*. It was sold both on disks, for slightly less than *Encarta*, and on the internet, for 159 francs per year. According to Havas, it was the first online encyclopedia to be published in France.[53] France's *Encyclopaedia universalis*, a co-production with Encyclopaedia Britannica, was published online for institutions in 1999 and then for individuals in 2002.[54] In Germany, two online services run by encyclopedia-makers opened around 2000. Brockhaus was behind Xipolis, a fee-based service, while Bertelsmann operated Wissen, a free service with advertising. Both allowed access to some of the publishers'

---

[47] *Information Today* 11 (May 1994): 50; *Tulsa World*, February 14, 1998: 8.
[48] Runte and Steuben, "*Encyclopaedia*," 97, 101. For different versions of *Britannica Online* see *Booklist* 108 (September 15, 2011): 50.
[49] *Booklist* 93 (August 1997): 1921.
[50] *Library Journal* 123 (November 15, 1998): S6. On the *New Book of Knowledge* see Walsh, *Anglo-American General Encyclopedias*, 112–13.
[51] *World Book* (2001), VI: 270.
[52] *Booklist* 92 (September 15, 1995): 192; *Library Journal* 123 (November 15, 1998), S6.
[53] *Publishers Weekly* 247 (May 1, 2000): 20; *Inside Multimedia* 207 (December 6, 1999): 1.
[54] Juanals, "Encyclopédies," 89–90.

encyclopedias.[55] Then in 2008, copying Bertelsmann, Brockhaus announced that it would offer its main encyclopedia free on a site supported by advertising, but the plan came to naught. Instead, Brockhaus was purchased by Bertelsmann in 2009.[56]

As these examples indicate, online encyclopedias were paid for in different ways. Early on, typically, they were sold by subscription. Unlike subscriptions to printed encyclopedias, a subscription to an electronic one did not lead toward ownership, but it did include updates. In a boon to consumers, the price of a subscription went steadily down. By around 2000, for example, the price of an annual subscription to *Britannica Online* had dropped almost 50 percent, to $85. At the time, online versions of the *Grolier Multi-Media Encyclopedia*, *World Book*, and *Compton's Multi-Media Encyclopedia* cost just $60, $50, and $30 per year respectively.[57]

Meanwhile, increasingly, encyclopedias were being offered online for free. In some cases, only a portion of their content was free. Whereas Microsoft charged for *Encarta*, for instance, it did not charge for the smaller *Encarta Concise Encyclopedia*. According to proponents of such schemes of pricing – later called "freemium" – users would like the free sample so well they would end up subscribing to get additional content. In other cases, a publisher would put its encyclopedia online and attempt to turn a profit by selling space for advertisements alongside the articles. The *Britannica*, among other works, was marketed this way from 1999 to 2001, but its free content was then scaled back because of financial losses.[58]

More generally, despite efforts to making advertising pay for encyclopedias, and despite continued purchases by institutions – responsible for two-thirds of the *Britannica*'s sales by 2012 – the business of selling encyclopedias continued to worsen.[59] The early twenty-first century saw not only the disappearance of printed encyclopedias but also the disappearance of electronic ones. Microsoft thus retired *Encarta* in 2009 after determining that it could neither be sold for a profit nor paid for by the advertising placed on its website.[60]

As we have seen, the fortunes of encyclopedia-makers had been in decline since the early 1990s, but the decline became definitive for all but a

[55] Keiderling, *F. A. Brockhaus*, 374–5; Winter, "Online-Lexika," 103.
[56] *New York Times*, March 16, 2008: WK3; Prodöhl, *Politik*, 4n.
[57] *Tulsa World*, February 14, 1998: 8; *PC* 19 (January 18, 2000): 160.
[58] *New York Times*, March 15, 2001: C4; *Link-Up* 18 (July–August 2001): 6.
[59] On the *Britannica*'s institutional sales see *Computerworld* 46 (March 26, 2012): 6.
[60] *New York Times*, May 3, 2009: BU3.

few of them because of an unexpected arrival in the early twenty-first century: Wikipedia. On this I will focus for the rest of the section, outlining its early history and distinctive characteristics.

Many histories of Wikipedia relate it to ideas and projects from decades before. Hyper-links, for example – a crucial element of Wikipedia and the World Wide Web as a whole – can be traced back to the ideas of Vannevar Bush in the mid twentieth century, if not further back to the textual cross-reference.[61] Likewise, according to Michael Hart – the creator of the "e-book," or digitized text – the idea of making a free encyclopedia for networked computers was already around in 1970 or so.[62] Regardless, it went nowhere until computers were widely networked at the end of the twentieth century. Even then, the first initiatives remained largely theoretical. In 1993, an encyclopedia called Interpedia was proposed for the internet, to be constructed by volunteers and legitimated by giving articles "seals of approval," but it never advanced beyond planning. Later in the 1990s, a poorly publicized Distributed Encyclopedia was imagined as a collection of articles from all over the internet.

While some of these ideas and precedents may have been inspirational, Wikipedia's immediate origins were more mundane, involving both traditional encyclopedias and their electronic successors. Specifically, by the late 1990s, disk-based encyclopedias had shown the way to a new kind of encyclopedism, and established encyclopedia-makers were putting their works on the internet, accepting the new order of far lower prices. Not only did Wikipedia – costing nothing at all – take the period's trends in pricing to their logical conclusion, but it was influenced by traditional encyclopedias in other ways too. Besides perpetuating a number of their conventions and premises, it borrowed from their content, notably from the eleventh edition of the *Britannica*, which was no longer under copyright.[63]

In any event, Wikipedia grew out of Nupedia, an online encyclopedia launched in 2000 by the entrepreneur Jimmy Wales. Wales planned to make money by allowing for advertising on Nupedia's website, so that consulting it would be free, but his assumption was that contributors would not need to be paid. As noted in Chapter 3, people had written for prestigious encyclopedias for little-to-no pay, but Nupedia was a new work of uncertain standing. Worse still, Wales and his editor, the philosopher

[61] Zimmer, "*Renvois*," 105–7.
[62] Reagle, *Good Faith Collaboration*, 32.
[63] *Ibid.*, 31–4. See also Schopflin, "Encyclopaedia," 292–3.

Larry Sanger, restricted their choices for possible contributors to recognized specialists, people almost inevitably swamped with responsibilities. Many such specialists agreed to contribute, but without necessarily making their contribution a priority. Nupedia was also a victim of its standards. Each submission had to go through a seven-step review. The process included an assessment by a second recognized specialist as well as an evaluation in a more open forum. In a remarkable enactment of editorial transparency, finished articles were dated, and featured the names of reviewers and copy-editors as well as authors. Not surprisingly, the combination of non-payment for authors and an arduous procedure for reviewing submissions made for slow progress. Fewer than two dozen articles were completed in the project's first year.[64]

Then, in 2001, Wales and Sanger decided to try using a "wiki" – a technology for facilitating the collaborative editing of websites – to accelerate the production of material for Nupedia. In "Wikipedia," as Sanger named the experiment, anyone could submit an article or revise others' articles. Content created there – it was originally expected – would be adapted for Nupedia if it was good enough, but the experts writing for Nupedia were uneasy about Wikipedia's openness. Within a week of its foundation, Wikipedia was split off from Nupedia. Over the following two years, while Nupedia stalled and was finally abandoned, Wikipedia flourished. Unemployment among technophiles after the collapse of the "Dot-Com Bubble" may have helped it take off, providing a pool of skilled contributors with time on their hands. A bigger factor, presumably, was excitement about sharing knowledge on an indefinite scale and contributing to an encyclopedia in an immediate way. Never before had such a prospect been placed before so many people. By the end of its first year, Wikipedia had 20,000 articles, far more than Nupedia would ever have.[65] By 2003, it was generating as much traffic online as the *Encyclopaedia Britannica*.[66]

It is worth dwelling a moment on the word "Wikipedia." From the beginning, it referred to both the encyclopedia and the community behind it. Printed encyclopedias too had depended on communities – that is, on groups of people sharing a sense of belonging. In the mid twentieth century, Brockhaus, for instance, encouraged a feeling of community among his employees by issuing an internal newsletter.[67] But the ties in such

---

communities were usually weak beyond a publisher's headquarters and staff. Even the famous gatherings in the home of the philosopher Paul-Henri Thiry d'Holbach – a social center for contributors to the *Encyclopédie* (1751–72) – brought together only a minority of authors of articles.[68] As encyclopedias came to rely on geographically scattered experts, many contributors interacted with an editor and no one else.

The community of Wikipedia was different. First, participants could contribute anonymously, or under assumed names or even identities. Second, while the community functioned with little face-to-face contact, interactions were frequent, since Wikipedians were permitted to revise one another's articles – and routinely did so. It was decided, moreover, to save all versions of articles as well as Wikipedians' discussions about them, so that anyone interested could trace an article's development and evaluate the reasoning behind each revision. The decision to link articles with all the "Talk" underpinning them resembled Bayle's decision to link articles with footnotes, since the latter presented arguments underpinning the articles, but citations aside, Bayle had not been talking with anyone else.[69] Though perhaps complete strangers, Wikipedians talked among themselves, and on matters in which the stakes could be high for all parties. The community of Wikipedia was thus both diffuse and at times highly personal.

For Wikipedians, then, Wikipedia was a community as well as an encyclopedia, but between 2001 and 2003, it was technically the property of Wales's company, Bomis. In 2003, though, it became a non-profit – a status better-suited to its volunteerism – and was housed within the larger organization of Wikimedia. Both are supported by fund-raising. Wikimedia's mission is to disseminate free, wiki-based educational content throughout the world. Besides Wikipedia, it operates Wiktionary – a multi-lingual dictionary – and Wikimedia Commons, a collection of freely usable images and other materials.

Wikipedia in fact anticipated the global aspirations of Wikimedia. By the end of 2001, it was already international, with articles in more than a dozen languages other than English. As of 2018, the encyclopedia had articles in almost 300 languages, though its offerings in languages with fewer speakers were haphazard and limited. From the beginning, articles in English have dominated Wikipedia, but the number of articles in each

---

[68] Kafker, *Encyclopedists*, 29–34.
[69] Compare Lih, *Wikipedia Revolution*, 75–6; Lieshout, *Making*, 12–13, 19–20, 68–72.

of the next eleven languages is at least 20 percent of the total in English. In many minor languages, Wikipedia is the first and only encyclopedia to date.[70]

Leaving aside Wikipedia's initial development, let us look now at what made it distinctive. Relative to other encyclopedias, what is most often cited as unique to it is that anyone can contribute. For supporters, this is a positive attribute, a step in the direction of democratic empowerment. For detractors, it is deplorable, a way of disregarding expertise in favor of amateurism. In reality, not everyone can contribute. Many lack the required equipment – a working computer and a connection to the internet – while others, judged rule-breakers, have been temporarily or permanently banned from the site. Furthermore, even if perhaps half the world's population could plausibly contribute, not everyone's contribution is likely to last.[71] Weak contributions can hang on for years, but their average lifespan is shorter than that of solid ones. In addition, despite Wikipedia's ideal of letting reasoned argument alone decide disputes about content, Wikipedians at least occasionally brandish credentials, academic and other, to override content by the apparently less expert.[72]

Regardless, the culture of amateurism with which Wikipedia is associated is more a revival than a novel development, since amateurs played a significant role in the production of knowledge through the early twentieth century.[73] In the case of encyclopedias, as shown in Chapter 7, the participation of experts was only gradually secured and was always mixed in with reliance on volunteers, celebrities, and editorial staffs composed of generalists.

In sum, the break between Wikipedia and earlier encyclopedias in the matter of expertise is undoubtedly real, but it should not be exaggerated. Furthermore, Wikipedia has ways of getting good material out of a pool of contributors that includes many non-experts. Four are worth mentioning.

First, Wikipedia has a high standard for documentation. Ideally, anyway, statements in articles are backed up by references to published sources. Whereas printed encyclopedias indicating sources used bibliographical lists, Wikipedia uses endnotes, a practice that lends itself to the validation of details.

---

[70] Jemielniak, *Common Knowledge?*, 11–12; Lih, *Wikipedia Revolution*, 10–11. I have updated Jemielniak's list of the dominant languages of Wikipedia using statistics from Wikipedia as of 2018.

[71] Tkacz, *Wikipedia*, 6, 46–7.

[72] See for example Chappey, *Ordres*, 344; Lih, *Wikipedia Revolution*, 198–9.

[73] Burke, *Social History … II*, 232.

Second, Wikipedia has strength in numbers. Presenting it as a product of collective intelligence may be misleading, but the abundance of editors allows errors unnoticed by one person to be corrected by another.[74]

Third, Wikipedia's ideal of the "neutral point of view" (NPOV) is not so different in principle from the ideals of objectivity behind previous encyclopedias, but it does differ in practice. Above all, it is pervasive within the culture of Wikipedia. Contributors bring it up in the everyday context of editing articles. Although NPOV can become a slogan to be wielded against contributors with opposing ideas, it can also help Wikipedians find common ground and create better articles than they might have without it.[75]

Fourth, debates about Wikipedia's human contributors miss something crucial, namely its dependence on non-human "bots." Bots – short for robots – are bits of software approved to do specific things for the encyclopedia. Bots can correct spelling, insert information from databases, check for plagiarism, verify cross-references, and deal with vandalism. By 2013, around a quarter of the editing on Wikipedia was being carried out by bots. The proportion was far less in English and more in little-spoken languages such as Ladino and Cornish.[76] Indeed, a bot designed by the physicist Sverker Johansson was responsible for almost 10 percent of Wikipedia's articles as of 2014. Johansson's bot combed through databases to get information for articles, notably on obscure animals. It focused on article-creation in Johansson's native Swedish and on two languages of the Philippines (Cebuano and Waray, one of which his wife speaks). As a result, the Wikipedias in these languages soon had more articles than nearly all others, though critics consider the bot's articles insignificant clutter.[77]

Wikipedia's openness to nearly everyone is not its only distinctive feature. Two others involve its content. First, independent as it is from the physical constraints of paper and bindings, Wikipedia has the space to cover trivia on a scale never imagined before. Furthermore, it has contributors who care about trivia, especially as related to popular culture. Thanks to them, it has numerous articles on songs, electronic games, and even specific episodes of programs on television. Printed encyclopedias had barely even touched on such matters.

[74] On Wikipedia and collective intelligence see Reagle, *Good Faith Collaboration*, 146–51.
[75] See *ibid.*, 15, 53–60. For a more cynical view of NPOV see Tkacz, *Wikipedia*, 49–50, 104–10.
[76] Niederer and van Dijck, "Wisdom," 1368–84; Livingstone, "Immaterial Editors," 13–15.
[77] *Wall Street Journal*, July 14, 2014: A1, A6.

Second, and more subtly, the possibility and reality of moment-to-moment adjustment pushed Wikipedia in the direction of journalism. A rule adopted early on required assertions in Wikipedia to be backed up with references to published material, not first-hand sources. In the abstract, the rule meant that Wikipedia could not cover news until it was reported in the media. In practice, however, the delay could be minuscule. In 2011, for example, an article on Japan's Tōhoku earthquake was created on Wikipedia eleven minutes after the disaster began, whereas *Britannica Online* only posted an article on it in the course of the day. Wikipedia became a trusted link in the assimilation of news. In one common schema, a person might hear of news through social networking, conduct a search on the internet to get more information, and end up being directed to a freshly edited article on Wikipedia. Indeed, monthly lists of the most-read articles on Wikipedia show a significant bias toward breaking news. From 2004 onward, Wikimedia sponsored Wikinews, a separate forum for collaborative journalism, but Wikipedia's incursions into journalism have turned out to be lasting.[78]

Wikipedia in Maturity

In the last section I narrated Wikipedia's development and sketched out its features. Here I will examine its successes and challenges, concentrating on the period after 2005. As in the previous sections, I will repeatedly evoke the printed encyclopedia as a point of comparison.

In the early 2000s, Wikipedia grew rapidly, adding articles and languages as well as contributors – or "editors," as Wikipedians call them. It soon grew beyond the *Grosses vollständiges Universal-Lexicon* (1732–50) and the *Encyclopédie méthodique* (1782–1832), the largest printed encyclopedias in the European tradition. Indeed, toward 2005, it overtook an unpublished eighteenth-century compilation, China's *Siku quanshu*, to become the largest encyclopedic work of all time.[79]

Wikipedia was also increasingly consulted and used, sometimes so uncritically as to provide matter for scandal. Teachers worried about how much – and how credulously – their students were using it. Complaints arose about how journalists used it. When drawing on

[78] Keegan, "High Tempo Knowledge Collaboration," 11–13, 95–116, 193–4. See also *New York Times*, June 22, 2009: B5. On *Britannica Online*'s coverage of the earthquake and its schedule for revising articles see *Booklist* 108 (September 15, 2011): 50; Kister, *Kister's Best Encyclopedias*, 262; *Booklist* 98 (September 15, 2001): 249.
[79] Dalby, *World*, 25, 42.

Wikipedia, as they frequently did, they rarely bothered to cite it. In extreme cases, they simply copied from it, neither citing it nor seeking corroboration from elsewhere. In 2009, for example, a student attributed a quotation to Maurice Jarre in the deceased composer's biography on Wikipedia. As it turned out, the quotation was fictional. Although it was cut from Wikipedia within a few days for not being documented, it made its way into an obituary in the *Guardian* and from there into other newspapers.[80]

Wikipedia, admittedly, is exposed in its own right to being an accomplice to plagiarism. Inexperienced contributors sometimes copy text from elsewhere and paste it into an article, oblivious to the possible ramifications of copyright. Happily for the project, bots have proven effective at detecting questionable copying and bringing it to editors' attention for review or deletion. The encyclopedia, nowadays, is a model of responsibility in its compliance with copyright.[81]

Students and journalists are not the only ones known to have borrowed from Wikipedia. On a broader scale, other websites have copied it wholesale. The encyclopedia's licensing, like that of free software, allows it to be copied as long as borrowers keep the terms of the original licensing. Two kinds of sites take advantage of the option. First, "mirrors" appropriate the entire encyclopedia, usually periodically. Supported by advertisers, mirrors try to draw readers away from Wikipedia, but because searches on Google regularly put Wikipedia ahead of its mirrors, they have thus far had little effect on the encyclopedia's popularity. Second, "forks" are derivative encyclopedias, spawned by rebellion among Wikipedians. By the terms of its licensing, anyone unhappy with Wikipedia can take over its content and establish a new encyclopedia on the same terms. Like the alleged right of societies to revolt against tyrants, the right to fork in Wikipedia has been presented as a check on leaders' power as well as a sign of legitimacy in how it is governed.[82]

The most rancorous fork was triggered in 2002 by Sanger and Wales's musings about putting advertisements on Wikipedia. Aghast at the prospect of their volunteerism being commercialized, Spanish Wikipedians seceded and launched their own Enciclopedia Libre ("Free Encyclopedia") from the thousand-odd Spanish-language articles then available on Wikipedia. Edgar Enyedy, the leader of the fork, had to prepare software and set up a computer to work as a server. In addition, with fellow rebels,

[80] *Ibid.*, 86–93.
[81] Jemielniak, *Common Knowledge?*, 22.
[82] Tkacz, *Wikipedia*, 127–39.

he was forced to transfer articles from Wikipedia one at a time, since he was unable to export the data automatically. Partly because of the mutiny, the idea of advertising on Wikipedia was dropped, but the damage was done. Enciclopedia Libre continues to exist, though it is dwarfed, at the present, by the revived and re-energized Spanish Wikipedia.[83] As Enyedy's experience indicates, forking requires dedication and technological resources. Indeed, because Wikipedia has grown and depends on hundreds of servers, not to mention paid programmers, the resources necessary for forking are much greater today than they were in 2002. For this reason alone, forking is unfeasible in most cases of discontent among Wikipedians.[84]

In addition to legally authorized mirrors and forks, Wikipedia has illegal ones, sites that copy its content without then allowing for further copying by others. A Chinese version of Wikipedia began in 2001, but it was repeatedly banned in China, perhaps to promote Chinese rivals supported by advertising and amenable to censorship. Two of these are currently, with Wikipedia, among the world's largest encyclopedic endeavors: Baike ("Encyclopedia," formerly Hudong), founded in 2005, and Baidu Baike ("Hundred-Fold Encyclopedia"), founded in 2006. Each has more articles than Wikipedia does in English. In some ways, they are "copycats." Not only do they rely on volunteers editing articles with a wiki, but they feature large amounts of material copied from Wikipedia and elsewhere. As we have seen, copying from Wikipedia can be legal and proper, but Chinese encyclopedias claim a copyright on content copied from Wikipedia, thereby violating the rules for such copying. Participants in Wikipedia have been vocal in denouncing the use of its articles by Baidu Baike in particular.[85]

Copying by Baidu Baike and other sites can be taken as a sign of Wikipedia's eminence. So can its synergy with the technological giant Google. In 2008, Google and Wales made forays into each other's territory – Google with a kind of encyclopedia called Knol, Wales with a service called Wikia Search – but overall, the relationship between Google and Wikipedia has been cooperative. From the beginning, searches on Google favored Wikipedia, placing it above its mirrors and displaying its articles as high-ranking results. On the surface, such favor might seem counter-productive for Google, since Wikipedia bans advertisements and cannot therefore earn Google a commission because of them. Yet

---

[83] *Ibid.*, 144–7, 173–6; Dalby, *World*, 47.
[84] Tkacz, *Wikipedia*, 148.
[85] Zhang, "Copycat," 135–45.

Google's searches are only valuable if they turn up helpful results, results of the sort that Wikipedia often provides. Another factor working in Wikipedia's favor is its centralization of content, since unlike the internet conceived as a whole, it does not allow a subject – or a keyword, at any rate – to give rise to more than one article per language. In addition, Google's searches are known to reward pages abundantly connected with hyper-links, internally and externally, as Wikipedia's are. Regardless, Google's preference for Wikipedia seems to have strengthened. In 2006, for example, Nicholas Carr predicted that a sample of Wikipedia's articles, already well placed on Google's searches, would continue moving upward, and so they did, all ten of them claiming first place by 2009. For Carr, a critic of the internet in general, Wikipedia's dominance among search-results is a significant worry, not only because of the encyclopedia's flaws, but also because it corresponds to a broader decline in the range of choices on the internet.[86]

Carr's views notwithstanding, perceptions of Wikipedia's quality improved over time. In 2005, the journal *Nature* published a comparison between Wikipedia and the *Encyclopaedia Britannica*. Experts evaluated forty-two scientific articles from the encyclopedias' websites, a few abridged for evenness or even concocted from a group of related articles. The choice of science for the test played to Wikipedia's advantage. Science had always been one of its strong points, presumably because the scientifically trained were more comfortable with computers and more inclined to contribute. The study's conclusion, that Wikipedia had just four errors for every three in the *Britannica*, was generally interpreted as a victory for Wikipedia. Incensed, the *Britannica*'s editors criticized the study's methods and its claims about specific "errors," but *Nature* stood by the article, refusing to retract it.[87]

Similarly, in 2007, the news magazine *Stern* published a comparison between Brockhaus's online encyclopedia and the German Wikipedia. The study dealt with fifty articles selected at random, all of them present in both encyclopedias. Experts compared the two versions of each of the articles, assigning ratings for accuracy, completeness, up-to-dateness, and understandability. On the whole, Wikipedia emerged as superior. In fact, the only criterion by which Brockhaus won was understandability.[88] This result echoed a complaint from the experts who evaluated Wikipedia

[86] Dalby, *World*, 82–6, 202–3.
[87] *Ibid.*, 56–8; Gourdain *et al.*, *Révolution*, 37–50.
[88] *Stern* 50 (December 6, 2007): 38–9.

against the *Britannica*. Specifically, in their view, articles on Wikipedia were poorly organized, whatever their accuracy.[89]

Indeed, because of Wikipedia's collaborative editing, in which authors build on or modify what others have written, many articles are disordered and brusque with transitions. Thus, even as the article on the cyclist Lance Armstrong was adjusted to reflect his doping and the annulment of his wins, it retained descriptions of his racing from earlier versions. One such vestige was this statement, still present in his biography in August 2018: "To complete his record-breaking feat, he crossed the line ... on July 24 [2005] to win his seventh consecutive Tour [de France]." Considered retrospectively, the statement is false, since authorities annulled the "feat" and do not recognize Armstrong as having broken a record for wins in the Tour. Just as importantly, the statement clashes with less heroic discourse elsewhere in the article.

Articles in printed encyclopedias were not immune to these ills. As shown in Chapter 4, later editions of the encyclopedias of Furetière (1690) and Bayle (1697), for example, suffered from a deficiency of holistic editing, since neither Bayle nor Furetière's successors liked to rewrite articles thoroughly. Instead, they added new material alongside the old, whether or not it was consistent – just as many authors in Wikipedia do. Nevertheless, such lapses in integration are more widespread in Wikipedia than they were in the final generation of printed encyclopedias, the ones with which Wikipedia is nearly always compared.

Studies comparing Wikipedia favorably with other encyclopedias continued to appear, though with progressively less impact than those in *Nature* and *Stern*. In any event, Wikipedia had long since become more popular than any established encyclopedia. Indeed, by 2006, it was among the world's ten most visited websites.[90] In English, criticism of encyclopedias had focused on the *Britannica* for more than a century, but it was now redirected toward Wikipedia. Some of the criticism was little different from criticism of printed encyclopedias. Teachers expressed dismay that their students were copying from Wikipedia, just as they had about copying from previous encyclopedias. Speaking for the most scandalized, Michael Gorman, a former president of the American Library Association, compared Wikipedia to a hamburger: "A professor who encourages the use of Wikipedia is the intellectual equivalent of a dietician who recommends a steady diet of Big Macs with everything."[91] Errors and

[89] Dalby, *World*, 57.
[90] Lih, *Wikipedia Revolution*, 95.
[91] Reagle, *Good Faith Collaboration*, 137–8.

horrendous articles were pointed out in Wikipedia, just as they had been in the twentieth-century *Britannica*. Whatever its validity, such criticism tended to idealize encyclopedias before Wikipedia and thereby contribute to a distorted impression.

Some criticism of Wikipedia was more specific to its character. Exaggerated though it was, the dichotomy between the experts of printed encyclopedias and Wikipedia's alleged amateurs was legitimately seized on as representing a shift in encyclopedia-making. Other complaints concerned libel and deliberately planted falsehoods. Most notoriously, in 2005, an anonymously editing prankster created a biography of the journalist John Seigenthaler, claiming, among other things, that Seigenthaler was a suspect in two assassinations. Months later, having discovered the biography, Seigenthaler denounced Wikipedia in an editorial in the newspaper *USA Today*. The event led to soul-searching and changes at Wikipedia. In the English-language community, anonymous users were no longer allowed to create articles, and articles at risk for vandalism could be "semi-protected," that is, limited to editing by registered editors with a certain amount of experience.[92]

Printed encyclopedias too had been subject to hoaxes. In 1959, for example, Larousse replaced pages from more than 100,000 unsold copies of the *Petit Larousse*, some already in book-stores, after learning of an anti-Semitic falsehood in the article on the politician Léon Blum. A temporary employee, apparently, had been directly responsible, but Larousse was judged negligent and forced to pay damages of 10,000 francs.[93] Similarly, in 1986, a recently fired sub-editor for the *Britannica* made a mockery of certain historical articles in an electronic draft, substituting "Allah" for "Jesus Christ," and inserting the names of his superiors as historical figures. Software caught the changes before they could be printed, however, so that it was the sub-editor responsible who was fined and not Encyclopaedia Britannica.[94] Wikipedia, for its part, is not liable for its contents under American law.[95] If it were, it would suffer, for it falls prey to vandalism more than printed encyclopedias, and it will continue to do so despite the best efforts of bots and human editors.

More worrying than vandalism for many Wikipedians is the possibility of using the encyclopedia for propaganda, commercial or otherwise. As

[92] Lih, *Wikipedia Revolution*, 191–4.
[93] Pruvost, *Dent-de-lion*, 140–2; Mollier and Dubot, *Histoire*, 568–9.
[94] *New York Times*, September 6, 1986: 8.
[95] Lih, *Wikipedia Revolution*, 227.

Wikipedia rose in visibility, so too did the interest of institutions and individuals in managing what the encyclopedia asserted about them. Once again, a comparison with printed encyclopedias is apt, for they too were occasionally used as promotional tools. The simplest possibility was for encyclopedias to advertise with their titles. Brockhaus, for instance, licensed its content to other companies, allowing them to print it with such titles as *DTV-Lexikon* (1966–8), for the German publisher DTV.[96] Another possibility was advertising on the wrappers of installments when an encyclopedia appeared serially. Few of these wrappers survive, since they were meant to be discarded, but we know that advertisements appeared on or within them, whether for work being serialized or other products.[97]

More seriously in conflict with the ideal of objectivity, articles in some encyclopedias endorsed particular products and firms. Harris, for example, praised the work of several instrument-makers in his *Lexicon Technicum* (1704), Coetlogon advertised his own medicines in the *Universal History* (1745), and William Osbaldiston ended the article "Mice and Rats" in his *British Sportsman; or, Nobleman, Gentleman, and Farmer's Dictionary* (1792) with the following recommendation for extermination: "But the Hampshire Miller's Rat Powder is the best of all; which may be bought where this book is sold, at 2s. 6d. per packet."[98] As mentioned in Chapter 2, a writer for *Johnson's New Universal Cyclopaedia* (1875–7) was accused of being paid to promote companies' products. Similarly, manufacturers apparently supplied the *Espasa* (1908–30) with technical drawings in exchange for acknowledgment, and Henry Ford's article "Mass Production" in the thirteenth edition (1926) of the *Britannica* defended its subject and implicitly promoted the Ford Motor Company.[99]

On Wikipedia, though, the potential for propaganda is greater, since interested parties can become contributors at will and then hide behind a pseudonym or no name at all. In 2007, a tool called Wikiscanner was devised to help identify the source of anonymous "edits," or acts of editing. On this basis, it was discovered that workers at the Central Intelligence Agency, Wal-Mart, and Sea World, for example, had all altered articles on their own institutions. The risk of exposure may have inhibited such activity, but since one can always edit articles from a public computer and

[96] Keiderling, *F. A. Brockhaus*, 362–3.
[97] See for example Rees, [*New*] *Cyclopaedia*, 1: iv; review of *Penny Cyclopaedia*, 75; Roberto, "Democratising," 50–1. More generally, see Brake, *Print*, 27–47.
[98] Loveland, *Alternative Encyclopaedia?*, 163, 167. On advertisements for periodicals in the *Grosses vollständiges Universal-Lexicon* (1732–50) see Lohsträter, "Periodische Presse," 46–9.
[99] Castellano, *Enciclopedia*, 416; *Encyclopaedia Britannica*, 13th edn., 11: 821–3.

thus confound Wikiscanner, propaganda will continue to seep into articles. Limiting its impact will depend, in large measure, on the number of people who are actively editing articles, since the most subtly placed propaganda can only be detected by humans.[100]

Vandalism and propaganda would not have troubled Wikipedia if it had not been so successful. The same can be said of concerns about its scope. As Wikipedia has matured and acquired millions of articles, its scope has become an issue for some Wikipedians, giving rise to opposed camps of Inclusionists and Deletionists. Inclusionists argue that since Wikipedia has the space, it will be useful to more people if it covers nearly everything that someone wishes to write about. Deletionists, on the contrary, think it has too many articles on trifling subjects, which should be deleted. They argue that trivia detracts from the work's seriousness, while an excess of articles impedes revision and searching. If articles were included on hundreds of people named George Washington, say, it might be hard to find information on the former American president.

In practice, the two camps have reached an uneasy compromise, with variations in different linguistic communities, so that German Wikipedians in particular are known for their Deletionism.[101] On the one hand, articles are deleted throughout Wikipedia as a matter of principle when they fail to meet the requirement of "notability." On the other hand, Wikipedia goes beyond any printed encyclopedia in the scope of its coverage, especially of popular culture. At one extreme, four-fifths of the articles in the Japanese Wikipedia were devoted to popular culture as of 2009.[102] More generally, Wikipedia is skewed toward the interests of its contributors.

Indeed, consternation has grown over the fact that Wikipedians are not representative of the populations around them, whether in a region, a country, or the world at large. Specifically, most Wikipedians are young, educated, and adept with computers. In addition, some 90 percent of them are men, though the percentage varies considerably from language to language. Not surprisingly, it correlates with the percentage of women speaking a given language who contribute to the production of knowledge.[103] Whatever its variance, the imbalance is striking, but it is less so when we look at contributors to printed encyclopedias. As we have seen, women encyclopedists were a rarity into the early twentieth century. Even

---

[100] *New York Times*, August 19, 2007: 1, 18; Foglia, "Wikipédia," 132–4.
[101] Lih, *Wikipedia Revolution*, 148.
[102] *New York Times*, August 31, 2009: B3.
[103] Massa and Zelenkauskaite, "Gender Gap," 85–95.

thereafter, few if any encyclopedias outdid Wikipedia in recruiting women contributors. By my estimation, in the opening years of the twenty-first century, more than 90 percent of the contributors to the *Britannica* and the *Encyclopaedia universalis* were men, for example. Fairly or not, Wikipedia has been criticized for being too homogeneous, not least by Sue Gardener, Wikimedia's director from 2007 to 2014. In Gardener's view, recruiting more women to write for Wikipedia would tip its coverage, beneficially, toward topics important to women.[104]

Research on Wikipedians has not been limited to demographics. Another strand of research, initiated early on, focused on the proportion of editing done by the few and the many. In response to Wales's finding that three-quarters of edits were made by just 2 percent of editors, Aaron Swartz thus contended that the most significant and durable edits were made by outsiders, not an inner elite.[105] The debate points to the difficulty of interpreting the abundant data that Wikipedia provides.

Whatever their importance within the project, Wikipedians are volunteers, free to leave if they want to. In fact, since 2007, the growth of Wikipedia has slowed, and the number of active Wikipedians has fallen.[106] To a degree, it is only natural, since adding or improving an article becomes harder as the encyclopedia grows. Furthermore, patrolling by bots has reduced the need for easy edits such as correcting misspellings. At the same time, problems within the community may have lessened the desire to be a member of Wikipedia. In the early 2000s, Wikipedians were a small, tightly knit group, but nowadays the community is often seen as a bureaucracy. It is still possible for contributors to be promoted in rank. In becoming "administrators," they acquire certain privileges, such as the ability to block users and delete articles. The barriers to administratorship have risen, however. In particular, candidates are expected to have made a large number of edits, and they need to campaign and network to have a chance of selection. Under these circumstances, resentment toward administrators has gradually accumulated. Toward 2010, Wales himself, long a "benevolent dictator," was pressed to cede power – and ultimately did so – by a community upset with his unilateral decisions. Newcomers, for their part, frequently feel unwelcome, or bewildered by the community's rules and acronyms.[107]

---

[104] *New York Times*, January 31, 2011: A1, A12
[105] Dalby, *World*, 143–5.
[106] *Time* 174 (September 28, 2009): 50.
[107] Jemielniak, *Common Knowledge?*, 24, 29–58, 87–9, 98–103, 153–80.

In spite of its problems and slackening growth, Wikipedia in maturity remains in a position of strength. On the one hand, encyclopedias founded before the twenty-first century have been put out of business or reduced to a shadow of what they once were. The few remaining encyclopedia-publishers are barely able to eke out a living, let alone threaten Wikipedia's dominance. Besides reducing their prices, several of them have resorted to copying Wikipedia, allowing participation by anyone interested. Users were thus invited to submit content to *Encarta* in 2005 and to the *Britannica* and Larousse's website in 2008. Larousse experimented with putting signed submissions by volunteers alongside its normal, solicited articles, but submissions to *Encarta* and the *Britannica* were only suggestions, since they had to be approved and perhaps edited by experts.[108] In this sense, the two encyclopedias were evolving not toward Wikipedia but toward Citizendium, an encyclopedia founded by Wikipedia's disillusioned co-founder, Sanger, in 2007. With Citizendium, Sanger sought to combine the energy of volunteerism with "gentle" oversight by experts.[109]

On the other hand, encyclopedias introduced since Wikipedia's founding have failed to take off or only succeeded in narrow markets. As we have seen, Chinese imitations of Wikipedia are huge, but they are limited to a single country and dependent on a framework of political repression. Sanger's Citizendium has developed so slowly, thanks to high standards for articles, that it remains little more than a sketch of an encyclopedia. Much the same fate has befallen the various ideological encyclopedias that ape Wikipedia. In the anglophone world, Conservapedia was meant to compensate for a supposed left-wing bias in Wikipedia, notably its hostility to "creationism" and other alternatives to evolution. At the other end of the spectrum, Liberapedia was launched on the premise that Wikipedia was conservative. If anything, Wikipedians would seem to incline leftward politically, in large part because Wikipedia is a collective, non-commercial, educational endeavor. Feeling outnumbered and thus frustrated in their efforts to influence articles, the most conservative of Wikipedians may be tempted to express themselves with acts of subversion. Such was the case, apparently, of the unknown Wikipedian who placed a reactionary study at the top of the bibliography in the article on the Dreyfus Affair in the French Wikipedia.[110] In any event, neither Conservapedia nor Liberapedia has grown beyond a selection of manifesto-like articles.

---

[108] Dalby, *World*, 200–2; Lih, *Wikipedia Revolution*, 204.
[109] Reagle, *Good Faith Collaboration*, 41.
[110] Jemielniak, *Common Knowledge?*, 5; Dalby, *World*, 68–81.

Meanwhile, some observers see the internet itself as the ultimate encyclopedia.[111] In theory, it has the power to compete with Wikipedia as an encyclopedic collection, since on many topics it includes resources that outdo Wikipedia's articles – and are equally free. The problem lies in recognizing these resources when they come up in searches. Here Wikipedia has an advantage. Not only does its name – like a brand – act as an assurance of quality, but it consolidates information into a single article per language on every subject. While other institutions have more authority in certain domains – the Mayo Clinic on diabetes, say, or the United States government on its citizens' passports – Wikipedia has authority across much of knowledge. Furthermore, although articles in Wikipedia vary significantly, they remain better summaries than most of the alternatives available on the internet. It is probably largely for these reasons that Wikipedia places so high in searches. Thanks to such rankings, its position appears strong against the backdrop of the internet.

Conclusion

The business of encyclopedia-publishing was one of the first to be upended in the linked revolutions of the personal computer and the internet. Not only did encyclopedias count among the most expensive of books, but they also stood to benefit from electronic links among articles and the possibility of searching throughout a full text. Trapped by a model that required high prices, established encyclopedia-publishers were reluctant to embrace electronic media except as accessories, but their hands were forced by *Encarta*. Prices for encyclopedias fell precipitously, as did demand for printed encyclopedias and employment at encyclopedia-publishers throughout the world.

The new order instituted by *Encarta* was short-lived, however. In less than a decade, it was swept away by Wikipedia, a free, non-commercial encyclopedia written by volunteers and consulted online. Wikipedia too may be displaced in its turn, though a successor is hard to conceive at the moment. If it survives – the most likely scenario for the indefinite future – nothing guarantees that it will continue to prosper. Although a well-funded Wikipedia sustained by its infrastructure and millions of articles will be hard to compete with, the encyclopedia may stagnate, only minimally maintained by bots and a core of devotees.

---

[111] Stickfort, "Internet," 272.

Regardless, much more than *Encarta* – which remained bound to tradition outside a sampling of multi-media – Wikipedia has created a new paradigm for encyclopedias. No printed encyclopedia was written by experts alone, despite what nostalgia would have us believe, but Wikipedia exceeds any previous encyclopedia in its openness to contributions from the public at large. Just as importantly, Wikipedia is the first socio-technical encyclopedia, dependent on software as well as humans; the first encyclopedia to exist as a brand in more than a handful of languages; and the first encyclopedia to test a new kind of comprehensiveness, one that puts popular knowledge on the same footing as the scientific and historical knowledge first brought together in eighteenth-century encyclopedias. For better or for worse, a new chapter of encyclopedism has begun to be written.

Despite Wikipedia's novelty, it is nonetheless an offshoot of the printed European encyclopedia. Although alphabetical order has almost vanished, Wikipedia remains an encyclopedia consisting of a numerous discrete articles arranged under keywords and connected with cross-references, now realized as hyper-links. While it includes illustrations, they are an adjunct to text. Like articles in printed encyclopedias from the mid nineteenth century onward, articles in Wikipedia are expected to conform to a uniform style, a style designed, among other things, to establish trust and authority. In addition, like the majority of modern encyclopedias – and unlike the encyclopedic dictionary, still a profitable genre in the twenty-first century – it does not offer entries on words considered as words, the subject of Wiktionary. Like the European encyclopedia, finally, Wikipedia is designed for consultation, but it is also an encyclopedia in which browsers can lose themselves, and in which the most dedicated can seek education.

Bibliography

Abbattista, Guido. "La 'Folie de la raison par alphabet': Le origini settecentesche dell'*Encyclopaedia Britannica* (1768–1801)." In *L'enciclopedismo in Italia nel XVIII secolo*. Ed. Guido Abbattista. Naples: Bibliopolis, 1996. 397–434.

ABC Sevilla.

Albertan, Christian. "Les Journalistes de Trévoux lecteurs de l'*Encyclopédie*." *Recherches sur Diderot et sur l'Encyclopédie* 13 (1992): 107–16.

Albrecht, Wolfgang. "Aufklärerische Selbstreflexion in deutschen Enzyklopädien und Lexika zur Zeit der Spätaufklärung." In *Enzyklopädien der frühen Neuzeit*. Ed. Franz M. Eybl *et al*. Tübingen: Niemeyer, 1995. 232–54.

Allgemeine Realencyklopädie; oder, Conversationslexicon für alle Stände. 3rd edn. 12 vols. Regensburg: Manz, 1865–73.

Almanach national: Annuaire de la République française pour 1852. Paris: Guyot and Scribe, 1852.

Alvarez de Miranda, Pedro. "Les projets encyclopédiques en Espagne." *Dix-huitième siècle* 38 (2006): 105–18.

Amelung, Iwo. "Zwischen 'Geschäft' und 'Aufklärung': Neue Enzyklopädien im China des späten 19. und frühen 20. Jahrhunderts." In *Wissenswelten: Historische Lexikographie und europäische Aufklärung*. Ed. Robert Charlier. Hanover: Wehrhahn, 2010. 99–116.

American Library Association. *Purchasing an Encyclopedia: 12 Points to Consider*. 4th edn. Chicago: Booklist, 1992.

Anderson, Wilda. *Between the Library and the Laboratory: The Language of Chemistry in Eighteenth-Century France*. Baltimore: Johns Hopkins University Press, 1984.

Appleton's Library Manual: Containing a Catalogue Raisonné of Upwards of Twelve Thousand of the Most Important Works in Every Department of Knowledge. New York: Appleton, 1847.

Arato, François. "Savants, philosophes, journalistes: L'Italie des dictionnaires encyclopédiques." *Dix-huitième siècle* 38 (2006): 69–82.

Archbold, Johanna. "'The Most Expensive Literary Publication Ever Printed in Ireland': James Moore and the Publication of the *Encyclopaedia Britannica* in Ireland, 1790–1800." In *Georgian Dublin*. Ed. Gillian O'Brien and Finola O'Kane. Dublin: Four Courts, 2008. 175–87.

Arendt, Hans-Jürgen. *Gustav Theodor Fechner und sein Hauslexikon, 1834 bis 1838: Ein Beitrag zur Fechner-Biographie und zur Geschichte der enzyklopädischen Literatur in Deutschland.* Leipzig: Fechner Gesellschaft, 1994.

Arner, Robert D. *Dobson's Encyclopaedia: The Publisher, Text, and Publication of America's First Britannica (1789–1803).* Philadelphia: University of Pennsylvania Press, 1991.

Baczko, Bronislaw. "Les trois temps de la *Méthodique*." In *L'Encyclopédie méthodique (1782–1832): Des Lumières au positivisme.* Ed. Claude Blanckaert et al. Geneva: Droz, 2006. 763–97.

Baker, Keith Michael. "Épistémologie et politique: Pourquoi l'*Encyclopédie* est-elle un dictionnaire?" In *L'Encyclopédie: Du réseau au livre et du livre au réseau.* Ed. Robert Morrissey and Philippe Roger. Paris: Champion, 2001. 51–58.

Baldwin, James. *A Guide to Systematic Readings in the Encyclopaedia Britannica.* Chicago: Werner, 1895.

Basnage de Beauval, Henri. Review of *Dictionnaire universel françois et latin.* *Histoire des ouvrages des savants* 20 (1704): 312–39.

Bauer, Wolfgang. "The Encyclopaedia in China." *Cahiers d'histoire mondiale* 9 (1966): 665–91.

Bayle, Pierre. *Dictionaire historique et critique.* 1st edn. 2 vols. Rotterdam: Leers, 1697.

Becq, Annie, ed. *L'Encyclopédisme: Actes du Colloque de Caen.* Paris: Aux Amateurs de Livres, 1991.

Behnke, Dorothea. *Furetière und Trévoux: Eine Untersuchung zum Verhältnis der beiden Wörterbuchserien.* Tübingen: Niemeyer, 1996.

Belgum, Kirsten. "Documenting the Zeitgeist: How the *Brockhaus* Recorded and Fashioned the World for Germans." In *Publishing Culture and the "Reading Nation."* Ed. Lynne Tatlock. Rochester: Camden House, 2010. 89–117.

Benhamou, Paul. "The Diffusion of Forbidden Books: Four Case Studies." *SVEC* 12 (2005): 259–81.

Benrekassa, Georges. "Didactique encyclopédique et savoir philosophique." In *L'Encyclopédisme: Actes du Colloque de Caen.* Ed. Annie Becq. Paris: Aux Amateurs de Livres, 1991. 291–308.

Berger, Gaston. Introduction to Vol. IV (*La Vie*) of *Encyclopédie française.* Paris: Société Nouvelle de l'Encyclopédie Française, 1960. v–x.

Bernabò, Massimo, and Rita Tarasconi. "L'epistolario Gentile-Ojetti ed un attacco vaticano all'*Enciclopedia italiana*." *Quaderni di storia* 53 (2001): 155–68.

Bernard, John Peter et al., eds. *A General Dictionary, Historical and Critical.* 10 vols. London: Roberts, 1734–41.

[Bewley, William]. Review of the 1st edn. of *Encyclopaedia Britannica*. *Monthly Review* 50 (April 1774): 301–9.

Beyer de Ryke, Benoît. "Les Encyclopédies médiévales: Un état de la question." *Pecia: Ressources en médiévistique* 1 (2002): 9–42.

Bibliographie de la France; ou, Journal général de la librairie et de l'imprimerie.

Biesterfeldt, Hans Hinrich. "Medieval Arabic Encyclopedias of Science and Philosophy." In *Medieval Hebrew Encyclopedias of Science and Philosophy.* Ed. Steven Harvey. Dordrecht: Kluwer, 2000. 77–98.

Birn, Raymond. "Les Mots et les images: *L'Encyclopédie*, le projet de Diderot et la stratégie des éditeurs." *Revue d'histoire moderne et contemporaine* 35 (1988): 637–51.

"The Profits of Ideas: *Privilèges en librairie* in Eighteenth-Century France." *Eighteenth-Century Studies* 4 (1970–1): 131–68.

Blair, Ann. "Annotating and Indexing Natural Philosophy." In *Books and the Sciences in History*. Ed. Marina Frasca-Spada and Nick Jardine. Cambridge: Cambridge University Press, 2000. 69–89.

"*Curieux, curieusement, curiosité.*" In *Le Dictionnaire universel d'Antoine Furetière*. Ed. Hélène Merlin-Kajman. Paris: Champion, 2002. 101–7.

"Le Florilège latin comme point de comparaison." In *Qu'était-ce qu'écrire une encyclopédie en Chine?* Ed. Florence Bretelle-Establet and Karine Chemla. Saint-Denis: Presses Universitaires de Vincennes, 2007. 185–204.

"Organizations of Knowledge." In *The Cambridge Companion to Renaissance Philosophy*. Ed. James Hankins. Cambridge: Cambridge University Press, 2007. 287–303.

"Reading Strategies for Coping with Information Overload, *ca.* 1550–1700." *Journal of the History of Ideas* 64 (2003): 11–28.

"Revisiting Renaissance Encyclopaedism." In *Encyclopaedism from Antiquity to the Renaissance*. Ed. Jason König and Greg Woolf. Cambridge: Cambridge University Press, 2013. 379–97.

Too Much to Know: Managing Scholarly Information before the Modern Age. New Haven: Yale University Press, 2011.

Blake, J. L. *Family Encyclopedia of Useful Knowledge and General Literature*. New York: Hill, 1834.

Blanchard, Gilles, and Mark Olsen. "Le Système de renvois dans l'*Encyclopédie*: Une cartographie des structures de connaissances au XVIIIe siècle." *Recherches sur Diderot et sur l'Encyclopédie* 31–32 (2002): 45–70.

Bléchet, Françoise. "Un précurseur de l'*Encyclopédie* au service de l'état: L'Abbé Bignon." In *L'Encyclopédisme: Actes du Colloque de Caen*. Ed. Annie Becq. Paris: Aux Amateurs de Livres, 1991. 395–415.

Blois, Julie de. "Le Dictionnaire *Petit Larousse*, d'hier à aujourd'hui: 'Toujours le même, toujours différent' ou l'évolution d'un produit dictionnairique." In *Pierre Larousse: Du Grand dictionnaire au Petit Larousse*. Ed. Jean Pruvost *et al*. Paris: Champion, 2002. 161–204.

Boner, Charles. *Memoirs and Letters of Charles Boner*. Ed. R. M. Kettle. 2 vols. London: Bentley, 1871.

Booklist.

Boston Globe.

Boulanger, Jean-Claude. "L'Epopée du *Petit Larousse illustré* au Québec de 1906 à 2005." In *Les Dictionnaires Larousse: Genèse et evolution*. Ed. Monique C. Cormier and Aline Francoeur. Montreal: Presses de l'Université de Montréal, 2005. 249–75.

"Quelques figures du panthéon des dictionnaires scolaires modernes (1856–2005)." In *Les Dictionnaires Larousse: Genèse et evolution*. Ed. Monique C.

Cormier and Aline Francoeur. Montreal: Presses de l'Université de Montréal, 2005. 91–128.

Bowen, Ralph H. "The *Encyclopédie* as a Business Venture." In *From the Ancient Régime to the Popular Front*. Ed. Charles K. Warner. New York: Columbia University Press, 1969. 1–22.

Boyles, Denis. *Everything Explained that Is Explainable: On the Creation of the Encyclopaedia Britannica's Celebrated Eleventh Edition, 1910–11*. New York: Knopf, 2016.

Bradshaw, Lael Ely. "Ephraim Chambers' *Cyclopaedia*." In *Notable Encyclopedias of the Seventeenth and Eighteenth Centuries*. Ed. Frank A. Kafker. Oxford: Voltaire Foundation, 1981. 123–40.

  "John Harris's *Lexicon Technicum*." In *Notable Encyclopedias of the Seventeenth and Eighteenth Centuries*. Ed. Frank A. Kafker. Oxford: Voltaire Foundation, 1981. 107–21.

  "Thomas Dyche's *New General English Dictionary*." In *Notable Encyclopedias of the Seventeenth and Eighteenth Centuries*. Ed. Frank A. Kafker. Oxford: Voltaire Foundation, 1981. 141–61.

Brake, L. *Print in Transition, 1850–1910: Studies in Media and Book History*. London: Palgrave, 2001.

Brandes, Helga. "Das *Frauenzimmer-Lexikon* von Amaranthes." *Das achtzehnte Jahrhundert* 22 (1998): 22–30.

Braunrot, Christabel P., and Kathleen Hardesty Doig. "The *Encyclopédie méthodique*: An Introduction." *SVEC* 327 (1995): 1–152.

Bretelle-Establet, Florence, and Karine Chemla, eds. *Qu'était-ce qu'écrire une encyclopédie en Chine?* Saint-Denis: Presses Universitaires de Vincennes, 2007.

Britannica Junior. 15 vols. Chicago: Encyclopaedia Britannica, 1957.

The British Encyclopaedia; or, Dictionary of Arts and Sciences. 6 vols. London: Longman *et al.*, 1809.

Brown, D. W. F. *Putting Minds to Work: An Introduction to Modern Pedagogy*. Sydney: Wiley, 1972.

Brown, Stephen W. "James Tytler's Misadventures in the Late Eighteenth-Century Edinburgh Book Trade." In *Printing Places*. Ed. John Hinks and Catherine Armstrong. New Castle: Oak Knoll, 2005. 47–63.

Buller, Christoph. "'Allgemeines Licht, allgemeiner Gebrauch': Carl Christoffer Gjörwells Projekt einer schwedischen Enzyklopädie (1777–1787)." *Leipziger Jahrbuch zur Buchgeschichte* 17 (2008): 9–57.

Bulliet, Richard W. "Of Encyclopedias and the End of the World." *Biblion: The Bulletin of the New York Public Library* 3 (1994): 49–58.

Burke, Peter. *A Social History of Knowledge from Gutenberg to Diderot*. Cambridge: Cambridge University Press, 2000.

  A Social History of Knowledge II: From the Encyclopédie to Wikipedia. Cambridge: Polity, 2012.

Burnand, Léonard, and Alain Cernuschi. "Circulation de matériaux entre l'*Encyclopédie* d'Yverdon et quelques dictionnaires spécialisés." *Dix-huitième siècle* 38 (2006): 253–67.

Burrell, Paul. "Pierre Bayle's *Dictionnaire historique et critique*." In *Notable Encyclopedias of the Seventeenth and Eighteenth Centuries*. Ed. Frank A. Kafker. Oxford: Voltaire Foundation, 1981. 83–103.

Cain, Julien. Introduction to Vol. x (*L'Etat*) of *Encyclopédie française*. Paris: Société Nouvelle de l'Encyclopédie française, 1964. v–viii.

Calvo, María Dolores. "The *Enciclopedia universal illustrada europeo-americana*: Its History and Content." M.A. thesis. Columbia University, 1951.

Carels, Peter E., and Dan Flory. "Johann Heinrich Zedler's *Universal Lexicon*." In *Notable Encyclopedias of the Seventeenth and Eighteenth Centuries*. Ed. Frank A. Kafker. Oxford: Voltaire Foundation, 1981. 165–96.

Castellano, Philippe. *Enciclopedia Espasa: Historia de una aventura editorial*. Trans. Caty Orero Saéz de Tejada. Madrid: Espasa, 2000.

"Catalogue des livres imprimés chez Denis Mariette." Vol. vii of Charles Le Bourg de Montmorel, *Homélies sur les évangiles des mystères de la sainte vierge*. Paris: Mariette, 1711. 1–18 [309–26].

Caullery, J. "Notes sur Samuel Chappuzeau." *Bulletin de la Societe de l'histoire du protestantisme français* 58 (1909): 141–55.

Cavaterra, Alessandra. *La rivoluzione culturale di Giovanni Gentile: La nascita della Enciclopedia Italiana*. Siena: Cantagalli, 2014.

The Century Dictionary and Cyclopedia. 10 vols. New York: Century, [1903].

Cernuschi, Alain. "L'ABC de l'*Encyclopédie* d'Yverdon ou la refonte encyclopédique de F.-B. De Felice à la lumière de ses lettres de 1771." *Recherches sur Diderot et sur l'Encyclopédie* 49 (2014): 123–43.

"L'Arbre encyclopédique des connaissances: Figures, opérations, métamorphoses." In *Tous les savoirs du monde*. Ed. Roland Schaer. Paris: Bibliothèque Nationale, 1996. 377–82.

"L'*Encyclopédie* d'Yverdon (1770–1780): Notes sur une refonte et quelques-unes de ses procédures." *Das achtzehnte Jahrhundert* 22 (1998): 102–13.

"Le Travail sur des sources non alphabétiques: L'Exemple de la compilation de l'*Histoire des mathématiques* (1758) de Montucla par l'*Encyclopédie* d'Yverdon." In *L'Encyclopédie d'Yverdon et sa résonance européenne*. Ed. Jean-Daniel Candaux *et al*. Geneva: Slatkine, 2005. 289–327.

Chambers, Ephraim. *Cyclopaedia; or, An Universal Dictionary of Arts and Sciences*. 1st edn. 2 vols. London: Knapton *et al*., 1728.

"Some Considerations Offered to the Public, Preparatory to a Second Edition of *Cyclopaedia; or, An Universal Dictionary of Arts and Sciences*." [London?]: [1733?].

Chambers, William. *Memoir of Robert Chambers with Autobiographical Reminiscences of William Chambers*. 5th edn. Edinburgh: Chambers, 1872.

Chambers's Encyclopaedia. 1st edn. 10 vols. London: Chambers, 1868.

Chambers's Encyclopaedia. New rev. edn. 15 vols. Oxford: Pergamon, 1966–8.

Changing Times: The Kiplinger Magazine.

Chapoutot-Remadi, Mounira. "L'Encyclopédie arabe au xᵉ siècle." In *L'Encyclopédisme: Actes du Colloque de Caen*. Ed. Annie Becq. Paris: Aux Amateurs de Livres, 1991. 37–46.

Chappey, Jean-Luc. *Ordres et désordres biographiques: Dictionnaires, listes de noms, réputation des Lumières à Wikipédia*. Seyssel: Champ Vallon, 2013.

"The Chartered Booksellers." *New Monthly Magazine and Literary Journal* 40 (1834): 65–75.

Chaudon, Louis-Mayeul. *Dictionnaire anti-philosophique*. New edn. 2 vols. Avignon: Girard and Seguin *et al.*, 1769.

[Chaudon, Louis-Mayeul]. *La Religion vengée; ou, Réfutation des auteurs impies*.

Chaumeix, Abraham-Joseph. *Préjugés légitimes contre l'Encyclopédie*. 8 vols. Brussels: 1758–9.

Chicago Sun-Times.

Chicago Tribune.

Christian Miscellany, and Family Visiter.

Ciclopedia ovvero dizionario universale delle arti e delle scienze. Trans. Giuseppe Maria Secondo. 8 vols. Naples: De Bonis, 1747–54.

Codoñer, Carmen. "De l'Antiquité au Moyen Age: Isidore de Séville." In *L'Encyclopédisme: Actes du Colloque de Caen*. Ed. Annie Becq. Paris: Aux Amateurs de Livres, 1991. 19–35.

[Coetlogon, Dennis de]. Prospectus to *An Universal History of Arts and Sciences*. In *Book Prospectuses before 1801 in the John Johnson Collection*. Ed. J. P. Feather. Oxford: Oxford Microform Publications, 1976.

Coleman, Patrick. "'Figure' in the *Encyclopédie*: Discovery or Discipline." In *Using the Encyclopédie*. Ed. Daniel Brewer and Julie Candler Hayes. Oxford: Voltaire Foundation, 2002. 63–79.

Coleridge, Samuel Taylor. *Collected Letters*. Ed. Earl Leslie Griggs. 2 vols. Oxford: Clarendon, 1956.

Collier's Encyclopedia. 20 volumes. New York: Collier and Son, 1950.

Collier's Encyclopedia. 24 vols. New York: Collier's, 1997.

Collison, Robert. *Encyclopaedias: Their History throughout the Ages*. 2nd edn. New York: Hafner, 1966.

Colman, George, the Younger. *Vagaries Vindicated; or, Hypercritick Hypercriticks: A Poem*. London: Longman *et al.*, 1813.

The Columbia Encyclopedia. 1st edn. Ed. Clarke F. Ansley. Morningside Heights: Columbia University Press, 1935.

The Columbia Encyclopedia. 2nd edn. Ed. William Bridgwater and Elizabeth J. Sherwood. Morningside Heights: Columbia University Press, 1956.

Complément du Dictionnaire de l'Académie française. Paris: Firmin Didot, 1842.

Computerworld.

Conrad, Ruth. *Lexikonpolitik: Die erste Auflage der RGG im Horizont protestantischer Lexikographie*. Berlin: De Gruyter, 2006.

Considine, John. *Academy Dictionaries, 1600–1800*. Cambridge: Cambridge University Press, 2014.

  "Cutting and Pasting Slips: Early Modern Compilation and Information Management." *Journal of Medieval and Early Modern Studies* 45 (2015): 487–504.

Dictionaries in Early Modern Europe: Lexicography and the Making of Heritage. Cambridge: Cambridge University Press, 2008.

"In Praise of Edward Phillips." *Studia linguistica universitatis Iagellonicae cracoviensis* 132 (2015): 211–28.

Considine, John, and Sylvia Brown. Introduction to N. H., *The Ladies Dictionary (1694)*. Burlington: Ashgate, 2010. vii–liii.

Cook, Nancy. "Reshaping Publishing and Authorship in the Gilded Age." In *Perspectives on American Book History*. Ed. Scott E. Casper *et al.* Amherst: University of Massachusetts Press, 2002. 223–54.

Cooney, Sondra Miley. "A Catalogue of Chambers's Encyclopaedia, 1868." *Bibliotheck: A Scottish Journal of Bibliography and Allied Topics* 24 (1999): 17–110.

"Die deutschen Wurzeln der 'Chambers Enzyklopädie: Ein Wörterbuch des universalen Wissens für das Volk.'" In *F. A. Brockhaus 1905–2005*. Ed. Thomas Keiderling. Leipzig: Brockhaus, 2005. 199–207.

Corbin, François. "Image-outil et image-spectacle: Sur la dualité de l'iconographie du *Petit Larousse illustré*." In *Pierre Larousse: Du Grand dictionnaire au Petit Larousse*. Ed. Jean Pruvost *et al.* Paris: Champion, 2002. 241–87.

Corneille, Thomas. *Le Dictionnaire des arts et des sciences*. 2 vols. Paris: Coignard, 1694.

Coronelli, Vincenzo. *Biblioteca universale sacro-profana, antico-moderna*. 7 vols. Venice: 1701–6.

Costabel, Pierre. "La Mécanique dans l'*Encyclopédie*." In *L'Encyclopédie et le progrès des sciences et des techniques*. Ed. Suzanne Delorme and René Taton. Paris: Presses Universitaires de France, 1952. 64–90.

Coste, Alain, and Pierre Crépel. "Prospectus pour une étude du dictionnaire de *Mathématiques* de l'*Encyclopédie méthodique*." In *L'Encyclopédie méthodique (1782–1832): Des Lumières au positivisme*. Ed. Claude Blanckaert *et al.* Geneva: Droz, 2006. 493–519.

Courrier des Alpes.

Coyne, John R. "The Effects of Continuous Revision on the Current Usefulness of Past Editions of *World Book Encyclopedia*." M.A. thesis. University of Chicago, 1973.

Craftsman.

Craik, Alex D. D. "Calculus and Analysis in Early 19th-Century Britain: The Work of William Wallace." *Historia mathematica* 26 (1999): 239–67.

Crews, Kambri. *Burn Down the Ground: A Memoir*. New York: Workshop Creations, 2012.

"Cyclopaedia Illustrations." In *The Cyclopaedia War: The Appletons against the Johnsons*. New York: Johnson, [1877?]. 1–18.

"The Cyclopaedia War: The Appletons against the Johnsons." In *The Cyclopaedia War: The Appletons against the Johnsons*. New York: Johnson, [1877?]. 1–14.

Daily Advertiser.

Dalby, Andrew. *The World and Wikipedia: How We are Editing Reality*. Draycott: Siduri, 2009.

Dale, Edgar, and Joseph O'Rourke. *The Living Word Vocabulary: The Words We Know.* Chicago: Field Enterprises, 1976.

Daly, Lloyd W. *Contributions to a History of Alphabetization in Antiquity and the Middle Ages.* Brussels: Latomas, 1967.

Darnton, Robert. *The Business of Enlightenment: A Publishing History of the Encyclopédie, 1775–1800.* Cambridge, MA: Harvard University Press, 1979.

The Great Cat Massacre and Other Episodes in French Cultural History. New York: Basic, 1984.

Daston, Lorraine. "Objectivity and the Escape from Perspective." *Social Studies of Science* 22 (1992): 597–618.

Daston, Lorraine, and Peter Galison. *Objectivity.* New York: Zone, 2007.

Daston, Lorraine, and Katharine Park. *Wonders and the Order of Nature, 1150–1750.* New York: Zone, 1998.

Database: The Magazine of Database of Reference and Review.

Decker, Uwe. "Die *Deutsche Encyclopädie* (1778–1807)." *Das achtzehnte Jahrhundert* 14 (1990): 147–51.

De Felice, Fortunato Bartolommeo, ed. *Encyclopédie; ou, Dictionnaire universel raisonné des connoissances humaines.* 58 vols. Yverdon: [Société Typographique], 1770–80.

De Kay, Drake. "*Encyclopedia Americana*, First Edition." *Journal of Library History* 3 (1968): 201–20.

Delavenay, Emile. "Quelques aspects pratiques de l'internationalisation d'une encyclopédie." *Cahiers d'histoire mondiale* 9 (1966): 835–44.

Denny, Joseph H., and Paul M. Mitchell. "Russian Translations of the *Encyclopédie.*" In *Notable Encyclopedias of the Late Eighteenth Century.* Ed. Frank A. Kafker. Oxford: Voltaire Foundation, 1994. 335–86.

Deseret Weekly.

Diccionario enciclopédico de la lengua española. Ed. Eduardo Chao Fernández. 2 vols. Madrid: Gaspar and Roig, 1853–5.

"Dictionaries of Arts and Sciences." *Eclectic Review* 5 (June 1809): 541–53.

Dictionnaire de la conversation et de la lecture. 52 vols. Paris: Belin-Mandar, 1832–9.

[*Dictionnaire de Trévoux*]. 1st edn. *Dictionnaire universel françois et latin.* 3 vols. Trévoux: Ganeau, 1704.

[*Dictionnaire de Trévoux*]. 2nd edn. *Dictionnaire universel françois et latin.* 5 vols. Trévoux: Delaulne *et al.*, 1721.

[*Dictionnaire de Trévoux*]. New edn. *Dictionnaire universel, français et latin.* 8 vols. Paris: Libraires Associés, 1771.

Dictionnaire encyclopédique des amusemens des sciences, mathématiques et physiques. Paris: Panckoucke, 1792.

Diderot, Denis. *Correspondance.* Ed. Georges Roth. 16 vols. Paris: Minuit, 1955–70.

[Diderot, Denis]. Prospectus to *Encyclopédie; ou, Dictionnaire raisonné des sciences, des arts et des métiers.* Paris: Briasson *et al.*, 1751 [1750].

Didier, Béatrice. *Alphabet et raison: Le Paradoxe des dictionnaires au XVIIIe siècle.* Paris: Presses Universitaires de France, 1996.

Diény, Jean-Pierre. "Les Encyclopédies chinoises." In *L'Encyclopédisme: Actes du Colloque de Caen.* Ed. Annie Becq. Paris: Aux Amateurs de Livres, 1991. 195–200.

Dierse, Ulrich. *Enzyklopädie: Zur Geschichte eines philosophischen und wissenschaftstheoretischen Begriffs.* Bonn: Bouvier, 1977.

Dirda, Michael. *Readings: Essays and Literary Entertainments.* Bloomington: Indiana University Press, 2000.

Dobson, John Blythe. "The Spurious Articles in Appleton's *Cyclopaedia of American Biography*: Some New Discoveries and Considerations." *Biography* 16 (1993): 388–408.

Doig, Kathleen Hardesty. "L'*Encyclopédie méthodique* et l'organisation des connaissances." *Recherches sur Diderot et sur l'Encyclopédie* 12 (1992): 59–69.

  From Encyclopédie to Encyclopédie méthodique: Revision and Expansion. Oxford: Voltaire Foundation, 2013.

  "The Quarto and Octavo Editions of the *Encyclopédie*." In *Notable Encyclopedias of the Late Eighteenth Century.* Ed. Frank A. Kafker. Oxford: Voltaire Foundation, 1994. 117–42.

Doig, Kathleen Hardesty, *et al.* "Colin Macfarquhar, George Gleig, and Possibly James Tytler's Edition (1788–97): The Attainment of Recognition and Eminence." In *The Early Britannica.* Ed. Frank A. Kafker and Jeff Loveland. Oxford: Voltaire Foundation, 2009. 156–251.

Doig, Kathleen Hardesty, *et al.* "James Tytler's Edition (1777–84): A Vast Expansion and Improvement." In *The Early Britannica.* Ed. Frank A. Kafker and Jeff Loveland. Oxford: Voltaire Foundation, 2009. 68–155.

Doig, Kathleen Hardesty, Frank A. Kafker, and Jeff Loveland. "George Gleig's *Supplement* to the Third Edition (1801–1803): Learned and Combative." In *The Early Britannica.* Ed. Frank A. Kafker and Jeff Loveland. Oxford: Voltaire Foundation, 2009. 252–97.

Donato, Clorinda. "Eighteenth-Century Encyclopedias and National Identity." *History of European Ideas* 16 (1993): 959–65.

  "Jean Henri Samuel Formey's Contribution to the *Encyclopédie* d'Yverdon." In *Schweizer in Berlin des 18. Jahrhunderts.* Ed. Martin Fontius and Helmut Holzhey. Berlin: Akademie, 1996. 87–98.

  "Übersetzung und Wandlung des enzyklopädischen Genres: Johann Georg Krünitz' *Oeconomische Encyklopädie* (1771–1858) und ihre französischsprachigen Vorläufer." In *Kuturtransfer im Epochenumbruch.* Ed. Hans-Jürgen Lüsebrink *et al.* Leipzig: Universitätsverlag, 1997. 539–65.

  "Writing the Italian Nation in French: Cultural Politics in the *Encyclopédie méthodique de Padoue.*" *New Perspectives on the Eighteenth Century* 10 (2013): 12–27.

Doody, Aude. *Pliny's Encyclopedia: The Reception of the Natural History.* Cambridge: Cambridge University Press, 2010.

Döring, Detlef. "Leipzig als Produktionsort enzyklopädischer Literatur bis 1750." In *Seine Welt wissen: Enzyklopädien in der frühen Neuzeit.* Ed. Ulrich Johannes Schneider. Darmstadt: Primus, 2006. 125–34.

Dorn, Nico, Lena Oetjens, and Ulrich Johannes Schneider. "Die sachliche Erschliessung von Zedlers *Universal-Lexicon*: Einblick in die Lexikographie des 18. Jahrhunderts." *Das achtzehnte Jahrhundert* 32 (2008): 96–125.

Downey, Margaret. "My 'Bye Bull' Story." In *50 Voices of Disbelief: Why We Are Atheists*. Ed. Russell Blackford and Udo Schüklenk. Oxford: Wiley-Blackwell, 2009. 10–15.

Draelants, Isabelle. "Le 'Siècle de l'encyclopédisme': Conditions et critères de définition d'un genre." In *Encyclopédire: Formes de l'ambition encyclopédique dans l'Antiquité et au Moyen Age*. Ed. Arnaud Zucker. Turnhout: Brepols, 2013. 81–106.

Drège, Jean-Pierre. "Des ouvrages classés par catégories: Les Encyclopédies chinoises." In *Qu'était-ce qu'écrire une encyclopédie en Chine?* Ed. Florence Bretelle-Establet and Karine Chemla. Saint-Denis: Presses Universitaires de Vincennes, 2007. 19–38.

Dreitzel, Horst. "Zedlers 'Grosses vollständiges Universallexikon.'" *Das achtzehnte Jahrhundert* 18 (1994): 117–24.

Duris, Pascal. "Entre Buffon et Linné: La Zoologie dans l'*Encyclopédie méthodique*." In *L'Encyclopédie méthodique (1782–1832): Des Lumières au positivisme*. Ed. Claude Blanckaert *et al.* Geneva: Droz, 2006. 579–604.

Durst, Margarete. *Gentile e la filosofia nell'Enciclopedia italiana: L'idea e la regola*. Rome: Pellicani, 1998.

L'Ecole normale: Journal d'éducation et d'instruction.

Edelstein, Dan, Robert Morrissey, and Glenn Roe. "To Quote or Not to Quote: Citation Strategies in the *Encyclopédie*." *Journal of the History of Ideas* 74 (2013): 213–36.

Edgerton, Ronald B. "How Difficult Are the Children's Encyclopedias?" *Elementary School Journal* 45 (1945): 379–85, 455–64.

Ehrard, Jean. "L'Arbre et le labyrinthe." In *L'Encyclopédie, Diderot, l'esthétique*. Ed. Sylvain Auroux *et al.* Paris: Presses Universitaires de France, 1991. 233–39.

Eick, David Michael. "Defining the Old Regime: Dictionary Wars in Pre-Revolutionary France." Ph.D. dissertation. University of Iowa, 2004.

    "Violence, Levity, and the Dictionary in Old Regime France: Chaudon's *Dictionnaire anti-philosophique*." In *An American Voltaire*. Ed. E. Joe Johnson and Byron R. Wells. Newcastle: Cambridge Scholars, 2009. 97–119.

Einbinder, Harvey. *The Myth of the Britannica*. New York: Grove, 1964.

Eisenstein, Elizabeth L. *The Printing Press as an Agent of Change: Communications and Cultural Transformations in Early Modern Europe*. Cambridge: Cambridge University Press, 1979.

Elman, Benjamin. "Collecting and Classifying: Ming Dynasty Compendia and Encyclopedias (*Leishu*)." In *Qu'était-ce qu'écrire une encyclopédie en Chine?* Ed. Florence Bretelle-Establet and Karine Chemla. Saint-Denis: Presses Universitaires de Vincennes, 2007. 131–57.

Enciclopedia [Einaudi]. 16 vols. Turin: Einaudi, 1977–84.

Enciclopedia italiana. Ed. Giovannia Gentile and Calogero Tumminelli. 36 vols. Rome: Treccani, 1929–39.

Encyclopaedia Americana: A Popular Dictionary of Arts, Sciences, Literature, History, Politics and Biography. 1st edn. Ed. Francis Lieber. 13 vols. Philadelphia: Carey *et al.*, 1829–33.

Encyclopaedia Britannica. 1st edn. 3 vols. Edinburgh: Bell and Macfarquhar, 1771.

Encyclopaedia Britannica. 2nd edn. 10 vols. Edinburgh: J. Balfour *et al.*, 1778–83.

Encyclopaedia Britannica. 3rd edn. 18 vols. Edinburgh: Bell and Macfarquhar, 1797.

Encyclopaedia Britannica. 3rd edn. Irish edn. 20 vols. Dublin: Moore, 1790–8.

Encyclopaedia Britannica. 5th edn. 20 vols. Ed. James Millar. Edinburgh: Encyclopaedia Press, 1817.

Encyclopaedia Britannica. 7th edn. 21 vols. Ed. Macvey Napier. Edinburgh: Black, 1842.

Encyclopaedia Britannica. 8th edn. 22 vols. Ed. Thomas Stewart Traill. Edinburgh: Black, 1853–60.

Encyclopaedia Britannica. 9th edn. 25 vols. Ed. Thomas Spencer Baynes and W. Robertson Smith. Edinburgh: Black, 1875–89.

Encyclopaedia Britannica. 9th edn. American reprint. Ed. D. O. Kellogg. 25 vols. Philadelphia: Stoddart, 1875–90.

Encyclopaedia Britannica. 11th edn. Ed. Hugh Chisholm. 29 vols. Cambridge: Cambridge University Press, 1910–11.

Encyclopaedia Britannica. 13th edn. 3 vols. London: Encyclopaedia Britannica, 1926.

Encyclopaedia Britannica. 14th edn. Ed. James Louis Garvin. 24 vols. London: Encyclopaedia Britannica, 1929.

Encyclopaedia Britannica. 14th edn. Ed. Walter Yust. 24 vols. Chicago: Encyclopaedia Britannica, 1960.

Encyclopaedia Perthensis; or, Universal Dictionary of Knowledge. Ed. Alexander Aitchison. 23 vols. Perth: Mitchel, [1796–1806].

Encyclopaedia universalis. 1st edn. Ed. Claude Grégory. 20 vols. Paris: Encyclopaedia Universalis France, 1970–5.

The Encyclopaedic Dictionary. Ed. Robert Hunter. 7 vols. London: Cassell *et al.*, 1879–88.

Encyclopedia Americana: International Edition. 30 vols. Danbury: Grolier, 1998.

Encyclopedia Americana: International Edition. 30 vols. Danbury: Grolier, 2003.

Encyclopédie des gens du monde, répertoire universel des sciences, des lettres et des arts. 22 vols. Paris: Treuttel and Würtz, 1833–44.

Encyclopédie française. 20 vols. Paris, 1935–66.

Encyclopédie méthodique: Manufactures, arts et métiers. Ed. Jean-Marie Roland de la Platière *et al*. 4 vols. Paris, 1785–1828.

Encyclopédie moderne; ou, Dictionnaire abrégé des sciences, des lettres et des arts. Ed. Eustache-Marie Courtin. 26 vols. Paris, 1823–32.

Encyclopédie nouvelle [originally *Encyclopédie pittoresque à deux sous*]. Ed. Pierre Leroux and Jean Reynaud. 8 vols. Paris, 1834–42.

Encyclopédie; ou, Dictionnaire raisonné des sciences, des arts et des métiers. Ed. Denis Diderot and Jean Le Rond D'Alembert. 28 vols. [Paris]: [Briasson *et al.*], 1751–72.

Encyclopédie progressive; ou, Collection de traités sur l'histoire, l'état actuel et les progrès des connaissances humaines. Paris: Bureau de l'Encyclopédie Progressive, 1826.

[Espasa]. *Enciclopedia universal ilustrada europeo-americana*. 72 vols. Madrid: Espasa et al., 1908–30.

[Espasa: Suplemento, 1934]. *Enciclopedia universal ilustrada europeo-americana: Suplemento anual, 1934*. Madrid: Espasa-Calpe, 1935.

L'Esprit des journaux, français et étrangers.

Estermann, Monika. "Lexika als biblio-kulturelle Indikatoren: Der Markt für Lexika in der ersten Jahrhunderthälfte." *Archiv für Geschichte des Buchhandels* 31 (1998): 247–58.

Estermann, Monika, and Georg Jäger. "Voraussetzungen und Entwicklungstendenzen." In *Das Kaiserreich, 1870–1918*. Vol. 1 of *Geschichte des deutschen Buchhandels in 19. und 20. Jahrhundert*. Ed. Georg Jäger et al. Frankfurt: Buchhändler-Vereinigung, 2001. 17–41.

Evenhuis, Neal L. "Dating and Publication of the *Encylopédie méthodique* (1782–1832), with Special Reference to the Parts of the *Histoire naturelle* and Details on the *Histoire naturelle des insectes*." *Zootaxa* 166 (2003): 1–48.

Farinella, Calogero. "Le traduzioni italiane della *Cyclopaedia* di Ephraim Chambers." In *L'Enciclopedismo in Italia nel XVIII secolo*. Ed. Guido Abbattista. Naples: Bibliopolis, 1996. 97–160.

Favre, Robert, and Michel Dürr. "Un Texte inédit de l'abbé de Gua de Malves concernant la naissance de l'*Encyclopédie*." *Mémoires de l'Académie des sciences, belles-lettres et arts de Lyon*, 3rd series 55 (2000 [2001]): 51–68.

Feather, John. "The Publishers and the Pirates: British Copyright Law in Theory and Practice, 1710–1775." *Publishing History* 22 (1987): 5–32.

Publishing, Piracy and Politics: An Historical Study of Copyright in Britain. London: Mansell, 1994.

Febvre, Lucien. "Une Encyclopédie française: Pourquoi, comment?" Vol. 1 (*L'Outillage mental*) of *Encyclopédie française*. Paris: Société de Gestion de l'Encyclopédie Française, 1937. Cahier 4, 11–14.

Introduction to Vol. VI (*L'Etre humain*) of *Encyclopédie française*. Paris: Société de Gestion de l'Encyclopédie Française, 1936. Cahier 4, 5–11.

Ferdinand, Christine. "Constructing the Frameworks of Desire: How Newspapers Sold Books in the Seventeenth and Eighteenth Centuries." In *News, Newspapers, and Society in Early Modern Britain*. Ed. Joad Raymond. London: Cass, 1999. 157–75.

Ferlin, Fabrice. "D'Alembert et l'optique: L'*Encyclopédie* comme banc d'essai de recherches originales." *Recherches sur Diderot et sur l'Encyclopédie* 43 (2008): 153–71.

Feuilleton du Journal de la librairie.

Feynman, Richard P. *Perfectly Reasonable Deviations from the Beaten Track*. Ed. Michelle Feynman. New York: Basic, 2005.

Fierro, Maribel. "El saber enciclopédico en el mundo islámico." In *Las enciclopedias en España antes de l'Encyclopédie*. Ed. Alfredo Alvar Ezquerra. Madrid: Consejo Superior de Investigaciones Científicas, 2009. 83–104.

Filliozat, Jean. "Les Encyclopédies de l'Inde." *Cahiers d'histoire mondiale* 9 (1966): 659–64.

"Fishing in St. Peter's Pond, and Other Criticisms on Appleton's Revised Cyclopaedia." Part II of *To Whom It May Concern! The Whys and Wherefores of the Cyclopaedia War*. New York: Johnson, 1875. 1–28.

Flagg, Gordon. "Online Encyclopedias: Are They Ready for Libraries? Are Libraries Ready for Them?" *American Libraries* 14 (1983): 134–6.

Flaubert, Gustave. *Madame Bovary*. Trans. Geoffrey Wall. London: Penguin, 2003.

Foglia, Marc. "Wikipédia, entre connaissance et démocratie." In *Les Encyclopédies: Construction et circulation du savoir de l'Antiquité à Wikipédia*. Ed. Martine Groult. Paris: Harmattan, 2011. 119–36.

Foligno, C. Review of *Enciclopedia italiana di scienze, lettere ed arti*. *Modern Language Review* 33 (1938): 446–7.

Fowler, Robert L. "Encyclopaedias: Definitions and Theoretical Problems." In *Pre-Modern Encyclopaedic Texts*. Ed. Peter Binkley. Leiden: Brill, 1997. 3–29.

Frank, Anne. *Het achterhuis: Dagboekbrieven, 12 juni 1942–1 augustus 1944*. Ed. Otto Frank and Mirjam Pressler. Amsterdam: Bakker, 2002.

Freeland, George E. *The Improvement of Teaching*. New York: Macmillan, 1924.

Freud, Sigmund. *Die Traumbedeutung*. 3rd edn. Leipzig: Franz Deuticke, 1911.

Fröhner, Annette. *Technologie und Enzyklopädismus im Übergang vom 18. zum 19. Jahrhundert: Johann Georg Krünitz (1728–1796) und seine oeconomisch-technologische Encyklopädie*. Mannheim: Palatium, 1994.

Fuchs, James. "Nationality and Knowledge in 18th-Century Italy." *Studies in Eighteenth-Century Culture* 21 (1991): 207–18.

"Vincenzo Coronelli and the Organization of Knowledge: The Twilight of Seventeenth-Century Encyclopedism." Ph.D. dissertation. University of Chicago, 1983.

Furetière, Antoine. *Dictionaire universel contenant généralement tous les mots françois tant vieux que modernes, et les termes de toutes les sciences et des arts*. Reprint edn. Ed. Alain Rey. 3 vols. Paris: SNL, 1978.

Essais d'un dictionaire universel. [Paris?]: 1684.

Furetière, Antoine, and Henri Basnage de Beauval. *Dictionnaire universel contenant généralement tous les mots françois tant vieux que modernes, et les termes des sciences et des arts*. Rev. edn. 3 vols. The Hague: Leers, 1701.

Furetière, Antoine, Henri Basnage de Beauval, and Jean-Baptiste Brutel de La Rivière. *Dictionnaire universel contenant généralement tous les mots françois tant vieux que modernes, et les termes des sciences et des arts*. 4 vols. The Hague: Husson *et al.*, 1727.

Garofalo, Silvano. *L'enciclopedismo italiano: Gianfrancesco Pivati*. Ravenna: Longo, 1980.

Gasparri, Giuliano. *Etienne Chauvin (1640–1725) and his "Lexicon philosophicum."* Trans. Federico Poole. Hildesheim: Georg Olms, 2016.

Geiger, Roger L. *Research and Relevant Knowledge: American Research Universities since World War II*. New York: Oxford University Press, 1993.

Genlis, Stéphanie Félicité du Crest de. *Mémoires inédits*. 10 vols. Brussels: De Mat, 1825.

Giacobbe, Mary Ellen. "Learning to Write and Writing to Learn in the Elementary School." In *The Teaching of Writing*. Ed. Anthony R. Petrosky and David Bartholomae. Chicago: University of Chicago Press, 1986. 131–47.

Gierl, Martin. "Compilation and the Production of Knowledge in the Early German Enlightenment." In *Wissenschaft als kulturelle Praxis, 1750–1900*. Ed. Hans Erich Bödeker *et al*. Göttingen: Vandenhoeck and Ruprecht, 1999. 69–103.

Giordano, Fausto. *Filologi e fascismo: Gli studi di letteratura latina nell'Enciclopedia italiana*. Naples: Arte Tipografica, 1993.

Globe and Mail.

Gluck, Carol. "The Fine Folly of the Encyclopedists." In *Currents in Japanese Culture*. Ed. Amy Vladeck Heinrich. New York: Columbia University Press, 1997. 223–51.

Godin, Christian. "Des encyclopédies chinoises à Wikipédia: Le Rêve d'empire." In *Encyclopédire: Formes de l'ambition encyclopédique dans l'antiquité et au Moyen Age*. Ed. Arnaud Zucker. Turnhout: Brepols, 2013. 33–53.

Goetschel, Willi, Catriona Macleod, and Emery Snyder. "The *Deutsche Encyclopädie*." In *Notable Encyclopedias of the Late Eighteenth Century*. Ed. Frank A. Kafker. Oxford: Voltaire Foundation, 1994. 257–333.

Gómez Aranda, Mariano. "Enciclopedias hebreas en la época medieval." In *Las enciclopedias en España antes de l'Encyclopédie*. Ed. Alfredo Alvar Ezquerra. Madrid: Consejo Superior de Investigaciones Científicas, 2009. 105–23.

Goodman, Katherine R. *Amazons and Apprentices: Women and the German Parnassus in the Early Enlightenment*. Rochester, NY: Camden, 1999.

Gordon, Douglas H., and Norman L. Torrey. *The Censoring of Diderot's Encyclopédie and the Re-Established Text*. New York: Columbia University Press, 1947.

Gostl, Igor. "Five Centuries of Croatian Encyclopaedism: A Short Historical Overview." *Journal of Croatian Studies* 36–7 (1997): 83–122.

Gourdain, Pierre *et al*. *La Révolution Wikipédia: Les Encyclopédies vont-elles mourir?* Paris: Mille et Une Nuits, 2007.

Gove, Philip Babcock. "Notes on Serialization and Competitive Publishing: Johnson's and Bailey's Dictionaries, 1755." *Proceedings and Papers of the Oxford Bibliographical Society* 5 (1939): 307–22.

Goyet, Francis. "Encyclopédie et 'lieux communs.'" In *L'Encyclopédisme: Actes du Colloque de Caen*. Ed. Annie Becq. Paris: Aux Amateurs de Livres, 1991. 493–504.

Gran enciclopedia Rialp: GER. 1st edn. 24 vols. Madrid: Rialp, 1971.

Grand Mémento encyclopédique Larousse. Ed. Paul Augé. 2 vols. Paris: Larousse, 1936–7.

La Grande Encyclopédie: Instructions du comité de direction à Mrs. les collaborateurs. Paris: Sociéte de la Grande Encyclopédie, [n.d.].

La Grande Encyclopédie: Inventaire raisonné des sciences, des lettres et des arts. 31 vols. Paris: Lamirault, 1885–1902.

Gray, Valerie. *Charles Knight: Educator, Publisher, Writer*. Aldershot: Ashgate, 2006.

Griffiths, David Albert. *Jean Reynaud, encyclopédiste de l'époque romantique, d'après sa correspondance inédite*. Paris: Rivière, 1965.

Grimal, Pierre. "Encyclopédies antiques." *Cahiers d'histoire mondiale* 9 (1966): 459–82.

Grimaldi, Elisabeth. "Interactions entre fonction encyclopédique et fonction linguistique: Les Réponses des 'grands dictionnaires' du XIXᵉ siècle." In *Pierre Larousse: Du grand dictionnaire au Petit Larousse*. Ed. Jean Pruvost *et al.* Paris: Champion, 2002. 77–113.

Groot algemeen historisch, geographisch, genealogisch, en oordeelkundig woorden-boek. Ed. David van Hoogstraten *et al.* 10 vols. Amsterdam: Brunel *et al.*, 1725–33.

[*Grosse Brockhaus*]. 1st edn. *Conversationslexikon mit vorzüglicher Rücksicht auf die gegenwärtigen Zeiten*. 6 vols. Leipzig: 1796–1808.

[*Grosse Brockhaus*]. 5th edn. 1st printing. *Allgemeine deutsche Real-Encyclopädie für die gebildeten Stände (Conversations-Lexikon)*. 10 vols. Leipzig: Brockhaus, 1819–20.

[*Grosse Brockhaus*]. 5th edn. 3rd printing. *Allgemeine deutsche Real-Encyclopädie für die gebildeten Stände (Conversations-Lexikon)*. 10 vols. Leipzig: Brockhaus, 1822.

[*Grosse Brockhaus*]. 10th edn. *Allgemeine deutsche Real-Encyklopädie für die gebildeten Stände: Conversations-Lexikon*. 15 vols. Leipzig: Brockhaus, 1851–5.

[*Grosse Brockhaus*]. 11th edn. *Allgemeine deutsche Real-Encyklopädie für die gebildeten Stände: Conversations-Lexikon*. 15 vols. Leipzig: Brockhaus, 1864–8.

[*Grosse Brockhaus*]. 15th edn. *Der grosse Brockhaus: Handbuch des Wissens*. 20 vols. Leipzig: Brockhaus, 1928–35.

[*Grosse Brockhaus*]. 16th edn. *Der grosse Brockhaus*. 14 vols. Wiesbaden: Brockhaus, 1952–63.

[*Grosse Brockhaus*]. 19th edn. *Brockhaus Enzyklopädie*. 25 vols. Mannheim: Brockhaus, 1986–94.

[*Grosse Herder*]. 4th edn. *Der grosse Herder: Nachschlagewerk für Wissen und Leben*. 12 vols. Freiburg: Herder, 1931–5.

[*Grosse Herder*]. 5th edn. *Der grosse Herder: Nachschlagewerk für Wissen und Leben*. 10 vols. Freiburg: Herder, 1952–6.

Grosses vollständiges Universal-Lexicon aller Wissenschafften und Künste. 64 vols. Halle and Leipzig: Zedler, 1732–50.

Groult, Martine, ed. *L'Encyclopédie; ou, La Création des disciplines*. Paris: CNRS, 2003.

Haechler, Jean. *L'Encyclopédie de Diderot et de … Jaucourt: Essai biographique sur le chevalier de Jaucourt*. Paris: Champion, 1995.

Hankins, Thomas L. *Science and the Enlightenment*. Cambridge: Cambridge University Press, 1985.

Hannah, Wanda Lee. "A Comparison of the Treatment of 'The Negro in the United States' in Four Major Adult Encyclopedias and their Yearbooks." M.A. thesis. Florida State University, 1959.

Harris, John. *Lexicon Technicum; or, An Universal English Dictionary of Arts and Sciences*. 1st edn. 2 vols. London: Brown *et al.*, 1704–10.

Harvey, Paul, and J. E. Heseltine, eds. *The Oxford Companion to French Literature.* Oxford: Clarendon Press, 1959.

Häseler, Jens. "Extraits – abrégés – encyclopédies." In *L'Encyclopédie d'Yverdon et sa résonance européenne.* Ed. Jean-Daniel Candaux *et al.* Geneva: Slatkine, 2005. 277–88.

Hass, Ulrike, ed. *Grosse Lexika und Wörterbücher Europas: Europäische Enzyklopädien und Wörterbücher in historischen Porträts.* Berlin: De Gruyter, 2011.

Hayes, Julie C. "Plagiarism and Legitimation in Eighteenth-Century France." *The Eighteenth Century: Theory and Interpretation* 34 (1993): 115–31.

Headrick, Daniel R. *When Information Came of Age: Technologies of Knowledge in the Age of Reason and Revolution, 1700–1850.* Oxford: Oxford University Press, 2000.

Heesen, Anke te. *The World in a Box: The Story of an Eighteenth-Century Picture Encyclopedia.* Trans. Ann M. Hentschel. Chicago: University of Chicago Press, 2002.

Heine, Heinrich. *Sämmtliche Werke: Bibliothek-Ausgabe.* 12 vols. Hamburg: Hoffman and Campe, 1885.

Henningsen, Jürgen. " 'Enzyklopädie': Zur Sprach- und Bedeutungsgeschichte eines pädagogischen Begriffs." *Archiv für Begriffsgeschichte* 10 (1966): 271–362.

Henry, Mary Kathryn. "A Survey of Selected Editions of *World Book Encyclopedia* as They Reflect Changing Trends in Curriculum Theories." M.A. thesis. University of Chicago, 1973.

Herren, Madeleine, and Ines Prodöhl. "Kapern mit Orangeblüten: Die globale Welt der Enzyklopädie." In *Seine Welt wissen: Enzyklopädien in der frühen Neuzeit.* Ed. Ulrich Johannes Schneider. Darmstadt: Primus, 2006. 42–53.

Hexelschneider, Erhard. "Der 'Brockhaus' erobert den russischen Markt: Zur Entstehungsgeschichte des 'Brockhaus-Efron.' " In *F. A. Brockhaus, 1905–2005.* Ed. Thomas Keiderling. Leipzig: Brockhaus, 2005. 207–18.

Hingst, Anja zum. *Die Geschichte des Grossen Brockhaus: Vom Conversationslexikon zur Enzyklopädie.* Wiesbaden: Harrassowitz, 1995.

Hofmann, James R. *André-Marie Ampère.* Cambridge: Cambridge University Press, 1995.

Hogg, Gordon E. "*Bolshaia sovetskaia entsiklopediia.*" In Vol. 61 (supplement 24) of *Encyclopedia of Library and Information Science.* Ed. Allen Kent. New York: Dekker, 1998. 17–62

Holmberg, Linn. *The Maurists' Unfinished Encyclopedia.* Oxford: Voltaire Foundation, 2017.

Hotson, Howard. *Johann Heinrich Alsted, 1588–1638: Between Renaissance, Reformation, and Universal Reform.* Oxford: Oxford University Press, 2000.

Howard, George Selby *et al. The New Royal Cyclopaedia, and Encyclopaedia.* 3 vols. London: Hogg, [1788].

Hübner, Johann. "Vorrede." In *Curieuses Natur- Kunst- Gewerck- und Handlungs-Lexicon.* 1st edn. Leipzig: Gleditsch, 1712.)(2r–)(5v (§§1–xlix).

Hüe, Dennis. "Structures et rhétoriques dans quelques textes encyclopédiques du Moyen Age." In *L'Encyclopédisme: Actes du Colloque de Caen*. Ed. Annie Becq. Paris: Aux Amateurs de Livres, 1991. 311–18.

Hughes, Arthur. "Science in English Encyclopaedias, 1704–1875: 1." *Annals of Science* 7 (1951): 340–70.

Hupka, Werner. *Wort und Bild: Die Illustrationen in Wörterbüchern und Enzyklopädien*. Tübingen: Niemeyer, 1989.

Iben, Icko. Review of *Der grosse Brockhaus*, 16th edn. *Journal of English and Germanic Philology* 56 (1957): 69–72.

Illich, Ivan. *In the Vineyard of the Text: A Commentary to Hugh's Didascalicon*. Chicago: University of Chicago Press, 1993.

Infelise, Mario. "Enciclopedie e pubblico a Venezia a metà Settecento: G. F. Pivati e i suoi dizionari." In *L'enciclopedismo in Italia nel XVIII secolo*. Ed. Guido Abbattista. Naples: Bibliopolis, 1996. 161–90.

Information Today.

InfoWorld.

Inside Multimedia.

Issitt, John. "From Gregory's Dictionary to Nicholson's Encyclopedia: Intrigue and Literary Craft in the Reshaping of Knowledge." *Publishing History* 65 (2009): 5–40.

[Jablonski, Johann Theodor]. *Allgemeines Lexicon der Künste und Wissenschafften*. Leipzig: Fritsch, 1721.

Jacobs, A. J. *The Know-It-All: One Man's Humble Quest to Become the Smartest Person in the World*. New York: Simon and Schuster, 2004.

Jacquet-Pfau, Christine. "Lexicographie et terminologie au détour du XIXe siècle: La *Grande Encyclopédie*." *Langages* 168 (2007): 24–38.

    "Naissance d'un projet lexicographique à la fin du XIXe siècle: *La Grande Encyclopédie, par une société de savants et de gens de lettres*." *Cahiers de lexicologie* 88 (2006): 97–111.

Jäger, Georg. "Der Lexikonverlag." In *Das Kaiserreich, 1870–1918*. Vol. 1 of *Geschichte des deutschen Buchhandels im 19. und 20. Jahrhundert*. Ed. Jäger *et al.* Frankfurt: Buchhändler-Vereinigung, 2001. 541–74.

Jemielniak, Dariusz. *Common Knowledge? An Ethnography of Wikipedia*. Stanford: Stanford University Press, 2014.

Jennings, Neil, and Margaret Jones. *A Biography of Samuel Chappuzeau, a Seventeenth-Century French Huguenot Playwright, Scholar, Traveller, and Preacher*. Lewiston: Edward Mellen, 2012.

Johns, Adrian. *The Nature of the Book: Print and Knowledge in the Making*. Chicago: University of Chicago Press, 1998.

Johnson's New Universal Cyclopaedia. Ed. Frederick A. P. Barnard and Arnold Guyot. 4 vols. New York: Johnson, 1875–7.

"*Johnson's New Universal Cyclopaedia*: A Dictionary, Gazetteer, and Directory." In *The Cyclopaedia War: The Appletons against the Johnsons*. New York: Johnson, [1877?]. 1–11.

Journal de l'Ain.

Juanals, Brigitte. "Encyclopédies en ligne: Un modèle du lecteur électronique." *Hermès* 39 (2004): 87–93.

Juntke, Fritz. *Johann Heinrich Zedler's Grosses vollständiges Universallexikon: Ein Beitrag zur Geschichte des Nachdruckes in Mitteldeutschland.* Halle: Universitäts- und Landesbibliothek Sachsen-Anhalt, 1956.

Kafker, Frank A. "Encyclopedias." In *Encyclopedia of the Enlightenment.* Ed. Alan Charles Kors. 4 vols. Oxford: Oxford University Press, 2003. 1: 398–403.

The Encyclopedists as a Group: A Collective Biography of the Authors of the Encyclopédie. Oxford: Voltaire Foundation, 1996.

"Epilogue: The Tortoise and the Hare: The Longevity of the *Encyclopaedia Britannica* and the *Encyclopédie* Compared." In *The Early Britannica.* Ed. Kafker and Jeff Loveland. 299–307.

"The Role of the *Encyclopédie* in the Making of the Modern Encyclopedia." In *The Encyclopédie and the Age of Revolution.* Ed. Clorinda Donato and Robert M. Maniquis. Boston, MA: Hall, 1992. 19–25.

Kafker, Frank A., and Serena L. Kafker. *The Encyclopedists as Individuals: A Biographical Dictionary of the Authors of the Encyclopédie.* Oxford: Voltaire Foundation, 1988.

Kafker, Frank A., and Jeff Loveland. "André-François Le Breton, initiateur et libraire en chef de l'*Encyclopédie.*" *Recherches sur Diderot et sur l'Encyclopédie* 51 (2016): 107–25.

"Antoine-Claude Briasson et l'*Encyclopédie.*" *Recherches sur Diderot et sur l'Encyclopédie* 35 (2003): 131–42.

eds. *The Early Britannica (1768–1803): The Growth of an Outstanding Encyclopedia.* Oxford: Voltaire Foundation, 2009.

"The Publisher James Moore and His Dublin Edition of the *Encyclopaedia Britannica*, a Notable Eighteenth-Century Irish Publication." *Eighteenth-Century Ireland* 26 (2011): 115–39.

"La Vie agitée de l'abbé De Gua de Malves et sa direction de l'*Encyclopédie.*" *Recherches sur Diderot et sur l'Encyclopédie* 47 (2012): 187–203.

"William Smellie's Edition (1768–71): A Modest Start." In *The Early Britannica: The Growth of an Outstanding Encyclopedia.* Ed. Frank A. Kafker and Jeff Loveland. Oxford: Voltaire Foundation, 2009. 10–67.

Kafker, Frank A., and Madeleine Pinault Sørensen. "Notices sur les collaborateurs du recueil de planches de l'*Encyclopédie.*" *Recherches sur Diderot et sur l'Encyclopédie* 18–19 (1995): 200–30.

Kaminski, Nicola. "Die Musen als Lexikographen: Zedlers *Grosses vollständiges Universal-Lexicon* im Schnittpunkt von poetischem, wissenschaftlichem, juristischem und ökonomischem Diskurs." *Daphnis* 29 (2000): 649–93.

Kaplan, Alice. *French Lessons: A Memoir.* Chicago: University of Chicago Press, 1993.

Katz, William A. *Basic Information Sources.* Vol. 1 of *Introduction to Reference Work.* 3rd edn. New York: McGraw-Hill, 1978.

Kavanagh, Nadine. *Conjuring Australia: Encyclopaedias and the Creation of Nations.* Saarbrücken: Südwestdeutscher Verlag für Hochschulschriften, 2009.

Keegan, Brian C. "High Tempo Knowledge Collaboration in Wikipedia's Coverage of Breaking News Events." Ph.D. dissertation. Northwestern University, 2012.

Keiderling, Thomas. "*Der Brockhaus.*" In *Grosse Lexika und Wörterbücher Europas: Europäische Enzyklopädien und Wörterbücher in historischen Porträts.* Ed. Ulrike Hass. Berlin: De Gruyter, 2011. 193–210.

F. A. Brockhaus 1905–2005. Leipzig: Brockhaus, 2005.

"Der Lexikonverlag." In *Die Weimarer Republik, 1918–1933.* Vol. 11 of *Geschichte des deutschen Buchhandels im 19. und 20. Jahrhundert.* Frankfurt: Saur, 2007. 441–62.

Kerr, Robert. *Memoirs of the Life, Writings, and Correspondence of William Smellie.* Reprint edn. Ed. Richard B. Sher. 2 vols. Bristol: Thoemmes, 1996.

Kewes, Paulina, ed. *Plagiarism in Early Modern England.* New York: Palgrave Macmillan, 2003.

Khan, M. A. *The Principles and Practice of Library Science.* New Delhi: Sarup and Sons, 1996.

Kister, Kenneth F. *Encyclopedia Buying Guide: A Consumer Guide to General Encyclopedias in Print.* 2nd edn. New York: Bowker, 1978.

Encyclopedia Buying Guide: A Consumer Guide to General Encyclopedias in Print. 3rd edn. New York: Bowker, 1981.

Kister's Best Encyclopedias: A Comparative Guide to General and Specialized Encyclopedias. 2nd edn. Phoenix: Oryx, 1994.

Kitto, John. *Memoirs of John Kitto.* Ed. J. E. Ryland. New York: Carter and Brothers, 1857.

Der kleine Brockhaus: Handbuch des Wissens in einem Band. 1st edn. Leipzig: Brockhaus, 1927.

Der kleine Herder: Nachschlagebuch über alles für alle. Freiburg: Herder, 1925.

Knight, Charles. *Passages of a Working Life during Half a Century.* 3 vols. London: Bradbury and Evans, 1864–5.

Kochanowska-Nieborak, Anna. "Konversationslexika aus der Perspektive der historischen Stereotypenforschung." In *Ältere Konversationslexika und Fachenzyklopädien.* Ed. Hans-Albrecht Koch and Gabriella Rovagnati. Frankfurt: Lang, 2013. 181–214.

Koepp, Cynthia J. "Advocating for Artisans: The Abbé Pluche's *Spectacle de la nature* (1732–51)." In *The Idea of Work in Europe from Antiquity to Modern Times.* Ed. Josef Ehmer and Catharina Lis. Surrey: Ashgate, 2009. 245–73.

"Making Money: Artisans and Entrepreneurs in Diderot's *Encyclopédie.*" In *Using the Encyclopédie.* Ed. Daniel Brewer and Julie Candler Hayes. Oxford: Voltaire Foundation, 2002. 119–41.

Kogan, Herman. *The Great EB: The Story of the Encyclopaedia Britannica.* Chicago: University of Chicago Press, 1958.

König, Jason, and Greg Woolf, eds. *Encyclopaedism from Antiquity to the Renaissance.* Cambridge: Cambridge University Press, 2013.

"Encyclopaedism in the Roman Empire." In *Encyclopaedism from Antiquity to the Renaissance.* Ed. König and Woolf. Cambridge: Cambridge University Press, 2013. 23–63.

Kossmann, Bernhard. "Deutsche Universallexika des 18. Jahrhunderts: Ihr Wesen und ihr Informationswert, dargestellt am Beispiel der Werke von Jablonski und Zedler." *Archiv für Geschichte des Buchwesens* 9 (1969): 1553–96.

Krünitz, Johann Georg *et al.*, eds. *Oeconomische Encyclopädie; oder, Allgemeines System der Land- Haus- und Staats-Wirthschaft* [later *Oeconomisch-technologische Encyklopädie*]. 242 vols. Berlin: Various, 1773–1858.

Kruse, Paul. "Piracy and the *Britannica*: Unauthorized Reprintings of the Ninth Edition." *Library Quarterly* 33 (1963): 313–28.

"The Story of the *Encyclopaedia Britannica*, 1768–1943." Ph.D. dissertation. University of Chicago, 1958.

Lambrechts, Chantal. "La Conception éditoriale d'un dictionnaire pédagogique." In *Les Dictionnaires Larousse: Genèse et evolution*. Ed. Monique C. Cormier and Aline Francoeur. Montreal: Presses de l'Université de Montréal, 2005. 153–76.

Lamoureux, Johanne. "Médium, référent et fonction dans les illustrations du *Petit Larouse illustré*." In *Les Dictionnaires Larousse: Genèse et evolution*. Ed. Monique C. Cormier and Aline Francoeur. Montreal: Presses de l'Université de Montréal, 2005. 177–98.

Larbaud, Valéry. *Journal*. Ed. Paule Moron. Paris: Gallimard, 2009.

Larousse mensuel.

Larousse, Pierre, ed. *Grand Dictionnaire universel du XIX*ᵉ *siècle*. 15 vols. Paris: [Larousse], 1866–76.

Law, Dorothy. "Indexing *Chambers's Encyclopaedia*." *Indexer* 7 (1970): 13–16.

Leca-Tsiomis, Marie. "Le Capuchon des cordeliers: Une légende de l'*Encyclopédie*." *Recherches sur Diderot et sur l'Encyclopédie* 50 (2015): 348–53.

"Du *Dictionnaire* de Furetière au *Grand vocabulaire français* de Panckoucke: La Joute confessionnelle des dictionnaires et des encyclopédies." In *L'Encyclopédie d'Yverdon et sa résonance européenne*. Ed. Jean-Daniel Candaux *et al.* Geneva: Slatkine, 2005. 13–29.

Ecrire l'Encyclopédie: Diderot. Oxford: Voltaire Foundation, 1999.

"L'*Encyclopédie* selon Jaucourt." In *Le Chevalier de Jaucourt*. Ed. Gilles Barroux and François Pepin. Paris: Société Diderot, 2015. 71–82.

"Langue et grammaire dans l'*Encyclopédie*." In *L'Encyclopédie; ou, La Création des disciplines*. Ed. Martine Groult. Paris: CNRS, 2003. 203–14.

"La Rhétorique de la recette: Remarques sur le *Dictionnaire oeconomique* de Chomel (1709) et l'*Encyclopédie*." *Recherches sur Diderot et sur l'Encyclopédie* 25 (1998): 115–34.

"Le 'Système figuré des connaissances humaines' de l'*Encyclopédie*: Théorie et pratique." In *L'Esprit de système au XVIIIe siècle*. Ed. Sophie Marchand and Elise Pavy-Guilbert. Paris: Hermann, 2017.

"The Use and Abuse of the Digital Humanities in the History of Ideas: How to Study the *Encyclopédie*." *History of European Ideas* 39 (2013): 467–76.

[Le Clerc, Jean]. Review of Antoine Furetière, *Dictionaire universel*. *Bibliothèque universelle et historique de l'année 1690*, 2nd edn. 16 (1698): 121–35.

Review of *Supplément ou troisième volume du Grand dictionaire historique*. *Bibliothèque universelle et historique*, 2nd edn. 14 (1689): 66–77.

Lehmann, Alise. "L'Evolution culturelle du *Petit Larousse*: L'Exemple de la sexualité." In *Pierre Larousse: Du Grand dictionnaire au Petit Larousse*. Ed. Jean Pruvost *et al.* Paris: Champion, 2002. 223–39.

Lehmann, Ernst Herbert. *Geschichte des Konversationslexikons*. Leipzig: Brockhaus, 1934.

Library Journal.

Lieshout, H. H. M. van. "Dictionnaires et diffusion du savoir." In *Commercium litterarium, 1600–1750*. Ed. Françoise Waquet and Hans Bots. Amsterdam: Holland University Press, 1994. 131–51.

The Making of Pierre Bayle's Dictionnaire historique et critique. Amsterdam: APA-Holland University Press, 2001.

Lieshout, H. H. M. van, and O. S. Lankhorst, eds. *Eleven Catalogues by Reinier Leers (1692–1709)*. Utrecht: HES, 1992.

Life.

Lih, Andrew. *The Wikipedia Revolution: How a Bunch of Nobodies Created the World's Greatest Encyclopedia*. New York: Hyperion, 2009.

Link-Up: The Newsmagazine for Users of Online Services, CD-ROM, and the Internet.

Lipták, Dorottya. "Die 'Sammlung gemeinnütziger Kenntnisse' von Otto Wigand: Zur Geschichte des ungarischen 'Brockhaus.'" In *F. A. Brockhaus, 1905–2005*. Ed. Thomas Keiderling. Leipzig: Brockhaus, 2005. 188–99.

Livingstone, Randall. "Immaterial Editors: Bots and Bot Policies across Global Wikipedia." In *Global Wikipedia*. Ed. Pnina Fichman and Noriko Hara. Lanham: Rowman and Littlefield, 2014. 7–23.

Livres hebdo.

Llana, James. "Natural History in the *Encyclopédie*." *Journal of the History of Biology* 33 (2000): 1–25.

Locke, John. *An Essay Concerning Human Understanding*. Ed. Alexander Campbell Fraser. 2 vols. New York: Dover, 1959.

Lockwood, Thomas. "Subscription-Hunters and Their Prey." *Studies in the Literary Imagination* 34 (2001): 121–35.

Löffler, Katrin. "Wer schrieb den Zedler? Eine Spurensuche." *Leipziger Jahrbuch zur Buchgeschichte* 16 (2007): 265–83.

Lohsträter, Kai. "Periodische Presse und Enzyklopädie: Friedrich Wilhelm Kraft und Zedlers Musen." In *Die gesammelte Welt: Studien zu Zedlers Universal-Lexicon*. Ed. Lohsträter and Flemming Schock. Wiesbaden: Harrassowitz, 2013. 41–72.

Los Angeles Times.

Lough, John. *The Encyclopédie*. London: Longman, 1971.

The Encyclopédie in Eighteenth-Century England, and Other Studies. Newcastle: Oriel, 1970.

Essays on the Encyclopédie of Diderot and D'Alembert. London: Oxford University Press, 1968.

"Le Breton, Mills et Sellius." *Dix-huitième siècle* 1 (1969): 267–87.

"Le Prospectus d'une nouvelle édition de l'*Encyclopédie* (Monaco, 1771)." *Recherches sur Diderot et sur l'Encyclopédie* 4 (1987): 111–16.

Loveland, Jeff. *An Alternative Encyclopedia? Dennis de Coetlogon's Universal History of Arts and Sciences (1745)*. Oxford: Voltaire Foundation, 2010.

"Animals in British and French Encyclopedias in the Long Eighteenth Century," *Journal for Eighteenth-Century Studies* 4 (2010): 507–23.

"Encyclopaedias and Genre, 1670–1750." *Journal for Eighteenth-Century Studies* 36 (2013): 159–75.

"How Serialisation Changed the Meanings of Encyclopaedias." In *From Text(s) to Book(s)*. Ed. Nathalie Collé *et al.* Nancy: Presses Universitaires de Nancy, 2014. 85–109.

"A *Laissez-Faire* Encyclopedia? A Comparative View of Diderot as Editor of the *Encyclopédie*." *Studies in Eighteenth-Century Culture* 46 (2017): 205–27.

"Louis-Jean-Marie Daubenton and the *Encyclopédie*." *SVEC* 12 (2003): 173–219.

"Two French 'Konversationslexika' of the 1830s and 1840s: The *Dictionnaire de la conversation et de la lecture* and the *Encyclopédie des gens du monde*." In *Translation and Transfer of Knowledge in Encyclopedic Compilations, 1680–1830*. Ed. Clorinda Donato and Hans-Jürgen Lüsebrink. Toronto: University of Toronto Press, forthcoming.

"Two Partial English-Language Translations of the *Encyclopédie*: The Encyclopedias of John Barrow and Temple Henry Croker." In *British–French Exchanges in the Eighteenth Century*. Ed. Kathleen Hardesty Doig and Dorothy Medlin. Newcastle: Cambridge Scholars, 2007. 168–87.

"Unifying Knowledge and Dividing Disciplines: The Development of Treatises in the *Encyclopaedia Britannica*." *Book History* 9 (2006): 57–87.

"Varieties of Authorship in Eighteenth-Century Encyclopedias." *Das achtzehnte Jahrhundert* 34 (2010): 81–102.

"Why Encyclopedias Got Bigger ... and Smaller." *Information and Culture* 47 (2012): 233–54.

Lucassen, Jan. "Wage Payments and Currency Circulation in the Netherlands from 1200 to 2000." In *Wages and Currency: Global Comparisons from Antiquity to the Twentieth Century*. Ed. Jan Lucassen. Bern: Lang, 2007. 221–63.

Luneau de Boisjermain, and Pierre-Joseph-François. *Mémoire pour Pierre-Joseph-François de Boisjermain, souscripteur de l'Encyclopédie*. Paris: [Grangé], 1771.

Lynch, Jack. "Johnson's Encyclopedia." In *Anniversary Essays on Johnson's Dictionary*. Ed. Jack Lynch and Anne McDermott. Cambridge: Cambridge University Press, 2005. 129–46.

You Could Look It Up: The Reference Shelf from Ancient Babylon to Wikipedia. New York: Bloomsbury, 2016.

Lyons, Martyn. *A History of Reading and Writing in the Western World*. Houndmills: Palgrave Macmillan, 2010.

Madrolle, Antoine. *Tableau de la dégénération de la France*. Paris: Aillaud, 1834.

Maître, Myriam. "Langue imprimée, savoir alphabétique, effractions de la voix." In *Le Dictionnaire universel d'Antoine Furetière*. Ed. Hélène Merlin-Kajman. Paris: Champion, 2002. 315–31.

Male, Thora van. "Ornamental Illustrations in French Dictionaries." *Dictionaries: Journal of the Dictionary Society of North America* 22 (2001): 31–84.

[Marperger, Paul Jacob]. *Curieuses Natur- Kunst- Gewerck- und Handlungs-Lexicon.* 1st edn. Leipzig: Gleditsch, 1712.

Martin, Henri-Jean. *Livre, pouvoirs et société à Paris au XVIIe siècle (1598–1701).* 2 vols. Geneva: Droz, 1969.

Martineau, Harriet. *Harriet Martineau's Autobiography.* 3rd edn. 3 vols. London: Smith, Elder, and Co., 1877.

Massa, Paolo, and Asta Zelenkauskaite. "Gender Gap in Wikipedia Editing: A Cross Language Comparison." In *Global Wikipedia.* Ed. Pnina Fichman and Noriko Hara. Lanham: Rowman and Littlefield, 2014. 85–96.

May, Louis-Philippe. "Documents nouveaux sur l'*Encyclopédie.*" *Revue de synthèse* 15 (1938): 31–110.

Mazière, Francine. "Cellule: Un discours de vulgarisations dans les dictionnaires encyclopédiques." *Langue française* 53 (1982): 62–77.

McArthur, Tom. *Worlds of Reference: Lexicography, Learning, and Language from the Clay Tablet to the Computer.* Cambridge: Cambridge University Press, 1986.

McKeon, Richard. "The Organization of Sciences and the Relations of Cultures in the Twelfth and Thirteenth Centuries." In *The Cultural Context of Medieval Learning.* Ed. John Emery Murdoch and Edith Dudley Sylla. Boston, MA: Reidel, 1975. 151–92.

McLaverty, James. "From Definition to Explanation: Locke's Influence on Johnson's Dictionary." *Journal of the History of Ideas* 47 (1986): 377–94.

Mémoires pour l'histoire des sciences et des beaux arts.

Meier, Christel. "Grundzüge der mittelalterlichen Enzyklopädik: Zu Inhalten, Formen und Funktionen einer problematischen Gattung." In *Literatur und Laienbildung.* Ed. Ludger Grenzmann and Karl Stackmann. Stuttgart: Metzler, 1984. 467–500.

"On the Connection between Epistemology and Encyclopedic *Ordo* in the Middle Ages and the Early Modern Period." In *Schooling and Society.* Ed. Alasdair A. MacDonald and Michael W. Twomey. Louvain: Peeters, 2004. 93–117.

"Organisation of Knowledge and Encyclopaedic *Ordo*: Functions and Purposes of a Universal Literary Genre." In *Pre-Modern Encyclopaedic Texts.* Ed. Peter Binkley. Leiden: Brill, 1997. 103–26.

Merit Students Encyclopedia. 20 vols. New York: Macmillan, 1990.

Merland, Marie-Anne, and Jehanne Reyniers. "La Fortune d'André-François Le Breton, imprimeur et libraire de l'*Encyclopédie.*" *Revue française d'histoire du livre* 22 (January–March 1979): 61–90.

Meyer, Georg. "Das Konversations-Lexikon, eine Sonderform der Enzyklopädie: Ein Beitrag zur Geschichte der Bildungsverbreitung in Deutschland." Ph.D. dissertation. Universität Göttingen, 1966.

[*Meyer's Konversations-Lexikon*]. "0th" edn. [*Wunder-Meyer*]. *Das grosse Conversations-Lexicon für die gebildeten Stände.* 46 vols. Hildburghausen: Bibliographisches Institut, 1840–53.

[*Meyer's Konversations-Lexikon*]. 6th edn. *Meyers grosses Konversations-Lexikon.* 20 vols. Leipzig: Bibliographisches Institut, 1902–8.

[*Meyer's Konversations-Lexikon*]. 9th edn. *Meyers enzyklopädisches Lexikon.* 25 vols. Mannheim: Bibliographisches Institut, 1971–9.

Michel, Paul, and Madeleine Herren. "Unvorgreifliche Gedanken zu einer Theorie des Enzyklopädischen: Enzyklopädien als Indikatoren für Veränderungen bei der Organisation und der gesellschaftlichen Bedeutung von Wissen." In *Allgemeinwissen und Gesellschaft.* Ed. Michel *et al.* Aachen: Shaker, 2007. 9–74.

Millar, James. Prospectus to *Encyclopaedia Edinensis.* Edinburgh: Hill *et al.*, 1819.

Miller, Arnold. "The Last Edition of the *Dictionnaire de Trévoux.*" In *Notable Encyclopedias of the Late Eighteenth Century.* Ed. Frank A. Kafker. Oxford: Voltaire Foundation, 1994. 5–50.

"Louis Moréri's *Grand Dictionnaire historique.*" In *Notable Encyclopedias of the Seventeenth and Eighteenth Centuries.* Ed. Frank A. Kafker. Oxford: Voltaire Foundation, 1981. 13–52.

Minghetti, François. *Vas-y mon kiki! Mémoires autobiographiques et considérations constituant un plaidoyer en faveur de l'oecuménisme des deux écoles.* Breteuil-sur-Iton: Presses Bretoliennes, 1984.

Mitterand, Henri. "Zola et le *Grand Dictionnaire universel du XIXe siècle* de Pierre Larousse." In *Pierre Larousse: Du Grand dictionnaire au Petit Larousse.* Ed. Jean Pruvost *et al.* Paris: Champion, 2002. 115–25.

Molitorisz, Joseph. *The Memoirs of an Immigrant.* Lincoln, NE: Authors Choice, 2001.

Mollier, Jean-Yves. *L'Argent et les lettres: Histoire du capitalisme d'édition, 1880–1920.* Paris: Fayard, 1988.

"Le Contexte éditoriale du XIXe siècle." *Revue Jules Verne* 26 (2007): 19–43.

"Editer au XIXe siècle." *Revue d'histoire littéraire de la France* 4 (2007): 771–90.

"Encyclopédie et commerce de la librairie du XVIIIe au XXe siècle." In *L'Entreprise encyclopédique.* Ed. Jean Bouffartigue and Françoise Mélonio. Nanterre: Centre des Sciences de la Littérature, Université Paris X, 1997. 295–310.

Mollier, Jean-Yves, and Bruno Dubot. *Histoire de la librairie Larousse (1852–2010).* Paris: Fayard, 2012.

Mollier, Jean-Yves, and Pascal Ory, eds. *Pierre Larousse et son temps.* Paris: Larousse, 1995.

Le Monde.

Monthly Review.

Monzie, Anatole de. "Pour une encyclopédie française." Vol. 1 (*L'Outillage mental*) of *Encyclopédie française.* Paris: Société de Gestion de l'Encyclopédie Française, 1937. Cahier 4, 5–9.

Moréri, Louis. *Le Grand Dictionaire historique; ou, Le Mélange curieux de l'histoire sainte et profane.* 1st edn. Lyon: Girin and Rivière, 1674.

Le Grand Dictionnaire historique; ou, Le mélange curieux de l'histoire sacrée et profane. New edn. 10 vols. Paris: Libraires Associés, 1759.

Morrisson, Christian, and Wayne Snyder. "Les Inégalités de revenus en France du début du xviiie siècle à 1985." *Revue économique* 51 (2000): 119–54.

Moyal, Gabriel. "Lexiques de l'histoire." In *Voyages dans le Grand Larousse*. Ed. Yannick Portebois and Maxime Prévost. Toronto: Centre d'Etudes du xixe Siècle Joseph Sablé, 2005. 25–35.

Mugglestone, Lynda. "Das *Oxford English Dictionary*." In *Grosse Lexika und Wörterbücher Europas: Europäische Enzyklopädien und Wörterbücher in historischen Porträts*. Ed. Ulrike Hass. Berlin: De Gruyter, 2011. 233–52.

Müller-Vollmer, Kurt. "*Encyclopaedia Americana*." In *Germany and the Americas*. Ed. Thomas Adam. 3 vols. Santa Barbara: ABC-CLIO, 2005. 1: 305–11.

Murray, William. *Adventures in the People Business: The Story of World Book*. Chicago: Field Enterprises, 1966.

Naas, Valérie. "L'*Histoire naturelle* de Pline l'Ancien: Texte fondateur de l'encyclopédisme? In *Les Encyclopédies: Construction et circulation du savoir de l'Antiquité à Wikipédia*. Ed. Martine Groult. Paris: Harmattan, 2011. 25–45.

Nault, William H. "Evaluating the Format of an Encyclopedia." In Padraig S. Walsh, *Anglo-American General Encyclopedias: A Historical Bibliography, 1703–1967*. New York: Bowker, 1968. 261–6.

The New American Cyclopaedia. Ed. George Ripley and Charles A. Dana. 16 vols. New York: Appleton, 1858–63.

New and Complete Dictionary of Arts and Sciences. 4 vols. London: Owen, 1754–5.

New Encyclopaedia Britannica. 30 vols. Chicago: Encyclopaedia Britannica, 1974.

New Encyclopaedia Britannica. 32 vols. Chicago: Encyclopaedia Britannica, 2002.

New Encyclopaedia Britannica. 32 vols. Chicago: Encyclopaedia Britannica, 2005.

New Scientist.

New York Times.

The New Yorker.

Nichols, Margaret I. *Handbook of Reference Sources and Services for Small and Medium-Sized Libraries*. 2nd edn. Austin: Texas State Library, 1994.

Niederer, Sabine, and José van Dijck. "Wisdom of the Crowd or Technicity of Content? Wikipedia as a Sociotechnical System." *New Media and Society* 12 (2010): 1368–87.

Nobre, Sergio. "La difusión de las matemáticas en la primera mitad del siglo xviii en Alemania a través de la gran enciclopedia universal." *Llull* 18 (1995): 113–33.

North, John. "Encyclopaedias and the Art of Knowing Everything." In *Pre-Modern Encyclopaedic Texts*. Ed. Peter Binkley. Leiden: Brill, 1997. 183–99.

Nuttall Encyclopaedia: Being a Concise and Comprehensive Dictionary of General Knowledge. Ed. James Wood. London: Warne, 1900.

Ory, Pascal. "Le *Grand Dictionnaire* de Pierre Larousse." In *Les Lieux de mémoire*. Ed. Pierre Nora. New edn. 3 vols. Paris: Gallimard, 1997. 1: 227–38.

Osselton, N. E. "The Early Development of the English Monolingual Dictionary." Vol. I (*General-Purpose Dictionaries*) of *The Oxford History of English Lexicography*. Ed. A. P. Cowie. Oxford: Oxford University Press, 2009. 131–81.

O'Sullivan, Thomas D. "Acquisition of Commissioned Articles in Encyclopedia Publishing." *Editors' Notes* 3 (1984): 28–30.

Panckoucke, Charles-Joseph. "Lettre de M. Panckoucke à messieurs les souscripteurs de *l'Encyclopédie.*" Vol. v of *Encyclopédie méthodique: Histoire.* Paris: Panckoucke, 1791. 1–29.

Prospectus et mémoires de l'Encyclopédie méthodique. 2 vols. Ed. Martine Groult. Saint-Etienne and Paris: 2011–13.

Parinet, Elisabeth, and Valérie Tesnière. "Une entreprise: La Maison d'édition." In *Le Livre concurrencé, 1900–1950.* Vol. iv of *Histoire de l'édition française.* Ed. Henri-Jean Martin *et al.* Paris: Promodis, 1986. 122–47.

Parmentier, Bérengère. "Abondance et singularité: Un *Dictionnaire universel* des variations du sens." In *Le Dictionnaire universel d'Antoine Furetière.* Ed. Hélène Merlin-Kajman. Paris: Champion, 2002. 63–81.

Paul, Ina Ulrike. "'Dieses Universal-Lexicon hat seines Gleichen nicht' – oder doch? Europas Enzyklopädien vor Zedlers *Universal-Lexicon.*" In *Die gesammelte Welt: Studien zu Zedlers Universal-Lexicon.* Ed. Kai Lohsträter and Flemming Schock. Wiesbaden: Harrassowitz, 2013. 19–40.

"Enzyklopädien der Aufklärung in europäischen Vernakularsprachen und der Wissenstransfer über 'Modell, Imitation und Kopie.'" *Cahiers d'études germaniques* 72 (2017): 23–34.

"'Wache auf und lies …': Zur Tradierung von Nationalstereotypen in europäischen Enzyklopädien des 18. Jahrhunderts." In *Populäre Enzyklopädien.* Ed. Ingrid Tomkowiak. Zürich: Chronos, 2002. 197–220.

PC: The Independent Guide to IBM Personal Computers.

Peche, Martin. *Bibliotheca lexicorum: Kommentiertes Verzeichnis der Sammlung Otmar Seemann. Eine Bibliographie der enzyklopädischen Literatur von den Anfängen bis zur Gegenwart.* Vienna: Antiquariat Inlibris, 2001.

Pellat, Charles. "Les Encyclopédies dans le monde arabe." *Cahiers d'histoire mondiale* 9 (1966): 631–58.

Penny Cyclopaedia of the Society for the Diffusion of Useful Knowledge. 27 vols. London: Knight, 1833–43.

Perla, George A. "The Unsigned Articles and Jaucourt's Biographical Sketches in the *Encyclopédie.*" SVEC 171 (1977): 189–95.

Perrot, Jean-Claude. "Les Dictionnaires de commerce au xviiie siècle." *Revue d'histoire moderne et contemporaine* 28 (1981): 36–67.

Pestana, Harold R. "Rees's *Cyclopaedia* (1802–1820), a Sourcebook for the History of Geology." *Journal of the Society for the Bibliography of Natural History* 9 (1979): 353–61.

Petit, Michael J. "Loose-Leaf Publications." Vol. iii of *Encyclopedia of Library and Information Science.* 2nd edn. Ed. Miriam A. Drake. New York: Dekker, 2003. 1700–11.

Petit Larousse illustré. Ed. Claude Augé. Paris: Larousse, 1923.

Petit Larousse illustré. Paris: Larousse, 2000.

Phelps, Rose B. "The *Encyclopaedia Britannica*, Ninth Edition: A Critical and Historical Study." M.S. thesis. Columbia University, 1930.

Philadelphia Daily News.

Pickstone, John V. *Ways of Knowing: A New History of Science, Technology and Medicine.* Chicago: University of Chicago Press, 2000.

[*Pierer's Universal-Lexikon*]. 1st edn. *Encyclopädisches Wörterbuch der Wissenschaften, Künste und Gewerbe*. 26 vols. Altenburg: 1824–36.

[*Pierer's Universal-Lexikon*]. 2nd edn. *Universal-Lexikon der Gegenwart und Vergangenheit oder neueste encyclopädisches Wörterbuch der Wissenschaften, Künste und Gewerbe*. 36 vols. Altenburg: Pierer, 1840–8.

[Piltz, Anton Ernst Oskar]. "Zur Geschichte und Bibliographie der enzyklopädischen Literatur insbesondere des Conversations-Lexikon." In *F. A. Brockhaus in Leipzig*. Ed. Heinrich Brockhaus. Leipzig: Brockhaus, 1872–5. i–lxxii.

Pinault [Sørensen], Madeleine. "Rôle et statut de l'image dans l'*Encyclopédie*." In *L'Encyclopédie; ou, La Création des disciplines*. Ed. Martine Groult. Paris: CNRS, 2003. 131–51.

"Sur les planches de l'*Encyclopédie* de D'Alembert et Diderot." In *L'Encyclopédisme: Actes du Colloque de Caen*. Ed. Annie Becq. Paris: Aux Amateurs de Livres, 1991. 355–62.

Pivati, Gianfrancesco. *Nuovo dizionario scientifico e curioso sacro-profano*. 10 vols. Venice: Milocco, 1746–51.

Pliny the Elder. *Natural History: Preface and Books 1–2*. Trans. H. Rackham. Cambridge, MA: Harvard University Press, 1949.

Political Dictionary: Forming a Work of Universal Reference. 2 vols. London: Knight, 1845.

Popkin, Richard H. *The History of Scepticism from Savonarola to Bayle*. Rev. edn. Oxford: Oxford University Press, 2003.

Popular Mechanics.

Popular Science.

Popular Science Monthly.

Porret, Michel. "Savoir encyclopédique, encyclopédie des savoirs." In *L'Encyclopédie méthodique (1782–1832): Des Lumières au positivisme*. Ed. Claude Blanckaert *et al*. Geneva: Droz, 2006. 13–56.

Porset, Charles. "L'Encyclopédie et la question de l'ordre: Réflexions sur la lexicalisation des connaissances au XVIIIe siècle." In *L'Encyclopédisme: Actes du Colloque de Caen*. Ed. Annie Becq. Paris: Aux Amateurs de Livres, 1991. 253–64.

Porter, Horace A. *The Making of a Black Scholar*. Iowa City: University of Iowa Press, 2003.

Preece, Warren E. "Notes toward a New Encyclopaedia." *Scholarly Publishing* 12 (1980–1): 13–30, 141–57.

The Press.

Prodöhl, Ines. "'Aus denen besten Scribenten': Zedlers *Universal-Lexicon* im Spannungsfeld zeitgenössischer Lexikonproduktion." *Das achtzehnte Jahrhundert* 29 (2005): 82–94.

Die Politik des Wissens: Allgemeine deutsche Enzyklopädien zwischen 1928 und 1956. Berlin: Akademie, 2011.

Prospectus to *Encyclopédie des gens du monde*. Vol. III of *Histoire du congrès de Vienne*. Paris: Treuttel and Würtz, 1829: 1–4 [455–8].

Proust, Jacques. "De quelques dictionnaires hollandais ayant servi de relais à l'encyclopédisme européen vers le Japon." *Dix-huitième siècle* 38 (2006): 17–38.

Diderot et l'Encyclopédie. New edn. Paris: Michel, 1995.

"L'Encyclopédie au Japon au XVIIIe siècle." In *Tous les savoirs du monde.* Ed. Roland Schaer. Paris: Bibliothèque Nationale, 1996. 411–15.

Marges d'une utopie: Pour une lecture critique des planches de l'Encyclopédie. Cognac: Le Temps qu'il Fait, 1985.

Pruvost, Jean. "De Diderot à Pierre Larousse: Un paysage lexicographique prémonitoire." In *Les Dictionnaires Larousse: Genèse et evolution.* Ed. Monique C. Cormier and Aline Francoeur. Montreal: Presses de l'Université de Montréal, 2005. 41–62.

La Dent-de-lion, la Semeuse et le Petit Larousse. Paris: Larousse, 2004.

"Dictionnaires de l'institution et dictionnaires de l'entreprise privée: Une stimulation caractéristique des dictionnaires français." In *Cultures et lexicographies.* Ed. Michaela Heinz. Berlin: Frank and Timme, 2010. 223–44.

"Du *Nouveau Dictionnaire de la langue française* (1856) au *Grand Dictionnaire universel du XIXe siècle* (1866–1876)." In *Pierre Larousse: Du Grand Dictionnaire au Petit Larousse.* Ed. Pruvost *et al.* Paris: Champion, 2002. 49–73.

"L'Illustration dictionnarique et les technolectes dans les dictionnaires sémasiologiques." *Meta* 39 (1994): 741–6.

"Pierre Larousse, genèse et épanouissement d'un lexicographe et éditeur hors du commun." In *Les Dictionnaires Larousse: Genèse et evolution.* Ed. Monique C. Cormier and Aline Francoeur. Montreal: Presses de l'Université de Montréal, 2005. 13–40.

Ptashnyk, Stefaniya. "*Enzyklopädie der Ukrainekunde,* hg. von Volodymyr Kubijovyč (1949–1995)." In *Grosse Lexika und Wörterbücher Europas: Europäische Enzyklopädien und Wörterbücher in historischen Porträts.* Ed. Ulrike Hass. Berlin: De Gruyter, 2011. 433–47.

Publishers Weekly.

Puschner, Uwe. "'Mobil gemachte Feldbibliotheken': Deutsche Enzyklopädien und Konversationslexika im 18. und 19. Jahrhundert." In *Literatur, Politik und soziale Prozesse: Studien zur deutschen Literatur von der Aufklärung bis zur Weimarer Republik.* Tübingen: Niemeyer, 1997. 62–77.

Quemada, Bernard. *Les Dictionnaires du français moderne, 1539–1863: Etude sur leur histoire, leurs types et leurs méthodes.* Paris: Didier, 1967.

Randall, Marilyn. *Pragmatic Plagiarism: Authorship, Profit, and Power.* Toronto: University of Toronto Press, 2001.

Rauch, Alan. *Useful Knowledge: The Victorians, Morality, and the March of Intellect.* Durham, NC: Duke University Press, 2001.

Raven, James. *The Business of Books: Booksellers and the English Book Trade, 1450–1850.* New Haven: Yale University Press, 2007.

Reagle, Joseph Michael. *Good Faith Collaboration: The Culture of Wikipedia.* Cambridge, MA: MIT Press, 2010.

Rees, Abraham, ed. *Cyclopaedia; or, An Universal Dictionary of Arts and Sciences.* 5 vols. London: Strahan *et al.*, 1778–88.

ed. *The [New] Cyclopaedia; or, Universal Dictionary of Arts, Sciences, and Literature.* 45 vols. London: Longman *et al.*, 1819–20.

Reich, Howard. *The First and Final Nightmare of Sonia Reich.* New York: Public Affairs, 2006.

Reinstein, Hagen. "Die *Oeconomische Encyclopädie* von Johann Georg Krünitz." In *Wissenswelten: Historische Lexikographie und europäische Aufklärung.* Ed. Robert Charlier. Hanover: Wehrhahn, 2010. 63–81.

"The Reply of the Johnsons to the Appletons." In *The Cyclopaedia War: The Appletons against the Johnsons.* New York: Johnson, [1877?]. 1–32.

Rétat, Pierre. "L'Age des dictionnaires." Vol. 11 *(Le Livre triomphant, 1660–1830)* of *Histoire de l'édition française.* Ed. Henri-Jean Martin *et al.* Paris: Promodis, 1984. 186–97.

Le Dictionnaire de Bayle et la lutte philosophique au XVIIIe siècle. Paris: Audin, 1971.

"Encyclopédies et dictionnaires historiques au XVIIIᵉ siècle." In *L'Encyclopédisme: Actes du Colloque de Caen.* Ed. Annie Becq. Paris: Aux Amateurs de Livres, 1991. 505–11.

Review of *Complete Dictionary of Arts and Sciences. Monthly Review* 40 (1769): 1–24.

Review of *Edinburgh Encyclopaedia. Blackwood's Edinburgh Magazine* 1 (1817): 186–8.

Review of *English Cyclopaedia. The Quarterly Review* 113 (January and April 1863): 354–87.

Review of *Grand Dictionaire historique. Bibliothèque universelle et historique* 21 (1691; 3rd edn., 1707): 109–22.

Review of *Penny Cyclopaedia. The Mechanics' Magazine, Museum, Register, Journal, and Gazette* 27 (1837): 74–9.

Review of *Penny Cyclopaedia* and other works. *Dublin University Magazine* 1 (March 1833): 337–8.

Review of *Science des personnes de la cour. Journal des sçavans* 76 (April 1725): 234–5.

Review of *Supplement to Mr. Chambers's Cyclopaedia. Monthly Review* 10 (1754): 51–7.

Revised Reports, Being a Republication of Such Cases in the English Courts of Common Law and Equity, from the Year 1785, as Are Still of Practical Utility.

Revue bibliographique belge.

Rey, Alain. "Antoine Furetière imagier de la culture classique." In *Le Dictionnaire universel d'Antoine Furetière.* Reprint edn. Ed. Alain Rey. 3 vols. Paris: SLN, 1984. 1: 5–95.

"Le Lexicographe." In *Pierre Larousse et son temps.* Ed. Jean-Yves Mollier and Pascal Ory. Paris: Larousse, 1995. 131–8.

Miroirs du monde: Une histoire de l'encyclopédisme. Paris: Fayard, 2007.

Richelet, César-Pierre. *Dictionnaire françois, contenant les mots et les choses.* Geneva: Widerhold, 1680.

Rivalan Guégo, Christine *et al. Gran enciclopedia gallega (1974–1991): La forja de una identidad.* Gijón: Trea, 2016.

Rivers, Isabel. "Biographical Dictionaries and Their Uses from Bayle to Chalmers." In *Books and Their Readers in Eighteenth-Century England: New Essays.* Ed. Isabel Rivers. London: Leicester University Press, 2001. 135–69.

Roberto, Rose. "Democratising Knowledge and Visualising Progress: Illustrations from *Chambers's Encyclopaedia*, 1859–1892." Ph.D. dissertation. University of Reading, 2018.

Robbins, Thomas. *Diary of Thomas Robbins, D. D., 1796–1854*. Ed. Increase N. Tarbox. 2 vols. Boston: Beacon, 1886–87.

Robichez, Jacques. "L'*Encyclopédie française*." *Cahiers d'histoire mondiale* 9 (1966): 819–31.

Rochefort, César de. *Dictionaire general et curieux, contenant les principaux mots, et les plus usitez en la langue françoise*. Lyon: Guillimin, 1685.

Ronsin, Albert. "Les Editions nancéiennes du *Dictionnaire de Trévoux* au XVIIIe siècle." *Le Pays lorrain* 4 (1960): 151–64.

Roosevelt, Eleanor. *The Autobiography of Eleanor Roosevelt*. New York: Harper, 1958.

Rose, Mark. "Technology and Copyright in 1735: The Engraver's Act." *The Information Society* 21 (2005): 63–66.

Ross, Walter W. "Thomas Corneille's *Dictionnaire des arts et des sciences*." In *Notable Encyclopedias of the Seventeenth and Eighteenth Centuries*. Ed. Frank A. Kafker. Oxford: Voltaire Foundation, 1981. 69–81.

Rouse, Mary A., and Richard H. Rouse. "La Naissance des index." Vol. 1. (*Le Livre conquérant: Du Moyen Age au milieu du XVIIᵉ siècle*) of *Histoire de l'édition française*. Ed. Henri-Jean Martin *et al*. Paris: Promodis, 1983. 76–85.

Rovigatti, Franca. "Gli anni della Enciclopedia." In *Storia di un'idea: L'Enciclopedia italiana tra memoria e progetto*. Rome: Enciclopedia Italiana, 1993. 3–26.

Rowe, Paul. "Tous les savoirs des gens du monde? Un précurseur du *GDU*." In *Voyages dans le Grand Larousse*. Ed. Yannick Portebois and Maxime Prévost. Toronto: Centre d'Études du XIXe Siècle Joseph Sablé, 2005. 11–23.

"Upwardly Mobile Footnotes: German References in the *Encyclopédie des gens du monde*." *Modern and Contemporary France* 14 (2006): 433–48.

Rüdiger, Bettina. "Der 'Ersch/Gruber': Konzeption, Drucklegung und Wirkungsgeschichte der *Allgemeinen Encyklopädie der Wissenschaften und Künste*." *Leipziger Jahrbuch zur Buchgeschichte* 14 (2005): 11–78.

Rudy, Seth. *Literature and Encyclopedism in Enlightenment Britain: The Pursuit of Complete Knowledge*. Houndmills: Palgrave Macmillan, 2014.

Runte, Maren, and Julia C. Steuben. "*Encyclopaedia Britannica*." In *Grosse Lexika und Wörterbücher Europas: Europäische Enzyklopädien und Wörterbücher in historischen Porträts*. Ed. Ulrike Hass. Berlin: De Gruyter, 2011. 79–104.

Sahl, Hans. *Memoiren eines Moralisten*. Darmstadt: Luchterhand, 1985.

Sainte-Soline, Claire. *Les Années fraîches*. Paris: Grasset, 1966.

Sarkowski, Heinz. *Das Bibliographische Institut: Verlagsgeschichte und Bibliographie: 1826–1976*. Mannheim: Bibliographisches Institut, 1976.

Sartre, Jean-Paul. *The Words*. Trans. Bernard Frechtman. New York: Braziller, 1964.

Saturday Review.

Saunders, David. *Authorship and Copyright*. London: Routledge, 1992.

Savary des Bruslons, Jacques, *et al*. *Dictionnaire universel de commerce*. 3 vols. Paris: Estienne, 1723–30.

Schaer, Roland, ed. *Tous les savoirs du monde: Encyclopédies et bibliothèques, de Sumer au XXIᵉ siècle*. Paris: Bibliothèque Nationale, 1996.

Schafroth, Elmar. "*Enciclopedia italiana di scienze, lettere ed arti.*" In *Grosse Lexika und Wörterbücher Europas: Europäische Enzyklopädien und Wörterbücher in historischen Porträts.* Ed. Ulrike Hass. Berlin: De Gruyter, 2011. 407–31.

Schmidt, Carole Hamner. "The Visionary Pedant: S. T. Coleridge, Abraham Rees, and the Encyclopaedia in the Romantic Period." Ph.D. dissertation. University of Virginia, 2008.

Schmidt-Biggemann, Wilhelm. "Enzyklopädie und Philosophia perennis." In *Enzyklopädien der frühen Neuzeit.* Ed. Franz M. Eybl *et al.* Tübingen: Niemeyer, 1995. 1–18.

Schmitt, Stéphane. "Inventaire des livraisons, des auteurs et du contenu de l'*Encyclopédie méthodique* (1782–1832)." *Recherches sur Diderot et sur l'Encyclopédie* 53 (2018): 207–70.

"Les voyages intertextuels de l'abada." *Recherches sur Diderot et sur l'Encyclopédie* 52 (2017): 23–38.

Schmitt, Stéphane, and Jeff Loveland. "Scientific Knowledge of Animals in Encyclopedias from around 1700 to 1860." *Erudition and the Republic of Letters* 2 (2017): 314–49.

Schneider, Ulrich Johannes. "Des transferts de savoir en format encyclopédique: Le *Dictionnaire historique* (1674–1759)." In *Transferts, circulations et réseaux savants franco-allemands au XVIIIe siècle.* Ed. Claire Gantet and Markus Meumann. Rennes: Presses Universitaires de Rennes, forthcoming.

Die Erfindung des allgemeinen Wissens: Enzyklopädisches Schreiben im Zeitalter der Aufklärung. Berlin: Akademie, 2013.

"Europea und der Rest der Welt: Zum geographischen Wissen in Zedlers 'Universal-Lexicon.'" In *Allgemeinwissen und Gesellschaft.* Ed. Paul Michel *et al.* Aachen: Shaker, 2007. 431–50.

"Die Konstruktion des allgemeinen Wissens in Zedlers 'Universal-Lexicon.'" In *Wissenssicherung, Wissensordnung und Wissensverarbeitung.* Ed. Theo Stammen and Wolfgang E. J. Weber. Berlin: Akademie, 2004. 81–101.

"Zedlers *Universal-Lexicon* und die Gelehrtenkultur des 18. Jahrhunderts." In *Die Universität Leipzig und ihr gelehrtes Umfeld, 1680–1780.* Ed. Hanspeter Marti and Detlef Döring. Basel: Schwabe, 2004. 195–213.

Schneider, Ulrich Johannes, and Helmut Zedelmaier. "Wissensapparate: Die Enzyklopädistik der frühen Neuzeit." In *Die Macht des Wissen.* Ed. Richard von Dülmen *et al.* Cologne: Böhlau, 2004. 349–63.

Schöpflin, Katharine. "The Encyclopaedia as a Form of the Book." Ph.D. dissertation. University College, London, 2013.

Schubring, Gert. "Mathematische Wörterbücher des 18. Jahrhunderts." *Das achtzehnte Jahrhundert* 22 (1998): 114–28.

Schwab, R. N., W. E. Rex, and J. Lough. *Inventory of Diderot's Encyclopédie.* 7 vols. Geneva: Institut et Musée Voltaire, 1971–84.

Seckel, Raymond-Josué, and Valérie Tesnière. "De Panckoucke à Queneau." In *Tous les savoirs du monde.* Ed. Roland Schaer. Paris: Bibliothèque Nationale, 1996. 420–41.

Sewell, William H., Jr. "Visions of Labor: Illustrations of the Mechanical Arts before, in, and after Diderot's *Encyclopédie.*" In *Work in France.* Ed. Steven

L. Kaplan and Cynthia Koepp. Ithaca: Cornell University Press, 1986. 258–86.

Sgard, Jean. "L'Echelle des revenus." *Dix-huitième siècle* 14 (1982): 425–33.

Shackleton, Robert. "The Encyclopaedic Spirit." In *Greene Centennial Studies*. Ed. Paul J. Korshin and Robert R. Allen. Charlottesville: University Press of Virginia, 1984. 377–90.

Sheirer, John. *Growing Up Mostly Normal in the Middle of Nowhere: A Memoir*. Cedarburg: Foremost, 2005.

Sher, Richard B. "Corporatism and Consensus in the Late Eighteenth-Century Book Trade: The Edinburgh Booksellers' Society in Comparative Perspective." *Book History* 1 (1998): 32–90.

The Enlightenment and the Book: Scottish Authors and their Publishers in Eighteenth-Century Britain, Ireland, and America. Chicago: University of Chicago Press, 2006.

Shiflett, Lee. *Louis Shores: Defining Educational Librarianship*. Lanham: Scarecrow, 1996.

Shores, Louis, and Richard Krzys. "Reference Books." *Encyclopedia of Library and Information Science* 25 (1978): 136–202.

Siegel, Steffen. "Die Orte des Bildes im Alphabet des enzyklopädischen Textes." In *Seine Welt wissen: Enzyklopädien in frühen Neuzeit*. Ed. Ulrich Johannes Schneider. Darmstadt: Primus, 2006. 164–79.

Silva Villar, Luis, and Susana Silva Villar. "Pérez Hervás: Borrado del mapa, y del *Espasa*." *Estudios de lingüística del español* 36 (2015): 485–95.

Smith, Margaret M. "Woodcut Illustration." Vol. 2 of *The Oxford Companion to the Book*. Ed. Michael F. Suarez and H. R. Wouldhuysen. 2 vols. Oxford: Oxford University Press, 2010. 1265–66.

Solovieff, Georges. *Une enfance berlinoise (1921–1931)*. Paris: Harmattan, 2002.

Southwestern Law Review.

The Spectator.

Spree, Ulrike. *Das Streben nach Wissen: Eine vergleichende Gattungsgeschichte der populären Enzyklopädie in Deutschland und Grossbritannien im 19. Jahrhundert*. Tübingen: Niemeyer, 2000.

"Die verhinderte 'Bürgerin'? Ein begriffsgeschichtlicher Vergleich zwischen Deutschland, Frankreich und Grossbritannien." In *Bürgerschaft*. Ed. Reinhart Koselleck and Klaus Schreiner. Stuttgart: Klett-Cotta, 1994. 274–306.

St. Clair, William. *The Reading Nation and the Romantic Period*. Cambridge: Cambridge University Press, 2004.

Stalnaker, Joanna. *The Unfinished Enlightenment: Description in the Age of the Encyclopedia*. Ithaca: Cornell University Press, 2010.

Stern.

Stern, Simon. "Copyright, Originality, and the Public Domain in Eighteenth-Century England." In *Originality and Intellectual Property in the French and English Enlightenment*. Ed. Reginald McGinnis. New York: Routledge, 2009. 69–101.

Stewart, Philip. "Illustrations encyclopédiques: De la *Cyclopaedia* à l'*Encyclopédie*." *Recherches sur Diderot et sur l'Encyclopédie* 12 (1992): 70–98.

Stickfort, Bernd. "Das Internet als enzyklopädische Utopie." In *Populäre Enzyklopädien*. Ed. Ingrid Tomkowiak. Zurich: Chronos, 2002. 271–95.

Stockwell, Foster. *A History of Information Storage and Retrieval*. Jefferson: McFarland, 2001.

Stross, Randall E. *The Microsoft Way: The Real Story of How the Company Outsmarts its Competition*. New York: Basic, 1996.

Sullivan, Lawrence E. "Circumscribing Knowledge: Encyclopedias in Historical Perspective." *The Journal of Religion* 70 (1990): 315–39.

Supplément au Dictionnaire historique, géographique, généalogique, etc. 3 vols. Basel: Christ, 1743–45.

Supplément au Grand Dictionnaire historique, généalogique, géographique, etc. de M. Louis Moreri. 2 vols. Paris: Lemercier *et al.*, 1735.

A Supplement to Dr. Harris's Dictionary of Arts and Sciences. London: The Authors, 1744.

Supplement to the Fourth, Fifth, and Sixth Editions of the Encyclopaedia Britannica. Ed. Macvey Napier. 6 vols. Edinburgh: Constable, 1824.

Die Tageszeitung.

Tammet, Daniel. *Embracing the Wide Sky: A Tour across the Horizons of the Mind*. New York: Free, 2009.

Tankard, Paul. "Reference Point: Samuel Johnson and the Encyclopedias." *Eighteenth-Century Life* 33 (2009): 37–64.

Taylor, Kennth L. "A Peculiarly Personal Encyclopedia: What Desmarest's *Géographie-Physique* tells us about his Life and Work." *Earth Sciences History* 32 (2013): 39–54.

Technology and Learning.

"Testimonials of Comparison." In *The Cyclopaedia War: The Appletons against the Johnsons*. New York: Johnson and Son [1877?]. 1–31.

Texas Monthly.

Théré, Christine, and Loïc Charles. "Un nouvel élément pour l'histoire de l'*Encyclopédie*: Le 'Plan' inédit du premier éditeur Gua de Malves." *Recherches sur Diderot et sur l'Encyclopédie* 39 (2005): 105–23.

Thomas, Gillian. *A Position to Command Respect: Women and the Eleventh Britannica*. Metuchen: Scarecrow, 1992.

Thomas, Keith. *Changing Conceptions of National Biography: The Oxford DNB in Historical Perspective*. Cambridge: Cambridge University Press, 2005.

Time.

The Times [of London].

Tkacz, Nathaniel. *Wikipedia and the Politics of Openness*. Chicago: University of Chicago Press, 2015.

Tracy, Michael. *The World of the Edwardian Child, as Seen in Arthur Mee's 'Children's Encyclopaedia,' 1908–1910*. York: Hermitage, 2008.

Tucoo-Chala, Suzanne. *Charles-Joseph Panckoucke et la librairie française, 1736–1798*. Pau: Marrimpouey, 1977.

Tulsa World.

Turi, Gabriele. *Il mecenate, il filosofo e il gesuita: L'Enciclopedia italiana, specchio della nazione*. Bologna: Mulino, 2002.

Twomey, Michael W. "Inventing the Encyclopedia." In *Schooling and Society*. Ed. Alasdair A. MacDonald and Twomey. Louvain: Peeters, 2004. 73–92.

"Towards a Reception History of Western Medieval Encyclopaedias in England before 1500." In *Pre-Modern Encyclopaedic Texts*. Ed. Peter Binkley. Leiden: Brill, 1997. 329–62.

Updike, John. *In the Beauty of the Lilies*. New York: Knopf, 1996.

Upton, Hilton R. "Some Landmarks in the Development of the English Encyclopedia." M.A. thesis. Columbia University, 1926.

US Census Bureau. *Population Profile of the United States: 1999*. Washington, DC: Government Printing Office, 2001.

Vanche-Roby, Mireille. "La Nomenclature comme manifestation et expression de l'idéologie dans trois encyclopédies de fin de siècle." In *Encyclopédies et dictionnaires français: Problèmes de norme(s) et de nomenclature*. Aix-en-Provence: Centre Dumarsais, 1993. 175–93.

Vasoli, Cesare. *L'Enciclopedismo del seicento*. Naples: Bibliopolis, 1978.

Viera, Lise. *L'Edition électronique: De l'imprimé au numérique*. Bordeaux: Presses Universitaires de Bordeaux, 2004.

Vogelgsang, Klaus. "Zum Begriff 'Enzyklopädie.'" In *Wissenssicherung, Wissensordnung, und Wissensverarbeitung*. Ed. Theo Stammen and Wolfgang E. J. Weber. Berlin: Akademie, 2004. 15–23.

Wald, James. "Periodicals and Periodicity." *A Companion to the History of the Book*. Ed. Simon Eliot and Jonathan Rose. Oxford: Blackwell, 2007. 421–33.

Wall Street Journal.

Wall Street Journal: Europe.

Walsh, S. Padraig. *Anglo-American General Encyclopedias: A Historical Bibliography, 1703–1967*. New York: Bowker, 1968.

Walters, Alice Nell. "Tools of Enlightenment: The Material Culture of Science in Eighteenth-Century England." Ph.D. dissertation. University of California, Berkeley, 1992.

Walters, Barrie. "Juigné Broissinière's Contribution to Moréri's *Grand Dictionnaire historique*." *SVEC* 256 (1988): 165–83.

Watts, George B. "The *Encyclopédie méthodique*." *PMLA* 73 (1958): 348–66.

Weedon, Alexis. *Victorian Publishing: The Economics of Book Production for a Mass Market, 1836–1916*. Aldershot: Ashgate, 2001.

Weijers, Olga. "Funktionen des Alphabets im Mittelalter." Trans. Ulrich Johannes Schneider. In *Seine Welt wissen: Enzyklopädien in der frühen Neuzeit*. Ed. Schneider. Darmstadt: Primus, 2006. 22–32.

Weil, Françoise. "L'*Encyclopédie* devant la censure." In *L'Encyclopédisme: Actes du Colloque de Caen*. Ed. Annie Becq. Paris: Aux Amateurs de Livres, 1991. 413–19.

Weiss, Gerhard. "The Americanization of Franz Lieber and the *Encyclopedia Americana*." In *German Culture in Nineteenth-Century America*. Ed. Lynne Tatlock and Matt Erlin. Rochester: Camden, 2005. 273–87.

Wellisch, Hans H. "Indexing." In *Encyclopedia of Library History*. Ed. Wayne A. Wiegand and Donald G. Davis, Jr. New York: Garland, 1994. 268–70.

Wellmon, Chad. *Organizing Enlightenment: Information Overload and the Invention of the Modern Research University.* Baltimore: Johns Hopkins University Press, 2015.

Wendt, Bernhard. *Idee und Entwicklungsgeschichte der enzyklopädischen Literatur: Eine literarisch-bibliographische Studie.* Würzburg-Aumühle: Triltsch, 1941.

Werner, Stephen. "Abraham Rees's Eighteenth-Century *Cyclopaedia.*" In *Notable Encyclopedias of the Late Eighteenth Century.* Ed. Frank A. Kafker. Oxford: Voltaire Foundation, 1994. 183–99.

"La Modernité de Chambers." In *L'Encyclopédisme: Actes du Colloque de Caen.* Ed. Annie Becq. Paris: Aux Amateurs de Livres, 1991. 161–67.

"Les Planches de Chambers." In *L'Encyclopédisme: Actes du Colloque de Caen.* Ed. Annie Becq. Paris: Aux Amateurs de Livres, 1991. 347–53.

Wiegand, Herbert Ernst. *Wörterbuchforschung: Untersuchungen zur Wörterbuchbenutzung, zur Theorie, Geschichte, Kritik und Automatisierung der Lexikographie.* Berlin: De Gruyter, 1998.

Wiles, R. M. *Serial Publication in England before 1750.* Cambridge: Cambridge University Press, 1957.

Williat, N. "Lucrative Learning: Encyclopedias Have Become a Source of Profit as Well as Knowledge." *Barron's National Business and Financial Weekly* 39 (6 July 1959): 5–6.

Winter, Matthias. "Online-Lexika." In *Die Zukunft der Printmedien.* Ed. Jörg Eberspächer. Berlin: Springer, 2002. 103–09.

Wionet, Chantal. "L'Esprit des langues dans le *Dictionnaire universel de Trévoux* (1704–1771)." *Dix-huitième siècle* 38 (2006): 283–302.

Wirth, Uwe. "Discursive Stupidity: Abduction and Comic in 'Monty Python's Flying Circus': From Peirce to Freud." In *Semiotics of the Media: State of the Art, Projects, and Perspectives.* Ed. Winfried Nöth. Berlin: De Gruyter, 1997. 279–89.

Wittmann, Reinhard. "Soziale und ökonomische Voraussetzungen des Buch- und Verlagswesens in der zweiten Hälfte des 18. Jahrhunderts." In *Buch- und Verlagswesen im 18. und 19. Jahrhundert.* Ed. Herbert G. Göpfert *et al.* Berlin: Camen, 1977. 5–25.

Wodehouse, P. G. *The Man with Two Left Feet and Other Stories.* London: Penguin, 1961.

Wootton, Charles W., and Carel M. Wolk. "The Evolution and Acceptance of the Loose-Leaf Accounting System, 1885–1935." *Technology and Culture* 41 (2000): 80–98.

[*World Book*]. *The World Book: Organized Knowledge in Story and Picture.* Ed. M. V. O'Shea. 8 vols. Chicago: *World Book*, 1918.

The World Book Encyclopedia. 20 vols. Chicago: Field Enterprises, 1960.

The World Book Encyclopedia. 22 vols. Chicago: World Book, 2001.

Wright, Willard Huntington. *Misinforming a Nation.* New York: Huebsch, 1917.

Yearbook: Commercial Arbitration.

Yeats, William Butler. *Reveries over Childhood and Youth.* New York: Macmillan, 1916.

Yeo, Richard. "Before Memex: Robert Hooke, John Locke, and Vannevar Bush on External Memory." *Science in Context* 20 (2007): 21–47.

Encyclopaedic Visions: Scientific Dictionaries and Enlightenment Culture. Cambridge: Cambridge University Press, 2001.

"Encyclopedism." In *New Dictionary of the History of Ideas.* Ed. Maryanne Cline Horowitz. 6 vols. New York: Scribner's Sons, 2005. 2: 669–73.

Introduction to *The Edinburgh Encyclopaedia.* Ed. David Brewster. Reprint edition. 18 vols. London: Routledge, 1999. 1: v-xix.

"Lost Encyclopedias: Before and After the Enlightenment." *Book History* 10 (2007): 47–68.

"Reading Encyclopedias: Science and the Organization of Knowledge in British Dictionaries of Arts and Sciences, 1730–1850." *Isis* 82 (1991): 24–49.

"A Solution to the Multitude of Books: Ephraim Chambers's *Cyclopaedia* (1728) as 'the Best Book in the Universe.'" *Journal of the History of Ideas* 64 (2003): 61–72.

Zachs, William. *The First John Murray and the Late Eighteenth-Century London Book Trade.* Oxford: British Academy, 1998.

Zelle, Carsten. "Auf dem Spielfeld der Autorschaft: Der Schriftsteller des 18. Jahrhunderts im Kräftefeld von Rhetorik, Medienentwicklung und Literatursystem." In *Spielräume des auktorialien Diskurses.* Ed. Klaus Städtke *et al.* Berlin: Akademie, 2003. 1–37.

Zhang, Gehao. "The Copycat of Wikipedia in China." In *Global Wikipedia.* Ed. Pnina Fichman and Noriko Hara. Lanham: Rowman and Littlefield, 2014. 135–46.

Zimmer, Michael. "*Renvois* of the Past, Present and Future: Hyperlinks and the Structuring of Knowledge from the *Encyclopédie* to Web 2.0." *New Media and Society* 11 (2009): 95–113.

Zischka, Gert A. *Index lexicorum: Bibliographie der lexikalischen Nachschlagwerke.* New York: Hafner, 1959.

Zorzi, Alessandro. *Prodromo della Nuova enciclopedia italiana (Siena, 1779).* Reprint edition. Ed. Giuliano Catoni *et al.* Siena: Monte dei Paschi, 1989.

Zucker, Arnaud, ed. *Encyclopédire: Formes de l'ambition encyclopédique dans l'Antiquité et au Moyen Âge.* Turnhout: Brepols, 2013.

Zurndorfer, Harriet T. "The Passion to Collect, Select, and Protect: Fifteen Hundred Years of the Chinese Encyclopaedia." In *Encyclopaedism from Antiquity to the Renaissance.* Ed. Jason Konig and Greg Woolf. Cambridge: Cambridge University Press, 2013. 505–28.

Index

For the most part, I have indexed books under their titles, not their authors. Because the titles of Brockhaus's, Herder's, Meyer's, and Pierer's encyclopedias varied, I have indexed editions under generic terms such as "Brockhaus's main encyclopedia."

Page numbers in **bold** refer to figures; those in *italics* to tables.

encyclopedias (*cont.*)

and schools, 35, 60, 97, 153–4, 325, 340–1
appearance, 50
   columns per page, 111–12, 113
   deluxe editions, 120–1, 298
   format, 92–3, 123, 128, 195
   layout and typography, 65–6, 185, 187, 222, 223, 243
   paper, 113, 120, 213, 216, 217, 298
   paperbacks, 113, 315
   type and type-size, 111
as dictionaries, 15, 18–19
as liberating, 8–9, 165–7
as prizes or gifts, 122, 314, 325
as sites for advertising, 383
authoritativeness, 79–80, 224–6, 253, 266–7, 284, 353; *see also* encyclopedias, objectivity
branding and prestige, 126, 141, 295, 315–16
by country
   Britain, 35, 79, 93–4, 96, 102, 103, 104–5, 176, 184, 188, 208, 231–2, 274–5, 291, 308, 309, 310
   China, 71–2, 89
   France, 35, 73, 78, 93–4, 96, 102, 104–5, 108, 140, 177–8, 208, 253, 309, 310
   Germany and German lands, 47, 65, 78, 95, 96, 102–3, 104–5, 123–4, 176–7, 197, 208–9, 250, 253–4, 258, 261–2, 275, 290, 309–10
   Japan, 89
   Netherlands, 365
   Spain, 35
   Ukraine, 88
   United States, 35, 158, 280, 291, 293, 303, 311
censorship, 38, 144, 248, 267–70, 284, 310
content, 10, 50–90, 91; *see also* encyclopedias, entries; encyclopedias, keywords
   biographies, 24, 105, 133, 237, 277, 329–30
   biographies of the living, 25–6, 80, 139, 276–7
   current events, 37, 42, 334
   cutting-edge knowledge, 9, 51
   dated, because of recycling from previous editions, 147, 150, 251, 282
   factual versus theoretical, 188, 231–2
   heraldry, 228–30, 265
   mathematics, 245, 343, 344, 346, 351, 352–3
   medicine, 66–8, 340
   natural history, 219, 231–4, 246, 266, 272, 326, 345, 348
   sexual, 45, 268, 329, 349
   technology, 60–4, 228, 230–1
contributors, 248–59, 372, 375, 388
   celebrities, 252, 253–4, 282–3

editorial staffs, 55, 254–5, 259, 266, 276, 289
foreigners, 83, 141
illustrators, 202
insiders, 81, 82, 139, 276–83, 284
named or anonymous, 80, 144–5, 202, 203, 248–53, 284
pay, 106, 116–18, 199, 254–5
professional backgrounds, 255–7, 284
relatives and friends of a biographical subject, 25, 276–7
specialists, 37, 51, 139, 141, 271–6, 278, 284
volunteers, some solicited with an invitation to the public, 25, 130, 137–40, 228, 271
women, 257–9, 277–8, 384–5
critical, 168, 354
demise as printed works, 2, 317, 358, 362–3, 366, 371–2, 386, 387
economics, 35, 73, 91–128, 209, 301, 320, 349; *see also* encyclopedias, pricing
editors, 129, 137, 162–3, 248, 259, 260–4; *see also* encyclopedias, preparation
   coordinating cross-references, 192–3, 261, 262, 263
   hierarchies and differentiation among, 264, 284
   managing contributors, 106, 115, 141–2, 144–5, 162–3, 252, 263
   revising submitted material, 252, 261, 262–3, 355
   versus compilers and authors, 259–60, 262, 263
entries; *see also* encyclopedias, content; encyclopedias, keywords
   doubled, to give two points of view, 75, 269, 279, 386
   geographical, 184, 187, 189, 256, 277, 299
   organization, 182, 355
   sub-entries, 132, 182–3
European, 2–3, 4–6
genres, 4, 6, 15–49, 50
historiography, 7, 10, 12, 89, 96, 99, 126–7, 148, 169–70, 171, 173–5, 193–4, 202, 285, 320, 321–2, 348, 349
ideological, 38, 42, 48, 72–3, 79
   communist, 39, 86–7, 166, 270
   fascist, 86, 268
   Nazi, 39, 269, 270
illustrations, 39, 92, 127, 147, 161, 162, 202–47, 270, 328–9, 369–70
   anatomy, 217, 220
   and paper, 213, 216, 239–41, 243
   colored, 214–16, 217–18, 222, 238, 239, 243
   cost, 110, 124, 207, 208, 215, 217, 219, 236, 241